ANNUAL REPORT

Houghton Mifflin
Accounting

Concepts/Procedures/Applications

Advanced Course

DONALD J. GUERRIERI
Norwin Senior High School

F. BARRY HABER
Valparaiso University

WILLIAM B. HOYT
Wilton High School

ROBERT E. TURNER
McNeese State University

Houghton Mifflin Company • BOSTON

Atlanta • Dallas • Geneva, Illinois •
Lawrenceville, New Jersey • Palo Alto • Toronto

Donald J. Guerrieri is a business instructor at Norwin Senior High School, North Huntingdon, Pennsylvania. He has taught accounting at both high school and college levels. He also has experience working for a firm of certified public accountants. Dr. Guerrieri has written numerous articles on the teaching of accounting in the high school classroom. He is a co-author of *Houghton Mifflin Accounting, Concepts/Procedures/Applications, First Year Course*.

F. Barry Haber is Dean of the College of Business Administration at Valparaiso University, Valparaiso, Indiana. In addition to his duties as Dean, he also serves as a professor of accounting. Dr. Haber is a certified public accountant and a member of the American Institute of Certified Public Accountants. He has authored two other textbooks, as well as various articles on accounting. He is a co-author of *Houghton Mifflin Accounting, Concepts/Procedures/Applications, First Year Course*.

William B. Hoyt is department chairperson of the Business Education Department at Wilton High School, Wilton, Connecticut. In addition to teaching accounting, he has been active in the development of microcomputer education for the state of Connecticut. In this endeavor, he has taken part in panel discussions, given workshops, and written on the use of microcomputers in the classroom. He is a co-author of *Houghton Mifflin Accounting, Concepts/Procedures/Applications, First Year Course*.

Robert E. Turner is the Vice-President for Business Affairs at McNeese State University, Lake Charles, Louisiana. Mr. Turner has taught accounting and other business subjects at the high school and college levels. Mr. Turner has appeared on the programs of a number of business education conferences. He is also a frequent speaker at educational seminars around the country. He is a co-author of *Houghton Mifflin Accounting, Concepts/Procedures/Applications, First Year Course*.

Contents

Preface

In the last few years, observers of both high school and college students have noted an increased seriousness toward preparing for future careers. One career area that continues to be popular with students is the field of accounting. The number of students who have selected accounting as a college major has increased steadily over the last several decades.

A glance at the classified ads in local newspapers indicates that there is a wide variety of jobs available to those who have an accounting education. These jobs vary from an entry-level accounting clerk to the comptroller of a corporation. Obviously, there is a great need to prepare both high school and college graduates for the many accounting jobs that are available in today's job market.

There are two basic reasons why students study a second year of accounting at the high school level. First, many students study advanced accounting because they plan to major in accounting in college and they want to be better prepared for their college courses. Second, high school graduates who will seek employment immediately after high school will be more qualified for entry-level accounting jobs if they have completed two years of study in accounting.

Houghton Mifflin Accounting, Concepts/Procedures/Applications, Advanced Course is designed to be used by the college-bound student as well as the vocational student. The textbook covers much of the same material that students will study in beginning college accounting, but at a depth and reading level that are suitable for high school students. The coverage of practical accounting procedures—such as those for uncollectible accounts and plant assets—will help prepare vocational students for the various tasks they will encounter on the job. Finally, the number and variety of problems and reinforcement activities will help all students to assimilate and apply the accounting principles and procedures presented in the textbook.

Course Objectives

Houghton Mifflin Accounting, Concepts/Procedures/Applications, Advanced Course is designed to be used in the second year of a complete two-year financial accounting course.

After studying this textbook and successfully completing activities in the textbook and the related working papers, students will be able to

1. Understand both the basic and advanced principles and procedures that are applied to accounting records kept for profit-oriented businesses.

2. Describe the differences in accounting for the three types of business organization: sole proprietorships, partnerships, and corporations.
3. Describe the accounting systems used by departmentalized, branch, and manufacturing businesses.
4. Use common techniques to analyze and interpret financial statements.
5. Apply accounting procedures to not-for-profit organizations.

Organization of the Textbook

Houghton Mifflin Accounting, Advanced Course is organized in six units of twenty-three chapters. The first unit of the textbook reviews the basic principles and procedures that students learned in their first-year study of accounting. In Chapter 1, students review the first five steps of the accounting cycle as they analyze, journalize, and post various business transactions. In Chapter 2, students review the final five steps of the accounting cycle as they complete the end-of-fiscal-period activities for a merchandising business operated as a sole proprietorship. This unit provides students with a solid base from which to expand their accounting knowledge.

Unit 2 elaborates upon transactions and procedures first introduced in the first-year accounting course. The topics discussed in the seven chapters in this unit include notes, uncollectible accounts receivable, inventory costs, the depreciation and disposal of plant assets, the voucher system, and deferrals and accruals. The final chapter in this unit pulls together all of the topics discussed in the unit and shows how these various financial events are reported in the financial statements of a business.

The first two chapters of Unit 3, Chapters 10 and 11, introduce students to the partnership form of business organization. Students learn how to account for the formation, dissolution, and liquidation of a partnership and how to divide partnership earnings. Chapters 12–14 cover the accounting procedures of a public corporation. Students learn to account for capital and treasury stock, dividends, bonds and interest, and corporate income taxes.

In Unit 4, students learn about the accounting systems and financial statements prepared by departmentalized businesses and businesses with branch operations. Students are also introduced to manufacturing businesses and the procedures followed in a cost accounting system.

The first chapter of Unit 5 discusses the basic accounting principles, concepts, and standards that influence the practice of accounting. By this point in their study of accounting, students should be able to recognize the effect these fundamental concepts, assumptions, principles, and guidelines have on financial reporting. Chapter 20 presents several different methods and techniques that can be used to analyze and interpret the information presented in various financial statements. The last chapter in this unit introduces students to the fourth major financial statement prepared by businesses, the statement of changes in financial position.

The final unit in this textbook, Unit 6, focuses on the accounting system used by not-for-profit organizations. Students learn about the budgeting process, a major tool of a fund accounting system. Students also learn about the financial statements prepared by not-for-profit organizations.

Special Features

Houghton Mifflin Accounting, Advanced Course continues the major features of the first-year textbook. These features are designed to ensure student involvement, achievement, and success in their study of accounting.

Accounting cycle approach. The textbook utilizes a traditional accounting cycle approach to introducing students to new concepts and procedures. This step by step development gives students the guidance they look for and clearly demonstrates the continuity and interrelationships of the accounting process.

Chapter objectives. Clearly defined and stated objectives are included at the beginning of each chapter to help students know exactly what they are expected to learn. The mastery of these objectives is evaluation through end-of-chapter activities, applications, and examinations.

Vocabulary emphasis. The new accounting terms that are defined in each chapter are listed on the first page of the chapter. This list should be used to "preview" the meaning of each term for students. This preview helps students achieve greater understanding and retention of the material in the chapter. End-of-chapter vocabulary reviews reinforce understanding of key terms.

Clear, conversational narrative. The textbook is written in a style that is appropriate for high school students. Simple analogies make concepts meaningful to students. Abundant illustrations and examples guide students through the preparation of accounting records.

Emphasis on transaction analysis. A solid review of the rules of debit and credit and a six-step method for analyzing transactions are presented early in the textbook. Understanding the "why" of transaction analysis ensures that the "how" comes naturally.

Frequent learning reinforcement. "Check Your Learning" reinforcement activities follow major sections in every chapter to help students assume the responsibility for their own learning. "Remember" notes summarize key points and help cement important facts in students' minds.

Chapter summaries. The key points in each chapter are presented, in a numbered list format, at the end of the narrative in each chapter.

Solid end-of-chapter activities. Vocabulary reviews reinforce key accounting terms. Review questions help students expand their understanding of accounting concepts. Decision-making cases teach students to make critical choices. A variety of problems, ranging from easy to challenging, gives students of all abilities the opportunity to gain practical accounting experience and to enjoy success.

Four comprehensive application activities. These applications, at appropriate points in the textbook, require students to integrate new knowledge with learned procedures and to apply their cumulative skills.

Glossary. A glossary of all accounting terms defined within the chapters is included in the back of the textbook.

Complete learning package. A complete package of student and teacher materials is available for the advanced accounting course. This package includes the textbook, student working papers, teacher's edition of the working papers, tests, simulations, and a teacher's manual.

Review of Learning Materials

To augment the proper presentation of basic accounting concepts and to promote greater accuracy of all statements and problem solutions, the content of *Houghton Mifflin Accounting, Concepts/Procedures/Applications, Advanced Course* has been reviewed by the professional accounting firm of Arthur Young & Company. We would especially like to acknowledge the assistance of Bruce E. Bezanson, Paul A. Hassie, Peter Kronenberg, and Gayle Howes of Arthur Young & Company, Boston, who reviewed the entire text and problem solutions. During the review process, the manuscript was checked to ensure that

1. Learning objectives for each chapter are met within the chapter.
2. New terms are correctly defined within each chapter.
3. Accounting material is conceptually and theoretically accurate and current.
4. Figures, tables, and similar examples are technically correct.
5. The questions in each ''Check Your Learning'' activity address material covered within related textbook narrative.
6. Answers to the ''Check Your Learning'' activities are appropriate.
7. Vocabulary, questions, cases, and problems relate to the material covered within the chapter.
8. Terms used within solutions are consistent with those used within the chapter narrative.
9. Vocabulary definitions and answers to questions, cases, and problems are technically correct and complete.

A letter from Arthur Young & Company acknowledging this review is shown on the next page.

Donald J. Guerrieri
F. Barry Haber
William B. Hoyt
Robert E. Turner

ARTHUR YOUNG

One Boston Place
Boston, Massachusetts 02102
Telephone: (617) 723-7570

Houghton Mifflin Company
School Division
One Beacon Street
Boston, MA 02108

We have reviewed the text of the first edition of HOUGHTON
MIFFLIN ACCOUNTING: CONCEPTS/PROCEDURES/APPLICATIONS,
ADVANCED COURSE by Guerrieri, Haber, Hoyt and Turner,
together with the Teacher's Edition of the Chapter Reviews
and Working Papers, for the purpose of ascertaining that the
material is accurate and up to date. Our review, among
other things, was directed at this work's technical and
mathematical accuracy, internal consistency and appropri-
ateness within the framework of basic accounting concepts
and techniques. This review was carried out during the
editing process and before final page proof. We communi-
cated to you our observations, suggestions and recommendations and found that such changes, that were needed, were
made to our satisfaction. In our opinion, the material in
this book is technically and mathematically accurate,
internally consistent and appropriate within the framework
of basic accounting concepts and techniques.

Arthur Young & Company

December 14, 1984

Unit 1
The Accounting Cycle

In the first unit of this textbook, you will review the basic principles and procedures you learned during your first-year study of accounting. You will review the accounting equation and the effect business transactions have on the equation. You will analyze transactions that are typical of a merchandising business operated as a sole proprietorship. You will journalize the transactions in special journals and post the entries to the general and subsidiary ledgers. You will also complete the end-of-period activities for the business.

By the time you have finished studying the chapters in this unit, you will have reviewed the complete accounting cycle. The chapters you study in this unit are listed below.

Chapter
1 Reviewing the First Five Steps of the Accounting Cycle
2 Reviewing the Final Five Steps of the Accounting Cycle

Counting and bagging pennies, U.S. Mint, Denver, Colorado

3

1 Reviewing the First Five Steps of the Accounting Cycle

Accounting, as you remember, is a systematic process of recording and reporting financial events, or transactions. A business transaction is an event that has a direct effect on the operation of a business. When a business transaction occurs, the financial position of the business changes. It is the responsibility of the accounting system to communicate this financial information to a wide variety of people.

In this chapter, you will review the basic accounting equation. You will also review the rules of debit and credit for the various types of accounts. Finally, you will review the first five steps of the accounting cycle.

Learning Objectives

When you have completed this chapter, you should be able to

1. Describe the effect of various business transactions on the basic accounting equation.

2. Record business transactions in special journals and in the general journal.

3. Post business transactions to the general ledger and the subsidiary ledger accounts.

4. Prove the accuracy of the subsidiary ledgers.

5. Prepare a trial balance.

6. Define the accounting terms presented in this chapter.

New Terms

assets / liabilities / owner's equity / basic accounting equation / account / double-entry accounting / debits / credits / revenue / cost of merchandise / expenses / withdrawals / general ledger / accounting cycle / source document / journal / sales journal / cash receipts journal / purchases journal / cash payments journal / general journal / contra account / posting / subsidiary ledger / controlling account / trial balance

Effects of Business Transactions on the Basic Accounting Equation

As you remember, assets are items of value owned or controlled by a business. Assets include such things as cash, accounts receivable, supplies, office equipment, buildings, and land.

The financial claims to these assets are referred to as *equity*. In accounting, there are two types of equity. First, the creditors' claims to the assets of a business are known as liabilities. Second, the owner's claims to these assets are known as owner's equity.

The Basic Accounting Equation

In accounting, total assets are always equal to total equities. The basic accounting equation shows this relationship.

ASSETS = LIABILITIES + OWNER'S EQUITY

As a business begins operations and business transactions are recorded, the financial position of the business changes. These changes are recorded in the business's accounts. An account, then, is a record of the increases and decreases for a specific item; for example, office equipment. Although each transaction affects the balances in two or more accounts, the basic accounting equation always remains in balance.

Double-entry Accounting

In double-entry accounting, every business transaction affects at least two accounts. In double-entry accounting, debits and credits are used to record the increases and decreases in the accounts affected by a business transaction. Each entry has a debit and a credit part. When the entry for a business transaction is completed, the total debit part must equal the total credit part. The rules of debit and credit for asset, liability, and owner's equity accounts are as follows.

ASSETS		=	LIABILITIES		+	OWNER'S EQUITY	
Debit	Credit		Debit	Credit		Debit	Credit
+	−		−	+		−	+
Increase Side	Decrease Side		Decrease Side	Increase Side		Decrease Side	Increase Side
Balance Side				Balance Side			Balance Side

Remember: **The debit and credit parts of each transaction must be equal.**

Asset, liability, and owner's equity accounts are permanent accounts. Their balances are carried forward from one accounting period to the next. A business also has temporary capital accounts. These temporary capital accounts are used to record increases and decreases in owner's equity. Temporary capital accounts include revenue, cost of merchandise, expense, and withdrawals accounts. Revenue is the income earned from the sale of goods and services. The cost of merchandise accounts are those used to record the actual cost to the business of merchandise to be resold to customers. Expenses are the amounts paid for goods and services used to operate a business. Withdrawals are the cash or other assets withdrawn from the business for the owner's personal use.

Temporary accounts are used for one accounting, or fiscal, period. At the end of the period, the balances of these accounts are transferred to the capital account.

The rules of debit and credit for the temporary capital accounts are as follows.

REVENUE		COST OF MERCHANDISE	
Debit	Credit	Debit	Credit
−	+	+	−
Decrease Side	Increase Side	Increase Side	Decrease Side
	Balance Side	Balance Side	

EXPENSE		WITHDRAWALS	
Debit	Credit	Debit	Credit
+	−	+	−
Increase Side	Decrease Side	Increase Side	Decrease Side
Balance Side		Balance Side	

The records of these accounts are maintained in the general ledger.

Remember: **The left side of an account is the debit side. The right side of an account is the credit side. The normal balance side is its increase side.**

The Steps in the Accounting Cycle

The accounting cycle is defined as the activities a business completes within a fiscal period to keep its accounting records in order. The accounting cycle consists of ten steps.

1. Collect and verify data on source documents.
2. Analyze business transactions.
3. Journalize business transactions.
4. Post each entry to the general ledger and subsidiary ledger accounts.
5. Prepare a trial balance.
6. Complete the work sheet.
7. Prepare the financial statements.
8. Journalize and post the adjusting entries.

9. Journalize and post the closing entries.

10. Prepare a post-closing trial balance.

In this chapter, you will review the first five steps of the accounting cycle. Steps six through ten will be reviewed in Chapter 2. In the two chapters, you will be examining the business transactions for Butler's Fishing & Tackle Shop, owned by Scott Butler. This shop is a merchandising business operated as a sole proprietorship. The chart of accounts for Butler's Fishing & Tackle Shop is shown in Figure 1–1.

Figure 1–1.
Chart of Accounts

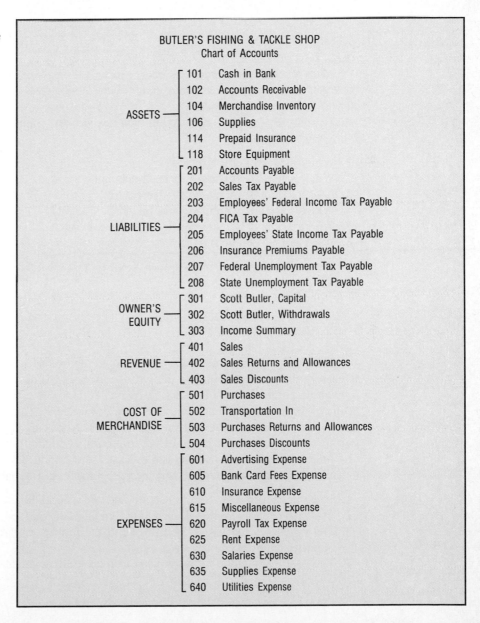

BUTLER'S FISHING & TACKLE SHOP
Chart of Accounts

ASSETS	101	Cash in Bank
	102	Accounts Receivable
	104	Merchandise Inventory
	106	Supplies
	114	Prepaid Insurance
	118	Store Equipment
LIABILITIES	201	Accounts Payable
	202	Sales Tax Payable
	203	Employees' Federal Income Tax Payable
	204	FICA Tax Payable
	205	Employees' State Income Tax Payable
	206	Insurance Premiums Payable
	207	Federal Unemployment Tax Payable
	208	State Unemployment Tax Payable
OWNER'S EQUITY	301	Scott Butler, Capital
	302	Scott Butler, Withdrawals
	303	Income Summary
REVENUE	401	Sales
	402	Sales Returns and Allowances
	403	Sales Discounts
COST OF MERCHANDISE	501	Purchases
	502	Transportation In
	503	Purchases Returns and Allowances
	504	Purchases Discounts
EXPENSES	601	Advertising Expense
	605	Bank Card Fees Expense
	610	Insurance Expense
	615	Miscellaneous Expense
	620	Payroll Tax Expense
	625	Rent Expense
	630	Salaries Expense
	635	Supplies Expense
	640	Utilities Expense

Collecting and Verifying Source Documents

The first step in the accounting cycle is to collect and verify the source documents. As each business transaction occurs, a paper is prepared as evidence that the transaction took place. This paper is called a source document. The accounting clerk begins the accounting cycle by collecting these source documents and checking the accuracy of the information and the calculations. Typical source documents used in a business are invoices, receipts, memorandums, check stubs, and sales slips.

Analyzing Business Transactions

After a source document has been verified, the accounting clerk analyzes the transaction and divides it into its debit and credit parts. This is the second step in the accounting cycle.

To analyze a business transaction, you need to determine the answers to the following six questions.

1. Which accounts are affected?
2. What is the classification of each account?
3. Is each account increased or decreased?
4. Which account is debited, and for what amount?
5. Which account is credited, and for what amount?
6. What is the complete entry?

When reviewing business transactions in this chapter, use this six-step method to analyze each transaction.

Journalizing Business Transactions

The third step in the accounting cycle is to record the debit and credit parts of each business transaction in a journal. A journal is a chronological record of a business's transactions. Butler's Fishing & Tackle Shop is a merchandising business that has a large number of business transactions. To operate efficiently, Scott Butler decided to record the transactions in special journals. A *special journal* is a multicolumn journal used to record a specific type of transaction. The four special journals used by Butler's are the sales journal, the cash receipts journal, the purchases journal, and the cash payments journal.

1. The sales journal is used to record sales of merchandise on account.
2. The cash receipts journal is used to record all cash received by the business.
3. The purchases journal is used to record the purchase of merchandise and other items on account.
4. The cash payments journal is used to record all payments of cash.

Butler's Fishing & Tackle Shop also has a general journal to record transactions not appropriate for the special journals.

Before reading further, do the following activity to check your understanding of the material you have just studied.

Check Your Learning

Write your answers to the following questions on a sheet of notebook paper.

1. The revenue account Sales normally has a __?__ balance.
2. Accounts Receivable is classified as a(n) __?__ account.
3. Assets = Liabilities + Owner's Equity is referred to as the __?__
4. Creditors' claims to the assets of a business are called __?__.
5. A __?__ is a chronological record of a business's transactions.

Compare your answers to those in the answers section. Re-read the preceding part of the chapter to find the correct answers to any questions you may have missed.

Journalizing Sales on Account

A **sales journal** is a special journal used only to record the sale of merchandise on account. The sales journal for Butler's Fishing & Tackle Shop has three special amount columns: Accounts Receivable Debit, Sales Tax Payable Credit, and Sales Credit. The source document for an entry in the sales journal is a sales slip.

Let's now look at a transaction and see how it is recorded in the sales journal.

December 2: *Sold merchandise on account to John Sawyer for $159.00 plus $11.13 sales tax, Sales Slip 63.*

In this transaction, Accounts Receivable is being increased, Sales Tax Payable is being increased, and Sales is being increased. To journalize this transaction, follow these steps.

1. Enter the sales slip date in the Date column.
2. Enter the sales slip number in the Sales Slip No. column.
3. Enter the name of the charge customer in the Customer's Account Debited column.
4. Enter the total amount to be received in the Accounts Receivable Debit column.
5. Enter the amount of sales tax in the Sales Tax Payable Credit column.
6. Enter the total selling price of the merchandise in the Sales Credit column.

The sales journal entry for this transaction is shown in Figure 1–2 on page 10. All sales of merchandise on account are journalized in the same manner.

Remember: Always journalize from left to right.

	DATE	SALES SLIP NO.	CUSTOMER'S ACCOUNT DEBITED	POST. REF.	ACCOUNTS RECEIVABLE DEBIT	SALES TAX PAYABLE CREDIT	SALES CREDIT	
1	19-- Dec. 2	63	John Sawyer		170 13	11 13	159 00	1
2	1	2	3		4	5	6	2

Figure 1–2. Journalizing a Sale on Account

Special journals simplify the journalizing and posting process. As you have seen, only one line was needed to record the December 2 entry in the sales journal. Special amount columns are provided to record debits and credits to frequently used accounts. The totals of these special amount columns are posted to the general ledger accounts rather than the individual entries. Therefore, at the end of each month, the special journals are totaled, proved, and ruled. To do this, follow these steps.

$ 242.40
+3,462.91
$3,705.31

1. Draw a single rule across all amount columns.
2. Pencil foot the amount columns.
3. Test for the equality of debits and credits. The total of the debit column ($3,705.31) must equal the total of the credit columns.
4. On the line below the single rule, enter the date the journal is being totaled in the Date column and the word "Totals" in the Customer's Account Debited column.
5. Enter the column totals just below the pencil footings.
6. Double rule the amount columns.

These same steps would be followed for any special journal. The totaled and ruled sales journal is shown in Figure 1–3.

	DATE	SALES SLIP NO.	CUSTOMER'S ACCOUNT DEBITED	POST. REF.	ACCOUNTS RECEIVABLE DEBIT	SALES TAX PAYABLE CREDIT	SALES CREDIT	
1	19-- Dec. 2	63	John Sawyer		170 13	11 13	159 00	1
2	4	64	Judy Drotos		90 95	5 95	85 00	2
3	7	65	Pat Porter		39 05	2 55	36 50	3
4	8	66	John Sawyer		32 04	2 09	29 95	4
5	11	67	Jose Mingles		122 51	8 01	114 50	5
9	27	71	John Sawyer		38 46	2 51	35 95	9
10	31		Totals		3705 31	242 40	3462 91	10

Figure 1–3. Completed Sales Journal

Remember: In the special journals, single and double rules are drawn across the amount columns only.

Journalizing Cash Receipts

The **cash receipts journal** is a special journal used to record all transactions in which cash is received. The number of special amount columns varies, depending upon a business's needs. However, every transaction recorded in the cash receipts journal requires a debit to the Cash in Bank account. The cash receipts journal, therefore, always contains a Cash in Bank Debit column. The cash receipts journal, in addition to the other special amount columns, also contains a General Credit column. This column is used to record amounts that cannot be entered in a special amount column. The source documents for cash receipts journal entries include receipts and cash register tapes.

The cash receipts journal used by Butler's Fishing & Tackle Shop is shown in Figure 1–4. Let's look at several transactions recorded in the journal.

December 3: *Received $45.00 cash from the Robins Company for an old adding machine, Receipt 205.*

In this transaction, Butler's sold an old adding machine to another business for $45.00 cash. Cash in Bank is being increased and Store Equipment is being decreased. The date and number of the source document are entered in the first two columns. The name of the account being credited is written in the Account Title column. Since there is no special amount column for store equipment, the amount of the decrease to the Store Equipment account is entered in the General Credit column. The amount of cash received is entered in the Cash in Bank Debit column.

December 4: *Received $50.00 from Mark Fowlings on account, Receipt 206.*

In this transaction, Butler's is receiving cash from a charge customer. Cash in Bank is being increased and Accounts Receivable is being decreased. The debit and credit amounts are entered in the special amount columns.

December 5: *Had cash sales of $1,529.80, plus sales tax of $107.09, Tape 107.*

The cash sales for the week were $1,529.80. The sales tax collected was $107.09. The total amount of cash received was $1,636.89. Notice that a check mark is entered in the Posting Reference column.

CASH RECEIPTS JOURNAL PAGE 13

	DATE	DOC. NO.	ACCOUNT TITLE	POST. REF.	GENERAL CREDIT	ACCOUNTS RECEIVABLE CREDIT	SALES TAX PAYABLE CREDIT	SALES CREDIT	SALES DISCOUNTS DEBIT	CASH IN BANK DEBIT	
1	Dec. 3	R205	Store Equipment		45 00					45 00	1
2	4	R206	Mark Fowlings			50 00				50 00	2
3	5	T107	Cash Sales	✓			107 09	1529 80		1636 89	3
4	5	T107	Bank Card Sales	✓			44 22	631 70		675 92	4
5	8	R207	John Sawyer			391 12			3 91	387 21	5
23	31		Totals		3232 28	1357 40	993 28	14189 66	13 57	19759 05	23

Figure 1–4. The Cash Receipts Journal

December 5: Recorded bank card sales of $631.70 plus $44.22 sales tax, Tape 107.

Bank card sales are considered to be a form of cash sales. The transaction, therefore, is recorded in the same way cash sales are recorded.

December 8: Received $387.21 from John Sawyer in payment of Sales Slip 53 for $391.12, less discount of $3.91, Receipt 207.

Some charge customers of Butler's are allowed a 1% discount if they pay the amounts owed within 10 days. For example, John Sawyer owes $391.12, but he is taking advantage of a sales discount of $3.91. Therefore, the total amount of cash received is $387.21.

At the end of the month, the cash receipts journal is totaled, proved, and ruled as shown in Figure 1–4.

Remember: **When a journal is totaled, the total of the debit columns of a special journal must equal the total of the credit columns.**

Journalizing Purchases on Account

Transactions in which items are bought on account are recorded in the **purchases journal**. Because items are being purchased on account, every transaction recorded in the purchases journal results in a credit to Accounts Payable. Butler's purchases journal also has a special amount column for recording purchases of merchandise for resale. The General columns are used to record purchases of all items other than merchandise.

Let's now look at two common transactions that would be recorded in the purchases journal. These transactions are illustrated in Figure 1–5. Remember to use the six-step method to analyze each transaction.

December 4: Received Invoice 2138 from Tackle Plus for merchandise purchased on account, $675.49.

In this transaction, merchandise that will be resold is being purchased. Purchases is being increased and is debited for $675.49. Accounts Payable is being increased and is credited for $675.49. These amounts are recorded in the two special amount columns.

	DATE	INVOICE NO.	CREDITOR'S ACCOUNT CREDITED	POST. REF.	ACCOUNTS PAYABLE CREDIT	PURCHASES DEBIT	GENERAL ACCOUNT DEBITED	POST. REF.	DEBIT	
PURCHASES JOURNAL									PAGE 12	
1	Dec. 4	2138	Tackle Plus		675 49	675 49				1
2	6	148	Babson Supply Co.		184 49		Supplies		184 49	2
24	31		Totals		9000 95	8391 45			609 50	24

Figure 1–5. The Purchases Journal

December 6: *Received Invoice 148 from Babson Supply Company for supplies bought on account, $184.49.*

In this transaction, supplies that will be used by the business are being purchased. Supplies is being increased and is debited for $184.49. Accounts Payable is being increased and is credited for $184.49. Since this is not a purchase of merchandise, the amount is entered in the General Debit column and the account title is entered in the General Account Debited column.

At the end of the month, the purchases journal is totaled, proved, and ruled as shown in Figure 1–5.

Journalizing Cash Payments

Transactions in which cash is paid out are recorded in the cash payments journal. Since every transaction entered in the journal involves a payment of cash, the Cash in Bank account will always be credited. There is, therefore, a Cash in Bank Credit column. Special amount columns are also provided in Butler's journal for debits to Accounts Payable and credits to Purchases Discounts. The journal also has a General Debit and a General Credit column. The source document for each transaction recorded in the cash payments journal is the check stub.

Butler's cash payments journal is shown in Figure 1–6.

Some common business transactions that are recorded in the cash payments journal are as follows.

December 3: *Paid $750.00 to Ashby Realty for the December rent, Check 4932.*

In this transaction, Rent Expense is being increased; it is debited for $750.00. Since there is no special column, the amount is entered in the General Debit column. Cash in Bank is being decreased; it is credited for $750.00.

CASH PAYMENTS JOURNAL   PAGE 14

DATE	CHK. NO.	ACCOUNT DEBITED	POST. REF.	GENERAL DEBIT	GENERAL CREDIT	ACCOUNTS PAYABLE DEBIT	PURCHASES DISCOUNTS CREDIT	CASH IN BANK CREDIT
Dec. 3	4932	Rent Expense		750 00				750 00
5	4933	G&S Corporation				943 27	9 43	933 84
6	4934	Store Equipment		79 85				79 85
7	4935	Purchases		741 63				741 63
12	4938	Salaries Expense		1481 00				1175 35
		Emp. Fed Inc Tax Payable			124 00			
		FICA Tax Payable			104 41			
		Emp State Inc Tax Payable			56 24			
		Insurance Prem Payable			21 00			
31		Totals		9494 62	611 30	6855 13	142 66	15595 79

Figure 1–6. The Cash Payments Journal

December 5: *Paid $933.84 to G & S Corporation for merchandise purchased on account, $943.27, less a discount of $9.43, Check 4933.*

In this transaction, a payment is being made to one of Butler's creditors. Accounts Payable is being decreased and is debited for $943.27, the total amount owed. Because Butler's is paying the invoice within the discount period, it may deduct a discount of $9.43. That amount is entered in the Purchases Discounts Credit column. Cash in Bank is being decreased and is credited for $933.84, the total amount of cash actually paid out.

December 6: *Purchased a new printing calculator for use in the shop, $79.85, Check 4934.*

Store Equipment is being increased and is, therefore, debited for $79.85. Cash in Bank is being decreased; it is credited for $79.85.

December 7: *Purchased merchandise from Fishing Hut for $741.63 cash, Check 4935.*

This transaction is not recorded in the purchases journal because it is a *cash* purchase of merchandise. However, the Purchases account is debited for $741.63. Since there is no special column for purchases, that amount is entered in the General Debit column. Cash in Bank is credited for $741.63.

December 12: *Paid the payroll of $1,481.00 (gross earnings) for the pay period. Amounts withheld include employees' federal income tax, $124.00; FICA tax, $104.41; employees' state income tax, $56.24; insurance premium, $21.00, Check 4938.*

The total amount earned by employees is debited to Salary Expense. Since it cannot be entered in a special column, the $1,481.00 is entered in the General Debit column. Cash in Bank is credited for the amount actually paid, $1,175.35. The deductions become liabilities of the business. Each liability is recorded on a separate line in the General Credit column.

At the end of the month, the cash payments journal is totaled, proved, and ruled as shown in Figure 1–6.

Journalizing General Journal Transactions

A business designs its special journals to handle particular kinds of transactions that occur frequently. Any transaction that cannot be recorded in a special journal is recorded in the general journal. The **general journal** is a two-column journal in which all types of transactions can be recorded. Examples of transactions that would be recorded in the general journal include correcting entries and transactions involving sales returns and allowances, purchases returns and allowances, bank service charges, and the recording of employer's payroll taxes.

Let's examine some of these transactions. The entries for these transactions are illustrated in Figure 1–7.

December 4: *Granted credit to Jose Mingles, $43.94, for merchandise of $41.00 returned, plus sales tax of $2.94, Credit Memo 24.*

	DATE	DESCRIPTION	POST. REF.	DEBIT	CREDIT	
1	Dec. 4	Sales Returns and Allowances		41 00		1
2		Sales Tax Payable		2 94		2
3		Accts. Receivable/Jose Mingles	/		43 94	3
4		Credit Memo 24				4
5	12	Accts. Pay./Parker's Fishing & Tackle	/	61 49		5
6		Purch. Returns and Allowances			61 49	6
7		Debit Memo 37				7
8	12	Payroll Tax Expense		156 25		8
9		FICA Tax Payable			104 41	9
10		State Unemploy. Tax Payable			39 99	10
11		Fed. Unemploy. Tax Payable			11 85	11
12		Payroll 12/12				12

Figure 1–7. Recording Transactions in the General Journal

Sales Returns and Allowances is a contra revenue account and is used to record merchandise returned by customers. A **contra account** is an account whose balance is a decrease to another account's balance. Sales Returns and Allowances has a normal debit balance. The account is being increased, so it is debited for $41.00, the original sales price of the merchandise. Sales Tax Payable is also debited for $2.94 because this amount is no longer owed to the state. Accounts Receivable and Jose Mingles' account are credited for $43.94, since Butler's no longer expects to receive this amount. A diagonal line is entered in the Posting Reference column. This line indicates that the amount will be posted to two accounts.

December 12: *Issued Debit Memo 37 for $61.49 to Parker's Fishing & Tackle for damaged merchandise returned to them.*

Accounts Payable and Parker's Fishing & Tackle account are being decreased; they are debited for $61.49. Purchases Returns and Allowances is a contra cost account and has a normal credit balance. Since Butler's is returning merchandise for credit and therefore no longer owes the money, Purchases Returns and Allowances is credited for $61.49.

December 12: *Recorded the employer's payroll taxes of FICA tax, $104.41; state unemployment taxes, $39.99; and federal unemployment taxes, $11.85.*

The taxes incurred by the employer during every payroll period are business expenses. The employer must pay FICA taxes at the same rate as paid by the employees (currently 7.05% of gross earnings). The employer must also pay both state and federal unemployment taxes. The state rate is 2.7% of gross earnings and the federal rate is .8% of gross earnings. The total of the three taxes is the total employer's payroll tax expense for the pay period. Butler's gross payroll for the period was $1,481.00. Total payroll taxes are $156.25.

Payroll Tax Expense is debited for $156.25. The payroll taxes are liabilities since they will be paid some time in the future. Each payroll liability account is credited for the amounts shown in Figure 1–7.

Before reading further, do the following activity to check your understanding of journalizing business transactions.

Check Your Learning

On a sheet of notebook paper, write your answers to the following questions.

1. All the transactions recorded in the sales journal require a debit to which account?
2. In which special journal are bank card sales recorded?
3. If merchandise is purchased on account, what accounts are debited and credited?
4. What is the source document for a transaction recorded in the cash payments journal?
5. Name two types of entries that would be recorded in the general journal.

Compare your answers to those in the answers section. Re-read the preceding part of the chapter to find the correct answers to any questions you may have missed.

Posting

The fourth step in the accounting cycle is posting. **Posting** is the process of transferring amounts from a journal to ledger accounts. In the accounting system used by Butler's Fishing & Tackle Shop, posting takes several forms:

1. Entries are posted from the special journals to the accounts in the subsidiary ledgers.
2. Amounts that cannot be posted as part of a special amount column total are individually posted to the appropriate general ledger accounts.
3. The totals of the special amount columns of the special journals are posted to the general ledger accounts named in the column headings.

Posting to the Subsidiary Ledgers

A **subsidiary ledger** is a ledger that is summarized in a controlling account in the general ledger. A **controlling account** is an account whose balance must equal the total of the balances in a subsidiary ledger. Butler's Fishing and Tackle Shop has two subsidiary ledgers. The accounts receivable subsidiary ledger contains accounts for all of Butler's charge customers. Accounts Receivable is the controlling account for the accounts receivable subsidiary ledger. The accounts payable subsidiary ledger contains accounts for all of Butler's creditors. Accounts Payable is the controlling account for the subsidiary ledger.

Amounts are posted to the subsidiary ledgers on a daily basis. Let's look at how a transaction in the sales journal is posted to an account in the accounts receivable subsidiary ledger. To post the December 2 transaction to John Sawyer's account, follow these steps.

1. Enter the date of the transaction listed in the journal in the Date column of the customer's account.
2. Enter the letter and page number of the journal on which the transaction was recorded in the Posting Reference column of the account. Use the letter "S" for the sales journal.
3. In the Debit column of the subsidiary ledger account, enter the amount recorded in the Accounts Receivable Debit column of the journal.
4. Compute the new balance and enter it in the Balance column.
5. Return to the sales journal and enter a check mark in the Posting Reference column.

$391.12
+170.13
———
$561.25

Remember: Always post from left to right.

The posting of the transaction is shown in Figure 1–8. All posting from a special journal to a subsidiary ledger account is done in a similar manner.

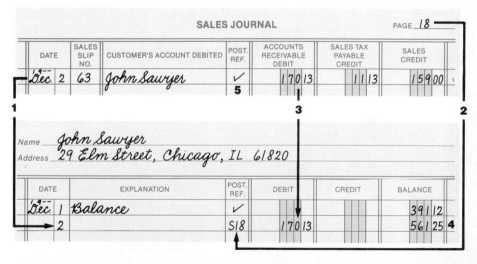

Figure 1–8. Posting from the Sales Journal to the Accounts Receivable Subsidiary Ledger

Transactions entered in the Accounts Receivable Credit column of the cash receipts journal are also posted to customers' accounts in the accounts receivable subsidiary ledger. For example, the December 4 cash receipt from Mark Fowlings would be posted as shown in Figure 1–9 on page 18. Notice that the same five steps are followed. However, the amount entered in the Accounts Receivable Credit column is recorded in the Credit column of the customer's account.

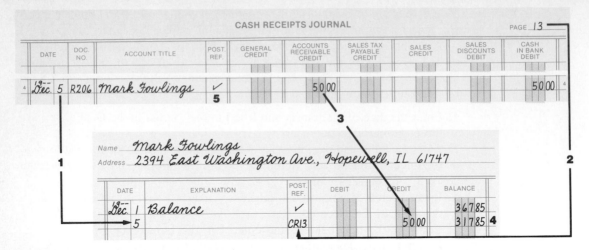

Figure 1-9. Posting from the Cash Receipts Journal to the Accounts Receivable Subsidiary Ledger

The amounts entered in the Accounts Payable Credit column of the purchases journal are posted daily to creditors' accounts in the accounts payable subsidiary ledger. The amounts entered in the Accounts Payable Debit column of the cash payments journal are posted daily to the creditors' accounts in the accounts payable subsidiary ledger. In both cases, the five-step procedure explained earlier is followed.

Before reading further, do the following activity to check your understanding of posting to the subsidiary ledger.

Check Your Learning

Write your answers to the following questions on a separate sheet of notebook paper.

1. What is a controlling account?
2. Name the two subsidiary ledgers.
3. How often are amounts posted to the subsidiary ledgers?

Compare your answers to those in the answers section. Re-read the preceding part of the chapter to find the correct answers to any questions you may have missed.

Posting to the General Ledger

As mentioned earlier, amounts that cannot be posted as part of a column total are posted individually to the general ledger accounts during the month. Such amounts are recorded in the General Debit and General Credit columns of the cash receipts, purchases, and cash payments journals.

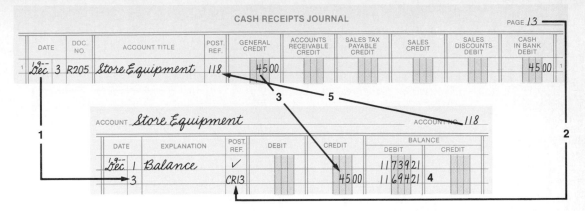

Figure 1–10. Posting from a Special Journal to the General Ledger

For example, the first transaction recorded in the cash receipts journal must be posted to the Store Equipment account in the general ledger. To do this, follow these steps.

1. Enter the date of the transaction listed in the journal in the Date column of the general ledger account.
2. Enter the letter and page number of the journal entry in the Posting Reference column of the account.
3. In the Credit column of the ledger account, record the amount entered in the General Credit column of the journal.
4. Compute and enter the new account balance.
5. Return to the journal and enter the ledger account number in the Posting Reference column.

The posting of this transaction is illustrated in Figure 1–10. This same procedure should be followed when posting an amount from the General Debit or General Credit column of any special journal.

Remember: When computing a new account balance, debit amounts are added to accounts having a normal debit balance. Credit amounts are subtracted from accounts with a normal debit balance. Likewise, credit amounts are added to and debit amounts are subtracted from accounts with a normal credit balance.

The general journal does not have any special amount columns. Each entry recorded in the general journal must be posted individually to the general ledger and the subsidiary ledgers. For example, the December 4 entry recorded earlier is posted as shown in Figure 1–11 on page 20.

Notice that the $43.94 amount was posted to both the Accounts Receivable account and to Jose Mingles' account in the accounts receivable subsidiary ledger. The Accounts Receivable account number and the check mark arc placed on either side of the diagonal line in the Posting Reference column of the general journal.

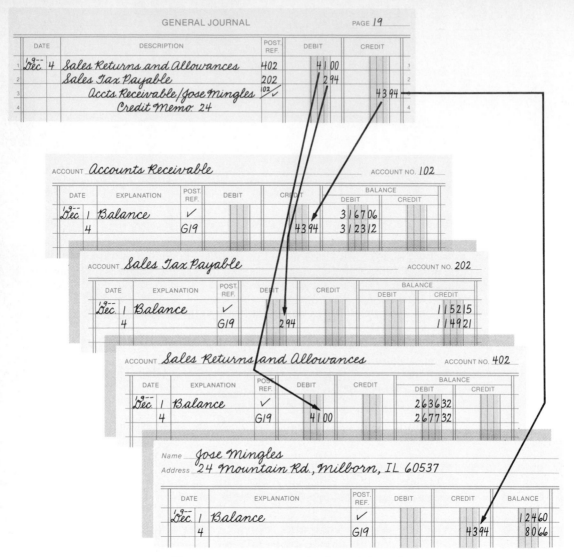

Figure 1–11. Posting from the General Journal

Posting Column Totals

As mentioned earlier, the special journals save time in posting since the totals of the special amount columns are posted to the appropriate general ledger accounts. At the end of the month, after the special journal has been totaled, proved, and ruled, the column totals are posted.

For example, to post the total of the Accounts Receivable Debit column of the sales journal to the ledger account, follow these steps.

1. In the Date column of the ledger account, enter the date.
2. Enter the letter and page number of the journal in the Posting Reference column of the general ledger account.

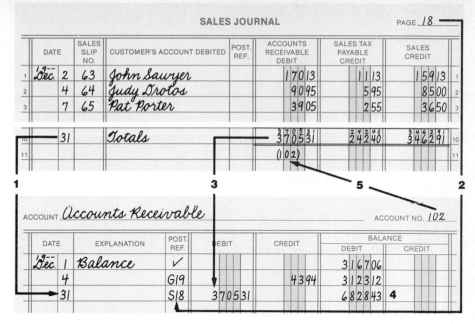

Figure 1–12. Posting Column Totals to the General Ledger

3. In the Debit column of the account, enter the total of the Accounts Receivable Debit column of the sales journal.

4. Compute the new balance and enter it in the correct Balance column.

5. Return to the journal and enter the number of the general ledger account—in parentheses—below the double rule in the column.

The posting of the column total is shown in Figure 1–12. From the sales journal, column totals will also be posted to the Sales Tax Payable and Sales accounts in the general ledger. The same procedure would be followed to post those column totals—and the column totals of any other special journal.

Remember: At the end of the month, the totals of the special amount columns of a special journal are posted to the general ledger accounts named in the column headings.

The entries in the General Debit and General Credit columns of the special journals are posted individually to the ledger accounts. As a result, the totals of these columns are *not* posted. To indicate that the totals of the General Debit and General Credit columns are not posted, check marks are placed in parentheses below the double rules in these columns. An example of this is shown in the cash receipts journal in Figure 1–13 on page 22.

Remember: After posting the total of a special amount column to a general ledger account, place the number of the account in parentheses below the double rule in the column. Place a check mark below the double rule under any column total that is not posted to a general ledger account.

DATE	DOC. NO.	ACCOUNT TITLE	POST. REF.	GENERAL CREDIT	ACCOUNTS RECEIVABLE CREDIT	SALES TAX PAYABLE CREDIT	SALES CREDIT	SALES DISCOUNTS DEBIT	CASH IN BANK DEBIT	
31		Totals		323228	135740	99328	1418966	1357	1975905	23
				(✓)	(102)	(202)	(401)	(403)	(101)	24

Figure 1–13. Posting References in the Cash Receipts Journal

Proving the Accuracy of the Subsidiary Ledgers

At the end of the month, after all posting has been completed, the balances of the accounts in a subsidiary ledger should equal the balance of its controlling account. To prove the accuracy of the subsidiary ledgers, a schedule of accounts receivable and a schedule of accounts payable are prepared.

Butler's schedule of accounts receivable for December is shown in Figure 1–14. As you can see, the schedule lists each customer, the balance of the customer's account, and the total amount to be received from all customers. The schedule of accounts payable is prepared in a similar manner.

Butler's Fishing + Tackle Shop
Schedule of Accounts Receivable
December 31, 19--

Judy Drotos	28391
Mark Fowlings	176184
Jose Mingles	243902
Pat Porter	57584
John Sawyer	41042
Total Accounts Receivable	547103

ACCOUNT Accounts Receivable   ACCOUNT NO. 102

DATE	EXPLANATION	POST. REF.	DEBIT	CREDIT	BALANCE DEBIT	BALANCE CREDIT
19-- Dec. 1	Balance	✓			316706	
4		G19		4394	312312	
31		S18	370531		682843	
31		CR13		135740	547103	

Figure 1–14. Schedule of Accounts Receivable

Remember: All accounts are listed—in alphabetical order—on the schedule of accounts receivable and schedule of accounts payable, even those with zero balances.

Preparing the Trial Balance

The fifth step in the accounting cycle is the preparation of the trial balance. A **trial balance** is prepared to prove the equality of debits and credits in the general ledger. It can be prepared at any time if posting has been completed.

At the end of a fiscal period, a trial balance is normally prepared using the first two amount columns of a work sheet. The accounts are listed in the trial balance in the order in which they appear in the chart of accounts. The balance of each account is entered in either the Trial Balance Debit or Credit column. After all balances have been entered, the debit and credit columns are totaled, proved, and ruled.

Remember: All general ledger accounts are listed in the trial balance, even if those accounts have a zero balance.

Butler's Fishing & Tackle Shop uses a ten-column work sheet. The Trial Balance section of the work sheet for the year ended December 31 is shown in Figure 1–15 on page 24.

Both the Debit and Credit columns of the Trial Balance section of the work sheet total $253,060.47. The general ledger is, therefore, proved and the amount columns are double ruled.

Accounting Tip

Dollar signs are not used when entering dollar amounts in journals or other accounting stationery. A poorly made dollar sign could be mistaken for a number, which could easily result in an error. Commas and decimal points also are not used when entering dollar amounts. The vertical lines in the amount columns take the place of commas and decimals.

Butler's Fishing & Tackle Shop
Work Sheet
For the Year Ended December 31, 19--

	ACCOUNT NAME	TRIAL BALANCE	
		DEBIT	CREDIT
1	Cash in Bank	17 021 65	
2	Accounts Receivable	5 471 03	
3	Merch. Inventory	26 347 91	
4	Supplies	3 148 60	
5	Prepaid Insurance	1 200 00	
6	Equipment	12 541 63	
7	Accounts Payable		5 271 80
8	Sales Tax Payable		1 235 68
9	Emp. Fed. Inc. Tax Pay.		248 00
10	FICA Tax Payable		417 64
11	Emp. State Inc. Tax Pay.		337 44
12	Insurance Prem. Pay.		42 00
13	Fed. Unempl. Tax Pay.		71 10
14	State Unempl. Tax Pay.		239 94
15	Scott Butler, Capital		30 445 76
16	Scott Butler, Withdr.	10 000 00	
17	Income Summary		
18	Sales		211 830 88
19	Sales Returns & Allow.	2 781 97	
20	Sales Discounts	1 364 67	
21	Purchases	100 697 40	
22	Transportation In	7 048 82	
23	Purchases Ret. & Allow.		1 208 37
24	Purchases Discounts		1 711 86
25	Advertising Expense	8 400 00	
26	Bank Card Fees Exp.	1 618 18	
27	Insurance Expense		
28	Miscellaneous Exp.	2 072 92	
29	Rent Expense	9 000 00	
30	Payroll Tax Expense	4 024 05	
31	Salaries Expense	38 142 64	
32	Supplies Expense		
33	Utilities Expense	2 179 00	
34		253 060 47	253 060 47

Figure 1–15.
Trial Balance
Section of the
Work Sheet

Summary of Key Points

1. The relationship between total assets and total equities is shown in the basic accounting equation: ASSETS = LIABILITIES + OWNER'S EQUITY. Assets are the items of value owned by a business. Liabilities are the debts of a business. Owner's equity is the owner's claims to the assets of a business.

2. In double-entry accounting, each business transaction affects at least two general ledger accounts.

3. The accounting cycle is the activities a business completes to keep its accounting records in an orderly fashion.

4. Special journals are multicolumn journals used to record specific types of business transactions.

5. A sales journal is used to record all sales of merchandise on account.

6. The cash receipts journal is used to record all cash received by the business.

7. The purchases journal is used to record all purchases on account made by a merchandising business.

8. The cash payments journal is used to record all transactions in which cash is paid out.

9. All transactions that cannot be recorded in the special journals are entered in the general journal.

10. The totals of the special amount columns of the special journals are posted at the end of the month to the general ledger accounts named in the column headings.

11. A subsidiary ledger is a ledger that is summarized in a controlling account in the general ledger. The accounts receivable subsidiary ledger contains accounts for a business's charge customers. The accounts payable subsidiary ledger contains accounts for a business's creditors.

12. The trial balance is prepared to prove the equality of debits and credits in the general ledger. The trial balance includes all accounts listed in the chart of accounts.

Review and Applications

Reviewing Your Accounting Vocabulary

In your own words, write the definition of each of the following accounting terms. Use complete sentences for your definitions.

account	credits	owner's equity
accounting cycle	debits	posting
assets	double-entry	purchases journal
basic accounting equation	accounting	revenue
cash payments journal	expenses	sales journal
cash receipts journal	general journal	source document
contra account	general ledger	subsidiary ledger
controlling account	journal	trial balance
cost of merchandise	liabilities	withdrawals

Reviewing Your Accounting Knowledge

1. Explain why liabilities and owner's equity are both considered to be equity.
2. What is the basic accounting equation?
3. What are the first five steps in the accounting cycle?
4. What are the six classifications of accounts found in a chart of accounts of a merchandising business?
5. What six questions can be used to analyze business transactions?
6. Name and describe four special journals.
7. Why must a general journal be used with the special journals?
8. What is a contra account?
9. Describe the steps for totaling, proving, and ruling a special journal.
10. Why is a schedule of accounts receivable prepared?
11. Why is a trial balance prepared?

Improving Your Decision-making Skills

Janet Kowalski, an accounting clerk for a merchandising store, does not understand how special journals can save time in posting. She feels that the general journal alone is fine even for businesses with larger sales volumes. Explain to Janet how the use of special journals can save time in posting.

Applying Accounting Procedures

Problem 1–1

The accounts at the top of page 27 are listed in the chart of accounts for the Milton Lamp Company.

Cash in Bank	Sales Returns and	Purchases Discounts
Salaries Expense	Allowances	Joan Murphy,
Sales Tax Payable	Transportation In	Withdrawals
Purchases	Accounts Payable	Sales
Prepaid Insurance	Bank Card Fees	Accounts Receivable
Merchandise Inventory	Expense	Purchases Returns
		and Allowances

Instructions: For each ledger account listed, indicate the classification of the account and its normal balance side. Use a form similar to the one shown below.

Account	Classification	Normal Balance
Cash in Bank	Asset	Debit

Problem 1–2

The Brotherton Music Shop uses special journals to record its transactions. The business had the following transactions during January.

Jan.
1 Sold sheet music on account to L. D. Langdon, $61.45 plus sales tax of $4.30, Sales Slip 1344.

2 Issued Check 416 to Longbrook Realty Company for the rent, $800.00.

5 Issued Credit Memo 16 for $14.50 to David Ifkovic, a charge customer, for merchandise returned. The amount includes $13.85 worth of merchandise plus sales tax of $.65.

8 Purchased merchandise on account from P. D. Springtime, $124.00, Invoice 904.

9 Harry Peterson sent a check for $100.00 to apply on account, Receipt 307.

11 Discovered that $15.00 worth of supplies bought on account in December from Executive Business Machines was incorrectly journalized and posted to the Purchases account, Memorandum 19.

15 Bought advertising on account from *The Evening Post,* $45.00, Invoice 349.

18 Recorded cash sales of $428.80 plus $30.02 sales tax, Tape 84.

18 Recorded bank card sales of $194.53 plus sales tax of $13.62, Tape 84.

23 The owner, Carl Porston, withdrew $500.00 for his personal use, Check 417.

26 Granted a $71.65 credit to Sandra Perkins for merchandise costing $67.25 returned by her plus sales tax of $4.40, Credit Memo 17.

27 Purchased merchandise for $1,496.50 cash, Check 418.

31 Recorded the bank card fee of $76.50, January bank statement.

31 Sold merchandise on account to Jennifer Paine, $18.50 plus sales tax of $1.30, Sales Slip 1345.

Instructions:

(1) Record the previous transactions in the sales journal, page 5; the cash receipts journal, page 7; the purchases journal, page 6; the cash payments journal, page 8; and the general journal, page 4.

(2) Total, prove, and rule the special journals.

Problem 1–3

The All-State Sport Shop uses special journals and subsidiary ledgers to record its business transactions. The general ledger and the subsidiary ledgers for the All-State Sport Shop are included in the working papers accompanying this textbook. The account balances have already been recorded.

The All-State Sport Shop had the following transactions during November.

Nov. 1 Issued Check 110 for $500.00 to Belmont Realty for the rent.
       2 Received a check for $28.00 from Carrie Laine to apply on her account, Receipt 107.
       4 Bought office supplies for cash, $215.59, Check 111.
       4 Returned $58.00 in merchandise to a creditor, Par Manufacturing, Debit Memo 48.
       9 Paid Townhouse, Inc., $149.49 for Invoice 401 for $151.00 less a discount of $1.51, Check 112.
      10 Sold merchandise on account to Judy Matinez, $79.95 plus sales tax of $5.60, Sales Slip 134.
      12 Received Invoice 4578 from T & N Supply for store equipment bought on account, $349.00.
      15 Sold store equipment for $40.00 cash, Receipt 108.
      15 Paid the weekly payroll of $1,495.59, Check 113. The amounts withheld include: employees' federal income taxes, $215.50, FICA taxes, $105.44; employees' state income taxes, $134.92.
      15 Recorded the employer's payroll taxes: FICA taxes, $105.44; state unemployment taxes, $40.38; federal unemployment taxes, $10.47, Memorandum 51.
      18 Sold merchandise on account to Max Stein, $121.50 plus sales tax of $8.50, Sales Slip 135.
      19 Sent Check 114 for $50.00 to the Baker Corp. to apply on account.
      22 Recorded cash sales of $132.93 plus sales tax of $2.24, Tape 86.
      24 Bought office supplies on account from McLaw & Sons for $285.40, Invoice 5896.
      26 Granted Lee Sonya an allowance of $20.00 for damaged merchandise purchased on account, Credit Memo 18.
      26 Sold supplies, as an accommodation, to Burn's Music Store for $20.00 cash, Receipt 109.
      29 Paid the telephone bill of $145.58, Check 115.
      29 Paid $600.00 for a three-month insurance policy, Check 116.
      30 Recorded the bank service charge of $5.00, November bank statement.

30 Purchased merchandise on account from Uptown Sports for $864.00, Invoice 30665.

Instructions:

(1) Record November's transactions in the special journals and in the general journal. Use these page numbers: sales journal, page 9; cash receipts journal, page 8; purchases journal, page 7; cash payments journal, page 12; and general journal, page 14.

(2) Post transactions to the subsidiary ledgers on a daily basis.

(3) Post transactions in the General columns of the cash receipts, purchases, cash payments, and general journals to the general ledger on a daily basis.

(4) Total, prove, and rule the special journals.

(5) Post the column totals of the special journals to the general ledger. Use the following order for posting: sales, cash receipts, purchases, cash payments.

Problem 1-4

Use the accounts receivable and accounts payable subsidiary ledgers from Problem 1-3 to prepare a schedule of accounts receivable and a schedule of accounts payable for the All-State Sport Shop. Use November 30 as the date. Compare the totals with the balances of the general ledger controlling accounts.

Problem 1-5

The Mandel Hardware Store had the following balances in its general ledger accounts on June 30.

Cash in Bank	$ 6,950.69
Accounts Receivable	2,395.59
Merchandise Inventory	29,435.30
Supplies	2,394.05
Prepaid Insurance	1,800.00
Office Equipment	8,348.45
Store Equipment	4,505.00
Accounts Payable	9,405.59
Sales Tax Payable	1,495.64
Employees' Federal Income Tax Payable	1,404.59
FICA Tax Payable	583.48
Employees' State Income Tax Payable	493.58
Gary Gula, Capital	36,120.08
Gary Gula, Withdrawals	1,300.00
Income Summary	
Sales	19,459.40
Sales Returns and Allowances	238.69
Sales Discounts	149.40
Purchases	7,056.00
Transportation In	149.40

Purchases Returns and Allowances	104.85
Purchases Discounts	39.05
Advertising Expense	785.00
Bank Card Fees Expense	218.69
Insurance Expense	
Miscellaneous Expense	205.96
Payroll Tax Expense	395.59
Rent Expense	900.00
Salaries Expense	1,384.86
Supplies Expense	
Utilities Expense	493.59

Instructions: Based on the account balances presented above, prepare a trial balance for the month ended June 30 using the first two columns of a ten-column work sheet. Total, prove, and rule the Debit and Credit columns.

Problem 1–6

The Adzima Auto Parts Store uses special journals and subsidiary ledgers to record its transactions. The general ledger and subsidiary ledgers for the business are included in the working papers accompanying this textbook. The account balances have already been recorded.

The following transactions occurred during October for the Adzima Auto Parts Store.

Oct. 1 Paid the October rent of $650.00, Check 474.

2 Issued Check 475 for $196.00 to Plantation Supply in payment of their invoice 5595 for $200.00, less $4.00 discount.

2 Sold merchandise on account to Linda Merkins, $139.49 plus sales tax of $9.76, Sales Slip 593.

3 Purchased $350.00 worth of merchandise on account from Reale Corporation, Invoice 345, dated October 3, terms 1/10, n/30.

5 Paid the monthly electric bill of $136.50, Check 476.

8 Issued Credit Memorandum 79 to Matthew Williams for the return of merchandise costing $76.95 plus sales tax of $5.38.

8 Received check for $75.00 from Valerie Burns to apply on account, Receipt 359.

10 Paid $59.65 for freight charges on merchandise bought from a supplier, Check 477.

11 Sold merchandise on account to Sam Kortor, $23.05 plus sales tax of $1.61, Sales Slip 594.

15 Purchased merchandise for $585.80 from American Manufacturing Company on account, Invoice 8019, dated October 5, terms n/30.

16 Bought an ad in the local paper for $125.00, Check 478.

17 Bought supplies on account from Kari's Office Supplies for $154.00; Invoice 673, dated October 8, terms 1/10, n/30.

18 Tona Toomey sent a check for $35.00 in payment of amount owed, Receipt 360.

19	Cash sales for the period October 1 through October 18 were $1,493.40 plus sales tax of $104.53, Tape 95.
19	Bank card sales for the same period were $704.56 plus sales tax of $49.31, Tape 95.
23	Purchased a new display rack for $395.00, Check 479.
23	Sold merchandise on account to Sharon Lewis, $18.50 plus sales tax of $.59, Sales Slip 595.
24	Paid the payroll of $1,595.50 for the pay period. The following amounts were deducted: employees' federal income tax, $305.69; FICA tax, $112.48; employees' state income tax, $131.38, Check 480.
24	Recorded the employer's tax liability for the payroll. The FICA tax rate is 7.05%; the federal unemployment tax rate is .8%; the state unemployment tax rate is 2.7%, Memorandum 45.
26	Discovered that a September purchase of $45.00 of supplies had been incorrectly journalized and posted as office equipment, Memorandum 46.
26	Sold an old adding machine for $20.00 cash, Receipt 361.
29	Wrote Check 481 to the owner, Stanley Hocter, as a cash withdrawal for personal use, $200.00.
29	Sold a tune-up kit on account to Jane Williams, $42.50 plus sales tax of $2.98, Sales Slip 596.
30	Received a check from Howard Steinberg for $183.75 in payment of a purchase on September 9, Receipt 362.
30	Bought a new typewriter on account from A & M Office Supply for $842.48, Invoice 957.
31	Received a check for $1,000.00 from the owner, Stanley Hocter, as an additional investment in the business, Receipt 363.
31	Purchased merchandise on account from Lampton Company, $2,157.59, Invoice 5474.
31	Returned defective merchandise purchased on account from American Manufacturing Company, $84.48, Debit Memo 24.

Instructions: The forms for this activity are included in the working papers accompanying this textbook.

(1) Record the previous transactions in the special journals and the general journal.
(2) Post the individual amounts from the five journals to the accounts receivable and accounts payable subsidiary ledgers daily.
(3) Post the individual amounts from the General columns of the cash receipts, purchases, cash payments, and general journals daily.
(4) Total, prove, and rule the special journals.
(5) Post the special journals' column totals to the general ledger. Use this order for posting: sales, cash receipts, purchases, and cash payments.
(6) Prepare a schedule of accounts receivable and a schedule of accounts payable.
(7) Prepare a trial balance in the first two columns of a work sheet.

2 Reviewing the Final Five Steps of the Accounting Cycle

In Chapter 1, you reviewed the first five steps in the accounting cycle. You reviewed various business transactions and journalized these transactions in special journals and the general journal. Those transactions were posted to accounts in the general ledger and the subsidiary ledgers. Finally, you proved the accuracy of the subsidiary ledgers and prepared a trial balance, using the first two columns of a ten-column work sheet.

In this chapter, you will review steps six through ten of the accounting cycle.

Learning Objectives

When you have completed this chapter, you should be able to

1. Determine which general ledger accounts must be adjusted and calculate the amounts of the adjustments needed.

2. Complete a ten-column work sheet.

3. Prepare an income statement for a merchandising business.

4. Prepare a statement of changes in owner's equity.

5. Prepare a balance sheet for a merchandising business.

6. Journalize and post adjusting entries.

7. Journalize and post closing entries.

8. Prepare a post-closing trial balance.

9. Define the accounting terms presented in this chapter.

New Terms

work sheet / adjustment / beginning inventory / ending inventory / income statement / net sales / cost of merchandise sold / net purchases / gross profit on sales / statement of changes in owner's equity / balance sheet / adjusting entries / closing entries / post-closing trial balance

End-of-fiscal-period Work

The balances of the general ledger accounts summarize the effects of business transactions during an accounting period. To properly evaluate a business's performance, the owner and creditors need more than just a list of account totals.

It is the purpose of end-of-period reports to provide essential information that shows the financial position of the business. These reports help the owner or manager make decisions and operate efficiently.

Preparing a Ten-column Work Sheet

The sixth step in the accounting cycle is to prepare a work sheet. A **work sheet** is a working paper used to collect information from the general ledger. The work sheet thus contains the information needed to prepare the financial statements for the period.

In Chapter 1, you prepared a trial balance using the first two columns of the work sheet. This trial balance was prepared to prove the equality of debits and credits in the general ledger. If the two amount columns do not prove equal, the errors must be found and corrected before the work sheet can be continued.

Common errors that may occur include the following:

1. Addition or subtraction errors
2. An omitted account
3. An account balance entered in the wrong amount column
4. A transposition error (reversing a number)
5. A slide error (moving the decimal place)

Once the Trial Balance section of the work sheet is proved equal, the next section of the work sheet can be prepared.

Calculating Adjustments

Not all changes in account balances result from a business's transactions. Some changes result from the passage of time or from the internal operation of the business. As a result, the balances of some general ledger accounts must be brought up to date at the end of the fiscal period. The updating of such accounts as Supplies, Prepaid Insurance, and Merchandise Inventory is calculated on the work sheet through adjustments. An **adjustment** is an amount that is added to or subtracted from an account balance to bring that balance up to date. Accounts whose balances are not up to date as of the last day of the fiscal period must be adjusted.

The adjustments are entered in the Adjustments section of the work sheet. Once the work sheet indicates how the account balances must be brought up to date, the net income or loss for the period can be calculated and the financial statements prepared using the data on the work sheet.

Remember: If an account balance is not up to date as of the last day of the fiscal period, it must be adjusted.

Adjusting the Merchandise Inventory Account

For a merchandising business, the first adjustment that must be made is for Merchandise Inventory. The balance for Merchandise Inventory entered in the Trial Balance section of the work sheet represents the beginning inventory. The **beginning inventory** is the merchandise a business has on hand at the beginning of the fiscal period. During the fiscal period, the balance of the Merchandise Inventory account does not change. Merchandise is bought and sold, but the transactions are recorded in other general ledger accounts, such as Sales and Purchases. Since the Merchandise Inventory account is not up to date, it must be adjusted. A physical inventory, an actual count of the merchandise on hand and available for sale, is taken. Then, the cost of the ending inventory is calculated. The **ending inventory** is the merchandise a business has on hand at the end of a fiscal period. The adjustment for Merchandise Inventory is done in two parts.

The first part of the adjustment is to remove the beginning inventory balance from the Merchandise Inventory account and enter that balance in the Income Summary account. This is done by crediting Merchandise Inventory for $26,347.91 and debiting Income Summary for the same amount. A small (a) is placed next to both amounts so that they can be easily identified later when the adjusting entries are journalized.

After the physical inventory was taken, Butler's Fishing & Tackle Shop determined that the cost of the ending inventory was $28,496.68. The second part of the adjustment is to enter this new balance in the Merchandise Inventory

	ACCOUNT NAME	TRIAL BALANCE		ADJUSTMENTS	
		DEBIT	CREDIT	DEBIT	CREDIT
3	Merch. Inventory	26347 91		(b) 28496 68	(a) 26347 91
17	Income Summary			(a) 26347 91	(b) 28496 68

Butler's Fishing & Tackle Shop
Work Sheet
For the Year Ended December 31, 19--

Figure 2–1. Recording the Adjustments to Merchandise Inventory on the Work Sheet

account and also in the Income Summary account. This is done by debiting Merchandise Inventory for $28,496.68 and crediting Income Summary for the same amount. The two parts of this adjustment are labeled (b). The adjustments to the Merchandise Inventory account are shown in Figure 2–1.

Both the beginning and ending inventory amounts are now included in the Income Summary account. The beginning inventory appears as a debit and the ending inventory appears as a credit.

Remember: Merchandise Inventory is adjusted in two steps. First, the beginning inventory is transferred to Income Summary. Second, the ending inventory is entered in Merchandise Inventory and Income Summary.

Adjusting the Supplies Account

As supplies are purchased, their cost is debited to the asset account Supplies. During the normal operations of the business, some of these supplies are consumed. To account for the supplies used during the period, an adjustment must be made at the end of the period.

The balance of the Supplies account recorded in the Trial Balance section is $3,148.60. This amount includes the supplies on hand at the beginning of the period and the cost of all supplies purchased during the period.

At the end of the period, an inventory of the supplies on hand is taken. This inventory shows that there are $934.55 worth of supplies still on hand. This means that $2,214.05 worth of supplies were consumed during the period ($3,148.60 − $934.55).

Butler's Fishing & Tackle Shop
Work Sheet
For the Year Ended December 31, 19--

ACCOUNT NAME	TRIAL BALANCE		ADJUSTMENTS	
	DEBIT	CREDIT	DEBIT	CREDIT
Supplies	3 1 48 60			(c) 2 2 1 4 05
Supplies Expense			(c) 2 2 1 4 05	

Figure 2–2. Recording the Adjustment to Supplies on the Work Sheet

To adjust the account, Supplies is credited for the amount of supplies consumed, $2,214.05. Supplies Expense is debited for the same amount. The two parts of the adjustment are labeled (c), as shown in Figure 2–2.

Adjusting the Prepaid Insurance Account

On November 28, Scott Butler paid $1,200.00 for a six-month insurance policy. The cost of the premium was debited to the Prepaid Insurance account. One month of the insurance coverage has now expired. The Prepaid Insurance account must be credited for $200.00, the amount of expired premium, to bring the balance up to date. The amount of the expired premium is an expense of doing business. Therefore, the Insurance Expense account is debited for $200.00. The two parts of the adjustment are labeled (d), as shown in Figure 2–3.

	ACCOUNT NAME	TRIAL BALANCE		ADJUSTMENTS	
		DEBIT	CREDIT	DEBIT	CREDIT
5	Prepaid Insurance	1 200 00			(d) 200 00
27	Insurance Expense			(d) 200 00	

Butler's Fishing & Tackle Shop
Work Sheet
For the Year Ended December 31, 19--

Figure 2–3. Recording the Adjustment to Prepaid Insurance on the Work Sheet

After all the adjustments have been entered on the work sheet, the Adjustments section is totaled, proved, and ruled. The total of the Debit column must equal the total of the Credit column.

Remember: The Adjustments section of the work sheet, like the Trial Balance section, must be proved before the work sheet can be continued.

Before reading further, do the following activity to check your understanding of adjustments.

Check Your Learning

Answer the following questions on a sheet of notebook paper.

1. When the beginning inventory amount is adjusted, it is entered as a __?__ to the Merchandise Inventory account.
2. The Trial Balance section of the work sheet shows a balance of $1,590.40 for Supplies. The actual amount of supplies on hand at the end of the period is $854.93. What is the amount of the adjustment? What account is debited? What account is credited?
3. In the Adjustments section of the work sheet, Income Summary is debited for $38,494.00 and credited for $35,496.06. The amount of the ending inventory is __?__.

Compare your answers to those in the answers section. Re-read the preceding part of the chapter to find the correct answers to any questions you may have missed.

Completing the Adjusted Trial Balance Section

The Adjusted Trial Balance section of the work sheet contains updated balances for all general ledger accounts. The section is completed by combining the balance of each account in the Trial Balance section with the adjustment, if any, in the Adjustments section. This section too must be totaled, proved, and ruled before continuing.

The Adjusted Trial Balance section of Butler's Fishing & Tackle Shop is shown in the completed work sheet in Figure 2–4 on pages 38–39. Make sure you understand how all balances are determined before going on to the next section.

Extending Amounts to the Balance Sheet and Income Statement Sections

Beginning with line 1, each account listed in the Adjusted Trial Balance section is extended to either the Balance Sheet section or the Income Statement section. The Balance Sheet section contains the balances of all permanent general ledger accounts. The Income Statement section contains the balances of all temporary general ledger accounts and the Income Summary account. Notice that both beginning and ending inventory amounts (recorded on the Income Summary line) are extended to the Income Statement section. Examine the work sheet in Figure 2–4 to identify the accounts that are extended to each section.

Completing the Work Sheet

After all amounts have been extended, the four amount columns are totaled and the net income or loss for the period calculated. A net income amount is entered in the Income Statement Debit column and in the Balance Sheet Credit column. Butler's net income, as shown on the work sheet in Figure 2–4, is $37,156.18.

Preparing the Financial Statements

The seventh step in the accounting cycle is the preparation of financial statements. A business prepares various reports at the end of each period that reflect the changes that have taken place during the period. In order to properly analyze the financial condition of the business, these reports must be prepared in a similar manner each period.

Butler's Fishing & Tackle Shop prepares three end-of-period financial statements, using the information on the work sheet.

The Income Statement

The net income or loss earned by a business during the fiscal period is reported on the income statement. An income statement for a merchandising business contains five sections: (1) Revenue, (2) Cost of Merchandise Sold, (3) Gross Profit on Sales, (4) Expenses, and (5) Net Income or Loss.

	ACCOUNT NAME	TRIAL BALANCE		ADJUSTMENTS	
		DEBIT	CREDIT	DEBIT	CREDIT
1	Cash in Bank	17021 65			
2	Accounts Receivable	5471 03			
3	Merch. Inventory	26347 91		(b) 28496 68	(a) 26347 91
4	Supplies	3148 60			(c) 2214 05
5	Prepaid Insurance	1200 00			(d) 200 00
6	Equipment	12541 63			
7	Accounts Payable		5271 80		
8	Sales Tax Payable		1235 68		
9	Emp. Fed. Inc. Tax Pay.		248 00		
10	FICA Tax Payable		417 64		
11	Emp. State Inc. Tax Pay.		337 44		
12	Insurance Prem. Pay.		42 00		
13	Fed. Unempl. Tax Pay.		71 10		
14	State Unempl. Tax Pay.		239 94		
15	Scott Butler, Capital		30445 76		
16	Scott Butler, Withdr.	10000 00			
17	Income Summary			(a) 26347 91	(b) 28496 68
18	Sales		211830 88		
19	Sales Ret. + Allow.	2781 97			
20	Sales Discounts	1364 67			
21	Purchases	100697 40			
22	Transportation In	7048 82			
23	Purchases Ret. + Allow.		1208 37		
24	Purchases Discounts		1711 86		
25	Advertising Expense	8400 00			
26	Bank Card Fees Exp.	1618 18			
27	Insurance Expense			(d) 200 00	
28	Miscellaneous Exp.	2072 92			
29	Payroll Tax Expense	4024 05			
30	Rent Expense	9000 00			
31	Salaries Expense	38142 64			
32	Supplies Expense			(c) 2214 05	
33	Utilities Expense	2179 00			
34		253060 47	253060 47	57258 64	57258 64
35	Net Income				
36					

Figure 2–4. Butler's Fishing & Tackle Shop's Work Sheet   (Left Side)

| ADJUSTED TRIAL BALANCE | | INCOME STATEMENT | | BALANCE SHEET | | |
DEBIT	CREDIT	DEBIT	CREDIT	DEBIT	CREDIT	
1702165				1702165		1
547103				547103		2
2849668				2849668		3
93455				93455		4
100000				100000		5
1254163				1254163		6
	527180				527180	7
	123568				123568	8
	24800				24800	9
	41764				41764	10
	33744				33744	11
	4200				4200	12
	7110				7110	13
	23994				23994	14
	3044576				3044576	15
1000000				1000000		16
2634791	2849668	2634791	2849668			17
	2183088		2183088			18
278197		278197				19
136467		136467				20
10069740		10069740				21
704882		704882				22
	120837		120837			23
	171186		171186			24
840000		840000				25
161818		161818				26
20000		20000				27
207292		207292				28
402405		402405				29
900000		900000				30
3814264		3814264				31
221405		221405				32
217900		217900				33
28155715	28155715	20609161	24324779	7546554	3830936	34
		3715618			3715618	35
		24324779	24324779	7546554	7546554	36

(Right Side)

The income statement is prepared using the information in the Income Statement section of the work sheet. The completed income statement for Butler's Fishing & Tackle Shop is shown in Figure 2–5.

Revenue Section

This section includes the Sales account and the contra revenue accounts Sales Returns and Allowances and Sales Discounts. Total sales minus the two contra accounts equals net sales for the period.

Cost of Merchandise Sold Section

Before a merchandising business can determine its gross profit, it must determine its cost of merchandise sold. The cost of merchandise sold is the actual cost to the business of the merchandise sold to customers. The cost of merchandise sold is calculated as follows.

$$
\begin{array}{l}
 \text{Beginning Merchandise Inventory} \\
+ \text{ Net Purchases During the Period} \\
\hline
= \text{Cost of Merchandise Available for Sale} \\
- \text{ Ending Merchandise Inventory} \\
\hline
= \text{Cost of Merchandise Sold}
\end{array}
$$

Net purchases is the amount of all costs related to merchandise purchased during the period. It is calculated as shown below.

$$
\begin{array}{l}
 \text{Purchases} \\
+ \text{ Transportation In} \\
\hline
= \text{Cost of Delivered Merchandise} \\
- \text{ Purchases Returns and Allowances} \\
- \text{ Purchases Discounts} \\
\hline
= \text{Net Purchases}
\end{array}
$$

Remember: **Transportation costs increase net purchases. Discounts, returns, and allowances decrease net purchases.**

Gross Profit on Sales

The amount of profit made during the period before expenses have been deducted is the gross profit on sales. Gross profit on sales is found by subtracting the cost of merchandise sold from the net sales for the period.

$$
\begin{array}{l}
 \text{Net Sales for the Period} \\
- \text{ Cost of Merchandise Sold} \\
\hline
= \text{Gross Profit on Sales}
\end{array}
$$

Expenses Section

In this section, all expenses are listed in the same order as they appear on the work sheet. The total of all expenses for the period is then extended to the fourth amount column.

Butler's Fishing & Tackle Shop
Income Statement
For the Year Ended December 31, 19--

Revenue:				
Sales			21 183 088	
Less: Sales Ret. + Allow.		278 197		
Sales Discounts		136 467	414 664	
Net Sales				20 768 424
Cost of Merchandise Sold:				
Merch. Inv., Jan. 1, 19--			2 634 791	
Purchases	10 069 740			
Plus: Transport. In	704 882			
Cost of Delivered Merch.		10 774 622		
Less: Purch. Ret. + Allow.	120 837			
Purch. Discounts	171 186	292 023		
Net Purchases			10 482 599	
Cost of Merch. Available			13 117 390	
Merch. Inv., Dec. 31, 19--			2 849 668	
Cost of Merch. Sold				10 267 722
Gross Profit on Sales				10 500 702
Expenses:				
Advertising Expense			840 000	
Bank Card Fees Exp.			161 818	
Insurance Expense			20 000	
Miscellaneous Exp.			207 292	
Payroll Tax Expense			402 405	
Rent Expense			900 000	
Salaries Expense			3 814 264	
Supplies Expense			221 405	
Utilities Expense			217 900	
Total Expenses				6 785 084
Net Income				3 715 618

Figure 2–5. Butler's Fishing & Tackle Shop's Income Statement

Net Income or Loss

The net income or loss for the period is calculated by subtracting the total expenses for the period from the gross profit on sales.

Gross Profit on Sales
− Total Expenses for the Period

= Net Income or Loss

The net income or loss shown on the income statement must agree with the amount shown on the work sheet.

Before reading further, do the activity on the next page to check your understanding of the income statement.

Statement of Changes in Owner's Equity

The changes that have occurred in the owner's capital account during the fiscal period are reported on the statement of changes in owner's equity. It is prepared from information contained on the work sheet and in the owner's capital account in the general ledger. The statement of changes in owner's equity for Butler's Fishing & Tackle Shop is presented in Figure 2–6.

Butler's Fishing & Tackle Shop Statement of Changes in Owner's Equity For the Year Ended December 31, 19--		
Beginning Capital, January 1, 19--		27445 76
Add: Investment by Owner	3000 00	
Net Income for Period	37156 18	
Total Increase in Capital		40156 18
Adjusted Capital Balance		67601 94
Less: Withdrawals by Owner		10000 00
Ending Capital, December 31, 19--		57601 94

Figure 2–6. Butler's Fishing & Tackle Shop's Statement of Changes in Owner's Equity

Notice that an additional investment by the owner and the net income for the period are added to the beginning capital amount. Withdrawals by the owner are subtracted from the adjusted capital balance.

The balance of Scott Butler, Capital entered on the work sheet is the balance of the account on December 31. The account itself must be examined to determine the beginning balance and the amount of any investments during the year. The net income and withdrawals amounts are taken from the work sheet.

The statement of changes in owner's equity is completed as a supporting document for the balance sheet. The ending balance in the owner's capital account, $57,601.94, will be reported on the balance sheet.

The final, updated balances of all asset, liability, and owner's equity accounts as of a specific date are reported on the **balance sheet**. It is prepared from the information contained in the Balance Sheet section of the work sheet and from the statement of changes in owner's equity.

A balance sheet may be prepared in either account form or report form. Butler's Fishing & Tackle Shop uses the report form, shown in Figure 2–7, which presents the classifications one under the other.

Notice that the amounts for the asset and liability sections are obtained from the work sheet. The balance of the Capital account, $57,601.94, is taken from the statement of changes in owner's equity. The total assets amount reported on the balance sheet, $65,465.54, must equal the total liabilities plus owner's equity amount, $65,465.54.

Remember: Total assets equal total liabilities plus owner's equity. This is the basic accounting equation.

Butler's Fishing & Tackle Shop
Balance Sheet
December 31, 19--

Assets		
Cash in Bank	1702165	
Accounts Receivable	547103	
Merchandise Inventory	2849668	
Supplies	93455	
Prepaid Insurance	100000	
Equipment	1254163	
Total Assets		6546554
Liabilities		
Accounts Payable	527180	
Sales Tax Payable	123568	
Employees' Federal Income Tax Payable	24800	
FICA Tax Payable	41764	
Employees' State Income Tax Payable	33744	
Insurance Premium Payable	4200	
Federal Unemployment Tax Payable	7110	
State Unemployment Tax Payable	23994	
Total Liabilities		786360
Owner's Equity		
Scott Butler, Capital		5760194
Total Liabilities and Owner's Equity		6546554

Figure 2–7. Butler's Fishing & Tackle Shop's Balance Sheet

The eighth step in the accounting cycle is to journalize and post the adjusting entries. The adjustments recorded on the work sheet do *not* update the account balances. Accounts can only be updated through journal entries. The adjusting entries update the balances in all general ledger accounts affected by the adjustments.

The work sheet is the source of the information for journalizing the adjusting entries. The two parts of each adjusting entry are found by matching the lettered amounts in the Adjustments section of the work sheet. The adjusting entries are recorded in the general journal. Be sure to enter the debit part of the entry first. The adjusting entries for Butler's Fishing & Tackle Shop are shown in Figure 2–8. Notice that the words "Adjusting Entries" are written in the Description column above the first entry.

GENERAL JOURNAL   PAGE 19

DATE	DESCRIPTION	POST. REF.	DEBIT	CREDIT
	Adjusting Entries			
Dec. 31	*Income Summary*		2634791	
	Merchandise Inventory			2634791
31	*Merchandise Inventory*		2849668	
	Income Summary			2849668
31	*Supplies Expense*		221405	
	Supplies			221405
31	*Insurance Expense*		20000	
	Prepaid Insurance			20000

Figure 2–8. Adjusting Entries for Butler's Fishing & Tackle Shop

After the adjusting entries have been recorded in the general journal, they must be posted to the accounts in the general ledger. After the adjusting entries are posted, the balances of the general ledger accounts are the same as those reported on the financial statements with the exception of Scott Butler, Capital. This account will be brought up to date when the closing entries have been posted.

Remember: The debit and credit parts of each adjusting entry are found by matching the lettered amounts in the Adjustments section of the work sheet.

The first adjusting entry would be posted as shown in Figure 2–9 on the next page.

All other adjusting entries are posted in a similar manner. Be sure to record the posting reference in both the general journal and the general ledger accounts.

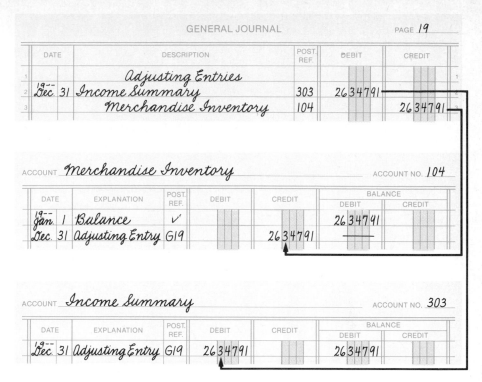

	DATE		DESCRIPTION	POST. REF.	DEBIT	CREDIT	
1			*Adjusting Entries*				1
2	19-- Dec.	31	Income Summary	303	26 34791		2
3			Merchandise Inventory	104		26 34791	3

ACCOUNT *Merchandise Inventory*   ACCOUNT NO. 104

DATE		EXPLANATION	POST. REF.	DEBIT	CREDIT	BALANCE DEBIT	BALANCE CREDIT
19-- Jan.	1	Balance	✓			26 34791	
Dec.	31	Adjusting Entry	G19		26 34791		

ACCOUNT *Income Summary*   ACCOUNT NO. 303

DATE		EXPLANATION	POST. REF.	DEBIT	CREDIT	BALANCE DEBIT	BALANCE CREDIT
19-- Dec.	31	Adjusting Entry	G19	26 34791		26 34791	

Figure 2–9. Posting the First Adjusting Entry to the General Ledger

Closing Entries

The ninth step in the accounting cycle is to journalize and post the closing entries. **Closing entries** transfer the balances of the temporary accounts to a permanent general ledger account. After all the closing entries are recorded, all temporary accounts will have a zero balance.

The Income Statement section of the work sheet is the source of information for the closing entries recorded in the general journal. For a merchandising business organized as a sole proprietorship, four separate closing entries are made. The first closing entry, shown in Figure 2–10 on the next page, closes the temporary revenue and contra cost accounts with credit balances into Income Summary. This entry includes Sales, Purchases Returns and Allowances, and Purchases Discounts.

The second closing entry is made to close the temporary contra revenue, cost, and expense accounts with debit balances into Income Summary.

The third closing entry closes the balance of the Income Summary account into the owner's capital account. The balance in Income Summary should be the net income for the period, $37,156.18. To close the account, Income Summary is debited for $37,156.18 and Scott Butler, Capital is credited for the same amount. When this entry is posted, the balance of Income Summary will be zero and the net income for the period will have been transferred to the capital account.

	DATE	DESCRIPTION	POST. REF.	DEBIT	CREDIT	
11		*Closing Entries*				11
12	19-- Dec. 31	Sales		21 183 088		12
13		Purchases Returns + Allowances		1 208 37		13
14		Purchases Discounts		1 711 86		14
15		Income Summary			21 475 111	15
16	31	Income Summary		17 974 370		16
17		Sales Returns + Allowances			2 781 97	17
18		Sales Discounts			1 364 67	18
19		Purchases			100 697 40	19
20		Transportation In			7 048 82	20
21		Advertising Expense			8 400 00	21
22		Bank Card Fees Expense			1 618 18	22
23		Insurance Expense			200 00	23
24		Miscellaneous Expense			2 072 92	24
25		Payroll Tax Expense			4 024 05	25
26		Rent Expense			9 000 00	26
27		Salaries Expense			38 142 64	27
28		Supplies Expense			2 214 05	28
29		Utilities Expense			2 179 00	29
30	31	Income Summary		37 156 18		30
31		Scott Butler, Capital			37 156 18	31
32	31	Scott Butler, Capital		1 000 000		32
33		Scott Butler, Withdrawals			1 000 000	33

Figure 2–10. Closing Entries for Butler's Fishing & Tackle Shop

The final closing entry closes the balance of the owner's withdrawals account into the capital account. Withdrawals by the owner, as you remember, decrease owner's equity.

Remember: The withdrawals account is closed separately into the owner's capital account.

After the four closing entries have been journalized, they must be posted to the general ledger. After all posting is completed, the temporary accounts will have zero balances and the capital account will be up to date. The equity, revenue, and cost of merchandise accounts for Butler's Fishing & Tackle Shop are shown in Figure 2–11 on pages 47–48.

After the posting of the closing entries is completed, all expense accounts will have zero balances. Advertising Expense is presented as an example in Figure 2–12, shown on page 48.

Remember: Be sure to write the words "Closing Entry" in the account.

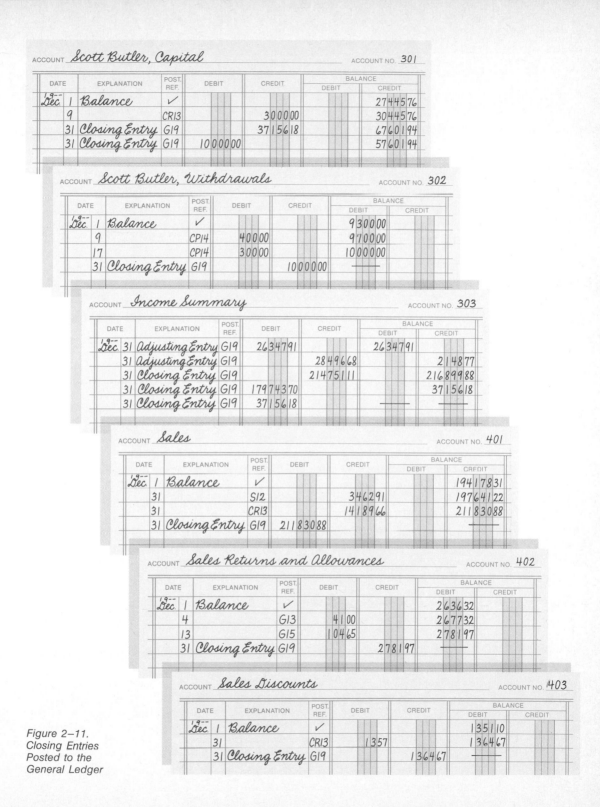

ACCOUNT Scott Butler, Capital   **ACCOUNT NO.** 301

DATE		EXPLANATION	POST. REF.	DEBIT	CREDIT	BALANCE DEBIT	BALANCE CREDIT
19-- Dec.	1	Balance	✓				2744576
	9		CR13		300000		3044576
	31	Closing Entry	G19		3715618		6760194
	31	Closing Entry	G19	1000000			5760194

ACCOUNT Scott Butler, Withdrawals   **ACCOUNT NO.** 302

DATE		EXPLANATION	POST. REF.	DEBIT	CREDIT	BALANCE DEBIT	BALANCE CREDIT
19-- Dec.	1	Balance	✓			930000	
	9		CP14	40000		970000	
	17		CP14	30000		1000000	
	31	Closing Entry	G19		1000000	—	

ACCOUNT Income Summary   **ACCOUNT NO.** 303

DATE		EXPLANATION	POST. REF.	DEBIT	CREDIT	BALANCE DEBIT	BALANCE CREDIT
19-- Dec.	31	Adjusting Entry	G19	2634791		2634791	
	31	Adjusting Entry	G19		2849668		214877
	31	Closing Entry	G19		21475111		21689988
	31	Closing Entry	G19	17974370			3715618
	31	Closing Entry	G19	3715618		—	

ACCOUNT Sales   **ACCOUNT NO.** 401

DATE		EXPLANATION	POST. REF.	DEBIT	CREDIT	BALANCE DEBIT	BALANCE CREDIT
19-- Dec.	1	Balance	✓				19417831
	31		S12		346291		19764122
	31		CR13		1418966		21183088
	31	Closing Entry	G19	21183088			—

ACCOUNT Sales Returns and Allowances   **ACCOUNT NO.** 402

DATE		EXPLANATION	POST. REF.	DEBIT	CREDIT	BALANCE DEBIT	BALANCE CREDIT
19-- Dec.	1	Balance	✓			263632	
	4		G13	4100		267732	
	13		G15	10465		278197	
	31	Closing Entry	G19		278197	—	

ACCOUNT Sales Discounts   **ACCOUNT NO.** 403

DATE		EXPLANATION	POST. REF.	DEBIT	CREDIT	BALANCE DEBIT	BALANCE CREDIT
19-- Dec.	1	Balance	✓			135110	
	31		CR13	1357		136467	
	31	Closing Entry	G19		136467	—	

Figure 2–11.
Closing Entries
Posted to the
General Ledger

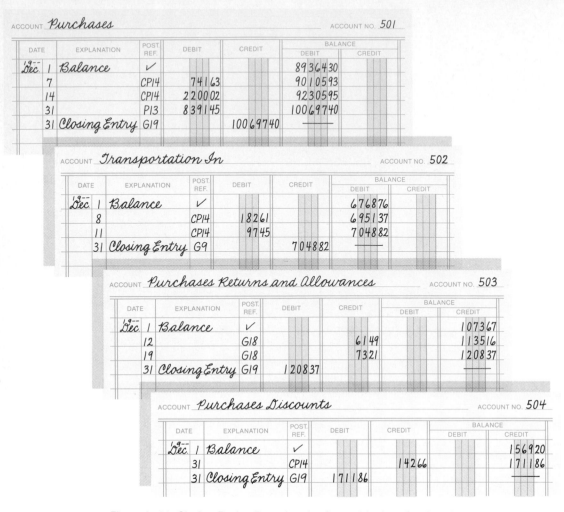

ACCOUNT *Purchases*   **ACCOUNT NO.** *501*

DATE		EXPLANATION	POST. REF.	DEBIT	CREDIT	BALANCE DEBIT	BALANCE CREDIT
19-- Dec.	1	Balance	✓			8936430	
	7		CP14	74163		9010593	
	14		CP14	220002		9230595	
	31		P13	839145		10069740	
	31	Closing Entry	G19		10069740		

ACCOUNT *Transportation In*   **ACCOUNT NO.** *502*

DATE		EXPLANATION	POST. REF.	DEBIT	CREDIT	BALANCE DEBIT	BALANCE CREDIT
19-- Dec.	1	Balance	✓			676876	
	8		CP14	18261		695137	
	11		CP14	9745		704882	
	31	Closing Entry	G9		704882		

ACCOUNT *Purchases Returns and Allowances*   **ACCOUNT NO.** *503*

DATE		EXPLANATION	POST. REF.	DEBIT	CREDIT	BALANCE DEBIT	BALANCE CREDIT
19-- Dec.	1	Balance	✓				107367
	12		G18		6149		113516
	19		G18		7321		120837
	31	Closing Entry	G19	120837			

ACCOUNT *Purchases Discounts*   **ACCOUNT NO.** *504*

DATE		EXPLANATION	POST. REF.	DEBIT	CREDIT	BALANCE DEBIT	BALANCE CREDIT
19-- Dec.	1	Balance	✓				156920
	31		CP14		14266		171186
	31	Closing Entry	G19	171186			

Figure 2–11. Closing Entries Posted to the General Ledger Continued

ACCOUNT *Advertising Expense*   **ACCOUNT NO.** *601*

DATE		EXPLANATION	POST. REF.	DEBIT	CREDIT	BALANCE DEBIT	BALANCE CREDIT
19-- Dec.	1	Balance	✓			770000	
	9		CP14	30000		800000	
	17		CP14	40000		840000	
	31	Closing Entry	G19		840000	——	

Figure 2–12. Closing Entry Posted to an Expense Account

Before reading further, do the following activity to check your understanding of adjusting and closing entries.

The Post-closing Trial Balance

At the end of the fiscal period, a post-closing trial balance is prepared to prove the equality of the debits and credits in the general ledger after all adjusting and closing entries have been posted. This is the tenth and final step in the accounting cycle. The post-closing trial balance for Butler's Fishing & Tackle Shop is shown in Figure 2–13.

Butler's Fishing & Tackle Shop
Post-Closing Trial Balance
December 31, 19--

Cash in Bank	1702165	
Accounts Receivable	547103	
Merchandise Inventory	2849668	
Supplies	93455	
Prepaid Insurance	100000	
Equipment	1254163	
Accounts Payable		527180
Sales Tax Payable		123568
Employees' Federal Income Tax Payable		24800
FICA Tax Payable		41764
Employees' State Income Tax Payable		33744
Insurance Premium Payable		4200
Federal Unemployment Tax Payable		7110
State Unemployment Tax Payable		23994
Scott Butler, Capital		5760194
Totals	6546554	6546554

Figure 2–13. Butler's Fishing & Tackle Shop's Post-closing Trial Balance

The post-closing trial balance lists only the balances of the permanent general ledger accounts. The temporary capital accounts have zero balances and are not listed on the post-closing trial balance.

The Accounting Cycle for a Merchandising Business

You have just completed your review of the accounting cycle for a merchandising business organized as a sole proprietorship. For review, the steps in the accounting cycle are as follows.

1. Collect and verify data on source documents.
2. Analyze business transactions.
3. Journalize business transactions.
4. Post each entry to the general ledger and subsidiary ledgers.
5. Prepare a trial balance.
6. Complete the work sheet.
7. Prepare the financial statements.
8. Journalize and post the adjusting entries.
9. Journalize and post the closing entries.
10. Prepare a post-closing trial balance.

Remember that the basic accounting cycle is the same no matter what type of ownership is involved or what type of accounting system is used.

Summary of Key Points

1. A work sheet is prepared to organize all the data needed to update the ledger accounts and to prepare the financial statements.
2. Changes in some accounts are not affected by daily business transactions. The end-of-fiscal-period adjustments to these accounts are planned and entered in the Adjustments section of the work sheet.
3. The net income for the period is first calculated on the work sheet.
4. A sole proprietorship prepares three financial statements. They are the income statement, the statement of changes in owner's equity, and the balance sheet.
5. Adjusting entries are journalized and posted to bring the general ledger accounts up to date.
6. The closing entries are journalized and posted to close the balances of the temporary capital accounts into a permanent general ledger account—the owner's capital account.
7. After the closing entries have been posted, a post-closing trial balance is prepared.
8. The basic steps in the accounting cycle are the same for all businesses, regardless of how they are organized or what type of accounting system they use.

Review and Applications

Building Your Accounting Vocabulary

In your own words, write the definition of each of the following accounting terms. Use complete sentences for your definitions.

adjusting entries   cost of merchandise sold   net sales
adjustment   ending inventory   post-closing trial balance
balance sheet   gross profit on sales   statement of changes in
beginning inventory   income statement   owner's equity
closing entries   net purchases   work sheet

Reviewing Your Accounting Knowledge

1. Why is a work sheet prepared before the financial statements?
2. Why must certain general ledger accounts be updated at the end of the fiscal period?
3. Why is the Merchandise Inventory account adjusted in two steps?
4. What three financial statements are usually prepared by a merchandising business operated as a sole proprietorship?
5. How is the cost of merchandise sold calculated?
6. How is the gross profit on sales calculated?
7. Why is the income statement prepared before the statement of changes in owner's equity?
8. What is the reason for journalizing and posting closing entries?
9. What is the purpose of a post-closing trial balance?
10. Name the ten steps in the accounting cycle.

Improving Your Decision-making Skills

Dale Rupurt, an accounting clerk for the Maplewood Bike Shop, prepared the end-of-period financial statements. In preparing the work sheet, Dale did not make any adjustments for supplies or prepaid insurance. The only adjustment that was recorded was for merchandise inventory. What effect will these omissions have on the income statement and the balance sheet for the period?

Applying Accounting Procedures

Problem 2–1

Instructions: Use a form similar to the one on the next page. For each item that follows, place a check mark in each section of the work sheet in which the amount would appear.

(1) Beginning merchandise inventory
(2) Expired portion of the insurance premium
(3) Amount owed to creditors
(4) Balance of Supplies account at the beginning of the period plus supplies purchased
(5) Supplies consumed during the period
(6) Ending merchandise inventory
(7) Revenue for the period
(8) Value of insurance premium at the beginning of the period
(9) Ending supplies inventory
(10) Value of insurance premium at the end of the period

Number of Item	Trial Balance	Adjustments	Adjusted Trial Balance	Income Statement	Balance Sheet
1	✓	✓	✓	✓	

Problem 2–2

The Trial Balance section of the work sheet for the Mariani Golf Shop has already been completed. A portion of that work sheet is shown below.

Mariani Golf Shop
Work Sheet
For the Month Ended April 30, 19--

	ACCOUNT NAME	TRIAL BALANCE DEBIT	TRIAL BALANCE CREDIT	ADJUSTMENTS DEBIT	ADJUSTMENTS CREDIT
3	Merch. Inventory	48 3 2 8 36			
4	Supplies	2 1 0 6 19			
5	Prepaid Insurance	1 8 0 0 00			
17	Income Summary				
27	Insurance Expense				
30	Supplies Expense				

Instructions: Based on the following information, record the adjustments in the Adjustments section of the work sheet.

(1) The value of the ending merchandise inventory is $45,495.40.
(2) The supplies on hand on April 30 are valued at $1,484.75.
(3) The six-month insurance premium of $1,800 was paid on April 1.

The December 31 balances of the general ledger accounts of Fox Business Supply Co. are listed below. Also listed are the data needed for the adjustments.

Cash in Bank	$ 9,830.31
Accounts Receivable	2,059.44
Merchandise Inventory	36,887.07
Supplies	4,408.05
Prepaid Insurance	1,680.00
Office Equipment	13,358.28
Accounts Payable	14,380.52
Sales Tax Payable	2,721.06
Employees' Federal Income Tax Payable	1,107.97
FICA Tax Payable	307.77
Employees' State Income Tax Payable	344.79
Federal Unemployment Tax Payable	283.64
State Unemployment Tax Payable	193.83
Martin Fox, Capital	46,321.52
Martin Fox, Withdrawals	2,100.00
Income Summary	
Sales	27,046.94
Sales Returns and Allowances	577.70
Sales Discounts	173.35
Purchases	11,748.03
Transportation In	867.78
Purchases Returns and Allowances	290.79
Purchases Discounts	125.44
Advertising Expense	980.00
Bank Card Fees Expense	256.43
Insurance Expense	
Miscellaneous Expense	300.17
Payroll Tax Expense	655.70
Rent Expense	1,000.00
Salaries Expense	5,347.16
Supplies Expense	
Utilities Expense	894.80

Data for Adjustments

Ending merchandise inventory	$39,895.35
Supplies on hand, December 31	2,707.60
Insurance premium expired	280.00

Instructions: Prepare a ten-column work sheet for the Fox Business Supply Co. for the year ended December 31. (The account titles have already been entered on the work sheet.)

Problem 2–4

Use the work sheet you prepared in Problem 2–3 to complete this problem.

Instructions:

(1) Prepare an income statement.
(2) Prepare a statement of changes in owner's equity. Martin Fox invested an additional $2,000 in the business during December, the only change for the year.
(3) Prepare a balance sheet.

Problem 2–5

Use the work sheet you prepared in Problem 2–3 to complete this problem.

Instructions:

(1) Journalize and post the adjusting entries. The ledger accounts appear in the working papers accompanying this textbook.
(2) Journalize and post the closing entries.

Problem 2–6

Using the documents you prepared earlier, prepare a post-closing trial balance for the Fox Business Supply Co.

Problem 2–7

The Rainbow's End Card Shop is owned and operated by Eileen Miller. It is a merchandising business selling greeting cards to retail customers. The business has a one-year fiscal period that ends on December 31.

The account balances in the general ledger on December 31 are listed below and on the next page.

Cash in Bank	$ 6,569.49
Accounts Receivable	4,357.29
Merchandise Inventory	27,348.50
Supplies	3,480.14
Prepaid Insurance	3,000.00
Store Equipment	7,495.29
Accounts Payable	12,406.42
Sales Tax Payable	1,294.04
Employees' Federal Income Tax Payable	1,035.13
FICA Tax Payable	704.48
Employees' State Income Tax Payable	613.56
Federal Unemployment Tax Payable	139.40
State Unemployment Tax Payable	348.85
Eileen Miller, Capital	27,502.65
Eileen Miller, Withdrawals	2,500.00

Income Summary	
Sales	48,682.80
Sales Returns and Allowances	1,041.34
Purchases	17,381.05
Transportation In	1,140.48
Purchases Discounts	686.89
Advertising Expense	1,130.91
Bank Card Fees Expense	284.30
Insurance Expense	
Miscellaneous Expense	374.48
Payroll Tax Expense	941.48
Rent Expense	8,500.00
Salaries Expense	6,484.18
Supplies Expense	
Utilities Expense	1,385.29

Instructions:

(1) Prepare a ten-column work sheet for the Rainbow's End Card Shop for the year ended December 31. The information needed for adjustments is as follows:

    (a) Ending merchandise inventory is $25,249.30.

    (b) Supplies on hand on December 31 are valued at $1,295.49.

    (c) The insurance premium of $3,000 paid on April 1 covers a one-year period.

(2) Based on the information contained on the work sheet, prepare an income statement.

(3) Prepare a statement of changes in owner's equity. During the period, Eileen Miller made an additional investment in the business of $750.00.

(4) Prepare a balance sheet as of December 31.

(5) Journalize and post the adjusting entries. The ledger accounts appear in the working papers accompanying this textbook.

(6) Journalize and post the closing entries.

(7) Prepare a post-closing trial balance.

A Complete Accounting Cycle for a Merchandising Business

In Unit 1, you reviewed the complete accounting cycle for a merchandising business organized as a sole proprietorship. Now you will have the opportunity to apply what you have reviewed as you work through the complete accounting cycle for MicroHelper.

When you have completed this activity, you will have

1. analyzed business transactions
2. journalized business transactions in the four special journals and in the general journal
3. posted journal entries to the general ledger and to the accounts receivable and accounts payable subsidiary ledgers
4. posted the totals of the special journals to the general ledger
5. proved cash
6. prepared a schedule of accounts receivable and a schedule of accounts payable
7. prepared a trial balance and a work sheet
8. prepared financial statements
9. journalized and posted adjusting and closing entries
10. prepared a post-closing trial balance

MicroHelper

Ann Lengyel owns and operates a sole proprietorship called MicroHelper. MicroHelper is a retail store that sells microcomputer accessories. It offers a wide variety of software, computer books and magazines, and various other computer accessories.

Because MicroHelper has a large number of business transactions, Ann has chosen to record daily business transactions in special journals and in a general journal.

The chart of accounts for MicroHelper follows.

MICROHELPER
Chart of Accounts

ASSETS	101	Cash in Bank
	102	Accounts Receivable
	105	Merchandise Inventory
	110	Supplies
	115	Prepaid Insurance
	120	Display Equipment
	125	Office Equipment
LIABILITIES	201	Accounts Payable
	202	Sales Tax Payable
	203	Employees' Federal Income Tax Payable
	204	FICA Tax Payable
	205	Employees' State Income Tax Payable
	208	Federal Unemployment Tax Payable
	209	State Unemployment Tax Payable
	212	Insurance Premium Payable
OWNER'S EQUITY	301	Ann Lengyel, Capital
	302	Ann Lengyel, Withdrawals
	303	Income Summary
REVENUE	401	Sales
	402	Sales Returns and Allowances
COST OF MERCHANDISE	501	Purchases
	502	Transportation In
	503	Purchases Returns and Allowances
	504	Purchases Discounts
EXPENSES	602	Advertising Expense
	604	Bank Card Fees Expense
	609	Insurance Expense
	615	Miscellaneous Expense
	620	Payroll Tax Expense
	625	Rent Expense
	630	Salaries Expense
	635	Supplies Expense
	640	Utilities Expense

Accounts Receivable Subsidiary Ledger

803	Carl Combs
808	Betty Foote
815	William Gillies
821	Ed Hibian
829	Nancy Pope
835	Stone High School
841	Deborah Vaughn

Accounts Payable Subsidiary Ledger

904	Hill's Supply Company
909	Kess Computer Supplies
916	Microworld, Inc.
919	Micro Products
927	R & T Electronics
931	Video Disk, Inc.
938	Winsted Micro Devices

Business Transactions

The following transactions took place during the month of December.

Dec. 2 Issued Check 395 for $750.00 to Randall's Realty for December rent.

2 Sold merchandise on account to Betty Foote, $57.75 plus sales tax of $4.04, Sales Slip 318.

3 Paid the monthly telephone bill of $84.71, Check 396.

4 Purchased computer software (merchandise) on account from Microworld, Inc. for $295.45, Invoice 574 dated December 3, terms 1/10, n/30.

4 Issued Check 397 for $285.14 to the Second City Bank in payment of employees' federal income taxes and FICA taxes withheld.

5 Sent Check 398 to Video Disk, Inc. in payment of Invoice 488 for $314.50, less discount of $6.29.

6 Bought an ad in the local paper for $65.00, Check 399.

6 Received a check for $25.00 from William Gillies to apply on his account, Receipt 283.

7 Sold some merchandise to Deborah Vaughn on account for $72.49 plus sales tax of $5.07, Sales Slip 319.

7 Purchased a new display rack for the store from H. Morton & Son for $147.47 cash, Check 400.

9 Issued Credit Memo 173 to Ed Hibian for the return of merchandise costing $31.00 plus $2.17 sales tax.

9 Paid $103.49 for freight charges on merchandise bought from a supplier, Check 401.

10   Purchased merchandise on account from R & T Electronics, $394.60, Invoice 573, terms n/30.

12   Sold four computer books on account to Stone High School for $58.50 (no sales tax), Sales Slip 320.

13   Received $50.00 from Nancy Pope to apply to her account, Receipt 284.

13   Wrote Check 402 for $292.50 to Microworld, Inc. in payment of Invoice 574 for $295.45, less $2.95 discount.

14   Wrote Check 403 for the amount of the total net pay due employees. Gross earnings for the pay period ended December 14 were $1,174.37. The following amounts were withheld: employees' federal income tax, $284.38; FICA tax, $82.79; employees' state income tax, $71.92; insurance premium, $26.50.

14   Calculated and recorded the employer's payroll taxes. Employer's payroll liabilities are as follows: FICA tax, 7.05%; state unemployment tax, 2.7%; federal unemployment tax, .8%.

14   Cash sales for December 2–14 were $2,484.93 plus sales tax of $173.94, T137.

14   Bank card sales for December 2–14 were $1,034.35 plus sales tax of $72.40, T137.

16   Paid $26.00 for stamps (Miscellaneous Expense), Check 404.

17   Purchased computer accessories on account from Kess Computer Supplies, $558.47, Invoice 4575, dated December 16, terms 1/30, n/60.

18   Bought office supplies on account from Hill's Supply Company for $138.48; Invoice 345, dated December 17, terms n/30.

18   Betty Foote sent a check for $50.00 to apply to her account, Receipt 285.

19   Sold computer magazines to Carl Combs on account for $29.58 plus sales tax of $2.07, Sales Slip 321.

20   Discovered that a November purchase of $36.00 worth of supplies had been incorrectly journalized and posted to display equipment, Memorandum 293.

21   Issued Check 405 for $391.25 to the state for the sales tax owed for the month of November.

21   Returned $45.60 worth of merchandise bought on account to Micro Products for full credit, Debit Memo 127.

23   Issued Check 406 for $137.10 to Kess Computer Supplies in payment of Invoice 3455 for $138.48 less discount of $1.38.

24   Purchased newspaper ads for $184.48, Check 407.

24   The owner, Ann Lengyel, withdrew $500.00 from the business for personal use, Check 408.

26   Recorded the bank charge of $69.48 for handling the company's bank card sales during November, taken from the December bank statement.

26   Recorded the $7.50 bank service charge from the December bank statement Miscellaneous Expense.

26 Purchased merchandise on account from Video Disk, Inc. for $494.28, Invoice 3756, dated December 24, terms 2/10, n/30.

27 Paid the electric bill of $95.48, Check 409.

28 Issued Check 410 for the total net pay due employees. Gross earnings for the pay period were $1,012.37. The following amounts were withheld: employees' federal income tax, $243.84; FICA tax, $71.37; employees' state income tax, $57.96; insurance premium, $26.50.

28 Recorded the employer's payroll liabilities as follows: FICA tax, 7.05%; state unemployment tax, 2.7%; federal unemployment tax, .8%.

28 Cash sales for December 16–28 were $4,596.86 plus sales tax of $321.78, T138.

28 Bank card sales for December 16–28 were $1,876.64 plus sales tax of $131.36, T138.

30 Sold computer disks to Deborah Vaughn on account for $68.95 plus sales tax of $4.83, Sales Slip 322.

30 Received $100.00 from Stone High School on account, Receipt 286.

31 Cash sales for December 30–31 were $766.57 plus sales tax of $53.66, T139.

31 Bank card sales for December 30–31 were $312.77 plus sales tax of $21.89, T139.

Instructions: The forms for this activity are included in the working papers accompanying this textbook.

(1) Record the December transactions in the sales, cash receipts, purchases, cash payments, and general journals.

(2) Post the individual amounts from the five journals to the accounts receivable and accounts payable subsidiary ledgers daily.

(3) Post the individual amounts from the General columns of the cash receipts, purchases, cash payments, and general journals daily.

(4) Total, prove, and rule the special journals.

(5) Post the special journals' column totals to the appropriate general ledger accounts. Use this order for posting: sales, cash receipts, purchases, and cash payments.

(6) Prove cash. After subtracting the total cash payments for the month, deduct the two bank charges that appeared on the December bank statement. The balance shown on check stub 410 is $15,060.39.

(7) Prepare a schedule of accounts receivable and a schedule of accounts payable.

(8) Prepare a trial balance on a ten-column work sheet.

(9) Complete the work sheet. Use the following adjustment information.

Merchandise inventory, December 31	$25,896.85
Supplies inventory, December 31	1,539.26
Expired insurance, December 31	235.00

(10) Prepare an income statement from the work sheet information.

(11) Prepare a statement of changes in owner's equity. Ann Lengyel did not make any additional investments during the year.

(12) Prepare a balance sheet.

(13) Record and post the adjusting entries.

(14) Record and post the closing entries.

(15) Prepare a post-closing trial balance.

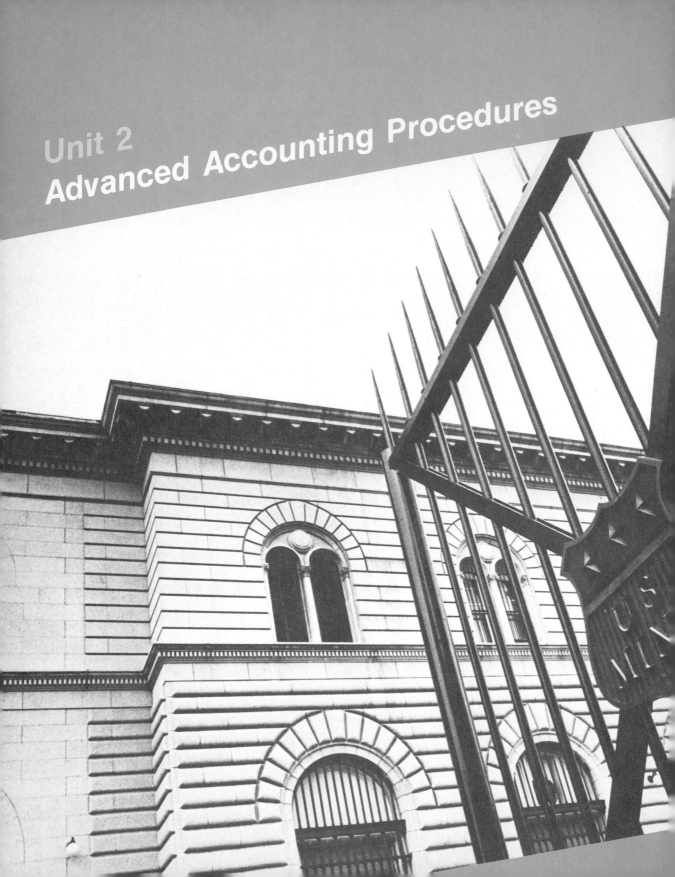

Unit 2
Advanced Accounting Procedures

In addition to the transactions presented in Unit 1, many businesses must also account for financial events that occur less frequently or only at the end of the fiscal period. In this unit, you will learn about the procedures followed in accounting for notes; accounting for uncollectible accounts receivable; accounting for the cost of inventories; accounting for property, plant, and equipment assets; and updating the balances of certain accounts at the end of the fiscal period. You will also learn about an accounting system that businesses can use to maintain better control over their purchases and cash payments. Finally, you will see how all of these financial events are brought together and reported on the financial statements.

In this unit, you will study the seven chapters listed below.

U.S. Mint, Denver, Colorado

3 Accounting for Accounts Receivable

The use of credit for both buying and selling goods and services has become standard practice for business firms of all types: retailers, wholesalers, and manufacturers. However, businesses that sell goods or services on credit find that not all the accounts receivable will be fully collected. The unpaid accounts must eventually be written off as uncollectible, or removed from the accounting records of the business. A firm that grants credit should provide for any such anticipated losses in its accounting records.

In this chapter you'll learn two methods of providing for anticipated losses from bad debts. You will also learn how to write off charge accounts that are no longer collectible.

Learning Objectives

When you have completed this chapter, you should be able to

1. Explain the difference between the direct write-off method and the allowance method of accounting for uncollectible accounts.

2. Calculate the amount of the adjustment for bad debts expense by using a percentage of net sales or net credit sales.

3. Determine the amount of the adjustment by using a percentage of accounts receivable or by aging Accounts Receivable.

4. Record the adjusting entry for estimated uncollectible accounts.

5. Journalize the entries to write off uncollectible accounts receivable using both the direct write-off method and the allowance method.

6. Journalize the entry to reinstate an account receivable previously written off.

7. Define the accounting terms presented in this chapter.

New Terms   **uncollectible account / direct write-off method / allowance method / book value of accounts receivable / percentage of net sales method / percentage of accounts receivable method / aging of accounts receivable method**

The Credit Department

The credit department, because it governs the extension of credit to charge customers, has to keep a watchful eye on present customers. It must also evaluate the debt-paying ability of prospective customers and determine the maximum amount of credit to be extended to each. Retail stores selling to individuals rely on reports from local retail credit bureaus. Wholesalers and manufacturers, when they grant credit to customers, use reports of national credit-rating institutions such as Dun and Bradstreet, wholesale credit bureaus, and the financial statements of prospective customers. Business firms that make many sales on credit find it worthwhile to subscribe to credit bureaus or credit-rating agencies. These organizations maintain files of current financial information on charge customers, establish credit ratings, and conduct special investigations.

But, no matter how careful the credit department is, there will always be some charge customers who will not or cannot pay their bills. An account receivable that cannot be collected becomes an expense to the business. These accounts, often called *bad debts*, decrease ownership equity by decreasing the revenue earned.

There are two methods that can be used to account for bad debts: the direct write-off method and the allowance method.

Direct Write-off Method

Accounts receivable that cannot be collected are known as uncollectible accounts. A simple system for writing off uncollectible accounts is the direct write-off method. With this method, when a firm decides that a charge account is not going to be paid, an entry is made in the general journal to remove the uncollectible amount from Accounts Receivable and the customer's account in the accounts receivable subsidiary ledger. The Accounts Receivable account should report only those accounts that are expected to be collected. The journal entry to write off an uncollectible account is made debiting an account called Bad Debts Expense and crediting Accounts Receivable and the customer's account. This method is used primarily by small businesses with few charge customers or by professional enterprises.

For example, on April 16 the Sloan Company sold merchandise on account to Carl Taylor for $42.50 plus sales tax of $1.70. The entry was recorded in the sales journal as a debit of $44.20 to Accounts Receivable and the customer's account, a credit of $42.50 to Sales, and a credit of $1.70 to Sales Tax Payable.

Taylor failed to pay his bill when it was due. Finally, on September 1 one year later, Sloan decided that Taylor was not going to pay the $44.20.

September 1: *Wrote off Carl Taylor's account as uncollectible, $44.20, Memorandum 86.*

Bad Debts Expense		Accounts Receivable		Carl Taylor	
Dr.	Cr.	Dr.	Cr.	Dr.	Cr.
+	–	+	–	+	–
$44.20		Bal. $44.20	$44.20	Bal. $44.20	$44.20

In the transaction, Bad Debts Expense is debited for $44.20, to show that the uncollectible amount has become an expense. Notice that the amount written off includes the sales tax amount. The bad debt expense, therefore, also includes the expense of having to pay the sales tax. Accounts Receivable and Taylor's account in the accounts receivable subsidiary ledger are credited for $44.20 to indicate the decrease in the amount to be received. The journal entry for the transaction is shown in Figure 3–1.

	DATE		DESCRIPTION	POST. REF.	DEBIT	CREDIT	
1	Sept.	1	Bad Debts Expense		44 20		1
2			Accounts Receivable/Carl Taylor	✓		44 20	2
3			Memo. 86				3

GENERAL JOURNAL PAGE 16

Figure 3–1. Journalizing the Direct Write-off of an Uncollectible Account

Reinstating an Account Previously Written Off

Occasionally the unexpected occurs, and an account previously written off as uncollectible may be collected. For example, suppose Carl Taylor suddenly decides on September 15 to pay his account in full, after the Sloan Company had already written it off. Before the cash receipt can be recorded, Taylor's account must be reinstated. As you can see in Figure 3–2, the entry to reinstate the account is the exact opposite of the write-off entry. After this entry is posted, the cash receipt can be recorded.

	DATE		DESCRIPTION	POST. REF.	DEBIT	CREDIT	
1	Sept.	15	Accounts Receivable/Carl Taylor	✓	44 20		1
2			Bad Debts Expense			44 20	2
3			Memo. 88				3

GENERAL JOURNAL PAGE 16

Figure 3–2. Journalizing the Reinstatement of an Account

Before reading further, do the following activity to check your understanding of the direct write-off method.

Check Your Learning

The Barnes Company uses the direct write-off method of accounting for uncollectible accounts. Record the following transactions in general journal form on a sheet of notebook paper.

Feb.   7   Wrote off the account of Andrew Almond as uncollectible, $170, Memorandum 22.

      18   Received $64 as payment in full from Betty Moreno, whose account had been written off as uncollectible during the previous year, Memorandum 23 and Receipt 1786.

Compare your answers to those in the answers section. Re-read the preceding part of the chapter to find the correct answers to any questions you may have missed.

Matching Bad Debt Losses with Sales

The matching principle of accounting states that revenue for a fiscal period must be matched against the expenses incurred in earning that revenue during that same accounting period. This principle is consistent with the earlier presentation of adjusting entries. For example, in adjusting for prepaid insurance, you debit Insurance Expense and credit Prepaid Insurance. In making the adjustment, you are allocating the insurance expense to the period the expense was incurred. By the same token, when a business sells merchandise on account to a customer who eventually fails to pay the amount owed, the business has incurred a bad debt expense that should be provided for in the year in which the sale is made.

When selling on account, the firm does not know for certain that it has incurred an expense. Nor does it know exactly which customers will fail to pay their bills. As a matter of fact, the firm will not be certain of the expense until it has repeatedly failed in attempts to collect the bill. So the actual recognition of the expense will probably occur many months after the sale, often during the next fiscal period. One way a business can match the bad debt expense for the period with the sales of the same period is to estimate the amount of the future bad debt losses.

The Allowance Method

Large firms and businesses that sell mainly on a credit basis use the allowance method of accounting for bad debts. The allowance method matches potential bad debt expenses with the sales made during the same year. At the end of the fiscal period, an estimate is made of the amount of uncollectible accounts. (There are various methods that can be used to determine the estimated uncollectible amount. They will be explained later in this chapter.) This involves an adjusting entry that is recorded first in the Adjustments section of the work sheet. The two accounts affected by the adjustment for the estimated uncollectible accounts are Bad Debts Expense and Allowance for Uncollectible Accounts.

A firm does not know with certainty which accounts it won't be able to collect fully. As a result, Accounts Receivable can't be credited directly for the estimated uncollectible amount. As you know, Accounts Receivable is a controlling account. Its balance must equal the total of the customers' accounts in the accounts receivable subsidiary ledger. Since a specific customer's account cannot be credited, neither can Accounts Receivable. You could compare this concept to a life insurance company that insures 1,000 newborn infants. The insurance company doesn't know who will be alive at age 21, but on the basis of experience, it can estimate how many will be alive at age 21. Since Accounts Receivable cannot be credited for the estimated uncollectible account, another account— Allowance for Uncollectible Accounts—is used. Allowance for Uncollectible Accounts is a contra asset account. Its balance represents the total estimated uncollectible accounts of the business. The account appears on the balance sheet as a deduction from Accounts Receivable. The difference between the two accounts is referred to as the book value of accounts receivable. It is the amount the business can reasonably expect to receive from its charge customers.

Based on its experience, a business firm can estimate what the year's bad debts expense will be. For example, Videosonics uses the allowance method of accounting for uncollectible accounts. On December 31, it determined that the adjustment for bad debts expense for the period was $704.

Bad Debts Expense		Allowance for Uncollectible Accounts	
Dr.	Cr.	Dr.	Cr.
+	−	−	+
Adj. $704			Bal. $172
			Adj. 704

Video
Work
For the Year Ended

	ACCOUNT NAME	TRIAL BALANCE		ADJUSTMENTS	
		DEBIT	CREDIT	DEBIT	CREDIT
1	Cash	1689100			
2	Notes Receivable	160000			
3	Accounts Receivable	2920000			
4	Allow. for Uncollect. Accts.		17200		(a) 70400
36	Bad Debts Expense			(a) 70400	

Figure 3–3. Adjustment for Bad Debts Expense   (Left Side)

In the adjustment, Bad Debts Expense is debited for $704, the estimated uncollectible amount for the period. Allowance for Uncollectible Accounts is credited for $704, the amount of current accounts receivable that Videosonics estimates to be uncollectible. The adjustment for bad debts expense is entered on the work sheet as shown in Figure 3–3 below.

Notice that prior to the adjustment Bad Debts Expense had no previous balance. With the allowance method, Bad Debts Expense is used only at the end of the period, when it is increased by the adjusting entry. It will be closed into Income Summary, along with the other expense accounts. However, Allowance for Uncollectible Accounts is a permanent account; its balance is carried over from previous periods.

Note that, in the Trial Balance section, Allowance for Uncollectible Accounts has a credit balance of $172. The $704 adjustment for the current period is added to the previous credit balance of $172, resulting in a new balance of $876 in the Adjusted Trial Balance section. This balance is extended to the Balance Sheet Credit column.

Reporting Estimated Uncollectible Accounts on the Financial Statements

The Bad Debts Expense account appears on the income statement in the Expenses section. A portion of Videosonics' income statement appears in Figure 3–4 on the next page, showing the placement of Bad Debts Expense.

Allowance for Uncollectible Accounts is listed immediately below Accounts Receivable in the Current Assets section of the balance sheet, as shown in Figure 3–5 on the next page. The $28,324 represents the book value of accounts receivable.

Remember: **Allowance for Uncollectible Accounts is a contra asset account. It is reported on the balance sheet as a deduction from Accounts Receivable.**

sonics
Sheet
December 31, 19--

ADJUSTED TRIAL BALANCE		INCOME STATEMENT		BALANCE SHEET		
DEBIT	CREDIT	DEBIT	CREDIT	DEBIT	CREDIT	
16891 00				16891 00		1
1600 00				1600 00		2
29200 00				29200 00		3
	876 00				876 00	4
704 00		704 00				36

(Right Side)

Figure 3–4. Placement of Bad Debts Expense on the Income Statement

Videosonics
Income Statement
For the Year Ended December 31, 19--

Revenue:		
Expenses:		
Advertising Expense	1362 00	
Bad Debts Expense	704 00	

Figure 3–5. Placement of Allowance for Uncollectible Accounts on the Balance Sheet

Videosonics
Balance Sheet
December 31, 19--

Assets		
Current Assets:		
Cash		16891 00
Notes Receivable		1600 00
Accounts Receivable	29200 00	
Less: Allow. for Uncollectible Accts	876 00	28324 00

Remember: **Accounts Receivable minus Allowance for Uncollectible Accounts represents the book value of accounts receivable.**

Journalizing the Adjusting Entry for Bad Debts

After the work sheet is completed and the financial statements are prepared, the adjusting entries are journalized. Figure 3–6 shows the adjusting entry for the estimated uncollectible amount for the period.

Bad Debts Expense will be closed, along with the other expense accounts, into Income Summary. Allowance for Uncollectible Accounts, since it is a permanent account, is not closed. Its balance is carried over to the beginning of the next period.

GENERAL JOURNAL   PAGE 26

	DATE	DESCRIPTION	POST. REF.	DEBIT	CREDIT	
1		Adjusting Entries				1
2	19-- Dec. 31	Bad Debts Expense		704 00		2
3		Allow. for Uncollectible Accts			704 00	3

Figure 3–6. Journalizing the Adjusting Entry for Bad Debts

Estimating the Amount of Bad Debts Expense

Management—on the basis of its judgment and past experience—has to make a reasonable estimate of the amount of its uncollectible accounts. Of course, any such estimate will be affected by economic conditions. In a period of prosperity and high employment, a business can expect fewer losses due to uncollectible accounts than in a period of recession.

There are several methods that can be used in estimating the amount of the adjustment for bad debts for the period.

The Percentage of Net Sales Method

The **percentage of net sales method** is a fairly simple method for estimating the amount of the adjustment for bad debts expense. With this method, a company assumes that a certain set percentage of the current period's net sales will be uncollectible. Net sales, you remember, is Sales less Sales Returns and Allowances and Sales Discounts. The amount of the adjustment is found by multiplying the current year's net sales by a set percentage.

For example, over the past few years the actual bad debt losses from sales on account for the Duncan Company have averaged approximately 1% of net sales. On the basis of this information, the company computes the amount of the current period's adjustment by using the 1% estimate.

The Duncan Company's net sales for the period are calculated as follows.

Sales		$640,000
Less: Sales Returns and Allowances	$26,000	
Sales Discounts	1,200	27,200
Net Sales		$612,800

To determine the amount of the adjustment, net sales are multiplied by the set percentage of 1%. The Duncan Company's estimated bad debts expense for the period, therefore, is $6,128. This amount is used as the amount of the adjustment recorded on the work sheet, as shown in Figure 3–7 on pages 72–73. Notice that the amount of the adjustment is *added to* the previous balance of Allowance for Uncollectible Accounts. After the adjusting entry is journalized and posted, Allowance for Uncollectible Accounts will have a credit balance of $6,344.

Some companies that make both cash and credit sales base their estimate of bad debts expense on net credit sales rather than net sales. For example, the Fenwick Company sells merchandise on both a cash and a credit basis. Charge sales, recorded in the sales journal, totaled $490,000. Sales Returns and Allowances and Sales Discounts on credit sales were $18,000 and $2,900 respectively. The Fenwick Company's net credit sales are calculated as shown below.

Credit Sales		$490,000
Less: Sales Returns and Allowances	$18,000	
Sales Discounts	2,900	20,900
Net Credit Sales		$469,100

Duncan
Work
For the Year Ended

	ACCOUNT NAME	TRIAL BALANCE DEBIT	TRIAL BALANCE CREDIT	ADJUSTMENTS DEBIT	ADJUSTMENTS CREDIT
3	Accounts Receivable	48 00 0 00			
4	Allow. for Uncollect. Accts.		2 16 00		(a) 6 12 8 00
24	Sales		64 00 0 0 00		
25	Sales Returns + Allow.	26 00 0 00			
26	Sales Discounts	1 20 0 00			
48	Bad Debts Expense			(a) 6 12 8 00	

Figure 3–7. Adjustment for Bad Debts Expense   (Left Side)

$469,100
× .02
$ 9,382

The Fenwick Company estimates that its bad debts expense for the period will be 2% of its net credit sales. The amount of the company's adjustment for bad debts expense is, therefore, $9,382. The amount of the adjustment for bad debts is *added to* the previous balance of Allowance for Uncollectible Accounts. After the adjusting entry is journalized and posted, Allowance for Uncollectible Accounts has a credit balance of $9,602.

Bad Debts Expense			Allowance for Uncollectible Accounts	
Dr.	Cr.		Dr.	Cr.
+	−		−	+
Adj. $9,382				Bal. $ 220
				Adj. 9,382

Remember: **When the estimated uncollectible amount is based on a set percentage of net sales or net credit sales, the total estimated uncollectible amount is added to the previous balance of Allowance for Uncollectible Accounts.**

The Percentage of Accounts Receivable Method

Some businesses estimate the amount of uncollectible accounts based on a set percentage of accounts receivable. These firms take an average of the actual bad debt losses for several previous years. Then the average bad debt loss—as a percentage of Accounts Receivable—is calculated. The balance of Accounts Receivable is multiplied by this percentage to determine the total estimated uncollectible amount. An adjustment is then made at the end of the fiscal period to bring the balance of Allowance for Uncollectible Accounts up to this estimated amount.

	ADJUSTED TRIAL BALANCE		INCOME STATEMENT		BALANCE SHEET		
	DEBIT	CREDIT	DEBIT	CREDIT	DEBIT	CREDIT	
	48 000 00				48 000 00		3
		6 344 00				6 344 00	4
		640 000 00		640 000 00			24
	26 000 00		26 000 00				25
	1 200 00		1 200 00				26
	6 128 00		6 128 00				48

(Right Side)

For example, Videosonics calculates the amount of the adjustment for bad debts expense as a set percentage of Accounts Receivable. The year-end balance of Accounts Receivable and the actual bad debt losses for the past three years were as follows.

	Balance of Accounts Receivable	Total Actual Bad Debt Losses (Accounts Receivable written off)
Year 1	$22,000	$ 770
Year 2	28,000	764
Year 3	24,000	686
	$74,000	$2,220

$\frac{\$ 2,220}{\$74,000} = 3\%$

By dividing $2,220 by $74,000, Videosonics determined that its average bad debt loss over the three previous years was 3% of the balance of Accounts Receivable.

Videosonics can now calculate the bad debts adjustment for the current period. At the end of the period, the balance of Videosonics' Accounts Receivable account is $29,200. This amount is multiplied by 3% to determine the total estimated uncollectible amount: $876. This $876 represents the updated, end-of-period balance that should be in Allowance for Uncollectible Accounts. An adjustment must be made to bring the balance of Allowance for Uncollectible Accounts up to the estimated amount of $876. The current balance of Allowance for Uncollectible Accounts shown in the Trial Balance section of the work sheet is $172. Allowance for Uncollectible Accounts must, therefore, be increased by $704 to bring the balance up to $876 ($876 − $172 = $704). Videosonics' adjustment on the work sheet was shown in Figure 3–4 on pages 68–69.

The Aging of Accounts Receivable Method

With the **aging of accounts receivable method**, each customer's account is examined and "aged," or classified according to the due date of the account. The accounts are then separated into age groups: not yet due, 1–30 days past due, 31–60 days past due, and so on. As an account grows older, the likelihood increases that it will prove to be uncollectible. Based on its past experience, a firm can estimate what percentage of each age group will be uncollectible. The total amount for each age group is then multiplied by the percentage considered to be uncollectible for that group. The resulting amounts are the estimated uncollectible amounts for each age group. The total of all the estimated uncollectible amounts by age groups represents the end-of-period balance of Allowance for Uncollectible Accounts. An adjustment is made at the end of the fiscal period to bring the balance of Allowance for Uncollectible Accounts up to the total estimated amount.

For example, the Winston Company estimated its bad debts expense by aging accounts receivable. At the end of the period, the company examined its accounts receivable and prepared an *accounts receivable aging schedule*. This schedule, which lists all customers' accounts by age group, is shown in Figure 3–8 below.

Accounts Receivable Aging Schedule			DATE December 31, 19--					
CUSTOMER'S NAME	BALANCE	NOT YET DUE	DAYS PAST DUE					
			1–30	31–60	61–90	91–180	181–365	OVER 365
Kate Allen	$722.00	$722.00						
John Baker	464.00				$464.00			
Laura Chase	136.90			$136.90				
Angie Dalton	914.00	914.00						
Totals	$90,000.00	$78,200.00	$4,030.00	$3,280.00	$1,975.00	$1,260.00	$834.00	$421.00

Figure 3–8. Accounts Receivable Aging Schedule

				Winston	
				Work	
				For the Year Ended	

ACCOUNT NAME	TRIAL BALANCE		ADJUSTMENTS	
	DEBIT	CREDIT	DEBIT	CREDIT
2 Accounts Receivable	90 000 00			
3 Allow. for Uncollect. Accts.		410 00		(a) 317 00
25 Bad Debts Expense			(a) 317 00	

Figure 3–9. Adjustment for Bad Debts Expense   (Left Side)

The amount for each age group is multiplied by the percentage the company estimates will be uncollectible. In the following table, for example, the company estimates that of the $78,200 of accounts receivable not yet due, 2% (or $1,564) will prove to be uncollectible. Of the $4,030 of accounts receivable 1–30 days past due, 4% ($161.20) are estimated to be uncollectible.

Age Group	Amount	Estimated Percentage Uncollectible	Estimated Uncollectible Amount
Not yet due	$78,200	2%	$1,564.00
1 to 30 days past due	4,030	4%	161.20
31 to 60 days past due	3,280	10%	328.00
61 to 90 days past due	1,975	20%	395.00
91 to 180 days past due	1,260	30%	378.00
181 to 365 days past due	834	50%	417.00
More than 365 days past due	421	80%	336.80
	$90,000		$3,580.00

As you can see, the firm estimates that a total of $3,580 of its accounts receivable will be uncollectible. An adjustment must now be made to bring the balance of Allowance for Uncollectible Accounts up to the estimated figure of $3,580. The balance of Allowance for Uncollectible Accounts shown in the Trial Balance is $410. The amount of the adjustment for bad debts expense is $3,170 ($3,580 − $410). The adjustment and its effect on the accounts are illustrated in the work sheet in Figure 3–9. After the adjusting entry is journalized and posted, the balance of Allowance for Uncollectible Accounts will be $3,580, the balance as determined by the aging procedure.

Remember: **When the adjustment for bad debts expense is based on a set percentage or aging of Accounts Receivable, Allowance for Uncollectible Accounts is adjusted to bring the balance up to the total estimated uncollectible amount.**

Company
Sheet
December 31, 19--

ADJUSTED TRIAL BALANCE		INCOME STATEMENT		BALANCE SHEET		
DEBIT	CREDIT	DEBIT	CREDIT	DEBIT	CREDIT	
90 000 00				90 000 00		2
	3 580 00				3 580 00	3
3 170 00		3 170 00				25

(Right Side)

Before reading further, do the following activity to check your understanding of the aging of accounts receivable method.

Check Your Learning

The Shafer Company estimates its bad debts expense by aging accounts receivable. The age groups and estimated uncollectible percentages are as shown below.

Age Group	Amount	Estimated Percentage Uncollectible
Not yet due	$60,000	1%
1 to 60 days past due	14,000	2%
61 to 120 days past due	6,000	5%
121 to 365 days past due	2,000	30%
More than 365 days past due	1,000	60%
	$83,000	

1. What is the estimated uncollectible amount for each age group?
2. What is the total estimated uncollectible amount?
3. If Allowance for Uncollectible Accounts has a balance of $1,100, what is the amount of the adjustment?

Compare your answers with those in the answers section. Re-read the preceding part of the chapter to find the correct answers to any questions you may have missed.

Writing off Uncollectible Accounts Using the Allowance Method

With the direct write-off method, when a customer's account proves to be uncollectible, it is written off. Bad Debts Expense is debited and Accounts Receivable and the customer's account are credited.

With the allowance method, however, the Bad Debts Expense account cannot be used when a customer's account is written off. The Bad Debts Expense account is used only at the end of the period, to record the adjusting and closing entries. Bad Debts Expense is closed, along with other expense accounts, into the Income Summary account at the end of the period.

Allowance for Uncollectible Accounts is not closed. Rather than having the balance continually increased through yearly adjustments, this account is used when writing off customers' accounts that are considered to be uncollectible. Allowance for Uncollectible Accounts can be compared to a reservoir. It is "filled up" at the end of the year by the adjusting entry. The estimated bad debt amount is saved until it is needed. When a charge customer's account proves to be uncollectible, the business can use the reservoir to write off the account.

For example, on March 12, after many attempts to collect the amount owed, Videosonics decided to write off the account of Ronald D. Oakes as uncollectible. The amount owed by Oakes is $71.40.

Allowance for Uncollectible Accounts		Accounts Receivable		Ronald D. Oakes	
Dr.	Cr.	Dr.	Cr.	Dr.	Cr.
−	+	+	−	+	−
$71.40	Bal. $876.00	Bal. $29,000.00	$71.40	Bal. $71.40	$71.40

In the transaction, Allowance for Uncollectible Accounts is debited for $71.40. The $71.40 is no longer part of the estimated bad debts; it *is* a bad debt. Allowance for Uncollectible Accounts is, therefore, decreased for the amount of the loss. Accounts Receivable and Oakes' account in the accounts receivable subsidiary ledger are credited for $71.40. Since Videosonics no longer expects to receive a payment, the amount must be removed from the company's books.

The journal entry to record the transaction is shown in Figure 3–10.

GENERAL JOURNAL   PAGE 46

	DATE	DESCRIPTION	POST. REF.	DEBIT	CREDIT	
1	19-- Mar 12	Allowance for Uncollectible Accounts		71 40		1
2		Accts. Receivable/Ronald D. Oakes	✓		71 40	2
3		Memo. 411				3

Figure 3–10. Journalizing the Write-off of an Uncollectible Account

Notice that an expense account is not involved in the entry to write off an account. The expense was recorded as part of the previous year's adjusting entry. Notice too that the entry does not change the book value of accounts receivable.

Account Name	Balance before Write-off	Balance after Write-off
Accounts Receivable	$29,200.00	$29,128.60
Less Allowance for Uncollectible Accounts	876.00	804.60
Book Value	$28,324.00	$28,324.00

Differences Between Write-offs and Estimates

The total amount of accounts receivable written off during a fiscal period does not ordinarily agree with the estimated uncollectible amount recorded in the adjusting entry. The accounts written off as uncollectible usually turn out to be less than the estimated amount. This means that, at the end of a fiscal period, there is a small credit balance in Allowance for Uncollectible Accounts. However, if (as sometimes happens) the accounts written off are greater than the estimated amount, Allowance for Uncollectible Accounts will temporarily have a debit balance. The debit balance will be eliminated by the adjusting entry at the end of the period, which results in an increase to Allowance for Uncollectible Accounts.

Reinstating an Account Previously Written Off

As with accounts written off by the direct write-off method, an account written off as uncollectible under the allowance method may later be paid. In such cases, the charge customer's account must first be reinstated by an entry that is the exact opposite of the write-off entry.

For example, on July 2 Videosonics received $71.40 from Ronald Oakes, whose account had been written off on March 12. Before the cash receipt can be recorded, Oakes' account is reinstated by the journal entry shown in Figure 3–11. Notice that this entry is the exact opposite of the entry to write off the account (shown in Figure 3–10). After this entry is posted, the cash receipt can be journalized.

	DATE	DESCRIPTION	POST. REF.	DEBIT	CREDIT	
1	July 2	Accounts Receivable/Ronald D. Oakes	/	71 40		1
2		Allow. for Uncollectible Accts.			71 40	2
3		Memo. 432				3

GENERAL JOURNAL   PAGE 47

Figure 3–11. Journalizing the Reinstatement of an Account

Summary of Key Points

1. A firm may account for bad debts by two different methods: the direct write-off method and the allowance method.
2. The direct write-off method of accounting for uncollectible accounts is used primarily by business firms with few charge customers and by professional enterprises. When using this method, Bad Debts Expense is debited and Accounts Receivable and the charge customer's account are credited.
3. The allowance method matches the bad debt expense with the sales for the same fiscal period. An adjustment is made at the end of the year debiting Bad Debts Expense and crediting Allowance for Uncollectible Accounts for the estimated amount of bad debt losses for the period.
4. Allowance for Uncollectible Accounts is a contra asset account. It appears as a deduction from Accounts Receivable in the Current Assets section of the balance sheet.
5. The book value of accounts receivable is the amount a business can reasonably expect to receive from its charge customers. It is the difference between the balance of Accounts Receivable and the balance of Allowance for Uncollectible Accounts.

6. A firm that uses the allowance method of accounting for uncollectible accounts can determine the amount of the adjustment by (1) taking a set percentage of net sales or net credit sales, or (2) taking a set percentage of Accounts Receivable, or (3) aging Accounts Receivable.

7. When a business estimates its bad debts expense based on a percentage of net sales or net credit sales, the amount of the adjustment is added to the balance of Allowance for Uncollectible Accounts.

8. When a business estimates its bad debts expense based on a percentage of or an aging of Accounts Receivable, the balance of Allowance for Uncollectible Accounts is adjusted to bring it up to the total estimated amount.

9. To write off a charge account as being uncollectible under the allowance method, the firm debits Allowance for Uncollectible Accounts and credits Accounts Receivable and the customer's account.

10. The entry to reinstate an account previously written off is the opposite of the entry to write off the account.

Review and Applications

Building Your Accounting Vocabulary

In your own words, write the definition of each of the following accounting terms. Use complete sentences for your definitions.

aging of accounts
receivable method
allowance method
book value of
accounts receivable

direct write-off
method
percentage of
accounts receivable
method

percentage of net
sales method
uncollectible account

Reviewing Your Accounting Knowledge

1. What two methods can be used to account for uncollectible accounts?
2. Why is the allowance method of handling bad debts considered to be more effective than the direct write-off method?
3. Why are bad debts considered to be an expense?
4. When a business uses the allowance method, why can't Accounts Receivable be credited for the estimated uncollectible amount?
5. How is Allowance for Uncollectible Accounts classified on financial statements?
6. How is the book value of Accounts Receivable calculated?
7. Explain the nature of Allowance for Uncollectible Accounts. How is it used?
8. What methods can be used to estimate the uncollectible amount?
9. What is meant by aging accounts receivable?
10. When an account is written off under the allowance method of accounting for bad debts, why doesn't the book value of Accounts Receivable decrease?
11. Why might Allowance for Uncollectible Accounts have a debit balance?

Improving Your Decision-making Skills

The Lafayette Company uses the percentage of net sales method for estimating its uncollectible amount. For the past three years, Allowance for Uncollectible Accounts, before adjusting entries, has had a debit balance. This debit balance has been increasing each year. What could management do to eliminate the increasing debit balance in Allowance for Uncollectible Accounts?

Applying Accounting Procedures

Problem 3–1

The Gibson Company uses the aging of accounts receivable method to estimate its uncollectible amount. Its aging schedule is at the top of page 81.

Instructions: Complete the schedule, using the form that is included in the working papers that accompany this textbook.

Age Group	Amount	Estimated Percentage Uncollectible	Estimated Uncollectible Amount
Not yet due	$124,320	2%	
1 to 30 days past due	6,340	5%	
31 to 60 days past due	5,752	10%	
61 to 90 days past due	3,280	20%	
91 to 180 days past due	1,920	25%	
181 to 365 days past due	432	40%	
More than 1 year past due	284	70%	
Totals	$142,328		

Problem 3–2

Garcia Imports uses the direct write-off method of accounting for uncollectible accounts. The following transactions took place during the accounting period.

Jan. 17 Sold merchandise on account to Jay Clayton for $1,200, terms n/30, Sales Slip 904.

Mar. 17 Received $400 from Jay Clayton on account, Receipt 646.

Dec. 1 Wrote off the account of Jay Clayton as uncollectible, Memorandum 1113.

20 Received a check for $200 on account from Jay Clayton, Memorandum 1120 and Receipt 1187.

Instructions:

(1) Record the transactions, in general journal form. Use page 34.
(2) Post the transactions to Clayton's subsidiary ledger account.

Problem 3–3

The Owens Company uses the allowance method of accounting for uncollectible accounts. On December 31, the following balances appear in the Trial Balance section of the work sheet.

Allowance for Uncollectible Accounts	$ 150
Sales	220,000
Sales Returns and Allowances	20,000

The Owens Company estimates that bad debt losses will be ½% of net sales.

Instructions:

(1) Determine the amount of the adjustment for bad debts.
(2) Record the adjusting entry on page 23 of the general journal.
(3) Post the adjusting entry to the Allowance for Uncollectible Accounts general ledger account.

Problem 3–4

On December 31, the following balances appeared in the Trial Balance section of the Martin Company's work sheet.

Accounts Receivable	$ 60,000
Allowance for Uncollectible Accounts	520
Sales	904,651
Sales Returns and Allowances	2,975
Sales Discounts	1,676

Instructions: Determine the amount of the adjusting entry to record the estimated bad debt expense under each of the following conditions.

(1) Bad debt losses are estimated at ½% of net sales.
(2) Bad debt losses are estimated to be 3½% of Accounts Receivable.

Problem 3–5

The Roth Company uses the allowance method of accounting for uncollectible accounts. During the year Roth completed the following selected transactions.

Feb. 11 Wrote off the $654.00 account of North Side Company as uncollectible, Memorandum 117.

May 6 Wrote off the account of John Graham, $348.32, as uncollectible, Memorandum 204.

19 Received $182.00 unexpectedly from Stella Wells, whose account had been written off two years earlier. Reinstated the account for $182.00 and recorded the collection of $182.00, Memorandum 205 and Receipt 531.

Aug. 3 Collected 10% of the $252.00 owed by Douglas Myers, a bankrupt. Wrote off the remainder as uncollectible, Receipt 622 and Memorandum 311.

Sept. 21 Received $180.00 from John Graham as part payment of the account written off on May 6. Accordingly, reinstated the account for the amount originally owed, $348.32, Memorandum 321 and Receipt 649.

Dec. 29 Journalized a compound entry to write off the following accounts: Nathan Ainsworth, $352.40; Todd Dowler, $228.00; Rachel Valdez, $248.72; Memorandum 400.

31 Recorded the adjusting entry for estimated bad debt losses at ½% of credit sales of $296,000.00.

31 Closed the Bad Debts Expense account.

Instructions:

(1) Record the entries, in general journal form. Use page 42.
(2) Post the entries to the general ledger accounts for Allowance for Uncollectible Accounts and Bad Debts Expense. The accounts have already been opened in the working papers that accompany this textbook.

Problem 3–6

Eastside Pool Supply uses the allowance method of accounting for uncollectible accounts. The following are among the transactions completed this year.

Jan. 8 Sold merchandise on account to Webber Motel, $1,480.00, Sales Slip 2116.

Feb. 6 Wrote off the account of Vaughn, Inc., $1,372.00, Memorandum 311.

Mar. 12 Reinstated the account of Newberry Apartments, which had been written off last year. Received $316.00 in full payment, Memorandum 319 and Receipt 402.

Aug. 17 Received $138.00 unexpectedly from Ruth Becker. The account had been written off last year in the amount of $138.00. Reinstated the account and recorded the collection of $138.00, Memorandum 800 and Receipt 912.

Sept. 28 Received 10% of the $1,480.00 balance owed by Webber Motel before it went out of business. Wrote off the remainder as uncollectible, Receipt 991 and Memorandum 866.

Oct. 15 Reinstated the account of Dillon Manor that had been written off two years earlier; received $652.00 in full payment of the amount owed, Memorandum 872 and Receipt 1004.

Dec. 29 Journalized a compound entry to write off the following accounts as uncollectible: Alexander Company, $1,968.00; Anderson Lodge, $328.00; Bannister Terrace, $1,568.40; Norman Watkins, $152.28; Memorandum 996.

31 By aging the $86,402.54 balance of Accounts Receivable, estimated that $4,592.00 of Accounts Receivable will be uncollectible. Recorded the adjusting entry.

31 Recorded the closing entry for Bad Debts Expense.

Instructions:

(1) Open the following accounts, recording any balance as of January 1.

> 114 Allowance for Uncollectible Accounts $6,352.00
> 313 Income Summary
> 605 Bad Debts Expense

(2) Beginning on page 41 of a general journal, record the transactions as well as the adjusting and closing entries described above. After each entry, post to the three general ledger accounts.

(3) Prepare the Current Assets section of the balance sheet. Balances of the other asset accounts are: Cash in Bank, $13,640.32; Supplies, $1,942.00; Merchandise Inventory, $98,652.00; Prepaid Insurance, $720.00.

4 Accounting for Notes

Credit plays a very important role in the operation of most businesses. Credit may be granted on a charge-account basis, with payment generally due within 30–60 days. This type of credit involves the Accounts Payable and Accounts Receivable accounts.

Credit may also be granted on the basis of short-term, written agreements. These formal written arrangements, called promissory notes, are usually used for credit transactions of more than 60 days. Most businesses at one time or another become involved with notes, either by issuing notes to creditors, receiving notes from customers, or issuing notes to banks when borrowing money.

In this chapter, you will learn how to record transactions involving promissory notes.

Learning Objectives

When you have completed this chapter, you should be able to

1. Explain how promissory notes are used by businesses.

2. Determine the interest expense and the due date of a promissory note.

3. Explain the difference between interest-bearing and non-interest-bearing promissory notes.

4. Record journal entries for notes payable and notes receivable.

5. Define the accounting terms presented in this chapter.

New Terms

promissory note / maturity date / term / principal / face value / payee / maker / interest / maturity value / note payable / interest-bearing note / non-interest-bearing note payable / bank discount / proceeds / note receivable / dishonored note / discounting notes receivable / discount period / contingent liability / protest fee

Promissory Notes

A **promissory note**, usually referred to simply as a ''note,'' is a written promise to pay a certain sum of money on a fixed or determinable date, the **maturity date**. The amount of time between the date of the note and the maturity date is the **term** of the note. The **principal** is the amount of money being borrowed. The **face value** is the amount written on the face of the note. In most cases, the principal and the face value are the same. As in the case of a check, a promissory note must be payable to the order of a particular person or firm, known as the **payee**. It must also be signed by the person or firm making the promise, known as the **maker**. In the promissory note shown in Figure 4–1, Hart Manufacturing is the payee and Videosonics is the maker.

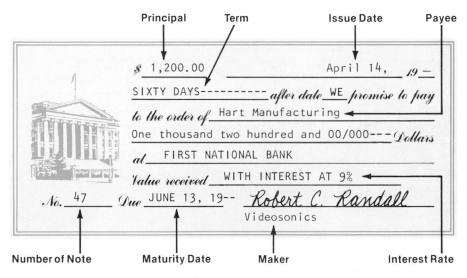

Figure 4–1. Promissory Note

Calculating Interest

When a promissory note is issued, the maker agrees to repay the principal with interest. **Interest** is a charge made for the use of money. To the maker of the note, interest is an expense. To the payee, interest is a form of revenue. The amount of interest a maker pays is expressed as a certain percentage of the principal of the note for a period of one year. The formula for calculating interest is as follows:

$$\text{Interest} = \text{Principal} \times \text{Interest Rate} \times \text{Time}$$

Time, or the term of the note, is expressed in terms of days or months. It is the period between the issue date of the note and the maturity date of the note. The time is stated in terms of a fraction of one year, such as:

$$3 \text{ months} = \frac{3}{12} \qquad 60 \text{ days} = \frac{60}{365}$$

$$6 \text{ months} = \frac{6}{12} \qquad 90 \text{ days} = \frac{90}{365}$$

Let's calculate the interest on the note in Figure 4–1. The principal is $1,200 and the interest rate of the note is 9% (.09). Since the term of the note is given in days, the time is expressed as a fraction of 365 days.

$$\begin{array}{cccc} \text{Principal} & \text{Interest Rate} & \text{Time} & \text{Interest} \\ \$1{,}200.00 \ \times & .09 & \times \ \dfrac{60}{365} = & \$17.75 \end{array}$$

$1,200.00
+ 17.75
―――――
$1,217.75

The interest on the note is $17.75. The **maturity value** of the note, which is the principal plus the interest that is repaid on the maturity date, is $1,217.75.

Remember: If the term of a note is less than a year, time is expressed as a fraction of one year.

In actual practice, banks and businesses generally use computers or interest tables to calculate interest. The interest computed in this way may differ by a few cents from interest calculated manually, since the factors are rounded off.

Before reading further, do the following activity to check your understanding of how to calculate interest.

Check Your Learning

Determine the interest for each of the following notes.

	Principal	Term	Interest Rate
1.	$1,200	30 days	10%
2.	900	60 days	11%
3.	1,600	90 days	9%
4.	1,550	75 days	9½%
5.	780	45 days	10½%

Compare your answers to those in the answers section. Re-read the preceding part of the chapter to find the correct answers to any questions you may have missed.

Determining the Maturity Date

As we have said, the term of a note may be expressed in either days or months. If the term is expressed in months, the maturity date is the same day of the month after the specified number of months have elapsed. For example, a note dated March 12 with a term of 3 months has a maturity date of June 12. If there is no date in the month of maturity that corresponds to the issue date, the maturity date becomes the last day of the month. For example, a 3-month note dated January 31 would be due on April 30.

But suppose that the term of a note is expressed in days. In counting the number of days, begin counting with the day *after* the date the note was issued, since the note states "after date." Do, however, count the last day. Let us assume that a promissory note issued on April 14 has a term of 60 days. To determine the due date, follow these steps:

30	April
− 14	Issue date
16	Left in April

1. Determine the number of days remaining in the month of issue (April) by subtracting the date of the note from the number of days in the month. In our example, the note was dated April 14. Therefore, 14 is subtracted from 30, leaving 16 days.

60	Term
− 16	April
44	

2. Determine the number of days the note has left after the first month. To do this, subtract the days calculated in Step 1 from the term of the note, 60 − 16 = 44.

− 31	May
13	June due date

3. Subtract the number of days in the second month (May) from the number of days left after Step 2, 44 − 31 = 13. The answer is the day of the next month (June) the note is due. The maturity date of the note is, therefore, June 13.

Before going on to a discussion of notes payable, do the following activity to check your understanding of how to determine the maturity date of a promissory note.

Check Your Learning

Determine the maturity dates for the following notes. Record your answers on a sheet of notebook paper.

	Date of Issue	Term
1.	March 28	60 days
2.	October 18	90 days
3.	June 26	30 days
4.	December 12	3 months
5.	July 1	120 days

Compare your answers to those in the answers section. Re-read the preceding part of the chapter to find the correct answers to any questions you may have missed.

Notes Payable

A promissory note issued by a person or business is a **note payable**. There are several reasons for issuing a note payable, including the following:

1. Note given to a supplier in return for an extension of time for payment of an account payable.
2. Note given in exchange for merchandise or other property purchased.
3. Note given as evidence of a loan.

The accounts particularly involved are Notes Payable (classified as a current liability on the balance sheet) and Interest Expense (classified as Other Expense on the income statement).

Interest-bearing Notes Payable

An **interest-bearing note** is a note that requires the face value (the principal) plus interest to be paid at maturity. On an interest-bearing note, the face value and the principal are the same. The note in Figure 4–1 on page 85 is an interest-bearing note and has a maturity value of $1,217.75 ($1,200.00 face value plus interest of $17.75).

Recording the Issuance of an Interest-bearing Note Payable

Occasionally, a business may want more time to pay for a charge purchase. The firm may ask a creditor to accept a note for all or part of the amount due. For example, on March 15 Videosonics bought merchandise on account from Hart Manufacturing, with terms of n/30. Videosonics recorded that transaction in its purchases journal as a debit to Purchases for $1,200 and a credit to Accounts Payable/Hart Manufacturing for $1,200.

Videosonics prefers not to pay for this purchase when it is due on April 14. Instead, Videosonics asks Hart to accept a note for the amount of its account payable. Hart agrees.

April 14: Issued a 60-day, 9% note payable to Hart Manufacturing for the $1,200 account payable, Note 47.

The accounts affected by this transaction are Accounts Payable and Notes Payable in the general ledger and the Hart Manufacturing account in the accounts payable subsidiary ledger. Notes Payable is classified as a current liability; it has a normal credit balance. In this transaction, Accounts Payable and Hart Manufacturing's account are debited for $1,200. Since a note is being issued in place of the amount recorded as an account payable, the $1,200 must be removed from the Accounts Payable account. Notes Payable is credited for $1,200 to show the increase in the liability.

Accounts Payable		Hart Manufacturing		Notes Payable	
Dr.	Cr.	Dr.	Cr.	Dr.	Cr.
–	+	–	+	–	+
$1,200.00	$1,200.00	$1,200.00	$1,200.00		$1,200.00

Notice that this transaction substitutes Notes Payable for the Accounts Payable account. The note does not pay the debt, but merely reclassifies the amount owed from Accounts Payable to Notes Payable. Hart prefers the note to the charge account because the note is written evidence of the debt and the amount owed. In addition, Hart is entitled to 9% interest. The general journal entry for this transaction is shown in Figure 4–2.

	DATE	DESCRIPTION	POST. REF.	DEBIT	CREDIT	
	GENERAL JOURNAL				PAGE 41	
1	19-- Apr. 14	Accounts Payable/Hart Mfg.	✓	1 200 00		1
2		Notes Payable			1 200 00	2
3		Note 47				3

Figure 4–2. Journalizing the Issuance of an Interest-Bearing Note Payable

Recording the Payment of an Interest-bearing Note Payable

When an interest-bearing note payable falls due, the maker prepares a check for the maturity value (principal plus interest) of the note.

June 13: *Issued Check 417 for $1,217.75 to Hart Manufacturing in payment of Note 47 issued April 14.*

This transaction can now be recorded. Notes Payable is debited for $1,200.00 because Videosonics no longer owes the liability. Videosonics must record the interest charge as an expense. Therefore, the Interest Expense account is debited for $17.75. Cash in Bank is credited for $1,217.75, the amount of the note plus the interest charge.

Notes Payable		Interest Expense		Cash in Bank	
Dr.	Cr.	Dr.	Cr.	Dr.	Cr.
–	+	+	–	+	–
$1,200.00	$1,200.00	$17.75			$1,217.75

The entry to record this transaction is shown in Figure 4–3. (This transaction could be recorded in the cash payments journal rather than in the general

	DATE	DESCRIPTION	POST. REF.	DEBIT	CREDIT	
	GENERAL JOURNAL				PAGE 42	
1	19-- June 13	Notes Payable		1 200 00		1
2		Interest Expense		1 7 75		2
3		Cash in Bank			1 2 1 7 75	3
4		Check 417				4

Figure 4–3. Journalizing the Payment of an Interest-Bearing Note Payable

journal. However, to simplify the discussion of the entries, all the transactions will be presented here in general journal form.)

Non-interest-bearing Notes Payable

Businesses often borrow money from banks, issuing notes payable as proof of the debt. In some cases, the bank may require the borrower to pay the interest on the note payable at the time the note is issued rather than at the maturity date. The bank deducts the interest charge from the face value of the note and gives the difference to the borrower. A note from which the interest has been deducted in advance is called a **non-interest-bearing note payable** because there is no interest rate stated on the note itself. On a non-interest-bearing note, the face value and the maturity value are the same. The amount deducted in advance by the bank is called the **bank discount**. The amount the borrower actually receives—the difference between the face value and the bank discount—is called the **proceeds**. This process is called *discounting a note payable*.

Remember: On interest-bearing notes, the face value is equal to the principal. On non-interest-bearing notes, the face value equals the maturity value.

Recording the Issuance of a Non-interest-bearing Note Payable

Now let's look at how a non-interest-bearing note payable would be recorded on the accounting records of Videosonics. On May 19, Videosonics had the following transaction.

May 19: Issued a $6,000, 60-day, non-interest-bearing note payable to Northwest National Bank, which was discounted at 10%, Note 48.

The first step is to calculate the amount of the bank discount. The bank discount is calculated the same way as the interest on an interest-bearing note payable is calculated. The interest rate used in the calculations is the bank's discount rate.

Principal	Interest Rate (Discount Rate)	Time	Bank Discount
$6,000.00 \times$	.10	$\times \dfrac{60}{365} =$	$98.63

$6,000.00
− 98.63
─────────
$5,901.37

The amount of the bank discount is deducted from the face value of the note to determine the proceeds. The amount of the proceeds, the amount Videosonics actually receives, is $5,901.37.

The accounts involved in recording this transaction are Cash in Bank, Discount on Notes Payable, and Notes Payable. Cash in Bank is debited for $5,901.37, the proceeds, or the amount of cash received. The amount of the bank discount, $98.63, represents future interest charges included in the face value of the note. To show the correct amount of the liability (the principal amount) on the accounting records, the $98.63 is debited to an account called Discount on Notes

Payable. Discount on Notes Payable is a contra liability account and has a normal debit balance. It will appear on the balance sheet as a deduction from Notes Payable. Notes Payable is credited for $6,000.00, the face value of the note.

Cash in Bank		Discount on Notes Payable		Notes Payable	
Dr.	Cr.	Dr.	Cr.	Dr.	Cr.
+	–	+	–	–	+
$5,901.37		$98.63			$6,000.00

The transaction is recorded in general journal form as shown in Figure 4–4.

	GENERAL JOURNAL			PAGE 41	
DATE	DESCRIPTION	POST. REF.	DEBIT	CREDIT	
19-- May 19	Cash in Bank		5 90 1 37		1
	Discount on Notes Payable		98 63		2
	Notes Payable			6 000 00	3
	Note 48				4

Figure 4–4. Journalizing the Issuance of a Non-Interest-Bearing Note Payable

Recording the Payment of a Non-interest-bearing Note Payable

When a non-interest-bearing note payable matures, a check is written for the face value of the note, which is also the maturity value of the note. In addition, the amount of the bank discount must be recognized as an expense. It is transferred from Discount on Notes Payable to the Interest Expense account.

July 18: Issued Check 599 for $6,000.00 to Northwest National Bank in payment of Note 48 issued on May 19.

In this transaction, Notes Payable is debited for $6,000.00 to show the decrease in the liability. Cash in Bank is credited for $6,000.00, the face value of the note. This removes the note payable from the accounting records of Videosonics. To show that the bank discount has now become an expense, Interest Expense is debited for $98.63 and Discount on Notes Payable is credited for $98.63.

Notes Payable		Cash in Bank	
Dr.	Cr.	Dr.	Cr.
–	+	+	–
$6,000.00	$6,000.00		$6,000.00

Interest Expense		Discount on Notes Payable	
Dr.	Cr.	Dr.	Cr.
+	–	+	–
$98.63		$98.63	$98.63

	DATE	DESCRIPTION	POST. REF.	DEBIT	CREDIT	
1	July 18	Notes Payable		6 00000		1
2		Interest Expense		98 63		2
3		Cash in Bank			6 00000	3
4		Discount on Notes Payable			98 63	4
5		Check 599				5

Figure 4–5. Journalizing the Payment of a Non-Interest-Bearing Note Payable

Two separate entries could be used to record: (1) the payment of the non-interest-bearing note payable and (2) the interest expense. However, it is much simpler to use one compound entry, as shown in Figure 4–5.

Renewal of an Interest-bearing Note at Maturity

What if the maker is unable to pay a note in full at maturity? Then he or she may arrange to renew all or part of the note. At this time, the maker usually pays the interest on the old note. For example, assume that on May 27 Videosonics issued a 60-day, 8% note to Danton, Inc., for $1,500 (Note 49). That transaction was recorded as a debit of $1,500 to Accounts Payable and to Danton, Inc. and a credit of $1,500 to Notes Payable.

When a firm renews an interest-bearing note, the interest must first be calculated on the existing note, up to the present date.

$$\text{Principal} \quad \text{Interest Rate} \quad \text{Time} \quad \text{Interest}$$
$$\$1,500.00 \times .08 \times \frac{60}{365} = \$19.73$$

An entry is then made to record the payment of the interest on the existing note and the issuance of a new note. In this case, the new note is for 30 days at 9% (the interest rate has been increased), as shown in the compound entry in Figure 4–6. The entry occurs on July 26, the maturity date of the old note.

	DATE	DESCRIPTION	POST. REF.	DEBIT	CREDIT	
1	July 26	Notes Payable		1 50000		1
2		Interest Expense		19 73		2
3		Notes Payable			1 50000	3
4		Cash in Bank			19 73	4
5		Note 50 / Check 610				5

Figure 4–6. Journalizing the Renewal of an Interest-Bearing Note at Maturity

Notes Receivable

A promissory note accepted by a person or business is called a **note receivable**. Business firms receive promissory notes for a variety of reasons. Companies frequently accept promissory notes from charge customers who request additional time to settle past-due accounts. Notes receivable may also come into being when a company grants loans to employees or preferred customers or suppliers. In some business fields, the credit period is often longer than the normal 30-day period. Here, the transactions are frequently evidenced by notes rather than open accounts. Some examples include the sale of farm machinery and construction equipment. The accounts involved are Notes Receivable (classified as a current asset if maturing within one year) and Interest Income (classified as other revenue).

Recording the Receipt of a Note Receivable

On March 6, Videosonics sold $480 worth of merchandise on account to Paul Henning. The transaction was recorded in its sales journal. On April 6, Videosonics had the following transaction:

April 6: *Received a $480, 30-day, 10% note from Paul Henning for the amount recorded as an account receivable (Note 413).*

The accounts affected by this transaction are Notes Receivable and Accounts Receivable in the general ledger and Paul Henning's account in the accounts receivable subsidiary ledger. Notes Receivable is a current asset account; it has a normal debit balance. To show the increase in the amount to be received by Videosonics, Notes Receivable is debited for $480. Since the note replaces the amount recorded as an account receivable, Accounts Receivable and Henning's account are credited for $480.

Notes Receivable		Accounts Receivable		Paul Henning	
Dr.	Cr.	Dr.	Cr.	Dr.	Cr.
+	−	+	−	+	−
$480.00		$480.00	$480.00	$480.00	$480.00

This transaction is recorded in the general journal as shown in Figure 4–7.

	DATE	DESCRIPTION	POST. REF.	DEBIT	CREDIT	
	19--					
1	Apr 6	Notes Receivable		480 00		1
2		Accts Receivable/Paul Henning	/		480 00	2
3		Note 413				3

GENERAL JOURNAL — PAGE 41

Figure 4–7. Journalizing the Receipt of a Note Receivable

Recording the Receipt of Cash for a Note Receivable at Maturity

On May 6 Henning paid Videosonics in full: principal plus interest. The interest Henning paid on the note is $3.95 ($480 \times .10 \times {}^{30}\!/_{365} = \$3.95$). Videosonics, therefore, received a check for $483.95.

The accounts affected by this transaction are Cash in Bank, Notes Receivable, and Interest Income. Cash in Bank is debited for $483.95, the total amount of cash received. Notes Receivable is credited for $480.00, to show the decrease in the asset. The interest a business receives on a note receivable is considered to be income. Therefore, the $3.95 is credited to an account called Interest Income.

Cash in Bank		Notes Receivable		Interest Income	
Dr.	Cr.	Dr.	Cr.	Dr.	Cr.
+	−	+	−	−	+
$483.95		$480.00	$480.00		$3.95

Videosonics recorded the transaction as shown in Figure 4–8.

	DATE	DESCRIPTION	POST. REF.	DEBIT	CREDIT	
1	19-- May 6	Cash in Bank		483 95		1
2		Notes Receivable			480 00	2
3		Interest Income			3 95	3
4		Receipt 459				4

GENERAL JOURNAL   PAGE 41

Figure 4–8. Journalizing the Receipt of Cash for a Note Receivable

Before reading further, do the following activity to check your understanding of how to record the receipt of cash for a note receivable.

Check Your Learning

Use a sheet of notebook paper to answer the following questions.

1. The Woodbury Company received a 90-day, 9½% note for $1,200, dated March 9, from Norman C. Hobson, a charge customer.
   a. Which accounts are debited and credited? For how much?
   b. Is this an interest-bearing or a non-interest-bearing note?
2. On June 7, a check was received from Hobson in payment of the note.
   a. Which accounts are debited and credited? For how much?
   b. What was the amount of Norman Hobson's check?

Compare your answers to those in the answers section. Re-read the preceding part of the chapter to find the correct answers to any questions you may have missed.

Dishonored Notes Receivable

When the maker of a note fails to pay or renew the note at maturity, the note is called a **dishonored note**. The maker of the note is still obligated to pay the principal plus interest, and the payee should take legal steps to collect the debt. However, the Notes Receivable account should show only the principals of notes that have not yet matured. Therefore, a note that is dishonored should be removed from the Notes Receivable account. The dishonored note is debited to an asset account called Notes Receivable Past Due. The amount entered in Notes Receivable Past Due is the principal plus interest earned on the note. The reason for this is that the maker owes both the principal and the interest, and the account should show the full amount to be received.

For example, Videosonics holds an $800, 7%, 60-day note, dated April 20, from Carl Baker. Baker fails to pay by the maturity date. Since Baker did not repay or renew the note at maturity, the note is considered to be dishonored. Therefore, Videosonics must remove the dishonored note from the Notes Receivable account.

June 19: Carl Baker dishonored his $800.00, 7%, 60-day note dated April 20, Memorandum 747.

Baker owes Videosonics both the $800.00 principal and $9.21 interest ($800 × .07 × $^{60}/_{365}$). The Notes Receivable Past Due account is therefore debited for $809.21, the full amount owed. Notes Receivable is credited for $800.00 to remove the dishonored note from the account. The Interest Income account is credited for $9.21 even though Baker didn't pay the interest. Revenue, as you know, is recorded when it is earned, rather than when it is received. This transaction is shown in general journal form in Figure 4–9.

Videosonics would continue to try to collect the amount due from Baker. If Baker does eventually pay the dishonored note, the transaction would be recorded as a debit to Cash in Bank and a credit to Notes Receivable Past Due.

If Videosonics determines that the note will not be paid, it must be written off as uncollectible. Most companies record the transaction as a debit to Bad Debts Expense and a credit to Notes Receivable Past Due.

Remember: A dishonored note receivable must be removed from the Notes Receivable account.

	DATE	DESCRIPTION	POST. REF.	DEBIT	CREDIT	
	19--	GENERAL JOURNAL			PAGE 42	
1	June 19	Notes Receivable Past Due		809 21		1
2		Notes Receivable			800 00	2
3		Interest Income			9 21	3
4		Memo: 747				4

Figure 4–9. Journalizing the Dishonor of a Note Receivable

Discounting Notes Receivable

One advantage a business gets from accepting notes receivable is that it can sell the notes to a bank for cash rather than holding them until maturity. This is known as **discounting notes receivable**.

The firm endorses the note and delivers it to the bank in exchange for cash. The bank discounts the note, deducting the interest in advance. As you know, this is called a bank discount. The amount the business receives—the proceeds— is the maturity value minus the bank discount. The bank holds the note until it becomes due and collects the maturity value directly from the maker of the note.

Recording a Discounted Note Receivable

Videosonics accepted an 8%, 60-day note for $540, dated April 20, from Clark Keller. On May 5, to raise cash to buy additional merchandise, Videosonics discounted the Keller note at the Valley National Bank. The bank charged a discount rate of 7%.

The amount of the proceeds that Videosonics receives is based on the *maturity value* of the note and on the amount of time between the date the note is given to the bank and the maturity date of the note. This is referred to as the **discount period**. The discount period is determined by subtracting the number of days the business held the note from the number of days in the term of the note. Look at the following diagram.

Period of the note (60 days)		
Date of note Apr. 20	Date discounted May 5	Maturity date June 19
Videosonics holds note	Discount Period (Bank holds note)	
15 days	45 days	

As you can see, the discount period is 45 days (May 5 to June 19).

Before the transaction can be recorded, the amount of the bank discount must be determined. The bank discount is calculated on the maturity value of the note. Since this is an interest-bearing note, the interest is calculated as follows.

$$\text{Principal} \quad \text{Interest Rate} \quad \text{Time} \quad \text{Interest}$$
$$\$540.00 \quad \times \quad .08 \quad \times \quad \frac{60}{365} \quad = \quad \$7.10$$

The maturity value is, therefore, $547.10 ($540.00 + $7.10).

The amount of the bank discount is calculated in the same way as the interest. The maturity value of the note, however, is used as the principal amount and the discount period is used as the time.

Maturity Value (Principal)	Discount Rate (Interest Rate)	Discount Period (Time)	Bank Discount (Interest)
$547.10 ×	.07 ×	$\dfrac{45}{365}$ =	$4.72

The amount of the proceeds is the maturity value minus the bank discount, or $542.38 ($547.10 − $4.72). This transaction can now be recorded.

Videosonics received proceeds of $542.38 from the bank; this amount is therefore debited to Cash in Bank. Notice that the amount of the proceeds is greater than the face value of the note. This difference represents interest income to Videosonics. The Interest Income account is, therefore, credited for $2.38. The face value of the note, $540.00, is credited to an account called Notes Receivable Discounted. Notes Receivable Discounted is a contra asset account and has a normal credit balance. It is used to report the face value of all discounted notes receivable. It is also used in determining the book value of notes receivable. It, therefore, appears on the balance sheet as a deduction from Notes Receivable.

Cash in Bank		Interest Income		Notes Receivable Discounted	
Dr.	Cr.	Dr.	Cr.	Dr.	Cr.
+	−	−	+	−	+
$542.38			$2.38		$540.00

In general journal form, the entry looks like that shown in Figure 4–10.

		GENERAL JOURNAL			PAGE 41	
	DATE	DESCRIPTION	POST. REF.	DEBIT	CREDIT	
1	19-- May 5	Cash in Bank		54238		1
2		Interest Income			238	2
3		Notes Receivable Discounted			54000	3
4		Receipt 1162				4

Figure 4–10. Journalizing a Discounted Note Receivable

As just explained, if the amount of the proceeds is larger than the face value, the difference represents interest income. Conversely, if the amount of the proceeds is less than the face value, the difference represents interest expense. The amount of the difference would be debited to the Interest Expense account.

Remember: Notes Receivable Discounted is a contra asset account and has a normal credit balance.

Before reading further, do the activity on page 98 to check your understanding of discounted notes receivable.

Contingent Liability

When Videosonics discounted Clark Keller's note at the bank, it had to endorse the note. By this endorsement, Videosonics was agreeing to pay the note when it became due, if it were not paid by the maker. Therefore, Videosonics has a **contingent liability** for payment of the note. If the note is dishonored by Keller, Videosonics is liable for the maturity value. In other words, the liability of the endorser is contingent, or depends, upon the possible dishonoring of the note by the maker. The endorser, by virtue of the endorsement, agrees to pay the note at maturity if it is not paid by the maker.

It is for this reason that the Notes Receivable Discounted account is used when discounting a note receivable. Since contingent liabilities may become actual liabilities, they affect the credit standing of the endorser. Therefore, when a note is discounted, the contingent liability should appear in the accounts and on the balance sheet of the endorser. By showing Notes Receivable Discounted on the balance sheet as a deduction from Notes Receivable, the contingent liability is apparent to a balance sheet reader.

When a discounted note receivable matures, the bank collects the principal plus the interest directly from the maker. When the maker pays the bank, the

DATE	DESCRIPTION	POST. REF.	DEBIT	CREDIT	
19-- June 19	Notes Receivable Discounted		540 00		1
	Notes Receivable			540 00	2
	Memo. 749				3

GENERAL JOURNAL   PAGE 42

Figure 4–11. Removing a Paid Discounted Note Receivable from the Accounting Records

endorser no longer has any contingent liability and should remove the note from its accounting records. Using the above example, Videosonics would make an entry on June 19 debiting Notes Receivable Discounted for $540.00 and crediting Notes Receivable for $540.00, as shown in Figure 4–11.

Dishonor of a Discounted Note Receivable

Suppose that the bank cannot get the maker of the note to pay the principal plus the interest of a discounted note. The bank immediately notifies the firm that endorsed and discounted the note. To take legal advantage of the contingent liability of the endorser, the bank must formally protest the note. It does so by preparing and mailing to the endorser a notice of dishonor and protest. This is a statement, signed by a notary public, identifying the note and stating that the note was duly presented to the maker for payment and that payment was refused. The bank charges the endorser a fee, known as a **protest fee**, which the endorser must pay along with the maturity value.

For example, let's say that Clark Keller dishonors his April 20 note, which was discounted at the bank by Videosonics. The bank issues a formal notice of dishonor and protest and charges Videosonics a protest fee of $3. As a consequence, the bank deducts $550.10 from the account of Videosonics ($540.00 principal + $7.10 interest + $3.00 protest fee). The journal entries Videosonics makes to record the payment of the dishonored discounted note receivable are shown in Figure 4–12.

GENERAL JOURNAL PAGE 42

DATE	DESCRIPTION	POST. REF.	DEBIT	CREDIT
19-- June 19	Notes Receivable Discounted		540 00	
	Notes Receivable			540 00
	Memo. 749			
19	Notes Receivable Past Due		547 10	
	Miscellaneous Expense		3 00	
	Cash in Bank			550 10
	Memo. 749			

Figure 4–12. Journalizing the Payment of a Dishonored Discounted Note Receivable

The first entry removes the discounted note receivable from Videosonics' accounting records. Videosonics is no longer *contingently* liable, it *is* actually liable. The second entry records the payment of the note receivable to the bank and the reclassification of the dishonored note. In the entry, Notes Receivable Past Due is debited for the maturity value of the note, $547.10. The protest fee charged by the bank is considered to be an administrative expense by some companies. The $3.00 is, therefore, debited to Miscellaneous Expense. Cash in Bank is credited for $547.10, the total amount Videosonics had to pay.

Summary of Key Points

1. A promissory note is a written promise to pay a certain sum on a fixed or determinable date.
2. Interest is the charge paid for the use of money. The formula for calculating interest is: Interest = Principal × Rate × Time. The interest rate is expressed as a percentage of the principal. Time is stated in terms of one year or a fraction of a year.
3. A promissory note issued by a person or business is called a note payable. Notes Payable is a current liability account.
4. The maturity value of an interest-bearing note equals the principal plus the interest.
5. A non-interest-bearing note payable is a note from which the interest has been deducted in advance. The amount deducted in advance is called the bank discount. The amount the borrower actually receives is called the proceeds.
6. A note receivable is a promissory note accepted by a business. Notes Receivable is a current asset account.
7. A dishonored note is one that is neither paid nor renewed at maturity. A dishonored note is removed from the Notes Receivable account and debited to the Notes Receivable Past Due account.
8. Notes receivable may be sold to a bank for cash; this procedure is known as discounting notes receivable.

Review and Applications

Building Your Accounting Vocabulary

In your own words, write the definition of each of the following accounting terms. Use complete sentences for your definitions.

bank discount	interest-bearing note	note receivable
contingent liability	maker	payee
discount period	maturity date	principal
discounting notes	maturity value	proceeds
receivable	non-interest-bearing	promissory note
dishonored note	note payable	protest fee
face value	note payable	term
interest		

Reviewing Your Accounting Knowledge

1. What is a promissory note? Why might promissory notes be issued by businesses?
2. What is the formula for the calculation of interest?
3. Why is a promissory note more acceptable than a charge account?
4. What is the difference between an interest-bearing note and a non-interest-bearing note?
5. How is the Discount on Notes Payable account classified? What is its normal balance?
6. What is meant by a dishonored note receivable? What must the payee do when a note receivable is dishonored?
7. How are the proceeds calculated when an interest-bearing note receivable is discounted?
8. What type of account is Notes Receivable Discounted? How and why is it reported on the balance sheet?
9. If the proceeds on a discounted note receivable are more than the face value of the note, in what account is the difference recorded?
10. Explain the contingent liability of an endorser of a note.

Improving Your Decision-Making Skills

In arranging for a loan from a bank, Harbor Machinery Company has two options:

(1) a $72,000, 10%, 60-day, interest-bearing note
(2) a $72,000, 60-day, non-interest-bearing note that the bank will discount at 10%

Which of the two alternatives is more favorable to Harbor Machinery Company? Why?

Problem 4–1

For each of the following notes, determine the maturity date, the interest amount, and the maturity value. Use a form similar to the one shown below.

(1) A $1,000, 60-day, 8% note dated February 16 (a 28-day month)
(2) A $750, 45-day, 9% note dated September 1
(3) A $1,750, 90-day, 10% note dated December 14 (February has 28 days.)
(4) A $4,200, 30-day, 8½% note dated May 9
(5) A $2,400, 4-month, 9% note dated January 31
(6) A $400, 2-month, 10% note dated May 8

Note	Principal	Term	Interest Rate	Maturity Date	Interest	Maturity Value
1	$1,000	60 Days	8%	April 17	$13.15	$1,013.15

Problem 4–2

On March 16, the Radach Company issued a $2,000, 90-day, 10% note payable to Lyon Company in place of the amount Radach had recorded as an account payable. Prepare the entries, on page 47 of the general journal, to record the following on Radach's books.

(1) The issuance of the note (Note 110)
(2) Payment of the note at maturity (Check 279)

Problem 4–3

The Gilbert Company borrowed $28,000 from the Hobbs State Bank, issuing a 90-day, non-interest-bearing note payable, which the bank discounted at 9½%. Prepare the entries, on page 60 of the general journal, to record the following.

(1) Issuance of the note payable (Note 47) on May 14
(2) Payment of the note at maturity (Check 306)

Problem 4–4

The following were among the transactions of the Salmon Company. Record these transactions on page 33 of the general journal.

Feb. 15 Sold merchandise on account to Jason Stevens, $2,400, Sales Slip 546.
Mar. 17 Received a 30-day, 11% note for $2,400 from Jason Stevens in place of the account receivable, Note 6.
Apr. 16 Stevens dishonored the note dated March 17, Memorandum 113.
May 24 Borrowed $6,000 from Pioneer National Bank, giving a 60-day, 10% interest-bearing note payable, Note 121.

July   23   Paid Pioneer National Bank the amount due on the note of May 24, Check 709.

Problem 4–5

The following were among the transactions of Hanson Motors during this year. Record these transactions on page 25 of the general journal.

Feb.   12   Sold merchandise on account to Jan Coe, $2,640, Sales Slip 443.

Mar.   13   Received a 90-day, 10½% note for $2,640 from Jan Coe to apply on account, Note 3.

Apr.   12   Discounted the Coe note at the bank at 11%, Receipt 401.

May   2   Bought merchandise on account from Harris Tool Company, $6,900, Invoice 4333.

June   3   Issued a 30-day, 10½% note to Harris Tool Company in place of the account payable, Note 37.

        12   Received word that Jan Coe paid the discounted note receivable on the maturity date, Memorandum 675.

July   3   Paid Harris Tool Company interest due on note of June 3 and renewed the obligation by issuing a new 60-day, 11% note for $6,900, Note 38/Check 3332.

Sept.   1   Paid Harris Tool for the July 3 note, Check 3396.

Problem 4–6

Here are some of the transactions carried out by Robinson and Company this year. Record these transactions on page 14 of the general journal.

Jan.   29   Sold merchandise on account to Todd Electronics, $2,640, terms 2/10, n/30, Sales Slip 106.

Feb.   28   Received a 60-day, 10% note for $2,640 from Todd Electronics in place of the account receivable, Note 4.

Mar.   10   Discounted the Todd note at the bank at 9%, Receipt 163.

Apr.   27   Sold merchandise on account to Peebles Electric, $3,300, terms 2/10, n/30, Sales Slip 211.

        29   Received notice that Todd Electronics had dishonored the note receivable discounted on Mar. 10. The bank charged a $5 protest fee, Memorandum 169.

May   27   Received a 45-day, 9% note from Peebles Electric in place of the account receivable, Note 5.

July   11   Received check from Peebles Electric for the amount owed on their note of May 27, Receipt 273.

Sept.   24   Borrowed $9,000 from Conrad National Bank for 90 days by issuing a non-interest-bearing note payable; the discount rate is 8%, Note 104.

Dec.   23   Paid Conrad National Bank the amount owed on the note of September 24, Check 669.

5 Accounting for Inventories

A merchandising business receives its revenue by selling merchandise. In terms of dollars, merchandise inventory is normally the largest current asset of a merchandising business. And, because merchandise is continually being bought and sold, the cost of goods sold is the largest deduction from sales. Therefore, accounting for merchandise is extremely important.

You have seen how purchases and sales of merchandise are recorded. You have also seen how Merchandise Inventory is adjusted at the end of the fiscal period. In this chapter, you'll learn how businesses determine the quantities of merchandise on hand and how they assign a cost value to the ending merchandise inventory.

Learning Objectives

When you have completed this chapter, you should be able to

1. Explain the importance of inventory valuation.

2. Explain the difference between the periodic and perpetual inventory systems.

3. Determine the cost of ending merchandise inventory using the following methods: specific identification; first in, first out; last in, first out; and weighted average cost.

4. Assign a value to merchandise inventory using the lower-of-cost-or-market rule.

5. Explain the reasons for estimating inventories and estimate the cost of ending inventory using the retail method and the gross profit method.

6. Define the accounting terms presented in this chapter.

New Terms

periodic inventory system / perpetual inventory system / specific identification method / first in, first out method / last in, first out method / weighted average cost method / lower-of-cost-or-market rule / retail method / markup / gross profit method

The Importance of Inventory Valuation

Merchandise Inventory is the only account that appears on both the balance sheet and the income statement. On the balance sheet, it appears in the Current Assets section. On the income statement, it is listed under Cost of Merchandise Sold. The reason that the valuation of merchandise inventory is so important is that in many business firms it is the current asset with the largest dollar amount. As a part of cost of merchandise sold, it vitally affects the net income, because the cost of merchandise sold is usually the largest deduction from sales. As a result, determining the cost of the inventory plays an important role in matching costs with revenue for a given period.

Inventory Management

Firms that want to satisfy their customers have to maintain large and varied inventories. Naturally, all of us would rather shop in stores that give us a wide selection of goods. The successful firm buys enough merchandise in advance to satisfy the demands of its customers.

To operate efficiently and produce accurate financial statements, a business should have an inventory control system that provides such information as the amount of merchandise on hand at a given time, the cost of that merchandise, what items are not selling, and the correct amount of merchandise to keep on hand. If the merchandise is incorrectly identified or counted, the amount of goods on hand may be too little or too much.

If the inventory is too small, the variety and choice will not be available for customers. Sales will be lost and customers will go elsewhere.

If the inventory is too large, other problems exist. First, a large amount of cash or credit power has been used to purchase unneeded merchandise. That cash or credit is now unavailable for other needs, and the excess merchandise must be stored and insured for a longer period of time. Second, the additional merchandise may soon be replaced by newer, better, or less expensive varieties. The excess merchandise may have to be sold at a loss in order to dispose of it. If styles change, it may be difficult to sell the merchandise at all.

By proper inventory control, a business should be able to maintain a sufficient inventory to satisfy the needs of its customers. A business should also be able to determine which items need to be reordered with sufficient time to receive the goods before running short. It will also be able to take advantage of discounts and special sales offered by suppliers.

Determining the Quantity of Inventories

There are two methods businesses use to determine the quantity of merchandise on hand: the periodic inventory system and the perpetual inventory system.

The Periodic Inventory System

Many merchandising firms, at a given time, have no record of the exact quantity and cost of merchandise on hand. They do make spot checks from time to time as part of inventory control, but they can determine exact amounts only by physically counting the goods on hand. The inventory system in which the amount of goods on hand is determined by periodically counting them is known as the **periodic inventory system**.

A physical inventory, or an actual count of the merchandise on hand, is usually taken when the amount of merchandise is at its lowest level. Many department stores, for example, choose to take a physical inventory of their stock toward the end of January, after the holiday rush and the post-holiday special sales. Today, many firms use an electronic recorder or a small hand-held computer. The inventory data is then recorded on inventory sheets, such as the one shown for Videosonics in Figure 5–1.

	VIDEOSONICS INVENTORY SHEET					

DATE 8/31/--   CLERK D. Alligood   PAGE 2

STOCK NO.	ITEM	UNIT	QUANTITY	UNIT PRICE	TOTAL VALUE
M368	Clock radio	each	16	34 50	552 00
V819	Videocassette tapes	box	9	79 20	712 80
S281	Speakers	each	12	56 45	677 40
C536	Cleanser	each	10	4 89	48 90

Figure 5–1. Inventory Sheet Used in a Periodic Inventory System

The Perpetual Inventory System

The increasing use of computers has enabled many businesses to maintain a perpetual inventory system. A **perpetual inventory system** is one in which the business keeps a constant, up-to-date record of the amount of merchandise on hand. Let's look at an example. In many stores today, each type of item in the inventory is assigned a product code number. When an item is sold, the code number, quantity, and price of the item are entered into an electronic cash register. The cash register is online with, or linked directly to, a computer. The computer updates the inventory information in its memory and determines the new balance on hand. Similarly, when inventory items are purchased, information concerning the purchases is also fed into the computer to update the inventory records. Thus the firm can determine the current status of any given item instantaneously. Whenever desired, the computer can list the balances of all the items in the inventory, in terms of both units and dollars. Some businesses that have their own computers or employ an independent data processing firm receive such a listing or printout daily.

A business that sells large items—items with a high unit cost—may use a manual perpetual inventory system. An appliance dealer, for example, could easily maintain a separate inventory card for each type of appliance in stock. The dollar cost per unit and the number of units sold and purchased would be recorded on the card continuously. An example of an inventory card that could be used in a perpetual inventory system is shown in Figure 5–2.

Item *Calculator, model 416C*

Date	Received			Sold			Balance		
	Units	Cost	Total	Units	Cost	Total	Units	Cost	Total
19-- June 1							60	10.00	600.00
5				10	10.00	100.00	50	10.00	500.00
6	100	10.00	1,000.00				150	10.00	1,500.00
16				25	10.00	250.00	125	10.00	1,250.00

Figure 5–2. Inventory Card Used in a Perpetual Inventory System

Even though sales and purchases are recorded on the inventory cards continually, a company using the perpetual inventory system must still take a physical inventory at least once a year. This is done to verify the balance shown on the inventory cards and to detect any losses due to breakage, spoilage, theft, or other causes.

Before reading further, do the following activity to check your understanding of periodic and perpetual inventory systems.

Check Your Learning

Write the answers to the following questions on a separate sheet of notebook paper.

1. The value of merchandise inventory is reported on the income statement in the __?__ section and on the balance sheet in the __?__ section.
2. In a __?__ inventory system, the merchandise on hand is physically counted at various times during the period.
3. In a __?__ inventory system, an up-to-date record of the amount of merchandise on hand is maintained, either on inventory cards or on a computer.

Compare your answers to those in the answers section. Re-read the preceding part of the chapter to find the correct answers to any questions you may have missed.

Assigning Costs to the Ending Inventory

After the items are identified and counted, the unit costs are inserted on the inventory sheet and the total cost of the inventory found. How do you determine unit cost? You might think that this would be rather elementary. Indeed, it would be—if all the purchases of a given article had been made at the same price per unit. To determine the total cost, you'd only need to look up one invoice, check the unit price, then multiply it by the number of items on hand. Unfortunately, nothing is ever that simple. Usually a firm makes several purchases of a given item during the year, and—especially these days—the unit cost varies from one purchase to another. A can of shoe polish that cost 50 cents in January may cost 53 cents in March. So which unit cost should one assign to the merchandise on hand?

There are four main methods of assigning costs to merchandise in the ending inventory: (1) specific identification, (2) first in, first out, (3) last in, first out, and (4) weighted average cost.

Specific Identification Method

When a firm sells "big-ticket" items (such as cars, appliances, or furniture), it can keep track of the purchase price of each individual article. With the specific identification method, the actual cost of each item in the ending inventory is determined and assigned to the item. To determine the exact cost of an item, the business simply looks at the purchase invoice.

Videosonics began the period with a beginning inventory of 22 portable stereos, which had been purchased at a cost of $57 each. During the year, Videosonics purchased 84 more at the following prices.

Jan. 1	Beginning inventory	22 units @ $57 =	$1,254
Mar. 16	Purchase	30 units @ 62 =	1,860
July 29	Purchase	36 units @ 65 =	2,340
Nov. 18	Purchase	18 units @ 68 =	1,224
Total available		106 units	$6,678

At the end of the year, when it takes an inventory, Videosonics finds that it has 26 stereos left in stock. Of these 26 stereos, 12 had been bought in November, 10 had been bought in July, and 4 had been bought back in March. Using the specific identification method, Videosonics can assign a cost to the ending inventory as follows.

12 units @ $68 =	$ 816
10 units @ 65 =	650
4 units @ 62 =	248
26 units	$1,714

The cost of Videosonics' ending inventory, then, is $1,714. Videosonics can determine the cost of merchandise sold by subtracting the cost of the ending inventory from the cost of the total merchandise available for sale.

Total stereos available (106 units)	$6,678
Less ending inventory (26 units)	1,714
Cost of merchandise sold (80 units)	$4,964

Remember: The cost of merchandise sold is determined by subtracting the cost of the ending inventory from the cost of merchandise available for sale. The cost of merchandise available for sale is the value of the beginning inventory plus net purchases.

First In, First Out Method

The **first in, first out (fifo) method** is based on the assumption that the first items purchased were the first items sold. The items in the ending inventory, then, are those that were purchased last. First in, first out is a logical way for a firm to rotate its stock of merchandise. As an example, think of the milk sold in a grocery store. Because milk will sour, the "oldest" milk, that purchased first, is moved up to the front of the shelf. As a result, the ending inventory consists of the freshest milk, that purchased most recently.

Let's return to the illustration of Videosonics' stereos. If you remember, 106 stereos were available for sale during the year.

Jan. 1	Beginning inventory	22 units @ $57 =	$1,254
Mar. 16	Purchase	30 units @ 62 =	1,860
July 29	Purchase	36 units @ 65 =	2,340
Nov. 18	Purchase	18 units @ 68 =	1,224
	Total available	106 units	$6,678

Videosonics has 26 units on hand in the ending inventory. Using the fifo method, the ending inventory consists of the items purchased most recently. In our example, the 26 stereos on hand were bought in July (8 units) and November (18 units). The cost of the ending inventory is calculated as shown in the following table.

18 units @ $68 =	$1,224
8 units @ 65 =	520
26 units	$1,744

Remember: With the fifo method, the ending inventory consists of those items purchased most recently.

With an ending inventory of $1,744, the cost of merchandise sold under the fifo method is:

Total stereos available (106 units)	$6,678
Less ending inventory (26 units)	1,744
Cost of merchandise sold	$4,934

Last In, First Out Method

The **last in, first out (lifo) method** is based on the assumption that the most recently purchased articles are sold first. The articles in the ending inventory are the oldest items. As an example, think of a business that sells coal. When the company buys coal from its supplier, the new coal is added to the top of the pile. When the company sells coal to its customers, coal is taken off the top of the pile. Consequently, the ending inventory consists of those first few tons at the bottom of the pile.

Videosonics has 26 units on hand in the ending inventory. Using the lifo method, the items in the ending inventory consist of 22 units in the beginning inventory and 4 units purchased in March. The cost of the ending inventory is calculated as follows.

```
22 units @ $57 = $1,254
 4 units @  62 =    248
26 units          $1,502
```

The cost of merchandise sold using the lifo method is as follows.

Total stereos available (106 units)	$6,678
Less ending inventory (26 units)	1,502
Cost of merchandise sold (80 units)	$5,176

Remember: When the lifo method is used, the ending inventory consists of those items purchased first.

Weighted Average Cost Method

An alternative to keeping track of the cost of each item purchased is to use the weighted average cost method. With the **weighted average cost method**, the cost of the ending inventory is determined by assigning an average unit cost to all like items in the ending inventory. Before the cost of the ending inventory can be determined, however, the average unit cost of the items must be calculated. For example, Videosonics first determines the total cost of all the stereos it had available for sale during the year.

```
 22 units @ $57 = $1,254
 30 units @  62 =  1,860
 36 units @  65 =  2,340
 18 units @  68 =  1,224
106 units          $6,678
```

According to this method, the cost of the ending inventory is affected by the number of units purchased at each price. In other words, the more units purchased at one time, the more influence—or weight—that purchase has on the average cost.

The average cost per stereo is found by dividing the total cost of merchandise available for sale by the total units available for sale.

$$\$6,678 \div 106 \text{ units} = \$63 \text{ weighted average cost per unit}$$

To find the value of the ending inventory, Videosonics multiplies the weighted average cost per unit of $63 by the number of stereos in the ending inventory.

$$26 \text{ units} \times \$63 = \$1,638$$

The cost of merchandise sold using the weighted average cost method is determined as follows.

Total stereos available (106 units)	$6,678
Less ending inventory (26 units)	1,638
Cost of merchandise sold	$5,040

The weighted average cost method is often used by companies dealing in fluids, such as oil. Since separate purchases usually are mixed together, it makes sense to average the costs.

Before reading further, do the following activity to check your understanding of how to calculate inventory costs.

Check Your Learning

The Renfro Company's beginning inventory of calendars on May 1 consisted of 34 units purchased at $3 each. Purchases and sales during May were as follows.

May   3   Sold 12 units
         9   Purchased 16 units @ $3.20
     14   Sold 22 units
     21   Purchased 19 units @ $3.10
     30   Sold 8 units

1. How many units are there in the ending inventory?
2. Determine the cost of the ending inventory using the specific identification method. Of the units on hand at the end of the month, 3 were purchased on May 9, 6 were purchased on May 21, and the remaining units were included in the beginning inventory.
3. Calculate the cost of the ending inventory of calendars by the fifo and lifo methods.

Compare your answers to those in the answers section. Re-read the preceding part of the chapter to find the correct answers to any questions you may have missed.

Comparing Inventory Methods

If prices don't change very much, all four inventory methods give just about the same results. However, in a market in which prices are constantly rising and falling, each method may yield different amounts. The following table compares the gross profit on the sale of the stereos using the four methods.

	Specific Identification	First In, First Out	Last In, First Out	Weighted Average Cost
Sales (@ $110 each)	$8,800	$8,800	$8,800	$8,800
Cost of Merchandise Sold	4,964	4,934	5,176	5,040
Gross Profit on Sales	$3,836	$3,866	$3,624	$3,760

The effects of the four methods are as follows:

1. Specific identification matches costs exactly with revenues.
2. Fifo is the most realistic method for valuing the ending merchandise inventory because the ending inventory is valued at the most recent costs.
3. Lifo offers the most realistic method for determining cost of merchandise sold because the items that have been sold will have to be replaced at the most recent costs. Lifo yields the smallest gross profit and, therefore, the smallest income tax obligation. This is true because lifo reflects rising prices, and the most recent costs are assigned to the cost of merchandise sold. For the past 30 years, since prices have generally been rising, there has been a built-in tax advantage for users of lifo. Because lifo results in a lower gross profit amount and a lower net income, lower income taxes are incurred. If prices were ever to start falling, lifo would become a disadvantage from the standpoint of taxes.
4. Weighted average cost is a compromise between lifo and fifo, both for the amount of the ending inventory and the cost of merchandise sold.

A firm can increase or decrease its gross profit, and therefore its net income and income tax obligation, by changing from one inventory costing method to another, such as a change from fifo to lifo. Although a firm may change its method of assigning inventory costs, it may not change back and forth repeatedly. That is, a firm can't switch back and forth in order to avoid its income tax obligation. If a firm does change its inventory costing method, that fact should be disclosed in the financial statements.

Lower-of-cost-or-market Rule

All four methods for determining the cost of the ending inventory are based on the cost per unit. In the examples, the prices were mostly rising. However, sometimes the market value of items in stock is less than the original cost. Market value refers to the current price that is being charged for similar items on the open market. It is the price at which, at the time the inventory is taken, the items could be replaced.

When reporting the cost of the ending inventory on the financial statements, a business must usually value the inventory at the cost calculated by one of the methods presented earlier or at market value, whichever is lower. Under the lower-of-cost-or-market rule, therefore, if the market value is lower than the cost, the inventory would be reported at its market value on the financial statements. For example, suppose Videosonics uses the lifo method to determine the cost of its inventory of portable stereos. Under this method, the cost of the ending inventory of 26 stereos was determined to be $1,502. Now assume that the current market value of the stereos is $62. Using the market value, the cost of the ending inventory is $1,240. Under the lower-of-cost-or-market rule, the inventory would be reported at $1,240.

Estimating the Value of Inventories

Management, in order to function efficiently, must have interim financial reports prepared monthly or quarterly. Merchandise inventory figures are an important part of these financial statements. However, the taking of a physical inventory is both time-consuming and expensive. Therefore, many businesses estimate the value of the ending inventories for their interim financial statements. In addition, natural disasters such as fire or flood may destroy a firm's inventory, making a physical count impossible. The value of any inventory destroyed must be estimated for insurance and tax purposes. Let's take a look at the two most frequently used methods of estimating the value of inventories— the retail method and the gross profit method.

Retail Method

As the name implies, the retail method is widely used by retail businesses, particularly department stores, to estimate the value of their inventories. When a business uses the retail method of estimating its inventory, it first calculates the cost of merchandise available for sale, both at cost and at retail. "At retail" refers to the selling (retail) price of the inventory items. A retailer buys merchandise at cost and adds a certain amount or percentage of the cost to arrive at the selling price. This added amount is referred to as the markup

Then the cost ratio, the ratio of cost to retail price, is calculated. This ratio provides an estimate of how much of the retail value of the merchandise is cost rather than markup. Next, the total sales for the period are subtracted from the retail price of the goods available for sale to find the *retail* value of the ending inventory. Finally, the retail value of the ending inventory is multiplied by the cost ratio to find the estimated cost of the ending inventory.

Videosonics takes a physical inventory at the end of each year. For its monthly financial statements, Videosonics estimates the value of its inventories by using the retail method, as shown in the table on page 114.

When a firm uses the retail method to estimate its inventory, the beginning inventory and net purchases must be recorded at both their cost and retail values. As you can see, Videosonics' total merchandise available for sale has a

	At Cost	At Retail
Merchandise Inventory (beginning)	$ 41,200	$ 68,600
Net Purchases	78,800	131,400
Merchandise available for sale	$120,000	$200,000

Cost ratio: $\dfrac{\$120,000}{\$200,000} = 60\%$

Deduct retail sales		142,000
Retail value of ending inventory		$ 58,000

Estimated cost of ending inventory: $58,000 × 60% = $34,800

cost of $120,000 and a retail value of $200,000. The cost of these goods was, therefore, an estimated 60% of the selling price. Since Videosonics' total retail sales for the month were $142,000, the retail value of the ending inventory is $58,000. The estimated cost of the ending inventory is found by multiplying the retail value of the ending inventory by the cost ratio: $58,000 × 60% = $34,800.

Gross Profit Method

Sometimes a firm finds that the retail prices of the beginning inventory and net purchases aren't readily available. In such cases, the firm can't use the retail method of estimating the value of the ending inventory. The **gross profit method** is an alternative procedure that achieves the same objective. As the name implies, the key element in this method of estimating the value of inventories is the percent of gross profit the firm makes over a given period of time. The gross profit percentage is found by dividing the gross profit by the net sales for the period. This is usually done by examining past financial statements.

If the gross profit percentage is known, the amount of net sales can be divided into its two parts: gross profit and cost of merchandise sold. The cost of merchandise sold can then be deducted from the cost of merchandise available for sale to determine the estimated cost of the ending merchandise inventory. If a company knows the net sales for the period, the cost of the beginning inventory, the net purchases, and the gross profit percentage, it can prepare an income statement and work backward to determine the cost of merchandise sold and the ending inventory. Let's look at an example.

On the night of April 29 the inventory of Midtown Hardware Store was destroyed by fire. However, the company's accounting records were saved. For insurance purposes, the owner must estimate the value of the inventory by the gross profit method. By looking at past income statements, the owner determines that the average gross profit percentage for the past five years was 32%. Using the information in the accounting records, a partial income statement, shown in Figure 5–3, can be prepared.

In order to find the value of the ending merchandise inventory, it is now necessary to work backward. The gross profit is estimated by multiplying the

Figure 5–3. Partial Income Statement

amount of net sales by the gross profit percentage: $200,000 × .32 = $64,000. The cost of merchandise sold is determined by subtracting the estimated gross profit from net sales.

Net sales	$200,000
Estimated gross profit	− 64,000
Cost of merchandise sold	$136,000

The value of the ending merchandise inventory is the difference between the value of the merchandise available for sale and the cost of merchandise sold.

Merchandise available for sale	$199,000
Cost of merchandise sold	−136,000
Estimated ending inventory	$ 63,000

Now the income statement can be completed, as shown in Figure 5–4.

Figure 5–4. Completed Portion of Income Statement

Before reading further, do the following activity to check your understanding of estimating inventory values.

Check Your Learning

Write your answers to the following questions on a separate sheet of paper.

1. In the __?__ method of estimating the value of inventories, records of the beginning inventory and purchases are maintained both at cost and at selling price.
2. __?__ is the amount or percentage added to the cost of an item to determine its selling price.
3. In the __?__ method of estimating the value of inventories, the cost of the ending inventory is found by working backward through an income statement.

Compare your answers to those in the answers section. Re-read the preceding part of the chapter to find the correct answers to any questions you may have missed.

Inventory Valuation and the Financial Statements

Merchandise Inventory, as you learned earlier in the chapter, is the only general ledger account that appears on both the income statement and the balance sheet. A mistake made in determining the cost of the ending inventory, then, results in incorrect amounts being reported on the two statements.

An error in determining the cost of the ending merchandise inventory has a dramatic effect on net income. You can see this in the following examples. Suppose that a firm had a beginning merchandise inventory of $84,000. Net sales for the period were $203,000 and net purchases for the year totaled $160,000. The cost of the ending merchandise inventory is $92,000. The net income for the period would then be determined as shown below.

Year 1 (With Correct Ending Inventory)

Net Sales		$203,000
Cost of Merchandise Sold:		
Beginning Merchandise Inventory	$ 84,000	
Net Purchases	160,000	
Cost of Merchandise Available	$244,000	
Less Ending Merchandise Inventory	92,000	
Cost of Merchandise Sold		152,000
Gross Profit on Sales		$ 51,000
Total Expenses		30,000
Net Income		$ 21,000

Now assume that the cost of the ending merchandise inventory had been incorrectly calculated at $82,000 instead of $92,000. The error would result in a decrease in net income of $10,000, as shown below.

Year 1 (With Incorrect Ending Inventory)

Net Sales		$203,000
Cost of Merchandise Sold:		
Beginning Merchandise Inventory	$ 84,000	
Net Purchases	160,000	
Cost of Merchandise Available	$244,000	
Less Ending Merchandise Inventory	82,000	
Cost of Merchandise Sold		162,000
Gross Profit on Sales		$ 41,000
Total Expenses		30,000
Net Income		$ 11,000

From this you can see that if the ending merchandise inventory is understated, the net income will be understated by the same amount, because the two are directly proportional to each other. Similarly, if the ending mechandise inventory is overstated, net income will be overstated.

But there's something else that must be taken into account. Since the ending inventory of one year becomes the beginning inventory of the following year, the net income of the following year is also affected, but in an opposite manner. To see this, let's continue our illustration into year 2. The $92,000 ending inventory of year 1 becomes the beginning inventory of year 2.

Year 2 (With Correct Ending Inventory)

Net Sales		$236,000
Cost of Merchandise Sold:		
Beginning Merchandise Inventory	$ 92,000	
Net Purchases	184,000	
Cost of Merchandise Available	$276,000	
Less Ending Merchandise Inventory	100,000	
Cost of Merchandise Sold		176,000
Gross Profit on Sales		$ 60,000
Total Expenses		35,000
Net Income		$ 25,000

However, if the incorrect ending inventory of $82,000 from year 1 becomes the beginning inventory for year 2, the income statement at the top of the next page will result.

From this you can see that if the beginning merchandise inventory is understated by $10,000, the net income will be overstated by $10,000, because the two are indirectly proportional to each other. Similarly, if the beginning merchandise inventory is understated, net income will be overstated.

Year 2 (With Incorrect Ending Inventory)

Net Sales		$236,000
Cost of Merchandise Sold:		
Beginning Merchandise Inventory	$ 82,000	
Net Purchases	184,000	
Cost of Merchandise Available	$266,000	
Less Ending Merchandise Inventory	100,000	
Cost of Merchandise Sold		166,000
Gross Profit on Sales		$ 70,000
Total Expenses		35,000
Net Income		$ 35,000

Notice, however, that over the two-year period, the two incorrect net income amounts will offset each other. The understatement of the first year is canceled out by the overstatement of the following year, as shown below.

Year	Correct Ending Inventory of $92,000	Incorrect Ending Inventory of $82,000
1	$21,000	$11,000
2	25,000	35,000
Total	$46,000	$46,000

The effect of an error in the ending inventory on the income statement can be summarized as follows:

1. If the ending inventory is overstated, net income for the period will be overstated.
2. If the ending inventory is understated, the net income for the period will be understated.
3. If the beginning inventory is overstated, net income for the period will be understated.
4. If the beginning inventory is understated, the net income for the period will be overstated.

Summary of Key Points

1. The correct valuation of inventory is important because it affects a firm's net income and the Current Assets section of the balance sheet.
2. The two inventory control systems used by businesses are the periodic inventory system and the perpetual inventory system.
3. There are four methods of calculating the cost of the ending inventory: specific identification, fifo, lifo, and weighted average cost.
4. A company's gross profit, net income, and income tax obligations are affected by the method used to determine the cost of the ending inventory.

5. Under the lower-of-cost-or-market rule, the ending inventory must usually be reported on the financial statements at cost or at its market value, whichever is lower.
6. Market value is the current price that is being charged for similar inventory items in the market. It is the price at which inventory items could be replaced.
7. Businesses often estimate the value of their ending inventories. Two methods of estimating the value of inventories are the retail method and the gross profit method.
8. Markup is the amount or percentage of the cost of an item that is added to the cost price to determine the selling price of an item.
9. An error in the ending inventory will affect the income statement and balance sheet for the current period and for the next period.
10. If the ending inventory is overstated, the net income will be overstated. If the ending inventory is understated, the net income will be understated. If the beginning inventory is overstated, the net income will be understated. If the beginning inventory is understated, the net income will be overstated.

Review and Applications

Building Your Accounting Vocabulary

In your own words, write the definition of each of the following accounting terms. Use complete sentences for your definitions.

first in, first out method
gross profit method
last in, first out method
lower-of-cost-or-market rule
markup

periodic inventory system
perpetual inventory system
retail method
specific identification method
weighted average cost method

Reviewing Your Accounting Knowledge

1. Why is the valuation of merchandise inventory so important?
2. Name two ways in which a business benefits by having effective inventory management procedures.
3. What is the difference between the periodic inventory system and the perpetual inventory system?
4. What is the most realistic method for determining inventory costs?
5. Name one advantage and one disadvantage of the lifo method of valuing inventories.
6. During periods of inflation, which inventory method results in the lowest reported profits?
7. Under what market conditions is the lower-of-cost-or-market rule applied?
8. Why might a firm estimate the value of its inventory rather than take a physical inventory?
9. Under what circumstances would the gross profit method be used instead of the retail method to estimate the value of the ending inventory?
10. If the beginning inventory is understated, what is the effect on net income?

Improving Your Decision-making Skills

On the income statement of the Shaw Company, the ending inventory was reported as $106,000 and gross profit was reported as $42,000. According to a recount of the ending inventory, the correct amount is $110,000. What effect does this have on cost of merchandise sold, gross profit, and net income?

Applying Accounting Procedures

Problem 5–1

Powell Wholesale Jewelers uses the fifo method to determine the cost of its inventory. It also maintains perpetual inventory records.

Jan. 1 Beginning inventory is 30 units @ $75 each
     20 Sold 16 units
Feb. 4 Purchased 20 units @ $78 each
     17 Sold 17 units
Mar. 4 Sold 10 units
     20 Purchased 16 units @ $80 each

Instructions: For each transaction, determine the following. Use a form similar to the one that follows.

(1) The total cost of the units purchased or sold.
(2) The balance of units on hand. If necessary, determine the number of units on hand at the different unit prices.
(3) The cost of the units on hand at the various unit prices.
(4) The total cost of the inventory.

Item Ring mounting #93								
	Received			Sold			Balance		
Date	Units	Cost	Total	Units	Cost	Total	Units	Cost	Total
19— Jan. 1							30	$75.00	$2,250

Problem 5–2

The Crimson Gift Shop uses the periodic inventory system. At the end of the fiscal period, the general ledger accounts had the following balances.

Merchandise Inventory, Jan. 1	$ 92,000
Purchases (net)	126,000
Sales (net)	169,000

The ending inventory, determined by physical count, is $81,000.

Instructions: Determine the cost of merchandise sold and the gross profit for the year ended December 31. Show your results on an income statement.

Problem 5–3

Barnes Radio and TV uses the periodic inventory system. Data pertaining to the beginning inventory of three items, purchases made during the year, and the December 31 inventory are as follows.

	CL311	DE243	6X16
Inventory, Jan. 1	11 @ $432	3 @ $786	21 @ $318
March 1	17 @ 444	7 @ 782	28 @ 322
June 14	22 @ 452	9 @ 788	30 @ 322
September 14	16 @ 452	6 @ 796	32 @ 330
November 30	12 @ 458		27 @ 332
Inventory, Dec. 31	14	8	32

Instructions:

(1) Assign a cost to the December 31 inventory using specific identification.
   (a) For Model CL311: Of the 14 units on hand, 12 had been purchased in November, 1 in September, and 1 in June.
   (b) For Model DE243: Of the 8 units on hand, 3 had been purchased in September, 3 in June, and 2 were part of the beginning inventory.
   (c) For Model 6X16: Of the 32 units on hand, 20 had been purchased in November, 5 in September, and 7 in March.
(2) Assign a cost to the December 31 inventory using the fifo method.
(3) Assign a cost to the December 31 inventory using the lifo method.
(4) Assign a cost to the inventory using the weighted average cost method.

Problem 5–4

The Ellis Company uses the periodic inventory system. On January 1, the Ellis Company's inventory of Product 9 was 16,000 gallons, which was bought at a cost of $.50 per gallon. Ellis made the following purchases.

Date	Quantity (gallons)	Cost per Gallon	Total Cost
Jan. 23	10,000	.51	$ 5,100
Feb. 5	12,000	.52	6,240
22	9,000	.52	4,680
Mar. 6	11,000	.51	5,610
29	8,000	.54	4,320
Apr. 17	9,000	.54	4,860
May 19	6,000	.54	3,240
June 18	4,000	.56	2,240
	69,000		$36,290

On June 30 the company had 9,000 gallons on hand. During this six-month period, Ellis sold all their Product 9 at $.60 per gallon.

Instructions:

(1) Assign a cost to the ending inventory by each of the following methods: weighted average cost; fifo; lifo.
(2) Determine the cost of merchandise sold according to the three methods.
(3) Determine the amount of the gross profit according to the three methods.

Problem 5–5

The Jefferson Sporting Goods Company assigns a value to its inventory using the lower-of-cost-or-market rule. A partial inventory record is shown on the next page. The complete inventory record is included in the working papers accompanying this textbook.

Instructions: Complete the inventory sheet.

INVENTORY RECORD						
Item No.	Item	Ending Inv.	Cost Per Unit	Current Market Value	Price To Be Used	Total Cost
1152	Sleeping bag	30	$100.00	$105.00	$100.00	$3,000.00

(1) To complete the sheet, select the lower of cost or market value and enter that amount in the Price to be Used column.
(2) Calculate the total cost of each item by multiplying the ending inventory amount by the price to be used.

Problem 5–6

At the end of the fiscal period, September 30, the accounting records of the Surfside Gift Shop provided the following information.

	At Cost	At Retail
Beginning inventory	$ 39,448	$ 65,416
Purchases (net)	102,548	171,256
Sales (net)		169,420

Instructions:

(1) Use the retail method to estimate the cost of the ending inventory.
(2) At the end of the fiscal period, the Surfside Gift Shop took a physical inventory of its merchandise at their retail prices. It found that the total retail value of its inventory was $65,968. There is a possibility that the difference between the estimated ending inventory and the actual ending inventory is due to shoplifting. Convert the retail value of the physical inventory into its cost value and determine the amount of the loss.

Problem 5–7

On the morning of July 21, the owner of Bell's Men's Store discovered that a robbery had taken place over the weekend. A large part of the stock had been stolen. However, the following information for the period January 1 through July 21 was available. Over the past four years, the store had earned an average 34% gross profit on sales.

Merchandise Inventory, Jan. 1	$126,838
Purchases (net)	288,930
Sales (net)	397,492

Instructions:

(1) Use the gross profit method to estimate the cost of the July 21 inventory.
(2) A physical inventory was taken and it was determined that the cost of the remaining inventory on hand was $53,960. What is the amount of loss?

6 Accounting for Property, Plant, and Equipment

Most businesses have many different assets they use in their operations. Cash, supplies, equipment, buildings, land, and merchandise are examples of assets. Some of these assets require special treatment in a business's accounting records, because they will be used to produce benefits for the business for a number of years. This group includes such assets as equipment, furniture, and buildings.

As assets are used up in the operation of a business, their costs are converted to expenses and matched against the revenue for the period. In this chapter, you will learn how the costs of long-term assets such as equipment are allocated, or spread, over the life of the assets. You will also learn how to account for the disposal of a long-term asset.

Learning Objectives

When you have completed this chapter, you should be able to

1. Identify property, plant, and equipment assets and record their initial costs.

2. Calculate the annual depreciation expense for a plant asset by the straight-line, units-of-production, double-declining-balance, and sum-of-the-years'-digits methods.

3. Calculate depreciation expense for a partial year.

4. Determine the book value of a plant asset.

5. Journalize the adjusting entries for depreciation.

6. Record the entries for the disposal of a plant asset.

7. Define the accounting terms presented in this chapter.

New Terms

current assets / property, plant, and equipment / appraisal value / depreciation / disposal value / depreciable cost / straight-line method / units-of-production method / double-declining-balance method / book value / accumulated depreciation / sum-of-the-years'-digits method

Property, Plant, and Equipment Assets

Most assets owned by a business can be classified as either current assets or property, plant, and equipment. **Current assets** are those assets that are either used up or will be converted to cash during one accounting period. Cash, notes and accounts receivable, supplies, prepaid insurance, and merchandise inventory are examples of current assets. **Property, plant, and equipment** are long-term tangible assets that are used for more than one accounting period in the production or sale of goods or services. These assets are purchased for use in the business rather than for resale. Examples of property, plant, and equipment assets include equipment, furniture, vehicles, machinery, tools, buildings, and land. Separate accounts are maintained for each type of property, plant, and equipment asset.

Remember: Property, plant, and equipment assets are expected to be used for more than one accounting period. Current assets are expected to be consumed or converted to cash in one accounting period.

Determining the Costs of Property, Plant, and Equipment

The introduction to this chapter mentioned that these property, plant, and equipment assets require special treatment in a business's accounting records. The first area of special treatment is in determining and recording the initial cost of a long-term asset.

Equipment

Assume that a business purchased a cash register for $550.00. The purchase is recorded in the accounting records of the business as a debit for $550.00 to the asset account Store Equipment and a credit for the same amount to Cash in Bank.

The original cost of the asset includes all normal costs necessary to acquire and install it. For example, the cost of the cash register includes not only its invoice price (less any discount), but also sales tax, freight charges, insurance costs while it is being transported, and costs of unpacking and assembling it. These additional charges are debited to the Store Equipment account.

Only normal and necessary costs are debited to the asset account. This rules out expenditures that result from carelessness, vandalism, or other unusual causes. For example, suppose that an employee who was unpacking the cash register dropped it. The cost of the repair is charged to an expense account, such as Repair Expense. This cost is an expense because the repair does not add to the usefulness of the cash register—it simply restores its usefulness.

Land

Land is considered to have an unlimited life—it does not wear out. As a result, its cost is not expensed, or written off over a number of years.

The cost of land includes the amount paid for the land plus other charges connected with the sale: real estate agents' commissions, legal fees, plus certain other costs for preparing the land for use. If a business buys land for a building site and the land happens to have old buildings standing on it, the firm debits the cost of the structures, as well as the costs of demolishing them, to the Land account.

Remember: **Land has an unlimited useful life. Its cost is not written off as an expense.**

Buildings

The cost of an existing building to be used in the business is debited to the Building account. The cost of constructing a building would also be debited to the Building account. The cost includes not only money spent for labor and materials, but also architectural and engineering fees, money spent for insurance premiums during construction, and all other necessary and normal expenditures applicable to the project. A buyer usually buys both land and a building for one price. But how should the price be allocated between the two?

When a firm is considering buying property, it wants to know whether the price being asked is appropriate. The firm may hire a qualified person to determine the appraisal value, or estimated worth, of the property. Suppose that a firm buys some property, including land and a building, for $500,000. An appraiser evaluated this property at $600,000, valuing the land at $120,000 and the building at $480,000. The value of the land is 20% of the appraisal value ($120,000 ÷ $600,000). The value of the building is 80% of the appraisal value ($480,000 ÷ $600,000). These percentages are used to determine the amounts to be allocated to the Land and Building accounts. The amount that the buyer should debit to Land is $100,000 ($500,000 × .20); the amount debited to Building is $400,000 ($500,000 × .80).

Remember: **When land and a building are purchased for one price, the value of the land must be separated from the value of the building.**

Land Improvements

Land improvements are expenditures for improvements that are (1) not as permanent as the land, or (2) not directly associated with a building. Land improvements include such things as driveways, parking lots, trees and shrubs, fences, and outdoor lighting systems. For accounting purposes, the cost of land improvements must be separated from the cost of land or buildings.

Before reading further, do the following activity to check your understanding of how to determine the cost of long-term assets.

Check Your Learning

1. Jacobsen Publications bought a printing press for $72,000, terms 2/10, n/30. Jacobsen paid the invoice within the discount period, along with $760 transportation charges. Jacobsen also paid installation costs of $990 and power connection costs of $832. How much should Jacobsen debit to its Equipment account?
2. The Frame Hut purchased land and a building for $240,000. Of the $300,000 appraisal value, 30% applies to the land and 70% to the building. What amount should the company debit to the Land account? to the Building account?

Compare your answers to those in the answers section. Re-read the preceding part of the chapter to find the correct answers to any questions you may have missed.

The Nature of Depreciation

The usefulness of all property, plant, and equipment except land decreases over time due to use, inadequacy, and obsolescence. **Depreciation** is a systematic procedure for allocating, or distributing, the cost of plant assets to the accounting periods in which the firm receives service from these assets.

An item of supplies may be bought and used up in one fiscal period. Its cost must be charged to that fiscal period. On the other hand, a depreciable, or plant, asset is used over several fiscal periods. To be consistent with the matching principle, the cost of the plant asset must be spread out over those accounting periods in which it is used. Accordingly, the amount that a plant asset depreciates in each fiscal period is an expense for that fiscal period.

It is difficult to predict accurately what the useful life of a plant asset will be. Any method of calculating depreciation provides only an estimate of how fast a plant asset is used up or loses its value. To determine the depreciation for an accounting period, three factors must be taken into account: (1) the depreciable cost, (2) the estimated useful life of the asset, and (3) the method of depreciation.

Depreciable Cost

Eventually a plant asset becomes used up or worn out and needs to be replaced or discarded. The estimated value of a plant asset at the time of its disposal is its **disposal value**. When a business buys a plant asset, it's hard to predict its disposal value. Many firms estimate the disposal value based on their own experience or on data supplied by trade associations or government agencies. If the firm expects the disposal value to be insignificant, compared to the cost of the asset, the firm often assumes the disposal value to be zero.

The total amount depreciated, the **depreciable cost** of an asset, is the original cost less any disposal value. For example, a cash register purchased for $550 has an estimated disposal value of $50. The depreciable cost of the cash register is $500 ($550 − $50). It is the depreciable cost of a plant asset that is written off over a number of periods.

Remember: The depreciable cost of a plant asset is its cost minus any disposal value.

Useful Life

For accounting purposes, the *useful life* of a plant asset is based on the expected use of the asset. The length of a plant asset's useful life is affected not only by physical wear and tear but also by technological change and innovation. An average car, for example, may have a useful life of five years. However, for reasons of competition, a car rental company may replace its cars every year, in order to offer customers the latest models. A company that has a fleet of cars for its sales force may replace the cars every three years.

Methods of Calculating Depreciation

The purpose of recording depreciation is to systematically spread out the cost of a plant asset over that asset's useful life. However, a firm doesn't need to use the same method of depreciation for all its assets. The four most common methods of computing depreciation are (1) the straight-line method, (2) the units-of-production method, (3) the double-declining-balance method, and (4) the sum-of-the-years'-digits method.

Straight-line Method

Using the **straight-line method** of calculating depreciation, a firm charges off, or converts to an expense, an equal amount of depreciation for each year of a plant asset's useful life. The annual depreciation expense amount is found by dividing the depreciable cost by the number of years of the asset's useful life.

$$\text{Depreciation expense} = \frac{\text{Depreciable cost}}{\text{Useful life (in years)}}$$

As an example, suppose a truck costs $15,000 and has an estimated useful life of 5 years. The estimated disposal value at the end of the 5 years is $1,500. The depreciable cost is, therefore, $13,500. The annual depreciation expense is found as follows.

$$\text{Depreciation expense} = \frac{\$13,500}{5} = \$2,700$$

Expressed as a percentage, the annual straight-line depreciation rate is 20% ($2,700 ÷ $13,500). That is, 20% of the depreciable cost of the truck is depreciated in each year of the asset's useful life.

Units-of-production Method

In some types of businesses, the use of a plant asset varies greatly from one accounting period to another. For example, a building contractor may use a certain piece of construction equipment only two months during a year. The units-of-production method of calculating depreciation is based on the idea that depreciation is the result of use and is not related to time. The useful life of the asset may be expressed in miles driven, hours used, or units produced. The formula for calculating depreciation using the units-of-production method is as follows.

$$\frac{\text{Depreciation expense}}{\text{per unit}} = \frac{\text{Depreciable cost}}{\text{Estimated units of production}}$$

Let's use the truck as our example again. Suppose the truck, which has a depreciable cost of $13,500, has an estimated useful life of 120,000 miles. The depreciation per mile would be:

$$\frac{\text{Depreciation expense}}{\text{per unit}} = \frac{\$13,500}{120,000 \text{ miles}} = \$.1125 \text{ per mile}$$

If the truck were driven 30,000 miles during the first year, the depreciation expense for that year would be 30,000 × $.1125 = $3,375. The depreciation expense for the remaining years of the truck's useful life will depend upon the number of miles the truck was driven in each year. For example, if the truck were driven only 20,000 miles in the second year, the depreciation expense for that year would be $2,250 (20,000 × $.1125).

Double-declining-balance Method

The double-declining-balance method allows larger amounts of depreciation to be taken during the early years of a plant asset's useful life. Some accountants reason that the depreciation expense of an asset should be greater during its early years in order to offset the higher repair and maintenance expenses during the asset's later years. In this way, the total annual expenses of the asset tend to be fairly equal over the life of the asset.

With the double-declining-balance method, the disposal value and depreciable cost are not used to determine the depreciation. The amount of depreciation is calculated using the asset's book value. The book value of an asset is the value of the asset according to the records (books) of the business. The book value of an asset is its cost minus the accumulated depreciation. **Accumulated depreciation** is the total amount of depreciation that has been recorded up to a specific point in time.

Remember: The book value of a plant asset is its cost minus the accumulated depreciation.

Under the double-declining-balance method, the annual depreciation expense is calculated by multiplying the asset's book value by the double-declining-balance rate, a rate that is twice the straight-line rate.

Depreciation expense = Book value × Double-declining-balance rate

The double-declining-balance depreciation rate is the same for each year the plant asset is depreciated. However, the book value—the amount on which the depreciation expense is based—decreases each year. The amount of depreciation, therefore, also decreases each year.

To compute the annual depreciation expense by the double-declining-balance method, follow these steps:

1. Determine the straight-line depreciation rate.
2. Multiply the straight-line depreciation rate by 2. The result is the double-declining-balance depreciation rate.
3. Multiply the book value of the asset at the beginning of the year by the double-declining-balance depreciation rate to determine the annual depreciation expense.

Using the double-declining-balance method, let's calculate the depreciation expense for the truck from previous examples. The straight-line depreciation rate, calculated earlier in the chapter, is 20%. Double the straight-line depreciation rate is 40% (20% × 2). The book value of the truck at the beginning of the first year is $15,000, which is also its cost. The first year's depreciation expense is determined by multiplying the book value by the double-declining-balance depreciation rate, as shown below.

Depreciation expense = $15,000 × .40 = $6,000

The depreciation expense for subsequent years is determined in the same way. Remember, however, that the book value of the asset decreases each year. At the beginning of the second year, the book value of the truck is $9,000 ($15,000 − $6,000 accumulated depreciation). The depreciation expense for the second year is calculated as follows.

Depreciation expense = $9,000 × .40 = $3,600

The table at the top of page 131 shows the book value, annual depreciation expense, and accumulated depreciation of the truck for its estimated useful life under the double-declining-balance method.

Year	Book Value	Depreciation Rate	Annual Depreciation Expense	Accumulated Depreciation
1	$15,000	40%	$6,000	$ 6,000
2	9,000	40%	3,600	9,600
3	5,400	40%	2,160	11,760
4	3,240	40%	1,296	13,056
5	1,944		444	13,500

Notice the amount of depreciation expense in the fifth year of the truck's life. The amount is $444.00, rather than $777.60 (40% of the book value of $1,944.00). The disposal value of the asset is not considered when calculating the depreciation expense by this method—until the last year of the asset's useful life. In that last year, the depreciation expense is limited to the amount necessary to reduce the asset's book value to its estimated disposal value. This is the end of the depreciation schedule; the asset cannot be depreciated below its disposal value.

Sum-of-the-years'-digits Method

The **sum-of-the-years'-digits method** uses fractions based on the number of years in a plant asset's estimated useful life to determine depreciation expense. Like the double-declining-balance method, this method allows higher amounts of depreciation expense to be taken during the early years of an asset's estimated useful life. The annual depreciation expense amount is calculated by multiplying the asset's depreciable cost by the yearly fraction.

Depreciation expense = Depreciable cost × Year's fraction

To calculate the depreciation expense by this method, follow these steps.

1. Determine the number of years in the asset's useful life. For example, our truck has an estimated useful life of 5 years.
2. Find the sum of the years' digits by adding the digits (numbers) of the years. The calculation for the truck is as follows.

$$1 + 2 + 3 + 4 + 5 = 15$$

The sum of the years' digits, 15 in the case of the truck, becomes the denominator of the fractions used in this method.
3. List the fractions in decreasing order using the year as the numerator and the sum of the year's digits as the denominator. For example,

$$\frac{5}{15} \quad \frac{4}{15} \quad \frac{3}{15} \quad \frac{2}{15} \quad \frac{1}{15}$$

4. Multiply the depreciable cost by the year's fraction to determine the annual depreciation expense. The 5/15 fraction is used to determine the first year's

depreciation expense. The $\frac{4}{15}$ fraction is used in the second year, the $\frac{3}{15}$ fraction in the third year, and so on. The depreciation expense for the first year is calculated as follows.

$$\$13,500 \times \frac{5}{15} = \$4,500$$

The following table shows the annual depreciation expense and the accumulated depreciation of the truck using the sum-of-the-years'-digits method.

Year	Depreciable Cost	Year's Fraction	Annual Depreciation Expense	Accumulated Depreciation
1	$13,500	5/15	$4,500	$ 4,500
2	13,500	4/15	3,600	8,100
3	13,500	3/15	2,700	10,800
4	13,500	2/15	1,800	12,600
5	13,500	1/15	900	13,500

Before reading further, do the following activity to check your understanding of how to calculate the annual depreciation expense.

Check Your Learning

At the beginning of the year, Herman's Pancake House bought cooking equipment for $6,720. The equipment had an estimated disposal value of $420 and an estimated useful life of 4 years. Determine the amount of the depreciation for the first year by each of the following methods. Write your answers on a sheet of notebook paper.

1. Straight-line method
2. Units-of-production method, assuming the equipment has a useful life of 14,000 hours and was used 3,500 hours during the first year
3. Double-declining-balance method
4. Sum-of-the-years'-digits method

Check your answers with those in the answers section. Re-read the preceding part of the chapter to find the correct answers to any questions you may have missed.

Comparison of the Four Methods

The straight-line method provides equal amounts of depreciation during an asset's useful life. The amounts of depreciation each year under the units-of-production method may vary widely from year to year, depending on how much the asset is used. The double-declining-balance method and the sum-of-the-years'-digits method yield higher depreciation charges during the early years of the plant asset's useful life. For this reason, they are called accelerated depreciation methods.

The table that follows compares the four depreciation methods, using the truck as the plant asset being depreciated.

	Straight-Line Method	Units-of-Production Method	Double-Declining-Balance Method	Sum-of-the-Years'-Digits Method
Year 1				
Book Value	$15,000	$15,000	$15,000	$15,000
Depreciation Expense	2,700	3,375*	6,000	4,500
Accumulated Depreciation	2,700	3,375	6,000	4,500
Year 2				
Book Value	$12,300	$11,625	$ 9,000	$10,500
Depreciation Expense	2,700	2,250*	3,600	3,600
Accumulated Depreciation	5,400	5,625	9,600	8,100
Year 3				
Book Value	$ 9,600	$9,375	$ 5,400	$ 6,900
Depreciation Expense	2,700	2,925*	2,160	2,700
Accumulated Depreciation	8,100	8,550	11,760	10,800
Year 4				
Book Value	$ 6,900	$ 6,450	$ 3,240	$ 4,200
Depreciation Expense	2,700	2,700*	1,296	1,800
Accumulated Depreciation	10,800	11,250	13,056	12,600
Year 5				
Book Value	$ 4,200	$ 3,750	$ 1,944	$ 2,400
Depreciation Expense	2,700	2,250*	444	900
Accumulated Depreciation	13,500	13,500	13,500	13,500

*Amount can vary greatly.

Calculating Depreciation for Less Than One Year

Businesses often acquire plant assets sometime during the year. In that case, the firm calculates the depreciation expense for the fraction of the year that the asset was actually owned. For example, if a firm owned a plant asset for 4 months, the depreciation would be calculated on $4/12$ of a full year's depreciation. If the firm owned the asset for less than half a month, that month is not counted when calculating the depreciation expense. But if the firm has owned it for more than half of a given month, the whole month is counted.

For example, suppose a firm buys an asset on June 11. The depreciation expense would be computed from June 1, counting the entire month. But if the company bought that asset on June 17, no depreciation expense would be computed for the month of June.

Other examples are shown in the table on the next page, assuming the fiscal period ends on December 31.

Date Acquired	Cost	Disposal Value	Depreciation Method	Useful Life	Depreciation Expense for First Year
Apr. 12	$9,000	$1,000	Straight-line	5 yrs.	$\dfrac{\$8,000}{5} = \$1{,}600$ per year $\$1{,}600 \times \tfrac{9}{12} = \$1{,}200$
Oct. 19	$6,000	$ 200	Double-declining-balance	8 yrs.	$\$6{,}000 \times .25 = \$1{,}500$ per year $\$1{,}500 \times \tfrac{2}{12} = \$250$
Aug. 8	$6,800	$ 500	Sum-of-the-year's-digits	6 yrs.	$\$6{,}300 \times \tfrac{6}{21} = \$1{,}800$ per year $\$1{,}800 \times \tfrac{5}{12} = \$750$

Recording Depreciation Expense

At the end of each accounting period, an adjusting entry is made to record the depreciation expense. Since the amount of depreciation is only an estimate, the plant asset account cannot be credited. Instead, a contra asset account, Accumulated Depreciation, is used to record the total amount of depreciation allocated to a plant asset. The corresponding expense account is Depreciation Expense. If a business has several types of plant assets, it will have several expense and contra asset accounts; for example, Accumulated Depreciation—Equipment and Accumulated Depreciation—Building. Now let's look at an example of how depreciation expense is recorded.

On January 1, Videosonics bought a typewriter for $1,000. It has an estimated useful life of 6 years and a disposal value of $100. The depreciable cost is, therefore, $900. On December 31, Videosonics must make an adjustment, entered first on the work sheet, for the annual depreciation expense on the typewriter. Videosonics uses the straight-line method of calculating depreciation. The annual depreciation expense is calculated as follows.

$$\text{Depreciation expense} = \frac{\$900}{6} = \$150$$

The two accounts affected are Depreciation Expense—Office Equipment and Accumulated Depreciation—Office Equipment. Depreciation Expense—Office Equipment is debited for $150, that portion of the cost of the typewriter that is being allocated as an expense for this fiscal period. The contra asset account Accumulated Depreciation—Office Equipment is credited for $150, since that account is used to record the total amount of depreciation allocated.

Depreciation Expense— Office Equipment		Accumulated Depreciation— Office Equipment	
Dr.	Cr.	Dr.	Cr.
+	−	−	+
Adj. $150			Adj. $150

The adjusting entry to record the first year's depreciation expense is shown in Figure 6–1.

	DATE	DESCRIPTION	POST. REF.	DEBIT	CREDIT	
1		*Adjusting Entries*				1
13	*19-- Dec. 31*	*Deprec Expense-Office Equipment*		1 50 00		13
14		*Accum Deprec-Office Equipment*			1 50 00	14

Figure 6–1. Adjusting Entry to Record Depreciation Expense

Remember: The cost of a plant asset minus its accumulated depreciation represents the book value of the asset.

Disposing of Plant Assets

Sooner or later a business disposes of its plant assets by (1) discarding them, (2) selling them, or (3) trading them in for other assets. When plant assets are disposed of, it is necessary to record the depreciation up to the date of the disposal and to remove the assets from the accounting records. Let's look at some examples.

Discarding Plant Assets

When plant assets are no longer useful to the business and have no disposal value, a firm discards them.

Discarding an Asset with No Book Value

On August 23, Videosonics discarded a display case that cost $1,400. The display case had no disposal value and had previously been fully depreciated. An asset is fully depreciated when its book value is zero. In this case, it is not necessary to record any additional depreciation since it has already been fully depreciated. The entry to record the disposal of the display case is a debit of $1,400 to Accumulated Depreciation—Store Equipment and a credit of $1,400 to Store Equipment. This entry reduces the balance of both accounts to zero. The entry to record the disposal of the display case is shown in Figure 6–2.

	DATE	DESCRIPTION	POST. REF.	DEBIT	CREDIT	
1	*19-- Aug. 23*	*Accum Deprec-Store Equipment*		1 400 00		1
2		*Store Equipment*			1 400 00	2
3		*Memo 26*				3

Figure 6–2. Journalizing the Disposal of a Fully Depreciated Plant Asset

Remember: Fully depreciated assets are retained on the company's records as long as they are still in use, but the company may not take any additional depreciation on them. Plant assets cannot be depreciated below their original cost.

Discarding an Asset with a Book Value

In October, Videosonics discarded a time clock that cost $1,600. The time clock had no disposal value. The total accumulated depreciation up to the end of the previous year was $1,450. Before the disposal of the time clock can be recorded, the depreciation expense for the current year, $90, must be recorded. This step is necessary because the time clock was used until October 1 and, under the matching principle, the cost must be allocated to the accounting periods the asset was used. The depreciation expense for the period from January 1 to September 30 is debited to Depreciation Expense—Office Equipment and credited to Accumulated Depreciation—Office Equipment as shown in the T accounts.

Depreciation Expense— Office Equipment		Accumulated Depreciation— Office Equipment	
Dr. + $90	Cr. –	Dr. –	Cr. + Bal. $1,450 90

The general journal entry to record the depreciation expense is shown in Figure 6–3.

GENERAL JOURNAL   PAGE 44

	DATE	DESCRIPTION	POST. REF.	DEBIT	CREDIT	
1	19-- Oct. 4	Deprec Expense–Office Equipment		90 00		1
2		Accum Deprec–Office Equipment			90 00	2
3		Memo 30				3

Figure 6–3. Journalizing Depreciation Expense for a Partial Year

Now let's determine the book value of the time clock. Book value, remember, is the original cost less the accumulated depreciation.

Original cost		Accumulated depreciation		Book value
$1,600	–	$1,540	=	$60

Since the business is discarding an asset that has a book value of $60, the accounting records should show a loss. This loss is recorded as an expense; the expense account used is Loss on Disposal of Plant Assets. Loss on Disposal of Plant Assets appears on the income statement in the Other Expenses section. The plant asset is then removed from the accounting records by a debit of $1,540 to

Accumulated Depreciation—Office Equipment and a credit of $1,600 to the Office Equipment account.

Accumulated Depreciation—Office Equipment		Loss on Disposal of Plant Assets		Office Equipment	
Dr.	Cr.	Dr.	Cr.	Dr.	Cr.
−	+	+	−	+	−
$1,540	Bal. $1,540	$60		Bal. $1,600	$1,600

The entry to record the disposal of the time clock is shown in Figure 6–4.

		GENERAL JOURNAL			PAGE 44	
	DATE	DESCRIPTION	POST. REF.	DEBIT	CREDIT	
1	19— Oct. 4	Accum. Deprec.–Office Equipment		1540 00		1
2		Loss on Disposal of Plant Assets		60 00		2
3		Office Equipment			1600 00	3
4		Memo. 30				4

Figure 6–4. Journalizing the Disposal of a Plant Asset at a Loss

Remember: Before the disposal of a plant asset can be recorded, the depreciation expense up to the date of disposal must be recorded.

Selling Plant Assets

Naturally, it's very hard to estimate the exact disposal value of a plant asset. So it's quite likely that when a firm sells a plant asset, the selling price may differ from the book value of the asset being sold. The difference between the book value and the selling price determines the amount of the gain or loss on the sale.

Sale of an Asset at a Loss

On August 21, Videosonics sold a desk for $135. This desk originally cost $1,900; the total accumulated depreciation recorded up to the end of the previous year was $1,560. The annual depreciation expense is $180.

First the depreciation expense for the current year is recorded. Depreciation for the year to date is $120 ($180 × 8/12). The total accumulated depreciation as of August 21 is $1,680, as shown in the T accounts.

Depreciation Expense—Office Equipment		Accumulated Depreciation—Office Equipment	
Dr.	Cr.	Dr.	Cr.
+	−	−	+
$120			Bal. $1,560
			120

The book value of the desk is $220 ($1,900 − $1,680). Videosonics, however, is receiving only $135 on the sale. Videosonics has, therefore, incurred a loss of $85 ($220 − $135). This loss is recorded in the Loss on Disposal of Plant Assets expense account. The complete transaction is shown in T account form below.

Cash in Bank		Accumulated Depreciation— Office Equipment	
Dr.	Cr.	Dr.	Cr.
+	−	−	+
$135		$1,680	Bal. $1,560
			120

Loss on Disposal of Plant Assets		Office Equipment	
Dr.	Cr.	Dr.	Cr.
+	−	+	−
$85		Bal. $1,900	$1,900

The entry to record the sale of the desk is shown in Figure 6–5.

GENERAL JOURNAL   PAGE 43

	DATE	DESCRIPTION	POST. REF.	DEBIT	CREDIT	
1	19-- Aug. 21	Cash in Bank		135 00		1
2		Accum. Deprec.-Office Equipment		1680 00		2
3		Loss on Disposal of Plant Assets		85 00		3
4		Office Equipment			1900 00	4
5		Receipt 243				5

Figure 6–5. Journalizing the Sale of a Plant Asset at a Loss

Sale of an Asset at a Gain

On January 10, Videosonics sold display equipment for $310. The equipment had originally cost $4,200; accumulated depreciation to date is $4,060. The book value of the display equipment is $140 ($4,200 − $4,060). Since Videosonics sold it for $310, it has a gain of $170. This gain is recorded in the Gain on Disposal of Plant Assets account. Gain on Disposal of Plant Assets is a revenue account that appears under Other Revenue on the income statement. The transaction in T account form is shown below.

Cash in Bank		Accumulated Depreciation— Display Equipment	
Dr.	Cr.	Dr.	Cr.
+	−	−	+
$310		$4,060	Bal. $4,060

Display Equipment		Gain on Disposal of Plant Assets	
Dr.	Cr.	Dr.	Cr.
+	–	–	+
Bal. $4,200	$4,200		$170

The entry to record the sale of the equipment is shown in general journal form in Figure 6–6.

GENERAL JOURNAL   PAGE 43

DATE	DESCRIPTION	POST. REF.	DEBIT	CREDIT	
1	19-- Jan. 10	Cash in Bank		310 00		1
2		Accum. Deprec.–Display Equipment		4060 00		2
3		Display Equipment			4200 00	3
4		Gain on Disposal of Plant Assets			170 00	4
5		Receipt 516				5

Figure 6–6. Journalizing the Sale of a Plant Asset at a Gain

Exchanging Plant Assets

Often a business trades in one plant asset for another similar asset. Usually, the business receives a trade-in allowance on the old asset and pays the balance in cash. The trade-in allowance often differs from the book value of the old asset. If the trade-in allowance is greater than the book value, the firm has a gain. If the trade-in allowance is less than the book value, the firm has a loss.

However, the gains and losses on the exchange of similar plant assets are handled differently than gains and losses on the sale of plant assets. When one plant asset is traded in for a similar asset, (1) losses are recognized, but (2) gains are *not* recognized. When gains are not recognized, the recorded value of the new asset should be equal to what the business gave up to acquire it. In other words, the recorded value of the new asset is the book value of the old asset plus any cash given. To illustrate accounting for the exchange of similar assets, we'll look at three examples.

1. The exchange of an asset when the trade-in allowance is less than the book value and cash is paid (a loss).
2. The exchange of an asset when the trade-in allowance is greater than the book value and no cash is paid (a gain).
3. The exchange of an asset when the trade-in allowance is greater than the book value and cash is paid (a gain).

Remember: When a plant asset is exchanged for a similar asset, losses are recognized in the accounting records but gains are not recognized.

Recognizing a Loss on the Exchange of an Asset

Metro Couriers owns a delivery truck, which had originally cost $50,000. The accumulated depreciation recorded to date is $41,000. The truck, therefore, has a book value of $9,000 ($50,000 − $41,000). Now assume that on January 12, Metro traded in the old truck for a new, smaller truck listed at $11,000. Metro received a trade-in allowance of $7,000 for the old truck and also paid $4,000 cash.

In this case, Metro has a loss on the transaction. While it has acquired an asset valued at $11,000, it has given up assets of $13,000 ($4,000 cash and a truck with a book value of $9,000). Metro, therefore, has a loss of $2,000 on the transaction ($13,000 − $11,000). This loss should be recognized in the accounting records. The loss is debited to the Loss on Disposal of Plant Assets account.

The transaction is illustrated in the T accounts that follow and in Figure 6–7. Note that the recorded value of the new truck is the list price of $11,000.

Delivery Equipment		Accumulated Depreciation— Delivery Equipment	
Dr. + Bal. $50,000 11,000 (new truck)	Cr. − $50,000 (old truck)	Dr. − $41,000	Cr. + Bal. $41,000

Loss on Disposal of Plant Assets		Cash in Bank	
Dr. + $2,000	Cr. −	Dr. +	Cr. − $4,000

GENERAL JOURNAL				PAGE 43	
DATE	DESCRIPTION	POST. REF.	DEBIT	CREDIT	
19-- Jan. 12	Delivery Equipment (new truck)		1 1 00 0 00		1
	Accum. Deprec-Delivery Equipment		41 00 0 00		2
	Loss on Disposal of Plant Assets		2 00 0 00		3
	Delivery Equipment (old truck)			50 00 0 00	4
	Cash in Bank			4 00 0 00	5
	Check 1066				6

Figure 6–7. Journalizing the Exchange of a Plant Asset at a Loss

Nonrecognition of a Gain on the Exchange of an Asset

We mentioned earlier that while losses on the exchange of plant assets are recognized, gains are not. For example, suppose that when Metro traded in the old truck, it received a trade-in allowance of $11,000. In other words, the truck dealer agreed to accept the old truck, which has a book value of $9,000, in full payment for the new truck.

$11,000
− 9,000
$ 2,000

In this transaction, Metro has a gain of $2,000. The business is acquiring an asset with a list price of $11,000 while giving up an asset with a book value of $9,000. This gain, however, is not recognized in the business's accounting records. The recorded value of the new truck will be the book value of the old truck plus any cash paid out. Since there was no cash involved in this transaction, the value of the new truck recorded in the Delivery Equipment account is $9,000. This transaction is illustrated in the following T accounts and in Figure 6–8.

Delivery Equipment		Accumulated Depreciation—Delivery Equipment	
Dr.	Cr.	Dr.	Cr.
+	−	−	+
Bal. $50,000	$50,000	$41,000	Bal. $41,000
9,000			

Figure 6–8. Journalizing the Exchange of a Plant Asset at a Gain

Now suppose that, instead of receiving a trade-in allowance of $11,000, Metro received a trade-in allowance of only $10,000 *and* paid $1,000 cash. Metro still has a gain on the transaction, but the gain is now $1,000. The company has acquired an asset worth $11,000 while giving up assets (the old truck and cash) of $10,000. Since the gain should not be recognized on the accounting records, the recorded value of the new truck is the book value of the old truck plus the amount of cash paid, or $10,000.

This transaction is illustrated in the T accounts that follow and in Figure 6–9 on page 142.

Delivery Equipment		Accumulated Depreciation—Delivery Equipment		Cash in Bank	
Dr.	Cr.	Dr.	Cr.	Dr.	Cr.
+	−	−	+	+	−
Bal. $50,000	$50,000	$41,000	Bal. $41,000		$1,000
10,000					

DATE	DESCRIPTION	POST. REF.	DEBIT	CREDIT	
19-- Jan. 12	Delivery Equipment (new truck)		10000 00		1
	Accum. Deprec.-Delivery Equipment		4100 00		2
	Delivery Equipment (old truck)			5000 00	3
	Cash in Bank			100 00	4
	Check 1066				5

Figure 6–9. Journalizing the Exchange of a Plant Asset at a Gain

Remember: When gains are not recognized, the recorded value of the new asset is equal to what the business gave up to acquire the asset.

Reporting Depreciation on the Financial Statements

We have seen that depreciation is regarded as an expense. Thus, the depreciation expense accounts are listed on the income statement in the Operating Expenses section. Their placement is shown in the partial income statement for Metro Couriers shown in Figure 6–10.

Gain on Disposal of Plant Assets and Loss on Disposal of Plant Assets are reported on the income statement in the Other Revenue and Other Expenses sections, as

Metro Couriers
Income Statement
For the Year Ended December 31, 19--

Revenue:			
Expenses:			
Advertising Expense	1750 00		
Deprec. Exp-Deliv Equip	2800 00		
Deprec. Exp-Store Equip.	2000 00		
Deprec. Exp-Office Equip.	1500 00		
Income from Operations			177825 00
Other Revenue:			
Gain on Disp of Pl. Assets			170 00
Subtotal			177995 00
Other Expenses:			
Loss on Disp of Pl. Assets			145 00
Net Inc. before Inc. Taxes			177850 00

Figure 6–10. Reporting Depreciation and Gains and Losses from Disposal on the Income Statement

shown in Figure 6–10. These accounts are not listed in the Revenue or Operating Expenses sections of Metro Couriers' income statement because the accounts summarize transactions that are not related to normal business operations.

The accumulated depreciation accounts are listed in the Property, Plant, and Equipment section of the balance sheet, immediately below their related asset accounts. A portion of Metro Couriers' balance sheet showing the Property, Plant, and Equipment section appears in Figure 6–11. The balances entered in the second amount column represent the book value of each of the property, plant, and equipment assets. As you can see, the balance of each contra asset account is subtracted from its related asset account to determine the book value.

Metro Couriers
Balance Sheet
December 31, 19--

Property, Plant, and Equipment:		
Delivery Equipment	20 000 00	
Less: Accum. Depreciation	12 000 00	8 000 00
Store Equipment	18 000 00	
Less: Accum. Depreciation	14 000 00	4 000 00
Office Equipment	6 000 00	
Less: Accum. Depreciation	4 500 00	1 500 00
Building	40 000 00	
Less: Accum. Depreciation	28 000 00	12 000 00
Land Improvements	3 000 00	
Less: Accum. Depreciation	2 300 00	700 00
Land		6 000 00
Total Property, Plant, and Equipment		32 200 00

Figure 6–11. Property, Plant, and Equipment Section of a Balance Sheet

Plant Asset Records

Plant asset records enable the firm to keep a record of the accumulated depreciation and book value for each asset, as well as to determine the amount of the adjusting entry for depreciation. Plant asset records are also invaluable if a firm has to prepare insurance claims in the event of insured losses.

To account for the depreciation of each item, a separate record card is kept for each plant asset. The assets are also divided according to type of plant assets; for example, Store Equipment includes such items as display cases, cash registers, counters, storage shelves, and so on. Store Equipment then becomes a controlling account, and the store equipment plant asset records become a subsidiary ledger. This relationship is similar to that of Accounts Receivable; it is a controlling account and the accounts receivable ledger is a subsidiary ledger, with an account for each individual charge customer. An illustration of a store equipment plant asset record is shown in Figure 6–12.

PLANT ASSET RECORD

ITEM _____Cash Register_____   ACCOUNT NO. _____122-1_____

SERIAL NO. _____ND37-4163_____   MANUFACTURER ____Security, Inc.____

PURCHASED FROM ____Rogers Equipment Company____

ESTIMATED LIFE _____5_____   EST. DISPOSAL VALUE _____$50_____

DEPRECIATION METHOD __Straight line__   DEPRECIATION PER YEAR __$150.00__   DEPRECIATION PER MONTH __$12.50__   RATE OF DEPRECIATION __20%__

DATE	EXPLANATION	ASSET			ACCUMULATED DEPRECIATION			BOOK VALUE
		DEBIT	CREDIT	BALANCE	DEBIT	CREDIT	BALANCE	
7/3/--		800		800				800
12/31/--						75	75	725
12/31/--						150	225	575
12/31/--						150	375	425

Figure 6–12. Plant Asset Record

Account 122 is the number of the general ledger account for Store Equipment. Account 122–1 is the first item of equipment classified under Store Equipment. The total amount of the adjusting entry for Depreciation Expense—Store Equipment is found by adding the current depreciation listed on each store equipment plant asset record.

Summary of Key Points

1. Property, plant, and equipment assets are assets that are expected to be used in the business for a number of years.
2. The original cost of a property, plant, and equipment asset includes all necessary and normal expenditures to acquire and install the asset.
3. Land has an unlimited life and is not depreciated. The value of land must be separated from the value of buildings when the two have been purchased as one package.
4. Land improvements are depreciable; these improvements include the costs of driveways, parking lots, trees and shrubs, and outdoor lighting systems.
5. All property, plant, and equipment assets, with the exception of land, are depreciable. That is, their costs must be spread out as expenses over their useful lives. Depreciation is a procedure for allocating the cost of a plant asset to the periods in which the firm receives service from the asset.
6. There are four methods of determining depreciation: the straight-line method, the units-of-production method, the double-declining-balance method, and the sum-of-the-years'-digits method.

7. The book value of a plant asset is equal to its cost minus the accumulated depreciation.
8. Depreciation is recorded at the end of the fiscal period in an adjusting entry as a debit to the Depreciation Expense account of the asset and a credit to the Accumulated Depreciation account of the asset.
9. A business may dispose of its plant assets by (1) discarding them, (2) selling them, or (3) trading them in for other assets.
10. Before the disposal of a plant asset can be recorded, the depreciation expense up to the date of disposal must be recorded.
11. If a business realizes a loss on the discarding or sale of a plant asset, that loss is recorded as an expense in the Loss on Disposal of Plant Assets account. If the business realizes a gain on the discarding or sale of a plant asset, the gain is recorded as revenue in the Gain on Disposal of Plant Assets account.
12. When a business exchanges a plant asset for a similar plant asset, losses are recognized in the accounting records, but gains are not. When a gain occurs, the recorded value of the new asset is the book value of the old asset plus any cash given.
13. Plant asset records are kept for each plant asset. These records usually list the date acquired, cost, and depreciation taken to date.

Review and Applications

Building Your Accounting Vocabulary

In your own words, write the definition of each of the following accounting terms. Use complete sentences for your definitions.

accumulated
  depreciation
appraisal value
book value
current assets
depreciable cost

depreciation
disposal value
double-declining-
  balance method
property, plant, and
  equipment

straight-line method
sum-of-the-years'-
  digits method
units-of-production
  method

Reviewing Your Accounting Knowledge

1. What is the difference between current assets and property, plant, and equipment assets?
2. What types of costs are included in the initial cost of a property, plant, and equipment asset?
3. Why is land handled differently from other property, plant, and equipment assets?
4. What kinds of expenditures are considered to be land improvements? Are land improvements depreciable?
5. List three things that must be known about a plant asset before its depreciation expense can be calculated.
6. Why is depreciation considered to be an estimate?
7. What is the advantage of using an accelerated depreciation method? Which two methods are considered to be accelerated depreciation methods?
8. What two accounts are involved when recording the adjusting entry for the depreciation of a plant asset?
9. Why are gains or losses on the sale of plant assets not listed in the Revenue or Operating Expenses sections of the income statement?
10. How are gains and losses on the exchange of similar plant assets handled in the accounting records?
11. Describe the use and operation of a plant asset ledger. What information is usually listed on each card in the plant asset ledger?

Improving Your Decision-making Skills

Case 1

Paul Jackson, a fellow accounting clerk, made the following statement: "A parking lot should not be depreciated because adequate repairs should make it last forever." Do you agree with Paul's statement? Why or why not?

Case 2

You have learned that depreciation is a process of allocating the cost of an asset to the accounting periods in which it is *used*. If usage is the most important characteristic in determining depreciation expense, which depreciation method would you consider most appropriate? Why? Why do you suppose all companies do not use this method?

Applying Accounting Procedures

Problem 6–1

Following is a list of the assets of the Hatfield Company.

Accounts Receivable	Land Improvements
Building	Machinery
Cash in Bank	Office Equipment
Delivery Equipment	Prepaid Insurance
Land	Supplies

Instructions: Use a form similar to the one that follows. For each asset, indicate whether it is a current asset or a property, plant, and equipment asset by placing a check mark in the correct column.

Asset	Current Asset	Property, Plant, and Equipment
Accounts Receivable	✓	

Problem 6–2

On June 1, Martin Manufacturing purchased a piece of land next to its offices. The company had the following costs: price of the land, $100,000; broker's fees, $6,000; legal fees, $500; demolition of a shack on the land, $2,000; grading and leveling the land, $1,500; parking lot, $10,000; lighting, $5,000.

Instructions: Record the transaction on page 41 of a general journal. Use Check 1163 as the source document.

Problem 6–3

On January 1, the Kramer Products Company bought a machine for $30,000. The machine has an estimated life of five years and an estimated disposal value of $3,000.

Instructions: Use a form similar to the one on the next page. Determine the annual depreciation of the machine for each of the five years of its life, the accumulated depreciation at the end of each year, and the book value of the machine at the end of each year by each of the following methods.

(1) straight-line method
(2) double-declining-balance method
(3) sum-of-the-years'-digits method

Year	Straight-line Method			Double-declining-balance Method			Sum-of-the-years'-digits Method		
	Depr. Exp.	Accum. Depr.	Book Value	Depr. Exp.	Accum. Depr.	Book Value	Depr. Exp.	Accum. Depr.	Book Value
1									

Problem 6–4

On April 4, Milly's Separates Shop sold some display equipment for $460 cash. The following details are from the display equipment plant asset records: Cost, $5,850; Accumulated depreciation as of the previous December 31, $4,240; Annual depreciation, $1,020.

Instructions:

(1) Record the general journal entry to record the depreciation up to April 4. Use Memorandum 109 as the source document.
(2) Record the entry, in general journal form, for the sale of the equipment. Use Receipt 442 as the source document.

Problem 6–5

On October 19, Cordova and Son, a machine shop, traded in a lathe (Machinery) on a new one that cost $9,440. Cordova got a trade-in allowance of $1,720 on the old lathe and issued Check 4101 for $7,720. The subsidiary account shows the following: Cost (of old lathe), $7,990; Accumulated depreciation to date, $7,024.

Instructions: Journalize the entry to record the exchange of plant assets.

Problem 6–6

During a three-year period, Jordan Oil Company completed the following transactions related to its oil delivery truck.

19X1
Jan.   6   Bought a used tanker truck for $24,800, Check 1011.
Oct. 21   Paid Artie's Repair Shop $252 for maintenance repairs to the truck, Check 1469.
Dec. 31   Recorded the adjusting entry for depreciation for the fiscal year. The estimated life of the truck is four years, and it has a disposal value of $5,200. Jordan uses the straight-line method of depreciation.
        31   Closed the appropriate accounts into Income Summary.

19X2

Mar. 9   Paid Artie's Repair Shop $104 for a tune-up on the truck, Check
          1709.
Aug. 27 Issued Check 1978 for $480 to Able Brothers for new tires.
Dec. 31 Recorded the adjusting entry for depreciation for the fiscal year.
      31 Closed the appropriate accounts into Income Summary.

19X3

Apr. 21 Paid $632 to Burke Auto Body for repairs to the truck, Check
          2497.
June 27 Traded in the old truck for a new one costing $39,200. Received a
          trade-in allowance of $15,600 and issued Check 2582 for the dif-
          ference. Recorded the entry to depreciate the truck to date (Memo.
          1173). Recorded the entry to record the exchange.
Dec. 31 Recorded the adjusting entry for depreciation on the new truck for
          the fiscal year. The estimated life of the truck is six years, and it
          has a disposal value of $2,550.
      31 Closed the appropriate accounts into Income Summary.

Instructions:

(1) Open the following general ledger accounts: Delivery Equipment, 120; Accumu-
     lated Depreciation—Delivery Equipment, 121; Depreciation Expense—Delivery Equip-
     ment, 640; Truck Repair Expense, 685.
(2) Record the transactions, beginning on page 12 of a general journal.
(3) Post the transactions to the accounts opened in Instruction 1.

7 The Voucher System of Accounting

The term *internal control* is often used in connection with cash receipts and cash payments. Internal control, as you recall, refers to those procedures a business takes to protect its assets, especially cash. These procedures are intended to prevent errors, safeguard cash and other assets, and provide for the efficient management of the business's resources. In a small business, internal control procedures require that one person, usually the owner or manager, approve all cash payments before they are made.

As a business grows, it becomes increasingly difficult for one person to handle all financial responsibilities. Therefore, duties are delegated. For example, more than one person is usually authorized to approve purchases and cash payments. As a result, internal control becomes even more important.

In this chapter, you will learn about one internal control system that can be used for a company's cash payments. You will also learn how to record a business's transactions within that system.

Learning Objectives

When you have completed this chapter, you should be able to

1. Explain how the voucher system is used to control a company's cash payments.

2. Describe the components of a voucher system.

3. Record vouchers in a voucher register.

4. Record the payment of vouchers in a check register.

5. Define the accounting terms presented in this chapter.

New Terms   **voucher system / voucher / voucher register / unpaid voucher file / voucher check / check register / paid voucher file / schedule of unpaid vouchers**

Objectives of the Voucher System

The **voucher system** is a system to control all purchases and cash payments. When a business uses the voucher system, authority can be delegated. At the same time, control can be maintained over these transactions through the medium of signatures. A person who signs a voucher has presumably read it and, by signing it, approved the purchase or the cash payment. That is why the voucher system provides for the efficient management of the company's resources. This is of vital importance, especially when large sums of money are involved.

The following four steps all involve the efficient management of resources. They aren't, of course, exclusive to the voucher system. However, when a firm is using the voucher system, these four steps are implied.

1. All expenditures must be supported by purchase orders or other authorizations.
2. Goods and services received must be inspected and approved.
3. Invoices from suppliers must be checked against respective purchase orders and the accuracy of the amounts, shipping costs, and credit terms verified.
4. All payments must be made by check, except for payments made from petty cash.

The voucher system focuses on these four steps and includes the following parts, each of which will be described in detail.

- Vouchers
- Voucher register
- Unpaid voucher file
- Voucher checks
- Check register
- Paid voucher file
- General journal

At the outset, bear in mind that the voucher system is appropriate only for a medium- to large-sized business. In other words, the business must have enough transactions to make the extra paperwork economically feasible. It must also customarily pay its bills when they are due instead of making part payments or installment payments. Also bear in mind that the voucher system has fixed channels in which to record routine types of transactions. Transactions that are not of a routine nature do not fit into these channels and therefore require special treatment by means of special entries in the general journal.

Vouchers

The dictionary defines a voucher as a piece of paper that serves as proof of a transaction. In the voucher system, a **voucher** is a written authorization for each cash payment and the source document for the entry.

When a business uses the voucher system, a voucher is prepared for every invoice or bill received, whether it is to be paid immediately or in the future. Videosonics has just begun using the voucher system. The voucher the company uses is shown in Figure 7–1. The front of the voucher describes the terms of the transaction. If merchandise is being purchased, the voucher lists the name and address of the supplier, the date of the invoice, the amount, and the credit

Front of Voucher

Videosonics				
Payee	Danton, Inc.		Voucher No. 117	
Address	1616 madlyn ave.		Date Prepared	10/1/--
	Los Angeles, CA 90026		Date Due	10/8/--
Terms	2/10, n/30		Date Paid	10/8/--
			Check No.	390

Date	Invoice No.	Description	Amount
10/1/--	3394	2,600 ft. speaker wire	715.00

Approved	RCR	Approved	MCl
	Controller		Treasurer

Back of Voucher

Account Debited	Acct. No.	Amount	
Purchases	501	715.00	Voucher No. 117
Transportation In	502		Payee Danton, Inc.
Rent Expense	630		Address 1616 madlyn ave.
Utilities Expense	640		Los Angeles, CA 90026
Salaries Payable	212		Invoice Amount 715.00
			Less Discount 14.30
			Net 700.70
			Date Due 10/8/--
			Date Paid 10/8/--
Total Vouchers Payable	202	715.00	Check No. 390

Figure 7–1. Front and Back of a Voucher

terms. The front of the voucher also has blanks for the signatures of those persons approving the amounts, terms, and so forth. The invoice or bill is attached to the voucher.

Characteristics of Vouchers

Just as invoices vary from one company to another, vouchers also vary from one company to another. Some businesses use a voucher that is in the form of a folder, with a pocket or envelope for the invoice. Although vouchers for different business firms or government units do vary, the following characteristics are usually present.

- Vouchers are prepared for every incoming bill and are numbered consecutively.
- The name and address of the payee or creditor appear on the vouchers.
- The amount and credit terms of the invoice appear on the vouchers.
- Vouchers list due dates so that firms can take advantage of cash discounts.
- For internal control, vouchers require signatures as approval for payment.
- The payment information (date paid and check number) are recorded on the voucher.

A completed voucher, with the invoice or bill stapled to it, describes an entire transaction, as well as the procedure for processing the voucher.

Preparation and Approval of Vouchers

Let's assume that Videosonics received from its supplier, Danton, Inc., the invoice shown in Figure 7–2.

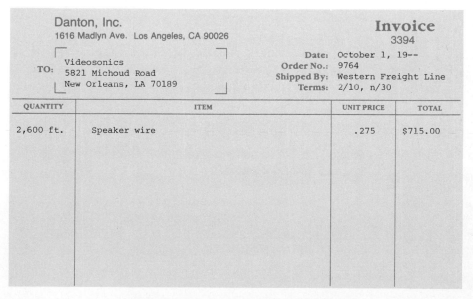

Figure 7–2. Invoice Received by Videosonics

With the invoice as the source of information, the voucher shown in Figure 7–1 is prepared. The front of the voucher lists the details of the transaction. The back of the voucher lists the accounts to be debited and credited; the name and address of the payee; the invoice amount, discount, and net amount; the due date; and the payment information. The invoice is stapled to the voucher and circulated for the required approval signatures.

The due date represents the last day on which Videosonics can take advantage of the cash discount (taking into consideration the time required for mail delivery). For example, the invoice of Danton, Inc., was dated October 1, with terms of 2/10, n/30. The discount period ends on October 11. However, if 3 days are necessary for mail delivery, the payment is prepared and sent on October 8, so that it will be in the hands of the creditor by October 11.

The accounts to be debited depend, of course, on the types of goods and services purchased. In the voucher system, the Vouchers Payable account replaces Accounts Payable. For example, when a firm buys merchandise on account, the accountant records it as a debit to Purchases and a credit to Vouchers Payable. Similarly, when a firm buys store equipment on account, the accountant records it as a debit to Store Equipment and a credit to Vouchers Payable. Each unpaid voucher requires a credit to Vouchers Payable. When the voucher is paid, the payment is recorded as a debit to Vouchers Payable and a credit to Cash in Bank. The date and number of the check are recorded on the voucher.

In the voucher system, a voucher is prepared every time a liability is incurred. This includes liabilities incurred for expenses as well as those incurred for purchases of merchandise or other assets. For example, when the telephone bill

VOUCHER

	DATE	VOU. NO.	CREDITOR	PAYMENT DATE	PAYMENT CK. NO.	VOUCHERS PAYABLE CREDIT	PURCHASES DEBIT
1	19—Oct. 1	117	Danton, Inc.	Oct. 8	390	715 00	715 00
2	1	118	Argel Mfg. Co.	Oct. 1	383	42 00	42 00
3	3	119	Davenport Office Supplies	Oct. 3	384	48 72	
4	5	120	Rockland Ins. Co.	Oct. 5	387	74 00	
5	9	121	Rogers + Simon Co.	Oct. 18	404	328 00	328 00
6	10	122	Reliable Express	Oct. 10	393	1690 00	
7	12	123	Northwest Journal			76 00	
8	12	124	Elwood Equipment Co.	Oct. 12	395	116 00	
9	15	125	Supersound, Inc.	Oct. 18	by note	421 00	421 00
33	29	149	Supersound, Inc.			714 00	714 00
34	30	150	Safety National Bank	Oct. 30	412	1507 50	
35							
36	31		Totals			10698 68	4553 20
37						(202)	(501)

Figure 7–3. Voucher Register   (Left Side)

is received, a voucher is prepared and the telephone bill attached to it. On the back of the voucher, the bill is recorded as a debit to Utilities Expense and a credit to Vouchers Payable. When a check is issued in payment of the voucher, the entry is recorded as a debit to Vouchers Payable and a credit to Cash in Bank.

Remember: A voucher is prepared for every invoice or bill received by the company.

The Voucher Register

The **voucher register** is a book of original entry in which all vouchers are recorded, in numerical order. It expands and replaces the purchases journal. The voucher register has only one credit column, Vouchers Payable Credit, but a number of debit columns. As in any special journal, the accounts listed in the debit columns are selected on the basis of their frequency of use. A merchandising business, for example, would always have a Purchases Debit column because it naturally buys a great volume of merchandise on account. The voucher register may vary widely, of course, depending on the size of the business and the number of accounts. In addition to the special amount columns, the voucher register also has a General section (for amounts that cannot be entered in special amount columns) and columns for recording the voucher number, name of creditor, date of payment, and check number. The voucher register for Videosonics is shown in Figure 7–3.

REGISTER   PAGE 3

TRANSPORTATION IN DEBIT	SUPPLIES DEBIT	MISCELLANEOUS EXPENSE DEBIT	GENERAL			
			ACCOUNT DEBITED	POST. REF.	DEBIT	
						1
						2
	48 72					3
			Prepaid Insurance	116	74 00	4
						5
1 690 00						6
			Advertising Expense	602	76 00	7
			Sales Returns & Allow.	402	1 16 00	8
						9
						33
			Notes Payable	211	1 500 00	34
			Interest Expense	621	7 50	35
3 314 00	1 21 79	83 69			2 626 00	36
(502)	(115)	(619)			(✓)	37

(Right Side)

Recording a Voucher

The first voucher recorded on page 3 of Videosonics' voucher register is the voucher illustrated earlier, Voucher 117 for Danton, Inc. The date and voucher number are recorded in the first two columns. The name of the creditor is entered in the Creditor column. (The payment columns are not filled in at this time; they are filled in when the voucher is paid.) The amount of the voucher, $715.00, is entered in the Vouchers Payable Credit column and in a special debit amount column, in this case the Purchases Debit column. Note that the total amount of the invoice is entered in the two amount columns. Any discount to be taken is not deducted when the voucher is recorded.

If the voucher cannot be recorded in a special debit column, it is entered in the General Debit column. For example, Voucher 120 is recorded in the General Debit column as a debit to Prepaid Insurance.

Remember: When a voucher is recorded in the voucher register, Vouchers Payable is always credited for the total amount of the voucher.

Posting from the Voucher Register

The entries in the General Debit column are posted individually to the general ledger during the month, just as the General columns of the other special journals are. At the end of the month, the voucher register is totaled, proved, and ruled like any special journal. The combined total of all the debit amount columns must equal the total of the Vouchers Payable Credit column.

After the voucher register has been proved and ruled, the totals of all the special amount columns are posted to the appropriate accounts in the general ledger. To indicate the posting of each total, the number of the account is written in parentheses immediately below the double rule. In the general ledger accounts, the letters ''VR'' and the page number are entered in the Posting Reference column.

Remember: At the end of the month, the voucher register is totaled, proved, and ruled and the totals of the special amount columns are posted to the appropriate general ledger accounts.

Filing Unpaid Vouchers

In the system used by Videosonics, an invoice is attached to the voucher and the voucher is circulated within the company for the necessary signatures of approval. After a voucher is recorded in the voucher register, it is filed in the unpaid voucher file. The unpaid voucher file contains all unpaid vouchers filed according to the dates on which they should be paid. In the voucher system, the unpaid voucher file takes the place of the accounts payable subsidiary ledger. As a result, the total of all the vouchers in the unpaid voucher file should equal the balance of the Vouchers Payable account after all posting has been completed.

The unpaid voucher file helps the company forecast how much cash is needed to pay outstanding bills. It also helps ensure that the firm will pay its bills promptly in order to take advantage of cash discounts.

Voucher Checks

When a voucher system is used, every cash payment is made by check. Although regular checks can be used with a voucher system, many businesses use voucher checks. A **voucher check** is a special check that has an attached stub. The stub is used to list the details of the cash payment. The voucher check used by Videosonics is shown in Figure 7–4. Voucher checks are prenumbered and are often prepared in duplicate. The original of the voucher check is sent to the payee. The company keeps the copy as a record of the payment.

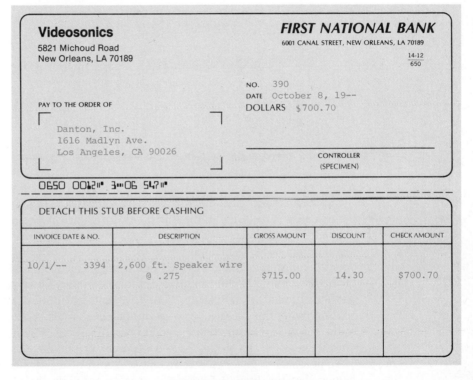

Figure 7–4. Voucher Check

Using a Check Register

Any business using a voucher system uses the check register as a book of original entry, along with the voucher register. The **check register**, shown in Figure 7–5 on page 158, replaces the cash payments journal in the voucher system. Every check written in payment of a voucher is recorded in the check register. As you can see, the check register has columns in which to record the date of the check, the check number, the name of the payee, and the number of the voucher being paid. There are also three amount columns: Vouchers Payable Debit, Purchases Discount Credit, and Cash in Bank Credit.

CHECK REGISTER   PAGE 11

	DATE	CK. NO.	PAYEE	VOU. NO.	VOUCHERS PAYABLE DEBIT	PURCHASES DISCOUNT CREDIT	CASH IN BANK CREDIT	
1	Oct. 1	383	Argel Mfg. Co.	118	42 00		42 00	1
2	3	384	Davenport Off. Supplies	119	48 72		48 72	2
3	3	385	Sinclair Mfg. Co.	114	206 00	2 06	203 94	3
4	4	386	Supersound, Inc.	115	540 00		540 00	4
5	5	387	Rockland Ins. Co.	120	74 00		74 00	5
6	6	388	Void					6
7	6	389	Rogers + Simon Co.	116	464 00	9 28	454 72	7
8	8	390	Danton, Inc.	117	715 00	14 30	700 70	8
30	30	412	Safety National Bank	150	1507 50		1507 50	30
31	31		Totals		2404 98	75 84	6329 14	31
32					(202)	(504)	(101)	32

Figure 7–5. Check Register

Under the voucher system, checks are issued only in payment of approved and recorded vouchers. As a result, each check recorded in the check register results in a debit to Vouchers Payable and a credit to Cash in Bank.

If Videosonics pays the voucher within the discount period, the amount of the discount is recorded in the Purchases Discount Credit column of the check register. For example, look at Check 390, written in payment of Voucher 117 to Danton, Inc. The total amount of the voucher, which was recorded in the voucher register, is entered in the Vouchers Payable Debit column. The amount of the discount, $14.30, is entered in the Purchases Discount Credit column, and the amount of the check, $700.70, is entered in the Cash in Bank Credit column. After the check is recorded in the check register, the date and number of the check are recorded on the appropriate line in the Payment columns of the voucher register and in the Record of Payment section of the voucher.

The check register is a consecutive record of all of a company's checks. Notice that, on line 6, Check 388 was recorded in the check register even though it was voided. By entering all checks in the check register, a company can maintain control over these important documents.

At the end of the month, the check register is totaled, proved, and ruled. The totals are posted to the general ledger accounts, and the account numbers are written in parentheses under the column totals as posting references.

Remember: When a cash payment is recorded in the check register, Vouchers Payable is debited and Cash in Bank is credited.

Before reading further, do the following activity to check your understanding of the voucher system.

Filing Paid Vouchers

After a payment has been recorded in the check register and in the Payment columns of the voucher register, the payment information is also recorded on the voucher. Then the voucher is marked paid and filed. The paid voucher file contains all paid vouchers, filed in numerical order. Many firms staple a copy of the voucher check to the paid voucher, which means that the paid voucher file contains a complete set of documents for every cash payment.

Schedule of Unpaid Vouchers

At the end of the month, Videosonics prepares a list of all unpaid vouchers, taking the information directly from the unpaid voucher file. The schedule of unpaid vouchers, shown in Figure 7–6, also lists the name of each creditor and the amount owed. As you can see, it is similar to the schedule of accounts payable.

	Videosonics Schedule of Unpaid Vouchers October 31, 19--		
Vou. No.	Name of Creditor		
123	Northwest Journal	76 00	
149	Supersound, Inc.	714 00	
	Total Vouchers Payable		790 00

Figure 7–6. Schedule of Unpaid Vouchers

Situations Requiring Special Treatment

A firm using the voucher system inevitably has some transactions that do not fit into the fixed channels of the voucher system. Such transactions require special treatment, generally in the form of a general journal entry. These transactions could be considered as adjustments to the voucher system. Let's look at four such types of transactions.

Handling Purchases Returns in the Voucher System

Normally a firm with an efficient purchasing department, if it's going to return merchandise, returns it before the vouchers are prepared and recorded in the voucher register. The purchases return can then be noted right on the invoice. The invoice would be recorded in the voucher register for the net amount (original amount of the invoice less the purchases return). For example, Videosonics bought $1,200 worth of merchandise on account. Before the voucher was prepared and recorded, Videosonics returned $100 worth of the merchandise to the supplier. The debit memorandum was attached to the invoice, and $100 was deducted from the original amount of the invoice. The voucher was recorded in the voucher register as a debit to Purchases for $1,100 and a credit to Vouchers Payable for $1,100.

Occasionally, however, merchandise is not returned until after the voucher has been recorded in the voucher register. For example, on September 29, Videosonics bought $566 worth of merchandise from Supersound, Inc. Videosonics prepared Voucher 115 and recorded the transaction in the voucher register on September 29 as a debit to Purchases for $566 and a credit to Vouchers Payable for $566.

A few days later, Videosonics returned $26 worth of defective merchandise to Supersound. Videosonics recorded this transaction in the general journal, as shown in Figure 7–7. This entry is very similar to purchases returns you recorded earlier. However, in this instance, Vouchers Payable is debited instead of Accounts Payable.

GENERAL JOURNAL PAGE 47

	DATE	DESCRIPTION	POST. REF.	DEBIT	CREDIT	
1	19-- Oct. 1	Vouchers Payable		26 00		1
2		Purchases Returns & Allowances			26 00	2
3		Debit Memo. 4611 (Voucher 115)				3

Figure 7–7. Journalizing a Purchases Return

Videosonics deducts the amount of the return ($26) on Voucher 115 and staples the debit memorandum to it. The purchases return is recorded in the Payment columns of the voucher register on the upper half of the line used to

| | DATE | VOU. NO. | CREDITOR | PAYMENT | | VOUCHERS PAYABLE CREDIT | PURCHASES DEBIT |
				DATE	CK. NO.		
20	Sept. 29	115	Supersound, Inc.	Oct. Oct. 4	1 DM 46 11 386	566 00	566 00

Figure 7–8. Recording a Purchases Return in the Voucher Register

record the original voucher. When Videosonics pays the voucher on October 4, it records the issuance of Check 386 in the check register as a debit to Vouchers Payable for $540.00, a credit to Purchases Discount for $10.80, and a credit to Cash in Bank for $529.20. The date and check number are also recorded in the Payment columns of the voucher register, as shown in Figure 7–8.

Issuing a Note Payable In Payment of a Voucher

Occasionally the firm may issue a note payable in payment of a voucher. This transaction is recorded in the general journal, debiting Vouchers Payable and crediting Notes Payable. For example, on October 15 Videosonics bought $421 worth of merchandise from Supersound, Inc., and issued Voucher 125, which was recorded in the voucher register. On October 18, to extend the payment period, Videosonics issued a 45-day, 8% note payable for $421, in payment of Voucher 125. The general journal entry is shown in Figure 7–9.

	DATE	DESCRIPTION	POST. REF.	DEBIT	CREDIT	
1	Oct. 18	Vouchers Payable		421 00		1
2		Notes Payable			421 00	2
3		Note 317				3

Figure 7–9. Journalizing a Note Payable in Payment of a Voucher

The issuance of the note is also recorded in the Payment columns of the voucher register. Look at line 9 of Figure 7–3 on pages 154–155. As you can see, "Oct. 18" is written in the Payment Date column and the words "by note" are entered in the Check Number column.

A notation is also made on the voucher indicating that it has been canceled by the issuance of a note. The voucher is then transferred from the unpaid voucher file to the paid voucher file.

On December 2, when the note is due, Videosonics must prepare a new voucher for the payment of the note. The new voucher is recorded in the voucher register as a debit to Notes Payable for $421, a debit to Interest Expense for

VOUCHER

	DATE		VOU. NO.	CREDITOR	PAYMENT DATE	PAYMENT CK. NO.	VOUCHERS PAYABLE CREDIT
12	19-- Dec.	2	163	Supersound, Inc.	Dec. 2	425	425 15
13							

Figure 7–10. Recording a Note Payable in the Voucher Register *(Left Side)*

$4.15 ($421, 8%, 45 days), and a credit to Vouchers Payable for $425.15. When the voucher is paid, the payment is recorded in the check register as a debit to Vouchers Payable for $425.15 and a credit to Cash in Bank for $425.15. The voucher register entries for the issuance and payment of Voucher 163 are illustrated in Figure 7–10.

Installment Payments

In a voucher system, vouchers generally are paid in full when they are due. Sometimes, however, management prefers to pay for an item in installments. When this happens, a separate voucher is prepared and recorded in the voucher register for each installment. For example, on November 2, Videosonics bought an office safe for $750 from the Newell Company. Videosonics made a down payment of $250 and agreed to make two installments of $250 each, payable on November 17 and December 2.

In the voucher system, a check can be written only in payment of an approved voucher. Since a total of three checks will be needed, three separate vouchers (numbered 154, 155, and 156) are prepared and recorded in the voucher register, as shown in Figure 7–11.

Each voucher has a due date that corresponds to the date the payment must be made. Voucher 154, which is for the November 2 down payment, is paid immediately. Vouchers 155 and 156 are filed in the unpaid voucher file according to their due dates.

VOUCHER

	DATE		VOU. NO.	CREDITOR	VOUCHERS PAYABLE CREDIT
5	19-- Nov.	2	154	Newell Co.	250 00
6		2	155	Newell Co.	250 00
7		2	156	Newell Co.	250 00

Figure 7–11. Recording Installment Payments in the Voucher Register *(Left Side)*

GENERAL		
ACCOUNT DEBITED	POST. REF.	DEBIT
Notes Payable	211	421 00
Interest Expense	621	4 15

(Right Side)

Correcting an Incorrect Voucher

The internal control of the voucher system will not entirely eliminate errors. However, errors should be kept to a minimum. If an error is discovered after a voucher has been recorded in the voucher register, it must be corrected by a general journal entry. The general journal entry cancels the original voucher by reversing the original voucher register entry. A new voucher is then prepared for the correct amount.

For example, on September 20 Videosonics bought merchandise on account from Supersound, Inc. The invoice amount was $546. Videosonics issued Voucher 102.

On October 19, an error was discovered in the price extensions. The correct amount of the invoice should have been $518. The general journal entry necessary to correct the error is shown in Figure 7–12, which appears at the top of the next page.

The general journal entry makes possible the issuance of a new voucher for the correct amount. The entry for the new voucher is shown in Figure 7–13 on page 164.

The cancellation of the original voucher must also be noted in the voucher register. As you can see in Figure 7–14 on page 164, the date and number of the new voucher are recorded in the Payment columns on the Voucher 102 line. This same notation is written on Voucher 102 itself. Voucher 102 is then placed in the paid voucher file.

GENERAL		
ACCOUNT DEBITED	POST. REF.	DEBIT
Office Equipment		750 00

(Right Side)

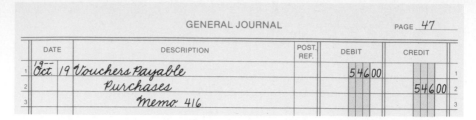

	DATE	DESCRIPTION	POST. REF.	DEBIT	CREDIT	
1	Oct. 19	Vouchers Payable		546 00		1
2		Purchases			546 00	2
3		Memo. 416				3

Figure 7–12. Recording a Correcting Entry

VOUCHER REGISTER   PAGE 3

	DATE	VOU. NO.	CREDITOR	PAYMENT DATE	CK. NO.	VOUCHERS PAYABLE CREDIT	PURCHASES DEBIT
20	Oct. 19	130	Supersound, Inc.			518 00	518 00

Figure 7–13. Recording the Issuance of a New Voucher

VOUCHER REGISTER   PAGE 2

	DATE	VOU. NO.	CREDITOR	PAYMENT DATE	CK. NO.	VOUCHERS PAYABLE CREDIT	PURCHASES DEBIT
15	Sept. 20	102	Supersound, Inc.	Oct. 19	V130	546 00	546 00

Figure 7–14. Recording the Cancellation of a Voucher

The Voucher System as a Management Tool

The voucher system is one example of how an accounting procedure can be used as an internal control. It provides a systematic record of cash disbursements and aids in the efficient management of financial resources. In this respect, it has the following advantages.

1. Financial managers use the information in the unpaid voucher file to plan for cash requirements.
2. Vouchers systematize the taking of cash discounts. Firms can save money by making payments within the discount period. The unpaid voucher file contains the information needed by the company to make timely payments.
3. Each cash payment corresponds to one specific voucher. This practice eliminates confusion that can lead to omitting payments or making duplicate payments for the same good or service.
4. Authority may be delegated and responsibility fixed. This advantage stems

from the system of requiring approval signatures. Because the approval is given when the goods arrive or the service is received, if something is not satisfactory, it is given immediate attention.

Before reading further, do the following activity to check your understanding of the material you have just read.

Check Your Learning

On a sheet of notebook paper, write your answers to the following questions. During April, the City Lights Company had the following transactions.

Apr. 6 Bought merchandise on account from the Larson Company, $9,600, terms 2/10, n/30, Voucher 3842.

9 Issued Debit Memo A326 to the Larson Company for the return of defective merchandise purchased April 6, $420.

15 Issued Check 4868 in payment of Voucher 3842, less the return and less the discount.

1. In which journal or register would each of these transactions be recorded?
2. How is the issuance of the debit memo noted in the voucher register?
3. For what amount is Check 4868 written?

Check your answers with those in the answers section. Re-read the preceding part of the chapter to find the answers to any questions you may have missed.

Summary of Key Points

1. The voucher system is a procedure for controlling all purchases and cash payments. The voucher system promotes internal control and the efficient management of financial resources.
2. A voucher is prepared for each invoice or bill received. The voucher, along with the invoice or bill, is circulated within the company for approval signatures. Then the voucher is recorded in the voucher register.
3. In the voucher system, the Vouchers Payable account replaces the Accounts Payable account.
4. In the voucher system, the unpaid voucher file replaces the accounts payable ledger. Unpaid vouchers are filed chronologically by due dates.
5. When the voucher system is used, all cash payments are made by check. Checks are issued only in payment of approved and recorded vouchers.
6. A voucher check is a special check with an attached stub on which the details of the cash payment are listed.
7. In the voucher system, all checks are recorded in a check register. The check register replaces the cash payments journal.
8. Nonroutine transactions that do not fit into fixed channels of the voucher system require special treatment, usually in the form of general journal entries.

Review and Applications

Building Your Accounting Vocabulary

In your own words, write the definition of each of the following accounting terms. Use complete sentences for your definitions.

check register	unpaid voucher	voucher check
paid voucher file	file	voucher register
schedule of unpaid	voucher	voucher system
vouchers		

Reviewing Your Accounting Knowledge

1. Explain why internal control is important.
2. Why might the voucher system not be appropriate for a small business?
3. What are the seven components of a voucher system?
4. When a business uses the voucher system, what types of transactions require the filling out of a voucher?
5. What is the value of maintaining an unpaid vouchers file?
6. When a voucher system is in use, is it necessary to have an accounts payable subsidiary ledger? Why or why not?
7. Why might a business prefer to use voucher checks, rather than regular checks, with a voucher system?
8. In the voucher system, what special journal does the check register replace?
9. Regarding the purchase of merchandise, what must be done when a debit memo is prepared after the original voucher has been recorded?
10. How are installment payments handled in the voucher system?
11. Explain briefly how the voucher system serves as a management tool.

Improving Your Decision-making Skills

Hector Ramos, the owner of a large department store, has asked for your help in evaluating his internal procedures. During your study of his operations, you notice that he occasionally pays invoices in cash, out of the cash register. You point out to him that all payments should be made by check, but he wants to know why. What explanation can you give him?

Applying Accounting Procedures

Problem 7–1

Buchanan and Sons uses the voucher system. On June 14, the invoice at the top of page 167 was received.

Housewares, Inc.

4856 Staples Mill Road, Richmond VA 23228

Invoice
H601

TO:
Buchanan and Sons
2425 Stuart Avenue
Richmond, VA 23220

Date: June 13, 19--
Order No.: 5863
Shipped By: Our truck
Terms: 2/10, n/30

QUANTITY	ITEM	UNIT PRICE	TOTAL
36	dinner plates	$15.00	$ 540.00
45	soup bowls	6.50	292.50
50	sets of glassware	20.00	1,000.00
	Total		$1,832.50

Instructions:

(1) Prepare Voucher 114, using the form in the working papers accompanying this textbook.

(2) Assume that Check 201 was written in payment of Voucher 114 on June 21, two days before the end of the discount period. Record the payment information on the voucher.

Problem 7–2

The Waterbury Company uses a voucher system. During March, the company had the following transactions.

Mar.   1   Issued Voucher 721 in favor of Lind Realty Company for the March rent, $1,100.00.

        2   Bought merchandise on account from Miller Manufacturing Company, $2,850.00, terms 2/10, n/30, Voucher 722.

        7   Issued Voucher 723 in favor of Regional Telephone Company for telephone bill, $108.00.

        9   Received Invoice 911 from Blake, Inc., for office supplies purchased on account, $425.50, terms n/30, Voucher 724.

     14   Bought merchandise on account from Great Lakes Products, $5,130.00, terms 2/10, n/EOM, Voucher 725.

     23   Issued Voucher 726 for a note payable previously recorded in the general journal: principal, $3,000.00, plus interest of $40.68. The note is payable to the First National Bank.

     25   Received a bill for $152.50 from the Midwest Ledger for advertisements published; issued Voucher 727.

31 Issued Voucher 728 for the net monthly salaries, $2,925.00, in favor of the payroll bank account (debit Salaries Payable).

Instructions:

(1) Record the transactions for March on page 14 of the voucher register.
(2) Total, prove, and rule the voucher register.

Problem 7–3

The Guthrie Company, which uses a voucher system, has the following unpaid vouchers on April 30.

Vou. No.	Creditor	For	Date of Invoice	Amount
7219	Huber and Ramsey	Merchandise	April 22	$11,680.00
7222	Hopkins Supplies	Store equipment	April 24	4,545.00
7223	Schultz & Co.	Merchandise	April 27	6,400.00

These vouchers appear in the voucher register in the working papers accompanying this textbook.

The Guthrie Company had the following transactions during May.

May 1 Issued Voucher 7226 in favor of Fidelity Insurance Company for a one-year premium on a fire insurance policy, $432.00.

1 Paid Voucher 7219 by issuing Check 9626 for $11,446.40 ($11,680.00 less 2% discount).

3 Issued Check 9627 for $432.00 in payment of Voucher 7226.

5 Issued Voucher 7227 in favor of Green Motor Freight for transportation charges on merchandise purchased, $84.00.

5 Paid Voucher 7227 by issuing Check 9628 for $84.00.

5 Issued Check 9629 for $6,272.00 in payment of Voucher 7223 ($6,400.00 less 2% discount).

10 Received the monthly utility bill of $174.60 from City Services, Inc., issued Voucher 7228.

10 Paid Voucher 7228 by issuing Check 9630 for $174.60.

11 Issued Voucher 7229 in favor of Reynolds and Howard for the purchase of merchandise on account, $10,240.00, terms 2/10, n/30.

12 Bought office stationery from Holland Stationers, $1,240.00, terms n/30; issued Voucher 7230.

19 Received a bill from Hughes County for 6 months' property taxes of $1,800.00, Voucher 7231.

19 Paid Voucher 7231 by issuing Check 9631 for $1,800.00.

19 Issued Check 9632 for $10,035.20 in payment of Voucher 7229 ($10,240.00 less discount).

24 Bought merchandise on account from Gross and Rogers, $9,632.00, terms 2/10, n/30; issued Voucher 7232.

24   Paid Voucher 7222 by issuing Check 9633 for $4,545.00.

31   Issued Voucher 7233 in favor of Payroll for the net monthly salaries of $7,720.00 (debit Salaries Payable).

31   Paid Voucher 7233 by issuing Check 9634 for $7,720.00, payable to Payroll.

Instructions:

(1) Enter the transactions for May on page 7 of the voucher register and on page 6 of the check register.

(2) Total, prove, and rule the voucher register and check register.

Problem 7–4

The Huffman Company uses a voucher system. During August of this year, it completed the following transactions.

Aug.   1   Issued Voucher 1079 in favor of Holliday Company for the purchase of merchandise costing $3,900.00, terms 30 days.

4   Purchased a computer for $2,925.00 from Hale Equipment, arranging to make three equal installment payments. Prepared Voucher 1080 for $975.00, Voucher 1081 for $975.00, and Voucher 1082 for $975.00. (Use three lines.)

4   Issued Check 1426 in payment of Voucher 1080.

7   Received Invoice 166 from Griffith Supply Co. for store supplies purchased on account, $243.00, terms n/30; issued Voucher 1083.

9   Prepared Voucher 1084 in favor of Townsend Products for the purchase of merchandise on account, $4,500.00, Invoice 1610, terms 2/10, n/30.

11   Prepared Voucher 1085 in favor of Burroughs Real Estate for the August rent, $1,425.00.

11   Wrote Check 1427 in payment of Voucher 1085.

14   Issued Voucher 1086 in favor of Hull Transportation for freight charges on merchandise purchased, $125.60.

14   Prepared Check 1428 in payment of Voucher 1086.

15   Canceled Voucher 1079 and arranged to pay the invoice in two installments as follows: $1,950.00 on September 1 and $1,950.00 on September 15; issued Vouchers 1087 and 1088, Memorandum 762.

16   Issued Debit Memorandum 211 to Townsend Products Company for $180.00 worth of merchandise returned.

17   Issued Check 1429 for $4,233.60 in payment of Voucher 1084.

22   Received the monthly telephone bill from National Telephone Co., $107.13; issued Voucher 1089.

22   Wrote Check 1430 in payment of Voucher 1089.

31   Prepared Voucher 1090 for the net monthly salaries of $2,940.00, in favor of Payroll (debit Salaries Payable).

31   Issued Check 1431 in payment of Voucher 1090.

Instructions:

(1) Record the transactions for August in the voucher register (page 8), the check register (page 7), and the general journal (page 8).

(2) Total, prove, and rule the voucher register and the check register at the end of the month.

(3) Post the amounts from the registers and the general journal to the Vouchers Payable account.

Problem 7–5

The Cunningham Company, which uses a voucher system, had the following unpaid vouchers on August 31.

Vou. No.	Creditor	For	Date of Invoice	Amount
4993	Robbins, Inc.	Store equipment	Aug. 26	$6,750.00
4998	Riggs Equipment	Office equipment	Aug. 28	7,905.00

The vouchers have already been recorded in the voucher register in the working papers accompanying this textbook.

The company made the following transactions during September.

Sept. 1 Received the monthly electric bill of $174.00 from Consolidated Power, issued Voucher 5003.

1 Paid Voucher 5003 by issuing Check 6815.

3 Issued Voucher 5004 to Carter, Inc. in payment of a $5,000, 12%, 60-day note payable previously recorded in the general journal.

3 Issued Check 6816 in payment of Voucher 5004.

4 Received Invoice A63, dated Sept. 3, for merchandise bought on account from Thompson Company, $8,100.00, terms 2/10, n/30; issued Voucher 5005.

9 Riggs Equipment agreed to accept a 60-day, 11% note, in payment of the August 28 invoice. Accordingly, canceled Voucher 4998 and issued Note 463.

10 Purchased office supplies on account from Taft Brothers, $67.95, terms n/30; issued Voucher 5006.

12 Issued Check 6817 for $7,938.00 in payment of Voucher 5005.

15 Prepared Voucher 5007 to the Sales Commissions account for $735.00 for sales commissions (Commissions Expense).

15 Issued Check 6818 in payment of Voucher 5007.

18 Purchased a three-year liability insurance policy from Sentry Insurance, $1,800.00; issued Voucher 5008.

18 Issued Check 6819 in payment of Voucher 5008.

19 Bought merchandise on account from the Tucker Company, $9,600.00, terms 1/10, n/30; issued Voucher 5009.

22   Issued Voucher 5010 in favor of Eastern Express Company for freight charges on the merchandise purchased from the Tucker Company, $162.95.

24   Discovered an error in the extensions on the invoice from the Tucker Company, reducing the amount by $360.00 (Memorandum 4012). Canceled Voucher 5009 and issued Voucher 5011 for $9,240.00.

25   Prepared Voucher 5012 for $916.33 in favor of Security Savings and Loan for the monthly mortgage payment; principal, $17.66, interest $898.67.

26   Issued Check 6820 in payment of Voucher 5012.

30   Prepared Voucher 5013 in favor of the payroll bank account for the net monthly payroll of $3,123.00 (debit Salaries Payable).

30   Paid Voucher 5013 by issuing Check 6821.

Instructions:

(1) Record the transactions for September in the voucher register (page 12), the check register (page 11), and the general journal (page 13).

(2) Total, prove, and rule the voucher register and the check register.

(3) Post the amounts from the registers and the general journal to the Vouchers Payable account.

(4) Prepare a schedule of unpaid vouchers.

8 Deferrals and Accruals

One of the purposes of accounting is to report, as accurately as possible, the financial condition of a business. This is done by matching the revenue earned during one accounting period with the expenses incurred to produce that revenue. As you remember, this is called the *matching principle* of accounting.

When revenue is collected in the accounting period in which it is earned and expenses are paid in the accounting period in which they are incurred, it is much easier to accurately report financial information. However, revenue is often received and expenses are often paid in an accounting period other than that in which they were earned or incurred. When this happens, the financial statements do not accurately report data because revenue and expenses are not properly matched.

In this chapter, you will learn how a business matches revenue and expenses to the proper accounting period by using the accrual basis of accounting.

Learning Objectives

When you have completed this chapter, you should be able to

1. Explain the difference between the cash basis and the accrual basis of accounting.

2. Explain the difference between an accrual and a deferral.

3. Record adjusting entries for deferred revenues and deferred expenses.

4. Record adjusting entries for accrued expenses and accrued revenues.

5. Define the accounting terms presented in this chapter.

New Terms

cash basis of accounting / accrual basis of accounting / deferral / accrual / prepaid expense / unearned revenue / accrued expense / accrued revenue

Cash Basis of Accounting

Some small businesses keep their financial records on a cash basis. The cash basis of accounting recognizes revenue and expenses only when cash is received or paid out. For example, the fee charged by a doctor is recorded as revenue when cash is received, not when the service was performed or when the patient was billed. Likewise, expenses are recorded in the accounting period in which they are paid, not when the expenses were actually incurred.

Businesses that earn revenue by providing a service often use the cash basis. Such businesses include professional offices of doctors, lawyers, and accountants, as well as service enterprises such as beauty salons, taxicab companies, and real estate offices. Their income is earned from the sale of their services, not from the sale of goods.

Accrual Basis of Accounting

The cash basis of accounting is not suitable for most businesses, particularly merchandising businesses. Merchandising businesses purchase goods on account from wholesalers and manufacturers. The merchandise is then sold to customers, often on credit. Often, payments are made to creditors and cash is received from charge customers in an accounting period *other than* the period in which the merchandise was purchased or sold. If net income is to be measured properly, revenue should be recognized when it is earned, regardless of when cash is received. Expenses should be reported in the fiscal period in which they are incurred, regardless of when they are paid. The accrual basis of accounting recognizes revenue when earned and expenses when incurred.

Remember: In the accrual basis of accounting, revenue is recorded when it is earned and expenses are recorded in the accounting period in which they are incurred.

In the accrual basis of accounting, adjusting entries are used to account for transactions that affect more than one accounting period. They are needed when deferrals or accruals exist. The word *defer* means to delay or postpone. In accounting, a deferral is the postponement of the expense or income recognition of a bill already paid or cash already received. Deferrals are needed when:

1. Already recorded costs must be allocated, or spread out, over two or more accounting periods. Two examples are the cost of supplies and prepaid insurance.

2. Already recorded revenues must be allocated over two or more accounting periods. Examples include rent received in advance and cash received in advance for magazine subscriptions or for season tickets to a sporting or cultural series.

The word *accrue* means to accumulate or grow in size. In accounting, an **accrual** is the recognition of an expense or revenue that has gradually increased over time but has not yet been recorded. Accruals are required when:

1. There are unrecorded revenues. An example is a fee or commission earned but not yet billed to or collected from a customer.
2. There are unrecorded expenses. Examples include property and income taxes and wages earned by employees in one period but not paid until the next period.

Remember: Adjusting entries must be recorded when (1) already recorded revenues and expenses must be allocated over two or more accounting periods and (2) there are unrecorded revenues and expenses at the end of the fiscal period.

Deferrals

Sometimes revenues are received before they are earned and expenses are paid before they are incurred. However, the receipt or outlay of this cash in an accounting period does not affect that period's net income. Instead, the recognition of these revenues or expenses is deferred to the proper accounting period so that a business can more accurately match its revenue and expenses. Deferrals are classified as either prepaid expenses or unearned revenues.

Prepaid Expenses

As its name implies, a **prepaid expense** is an expense paid in advance. Examples of prepaid expenses include the purchase of office supplies, premiums paid on insurance policics, rent paid in advance for the use of buildings or cars, and the bank discounts on non-interest-bearing notes payable.

A prepaid expense is usually recorded in the accounting records as an asset. During the accounting period, a portion (or all) of the asset is used up or expires. That portion of the asset that is used up or expires is an expense for the accounting period. The portion of the asset that has not been used up or expired is an asset that applies to the next accounting period. At the end of the accounting period, an adjusting entry is made to record the amount of the expense.

Office Supplies

Throughout the accounting period, a business purchases office supplies when needed. When a business purchases office supplies, the transaction is recorded as a debit to Office Supplies and a credit to Cash in Bank or Accounts Payable.

During the accounting period, the office supplies are used up in the business's normal operations. Rather than recording the expense during the year as each item of supplies is used up, an adjusting entry is made at the end of the accounting period to record the total amount of the supplies expense for the period.

For example, the Chaddock Corporation records the purchase of office supplies in the current asset account Office Supplies. At the end of the accounting period, the Office Supplies account has a balance of $1,942. On December 31, a physical inventory is taken and it is found that $175 of office supplies are still on hand. By subtracting the ending supplies inventory from the balance of the Office Supplies account, the amount of supplies used during the fiscal period, the supplies expense, is determined.

Balance of Office Supplies account	$1,942
Ending inventory	− 175
Office supplies used	$1,767

As you can see, the office supplies expense for the period is $1,767. At the end of the period, an adjusting entry—entered first on the work sheet—is made to record the office supplies expense. This entry is shown in Figure 8–1.

Figure 8–1. Adjusting Entry for Office Supplies Expense

Remember: **Adjustments are first planned and recorded on the work sheet.**

Prepaid Rent

Some businesses pay their office rent several months in advance. For example, the Garry Real Estate Agency pays its office rent three months in advance. On December 1, James Garry, the owner, wrote a $1,500 check to Holly Realty for rent for the months of December, January, and February. The transaction was recorded as a debit of $1,500 to the current asset account Prepaid Rent and a credit of $1,500 to Cash in Bank.

As each day goes by, a portion of the prepaid rent expires. The expired amount becomes an expense to the business. On December 31, the end of Garry's accounting period, one month's rent, or $500 ($1,500 ÷ 3), has expired and should be recorded as an expense for the fiscal period. The adjusting entry made on December 31 is shown in Figure 8–2 on page 176.

DATE	DESCRIPTION	POST. REF.	DEBIT	CREDIT	
	Adjusting Entries				1
19-- Dec. 31	Rent Expense		5 00 00		2
	Prepaid Rent			5 00 00	3

Figure 8–2. Adjusting Entry for Rent Expense

Interest on Non-interest-bearing Notes Payable

In Chapter 4, you learned that when a business issues a non-interest-bearing note payable the bank deducts the amount of the interest in advance. The amount deducted in advance is called the bank discount and the amount the business actually receives is called the proceeds. The amount of the bank discount is debited to a contra liability account called Discount on Notes Payable. Since the business is paying the interest expense in advance, the amount recorded in Discount on Notes Payable is actually a prepaid expense.

A business may issue a non-interest-bearing note payable in one fiscal period that does not come due until the next fiscal period. When this happens, an adjusting entry must be made at the end of the fiscal period to record the portion of the prepaid interest that is an expense of the current fiscal period. Let's look at an example.

On December 16, Pick a Stitch borrowed $5,000 from the National Bank of Commerce by issuing a 30-day non-interest-bearing note payable that was discounted at 10%. The amount of the bank discount was calculated as follows.

$$\text{Principal} \quad \text{Discount Rate} \quad \text{Time} \quad \text{Bank Discount}$$
$$\$5{,}000.00 \times \quad .10 \quad \times \frac{30}{365} = \quad \$41.10$$

When the transaction was journalized, Cash in Bank was debited for $4,958.90, the amount of the proceeds received ($5,000.00 − $41.10). Discount on Notes Payable was debited for $41.10, the amount of the interest deducted in advance. Notes Payable was credited for $5,000.00, the face amount of the note. This transaction is shown in the following T accounts.

Cash in Bank		Discount on Notes Payable		Notes Payable	
Dr.	Cr.	Dr.	Cr.	Dr.	Cr.
+	−	+	−	−	+
$4,958.90		$41.10			$5,000.00

At the end of the fiscal period, a portion of the bank discount has become an expense. Since the term of the note is 30 days, 15 days of interest must be charged to the current fiscal period. The amount of the interest expense is calculated as shown at the top of the next page.

$$\begin{array}{cccc} \text{Principal} & \text{Interest Rate} & \text{Time} & \text{Interest} \\ \$5,000.00 \times & .10 & \times \dfrac{15}{365} = & \$20.55 \end{array}$$

An adjusting entry must be made on December 31 to record the amount of the interest expense for the period.

Interest Expense is debited for $20.55, the amount of the bank discount that has now become an expense. Discount on Notes Payable is credited for $20.55 to remove the actual amount of interest expense for the period. Discount on Notes Payable now has a balance of $20.55.

Interest Expense		Discount on Notes Payable	
Dr.	Cr	Dr.	Cr.
+	−	+	−
Adj. $20.55		Bal. $41.10	Adj. $20.55

The adjusting entry is shown in Figure 8–3.

	DATE	DESCRIPTION	POST. REF.	DEBIT	CREDIT	
1		*Adjusting Entries*				1
2	19-- Dec. 31	*Interest Expense*		20 55		2
3		*Discount on Notes Payable*			20 55	3

GENERAL JOURNAL   PAGE 31

Figure 8–3. Adjusting Entry for Interest Expense

On the due date of the note, January 15, Pick a Stitch will issue a check for $5,000 (the face value of the note) to the National Bank of Commerce. That transaction will be recorded as a debit of $5,000 to Notes Payable and a credit of $5,000 to Cash in Bank.

At the same time, an entry must be made transferring the amount in the Discount on Notes Payable account to the Interest Expense account. The balance of the Discount on Notes Payable account, $20.55, represents the amount of the bank discount that is an expense of the current fiscal period. That account is therefore credited for $20.55. Interest Expense is debited for $20.55.

Interest Expense		Discount on Notes Payable	
Dr.	Cr.	Dr.	Cr.
+	−	+	−
$20.55		$41.10	Adj. $20.55
			$20.55

The entry is shown, in general journal form, in Figure 8–4 at the top of the next page.

DATE	DESCRIPTION	POST. REF.	DEBIT	CREDIT	
19-- Jan. 15	Interest Expense		20 55		1
	Discount on Notes Payable			20 55	2
	Memo. 15				3

Figure 8–4. Recording the Interest Expense on a Discounted Note

Remember: **When a non-interest-bearing note payable is paid, the amount recorded in the Discount on Notes Payable account must be transferred to the Interest Expense account.**

Unearned Revenues

Businesses often receive revenue before it is earned. Some examples include cash received in advance for rental properties, magazine subscriptions, season tickets, advertising, insurance premiums, and work to be completed in the future. Revenue received in advance but not yet earned is referred to as unearned revenue. When revenues are received in advance, the business has an obligation to deliver the goods or perform the services. Therefore, these unearned revenues normally represent a current liability to the business. As the business delivers the merchandise or performs the service, it earns a part of the advance payment. The earned portion must be transferred from the liability account to a revenue account. This is done through an adjusting entry at the end of the fiscal period.

Remember: **Unearned revenue is a liability of the business.**

Accounting for Rent Received in Advance

The LaSalle Jewelry Company rents desk space in its store to a manufacturer's representative. On November 1, the representative paid LaSalle $450 for rent for the months of November, December, and January.

November 1: *Received $450 cash for the rental of desk space for 3 months, Receipt 181.*

In this transaction Cash in Bank is debited for $450. Since the $450 has not yet been earned, it is credited to the current liability account Unearned Rent. LaSalle has an obligation to provide the desk space for the three months.

Cash in Bank		Unearned Rent	
Dr.	Cr.	Dr.	Cr.
+	–	–	+
$450			$450

The entry to record this transaction is shown in general journal form in Figure 8–5 on page 179.

DATE	DESCRIPTION	POST. REF.	DEBIT	CREDIT	
1	*19-- nov. 1*	*Cash in Bank*		450 00		1
2		*Unearned Rent*			450 00	2
3		*Receipt 181*				3

Figure 8–5. Recording Rent Received in Advance as Unearned Revenue

The LaSalle Company's fiscal period ends on December 31. On that date, LaSalle has earned two of the three months' rental income. An adjusting entry must be made on December 31 to record the amount of rental income earned to that date.

Since $300 of the $450 has been earned by December 31 ($450 $\times$ ⅔), Unearned Rent is debited for that amount to record the decrease in the liability. The $150 credit balance in the account represents one month's rent that has been deferred to the next accounting period. The other revenue account Rental Income is credited for $300 to record the increase in revenue for the accounting period.

Unearned Rent			Rental Income	
Dr.	Cr.		Dr.	Cr.
−	+		−	+
Adj. $300	Bal. $450			Adj. $300

The adjusting entry made on December 31 is shown in Figure 8–6.

DATE	DESCRIPTION	POST. REF.	DEBIT	CREDIT	
1		*Adjusting Entries*				1
2	*19-- Dec. 31*	*Unearned Rent*		300 00		2
3		*Rental Income*			300 00	3

Figure 8–6. Adjusting Entry for Rental Income

Accounting for Subscription Income Received in Advance

A magazine publishing company earns revenue by selling issues of its magazine, often on a subscription basis. When a magazine subscription is sold, cash is received in advance. The company incurs a liability to the subscribers for a certain number of magazine issues. The company earns a portion of the revenue received in advance as each issue is published and sent to the subscriber.

For example, the Jason Publishing Company publishes a magazine called *The Outdoor Athlete*. The company received $48,000 for subscriptions covering a 24-month period.

October 1: Received $48,000 cash for magazine subscriptions, Receipt 550.

In this transaction, Cash in Bank is debited for $48,000, the amount of cash received for 24 months of magazine subscriptions. Since the $48,000 has not yet been earned, it is credited to the current liability account Unearned Subscriptions Income. Jason Publishing is liable to its subscribers for the amount received until it is earned.

Cash in Bank		Unearned Subscriptions Income	
Dr.	Cr.	Dr.	Cr.
+	−	−	+
$48,000			$48,000

The entry to record this transaction is shown in general journal form in Figure 8–7.

	GENERAL JOURNAL			PAGE 63
DATE	DESCRIPTION	POST. REF.	DEBIT	CREDIT
19-- Oct. 1	Cash in Bank		48 000 00	
	Unearned Subscriptions Income			48 000 00
	Receipt 550			

Figure 8–7. Recording Subscriptions Income as Unearned Revenue

Jason's fiscal period ends on December 31. On that date, three months of subscription income, $6,000, has been earned ($48,000 × $3/24$ = $6,000). An adjusting entry must be made on December 31 to record the amount of subscription income earned.

Since $6,000 in subscription income was earned during the fiscal period, that amount is debited to the Unearned Subscriptions Income account to record the decrease in the liability. The $42,000 credit balance in the account represents the amount Jason is liable to subscribers for until it is earned. The revenue account Subscriptions Income is credited for $6,000 to record the amount of income earned during the accounting period.

Unearned Subscriptions Income		Subscriptions Income	
Dr.	Cr.	Dr.	Cr.
−	+	−	+
Adj. $6,000	Bal. $48,000		Adj. $6,000

The adjusting entry is shown in Figure 8–8 on page 181.

Remember: Revenue received in advance is recorded in a liability account. That account must be adjusted at the end of the fiscal period to recognize the revenue earned during the period.

	DATE	DESCRIPTION	POST. REF.	DEBIT	CREDIT	
1		*Adjusting Entries*				1
2	*19-- Dec. 31*	*Unearned Subscriptions Income*		6 00 00 0		2
3		*Subscriptions Income*			6 00 00 0	3

Figure 8–8. Adjusting Entry for Subscription Income

Before reading further, do the following activity to check your understanding of deferrals.

Check Your Learning

Answer the following questions on a separate sheet of paper.

1. In the __?__ basis of accounting, revenues and expenses are recognized when cash is paid out or received.
2. In the __?__ basis of accounting, revenues are recognized when they are earned and expenses are recognized when they are incurred.
3. A(n) __?__ is the postponement of the recognition of an expense already paid or a revenue already received.
4. Deferred expenses are called __?__.
5. Unearned revenues are reported on the balance sheet as __?__.

Compare your answers to those in the answers section. Re-read the preceding part of the chapter to find the correct answers to any questions you may have missed.

Accruals

As mentioned earlier, accruals are expenses or revenues that gradually increase with the passage of time. In order to accurately report a company's financial position, accruals should be recognized in the accounting period in which they occur. Let's first look at accrued expenses.

Accrued Expenses

Most expenses are recorded at the time they are paid. For example, when the business receives the telephone bill, a check is written, and the transaction is recorded as a debit to Utilities Expense and a credit to Cash in Bank. There are, however, some business expenses that accrue on a day-to-day basis but have not been recorded at the end of the accounting period. These expenses include salaries and wages earned by employees, interest incurred on unpaid notes, and property taxes. These items are examples of accrued expenses. An accrued expense is an expense that is incurred in one fiscal period but will not be paid until a later fiscal period. In order to recognize all expenses for the fiscal period, an adjusting entry is made at the end of the period to record any expense that has been incurred but is not yet due to be paid.

December
S M T W T F S
1 2 3 4 5 6 7
8 9 10 11 12 13 14
15 16 17 18 19 20 21
22 23 24 25 26 27 28
29 30 31

Accrued Salaries Expense

Pickett Products Company pays its employees weekly. The weekly payroll is $1,500. At the end of the fiscal period, Pickett owes its employees $600 for salaries earned on December 30–31 ($1,500 × ⅖). Although Pickett has incurred the $600 salaries expense during this fiscal period, it will not be paid until January 3, during the next fiscal period. If the accounting records for Pickett are to show the correct amount of the salaries expense for the fiscal period, an adjusting entry must be made on December 31.

Salaries Expense is debited for $600 to show the total salaries expense incurred but not yet paid. It is an accrued expense for the current fiscal period, and it will appear on the income statement. Salaries Payable is credited for $600 to show the amount owed to employees. This amount will appear on the balance sheet as a current liability.

Salaries Expense			Salaries Payable	
Dr.	Cr.		Dr.	Cr.
+	−		−	+
Bal. $76,500				Adj. $600
Adj. 600				

The adjusting entry is shown in Figure 8–9.

GENERAL JOURNAL   PAGE 47

	DATE	DESCRIPTION	POST. REF.	DEBIT	CREDIT	
1		Adjusting Entries				1
2	19-- Dec. 31	Salaries Expense		600 00		2
3		Salaries Payable			600 00	3

Figure 8–9. Adjusting Entry for Accrued Salaries Expense

Remember: **An adjusting entry must be made at the end of the fiscal period for expenses that have accrued but have not yet been recorded.**

On January 3, Pickett prepares the weekly payroll of $1,500.

January 3: *Paid the weekly payroll of $1,500 by issuing Check 101.*

Of this amount, $600 is an expense charged to the prior fiscal period and $900 is an expense charged to the current accounting period. Salaries Expense is, therefore, debited for $900, the amount of the expense for the current accounting period. Salaries Payable is debited for $600 to show the decrease in the liability. Cash in Bank is credited for $1,500, the total amount of the check written for the weekly payroll.

Salaries Expense		Salaries Payable		Cash in Bank	
Dr.	Cr.	Dr.	Cr.	Dr.	Cr.
+	−	−	+	+	−
$900		$600	Adj. $600		$1,500

The entry to record this transaction is shown in general journal form in Figure 8–10.

	DATE	DESCRIPTION	POST. REF.	DEBIT	CREDIT	
	GENERAL JOURNAL				PAGE 48	
1	19‑‑ Jan. 3	Salaries Expense		900 00		1
2		Salaries Payable		600 00		2
3		Cash in Bank			1500 00	3
4		Check 101				4

Figure 8–10. Recording Payment of the Weekly Payroll

Accrued Interest Expense

Occasionally, Pickett borrows money by issuing a promissory note. The transaction is recorded by debiting Cash in Bank and crediting Notes Payable.

Sometimes a note is issued in one accounting period but is not due until the next accounting period. For example, Pickett issued a $10,000, 60-day, 10% note payable on November 30. That note does not mature until January 29. However, interest expense has accrued on the note from November 30 to December 31 and must be recorded. There are 31 days between November 30 and December 31. The amount of the accrued interest expense is calculated as follows.

$$\text{Principal} \quad \text{Interest Rate} \quad \text{Time} \quad \text{Interest}$$
$$\$10{,}000 \times .10 \times \frac{31}{365} = \$84.93$$

Interest Expense is debited for $84.93, the amount of accrued interest chargeable to the current fiscal period. Interest Payable is credited for $84.93 to show the amount of interest owed but not yet paid at the end of the fiscal period. It will be reported as a current liability on the balance sheet.

Interest Expense		Interest Payable	
Dr.	Cr.	Dr.	Cr.
+	−	−	+
Adj. $84.93			Adj. $84.93

The adjusting entry is shown in Figure 8–11.

	GENERAL JOURNAL			PAGE 47	
DATE	DESCRIPTION	POST. REF.	DEBIT	CREDIT	
1	*Adjusting Entries*				1
8	Dec. 31 *Interest Expense*		84 93		8
9	*Interest Payable*			84 93	9

Figure 8–11. Adjusting Entry for Accrued Interest Expense

On the due date of the note, Pickett will issue a check for the maturity value of the bank note. As you remember, the maturity value is the amount of the principal plus the interest. The amount of the interest on the note for the full term is calculated as follows.

$$\text{Principal} \quad \text{Interest Rate} \quad \text{Time} \quad \text{Interest}$$
$$\$10,000 \times .10 \times \frac{60}{365} = \$164.38$$

The maturity value of the note, therefore, is $10,164.38 ($10,000.00 + $164.38).

January 29: *Issued Check 115 for $10,164.38 to National Bank of Commerce in payment of the note payable issued November 30.*

In this transaction, Notes Payable is debited for $10,000.00 to show a decrease in the liability. The total amount of interest expense on the note payable is $164.38. Of that amount, $84.93 is an expense charged to and recorded in the prior fiscal period. The remaining $79.45 ($164.38 − $84.93) is an expense of the current fiscal period. Interest Payable is, therefore, debited for $84.93 to decrease the liability since the interest owed is now being paid. Interest Expense is debited for $79.45, the amount of the expense for the current fiscal period. Cash in Bank is credited for $10,164.38, the total amount that is being paid out.

Notes Payable			Interest Payable		
Dr.	Cr.		Dr.	Cr.	
−	+		−	+	
$10,000.00	Bal. $10,000.00		$84.93	Adj. $84.93	

Interest Expense			Cash in Bank		
Dr.	Cr.		Dr.	Cr.	
+	−		+	−	
$79.45				$10,164.38	

The entry to record this transaction is shown in general journal form in Figure 8–12.

GENERAL JOURNAL   PAGE 49

DATE	DESCRIPTION	POST. REF.	DEBIT	CREDIT
19-- Jan. 29	Notes Payable		10000 00	
	Interest Payable		84 93	
	Interest Expense		79 45	
	Cash in Bank			10164 38
	Check 115			

Figure 8–12. Recording Payment of a Note Payable

Accrued Federal Income Taxes

A corporation is considered to be a separate legal entity. As such, it must pay federal income tax on its corporate net income. A corporation is put on a pay-as-you-go basis. That is, the corporation is required to estimate in advance its federal income taxes for the year. The corporation pays that estimated amount to the federal government in quarterly installments during the year. At the end of the fiscal year, the exact amount of net income and the tax on that income are determined. If the corporation owes additional taxes (as is usually the case), an adjusting entry must be made to record the amount of accrued income taxes. (An adjusting entry would also be made if the corporation over-paid its federal income taxes.)

At the beginning of the fiscal period, Pickett Products Company estimated that its federal income taxes would be $4,000. The business made quarterly payments of $1,000 in April, June, September, and December. These cash payments were recorded as debits to Income Tax Expense and credits to Cash in Bank.

At the end of the fiscal period, Pickett determined that its actual federal income taxes for the year were $4,200. Since Pickett had already paid $4,000, it owes an additional $200. The adjusting entry made at the end of the fiscal period is shown in Figure 8–13.

GENERAL JOURNAL   PAGE 47

DATE	DESCRIPTION	POST. REF.	DEBIT	CREDIT
	Adjusting Entries			
19-- Dec. 31	Income Tax Expense		200 00	
	Corporate Income Tax Payable			200 00

Figure 8–13. Adjusting Entry for Accrued Federal Income Tax Expense

Accrued Revenues

A business may earn revenue in one fiscal period but not record the transaction until the next fiscal period. **Accrued revenue** is revenue that has been earned but not yet received and recorded. For example, an advertising agency may bill a client for its services only after a series of advertisements have been completed. The work on those advertisements may extend beyond the end of the fiscal period. An adjusting entry must be made at the end of the fiscal period to record the amount of the revenue earned during the period but not yet recorded. Another example of accrued revenue is the interest earned on a note receivable.

On December 5 the Stanlewicz Distributing Company accepted a $2,000, 90-day, 9% note receivable from a charge customer, Joy Peterson. The note was in payment of her charge account. The transaction was recorded as a debit of $2,000 to Notes Receivable and a credit of $2,000 to Accounts Receivable and Joy Peterson's account in the subsidiary ledger.

On December 31, 26 days of interest income have accrued on the note receivable. An adjusting entry must be made on December 31 to record the amount of the interest income earned during the period. The amount of the interest earned is calculated as follows.

$$\underset{\text{Principal}}{\$2,000} \times \underset{\text{Interest Rate}}{.09} \times \underset{\text{Time}}{\frac{26}{365}} = \underset{\text{Interest}}{\$12.82}$$

Interest Receivable is debited for $12.82, the amount of interest earned for 26 days. Interest Receivable will be reported as a current asset on the balance sheet. Interest Income is credited for $12.82 to show the amount of interest earned on the note in the current fiscal period. Interest Income will be reported in the Other Revenue section of the income statement.

Interest Receivable		Interest Income	
Dr.	Cr.	Dr.	Cr.
+	−	−	+
Adj. $12.82			Adj. $12.82

The adjusting entry is shown in Figure 8–14.

	DATE	DESCRIPTION	POST. REF.	DEBIT	CREDIT	
1		*Adjusting Entries*				1
2	19-- Dec. 31	Interest Receivable		1282		2
3		Interest Income			1282	3

GENERAL JOURNAL — PAGE 50

Figure 8–14. Adjusting Entry for Accrued Interest Income

On March 5, Stanlewicz received a check from Joy Peterson for the maturity value of the 90-day note issued on December 5. The maturity value of the note (principal plus interest) is calculated as follows.

$$\text{Principal} \quad \text{Interest Rate} \quad \text{Time} \quad \text{Interest}$$
$$\$2,000 \;\times\; .09 \;\times\; \frac{90}{365} = \$44.38$$

The maturity value is, therefore, $2,044.38.

March 5: Received a check for $2,044.38 from Joy Peterson in full payment of the note dated December 5, Receipt 416.

In this transaction, Cash in Bank is debited for $2,044.38, the total amount of cash received. The collection of the note reduces the balance in the Notes Receivable account, so Notes Receivable is credited for $2,000.00. The total amount of interest earned for 90 days is $44.38. However, $12.82 of interest was earned and reported in the last fiscal period. The interest earned during the current fiscal period is $31.56. Interest Income is credited for $31.56. Interest Receivable is credited for $12.82 because the interest to be received has now been collected.

Cash in Bank		Interest Income	
Dr.	Cr.	Dr.	Cr.
+	–	–	+
$2,044.38			$31.56

Interest Receivable		Notes Receivable	
Dr.	Cr.	Dr.	Cr.
+	–	+	–
Adj. $12.82	$12.82	Bal. $2,000.00	$2,000.00

The entry to record the collection of the note is shown in general journal form in Figure 8–15.

GENERAL JOURNAL   PAGE 62

DATE	DESCRIPTION	POST. REF.	DEBIT	CREDIT
19-- mar. 5	Cash in Bank		2 04438	
	Notes Receivable			2 00000
	Interest Income			31 56
	Interest Receivable			12 82
	Receipt 416			

Figure 8–15. Recording Collection of a Note Receivable

Before reading further, do the activity on page 188 to check your understanding of accruals.

Summary of Key Points

1. The cash basis of accounting recognizes revenues and expenses only when cash is received and paid out.
2. The accrual basis of accounting recognizes revenues when they are earned and expenses when they are incurred.
3. In the accrual basis of accounting, adjusting entries are recorded to account for transactions that affect more than one accounting period.
4. A deferral is the postponement of the recognition of an expense already paid or a revenue already received.
5. There are two types of deferrals: prepaid expenses and unearned revenues.
6. An accrual is the recognition of an expense or revenue that has gradually increased over time but has not yet been recorded.
7. An accrued expense is an expense that has been incurred but has not yet been paid. Accrued revenue is revenue that has been earned but has not yet been received and recorded.

Review and Applications

Building Your Accounting Vocabulary

In your own words, write the definition of each of the following accounting terms. Use complete sentences for your definitions.

accrual   accrued revenue   deferral
accrual basis of   cash basis of   prepaid expense
  accounting   accounting   unearned revenue
accrued expense

Reviewing Your Accounting Knowledge

1. Explain the difference between the cash basis of accounting and the accrual basis of accounting.
2. Why is the cash basis of accounting not suitable for businesses that maintain inventories?
3. Which accounting principle requires that revenues be recognized in the accounting period in which they were earned and expenses recognized in the accounting period in which they were incurred?
4. What is the difference between an accrual and a deferral?
5. List three examples of prepaid expenses.
6. To what account is the bank discount on a non-interest-bearing note payable debited?
7. When recording an adjusting entry at the end of a fiscal period for interest expense on a non-interest-bearing note payable, which accounts are debited and credited?
8. Under what circumstances might a company have unearned revenue? Give one example.
9. Classify the following accounts: Discount on Notes Payable, Unearned Rent, and Prepaid Insurance.
10. What is an accrued expense? Give three examples.
11. Under what circumstances might a company have accrued revenue? Give one example.

Improving Your Decision-making Skills

The Weatherford Company, a small merchandising business, uses the cash basis of accounting. It records revenue when it is collected and expenses when they are paid.

The new company accountant has recommended that the company change to the accrual basis of accounting. What reasons can the new accountant offer to justify this change?

Problem 8–1

Use a form similar to the one that follows. For each item listed below, indicate whether the item is a prepaid expense, unearned revenue, accrued expense, or accrued revenue by placing a check mark in the correct column.

(1) A three-year premium paid on a fire insurance policy
(2) Cash received for season tickets to a concert series
(3) Interest on a note receivable that is not yet due
(4) Office supplies on hand
(5) Additional corporate federal income taxes owed
(6) Salaries owed but not yet paid
(7) Cash received for a five-year magazine subscription
(8) The bank discount deducted on a non-interest-bearing note payable
(9) The commission due for completing the redecoration of three floors of a five-story building
(10) Tuition collected in advance by a school
(11) Interest on an interest-bearing note payable due in the next fiscal period
(12) Property taxes incurred for the last two months of the fiscal period

Item	Prepaid Expense	Unearned Revenue	Accrued Expense	Accrued Revenue
1	✓			

Problem 8–2

Hanover Distributors uses the accrual basis of accounting. On June 15, Hanover accepted a $2,000, 90-day, 10% interest-bearing note from Cyrus Long, a charge customer. The note was accepted in place of the amount recorded as an account receivable. Hanover Distributors' fiscal period ends on June 30.

Instructions: In general journal form, prepare the entries to record the following transactions.

(1) The receipt of the note from Cyrus Long (Memorandum 1114).
(2) The adjusting entry to record the amount of accrued interest income for the period.
(3) The receipt of cash in payment of the note (Receipt 42).

Problem 8–3

The Lynx Corporation uses the accrual basis of accounting. Its fiscal period ends on December 31.

On November 20, the Lynx Corporation borrowed $10,000 from the Commonwealth Bank by issuing a 60-day, non-interest-bearing note payable, which was discounted at 10%.

Instructions: In general journal form, prepare the entries to record the following transactions.

(1) The issuance of the note (Note 16).
(2) The adjusting entry to record the amount of accrued interest expense.
(3) The payment of the note on the maturity date (Check 245 and Memorandum 1663).

Problem 8–4

The Brooks Advertising Agency uses the accrual basis of accounting. Its fiscal period ends on June 30. The balances of the following accounts appear in the agency's general ledger as of June 30.

Commissions Receivable	
Office Supplies	$ 1,953.00
Salaries Payable	
Unearned Advertising Income	10,000.00
Advertising Income	18,650.00
Commissions Income	31,700.50
Salaries Expense	38,250.00
Supplies Expense	

Instructions: Record the adjusting entries using the following information.

(1) The office supplies on hand on June 30 are valued at $395.00.
(2) Brooks' weekly payroll is $750.00. Salaries have been earned, but not yet recorded, for June 28–30.
(3) The agency is to be paid a $4,000.00 commission for preparing eight advertisements. As of June 30, five of the advertisements had been completed.
(4) Of the $10,000.00 recorded in the Unearned Advertising Income account, $4,000.00 had been earned as of June 30.

Problem 8–5

Culver City Enterprises uses the accrual basis of accounting. Its fiscal period ends on December 31.

The following balances appear in selected general ledger accounts of the company as of December 1.

Cash in Bank	$6,219.40
Supplies	2,596.00
Prepaid Insurance	
Notes Payable	
Corporate Income Tax Payable	
Interest Payable	
Insurance Expense	
Supplies Expense	
Income Tax Expense	2,137.50
Interest Expense	

Some transactions that occurred during December for Culver City Enterprises are listed below.

Dec.   3   Issued Check 1278 for $1,200 to Great Western Insurance Company for the premium on a two-year fire insurance policy.

      15   Issued Check 1293 for $712.50 for the final quarterly estimated income tax installment.

      24   Borrowed $6,000 from the First National Bank by issuing a 30-day, 12% note payable, Note 15.

Instructions:

(1) Journalize the three transactions on page 8 of a general journal.

(2) Post the transactions to the accounts listed earlier. The balances have already been recorded in the accounts.

(3) Using the following data, journalize and post the adjusting entries.

    (a) The supplies inventory on December 31 is $319.50.

    (b) A month of the insurance premium paid on December 1 has expired.

    (c) Interest expense has accrued on the note issued December 24.

    (d) The total federal income taxes for the year are $3,075.00.

Problem 8–6

The Dillon Publishing Company uses the accrual basis of accounting. Its fiscal period ends on December 31.

The following accounts appear in Dillon's December 31 trial balance.

Office Supplies	$ 3,050.25
Prepaid Insurance	900.00
Interest Receivable	
Advertising Receivable	
Discount on Notes Payable	295.89
Unearned Subscriptions	26,400.00
Salaries Payable	
Corporate Income Tax Payable	
Advertising Income	89,900.00
Subscriptions Income	32,100.00
Insurance Expense	
Salaries Expense	61,200.00
Supplies Expense	
Income Tax Expense	4,110.00
Interest Income	6.57
Interest Expense	

Instructions: Using the following information, journalize and post the adjusting entries for Dillon Publishing Company. The opened accounts appear in the working papers accompanying this textbook. Record the entries on page 12 of the general journal.

(1) The supplies on hand on December 31 were $435.

(2) The insurance premium of $900 was paid on October 2. The insurance coverage was for one year.

(3) On December 1, the Dillon Company accepted a $4,000, 60-day, 12% promissory note from one of its clients in payment for advertisements published in November.

(4) Advertising income totaling $2,500 has been earned for which the clients have not yet been billed.

(5) Of the $26,400 received for subscriptions, $6,600 has been earned by the end of the fiscal period.

(6) On November 28, Dillon borrowed $10,000 from the Clarion National Bank by issuing a 90-day non-interest-bearing note payable that was discounted at 12%.

(7) Dillon's weekly payroll is $1,200. Salaries have been earned, but not yet paid, for December 29–31.

(8) The total federal income taxes for the year are $4,495.

9 Work Sheet and Financial Statements

A variety of advanced accounting procedures have been presented in this unit. You learned how to analyze and record transactions affecting uncollectible accounts; promissory notes; inventories; property, plant, and equipment; vouchers; and deferrals and accruals.

Each of these procedures was presented as a separate accounting activity. However, each accounting procedure plays a vital part in the total operation of the business.

In this chapter, you will learn how all of the accounting data for these procedures are pulled together on the work sheet. You'll use that work sheet as a tool to prepare the business's financial statements.

Learning Objectives

When you have completed this chapter, you should be able to

1. Determine which general ledger accounts must be adjusted.

2. Prepare a ten-column work sheet for a merchandising corporation.

3. Prepare an income statement for a merchandising corporation.

4. Prepare a statement of retained earnings for a merchandising corporation.

5. Prepare a balance sheet for a merchandising corporation.

6. Define the accounting terms presented in this chapter.

New Terms

gross profit from operations / other revenue / other expenses / stockholders' equity / capital stock / retained earnings / statement of retained earnings

The Ten-column Work Sheet

As you know, the general ledger accounts summarize the changes caused by business transactions during an accounting period. They do not, however, summarize the overall performance of a company. To evaluate performance, managers, stockholders, and creditors need more than a list of account balances. They need to know net income, the value of stockholders' equity, and the company's financial strength. This information is reported on the financial statements. The purpose of the work sheet is to assemble all the financial data needed to prepare the end-of-period financial statements and journal entries.

The Trial Balance Section

At the end of the fiscal period, a trial balance is prepared using the first two columns of the work sheet. The trial balance is prepared to prove the equality of debits and credits in the general ledger. The title and balance of each account in the general ledger are entered on the work sheet. Then, the debit and credit columns are totaled, proved, and ruled.

The completed work sheet for Videosonics is illustrated in Figure 9–1 on pages 198–201. Notice that, in the Trial Balance section, every general ledger account is listed, even those with zero balances. Notice also that, on this two-page work sheet, the account balances are totaled at the bottom of the first page. The totals are then carried forward to the first line of the second page.

The Adjustments Section

As you have learned, most businesses have certain accounts that do not show up-to-date balances at the end of the accounting period. Therefore, adjustments must be made to those accounts to bring them up to date. In Chapter 2, you planned and recorded the adjustments for merchandise inventory, supplies used during the period, and the expired portion of the prepaid insurance premium. Although they are included on the work sheet, there is no discussion of those adjustments in this chapter. If necessary, review pages 34–36 of Chapter 2 for the discussion of these adjustments.

Videosonics has additional accounts that require adjustments at the end of the accounting period. Videosonics must record adjustments for estimated bad debt losses, depreciation on plant assets, interest expense on notes payable, interest income on notes receivable, accrued salaries, deferred rental income, and corporate income taxes.

Adjustment for Estimated Bad Debt Losses

As you learned in Chapter 3, not all charge customers can or will pay their bills. An account receivable that cannot be collected becomes an expense to the business. In order to match potential bad debt losses with revenue earned, Videosonics uses the allowance method of accounting for uncollectible accounts. At the end of the fiscal period, Videosonics estimates the amount of its bad debt losses by taking a set percentage of Accounts Receivable. Based on its experience, Videosonics estimates that 3% of the balance of Accounts Receivable will prove to be uncollectible.

$27,564.00
× .03
———————
$ 826.92

At the end of the fiscal period, the balance of Videosonics' Accounts Receivable account is $27,564.00. Multiplying this amount by 3%, Videosonics determines that the total estimated uncollectible amount is $826.92. This amount, remember, represents the updated, end-of-period balance that should be in Allowance for Uncollectible Accounts. An adjustment must be made to bring that account *up to* the $826.92 amount.

Bad Debts Expense		Allowance for Uncollectible Accounts	
Dr.	Cr.	Dr.	Cr.
+	−	−	+
Adj. $702.88			Bal. $124.04
			Adj. 702.88

The current balance of Allowance for Uncollectible Accounts is $124.04. It must, therefore, be credited for $702.88 ($826.92 − $124.04). Bad Debts Expense is also debited for $702.88. This adjustment is labeled (e) on the work sheet in Figure 9–1 on pages 198–201.

Remember: When the adjustment for bad debts expense is based on a set percentage of Accounts Receivable, Allowance for Uncollectible Accounts is adjusted to bring the balance up to the estimated uncollectible amount.

Adjustment for the Depreciation of Store Equipment

In Chapter 6, you learned that all plant, property, and equipment assets—except land—are depreciated. That is, their costs are spread out over the accounting periods in which they are used. There are several methods of calculating the amount of depreciation. Whichever method is used, an adjusting entry is made at the end of the fiscal period to record the depreciation expense.

Videosonics uses the straight-line method of calculating depreciation. The balance of the Store Equipment account in the Trial Balance section of the work sheet is $15,882.90. This amount, you remember, represents the cost of all the store equipment items. The balance of the Accumulated Depreciation—Store Equipment account is $8,891.73. This amount represents the total amount of depreciation on store equipment allocated to previous fiscal periods. Videosonics determined that the annual estimated depreciation on its store equipment is $2,500.00. An adjustment must be made on the work sheet to record this amount.

Depreciation Expense—Store Equipment is debited for $2,500.00, the amount of depreciation expense for the current fiscal period. Accumulated Depreciation—Store Equipment is credited for $2,500.00. After the adjusting entry is posted, the account will have a balance of $11,391.73. This adjustment is labeled (f) in Figure 9–1.

Depreciation Expense— Store Equipment		Accumulated Depreciation— Store Equipment	
Dr.	Cr.	Dr.	Cr.
+	–	–	+
Adj. $2,500.00			Bal. $8,891.73
			Adj. 2,500.00

Adjustment for the Depreciation of Office Equipment

In the Trial Balance section of the work sheet, Office Equipment has a balance of $4,200.00. Accumulated Depreciation—Office Equipment has a balance of $2,350.00. Videosonics estimates that the annual depreciation on its office equipment is $840.00.

In the adjustment, Depreciation Expense—Office Equipment is debited for $840.00. Accumulated Depreciation—Office Equipment is credited for $840.00. After the adjusting entry is posted, the account will have a balance of $3,190.00. This adjustment is labeled (g) in Figure 9 1.

Depreciation Expense— Office Equipment		Accumulated Depreciation— Office Equipment	
Dr.	Cr.	Dr.	Cr.
+	–	–	+
Adj. $840.00			Bal. $2,350.00
			Adj. 840.00

Adjustment for the Depreciation of a Building

The balance of the Building account in the Trial Balance section of the work sheet is $62,300.00. The balance of the Accumulated Depreciation—Building account is $33,000.00. On December 31, Videosonics estimates that the annual depreciation for its building is $5,000.00.

In the adjustment, Depreciation Expense—Building is debited for $5,000.00. Accumulated Depreciation—Building is credited for $5,000.00. After the adjusting entry is posted, the account will have a balance of $38,000.00. The adjustment for the depreciation of Videosonics' building is labeled (h) on the work sheet in Figure 9–1.

Depreciation Expense— Building		Accumulated Depreciation— Building	
Dr.	Cr.	Dr.	Cr.
+	–	–	+
Adj. $5,000.00			Bal. $33,000.00
			Adj. 5,000.00

ACCOUNT NAME	TRIAL BALANCE DEBIT	TRIAL BALANCE CREDIT	ADJUSTMENTS DEBIT	ADJUSTMENTS CREDIT
1 Cash in Bank	12747 29			
2 Notes Receivable	5000 00			
3 Interest Receivable			(i) 124 93	
4 Accounts Receivable	27564 00			
5 Allow. for Uncoll. Accts.		124 04		(e) 702 88
6 Merch. Inventory	88890 67		(b) 78543 22	(a) 88890 67
7 Supplies	3575 00			(c) 3025 00
8 Prepaid Insurance	1300 00			(d) 900 00
9 Store Equipment	15882 90			
10 Accum. Depr.-Store Equip.		8891 73		(f) 2500 00
11 Office Equipment	4200 00			
12 Accum. Depr.-Office Equip.		2350 00		(g) 840 00
13 Building	62300 00			
14 Accum. Depr. -Bldg.		33000 00		(h) 5000 00
15 Land	20000 00			
16 Notes Payable		15000 00		
17 Discount on Notes Pay.	493 15			(j) 123 29
18 Vouchers Payable		3987 53		
19 Salaries Payable				(k) 900 00
20 Emp. Fed. Inc. Tax Pay.		251 18		
21 FICA Tax Payable		423 00		
22 Emp. State Inc. Tax Pay.		683 52		
23 Fed. Unemploy. Tax Pay.		154 80		
24 State Unemploy. Tax Pay.		522 45		
25 Sales Tax Payable		1618 30		
26 Corp. Inc. Tax Payable				(m) 400 39
27 Unearned Rent		7500 00	(l) 5000 00	
28 Capital Stock		60000 00		
29 Retained Earnings		54508 38		
30 Income Summary			(a) 88890 67	(b) 78543 22
31 Sales		328067 09		
32 Sales Returns + Allow.	2427 45			
33 Carried Forward	240380 46	517082 02	168558 82	177825 45

Figure 9–1. Completed Work Sheet

(Left Side)

sonics
Sheet
December 31, 19--

	ADJUSTED TRIAL BALANCE		INCOME STATEMENT		BALANCE SHEET		
	DEBIT	CREDIT	DEBIT	CREDIT	DEBIT	CREDIT	
1	1274729				1274729		
2	500000				500000		
3	12493				12493		
4	2756400				2756400		
5		82692				82692	
6	7854322				7854322		
7	55000				55000		
8	40000				40000		
9	1588290				1588290		
10		1139173				1139173	
11	420000				420000		
12		319000				319000	
13	6230000				6230000		
14		3800000				3800000	
15	2000000				2000000		
16		1500000				1500000	
17	36986				36986		
18		398753				398753	
19		90000				90000	
20		25118				25118	
21		42300				42300	
22		68352				68352	
23		15480				15480	
24		52245				52245	
25		161830				161830	
26		40039				40039	
27		250000				250000	
28		6000000				6000000	
29		5450838				5450838	
30	8489067	7854322	8489067	7854322			
31		32806709		32806709			
32	242745		242745				
33	31500032	60096851	8731812	40661031	22768220	19435820	

(Right Side)

	ACCOUNT NAME	TRIAL BALANCE		ADJUSTMENTS	
		DEBIT	CREDIT	DEBIT	CREDIT
1	Brought Forward	2403804 6	5170820 2	1685588 2	1778254 5
2	Sales Discounts	20736 9			
3	Purchases	1852290 2			
4	Purch Returns & Allow.		15750 0		
5	Purchases Discounts		22781 5		
6	Bad Debts Expense			(e) 7028 8	
7	Bank Card Fees Exp.	16863 0			
8	Depr. Exp.-Building			(h) 50000 0	
9	Depr. Exp.-Office Equip.			(g) 8400 0	
10	Depr. Exp.-Store Equip.			(f) 25000 0	
11	Insurance Expense			(d) 9000 0	
12	Payroll Tax Expense	81657 0			
13	Salaries Expense	774000 0		(k) 9000 0	
14	Supplies Expense			(c) 30250 0	
15	Rental Income				(l) 50000 0
16	Interest Income				(i) 1249 3
17	Interest Expense			(j) 1232 9	
18	Income Tax Expense	60000 0		(m) 4003 9	
19		5209351 7	5209351 7	1829503 8	1829503 8
20	Net Inc. after Inc. Taxes				
21					

Figure 9–1. Completed Work Sheet (continued)   (Left Side)

Adjustment for Accrued Interest Income

On October 16, Videosonics accepted a $5,000.00, 12%, 90-day note from a charge customer in payment of a charge account. Even though the note will not mature until January 14, interest has accrued and must be reported as income in this fiscal period. The amount of the accrued interest income is determined as follows.

$$\underset{\$5,000.00}{\overset{\text{Principal}}{}} \times \underset{.12}{\overset{\text{Interest Rate}}{}} \times \underset{\frac{76}{365}}{\overset{\text{Time}}{}} = \underset{\$124.93}{\overset{\text{Interest}}{}}$$

The current asset account Interest Receivable is debited for $124.93. This is the amount of interest earned, but not yet received, as of December 31. The same amount is credited to the Interest Income account. The adjustment for accrued interest income is labeled (i) on the work sheet in Figure 9–1.

sonics
(Continued)
December 31, 19--

	ADJUSTED TRIAL BALANCE		INCOME STATEMENT		BALANCE SHEET	
	DEBIT	CREDIT	DEBIT	CREDIT	DEBIT	CREDIT
1	315000 32	600968 51	8731 8 12	406610 31	227682 20	194358 20
2	2073 69		2073 69			
3	185229 02		185229 02			
4		1575 00		1575 00		
5		2278 15		2278 15		
6	702 88		702 88			
7	1686 30		1686 30			
8	5000 00		5000 00			
9	840 00		840 00			
10	2500 00		2500 00			
11	900 00		900 00			
12	8165 70		8165 70			
13	78300 00		78300 00			
14	3025 00		3025 00			
15		5000 00		5000 00		
16		124 93		124 93		
17	123 29		123 29			
18	6400 39		6400 39			
19	609946 59	609946 59	382264 39	415588 39	227682 20	194358 20
20			33324 00			33324 00
21			415588 39	415588 39	227682 20	227682 20

(Right Side)

	Interest Receivable			Interest Income	
	Dr.	Cr.		Dr.	Cr.
	+	−		−	+
	Adj. $124.93				Adj. $124.93

Adjustment for Prepaid Interest Expense

On December 1, Videosonics borrowed $15,000.00 from the Commerce National Bank by issuing a 120-day, non-interest-bearing note. The $15,000.00 is listed in the Trial Balance section as a credit to Notes Payable. The bank discounted the note at 10%, deducting $493.15 in advance. This amount was recorded in the contra liability account Discount on Notes Payable. Since the note will not mature until the next fiscal period (on March 31), only a portion of the discount amount can be charged as an expense to the current fiscal period.

The amount of the interest expense for the current period is determined as follows.

$$\text{Principal} \quad \text{Discount Rate} \quad \text{Time} \quad \text{Interest}$$
$$\$15{,}000.00 \quad \times \quad .10 \quad \times \quad \frac{30}{365} \quad = \quad \$123.29$$

Interest Expense is debited for $123.29, the actual amount of interest expense chargeable to the current accounting period. Since $123.29 of the $493.15 is an expense for the current fiscal period, that amount must be removed from Discount on Notes Payable. It is credited for that amount. After the adjusting entry is journalized and posted, Discount on Notes Payable will have a debit balance of $369.86. This amount is the prepaid interest expense chargeable to the next fiscal period. The adjustment for prepaid interest expense is labeled (j) in Figure 9–1.

Interest Expense		Discount on Notes Payable	
Dr.	Cr.	Dr.	Cr.
+	−	+	−
Adj. $123.29		Bal. $493.15	Adj. $123.29

Adjustment for Accrued Salaries Expense

The Salaries Expense account has a balance of $77,400.00 in the Trial Balance section. This is the total amount of employees' salaries paid during the fiscal period. However, by December 31, an additional $900.00 in salaries have accrued (for December 29–31). That is, salaries have been earned by employees but have not yet been paid. In the adjustment, Salaries Expense is debited for $900.00 to show the amount of accrued salaries expense for December 29–31. Since the salaries have not yet been paid, they represent a liability. Therefore, Salaries Payable is credited for $900.00. The adjustment for accrued salaries expense is labeled (k) in Figure 9–1.

Salaries Expense—		Salaries Payable	
Dr.	Cr.	Dr.	Cr.
+	−	−	+
Bal. $77,400.00			Adj. $900.00
Adj. 900.00			

Adjustment for Unearned Rental Income

Since Videosonics is a merchandising business, its primary source of revenue is from the sale of merchandise. It does, however, have an additional source of revenue. Videosonics owns the land and building in which it operates. Since the building is large, Videosonics leases office space to another business for an annual rent of $7,500.00 ($625.00 a month). According to the lease agreement, the rent must be paid in advance. When Videosonics received the $7,500.00, it recorded the transaction in the liability account Unearned Rent. That amount appears as a credit to Unearned Rent in the Trial Balance section of Videosonics' work sheet.

At the end of the accounting period, eight months of the lease have expired. Videosonics has, therefore, earned $5,000.00 of the rent received in advance ($625.00 × 8). In the adjustment, Unearned Rent is debited for $5,000.00. Rental Income is credited for $5,000.00, the amount of rent earned during the accounting period. The adjustment for unearned rental income is labeled (l) on the work sheet in Figure 9–1.

Unearned Rent				Rental Income	
Dr.	Cr.			Dr.	Cr.
−	+			−	+
Adj. $5,000.00	Bal. $7,500.00				Adj. $5,000.00

Adjustment for Federal Income Taxes

As you learned in Chapter 8, a corporation is required to estimate in advance its federal income taxes for the year. The corporation then pays the estimated amount in equal quarterly installments. At the end of the fiscal year, the exact amount of the pre-tax net income and the tax on that income are determined. An adjustment is entered on the work sheet to record the amount owed or overpaid.

In the Trial Balance section, Income Tax Expense has a balance of $6,000.00. This represents the amount of income taxes Videosonics estimated and paid during the year.

At the end of the fiscal period, Videosonics determined that its federal income tax liability for the year was $6,400.39. Since Videosonics has already paid $6,000.00 in taxes, the business owes an additional $400.39. In the adjustment, Income Tax Expense is debited for $400.39, the amount of additional taxes owed. Corporate Income Tax Payable is credited for $400.39. The adjustment for federal income taxes is labeled (m) in Figure 9–1.

Income Tax Expense				Corporate Income Tax Payable	
Dr.	Cr.			Dr.	Cr.
+	−			−	+
Bal. $6,000.00					Adj. $400.39
Adj. 400.39					

Completing the Adjustments Section

After all the adjustments have been entered, the Adjustments section of the work sheet is totaled and ruled. Since each adjustment has an equal debit and credit, the total of the Adjustments Debit and Credit columns should be the same.

Remember: **The Adjustments section of the work sheet, like the Trial Balance section, must be proved for equality before the work sheet can be continued.**

Before continuing, do the activity at the top of the next page to check your understanding of the material you have just read.

Completing the Adjusted Trial Balance Section

After the Adjustments section is totaled and ruled, the Adjusted Trial Balance section is completed. The Adjusted Trial Balance section has a twofold purpose. First, this section shows the updated balances of all the general ledger accounts. Second, this section proves the equality of debits and credits after all adjustments have been recorded.

When completing this section, combine the balance of each account in the Trial Balance section with the adjustment, if any, in the Adjustments section. Then enter the new balance in the appropriate Adjusted Trial Balance column. After all balances have been entered, the Adjusted Trial Balance section is totaled, proved, and ruled.

Remember: **The Adjusted Trial Balance section of the work sheet must be proved for equality before the work sheet can be continued.**

Extending Amounts to the Balance Sheet and Income Statement Sections

Next, each account balance in the Adjusted Trial Balance section is extended either to the Balance Sheet section or to the Income Statement section.

The Balance Sheet section, remember, contains the balances of all permanent general ledger accounts. Here you will find all of the asset and liability accounts and the two stockholders' equity accounts, Capital Stock and Retained Earnings. The Income Statement section contains the balances of all temporary general ledger accounts. This section includes all revenue, cost, and expense accounts, as well as Income Summary. Look at Figure 9–1 again. Notice that both the beginning and ending inventory amounts recorded in Income Summary were extended to the Income Statement section. Both amounts are needed to determine the net income or net loss.

Completing the Work Sheet

After all amounts have been extended to the Balance Sheet and Income Statement sections, the last four columns are totaled. Then the net income (or loss) for the fiscal period is calculated and recorded. As you can see, Videosonics had a net income after income taxes of $33,324.00.

After the net income is recorded, the last four columns are totaled and ruled. Finally, the words "Net Income after Income Taxes" are written in the Account Name column on the same line as the net income amount.

Remember: **As a check on the accuracy of the net income amount, compare the net income calculated by subtracting the Income Statement Debit column from the Credit column to the amount found by subtracting the Balance Sheet Credit column from the Debit column. They must agree.**

Preparing End-of-period Financial Statements

As you know, the work sheet is used to prepare a corporation's income statement, statement of retained earnings, and balance sheet. These statements are useful to management, creditors, and governmental agencies. Management uses the financial statements to evaluate past performance and to help make future business decisions. Since creditors have a vested interest in the business, they want to know whether Videosonics will be able to pay its debts. In addition, governmental agencies, employees, and consumer groups are also interested in determining the financial strength of the business.

The Income Statement

Since the income statement reports the financial progress of the business, it is the first financial statement a business prepares. The Income Statement section of the work sheet contains the data needed to prepare this financial statement. Videosonics' income statement is shown in Figure 9–2 on page 206.

The income statement shows sources of business revenue, cost of merchandise sold, expenses, and net income before and after federal income taxes. Look at Figure 9–2. Notice that the gross profit has been labeled "from operations." The normal source of revenue for a merchandising business, recall, is the sale of merchandise. Therefore, gross profit from operations is net sales minus the cost of merchandise sold. If a business has additional sources of revenue, they

Figure 9–2.
Income Statement

Videosonics
Income Statement
For the Year Ended December 31, 19--

Revenue:				
Sales			3280 67 09	
Less: Sales Ret.+ Allow.		2427 45		
Sales Discounts		2073 69	4501 14	
Net Sales				3235 65 95
Cost of Merchandise Sold:				
Merch. Inv., Jan. 1, 19--			8489 67	
Purchases		18522 902		
Less: Purch. Ret.+ Allow.	1575 00			
Purch. Discounts	2278 15	3853 15		
Net Purchases			18137 587	
Cost of Merch. Available			26626 654	
Merch. Inv., Dec. 31, 19--			7854 322	
Cost of Merch. Sold				18772 332
Gross Profit fr. Operations				13584 263
Operating Expenses:				
Bad Debts Expense			702 88	
Bank Card Fees Exp.			1686 30	
Deprec. Exp.– Building			5000 00	
Deprec. Exp.–Office Equip.			840 00	
Deprec. Exp.–Store Equip.			2500 00	
Insurance Expense			900 00	
Payroll Tax Expense			8165 70	
Salaries Expense			78300 00	
Supplies Expense			3025 00	
Total Operating Exp.				10111 988
Net Inc. from Operations				3472 275
Other Revenue:				
Rental Income		5000 00		
Interest Income		124 93	5124 93	
Other Expenses:				
Interest Expense			123 29	
Net Addition				5001 64
Net Inc. before Inc. Taxes				3972 439
Income Taxes				6400 39
Net Inc. after Inc. Taxes				3332 400

are listed in a separate section of the income statement. For example, Videosonics' income statement in Figure 9–2 has two additional sections. The first section is for Other Revenue and includes Rental Income and Interest Income. The second section is for Other Expenses and includes Interest Expense. **Other revenue** and **other expenses** are non-operating revenue or expenses. That is, other revenue and other expenses do not result from the normal operations of the business.

The difference between Other Revenue and Other Expenses is either a net addition to or a net deduction from income. Since Videosonics' other revenue is greater than its other expenses, there is a net addition of $5,001.64.

Notice also that the amount of income taxes is listed separately on the income statement. Although income taxes are a normal expense for a corporation, they are not included with the operating expenses. In this way, the amount of taxable income is more easily seen on the income statement.

Remember: **Net income after taxes shown on the income statement must agree with the net income reported on the work sheet.**

The Statement of Retained Earnings

The owner's equity of a corporation is called **stockholders' equity**. Stockholders' equity is the value of the stockholders' claims to the assets of the corporation. (Stockholders are the owners of a corporation.) A corporation has two types of stockholders' equity: capital stock and retained earnings. **Capital stock** represents the total amount of investment in the corporation by its stockholders. **Retained earnings** represents the profits that have been kept by the company and not distributed to stockholders.

Videosonics has two stockholders' equity accounts: Capital Stock and Retained Earnings. The Capital Stock account reports the stockholders' investment in the corporation. Videosonics is a closely held corporation owned by the Clay family. It does not sell its stock to the general public, nor does it pay its owners dividends. The Retained Earnings account summarizes Videosonics' earnings, or profits, that have been retained by the business for future use.

At the end of the fiscal period, a **statement of retained earnings** is prepared to report the changes that have taken place in the Retained Earnings account during the accounting period. Changes in the Retained Earnings account are a result of net income or loss and the distribution of dividends. Since Videosonics does not pay dividends, its statement of retained earnings reports only the net income for the period. The statement of retained earnings is prepared as a supporting document for the balance sheet. The data needed to prepare the statement are taken from the Balance Sheet section of the work sheet.

The statement of retained earnings for Videosonics is shown in Figure 9–3.

Videosonics			
Statement of Retained Earnings			
For the Year Ended December 31, 19--			
Retained Earnings, January 1, 19--			54 50 8 38
Net Income after Income Taxes			33 32 4 00
Retained Earnings, December 31, 19--			87 83 2 38

Figure 9–3. Statement of Retained Earnings

Remember: **A net income increases the balance of the Retained Earnings account. A net loss and any dividends paid decrease the balance of the Retained Earnings account.**

The Balance Sheet

The balance sheet reports what the business owns, owes, and is worth as of the date it is prepared. Specifically, it shows the updated balances of all asset, liability, and stockholders' equity accounts. The information needed to prepare the balance sheet is taken from two different sources. The balances of the asset, liability, and Capital Stock accounts are taken from the Balance Sheet section of the work sheet. The balance of the Retained Earnings account is taken from the statement of retained earnings.

Videosonics' balance sheet is illustrated in Figure 9–4. Notice that the Assets section is divided into two parts. The first part lists the business's current assets; the second part lists the property, plant, and equipment assets. Each type of plant asset is presented, along with its accumulated depreciation account. The difference between the balances of the plant asset and accumulated depreciation accounts is the book value of the plant asset.

Remember: **When preparing the balance sheet, the amount reported for Retained Earnings is taken from the statement of retained earnings, not the work sheet.**

Before reading further, do the following activity to check your understanding of the material you have just read.

Check Your Learning

Write your answers to the following questions on a separate sheet of notebook paper.

1. The information needed to prepare the income statement is taken from the __?__ section of the work sheet.
2. Rental Income and Interest Income are listed in the __?__ section of the income statement.
3. Interest Expense is listed in the __?__ section of the income statement.
4. The information needed to prepare the statement of retained earnings is taken from the __?__ section of the work sheet.
5. The balance of the Retained Earnings account on the balance sheet is taken from the __?__.

Compare your answers to those in the answers section. Re-read the preceding part of the chapter to find the correct answers to any questions you may have missed.

Videosonics
Balance Sheet
December 31, 19--

Assets			
Current Assets:			
Cash in Bank		12 74 7 29	
Notes Receivable		5 000 00	
Interest Receivable		1 24 93	
Accounts Receivable	2 7 5 6 4 00		
Less: Allow. for Uncoll. Accts.	8 26 92	2 6 7 3 7 08	
Merchandise Inventory		7 8 5 4 3 22	
Supplies		5 5 000	
Prepaid Insurance		4 000 0	
Total Current Assets			12 4 1 0 2 52
Property, Plant, and Equipment:			
Store Equipment	15 88 2 90		
Less: Accum. Deprec-Store Equip.	11 39 1 73	4 49 1 17	
Office Equipment	4 200 00		
Less: Accum. Deprec-Office Equip.	3 190 00	1 010 00	
Building	6 2 300 00		
Less: Accum. Deprec.-Bldg.	3 8 000 00	2 4 300 00	
Land		2 0 000 00	
Total Property, Plant, & Equip.			4 9 8 0 1 17
Total Assets			17 3 9 0 3 69
Liabilities			
Notes Payable	15 000 00		
Less: Discount on Notes Payable	3 69 86	1 4 6 3 0 14	
Vouchers Payable		3 9 8 7 53	
Salaries Payable		9 00 00	
Emp. Federal Income Tax Payable		2 51 18	
FICA Tax Payable		4 23 00	
Emp. State Income Tax Payable		6 83 52	
Federal Unemployment Tax Payable		1 54 80	
State Unemployment Tax Payable		5 22 45	
Sales Tax Payable		1 6 1 8 30	
Corporate Income Tax Payable		4 00 39	
Unearned Rent		2 500 00	
Total Liabilities			2 6 0 7 1 31
Stockholders' Equity			
Capital Stock		6 0 000 00	
Retained Earnings		8 7 8 3 2 38	
Total Stockholders' Equity			14 7 8 3 2 38
Total Liabilities & Stockholders' Equity			17 3 9 0 3 69

Figure 9–4. Balance Sheet

Completing the Accounting Cycle

After the financial statements are prepared, the work sheet is used as the source document to journalize the adjusting and closing entries. The data needed for the adjusting entries are taken from the Adjustments section of the work sheet. The data needed for the closing entries are taken from the Income Statement section of the work sheet.

After the adjusting and closing entries have been posted, a post-closing trial balance is prepared. Videosonics' post-closing trial balance appears in Figure 9–5.

Videosonics Post-Closing Trial Balance December 31, 19--		
Cash in Bank	12 747 29	
Notes Receivable	5 000 00	
Interest Receivable	124 93	
Accounts Receivable	27 564 00	
Allowance for Uncollectible Accounts		826 92
Merchandise Inventory	78 543 22	
Supplies	550 00	
Prepaid Insurance	400 00	
Store Equipment	15 882 90	
Accum. Depreciation – Store Equipment		11 391 73
Office Equipment	4 200 00	
Accum. Depreciation – Office Equipment		3 190 00
Building	62 300 00	
Accum. Depreciation – Building Equipment		38 000 00
Land	20 000 00	
Notes Payable		15 000 00
Discount on Notes Payable	369 86	
Vouchers Payable		3 987 53
Salaries Payable		900 00
Employees' Federal Income Tax Payable		251 18
FICA Tax Payable		423 00
Employees' State Income Tax Payable		683 52
Federal Unemployment Tax Payable		154 80
State Unemployment Tax Payable		522 45
Sales Tax Payable		1 618 30
Corporate Income Tax Payable		400 39
Unearned Rent		2 500 00
Capital Stock		60 000 00
Retained Earnings		87 832 38
Total	227 682 20	227 682 20

Figure 9–5. Post-Closing Trial Balance

Summary of Key Points

1. The work sheet is prepared to organize all the data needed to update the general ledger accounts, to prepare financial statements, and to record the adjusting and closing entries.
2. Adjustments recorded on the work sheet may include those for estimated bad debts, depreciation, accrued interest, deferred revenue, accrued salaries, and corporate income taxes.
3. The three financial statements prepared by a merchandising corporation are the income statement, the statement of retained earnings, and the balance sheet.
4. If a business has revenue or expenses that are not a result of its normal business operations, they are reported in separate sections of the income statement.
5. On the income statement, corporate federal income taxes are listed separately so that taxable income can be more easily recognized.
6. The statement of retained earnings shows the changes that took place in the Retained Earnings account during the fiscal period.

Review and Applications

Building Your Accounting Vocabulary

In your own words, write the definition of each of the following accounting terms. Use complete sentences for your definitions.

capital stock
gross profit from
 operations

other expenses
other revenue
retained earnings

statement of retained
 earnings
stockholders' equity

Reviewing Your Accounting Knowledge

1. List three adjustments normally made by a merchandising business at the end of its fiscal period.
2. If a business uses the allowance method of accounting for uncollectible accounts, which accounts are affected by an adjustment for the period's estimated uncollectible amount?
3. What does the balance of the Office Equipment account in the Trial Balance section of the work sheet represent?
4. What account is debited at the end of the fiscal period for the prepaid interest expense on a non-interest-bearing note payable?
5. If a business makes an adjustment for accrued salaries, what accounts will be debited and credited?
6. What three financial statements are prepared at the end of a fiscal period by a merchandising corporation?
7. What are other revenue and other expenses? Give an example of each.
8. If a business's other expenses are greater than its other revenue, is there a net addition to or net deduction from income?
9. What information is reported on the statement of retained earnings?
10. Where are the data needed to prepare the balance sheet found?

Improving Your Decision-making Skills

Case 1

The new accounting clerk you have been training does not understand why the income statement, statement of retained earnings, and balance sheet are to be prepared in that order. What explanation can you offer?

Case 2

The Humboldt Lumber Company lists all plant assets on the balance sheet at their book value. The company believes that this eliminates work because it is not necessary to list the plant asset at cost and then subtract the accumulated depreciation. Do you agree with Humboldt's procedure? Why or why not?

Applying Accounting Procedures

Problem 9–1

Each of the following debits and credits represents one half of an adjustment recorded on the work sheet.

(1) Unearned Subscriptions is debited.
(2) Prepaid Insurance is credited.
(3) Salaries Expense is debited.
(4) Interest Income is credited.
(5) Allowance for Uncollectible Accounts is credited.
(6) Discount on Notes Payable is credited.
(7) Rental Income is credited.

Instructions: Use a form similar to the one that follows. For each item, indicate the title of the account that would appear in the other half of the adjustment.

Item	Account Debited	Account Credited
1	Unearned Subscriptions	Subscriptions Income

Problem 9–2

Several accounts that must be adjusted at the end of a fiscal period are listed below. The current balance (before any adjustment) is given for each account.

Allowance for Uncollectible Accounts	$ 125
Interest Receivable	
Accum. Depr.—Delivery Equipment	6,000
Discount on Notes Payable	275
Corporate Income Tax Payable	
Unearned Rent	1,200
Bad Debts Expense	
Depr. Exp.—Delivery Equipment	
Rental Income	
Interest Income	
Interest Expense	
Income Tax Expense	3,197

Data for the adjustments are as follows.

(a) Uncollectible accounts are estimated to be 2% of the Accounts Receivable balance of $17,900.

(b) Accrued interest on an interest-bearing note receivable is $85.

(c) Estimated annual depreciation on the company's delivery equipment is $2,000.

(d) Prepaid interest expense on a non-interest-bearing note payable is $150.

(e) The company received $1,200 rent in advance for desk space rented for one year. Three months of the rental agreement have expired.

(f) The total income tax liability for the year is $3,495.

Instructions: Use a form similar to the one that follows.

(1) Determine the amount of the adjustment for each account.

(2) Enter the adjustment in the Adjustments Debit or Credit column. Label each adjustment (a), (b), (c), and so on.

(3) Determine the new account balance and enter that amount in the Adjusted Trial Balance Debit or Credit column.

Account Title	Trial Balance Dr.	Trial Balance Cr.	Adjustments Dr.	Adjustments Cr.	Adjusted Trial Balance Dr.	Adjusted Trial Balance Cr.
Allow. for Uncoll. Accts.		125				

Problem 9–3

The December 31 trial balance for J & M Enterprises is listed below and on page 215. Also listed are the data needed for the adjustments.

Cash in Bank	$ 3,268.49	
Notes Receivable	5,000.00	
Interest Receivable		
Accounts Receivable	8,650.97	
Allow. for Uncollectible Accounts		$ 173.02
Merchandise Inventory	38,443.15	
Office Supplies	250.00	
Prepaid Insurance	370.00	
Prepaid Rent	3,600.00	
Store Equipment	17,700.00	
Accumulated Depr.—Store Equipment		4,000.00
Notes Payable		3,500.00
Discount on Notes Payable	103.56	
Accounts Payable		1,575.00
Salaries Payable		
Employees' Federal Income Tax Payable		1,800.00
FICA Tax Payable		630.00
Employees' State Income Tax Payable		360.00

Federal Unemployment Tax Payable		90.00
State Unemployment Tax Payable		278.00
Sales Tax Payable		1,200.00
Corporate Income Tax Payable		
Unearned Fees		2,500.00
Capital Stock		50,000.00
Retained Earnings		13,689.50
Income Summary		
Sales		41,160.15
Sales Returns and Allowances	1,500.00	
Sales Discounts	650.00	
Purchases	35,000.00	
Purchases Returns and Allowances		4,700.00
Purchases Discounts		780.00
Advertising Expense	450.00	
Bad Debts Expense		
Depreciation Expense—Store Equipment		
Insurance Expense		
Office Supplies Expense		
Payroll Tax Expense	949.50	
Rent Expense		
Salaries Expense	9,000.00	
Fees Income		
Interest Income		
Interest Expense		
Income Tax Expense	1,500.00	
	$126,435.67	$126,435.67

Data for Adjustments

Accrued interest on note receivable	$ 75.00
Additional estimated bad debt losses	112.00
Merchandise Inventory, December 31	55,500.00
Ending office supplies inventory	100.00
Expired insurance	275.00
Expired rent	2,500.00
Depreciation on store equipment	1,850.00
Interest incurred on discounted note payable	42.00
Accrued salaries	668.00
Deferred fees income earned	1,500.00
Additional income taxes owed	308.25

Instructions: Complete the ten-column work sheet for J & M Enterprises for the year ended December 31. The trial balance has already been entered on the work sheet.

Problem 9–4

Instructions: Use the work sheet you prepared in Problem 9–3 to complete this problem.

(1) Prepare an income statement.
(2) Prepare a statement of retained earnings. No dividends were declared and paid during the year.
(3) Prepare a balance sheet.

Problem 9–5

The balances of the general ledger accounts of Microdata Products, Inc., as of December 31 are listed below.

Cash in Bank	$ 3,456.98
Notes Receivable	4,000.00
Interest Receivable	
Accounts Receivable	16,420.74
Allowance for Uncollectible Accounts	67.12
Merchandise Inventory	42,583.16
Store Supplies	375.00
Prepaid Insurance	1,200.00
Prepaid Rent	3,600.00
Furniture and Fixtures	12,500.00
Accum. Depr.—Furniture and Fixtures	4,000.00
Store Equipment	18,000.00
Accum. Depr.—Store Equipment	6,000.00
Vouchers Payable	4,478.76
Notes Payable	7,000.00
Discount on Notes Payable	460.27
Salaries Payable	
Employees' Federal Income Tax Payable	162.50
FICA Tax Payable	141.00
Employees' State Income Tax Payable	139.21
Federal Unemployment Tax Payable	47.00
State Unemployment Tax Payable	168.00
Corporate Income Tax Payable	
Unearned Subscriptions Income	6,600.00
Capital Stock	40,000.00
Retained Earnings	16,010.52
Income Summary	
Sales	87,000.00
Sales Returns and Allowances	1,570.00
Sales Discounts	1,240.00
Purchases	35,000.00
Transportation In	657.71
Purchases Returns and Allowances	700.00

Purchases Discounts	640.00
Advertising Expense	1,500.00
Bad Debts Expense	
Depr. Exp.—Furniture and Fixtures	
Depr. Exp.—Store Equipment	
Insurance Expense	
Payroll Tax Expense	2,690.25
Rent Expense	
Salaries Expense	25,500.00
Store Supplies Expense	
Interest Income	
Subscriptions Income	
Interest Expense	
Income Tax Expense	2,400.00

Instructions:

(1) Prepare a ten-column work sheet for Microdata Products, Inc. for the year ended December 31. The account titles have already been recorded on the work sheet. Data for the adjustments are as follows.

- **(a)** Microdata accepted a $4,000.00, 9%, 60-day note receivable from a charge customer on December 1.
- **(b)** Uncollectible accounts are estimated to be 2% of the balance of Accounts Receivable.
- **(c)** The ending merchandise inventory is $44,623.81.
- **(d)** The ending store supplies inventory is $50.00.
- **(e)** Microdata paid $1,200.00 on May 1 for a one-year fire insurance policy.
- **(f)** Microdata signed a one-year lease on March 1, paying the full year's rent in advance.
- **(g)** The estimated depreciation on the company's furniture and fixtures is $1,500.00.
- **(h)** Estimated depreciation for the company's store equipment is $2,000.00.
- **(i)** On November 1, Microdata borrowed $7,000.00 from the Peoples National Bank, issuing a 240-day non-interest-bearing note, which the bank discounted at 10%.
- **(j)** On January 1, Microdata received $6,600.00 for 3-year subscriptions to a magazine the company publishes.
- **(k)** Microdata's weekly payroll is $500.00. Salaries have accrued for December 30–31.
- **(l)** The income tax liability for the year is $2,533.16.

(2) Prepare an income statement.

(3) Prepare a statement of retained earnings. No dividends were declared and paid during the year.

(4) Prepare a balance sheet.

In Unit 2, you learned about several different types of advanced accounting procedures. Now you will have the opportunity to review and apply what you have learned by keeping the records for Three Rivers Kitchen Wares.

When you have completed this activity, you will have

1. analyzed business transactions
2. journalized business transactions in the sales journal, the cash receipts journal, the voucher register, the check register, and the general journal
3. posted entries to the general ledger and the accounts receivable ledger
4. posted the totals of the journals and registers to the general ledger
5. prepared schedules of accounts receivable and vouchers payable
6. prepared a trial balance and a work sheet
7. prepared financial statements
8. journalized and posted adjusting and closing entries
9. prepared a post-closing trial balance

Three Rivers Kitchen Wares

Three Rivers Kitchen Wares is a closely held merchandising corporation owned and operated by Jim and Joanna Barnes. The business earns revenue by selling kitchen items to the general public and to local restaurants.

Chart of Accounts

The chart of accounts for Three Rivers is shown on page 219.

Business Transactions

In order to maintain better control over its purchases and cash payments, Three Rivers uses the voucher system of accounting. On December 1 the vouchers listed at the top of page 220 were still unpaid. (The vouchers have already been recorded in the voucher register.)

Chart of Accounts

ASSETS	101	Cash in Bank	REVENUE	401	Sales
	105	Accounts Receivable		402	Sales Discounts
	110	Allowance for Uncollectible Accounts		403	Sales Returns and Allowances
	115	Notes Receivable			
	120	Interest Receivable	COST OF	501	Purchases
	125	Merchandise Inventory	MERCHANDISE	502	Transportation In
	130	Supplies		503	Purchases Discounts
	135	Prepaid Insurance		504	Purchases Returns and Allowances
	140	Store Equipment			
	145	Accumulated Depreciation—Store Equipment	EXPENSES	601	Advertising Expense
				605	Bad Debts Expense
	150	Office Equipment		610	Depreciation Expense—Office Equipment
	155	Accumulated Depreciation—Office Equipment		615	Depreciation Expense—Store Equipment
LIABILITIES	201	Vouchers Payable		620	Insurance Expense
	202	Notes Payable		625	Miscellaneous Expense
	203	Discount on Notes Payable		630	Office Expense
	204	Employees' Federal Income Tax Payable		635	Payroll Tax Expense
				640	Rent Expense
	205	FICA Tax Payable		645	Salaries Expense
	206	Employees' State Income Tax Payable		650	Supplies Expense
				655	Utilities Expense
	207	Federal Unemployment Tax Payable		660	Income Tax Expense
	208	State Unemployment Tax Payable	OTHER REVENUE	701	Interest Income
	209	Corporate Income Tax Payable	OTHER EXPENSES	801	Interest Expense
	210	Salaries Payable			
	211	Sales Tax Payable			
STOCKHOLDERS' EQUITY	301	Common Stock			
	302	Retained Earnings			
	303	Income Summary			

Accounts Receivable Subsidiary Ledger

905   The Cloverleaf Restaurant
920   Inn on the Square
940   The Oak Leaf Restaurant
945   Parson's
960   Shearson's Steak House
980   The Weeping Willow Restaurant

Voucher No.	Creditor	For	Date of Invoice	Amount
115	Sonoma Appliances	Merchandise	Nov. 25	$3,595.50
116	Quality Glass Products	Merchandise	Nov. 28	4,375.00

The following transactions took place during the month of December.

Dec. 1 Received a check for $4,238.49 from Inn on the Square in payment of Sales Slip 1193 for $4,320.00 less a discount of $81.51, Receipt 479.

1 Issued Voucher 117 for $1,500.00 to Barker Realty for the December rent.

1 Issued Check 322 in payment of Voucher 117.

1 Sold merchandise for $5,069.00, plus sales tax of $304.14, on account to The Weeping Willow Restaurant, Sales Slip 1201.

1 Bought store equipment for $12,000.00 from Norris Equipment Co. and issued a 30 day, 10% note payable (Note 117) in payment.

2 Received Invoice A49 for $5,500.00 from United Kitchen Products for merchandise purchased on account, terms 2/10, n/30, dated December 1; issued Voucher 118.

2 Purchased merchandise on account for $8,200.00 from Williams, Inc., Invoice 1145, dated December 2, terms 3/10, n/30; issued Voucher 119.

3 Sold merchandise on account to The Cloverleaf Restaurant, $16,600.00 plus sales tax of $990.00, Sales Slip 1202.

4 Bought $150.00 worth of supplies on account from Parker's, Invoice 15, dated December 2, terms n/30; issued Voucher 120.

5 Issued Check 323 for $3,523.59 to Sonoma Appliances in payment of Voucher 115 for $3,595.50 less discount of $71.91.

5 Received a check for $8,437.74 from The Oak Leaf Restaurant in payment of Sales Slip 1197 for $8,600.00 less discount of $162.26, Receipt 480.

8 Sold merchandise on account to Parson's, $3,122.00 plus sales tax of $187.32, Sales Slip 1203.

8 Wrote Check 324 for $4,243.75 to Quality Glass Products in payment of Voucher 116 for $4,375.00 less a 3% discount of $131.25.

9 Sold merchandise on account, $5,500.00 plus sales tax of $330.00, to Shearson's Steak House, Sales Slip 1204.

10 Received Invoice 2119B from Mancini Imports for $1,282.00 worth of merchandise purchased on account, terms 2/10, n/30, dated December 10; issued Voucher 121.

10 Received a check for $5,271.76 from The Weeping Willow Restaurant in payment of Sales Slip 1201 for $5,373.14 less a discount of $101.38, Receipt 481.

11 Issued Check 325 for $5,390.00 to United Kitchen Products in payment of Voucher 118 for $5,500.00 less a discount of $110.00.

12 Recorded the payroll (in the general journal) of $3,800.00. The

following amounts were withheld: employees' federal income tax, $318.16; FICA tax, $267.90; employees' state income tax, $144.30 (credit Salaries Payable for the net pay), Memorandum 416.

12 Issued Voucher 122 for $3,069.64 in favor of the payroll bank account for the salaries owed employees.

12 Issued Check 326 in payment of Voucher 122.

12 Cash sales for December 1–12 were $10,130.50 plus sales tax of $607.83, T119.

12 Recorded the employer's payroll taxes as follows: FICA tax, $267.90; federal unemployment tax, $30.40; state unemployment tax, $102.60, Memorandum 417.

12 Issued Check 327 for $7,954.00 to Williams, Inc. in payment of Voucher 119 for $8,200.00 less a discount of $246.00.

12 Issued Voucher 123 to Speedy Delivery Service for freight charges on merchandise purchased from a supplier, $72.00.

12 Wrote Check 328 in payment of Voucher 123.

15 Received a check for $17,258.00 from The Cloverleaf Restaurant in payment of Sales Slip 1202 for $17,590.00 less a discount of $332.00, Receipt 482.

15 Issued Voucher 124 to the Internal Revenue Service for the final quarterly income tax installment of $11,037.50.

15 Paid Voucher 124 by issuing Check 329.

16 Received Invoice L101 for $3,200.00 from NordicWares for merchandise purchased on account, terms 2/10, n/30, dated December 15; issued Voucher 125.

16 Sold merchandise on account to Inn on the Square, $2,130.00 plus sales tax of $127.80, Sales Slip 1205.

17 Received a check for $3,246.88 from Parson's in payment of Sales Slip 1203 for $3,309.32 less a discount of $62.44, Receipt 483.

17 Issued Voucher 126 for $125.00 to Parker's for supplies purchased on account, Invoice 63, dated December 15, terms n/30.

18 Received Invoice MP47 for $4,200.00 from Perfetti's for merchandise purchased on account, terms 2/10, n/30, dated December 17; issued Voucher 127.

18 Sold merchandise on account to The Weeping Willow Restaurant, $6,015.00 plus sales tax of $360.00, Sales Slip 1206.

19 Issued Voucher 128 for $500.00 to Duke Electric for the monthly electric bill.

19 Received a check for $5,720.00 from Shearson's Steak House in payment of Sales Slip 1204 for $5,830.00 less a discount of $110.00, Receipt 484.

19 Wrote Check 330 for $1,256.36 to Mancini Imports in payment of Voucher 121 for $1,282.00 less a 2% discount of $25.64.

22 Issued Voucher 129 for $300.00 to City Water Co. for the monthly water bill.

22 Sold merchandise on account to The Cloverleaf Restaurant, $7,044.00 plus sales tax of $422.64, Sales Slip 1207.

22	Wrote Check 331 for $500.00 in payment of Voucher 128.
23	Wrote Check 332 for $300.00 in payment of Voucher 129.
23	Purchased $2,000.00 worth of merchandise on account from United Kitchen Products, Invoice A63, dated December 23, terms 2/10, n/30; issued Voucher 130.
23	Sold merchandise on account, $10,495.00 plus sales tax of $629.70, to The Oak Leaf Restaurant, Sales Slip 1208.
24	Issued Voucher 131 to Rapid Delivery for freight charges on merchandise purchased, $75.00.
24	Issued Check 333 in payment of Voucher 131.
24	Issued Check 334 for $3,136.00 to NordicWares in payment of Voucher 125 for $3,200.00 less a 2% discount of $64.00.
26	Recorded the payroll of $3,900.00. The following amounts were withheld: employees' federal income tax, $326.54; FICA tax, $274.95; employees' state income tax, $148.10; Memorandum 418.
26	Issued Voucher 132 for $3,150.41 in favor of the payroll bank account for the net amount due employees.
26	Recorded the employer's payroll taxes: FICA tax, $274.95; federal unemployment tax, $31.20; state unemployment tax, $105.30; Memorandum 419.
26	Issued Check 335 in payment of Voucher 132.
26	Cash sales for December 15–26 were $12,040.50 plus sales taxes of $722.43, T120.
26	Issued Debit Memo 57 for $100.00 to United Kitchen Products for merchandise returned (originally recorded on Voucher 130).
26	Received a check for $6,254.70 from The Weeping Willow Restaurant in payment of Sales Slip 1206 for $6,375.00 less a discount of $120.30, Receipt 485.
26	Sold merchandise on account to Parson's, $2,470.00 plus sales tax of $148.20, Sales Slip 1209.
26	Issued Credit Memo 85 for $212.00 to The Cloverleaf Restaurant for $200.00 worth of merchandise returned to us plus sales tax of $12.00.
29	Sold merchandise on account, $2,575.00 plus sales tax of $154.50, to Shearson's Steak House, Sales Slip 1210.
29	Received Invoice 2208B from Mancini Imports for merchandise purchased on account, $1,500.00, terms 2/15, n/30, dated December 26; issued Voucher 133.
29	Issued Voucher 134 for $276.00 to Rockland Insurance Co. for the premium on a three-month fire insurance policy.
29	Issued Check 336 in payment of Voucher 134.
30	Purchased $5,700.00 worth of merchandise on account from NordicWares, Invoice L136, dated December 29, terms 2/10, n/30; issued Voucher 135.
30	Issued Voucher 136 for Invoice 1209 from Williams, Inc. for $9,300.00 worth of merchandise purchased on account, terms 3/10, n/30, dated December 29.

31   Sold $5,067.00 worth of merchandise on account to Inn on the Square, plus sales tax of $304.02, Sales Slip 1211.

31   Issued Voucher 137 to Norris Equipment Co. in payment of Note 317 for $12,000.00, plus interest of $98.63.

31   Issued Check 337 in payment of Voucher 137.

31   Cash sales for December 27–31 were $1,129.00 plus sales tax of $67.74, T121.

Instructions: The forms for this activity are included in the working papers.

(1) Record the December transactions in the sales journal, cash receipts journal, voucher register, check register, and general journal.

(2) Post the individual amounts from the five journals and registers to the accounts receivable subsidiary ledger daily.

(3) Post the individual amounts from the General columns of the journals and registers to the general ledger daily.

(4) Total, prove, and rule the special journals and registers at the end of the month.

(5) Post the column totals of the special journals and registers to the general ledger accounts. Use this order for posting: sales journal, cash receipts journal, voucher register, and check register.

(6) Prepare a schedule of accounts receivable and a schedule of vouchers payable.

(7) Prepare a trial balance on a ten-column work sheet. Be sure to total the Trial Balance columns at the bottom of the first page and carry those totals forward to the first line of the second page.

(8) Complete the work sheet. Data for the adjustments are as follows.

    (a) The ending merchandise inventory on December 31 is $38,500.

    (b) Uncollectible accounts are estimated to be 3% of the balance of Accounts Receivable.

    (c) On November 15, Three Rivers accepted a $37,000, 9%, 90-day note receivable in payment for merchandise sold.

    (d) The ending supplies inventory on December 31 is $625.00.

    (e) On March 1, Three Rivers purchased a one-year liability insurance policy, paying a premium of $1,500.00.

    (f) Estimated annual depreciation on store equipment is $1,500.00.

    (g) Estimated annual depreciation on office equipment is $600.00.

    (h) On November 30, Three Rivers borrowed $20,000 from the American State Bank, issuing a 60-day, non-interest-bearing note, which the bank discounted at 9%.

    (i) Accrued salaries for December 29–31 are $1,170.00.

    (j) The income tax liability for the year is $47,719.00.

(9) Prepare an income statement for the year ended December 31.

(10) Prepare a statement of retained earnings.

(11) Prepare a balance sheet.

(12) Journalize and post the adjusting and closing entries.

(13) Prepare a post-closing trial balance.

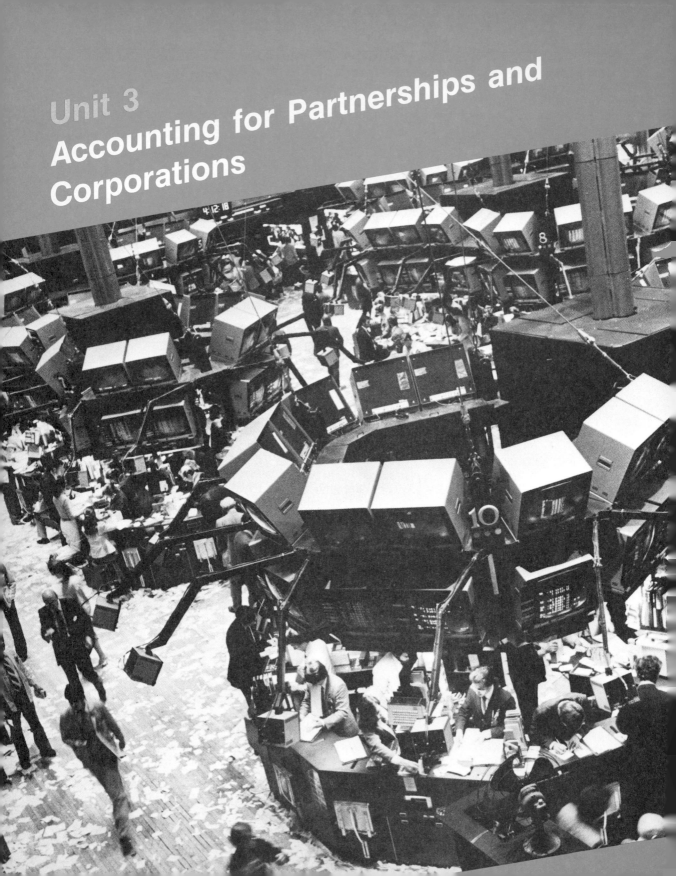

Sole proprietorships, partnerships, and corporations all account for every-day business transactions in much the same manner. One major difference in the accounting procedures of these three forms of business organization lies in accounting for ownership equity. In this unit, you will learn how financial events affecting the ownership equity of partnerships and publicly held corporations are recorded and reported. You will also learn about two situations unique to corporations: accounting for corporate income taxes and accounting for long-term liabilities in the form of bonds.

The chapters you will study in this unit are listed below.

New York Stock Exchange

10 Partnerships: Formation, Dissolution, and Liquidation

The three forms of business organization are, as you know, the sole proprietorship, the partnership, and the corporation. Most of the accounting procedures you have studied thus far in the textbook can be applied to any of these three types of businesses. For example, the sale of merchandise on account would be handled in the same manner by a sole proprietorship, a partnership, or a corporation.

The major difference in accounting for the three types of business organization lies in accounting for ownership equity. In this chapter and the next, you will examine the accounting procedures that are applicable to the partnership form of organization.

In this chapter, you will learn about the characteristics of a partnership. You will learn how partnerships are formed and how they may be dissolved. You will also learn how to record the journal entries necessary when a partnership is formed, dissolved, or liquidated.

Learning Objectives

When you have completed this chapter, you should be able to

1. List the major characteristics of a partnership.

2. List some of the advantages and disadvantages of the partnership form of organization.

3. Journalize entries to record the initial investment of partners.

4. Journalize transactions pertaining to the dissolution of a partnership.

5. Journalize entries involving the sale of assets when a partnership is liquidated.

6. Define the accounting terms presented in this chapter.

New Terms partnership / mutual agency / partnership agreement / dissolution / liquidation / realization

Accounting for Partnerships

A partnership, as defined by the Uniform Partnership Act, is an association of two or more persons to carry on, as co-owners, a business for profit. It is a voluntary association, freely entered into by the parties. Any type of business can be organized as a partnership. However, partnerships are often found in the professions, such as law or medicine, and in firms that stress personal service. Each partner can maintain her or his own clients, yet share with the other partners the expenses of operating an office.

Characteristics of a Partnership

Certain features of a partnership affect just the partners. Other features affect the partners as well as others who are not members of the partnership. Let us examine some of these features.

Co-ownership of Partnership Property

All partners are co-owners of the assets of the partnership. For example, Dobbs and Sutter formed a partnership to operate a delivery service. The partnership owns two delivery vans. According to the co-ownership concept, each partner owns half of each van, as well as half of all other assets of the firm.

Limited Life

A partnership is ended by the death or withdrawal of any partner. Other factors that may bring about the end of a partnership include the bankruptcy or incapacity of a partner, the addition of a new partner, the expiration of the period of time specified in the partnership agreement, or the completion of the project for which the partnership was formed.

Unlimited Liability

Just as a sole proprietor is personally liable for the debts of a proprietorship, each partner is personally liable for the debts of the partnership. A new partner who joins an existing firm may or may not assume liability for debts incurred by the firm prior to admission. A partner who withdraws from a firm must give adequate public notice of withdrawal, or he or she may be held liable for debts the partnership incurs after withdrawal.

Mutual Agency

The right of any partner to enter into valid contracts in the name of the firm for the purchase or sale of goods or services within the normal scope of the firm's business is known as **mutual agency**. The partners may agree among themselves to limit the right of any partner to enter into certain contracts in the name of the firm. This agreement, however, is not binding on outsiders dealing with the firm who are unaware of its existence.

Advantages of a Partnership

The partnership form of business organization has several advantages.

1. Partnerships offer an opportunity to pool the abilities and capital of two or more persons.
2. It is fairly easy to form a partnership. The only requirement is an agreement or mutual understanding by the partners.
3. There are few legal restrictions. Although the purpose of a partnership must be legal, there are no other limitations on the types of business activities.
4. Federal income taxes are not levied against a partnership as an entity. A partnership, however, must file an informational tax return (Form 1065). This return contains an income statement, a balance sheet, and a report showing how the year's net income was allocated to each partner (Schedule K-1). Each partner must include his or her share of the net income, whether this share is taken out of the business or not, on his or her personal income tax return.

Disadvantages of a Partnership

The partnership form of business organization also has some disadvantages that should be considered.

1. General partners—those who actively and publicly participate in transactions of the firm—have unlimited liability.
2. A partnership has a limited life.
3. The actions of one partner are binding on the other partners (mutual agency).
4. It is difficult to raise large amounts of capital since it depends entirely on the partners themselves.
5. It is hard to transfer a partial or entire partnership interest to another person, as the transfer must be agreed to by all partners.

The Partnership Agreement

Although generally a partnership may be formed on the basis of an oral understanding, it is much better to have a written partnership agreement. A partnership agreement is a written document that sets out the terms under which the partnership will operate. Although there is no standard form of partnership agreement, the following provisions are usually included.

- Effective date of the agreement
- Names and addresses of the partners
- Name, location, and nature of the business
- Duration of the agreement
- Investment of each partner
- Duties, rights, and responsibilities of each partner
- Withdrawals of capital to be allowed each partner
- Procedure for sharing profits and losses
- Provision for division of assets when the partnership is dissolved

A typical partnership agreement is shown in Figure 10–1 on page 230.

Accounting for Partners' Equity

The only difference between accounting for a sole proprietorship and accounting for partnerships is in the owners' equity accounts. Otherwise, the same types of asset, liability, revenue, and expense accounts are used as have been discussed before. But because there is more than one owner, it is necessary to have one capital account and one withdrawals account for each partner. As in the case of a sole proprietorship, the capital accounts are involved only when there is a change in the partners' investments or when the Income Summary account and the Withdrawals account are closed.

Remember: **In a partnership, there is a separate capital account and a separate withdrawals account for each partner.**

Recording the Partners' Investments

When a partnership is formed, the investment of each partner is listed in the partnership agreement. Then, a separate entry is made to record the investment of each partner. All assets contributed by a given partner are debited to the appropriate asset accounts. If the partnership also assumes liabilities, the amounts are credited to the proper liability accounts. Each partner's capital account is credited for the net amount of his or her investment.

Let's look at an example. Penny Wolfburg and Ingrid Swenson decide to form a partnership to operate a jewelry store. Wolfburg presently owns and operates Wolfburg's Jewelry Store. She is contributing the assets and liabilities of her store to the new firm. Swenson's investment is $20,000 in cash.

PARTNERSHIP AGREEMENT

This agreement, made June 20, 19--, between Penelope Wolfburg of 783A South Street, Hazelton, Idaho, and Ingrid Swenson of RR 5, Box 96, Hazelton, Idaho.

1. The above named persons have this day formed a partnership that shall operate under the name of W-S Jewelers, located at 85 Broad Street, Hazelton, Idaho 83335, and shall engage in jewelry sales and repairs.

2. The duration of this agreement will be for a term of fifteen years, beginning on June 20, 19--, or for a shorter term if agreed upon in writing by both partners.

3. The initial investment by each partner will be as follows: Penelope Wolfburg, assets and liabilities of Wolfburg's Jewelry Store, valued at a capital investment of $40,000; Ingrid Swenson, cash of $20,000. These investments are partnership property.

4. Each partner will give her time, skill, and attention to the operation of this partnership and will engage in no other business enterprise unless permission is granted in writing by the other partner.

5. The salary for each partner will be as follows: Penelope Wolfburg, $40,000 per year; Ingrid Swenson, $30,000 per year. Neither partner may withdraw cash or other assets from the business without express permission in writing from the other partner. All profits and losses of the business will be shared as follows: Penelope Wolfburg, 60 percent; Ingrid Swenson, 40 percent.

6. Upon the dissolution of the partnership due to termination of this agreement, or to written permission by each of the partners, or to the death or incapacitation of one or both partners, a new contract may be entered into by the partners or the sole continuing partner has the option to purchase the other partner's interest in the business at a price that shall not exceed the balance in the terminating partner's capital account. The payment shall be made in cash in equal quarterly installments from the date of termination.

7. At the conclusion of this contract, unless it is agreed by both partners to continue the operation of the business under a new contract, the assets of the partnership, after the liabilities are paid, will be divided in proportion to the balance in each partner's capital account on that date.

<table>
<tr><td>Penelope Wolfburg</td><td>Ingrid Swenson</td></tr>
<tr><td>Penelope Wolfburg</td><td>Ingrid Swenson</td></tr>
<tr><td>June 20, 19--</td><td>June 20, 19--</td></tr>
<tr><td>Date</td><td>Date</td></tr>
</table>

Figure 10–1. Partnership Agreement

Both partners have to agree on the amounts at which Wolfburg's noncash assets are to be recorded. For example, Wolfburg's Jewelry Store has the following account balances.

Cash in Bank	$ 2,900
Accounts Receivable	18,000
Allowance for Uncollectible Accounts	200
Merchandise Inventory	20,400
Equipment	16,000
Accumulated Depreciation—Equipment	4,500
Accounts Payable	8,400
Notes Payable	1,600

The partners agree that $400 of the accounts receivable is definitely uncollectible and should not be recorded on the books of the new partnership. Of the remaining $17,600 of accounts receivable, there is some doubt as to the collectibility of $500. The present appraised value of Wolfburg's merchandise is $21,000. The present appraised value of Wolfburg's equipment is $9,000. The entries to record each partner's investment are shown in Figure 10–2.

GENERAL JOURNAL   PAGE _____

	DATE	DESCRIPTION	POST. REF.	DEBIT	CREDIT	
1	19— Feb. 2	Cash in Bank		20 000 00		1
2		Ingrid Swenson, Capital			20 000 00	2
3		Memo. 1				3
4	2	Cash in Bank		2 900 00		4
5		Accounts Receivable		17 600 00		5
6		Merchandise Inventory		21 000 00		6
7		Equipment		9 000 00		7
8		Allow. for Uncollectible Accts.			500 00	8
9		Notes Payable			1 600 00	9
10		Accounts Payable			8 400 00	10
11		Penny Wolfburg, Capital			40 000 00	11
12		Memo. 1				12

Figure 10–2. Journalizing the Partners' Initial Investments

Notice that Accounts Receivable is debited for the full amount of the accounts taken over by the new partnership. Allowance for Uncollectible Accounts is credited for the amount the partners estimate to be uncollectible. Any customer accounts that are definitely uncollectible are not recorded in the accounting records of the new business.

The new firm's Merchandise Inventory and Equipment accounts are debited for the amount of their appraised present values. The accumulated depreciation is not recorded, because the appraised value represents the new book value for the partnership.

Remember: **When a partner invests noncash assets in the business, they are recorded in the partnership records at their present appraised values.**

Recording Additional Investments

Now let's say that eight months have gone by and the new partnership needs more cash. On October 1, the partners each invest an additional $4,000. The entry is shown in Figure 10–3.

	DATE		DESCRIPTION	POST. REF.	DEBIT	CREDIT	
1	Oct.	1	Cash in Bank		8 000 00		1
2			Penny Wolfburg, Capital			4 000 00	2
3			Ingrid Swenson, Capital			4 000 00	3
4			Memo 41				4

GENERAL JOURNAL — PAGE 28

Figure 10–3. Journalizing the Additional Investments by the Partners

At the end of the year, before the books are closed, the capital accounts of the partners will appear as shown in Figure 10–4.

ACCOUNT _Penny Wolfburg, Capital_ — ACCOUNT NO. 301

DATE	EXPLANATION	POST. REF.	DEBIT	CREDIT	BALANCE DEBIT	BALANCE CREDIT
Feb. 2		G1		40 000 00		40 000 00
Oct. 1		G28		4 000 00		44 000 00

ACCOUNT _Ingrid Swenson, Capital_ — ACCOUNT NO. 303

DATE	EXPLANATION	POST. REF.	DEBIT	CREDIT	BALANCE DEBIT	BALANCE CREDIT
Feb. 2		G1		20 000 00		20 000 00
Oct. 1		G28		4 000 00		24 000 00

Figure 10–4. Partners' Capital Accounts at End of Year

Recording Partners' Withdrawals

The withdrawals accounts of partners serve the same purpose as the withdrawals account of the owner of a sole proprietorship. Debits to the withdrawals accounts may be in the form of cash or other assets. The amount of the withdrawal is debited to the partner's withdrawals account and credited to the appropriate asset account.

November 9: *Penny Wolfburg withdrew $200 for personal use (Check 93) and Ingrid Swenson withdrew $148 in supplies for personal use (Memo 17).*

This transaction is illustrated in Figure 10–5.

	DATE	DESCRIPTION	POST. REF.	DEBIT	CREDIT	
	GENERAL JOURNAL				PAGE 33	
1	Nov. 9	Penny Wolfburg, Withdrawals		200 00		1
2		Cash in Bank			200 00	2
3		Check 93				3
4	9	Ingrid Swenson, Withdrawals		148 00		4
5		Supplies			148 00	5
6		Memo 17				6

Figure 10–5. Journalizing Withdrawals by the Partners

Before reading further, do the following activity to check your understanding of how to record partners' investments.

Check Your Learning

John LeBrand and Jan Wolek agree to form a partnership. As his investment in the new firm of LeBrand and Wolek, LeBrand invests equipment that had been recorded on the books of his own business as costing $40,000, with accumulated depreciation of $26,000. The partners agree on a valuation of $18,000 for the equipment. They also agree to accept LeBrand's accounts receivable of $20,000, collectible to the extent of 80%.

On a separate piece of paper, record LeBrand's investment in the partnership of LeBrand and Wolek in general journal form. The date is May 7 and the source document is Memo. 247.

Check your answer with that in the answers section. Re-read the preceding part of the chapter to find the answers to any portion of the entry you may have missed.

Dissolution of a Partnership

As mentioned earlier in the chapter, one of the disadvantages of a partnership is that it has a limited life. Any change in the personnel of the membership technically ends the partnership. When a partnership dissolves, the main visible result is a change in the names listed in the partnership agreement and a change in the division of net income. The routine transactions of the business go on as usual. For example, suppose that a partnership originally consists of A, B, and C. Then C withdraws his or her investment from the firm, and a new partnership emerges: A and B. During the transition, business is carried on as usual. In other words, in a **dissolution**, the original partnership is dissolved by the admission of a new partner, the withdrawal of a partner, or the death of a partner, and the firm continues to operate.

Remember: **When a partnership dissolves, the business continues in operation. The change occurs in the personnel of the partnership.**

Admission of a New Partner

The admission of a new partner dissolves an existing partnership because a new association has been formed. However, a new partner cannot be admitted without the consent of all the old partners. When a new partner is admitted, a new partnership agreement should be drawn up describing the new arrangement.

An individual may be admitted to a partnership in one of two ways: (1) by purchasing an interest in the partnership from one or more of the original partners or (2) by investing assets in the partnership.

Purchase of a Partnership Interest with No Increase in Capital

A partner may choose to sell his or her interest to a person outside the firm who is acceptable to the remaining partners. For example, Robin Easely and Linda Dodd are partners in the firm of Dodd & Easely. Let's say that at the end of a given year Robin Easely has a capital balance of $31,760. She decides to sell her interest in the partnership to Paul Falkner for $40,000. The entry to record the transfer of ownership is shown in Figure 10–6.

	GENERAL JOURNAL		PAGE _53_	
DATE	DESCRIPTION	POST. REF.	DEBIT	CREDIT
Dec. 31	Robin Easely, Capital		31 760 00	
	Paul Falkner, Capital			31 760 00
	Memo 167			

Figure 10–6. Journalizing the Admission of a New Partner with No Increase in Capital

The difference between $40,000 and $31,760 represents a personal profit to Easely, not to the firm. There has been no change in the partnership's assets or liabilities, and consequently there is no change in the total owners' equity. However, remember that if the firm is to continue, Linda Dodd (the other original partner) must be willing to accept Falkner as a new partner.

The Investment of Assets by a New Partner

When a new partner is admitted and invests assets in the partnership, both the assets and the owners' equity of the firm are increased. This is so because, in contrast to the case of buying a partner out, the assets that the new partner invests become partnership assets. This increase in assets creates a corresponding increase in owners' equity.

For example, Cathy Barton and Andrew Stevens are partners with capital accounts of $70,000 and $80,000 respectively. James Connolly wishes to invest $75,000 in the partnership of Barton and Stevens. The two partners agree to admit Connolly to the firm for a $75,000 investment. The entry to record this investment is shown in Figure 10–7.

	GENERAL JOURNAL			PAGE 19	
DATE	DESCRIPTION	POST. REF.	DEBIT	CREDIT	
19— July 1	Cash in Bank		75 00 00		1
	James Connolly, Capital			75 00 00	2
	Memo. 114				3

Figure 10–7. Journalizing the Investment of a New Partner

With the admission of Connolly, the total equity of the business becomes $225,000.

Remember: If a new partner invests assets in a partnership, the owners' equity of the business increases.

Withdrawal of a Partner

The partnership agreement should provide for a set procedure to be followed when one of the partners withdraws. Such a procedure usually requires an audit of the books and a revaluation of the partnership's assets to reflect current market values.

When a partner withdraws from the firm, he or she may withdraw (1) the book value of his or her equity, (2) more than the book value of his or her equity, or (3) less than the book value of his or her equity.

Partner Withdraws Book Value of Equity

Suppose that Sally Hogan is retiring from the partnership of Gray, Hogan, and Insell. The partnership agreement states that net income and net loss shall be shared on an equal basis. It also provides for an audit and revaluation of assets if a partner retires. After the audit and revaluation of assets, the partners' capital accounts look like this.

Rachel Gray, Capital			Sally Hogan, Capital			Donald Insell, Capital	
Dr.	Cr.		Dr.	Cr.		Dr.	Cr.
−	+		−	+		−	+
	Bal. $48,400			Bal. $26,400			Bal. $24,400

Hogan can now withdraw cash from the partnership equal to her equity, which leads to the entry shown in Figure 10–8.

GENERAL JOURNAL   PAGE 26

DATE	DESCRIPTION	POST. REF.	DEBIT	CREDIT
¹⁹⁻⁻Sept. 30	Sally Hogan, Capital		26400 00	
	Cash in Bank			26400 00
	Check 1732			

Figure 10–8. Journalizing the Withdrawal of a Partner

After Hogan's withdrawal, the total equity of the business is $72,800.

Partner Withdraws More Than Book Value of Equity

Sometimes a partner may withdraw more cash than the amount of his or her capital account. There are two possible reasons for this: (1) The business is prosperous and shows excellent potential for growth, or (2) the remaining partners are so anxious for the partner to retire that they are willing to buy him or her out.

Suppose that, in the firm of Gray, Hogan, and Insell, when Hogan announces that she's going to retire, Gray and Insell agree to pay her $27,000 for her interest in the partnership. Because the balance of Hogan's capital account after the revaluation is $26,400, the additional $600 must be deducted from the capital accounts of the remaining partners, in accordance with their basis for sharing profits and losses. The entry to record Hogan's withdrawal appears in Figure 10–9.

GENERAL JOURNAL   PAGE 26

DATE	DESCRIPTION	POST. REF.	DEBIT	CREDIT
¹⁹⁻⁻Sept. 30	Sally Hogan, Capital		26400 00	
	Rachel Gray, Capital		300 00	
	Donald Insell, Capital		300 00	
	Cash in Bank			27000 00
	Check 1732			

Figure 10–9. Journalizing a Partner's Withdrawal That Is Greater than Book Value of Equity

After Hogan's withdrawal, the total capital of the business is $72,200.

Partner Withdraws Less Than Book Value of Equity

Sometimes a partner may be so anxious to retire that he or she is willing to take less than the current value of his or her equity. In the firm of Gray, Hogan, and Insell, let's say that Hogan is willing to withdraw from the partnership for a

$21,000 settlement. Because the balance of Hogan's capital account after the revaluation is $26,400, the difference ($5,400) represents a profit to the remaining partners. That profit is recorded in the remaining partners' capital accounts. The entry to record this is shown in Figure 10–10.

	GENERAL JOURNAL			PAGE 26

	DATE	DESCRIPTION	POST. REF.	DEBIT	CREDIT	
1	19-- Sept 30	Sally Hogan, Capital		26 400 00		1
2		Rachel Gray, Capital			2 700 00	2
3		Donald Insell, Capital			2 700 00	3
4		Cash in Bank			21 000 00	4
5		Check 1732				5

Figure 10–10. Journalizing a Partner's Withdrawal That Is Less than Book Value of Equity

After Hogan's withdrawal, the total equity of the business is $78,200.

Death of a Partner

The death of a partner automatically ends the partnership, and the partner's heirs are entitled to receive the amount of his or her equity. Normally, the partnership's books are closed immediately, so that the firm's net income for the current fiscal period can be determined. Partnership agreements usually also provide for an audit and revaluation of the assets at this time. Then, after the current value of the deceased partner's capital account is determined, the remaining partners and the executor of the deceased partner's estate must agree on the method of payment. The journal entries are similar to those made for the withdrawal of a partner. To be sure that they have enough cash to meet such a demand, partnerships often carry life insurance policies on each of the partners.

Liquidation of a Partnership

A **liquidation** means an end of the partnership as well as of the business itself. This final winding-up process involves selling assets, paying off liabilities, and distributing the remaining cash to the partners. The closing entries are journalized and posted prior to the liquidation.

Occasionally it takes a long time to convert merchandise inventory and other assets into cash; on the other hand, the conversion could move quickly. One can never predict how long the liquidation process may take. In the process, several things may happen. We shall discuss only two possibilities in this chapter.

The four steps listed on the next page are necessary to liquidate a partnership.

1. Sale of the assets, using the Loss or Gain from Realization account. This account is a temporary account that is used only during the liquidation process. This account is debited for losses and credited for gains. In this respect the account is comparable to the Income Summary account. The word realization refers to the sale of the assets for cash.

2. Allocation of loss or gain. The Loss or Gain from Realization account is closed into the partners' capital accounts according to the partnership agreement on sharing profits and losses. The account must be closed separately because it came into being after the regular closing entries had been journalized and posted.

3. Payment of liabilities. The company makes a final settlement to all of its creditors.

4. Distribution of remaining cash to the partners, according to the balances of their capital accounts.

For example, in the partnership of Jacobs, King, and Lowell, the partners share profits and losses as follows: Jacobs, one half; King, one fourth; Lowell, one fourth.

Let us now have a look at the account balances for this firm.

Cash in Bank	$10,000
Merchandise Inventory	20,000
Other Assets	40,000
Accounts Payable	7,000
Ronald Jacobs, Capital	27,000
Miranda King, Capital	24,000
Craig Lowell, Capital	12,000

Gain on Sale of Assets

Assume that the firm sells its merchandise inventory for $26,000 and the other assets for $48,000, for a total of $74,000. First, the sale of assets is recorded, showing a gain on realization of $14,000 ($74,000 − $60,000 recorded value). Then the Loss or Gain from Realization account is closed into the partners' capital accounts, according to the partnership agreement. Next, the creditors are paid, and the remaining cash is distributed to the partners. The journal entries to cover these transactions are shown in Figure 10–11 on the next page.

After these entries are journalized and posted, the Cash in Bank and capital accounts appear as shown in the T accounts below and on the next page.

Cash in Bank			Ronald Jacobs, Capital	
Dr.	Cr.		Dr.	Cr.
+	−		−	+
Bal. $10,000	$ 7,000		$34,000	Bal. $27,000
74,000	77,000			7,000

Miranda King, Capital			Craig Lowell, Capital	
Dr.	Cr.		Dr.	Cr.
–	+		–	+
$27,500	Bal. $24,000		$15,500	Bal. $12,000
	3,500			3,500

GENERAL JOURNAL   PAGE 19

	DATE	DESCRIPTION	POST. REF.	DEBIT	CREDIT	
1	19-- June 30	Cash in Bank		74 00 00		1
2		Merchandise Inventory			20 00 00	2
3		Other Assets			40 00 00	3
4		Loss or Gain from Realization			14 00 00	4
5		Receipt 1117				5
6	30	Loss or Gain from Realization		14 00 00		6
7		Ronald Jacobs, Capital			7 00 00	7
8		Miranda King, Capital			3 50 00	8
9		Craig Lowell, Capital			3 50 00	9
10		Memo. 462				10
11	30	Accounts Payable		7 00 00		11
12		Cash in Bank			7 00 00	12
13		Check 2173				13
14	30	Ronald Jacobs, Capital		34 00 00		14
15		Miranda King, Capital		27 50 00		15
16		Craig Lowell, Capital		15 50 00		16
17		Cash in Bank			77 00 00	17
18		Memo. 463				18

Figure 10–11. Journalizing a Partnership Liquidation with a Gain on Sale of Assets

Remember: When a partnership is liquidated, the cash is distributed to the partners according to the balances in their capital accounts.

Loss on Sale of Assets

Now suppose that the partnership of Jacobs, King, and Lowell sells its merchandise inventory for only $16,000. The other assets are sold for only $32,000. The company has realized a total of $48,000. Again, the sale of the assets is recorded. In this case, however, there is a loss on realization of $12,000 ($60,000 − $48,000).

The Loss or Gain from Realization account is closed into the three partners' capital accounts. All creditors are paid. Finally, the remaining cash is distributed to the partners. The journal entries are shown in Figure 10–12 on page 240.

	DATE	DESCRIPTION	POST. REF.	DEBIT	CREDIT	
1	19-- June 30	Cash in Bank		48 00 0 00		1
2		Loss or Gain from Realization		12 00 0 00		2
3		Merchandise Inventory			20 00 0 00	3
4		Other Assets			40 00 0 00	4
5		Receipt 1117				5
6	30	Ronald Jacobs, Capital		6 00 0 00		6
7		Miranda King, Capital		3 00 0 00		7
8		Craig Lowell, Capital		3 00 0 00		8
9		Loss or Gain from Realization			12 00 0 00	9
10		Memo. 462				10
11	30	Accounts Payable		7 00 0 00		11
12		Cash in Bank			7 00 0 00	12
13		Check 2173				13
14	30	Ronald Jacobs, Capital		21 00 0 00		14
15		Miranda King, Capital		21 00 0 00		15
16		Craig Lowell, Capital		9 00 0 00		16
17		Cash in Bank			51 00 0 00	17
18		Memo 463				18

Figure 10–12. Journalizing a Partnership Liquidation with a Loss on Sale of Assets

After these entries are journalized and posted, the Cash in Bank and capital accounts appear as shown in the following T accounts.

Cash in Bank			Ronald Jacobs, Capital	
Dr.	Cr.		Dr.	Cr.
+	–		–	+
Bal. $10,000	$ 7,000		$ 6,000	Bal. $27,000
48,000	51,000		21,000	

Miranda King, Capital			Craig Lowell, Capital	
Dr.	Cr.		Dr.	Cr.
–	+		–	+
$ 3,000	Bal. $24,000		$3,000	Bal. $12,000
21,000			9,000	

Remember: **The Loss or Gain from Realization account is used in the liquidation process only when a gain or loss from the sale of partnership assets is realized.**

Before reading further, do the activity at the top of the following page to check your understanding of how to record the liquidation of a partnership.

Summary of Key Points

1. A partnership is an association of two or more persons to carry on, as co-owners, a business for profit.
2. The actions of one partner acting on behalf of the partnership are binding on all the partners. This is known as mutual agency.
3. The main advantage of a partnership is that it makes possible the combining of people's abilities and investments to carry on a business.
4. The main disadvantage of a partnership is the unlimited liability assumed by each partner.
5. In a partnership, separate capital and withdrawals accounts are set up for each partner.
6. A partnership is dissolved and reformed whenever there is any change in the composition of its membership. The effect on the business may simply be a change in the members listed in the partnership agreement and in the capital accounts. The normal transactions of the business go on as usual.
7. When a partnership liquidates, the business ends. Assets are sold, all liabilities are paid, and the remaining cash is distributed to the partners.

Review and Applications

Building Your Accounting Vocabulary

In your own words, write the definition of each of the following accounting terms. Use complete sentences for your definitions.

dissolution   mutual agency   partnership agreement
liquidation   partnership   realization

Reviewing Your Accounting Knowledge

1. What is meant by the concept of co-ownership of partnership property?
2. List three advantages and three disadvantages of the partnership form of organization.
3. Paul Cary and Gina Furillo are partners in the firm of Cary & Furillo. Paul signed a contract to purchase a word processing system for the business. Is the contract binding on the partnership? Why or why not?
4. Are partnerships required to pay federal income taxes? Why or why not?
5. Is it possible for one owner to lose a greater amount than the amount of his or her investment in the partnership? Why or why not?
6. What kind of information is usually included in a partnership agreement?
7. When assets other than cash are invested in a partnership by one of the partners, at what value are those assets recorded on the books of the partnership?
8. Name three situations that cause the dissolution of a partnership.
9. In what two ways may an individual be admitted to an already existing partnership?
10. How does the dissolution of a partnership differ from a liquidation?
11. What four steps are followed in the liquidation of a partnership?

Improving Your Decision-making Skills

Case 1

Earl Rowe and Claire Pound are considering forming a partnership to operate a gift shop. They don't think that it is necessary to prepare a formal partnership agreement; their oral agreement, they think, is enough. Do you agree or disagree with Earl and Claire?

Case 2

Jane Dittrich and John Dayton are partners in the firm of D & D Sales. When John Dayton dies, his daughter Anna claims that she has the right to take her father's place in the partnership. Do you agree with Anna? Why or why not?

Problem 10–1

Marie Iosa and John Quintel agree to form a partnership to operate a business called The Light House. Marie Iosa plans to invest the assets and liabilities of her current business. John Quintel plans to invest cash and other assets. The investments of the two partners are shown in the following table. All assets have been valued at their present appraised value.

	Marie Iosa	John Quintel
Cash	$12,000	$25,000
Accounts Receivable	3,000	
Allowance for Uncollectible Accounts	150	
Merchandise Inventory	15,000	
Supplies	100	500
Equipment	3,000	5,000
Accounts Payable	4,500	

Instructions: Prepare the entries in general journal form to record the initial investments of the partners on June 1. Use page 1 of the general journal and Memorandum 1 as the source document.

Problem 10–2

Judy O'Connor and Irene Madison are partners in Holiday Travel Services. The following transactions took place during the month of February.

Feb. 4 O'Connor withdrew $500 in cash from the business, Check 203.
11 Madison invested an additional $3,000 in the business, Receipt 219.
20 Madison withdrew $1,000 in cash from the business, Check 216.
25 O'Connor invested filing cabinets (Equipment) valued at $125 and an electronic typewriter (Equipment) valued at $1,200 in the business, Memorandum 41.

Instructions: Record the transactions on page 11 of a general journal.

Problem 10–3

Barbara Stanfield and Jay Delaney are partners in the firm of Stanfield & Delaney. Their capital balances are $35,000 and $24,000, respectively. Jay and Barbara agree to admit Jan Brooks to the partnership for an investment of $40,000 cash (Receipt 1145).

Instructions:

(1) Journalize the entry to record the admission of Brooks on July 1. Use page 33 of the general journal.
(2) Determine the total equity of the new partnership.

Problem 10-4

Joe Abbott, Carol Barker, and Arthur Cannon are partners in the firm of ABC Enterprises. The balances of their capital accounts are $30,000, $40,000, and $25,000, respectively. The three partners share profits and losses equally.

Cannon wishes to retire from the partnership. Abbott and Barker agree to pay Cannon $30,000 for his interest in the business. Cannon agrees to accept $20,000 cash (Check 4167) and a $10,000 note payable (Note 41).

Instructions:

(1) Journalize the entry to record the withdrawal of Cannon on March 1. Use page 54 of the general journal.
(2) Determine the total equity of the partnership after Cannon's withdrawal.

Problem 10-5

Joan Bauer, Mary Chester, and Len Dawson are partners in the firm of Bauer, Chester, and Dawson. Their capital balances are $75,000, $90,000, and $100,000, respectively. The partners share profits and losses equally.

When Bauer dies, the firm's accountant conducts a revaluation of the firm's assets. The revaluation indicates that the following assets have increased in value by these amounts:

Merchandise Inventory	$22,000
Building	62,000

The asset Equipment, however, has decreased in value by $6,000.

Instructions:

(1) Journalize the entry to record the revaluation of the firm's assets on November 28. Use page 41 of the general journal. The source document is Memorandum 148.
(2) Journalize the entry to record the payment of Bauer's share of the partnership to her heirs (Check 5039).
(3) Determine the total equity of the partnership.

Problem 10-6

The partnership of Lane, Morgan, and Shoemaker is being liquidated as of April 30. The partners share profits and losses equally. The balances of the firm's accounts are as follows.

Cash in Bank	$58,840
Merchandise Inventory	76,500
Other assets	57,500
Accounts Payable	16,840
Marcia C. Lane, Capital	72,000
Rhoda Morgan, Capital	56,000
Ron Shoemaker, Capital	48,000

Instructions: Journalize the entries, on page 46 of the general journal, to record the following. Use April 30 as the date.

(1) The sale of the merchandise inventory for $72,000 and the other assets for $56,000 (Receipt 814)
(2) The allocation of the gain or loss from realization to the partners' capital accounts (Memorandum 527)
(3) The payment of creditors (Check 2821)
(4) The distribution of cash to the partners (Checks 2822–2824)

Problem 10–7

Paula Rogers, Laura Masters, and Steven Mallory are partners in the firm of The Crystal Cave. Their capital balances are $53,800, $43,680, and $39,600, respectively. They share profits and losses in a 2:2:1 ratio.

By mutual agreement, the three partners decide to liquidate their partnership. The balances of the other partnership accounts are as follows.

Cash in Bank	$57,920
Accounts Receivable	8,900
Merchandise Inventory	67,240
Equipment	15,620
Accounts Payable	12,600

Instructions: Journalize and post the following entries to liquidate the partnership. Use page 89 of the general journal. The opened general ledger accounts appear in the working papers accompanying this textbook.

(1) The sale of the assets and the collection of accounts receivable (Journalize separately.)
    (a) Merchandise was sold on December 1 for $69,500 (Receipt 1133).
    (b) Equipment was sold on December 4 for $12,000 (Receipt 1134).
    (c) Collected 90% of Accounts Receivable (Receipt 1135) on December 10.
(2) The allocation of the gain or loss from realization to the partners' capital accounts on December 10 (Memorandum 1279)
(3) The payment of creditors on December 12 (Check 3281)
(4) The distribution of cash to the partners on December 14 (Checks 3282–3284)

11 Partnerships: Division of Profits and Losses

In Chapter 10, you were introduced to the partnership form of business organization. You learned that the basic difference in partnership accounting is in accounting for partners' equity. Each partner has her or his own capital account and withdrawals account. The capital accounts are used to record each partner's investment in the business.

Capital accounts are also used to record the net income or loss for a fiscal period. For a sole proprietorship, this is simple. The balance of the Income Summary account is closed into the owner's capital account. In a partnership, however, there are several owners. The amount of the net income or loss must be divided among those partners.

In this chapter, you will learn about the various methods that can be used to divide a partnership's earnings among the partners. You'll learn how to record the closing entries for the division of net income or loss and how to prepare the financial statements for a partnership.

Learning Objectives

When you have completed this chapter, you should be able to

1. List five methods of distributing a partnership's net income or loss.

2. Journalize the closing entry for a partnership pertaining to the division of net income or loss.

3. Prepare the financial statements for a partnership.

4. Define the accounting terms presented in this chapter.

New Terms   salary allowance / interest allowance

Division of Net Income or Net Loss

As you remember, the closing entries for a sole proprietorship consist of the following steps.

1. Close the revenue and contra cost accounts into Income Summary.
2. Close the contra revenue, cost, and expense accounts into Income Summary.
3. Close Income Summary into the capital account by the amount of the net income or loss.
4. Close the withdrawals account into the capital account.

The only differences in closing entries for a partnership, as opposed to those for a sole proprietorship, pertain to steps 3 and 4. Instead of a single capital account and a single withdrawals account, in a partnership each partner has a capital account and a withdrawals account. Income Summary is closed into the capital accounts by the amount of the net income or loss, and the withdrawals accounts are closed into the respective capital accounts.

Let's look at step 3, which deals with the division of net income or loss. The partners are free to make whatever arrangements they wish to divide any profits and losses among them. They may even provide for losses to be handled differently from profits. Wise partners record these arrangements in written partnership agreements. The law provides that partners share profits and losses equally unless they agree otherwise.

Partners may use any one of a number of methods to determine the distribution of earnings, or they may use a combination of methods. Each method reflects the differences in the value of the services or investments contributed by individual partners. We shall discuss the following methods.

1. Division of net income (or loss) equally
2. Division of net income on a fractional-share basis
3. Division of net income based on the ratio of capital investments
4. Division of net income based on salary allowances
5. Division of net income based on interest allowances

Remember: **If the partnership agreement fails to specify how net income or loss is to be distributed, then net income or loss is shared equally among the partners.**

To illustrate the various methods, we'll look at two examples of each. In the first example of each method, the partnership of Dodd and Easely has a net income of $48,000. In the second example of each method, the partnership has a net loss of $2,000 instead of a net income. We'll use the same balances of the capital accounts for each example, and consider that each method used for the division of net income represents a separate partnership agreement.

The balances of the capital accounts represent the partners' shares in the equity of the business. On December 31, the capital accounts for the partnership of Dodd and Easely have the following balances.

Cindy Dodd, Capital			Robin Easely, Capital	
Dr.	Cr.		Dr.	Cr.
−	+		−	+
	Bal. $55,000			Bal. $35,000

Division of Net Income or Loss Equally

The easiest way to divide a partnership's net income or loss is equally. This method is frequently used when all partners spend the same amount of time in the business, contribute equal amounts of capital, and have similar managerial talents.

Net Income of $48,000

When the partnership has a net income of $48,000, the first step is to divide that amount equally between the two partners.

Dodd's share	$48,000	÷ 2 =	$24,000
Easely's share	$48,000	÷ 2 =	$24,000

The effect of this division of net income is shown in the T accounts that follow.

Cindy Dodd, Capital			Robin Easely, Capital	
Dr.	Cr.		Dr.	Cr.
−	+		−	+
	Bal. $55,000			Bal. $35,000
	Clo. 24,000			Clo. 24,000

The closing entry to record this distribution of net income is shown in Figure 11–1.

GENERAL JOURNAL   PAGE 33

	DATE		DESCRIPTION	POST. REF.	DEBIT	CREDIT	
1	19-- Dec	31	Income Summary		4800000		1
2			Cindy Dodd, Capital			2400000	2
3			Robin Easely, Capital			2400000	3

Figure 11–1. Closing Entry to Distribute Net Income Equally

Net Loss of $2,000

The division of a net loss is calculated in the same manner as the division of a net income.

$$\text{Dodd's share} \quad (\$2,000) \div 2 = (\$1,000)$$
$$\text{Easely's share} \quad (\$2,000) \div 2 = (\$1,000)$$

The effect of this division of net loss on the partners' capital accounts is shown in the following T accounts.

Cindy Dodd, Capital			Robin Easely, Capital	
Dr.	Cr.		Dr.	Cr.
−	+		−	+
Clo. $1,000	Bal. $55,000		Clo. $1,000	Bal. $35,000

The closing entry to record the equal division of the net loss is shown in Figure 11–2.

	GENERAL JOURNAL			PAGE 33	
DATE	DESCRIPTION	POST. REF.	DEBIT	CREDIT	
Dec. 31	Cindy Dodd, Capital		1 000 00		1
	Robin Easely, Capital		1 000 00		2
	Income Summary			2 000 00	3

Figure 11–2. Closing Entry to Distribute Net Loss Equally

Division of Net Income or Loss on a Fractional-Share Basis

The second simplest way to divide net income or loss is to allot each partner a stated fraction of the total. The size of the fraction may take into consideration (1) the amount of each partner's investment, and (2) the value of services rendered by each partner.

Net Income of $48,000

Assume that the partnership agreement stipulates that profits and losses are to be divided this way: three fourths for Dodd and one fourth for Easely. The division of net income would be calculated as follows. The net income amount is multiplied by each partner's fractional share.

$$\text{Dodd's share} \quad \$48,000 \times \frac{3}{4} = \$36,000$$

$$\text{Easely's share} \quad \$48,000 \times \frac{1}{4} = \$12,000$$

This fractional-share division of net income is shown in the T accounts at the top of the next page.

Cindy Dodd, Capital			Robin Easely, Capital	
Dr.	Cr.		Dr.	Cr.
−	+		−	+
	Bal. $55,000			Bal. $35,000
	Clo. 36,000			Clo. 12,000

The division of net income is recorded as a closing entry as shown in Figure 11–3.

GENERAL JOURNAL — PAGE 33

	DATE	DESCRIPTION	POST. REF.	DEBIT	CREDIT	
1	19— Dec. 31	Income Summary		4800000		1
2		Cindy Dodd, Capital			3600000	2
3		Robin Easely, Capital			1200000	3

Figure 11–3. Closing Entry for the Fractional-Share Division of Net Income

Net Loss of $2,000

The net loss is divided just as the net income was divided.

Dodd's share $\quad$ ($2,000) $\times \dfrac{3}{4}$ = ($1,500)

Easely's share $\quad$ ($2,000) $\times \dfrac{1}{4}$ = ($ 500)

This fractional-share division of net loss appears in the T accounts as shown below.

Cindy Dodd, Capital			Robin Easely, Capital	
Dr.	Cr.		Dr.	Cr.
−	+		−	+
Clo. $1,500	Bal. $55,000		Clo. $500	Bal. $35,000

The closing entry for the fractional-share division of the net loss is recorded as shown in Figure 11–4.

GENERAL JOURNAL — PAGE 33

	DATE	DESCRIPTION	POST. REF.	DEBIT	CREDIT	
1	19— Dec. 31	Cindy Dodd, Capital		150000		1
2		Robin Easely, Capital		50000		2
3		Income Summary			200000	3

Figure 11–4. Closing Entry for the Fractional-Share Division of Net Loss

250   Unit 3   Accounting for Partnerships and Corporations

Division of Net Income or Loss Based on the Ratio of Capital Investments

Often, net income or loss is divided among the partners on the basis of their capital investment in the business. This method works well for businesses whose profits are closely related to the amount of money invested, such as businesses that buy and sell real estate. Suppose that Dodd and Easely have agreed to share profits or losses according to the ratio of their investments at the *beginning* of the year. Let's say that Dodd originally invested $50,000 and Easely $30,000. The respective shares of the two partners are calculated as follows.

Dodd	$50,000	Dodd's share	$\frac{\$50,000}{\$80,000} = \frac{5}{8}$
Easely	30,000		
Total	$80,000	Easely's share	$\frac{\$30,000}{\$80,000} = \frac{3}{8}$

Net Income of $48,000

The distribution of the net income is determined as follows.

$$\text{Dodd's share} \qquad \$48,000 \times \frac{5}{8} = \$30,000$$

$$\text{Easely's share} \qquad \$48,000 \times \frac{3}{8} = \$18,000$$

The division of net income based on the capital investment ratio is shown in the T accounts that follow.

Cindy Dodd, Capital			Robin Easely, Capital	
Dr.	Cr.		Dr.	Cr.
–	+		–	+
	Bal. $55,000			Bal. $35,000
	Clo. 30,000			Clo. 18,000

The closing entry is shown in Figure 11–5.

	DATE	DESCRIPTION	POST. REF.	DEBIT	CREDIT	
1	19-- Dec. 31	Income Summary		48 00 00		1
2		Cindy Dodd, Capital			30 00 00	2
3		Robin Easely, Capital			18 00 00	3

GENERAL JOURNAL PAGE 33

Figure 11–5. Closing Entry for the Divison of Net Income Based on Capital Investments Ratio

Net Loss of $2,000

When the partnership has a net loss of $2,000, the distribution of the loss is calculated as follows.

Dodd's share $\quad$ ($2,000) $\times \dfrac{5}{8}$ = ($1,250)

Easely's share $\quad$ ($2,000) $\times \dfrac{3}{8}$ = ($ 750)

The effect of this division of the net loss on the capital accounts is shown in the following T accounts.

Cindy Dodd, Capital	
Dr.	Cr.
–	+
Clo. $1,250	Bal. $55,000

Robin Easely, Capital	
Dr.	Cr.
–	+
Clo. $750	Bal. $35,000

The closing entry for the net loss based on the capital investment ratio is shown in Figure 11–6.

	DATE	DESCRIPTION	POST. REF.	DEBIT	CREDIT	
1	19-- Dec. 31	Cindy Dodd, Capital		1 25 0 00		1
2		Robin Easely, Capital		75 0 00		2
3		Income Summary			2 00 0 00	3

GENERAL JOURNAL PAGE 33

Figure 11–6. Closing Entry for the Division of Net Loss Based on Capital Investments Ratio

Before reading further, do the activity at the top of the next page to check your understanding of how to divide net income or loss based on the ratio of capital investments.

Division of Net Income or Loss Based on Salary Allowances

Partners do not always contribute equally to the partnership. For example, one partner might devote his or her full time to the partnership while another may participate only part time. Further, the services of one partner may be more valuable to the partnership than the services of the other partners. To account for these unequal contributions, some partnership agreements provide for salary allowances to the partners.

Salary allowances are allocations of net income. They are used as a means of recognizing and rewarding differences in ability and time devoted to the business. Salary allowances are not a business expense nor are they the same as withdrawals by the partners.

Legally, partners do not work for salaries; they invest and work in the partnership in order to share in the business's earnings. As a result, when a partnership agreement provides for salary allowances, the partners must realize that the salary allowances are a means of sharing the profits and losses of the business.

Suppose that Dodd and Easely have a partnership agreement that provides for yearly salary allowances of $12,000 and $8,000, respectively, with the remaining net income to be divided equally. It would also be possible to divide the remainder on the basis of the ratio of capital investments, or any other ratio agreed on by the partners.

Remember: Salary allowances to partners are not expenses of the business. They are allocations of net income or loss.

Net Income of $48,000

To distribute the net income, the salary allowances must first be subtracted from the net income of $48,000. The remaining amount is then divided equally, as shown in the calculations at the top of the next page.

Net income	$48,000
Less salary allowances	
Dodd	$12,000
Easely	8,000 −20,000
Net income after salary allowances	$28,000

$$\$28,000 \div 2 = \$14,000$$

Each partner's share of the net income of $48,000 is determined by adding her or his salary allowance and her or his share of the remaining net income.

Dodd's share	$12,000 + $14,000 = $26,000
Easely's share	$ 8,000 + $14,000 = $22,000

This division of net income is shown in the T accounts that follow.

Cindy Dodd, Capital		Robin Easely, Capital	
Dr.	Cr.	Dr.	Cr.
−	+	−	+
	Bal. $55,000		Bal. $35,000
	Clo. 26,000		Clo. 22,000

The closing entry is shown in Figure 11–7.

	GENERAL JOURNAL			PAGE *33*
DATE	DESCRIPTION	POST. REF.	DEBIT	CREDIT
19-- Dec. 31	Income Summary		48 000 00	
	Cindy Dodd, Capital			26 000 00
	Robin Easely, Capital			22 000 00

Figure 11–7. Closing Entry for the Division of Net Income with Salary Allowances

Net Loss of $2,000

When salary allowances are stipulated in the partnership agreement, they must be allocated (not necessarily paid) regardless of whether there is enough net income to take care of them. The calculation for the partnership's net loss of $2,000 is as follows. The amounts enclosed in parentheses in the following calculations represent *negative* amounts.

Net loss	($ 2,000)
Less salary allowances	
Dodd	$12,000
Easely	8,000 −20,000
Net loss after salary allowances	($22,000)

$$(\$22,000) \div 2 = (\$11,000)$$

Each partner's share of the net loss of $2,000 is determined by adding her or his salary allowance and her or his share of the total net loss.

Dodd's share $12,000 + ($11,000) = $1,000
Easely's share $ 8,000 + ($11,000) = ($3,000)

The distribution of the net loss has the following effect on the owners' capital accounts.

Cindy Dodd, Capital			Robin Easely, Capital	
Dr.	Cr.		Dr.	Cr.
–	+		–	+
	Bal. $55,000		Clo. $3,000	Bal. $35,000
	Clo. 1,000			

Even though there was a $2,000 net loss for the year, Dodd's capital account increased by $1,000. Easely's capital account, however, decreased by $3,000. The closing entry is shown in Figure 11–8.

	DATE	DESCRIPTION	POST. REF.	DEBIT	CREDIT	
1	Dec. 31	Robin Easely, Capital		3 0 0 0 00		1
2		Income Summary			2 0 0 0 00	2
3		Cindy Dodd, Capital			1 0 0 0 00	3

GENERAL JOURNAL   PAGE _33_

Figure 11–8. Closing Entry for the Division of Net Loss with Salary Allowances

Before reading further, do the following activity to check your understanding of how to calculate the division of net income or loss based on salary allowances.

Check Your Learning

Write your answer to the following situation on a sheet of notebook paper.

The partnership agreement of Milo and Bower provides for salary allowances of $19,000 per year for Milo and $17,000 per year for Bower. They share the remaining net income on the basis of three fifths for Milo and two fifths for Bower. If the net income for the year is $38,000, calculate the total share for each partner.

Check your answer with that in the answers section. Re-read the preceding part of the chapter to find the correct answers to any portion of the calculation you may have missed.

Sometimes a partnership agreement provides an allowance for interest on the capital investments of the partners. This provision acts as an incentive for partners not only to leave their investments in the business but even to increase them. For example, suppose that Dodd and Easely, in addition to their salary allowances of $12,000 and $8,000, are allowed 8% interest on their capital balances at the beginning of the fiscal year. The remaining net income is to be divided equally. Interest allowances are also distributions of net income.

Remember: An interest allowance is a distribution of net income. It is calculated on the balances of the partners' capital accounts.

Net Income of $48,000

Under this method, the interest allowances must be calculated first. Dodd's and Easely's capital balances at the beginning of the year were $50,000 and $30,000, respectively.

Dodd's interest allowance	$50,000 × .08 = $4,000
Easely's interest allowance	$30,000 × .08 = $2,400

Then both the salary and interest allowances are subtracted from the net income amount. The remainder is divided equally between the partners.

Net income		$48,000
Less:		
Salary allowances		
($12,000 + $8,000)	$20,000	
Interest allowances		
($4,000 + $2,400)	6,400	−26,400
Net income after salary and		
interest allowances		$21,600

$$\$21,600 \div 2 = \$10,800$$

Each partner's share of the net income is determined by adding the following: salary allowance, interest allowance, and share of remaining net income.

Dodd's share	$12,000 + $4,000 + $10,800 = $26,800
Easely's share	$ 8,000 + $2,400 + $10,800 = $21,200

The distribution of net income has the following effect on the partners' capital accounts.

Cindy Dodd, Capital			Robin Easely, Capital	
Dr.	Cr.		Dr.	Cr.
−	+		−	+
	Bal. $55,000			Bal. $35,000
	Clo. 26,800			Clo. 21,200

The closing entry for this distribution of the net income would appear as in Figure 11–9.

	DATE	DESCRIPTION	POST. REF.	DEBIT	CREDIT	
1	Dec 31	Income Summary		4800000		1
2		Cindy Dodd, Capital			2680000	2
3		Robin Easely, Capital			2120000	3

GENERAL JOURNAL   PAGE 33

Figure 11–9. Closing Entry for the Division of Net Income with Interest Allowances

Net Loss of $2,000

Interest allowances are handled the same way as salary allowances. Both must be allocated, regardless of whether there is enough net income to take care of them.

Net loss		($ 2,000)
Less:		
Salary allowances		
($12,000 + $8,000)	$20,000	
Interest allowances		
($4,000 + $2,400)	6,400	−26,400
Net loss after salary and		
interest allowances		($28,400)

$$($28,400) \div 2 = ($14,200)$$

The total amount to be allocated to each partner's capital account is determined by adding each partner's salary allowance, interest allowance, and proportional share of the total net loss.

Dodd's share $12,000 + $4,000 + ($14,200) = $1,800
Easely's share $ 8,000 + $2,400 + ($14,200) = ($3,800)

The distribution of the net loss and the salary and interest allowances have the following effect on the partners' capital accounts.

Cindy Dodd, Capital		Robin Easely, Capital	
Dr.	Cr.	Dr.	Cr.
−	+	−	+
	Bal. $55,000	Clo. $3,800	Bal. $35,000
	Clo. 1,800		

As you can see, Dodd's capital account is increased by $1,800, but Easely's capital account is decreased by $3,800. The closing entry is shown in Figure 11–10 at the top of the next page.

GENERAL JOURNAL					PAGE 33
DATE	DESCRIPTION	POST. REF.	DEBIT	CREDIT	
19-- Dec. 31	Robin Easely, Capital		3800 00		1
	Income Summary			2000 00	2
	Cindy Dodd, Capital			1800 00	3

Figure 11–10. Closing Entry for the Division of Net Loss with Interest Allowances

Remember: Salary and interest allowances must be allocated to the partners regardless of whether there is enough net income available.

Financial Statements for a Partnership

At the end of the fiscal period, financial statements for the partnership are prepared. For the partnership of Dodd and Easely, these include an income statement, a statement of changes in partners' equity, and a balance sheet. The income statement for a partnership is prepared in the same way as an income statement for a sole proprietorship. The differences in the financial statements for a partnership occur in the statement of changes in partners' equity and the balance sheet.

Statement of Changes in Partners' Equity

Changes in the balances of the partners' capital accounts are recorded in the statement of changes in partners' equity, shown in Figure 11–11. This is just like a statement of changes in owner's equity for a sole proprietorship, except that there is a separate column for each partner.

When the partners make an additional investment during the fiscal period, it is reported immediately below the beginning balances of the capital accounts.

Dodd and Easely
Statement of Changes in Partners' Equity
For the Year Ended December 31, 19--

	Dodd	Easely	Total
Beginning Capital, January 1, 19--	50000 00	30000 00	80000 00
Add: Investments by Partners	5000 00	5000 00	10000 00
Net Income from Operations	26800 00	21200 00	48000 00
Subtotal	81800 00	56200 00	138000 00
Less: Withdrawals by Partners	19000 00	10000 00	29000 00
Ending Capital, December 31, 19--	62800 00	46200 00	109000 00

Figure 11–11. Statement of Changes in Partners' Equity

A partnership does not pay income taxes as a separate entity. Partners have to pay federal income taxes on the basis of their shares of net income from the business. For example, Cindy Dodd's taxable income from the partnership is $26,800, even though she withdrew only $19,000. She lists $26,800 on her personal income tax return.

Balance Sheet

Each partner's capital account is listed separately in the Partners' Equity section of the balance sheet, as shown in Figure 11–12. The balances of the accounts are taken from the statement of changes in partners' equity.

Figure 11–12. Balance Sheet for a Partnership

Summary of Key Points

1. The partnership agreement should specify how the net income or net loss is to be distributed to the partners. If it does not, net income or loss is shared equally.
2. The net income for a partnership can be divided by any of the following methods or by any combination of these methods: equal division, fractional-share basis, ratio of capital investments, salary allowances, and interest allowances.
3. Salary allowances and interest allowances are distributions of net income or loss. They are not business expenses.
4. Salary and interest allowances must be allocated to the partners regardless of whether there is net income available.
5. The financial statements for a partnership include the income statement, statement of changes in partners' equity, and balance sheet.
6. The division of net income or loss among partners is reported on the statement of changes in partners' equity.

Review and Applications

Building Your Accounting Vocabulary

In your own words, write the definition of each of the following accounting terms. Use complete sentences for your definitions.

interest allowance   salary allowance

Reviewing Your Accounting Knowledge

1. What are the differences between the closing entries for a sole proprietorship and those for a partnership?
2. How is net income or loss allocated to partners if there is no method specified in the partnership agreement?
3. Name five methods by which partners can divide the partnership's net income or loss.
4. Under what circumstances might partners choose to divide net income or loss equally rather than by some other method?
5. When net income or loss is divided on a fractional-share basis, what factors are considered in establishing the sizes of the fractions?
6. What is the difference between a salary allowance and salary expense?
7. What is the advantage to the partnership of providing an allowance for interest on the capital investment of the partners?
8. Hunt and Wright are partners who share profits and losses in a 3:2 ratio. If the net income is $64,000, what is each partner's share?
9. What three financial statements are prepared for a partnership at the end of the fiscal period?
10. Must a partnership file a federal income tax return and pay federal income taxes? Explain.

Improving Your Decision-making Skills

Donna Hess and Melissa Akers are forming a partnership to operate an interior decorating business. Both plan to work full time in the firm. Hess will make an initial investment of $30,000 and Akers, $45,000. They are considering the following plans for the division of net income or loss.

1. Division in the same ratio as the balances of their capital accounts
2. Interest of 10% on the balances of their capital accounts at the beginning of the year and the remainder of the net income divided equally
3. Salary allowances of $15,000 to Hess and $13,500 to Akers (according to value of services); interest of 8% on the balances of their capital accounts at the beginning of the year; and the remainder of the net income divided equally

Calculate the division of net income under each of the three plans, assuming a net income of $45,000. Which plan seems to be the fairest? Give reasons for your opinion.

Applying Accounting Procedures

Problem 11-1

John Kennedy, Paul Porter, and Denise Folke are partners in the firm of Avon Fabrics. Their partnership agreement states that profits will be shared equally but does not say anything about how losses are to be allocated. The firm had a net loss of $11,175 for the current fiscal year.

Instructions:

(1) Journalize the closing entry to allocate the net loss among the partners.
(2) Post the closing entry to the partners' capital accounts. The opened accounts are included in the working papers that accompany this textbook.

Problem 11-2

Ted Ames, Karen Boyd, and Betty Cohen are partners in the firm of Milton Garden Center. The balances in their capital accounts on December 31, the end of the fiscal period, are $30,000, $30,000, and $15,000, respectively. According to their partnership agreement, profits and losses are to be shared in a 2:2:1 ratio. The Milton Garden Center had a net profit of $89,700 for the year.

Instructions:

(1) Open the partners' capital accounts in the general ledger, using the balances listed above.
(2) Journalize the closing entry to allocate the net profit among the partners.
(3) Post the closing entry to the partners' capital accounts.

Problem 11-3

Fred Irving and Amy Sharp are partners in the firm of The Jewel Shoppe. The partners started the business on January 1 by investing $50,000 and $60,000, respectively. Their partnership agreement states that profits and losses are to be allocated according to the balance of the capital accounts at the beginning of the year. The balances of their capital accounts at the end of the fiscal period were $45,000 and $62,000, respectively.

The Jewel Shoppe had a net profit of $22,000 at the end of its first year of operations.

Instructions:

(1) Open the partners' capital accounts in the general ledger, using the December 31 balances.

(2) Journalize the closing entry to allocate the net profit between the partners.

(3) Post the closing entry to the partners' capital accounts.

Problem 11–4

Larry Kline and Nadine Simpson are partners in the firm of Marathon Delivery Service. The balances of their capital accounts on December 31 are $32,000 and $29,000, respectively.

The partnership agreement states that Kline is to receive a salary allowance of $12,000 and Simpson a salary allowance of $15,000. The partnership agreement also provides for an interest allowance of 8% on the balances of the capital accounts at the end of the period. The remaining profits are to be divided equally.

Marathon Delivery Service had a net profit of $32,000 for the current fiscal period.

Instructions:

(1) Open the partners' capital accounts in the general ledger, using the December 31 balances.

(2) Journalize the closing entry to allocate the net profit between the partners.

(3) Post the closing entry to the partners' capital accounts.

Problem 11–5

Cindy Taylor and David Sanders plan to form a partnership to operate a picture framing business. Taylor plans to work in the firm on a full-time basis, while Sanders will work part time. Taylor's initial investment is $27,000 and Sanders' investment is $39,000. They are considering the following plans for the division of profits and losses.

(a) Division in the same ratio as their capital accounts.

(b) Interest of 9% on the balances of their capital accounts at the beginning of the year and the remainder divided equally.

(c) Salary allowances of $18,000 to Taylor and $13,000 to Sanders, interest of 9% on the balances of their capital accounts at the beginning of the year, and the remainder divided equally.

Instructions: Use the form provided in the working papers that accompany this textbook. Record the allocation of net profit to the partners if the business earned a profit of $33,000.

Problem 11–6

The partnership of Sandra Dorsey, Ralph Ewell, and Doug Ferguson had a net income of $92,850 for the current year. The balances in the capital accounts at the beginning of the year were $34,500, $39,000, and $48,000, respectively. At the end of the year, the balances of the partners' withdrawals accounts were $16,500, $19,800, and $18,000, respectively.

The partnership agreement provides for salary allowances as follows: Dorsey, $16,500; Ewell, $21,000; and Ferguson, $18,000. The partnership agreement also provides for an interest allowance of 10% on the balances of the partners' capital accounts at the beginning of the year. The remainder is to be divided equally.

Instructions: Prepare the statement of changes in partners' equity for the partnership of Dorsey, Ewell & Ferguson for the year ended December 31.

Problem 11–7

The following balances appear in the Adjusted Trial Balance section of the work sheet for the partnership of Allman and Watson.

Cash in Bank	$ 3,658	
Accounts Receivable	53,438	
Allowance for Uncollectible Accounts		$ 1,842
Merchandise Inventory	129,452	
Prepaid Insurance	720	
Equipment	73,838	
Accumulated Depreciation—Equipment		45,380
Accounts Payable		67,432
Notes Payable		20,000
Dennis Allman, Capital		60,000
Dennis Allman, Withdrawals	32,000	
Tracy Watson, Capital		48,000
Tracy Watson, Withdrawals	24,000	
Income Summary	141,234	129,452
Sales		700,490
Sales Returns and Allowances	36,838	
Purchases	551,180	
Purchases Discounts		4,220
Purchases Returns and Allowances		25,452
Selling Expenses	37,832	
Administrative Expenses	14,646	
Interest Expense	3,432	

There were no changes in the capital accounts of any of the partners during the year.

The partnership agreement provides for salary allowances of $32,000 for Allman and $28,000 for Watson. It also provides for an interest allowance of 7% on the balances of the capital accounts at the beginning of the year, with the remainder to be divided equally.

Instructions:

(1) Prepare an income statement for the year ended December 31.
(2) Prepare a statement of changes in partners' equity.
(3) Prepare a balance sheet.

12 Corporations: Organization and Capital Stock

There are fewer corporations than sole proprietorships or partnerships. Although corporations are fewer in number, they account for more business activity than the other two combined. Frequently, a firm begins as a sole proprietorship or a partnership. As it grows and prospers, it usually needs more investment capital. As a means of raising that additional capital, the firm incorporates, which allows it to sell stock. In other cases, businesses are organized as corporations from the start. Because of the importance of corporations, everyone entering the business world should be familiar with the corporate form of organization.

In this chapter, you will learn about the characteristics, advantages, and disadvantages of corporations. You will also learn how corporations raise capital and how to journalize transactions for the issuance of stock.

Learning Objectives

When you have completed this chapter, you should be able to

1. Define a corporation and list some of its advantages and disadvantages.

2. Describe the organization and management of a corporation.

3. Describe the different types of capital stock.

4. Journalize transactions for the issuance of par-value and no-par stock.

5. Define the accounting terms presented in this chapter.

New Terms

corporation / stockholders / stock / stock certificate / double taxation / articles of incorporation / charter / privately held corporation / publicly held corporation / dividends / pre-emptive right / authorized capital stock / issued shares / outstanding stock / treasury stock / common stock / par-value stock / no-par stock / preferred stock / stockholders' ledger / legal capital / stated value / stock subscription

The Nature of a Corporation

In 1819 Chief Justice of the U. S. Supreme Court John Marshall defined a corporation as "an artificial being, invisible, intangible, and existing only in contemplation of the law."

A **corporation** is an artificial legal being that may own property, enter into contracts, sue and be sued in the courts, and so forth. In every respect it is a separate legal entity, having a continuous existence apart from that of its owners. The owners of a corporation are called **stockholders**.

In the remaining chapters of this unit, you will learn about for-profit corporations. For-profit corporations issue stock and carry out business activities for the purpose of making profits and distributing the profits to their owners. Not-for-profit corporations are those corporations that do not issue stock or distribute profits, but carry out activities for charitable, educational, or other philanthropic purposes.

Advantages of a Corporation

The corporation offers a number of advantages over the sole proprietorship and the partnership forms of organization.

1. Limited liability. As a separate legal entity, a corporation is responsible for its own debts. All that stockholders can lose is the amount of their investment. Since the stockholders are the owners, this is the most important advantage. On the other hand, the owners of sole proprietorships and partnerships can be held personally liable for the debts of the business.
2. Ease of raising capital. A corporation can raise greater amounts of investment capital than a sole proprietorship or partnership, because a corporation can sell stock. Some corporations have more than one million stockholders. Sole proprietorships and partnerships are limited to the investments of their individual owners.
3. Ease of transferring ownership rights. **Stock**, the shares of ownership in a corporation, can easily be transferred from one person to another without the permission of other stockholders. All that is required for transfer of ownership is to transfer the **stock certificate**, a document that shows how many shares of corporation stock are owned by a particular shareholder. In a partnership, the other partners must approve changes in ownership in order for the business to continue.
4. Continuous existence. The length of life of a corporation is stipulated in its

charter. When the charter expires, it may be renewed. The death, incapacity, or withdrawal of an owner does not affect the life of a corporation. Such a circumstance would cause a partnership to be dissolved or liquidated.

5. No mutual agency. Individual stockholders do not have the power to bind the corporation to contracts, unless a given stockholder is also an officer. Since owners need not participate in management, the corporation is free to employ the managerial talent it believes best to accomplish its objectives.

Disadvantages of a Corporation

The corporation also has a number of disadvantages.

1. Additional taxation. In addition to the usual property and payroll taxes, corporations must pay income taxes and charter fees. Since corporations are separate legal entities, they may be subject to federal and state income taxes in their own names. Part of the corporation's profits may be distributed to the stockholders in the form of dividends. This money is personal income to the stockholders; the stockholders have to pay personal income taxes on it. This is known as the double taxation of corporations. It represents their greatest disadvantage.

    Charter fees (fees paid by the corporation for the right to exist) may be considered additional taxes, because they are paid to a state in return for the issuance of a charter.

2. Government regulation. Since states create corporations by granting charters, states can exercise closer control and supervision over corporations than over sole proprietorships and partnerships. States often regulate even the amount of net income that a corporation may retain, the extent to which it may buy back its own stock, and the amount of real estate it may own. By contrast sole proprietorships and partnerships need only have legal purposes; states impose no further regulations on them.

Forming a Corporation

To organize a corporation, a person or persons must submit an application to the appropriate official (usually the corporation commissioner or secretary of state) of the state in which the company is to be incorporated. The application is called the articles of incorporation. Generally the application must include the following items.

- Name and address of the corporation
- Nature of the business to be conducted
- Amount and description of the capital stock to be issued
- Names and addresses of the subscribers and the amount of stock subscribed by each
- Names of the promoters (or temporary officers) who will serve until the first meeting of the stockholders is held

The articles of incorporation must be signed by three of the promoters and must be accompanied by a charter fee.

When the state officials approve them, the articles of incorporation become the charter of the corporation. Shortly after receiving the charter, the stock subscribers hold a meeting to elect an acting board of directors and to develop bylaws. The charter and the bylaws provide the basic rules for conducting the corporation's affairs. Next, the directors meet to appoint officers to serve as active managers of the business. Then the corporation issues capital stock certificates to the subscribers who have paid in full. Since stockholders have now come into existence, the stockholders can elect a permanent board of directors.

The size of the corporation may vary as to number of stockholders and amounts of investment. It may be a small corporation with only three stockholders and a minimum investment of $1,000. It may be a giant corporation, consisting of more than one million stockholders and an investment of more than a billion dollars. In the small corporation, the three stockholders may also be the directors and officers. A corporation whose ownership is confined to a small group of stockholders is called a privately held corporation. A corporation whose stock is publicly traded on a stock exchange or over the counter is called a publicly held corporation.

Organization Costs

Let us suppose that the Richey Corporation is forming. The organizers hire an accountant to set up the books. The accountant debits the costs of organizing the corporation—such as fees paid to the state, attorneys' fees, promotional costs, travel outlays, costs of printing stock certificates, and so on—to an account entitled Organization Costs. This account is classified as an intangible asset. Intangible assets, which are long term in nature, appear on the balance sheet as a separate category, below plant assets. The Organization Costs account is like the Prepaid Insurance account in that it will eventually be written off as an expense over a period of years. Organization costs are paid only once, although they benefit the corporation during its entire life.

Remember: Organization Costs is classified as an intangible asset. The amount debited to the account will be written off as an expense over a number of years.

Stock Certificates

One necessary element of organization costs is the printing of stock certificates. A corporation issues stock certificates only when the stock has been paid for in full. In a small corporation the certificates often have stubs attached. The certificates and stubs are bound in a stock certificate book, rather like a checkbook. Each certificate must list the name of the stockholder, the number of shares issued, and the date of issuance. The stub must also show the name and address of the stockholder, the number of shares listed on the stock certificate,

Figure 12–1. Stock Certificate

and the date of issuance. Both certificates and stubs are numbered consecutively. An example of a stock certificate is shown in Figure 12–1.

When a transfer of ownership takes place, the stockholder surrenders the stock certificate to the corporation, which cancels it. The corporation also cancels the matching stub and issues one or more new certificates in the place of these documents. This procedure enables the corporation to maintain an up-to-date record of the name of each stockholder and the number of shares owned by each.

Large corporations whose stocks are listed on major stock exchanges are required to have independent registrars and transfer agents maintain their records of stock ownership. Banks and trust companies perform this service.

Management of a Corporation

The stockholders are the owners of the corporation. They delegate authority to the board of directors, who oversee the corporation's affairs. (Generally the directors are also stockholders, although this is not always so.) The board of directors, in turn, delegates authority to the officers, who do the actual work of running the business. The officers themselves may also be members of the board of directors. A typical organization chart for a corporation is shown in Figure 12–2.

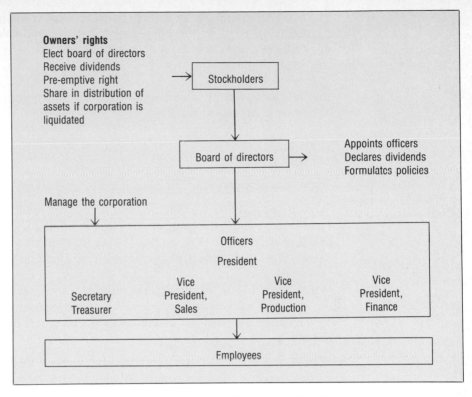

Figure 12–2. Corporation Organization Chart

Dividends are the share of the corporation's earnings distributed to stockholders. The sources of dividends are the current year's net income after income taxes and the retained earnings of prior years.

Suppose the Richey Corporation issues additional stock. Each original stockholder then has the right to subscribe to, or purchase, additional shares, in proportion to his or her present holding. This is known as the stockholders' **pre-emptive right**. For example, assume that the corporation's new issue consists of 1,000 shares. The number of shares of stock originally issued was 10,000 shares, of which Laura Tickner owns 2,000. She currently owns one fifth (2,000 ÷ 10,000) of the total number of shares issued. Therefore, she has the right to subscribe to 200 shares (1,000 shares × ⅕) of the new issue.

Stockholders' Equity

Ownership equity in a corporation is called *stockholders' equity*. Just as in sole proprietorships and partnerships, stockholders' equity represents the value of the owners' claims to the assets of the firm. Of the five major classifications of accounts, the main difference with corporations occurs in the stockholders' equity classification. The Capital Stock account summarizes the owners' original investment, and the Retained Earnings account is used to summarize earnings held by the business and not distributed as dividends.

Remember: **Ownership equity in a corporation consists of capital stock (the total amount invested in the corporation by stockholders) and retained earnings (the earnings kept by a corporation and not distributed to stockholders as dividends).**

Before reading further, do the following activity to check your understanding of corporate organization.

Check Your Learning

Write your answers to the following questions on a sheet of notebook paper.

1. What is meant by the double taxation of corporations?
2. Rose Burke owns 500 shares of stock in the Bradbury Corporation, which has already issued 10,000 shares. The company plans to issue 2,000 more shares. How many shares of stock does Rose Burke have the right to subscribe to?
3. Which stockholders' equity account represents the total amount invested in the company by stockholders? Which account represents the amount held by the corporation and not distributed to stockholders in the form of dividends?

Check your answers with those in the answers section. Re-read the preceding part of the chapter to find the correct answers to any questions you may have missed.

Capital Stock

The shares of ownership in a corporation are referred to as *capital stock*. Authorized capital stock is the maximum number of shares a corporation may sell, according to its charter. Issued shares are those shares sold to the stockholders. Stock that is actually in the hands of stockholders is called outstanding stock.

Occasionally, a corporation may reacquire some of the stock it has issued by buying it back or by receiving it as a donation from someone. This reacquired stock is known as treasury stock. As a result, the number of shares that have been issued may differ from the number of shares outstanding.

Classes of Capital Stock

In order to appeal to as many investors as possible, a corporation may issue more than one kind of capital stock, just as a manufacturer of refrigerators may make different models to please different groups of potential buyers. The two main types of capital stock are common and preferred. Each type may have a variety of characteristics.

Common Stock

When a corporation issues only one type of stock, it is called common stock. Holders of common stock have all the rights listed in Figure 12–2. In addition, common stockholders may vote on issues at the corporation's annual meetings. They are allowed one vote for each share of stock owned. Common stock may be either par or no-par stock. Par-value stock is stock that has a face value printed on the stock certificates, such as $50. No-par stock is stock that does not have a value printed on the stock certificates.

Preferred Stock

As its name implies, preferred stock has certain preferences over common stock. Preferred stock is generally par-value stock and is preferred in two ways: (1) the corporation pays dividends to preferred stockholders before it pays them to common stockholders, and (2) it pays them at a uniform, stated rate. The dividend on preferred stock is stated as a percentage of the par value of the stock; for example, 8%. (The stock itself is then referred to as "Preferred 8% Stock.") If the corporation is liquidated, holders of preferred stock receive their share of the corporation's assets before holders of common stock. In most circumstances, however, holders of preferred stock do not have voting privileges. There are several specific types of preferred stock.

Cumulative and Noncumulative Preferred Stock

Suppose that a corporation has a bad year and finds that it is not able to pay the dividend on its preferred stock. (This is known as passing a dividend.) Stockholders who own *cumulative preferred stock* accumulate any dividends passed in former years. The corporation must pay these dividends in full before it can pay any dividends to common stockholders. If stockholders own *noncumulative preferred stock,* any passed dividends owed do not accumulate. In other words, if the corporation passes a dividend, it is gone forever. Since preferred stockholders naturally want a regular dividend, most preferred stock is cumulative.

Participating and Nonparticipating Preferred Stock

As mentioned earlier, the dividend on preferred stock consists of a set percentage of the par value of that stock. Some preferred stock, however, provides for dividends in excess of this established amount. This kind of preferred stock is called *participating preferred stock*. Holders of participating preferred stock first receive their regular dividend. Next, the corporation allocates a certain amount to holders of its common stock. Then the holders of participating preferred stock are allowed to participate, or share, in any further distributions. The dividends of *nonparticipating preferred stock,* on the other hand, are limited to the regular rate. Most preferred stock is nonparticipating.

Remember: **The capital stock of a corporation may consist of both common stock and preferred stock.**

Issuing Stock

Stock is issued when the buyer has paid for it in full or when the corporation has received noncash assets in exchange for the stock. Let us first discuss the issuance of par-value stock and then the issuance of no-par stock.

Issuing Stock at Par for Cash

A separate general ledger account is maintained for each class of stock, for example, Common Stock and Preferred 8% Stock. The capital stock accounts are used to record the par value of the stock issued. When stock is sold at par for cash, the transaction is recorded as a debit to Cash in Bank and a credit to the appropriate stock account. Remember that par value is the face value printed on each stock certificate.

For example, the Richey Corporation is organized on July 16 with an authorized capital of 4,000 shares of $50-par preferred 8% stock and 20,000 shares of $25-par common stock. On August 1, Richey had the following transaction.

August 1: Issued 1,000 shares of preferred 8% stock at par and 10,000 shares of common stock at par, Memorandum 4.

In this transaction, Richey received a total of $300,000 cash in return for the shares. When stock is sold at its par value, the amount credited to the capital stock account is determined by multiplying the number of shares issued by the par value. In this transaction, therefore, Preferred 8% Stock is credited for $50,000 (1,000 shares × $50) and Common Stock is credited for $250,000 (10,000 shares × $25). Cash in Bank is debited for $300,000, the total amount of cash received.

Cash in Bank		Preferred 8% Stock		Common Stock	
Dr.	Cr.	Dr.	Cr.	Dr.	Cr.
+	−	−	+	−	+
$300,000			$50,000		$250,000

This transaction is shown in general journal form in Figure 12–3. (This transaction could also be recorded in the cash receipts journal.)

GENERAL JOURNAL PAGE 1

	DATE	DESCRIPTION	POST. REF.	DEBIT	CREDIT	
1	Aug. 1	Cash in Bank		300000 00		1
2		Preferred 8% Stock			50000 00	2
3		Common Stock			250000 00	3
4		Memo 4				4

Figure 12–3. Journalizing the Issuance of Stock at Par

Remember: The amount credited to the capital stock account is the par value of the stock issued.

The capital stock accounts (Preferred 8% Stock and Common Stock) are controlling accounts. The subsidiary ledger for each may consist of the stock certificate book, or it may be a supplementary record showing the name and address of each stockholder and the number of shares owned. This is known as a stockholders' ledger

Issuing Stock at Par for Noncash Assets

Corporations often accept assets other than cash in exchange for their stock. The Richey Corporation received equipment, a building, and land from stockholders, in exchange for 2,640 shares of common stock. The journal entry is shown in Figure 12–4.

	DATE	DESCRIPTION	POST. REF.	DEBIT	CREDIT	
1	19-- Aug. 1	Office Equipment		6 000 00		1
2		Building		50 000 00		2
3		Land		10 000 00		3
4		Common Stock			66 000 00	4
5		Memo. 5				5

GENERAL JOURNAL — PAGE 1

Figure 12–4. Journalizing the Issuance of Stock for Noncash Assets

When a corporation accepts an asset other than cash, the asset is recorded at its fair market value. This presents a current balance sheet and provides a realistic base on which to calculate future depreciation.

A corporation may give shares of its stock to its organizers in exchange for their services in organizing the corporation. In this instance, the corporation receives the intangible asset Organization Costs. Suppose that the Richey Corporation issues 200 shares of common stock to its organizers. The journal entry to record this transaction is shown in Figure 12–5.

	DATE	DESCRIPTION	POST. REF.	DEBIT	CREDIT	
1	19-- Aug. 1	Organization Costs		5 000 00		1
2		Common Stock			5 000 00	2
3		Memo. 6				3

GENERAL JOURNAL — PAGE 1

Figure 12–5. Journalizing the Issuance of Stock to Organizers

A corporation, such as the Richey Corporation, generally issues its stock at a price other than par. The price at which stock can be sold is usually influenced by the following factors.

1. The earnings record, financial condition, and dividend record of the corporation
2. The potential for growth in earnings of the corporation
3. The supply of and demand for money for investment purposes in the economy
4. General business conditions and prospects for the future

Issuing stock at a discount, or at a price below its par value, is illegal in most states and rarely occurs. (Only two states still allow corporations to issue stock below par.) It will not, therefore, be discussed in this chapter.

When a corporation issues stock at a price above par value, the stock is said to be issued "in excess of par." This higher price may be due to the fact that the corporation has been successful in the past and has good prospects for growth in the future.

When a corporation issues stock at a price above its par value, Cash in Bank or other noncash asset accounts are debited for the amount of cash received. The capital stock account is credited for the par value of the stock issued. The difference between the amount received and the par value is credited to an account called Paid-in Capital in Excess of Par. Paid-in Capital in Excess of Par is a stockholders' equity account. It appears immediately below the capital stock account in the Paid-in Capital section of the balance sheet. The amounts recorded in this account do not represent a profit to the corporation. Rather, the account represents part of the stockholders' investment in the corporation. A separate paid-in account is kept for each class of stock.

Paid-in Capital
in Excess of Par

Dr.	Cr.
−	+
Decrease Side	Increase Side
	Balance Side

Remember: The Paid-in Capital in Excess of Par account is used to record the difference between the total amount received from stockholders and the par value of the stock issued.

The Richey Corporation had the following transaction.

September 1: *Issued 2,000 shares of $25-par common stock at $28.*

In this transaction, the Richey Corporation received $56,000 for 2,000 shares of common stock (2,000 shares × $28). Before the transaction can be journalized, the corporation must determine how much of the $56,000 should be credited to Common Stock and how much should be credited to Paid-in Capital in Excess of Par. Since the par value of the stock is $25, Richey received an excess of $3 over par for each share, or $6,000.

Common Stock, 2,000 shares @ $25 par = $50,000
Excess, 2,000 shares @ 3.00 per share = 6,000
Total received $56,000

In this transaction, Cash in Bank is debited for $56,000, the total amount of cash received. Common Stock is credited for $50,000, the par value of the 2,000 shares issued. The Paid-in Capital in Excess of Par account is credited for $6,000, the amount of the difference between the cash received and the par value of the stock being issued.

Cash in Bank		Common Stock		Paid-in Capital in Excess of Par—Common	
Dr.	Cr.	Dr.	Cr.	Dr.	Cr.
+	−	−	+	−	+
$56,000			$50,000		$6,000
(2,000 shares			(2,000 shares		(2,000 shares
× $28 each)			× $25 each)		× $3 each)

The transaction is shown in general journal form in Figure 12–6.

GENERAL JOURNAL   PAGE _____

	DATE	DESCRIPTION	POST. REF.	DEBIT	CREDIT	
1	'9— Sept. 1	Cash in Bank		56 00 00		1
2		Common Stock			50 00 00	2
3		Paid-in Cap in Exc. of Par—Common			6 000 00	3
4		Memo. 46				4

Figure 12–6. Journalizing the Issuance of Common Stock in Excess of Par Value

Preferred stock issued at a price above its par value would be recorded in a similar manner. The difference between the total amount of cash received and the total par value of the shares issued would be credited to Paid-in Capital in Excess of Par—Preferred.

Remember: **In the case of par-value stock, the capital stock account is credited for the total par value of the stock issued.**

Before reading further, do the activity at the top of the following page to check your understanding of how to record transactions involving the sale of par-value stock.

No-par Stock

No-par stock, as you recall, does not have a par value printed on the stock certificates. At one time all stock had to have a par value. Today, corporations in all 50 states can issue no-par stock. Some of the advantages claimed for no-par stock are as follows.

1. No-par stock, since it does not have a par value, may be issued at any price.
2. No-par stock prevents confusion on the part of stockholders as to the value of the stock. In the case of par-value stock, investors might believe that the stock is worth the amount printed on the face of the stock certificate.
3. The use of no-par stock results in more realistic values being placed on the noncash assets acquired by the corporation in exchange for stock. As you remember, the business records the noncash assets at values that reflect current market prices. A corporation's directors determine the values of the noncash assets. The use of no-par stock greatly reduces the possibility of placing an inflated, or overestimated, value on the noncash assets.

Stated Value

Because of the limited liability of a corporation, the creditors of a corporation have no claim against the personal assets of stockholders. They must rely solely on the assets of the corporation. To give some protection to creditors, corporations are required to retain in the business a minimum amount of the capital contributed by the stockholders. This amount is called the **legal capital**. Legal capital varies among the states, but it is usually the par value of the shares of capital stock issued. A corporation's legal capital, then, is the amount recorded in its capital stock accounts.

When various state legislatures passed laws permitting corporations to issue no-par stock, they tried to continue to protect creditors by requiring that all or part of the amount the corporation receives for its no-par shares be retained by the corporation. In order to comply with such requirements, the board of directors of a corporation may set a stated value per share on the stock being issued. Stated value is not a true par value, but simply the value assigned to the shares by the board of directors. The board of directors may set whatever stated value it chooses, provided that the state's legal capital requirements have been met.

If a corporation issues no-par stock with a stated value, the corporation may choose to record the total amount received in the Common Stock account. The corporation may also choose to record any amount received over the stated value in a separate paid-in capital account. If the second method is chosen, the journal entries are very similar to those recorded when par-value common stock is issued in excess of par.

Remember: **The stated value of no-par stock is the value that has been assigned to the stock by the board of directors.**

Issuing No-par Stock Without a Stated Value

If a corporation issues no-par stock without a stated value, the entire amount the corporation receives for the stock is credited to the capital stock account.

For example, the Malone Corporation is authorized to issue 25,000 shares of no-par stock without a stated value. On April 30 the Malone Corporation issued 1,000 shares of no-par stock at $49 per share. On May 10 it issued an additional 1,000 shares at $51 per share. In both instances, the total amount the corporation received for its stock is credited to the Common Stock account. These transactions are recorded in general journal form in Figure 12–7.

	DATE	DESCRIPTION	POST. REF.	DEBIT	CREDIT	
1	Apr. 30	Cash in Bank		49 00 0 00		1
2		Common Stock			49 00 0 00	2
3		Memo. 67				3
15	May 10	Cash in Bank		51 00 0 00		15
16		Common Stock			51 00 0 00	16
17		Memo. 73				17

GENERAL JOURNAL — PAGE 2

Figure 12–7. Journalizing the Issuance of No-par Stock Without a Stated Value

Issuing No-par Stock in Excess of Stated Value

Augusta Modern Homes is authorized to issue 50,000 shares of no-par stock. The board of directors of Augusta Modern Homes chose a stated value of $25 per share for its no-par common stock. The corporation has also decided to record any amount received over the stated value in a separate paid-in capital account. Augusta had the following stock transactions.

June 20: Issued 1,000 shares of no-par common stock (stated value $25) at $28 per share, receiving cash, Memorandum 68.

September 10: Issued 1,000 shares of no-par common stock at $30 per share, receiving cash, Memorandum 91.

These transactions are similar to the issuance of par-value stock in excess of par. Just as for par-value stock, the excess is credited to a separate stockholders' equity account, Paid-in Capital in Excess of Stated Value. For example, in the June 20 transaction, Cash in Bank is debited for the total amount of cash received, $28,000. The Common Stock account is credited for the stated value of the shares issued, $25,000. The amount received in excess of the stated value, $3,000 ($3 per share), is credited to Paid-in Capital in Excess of Stated Value. The September 10 transaction is handled in the same way, as shown in the following T accounts.

Cash in Bank		Common Stock		Paid-in Capital in Excess of Stated Value	
Dr.	Cr.	Dr.	Cr.	Dr.	Cr.
+	−	−	+	−	+
$28,000			$25,000		$3,000
30,000			25,000		5,000

The entries to record these transactions are shown in general journal form in Figure 12–8.

GENERAL JOURNAL — PAGE 2

DATE	DESCRIPTION	POST. REF.	DEBIT	CREDIT
19-- June 20	Cash in Bank		28 000 00	
	Common Stock			25 000 00
	Paid-in Cap. in Exc. of Stated Value			3 000 00
	Memo. 68			
Sept. 10	Cash in Bank		30 000 00	
	Common Stock			25 000 00
	Paid-in Cap. in Exc. of Stated Value			5 000 00
	Memo. 41			

Figure 12–8. Journalizing the Issuance of No-par Stock in Excess of Stated Value

Remember: **The Paid-in Capital in Excess of Stated Value account may be used to record the difference between the total amount received from stockholders and the stated value of the no-par stock issued.**

Now let's compare the accounting for no-par stock with a stated value and the accounting for par-value stock. When a firm issues no-par stock with a stated value, the account Paid-in Capital in Excess of Stated Value is used instead of Paid-in Capital in Excess of Par. Although the two accounts are similar, there is a definite distinction between par value and stated value. The corporation's charter sets the par value of its stock. The corporation can change this value only with the approval of the state. On the other hand, the board of directors of a corporation can change the stated value of no-par stock by passing a resolution.

Stock Subscriptions

A corporation often sells its stock directly to investors on a contract (installment) basis. Under this procedure, known as a stock subscription, the investor enters into a contract with the corporation. The subscriber promises to pay at a later date for a specified number of shares at an agreed price. The corporation agrees to issue the shares when the investor has finished paying for them in full.

The amount of the subscription represents an asset to the corporation. Therefore, the amount of the subscription is debited to a current asset account called Subscriptions Receivable. The total par value or stated value of the stock is credited to Common Stock Subscribed, a temporary stockholders' equity account. This account represents the par or stated value of the stock not yet fully paid for and issued. The difference between the subscription price and the par value or stated value is recorded in the paid-in capital account.

As the investor sends in payments, they are recorded as debits to Cash in Bank and credits to Subscriptions Receivable. When the investor finishes paying for all the shares in full, the stock is issued. The entry is recorded as a debit to Common Stock Subscribed and a credit to the capital stock account. When corporations have investors who want subscriptions to both common and preferred stock, separate accounts are kept for each class of stock; for example, Common Stock Subscribed and Preferred 8% Stock Subscribed. Let's look at some examples.

Remember: The Common Stock Subscribed account is a temporary stockholders' equity account. It is used to record the par or stated value of the stock subscribed to but not yet issued.

Subscription Transactions for No-par Stock

The Reikert Manufacturing Corporation, a newly organized company, had the following stock subscription transactions.

May 1: Received subscriptions to 10,000 shares of no-par common stock (stated value $10 per share) from various subscribers at $16 per share, with a down payment of 50% of the subscription price, Memorandum 27.

Two journal entries are required to record this transaction. The first entry records the total stock subscription. The second entry records the receipt of one half of the subscription price from the subscribers.

The entries to record these transactions are shown in general journal form in Figure 12–9.

GENERAL JOURNAL PAGE 2

	DATE		DESCRIPTION	POST. REF.	DEBIT	CREDIT	
1	19-- May	1	Sub. Rec.- Common Stock		160 00 00		1
2			Common Stock Subscribed			100 00 00	2
3			Paid-in Cap. in Exc. of Stated Value			60 00 00	3
4			Memo. 27				4
5		1	Cash in Bank		80 00 00		5
6			Sub. Rec.-Common Stock			80 00 00	6
7			Memo. 27				7

Figure 12–9. Journalizing the Subscription of No-par Stock

In June, Reikert received an additional portion of the subscription price from subscribers.

June 1: *Received an additional 30% of the subscription price from all subscribers, Memorandum 35.*

The entry to record this transaction is shown in general journal form in Figure 12–10.

GENERAL JOURNAL PAGE 3

	DATE		DESCRIPTION	POST. REF.	DEBIT	CREDIT	
1	19-- June	1	Cash in Bank		48 00 00		1
2			Sub. Rec.-Common Stock			48 00 00	2
3			Memo. 35				3

Figure 12–10. Journalizing the Receipt of Payment on a Stock Subscription

Finally, in July, Reikert received the balance of the subscription price due from subscribers. Only when the stock has been completely paid for will the corporation issue the stock.

July 1: *Received the final 20% of the subscription price from all subscribers; issued 10,000 shares of no-par stock, Memorandum 43.*

Again, two journal entries are required to record this transaction. In the first journal entry, the receipt of the final payment of $32,000 due from subscribers is recorded. In the second journal entry, the issuance of the 10,000 shares of no-par stock by the corporation is recorded. The effects of this transaction—as well as the effects of the earlier stock subscription transactions—are shown in the T accounts at the top of the next page.

Cash in Bank		Subscriptions Receivable— Common Stock		Common Stock	
Dr.	Cr.	Dr.	Cr.	Dr.	Cr.
+	−	+	−	−	+
$80,000		$160,000	$80,000		$100,000
48,000			48,000		
32,000			32,000		

Common Stock Subscribed		Paid-in Capital in Excess of Stated Value	
Dr.	Cr.	Dr.	Cr.
−	+	−	+
$100,000	$100,000		$60,000

The entries to record these transactions are shown in general journal form in Figure 12–11.

GENERAL JOURNAL   PAGE 4

	DATE	DESCRIPTION	POST. REF.	DEBIT	CREDIT	
1	19— July 1	Cash in Bank		32 000 00		1
2		Sub. Rec. – Common Stock			32 000 00	2
3		Memo. 43				3
4	1	Common Stock Subscribed		100 000 00		4
5		Common Stock			100 000 00	5
6		Memo. 43				6

Figure 12–11. Journalizing the Final Payment on a Stock Subscription and the Issuance of Stock

Common Stock Subscribed, remember, represents the total par value or stated value of the shares subscribed. It is used to record the shares that have been subscribed for, but not yet paid for in full. When the investors have completely paid for all the shares, the firm records the issuing of the stock by debiting the Common Stock Subscribed account and crediting the Common Stock account.

Subscription Transactions for Par-value Stock

The Fidelity Service Corporation, a newly organized company, had the following subscription transactions involving its preferred stock.

June 15: Received subscriptions to 2,000 shares of preferred 9% stock ($100 par value) from various subscribers at $103 per share, with a down payment of 40% of the subscription price, Memorandum 72.

The entries to record this transaction are shown in general journal form in Figure 12–12 on the next page.

DATE	DESCRIPTION	POST. REF.	DEBIT	CREDIT	
19-- June 15	Sub. Rec. - Preferred 9% Stock		206 000 00		1
	Preferred 9% Stock Subscribed			200 000 00	2
	Paid-in Cap. in Exc. of Par-Preferred			6 000 00	3
	Memo. 72				4
15	Cash in Bank		82 400 00		5
	Sub. Rec.-Preferred 9% Stock			82 400 00	6
	Memo. 72				7

Figure 12-12. Journalizing the Subscription of Preferred Stock

July 1: *Received 30% of the subscription price from all subscribers (2,000 shares), Memorandum 89.*

The entry to record this is shown in general journal form in Figure 12-13.

DATE	DESCRIPTION	POST. REF.	DEBIT	CREDIT	
19-- July 1	Cash in Bank		61 800 00		1
	Sub. Rec.-Preferred 9% Stock			61 800 00	2
	Memo. 89				3

Figure 12-13. Journalizing the Receipt of Payment on a Preferred Stock Subscription

July 15: *Received 30% of the subscription price from subscribers to 500 shares; issued 500 shares of preferred 9% stock, Memorandum 103.*

The entries to record this transaction are shown in general journal form in Figure 12-14.

DATE	DESCRIPTION	POST. REF.	DEBIT	CREDIT	
19-- July 15	Cash in Bank		15 450 00		1
	Sub. Rec.-Preferred 9% Stock			15 450 00	2
	Memo. 103				3
15	Preferred 9% Stock Subscribed		50 000 00		4
	Preferred 9% Stock			50 000 00	5
	Memo. 103				6

Figure 12-14. Journalizing the Final Payment on a Portion of a Preferred Stock Subscription

These transactions show that the Preferred 9% Stock Subscribed account represents the total par value of the shares subscribed. It also points up the fact that a firm does not issue stock until the investor has paid for it in full. Since only 500 shares were paid for in full, Fidelity issued only 500 shares.

Before reading further, do the following activity to check your understanding of how to record transactions involving stock subscriptions.

Check Your Learning

On a separate piece of paper, describe the five transactions recorded in the following T accounts of Finch Cedar Shingle Company, Inc. Match the bold numbers in parentheses to determine the amount of the transaction.

Cash in Bank		Subscriptions Receivable— Common Stock		Common Stock	
Dr.	Cr.	Dr.	Cr.	Dr.	Cr.
+	–	+	–	–	+
(1) $14,000		(2) $26,000	(3) $14,800		(1) $10,000
(3) 14,800			(4) 11,200		(5) 20,000
(4) 11,200					

Common Stock Subscribed		Paid-in Capital in Excess of Stated Value	
Dr.	Cr.	Dr.	Cr.
–	+	–	+
(5) $20,000	(2) $20,000		(1) $4,000
			(2) 6,000

Check your answers with those in the answers section. Re-read the preceding part of the chapter to find the correct answers to any questions you may have missed.

Controlling Accounts and Subsidiary Ledgers

Because investors may finish paying for subscriptions at varying times and because a firm issues stock only when the individual subscriber has paid in full, the firm has to maintain an account for each individual subscriber. As a result, the Subscriptions Receivable accounts are controlling accounts with subsidiary ledgers, as shown below.

Controlling Account	Subsidiary Ledger
Subscriptions Receivable—Preferred 9% Stock	Preferred 9% Stock Subscribers' Ledger
Subscriptions Receivable—Common Stock	Common Stock Subscribers' Ledger

This is similar to the Accounts Receivable controlling account and the accounts receivable subsidiary ledger.

The firm also has to keep an accurate record of the number of shares owned by each stockholder. Consequently, each capital stock account is also a controlling account, as shown below.

Controlling Account	Subsidiary Ledger
Preferred 9% Stock	Preferred 9% Stockholders' Ledger
Common Stock	Common Stockholders' Ledger

As we have said, a small corporation may use its stock certificate book as a subsidiary ledger. The information must be complete so that the company can declare and pay dividends correctly. Dividends are paid on outstanding stock only.

Reporting Stock on a Corporation Balance Sheet

The balance sheet for the Richey Corporation, illustrated in Figure 12–15, shows the placement of the various accounts related to capital stock that were introduced in this chapter. The Subscriptions Receivable accounts are listed in the Current Assets section of the balance sheet. The capital stock accounts are listed under the Paid-in Capital heading of the Stockholders' Equity section. Notice that each stock account lists the par value, the number of shares authorized, and the number of shares issued. Preferred stock and its related subscription and premium accounts are always listed before common stock. Preferred stock is assumed to be noncumulative and nonparticipating, unless otherwise stated.

Summary of Key Points

1. A corporation is defined as "an artificial being, invisible, intangible, and existing only in the contemplation of the law."
2. As a form of business organization, the corporation has the following advantages over a sole proprietorship or a partnership: limited liability of stockholders, ease of raising capital, ease of transferring ownership rights, continuous existence, and no mutual agency.
3. The disadvantages of a corporation are additional taxation and government regulation.
4. In a corporation, the stockholders—the owners of the corporation—elect the board of directors. The board of directors in turn appoints the officers to manage the corporation.
5. Ownership equity in a corporation is called stockholders' equity. Stockholders' equity consists of capital stock (the amount invested in the corporation by stockholders, including additional paid-in capital) and retained earnings (the earnings held by the corporation and not distributed to stockholders as dividends).
6. There are two types of capital stock: common stock and preferred stock.

Figure 12–15.
Corporate
Balance Sheet

Richey Corporation
Balance Sheet
June 30, 19—

Assets

Current Assets:

Cash		$ 48,000
Accounts Receivable	$219,000	
Less: Allowance for Uncollectible Accounts	2,380	216,620
Subscriptions Receivable—Preferred 8% Stock		14,000
Subscriptions Receivable—Common Stock		30,000
Merchandise Inventory		179,000
Supplies		3,000
Prepaid Insurance		500
Total Current Assets		$491,120

Property, Plant, and Equipment:

Delivery Equipment	$ 60,000		
Less Accumulated Depreciation	7,200	$ 52,800	
Store Equipment	$ 82,000		
Less Accumulated Depreciation	9,840	72,160	
Office Equipment	$ 12,000		
Less Accumulated Depreciation	1,440	10,560	
Building	$ 50,000		
Less Accumulated Depreciation	2,000	48,000	
Land		10,000	
Total Property, Plant, and Equipment			193,520

Intangible Assets:

Organization Costs		5,000
Total Assets		$689,640

Liabilities

Notes Payable		$ 20,000
Accounts Payable		82,150
Salaries Payable		3,000
Interest Payable		1,000
Corporate Income Tax Payable		6,100
Total Liabilities		$112,250

Stockholders' Equity

Paid-in Capital:

Preferred 8% Stock, $50 par (4,000 shares authorized, 1,000 shares issued)	$ 50,000	
Preferred 8% Stock Subscribed (500 shares)	25,000	
Paid-in Capital in Excess of Par—Preferred	1,500	$ 76,500
Common Stock, $25 par (20,000 shares authorized, 14,840 shares issued)	$371,000	
Common Stock Subscribed (1,000 shares)	25,000	
Paid-in Capital in Excess of Par—Common	15,000	411,000
Total Paid-in Capital		$487,500
Retained Earnings		89,890
Total Stockholders' Equity		577,390
Total Liabilities and Stockholders' Equity		$689,640

Preferred stock has a preference over common stock in receiving dividends. Preferred stockholders, however, do not usually have voting privileges.

7. Par-value stock is stock that has a certain value printed on the stock certificate. No-par stock does not have a value printed on the stock certificate. No-par stock may or may not have a stated value, a value assigned by the corporation's board of directors.

8. When stock is issued at a price above its par or stated value, the difference between the total amount received and the par or stated value of the stock is credited to the Paid-in Capital in Excess of Par (or Stated Value) account.

9. Corporations may issue stock to investors on a subscription basis. The amount to be received from subscribers is debited to the Subscriptions Receivable account, an account similar to Accounts Receivable.

10. Stock is not issued by a corporation until it has been paid for in full.

11. Separate general ledger accounts are maintained for the different classes of capital stock and for their related premium and subscription accounts.

Review and Applications

Building Your Accounting Vocabulary

In your own words, write the definition of each of the following accounting terms. Use complete sentences for your definitions.

articles of
  incorporation
authorized capital
  stock
charter
common stock
corporation
dividends
double taxation

issued shares
legal capital
no-par stock
outstanding stock
par-value stock
pre-emptive right
preferred stock
privately held
  corporation

publicly held
  corporation
stated value
  stock
stock certificate
stockholders
stockholders' ledger
stock subscription
treasury stock

Reviewing Your Accounting Knowledge

1. In what respect is a corporation a separate legal entity?
2. List at least two advantages and two disadvantages of the corporate form of business organization. In your opinion, which is the greatest advantage and the greatest disadvantage?
3. List three types of organization costs. How is Organization Costs classified? What eventually happens to Organization Costs?
4. What is the difference between capital stock and retained earnings?
5. What is the difference between issued stock and outstanding stock?
6. What advantages do preferred stockholders have over common stockholders? What disadvantages do they have?
7. If a corporation sells its stock at a price above par, does the amount of the excess represent revenue to the firm?
8. What is the difference between par value and stated value?
9. What is a stock subscription?
10. What is the purpose of the Common Stock Subscribed account? What happens to the account?

Improving Your Decision-making Skills

Case 1

Barbara Baker, Carl Owens, and John Young each own their own businesses. They would like to combine their various talents and operate one business. They have been considering forming a partnership. However, their lawyers have suggested that they form a corporation. What reasons would the lawyers have given them for forming a corporation rather than a partnership?

Case 2

Laws do not limit the amount partners may withdraw from a partnership. However, various state laws do place a limit on the amounts corporations may withdraw in the form of dividends. Why is there a difference?

Applying Accounting Procedures

Problem 12-1

Dick Carlson, Joanne Potter, and Irene Draper have formed a corporation, Sports, Inc. The corporation is authorized to issue 10,000 shares of no-par stock with a stated value of $20.

The three incorporators are to receive shares of stock in exchange for assets contributed to the corporation. Carlson will provide $10,000 worth of merchandise. Potter will provide $7,500 in office equipment. Draper will provide $9,500 worth of store equipment. In addition, Potter will pay the organization costs of $3,200 in return for additional shares of stock.

Instructions: Based on this information, how much stock should be issued to each person?

Problem 12-2

Pinecrest Estates, organized on February 7 of this year, was authorized to issue 700 shares of $100-par cumulative preferred 8% stock and 7,000 shares of $25-par common stock. The following transactions were completed during Pinecrest's first year of operation.

Feb.   7   Issued 3,000 shares of common stock at par for cash, Memorandum 105.

       7   Issued 70 shares of common stock to an attorney, Paula Kerr, in return for legal services during the incorporation, Memorandum 106.

May   6   Issued 500 shares of preferred stock at par for cash, Memorandum 235.

Aug.   6   Issued 2,200 shares of common stock in exchange for land with a fair market value of $55,000, Memorandum 351.

Instructions: Record the transactions, in general journal form, on page 1 of a general journal.

Problem 12-3

The Midwest Implement Company, Inc, has authorized capital consisting of 1,500 shares of $50-par preferred 9% stock and 15,000 shares of $10-par common stock. During its first year of operations, Midwest Implement completed the following transactions that affected stockholders' equity.

Mar.	1	Issued 3,000 shares of common stock at par for cash, Memorandum 106.
	1	Acquired equipment valued at $39,000 in exchange for 3,900 shares of common stock, Memorandum 107.
	1	Acquired land and a building in exchange for shares of common stock. The land is valued at $14,250 and the building at $57,750. There is an outstanding mortgage on the property of $24,000, held by Commercial Savings and Loan Association. The corporation assumed responsibility for the mortgage, Memorandum 108.
	4	Paid an attorney $3,600 for paying the charter fees and for legal services to incorporate the firm, Check 1015.
	6	Issued 75 shares of common stock at par in exchange for promotional services, Memorandum 116.
Apr.	9	Issued 600 shares of preferred 9% stock at $52 per share for cash, Memorandum 133.
May	27	Issued 450 shares of preferred 9% stock at $51 per share for cash, Memorandum 170.
	29	Issued 500 shares of common stock at $12 for cash, Memorandum 173.

Instructions: Record the transactions on page 3 of a general journal.

Problem 12–4

The Kendall Refrigeration and Air Conditioning Company, Inc. is authorized to issue 3,000 shares of $100-par preferred 8% stock and 37,500 shares of $25-par common stock. Kendall completed the following transactions concerning stock subscriptions.

May	6	Received subscriptions to 12,000 shares of common stock at $25 per share; collected 60% of the subscription price, Memorandum 415.
June	6	Subscribers to 12,000 shares of common stock paid an additional 20% of the subscription price, Memorandum 454.
July	6	Received an additional 20% of the subscription price from all subscribers; issued 12,000 shares of stock, Memorandum 480.
Sept.	11	Received subscriptions to 3,000 shares of common stock at $26 per share; collected 50% of the subscription price, Memorandum 532.
Oct.	19	Received subscriptions to 300 shares of preferred 8% stock at $105 per share; collected 20% of the subscription price, Memorandum 558.

Instructions: Record these transactions on page 29 of a general journal.

Problem 12–5

The Woodward Bakery was incorporated on October 1 of this year with authorized capital as follows: 1,500 shares of $50-par preferred 8% stock and 30,000 shares of no-par common stock with a stated value of $5. During the first year of operations, the Woodward Bakery completed the following transactions.

Oct. 2 Received subscriptions to 6,000 shares of no-par stock at $12 per share, collecting 30% of the subscription price from all subscribers, Memorandum 104.

2 Acquired equipment valued at $36,000 in exchange for 2,000 shares of no-par stock, Memorandum 105.

14 Subscribers to 6,000 shares of no-par stock paid an additional 30% of the subscription price, Memorandum 117.

16 Issued 150 shares of no-par stock in return for promotional services valued at $1,800, Memorandum 119.

20 Received subscriptions to 600 shares of preferred 8% stock at $53 per share, collecting 40% of the subscription price, Memorandum 123.

23 Paid an attorney $1,960 for paying charter fees and for legal services needed for incorporating the firm, Check 1152.

30 Subscribers to 6,000 shares of no-par stock paid the remaining 40% of the subscription price; issued the 6,000 shares, Memorandum 134.

Nov. 5 Received subscriptions to 3,000 shares of no-par stock at $14 per share, collecting 50% of the subscription price, Memorandum 140.

10 Subscribers to 600 shares of preferred 8% stock paid an additional 30% of the subscription price, Memorandum 145.

16 Sold 150 shares of preferred 8% stock at $51 per share for cash, Memorandum 151.

25 Subscribers to 3,000 shares of no-par stock paid the remaining 50% of the subscription price; issued the 3,000 shares, Memorandum 160.

Instructions: Record the above transactions on page 51 of a general journal.

Problem 12–6

The Fleming Corporation's charter authorized it to issue 1,200 shares of $50-par preferred 9% stock and 12,000 shares of no-par common stock with a stated value of $10. The following balances are taken from the Balance Sheet section of the work sheet.

Common Stock	$80,000
Common Stock Subscribed (2,000 shares)	20,000
Paid-in Capital in Excess of Stated Value	22,000
Preferred 9% Stock	50,000
Retained Earnings (credit balance)	31,000

Instructions: Prepare the Stockholders' Equity section of the balance sheet as of December 31.

Problem 12–7

Pitts Sporting Goods, Inc., has authorized capital of 1,500 shares of $100-par preferred 9% stock and 15,000 shares of no-par common stock with a stated value of $20. The following account balances are taken from the Balance Sheet section of the work sheet for the fiscal year ended December 31.

Accounts Payable	$281,460
Accounts Receivable	332,760
Accumulated Depreciation—Building	30,900
Accumulated Depreciation—Equipment	62,475
Allowance for Uncollectible Accounts	10,380
Building	192,000
Cash in Bank	41,400
Common Stock	180,000
Common Stock Subscribed	30,000
Equipment	138,000
Land	45,000
Merchandise Inventory	216,750
Mortgage Payable (a long-term liability)	63,000
Notes Payable	24,600
Organization Costs	9,630
Paid-in Capital in Excess of Par—Preferred	2,700
Paid-in Capital in Excess of Stated Value	52,500
Preferred 9% Stock	120,000
Preferred 9% Stock Subscribed	15,000
Retained Earnings	126,000
Subscriptions Receivable—Common Stock	13,050
Subscriptions Receivable—Preferred 9% Stock	7,650
Supplies	2,775

Instructions:

(1) Determine the number of shares of preferred 9% stock subscribed and issued.

(2) Determine the number of shares of no-par stock subscribed and issued.

(3) Prepare a balance sheet. Place the Assets section on the front of the form and the Liabilities and Stockholders' Equity sections on the back of the form.

13 Corporations: Taxes, Dividends, and Retained Earnings

In Chapter 12, you learned how corporations are organized and about the legal requirements that must be met to start a corporation. You also learned that ownership in a corporation is represented by shares of stock. You recorded transactions relating to the issuance of common and preferred stock. You also saw how capital stock is reported in the Stockholders' Equity section of the balance sheet.

In this chapter, we will first look at a situation unique to corporations: the payment of corporate income taxes. Then, we will continue our study of the stockholders' equity of a corporation. You will see how a corporation distributes its earnings to stockholders. You will also see how a corporation acquires and reissues shares of its own stock.

Learning Objectives

When you have completed this chapter, you should be able to

1. Record journal entries for the payment of corporate income taxes.

2. Explain the difference between a cash dividend and a stock dividend.

3. Record journal entries relating to the declaration and payment of dividends.

4. Record journal entries relating to the acquisition and reissue of treasury stock.

5. Define the accounting terms presented in this chapter.

New Terms

taxable income / cash dividend / stock dividend / stock split

Recording and Paying Income Taxes

The net income of a sole proprietorship and the partners' shares of net income of a partnership are taxable as part of the owners' personal incomes. However, since the corporation is a separate legal entity, it must pay income taxes in its own name. Corporations are subject to federal income taxes; most states and many cities also impose an income tax on them. In this chapter, we'll talk just about the income tax levied by the federal government. The same basic principles apply to state and city income taxes.

As you learned earlier, corporations are placed on a pay-as-you-go basis. Most corporations are required to estimate in advance the amount of their federal income taxes for the fiscal year. The corporations must then pay the estimated amount in four installments during the year in which revenues are earned. The installments are due on the 15th day of April, June, September, and December.

At the end of the fiscal year, after the corporation determines the exact amount of its net income, it calculates the actual amount of the income tax. If the amount of income tax the corporation has paid in advance exceeds its tax liability for the year, the firm has made an overpayment. Usually, however, the amount of income tax paid in advance is less than the amount of the tax liability. (Note: The Internal Revenue Service provides income tax rate tables that corporations can use to determine both their estimated and actual income tax liabilities. The federal income tax rates for corporations in effect at the time this book was written were used to calculate the federal income taxes for the various corporations in the chapter.)

Remember: **Corporations are required to pay income taxes on the amount of their net income; sole proprietorships and partnerships are not taxed directly.**

Recording the Payment of Income Taxes

The Cardoza Corporation's fiscal year extends from January 1 through December 31. Its authorized capital consists of 200,000 shares of $20-par common stock. For the fiscal year, the corporation estimated that its net income would be $80,625 and that its income tax would be $18,000. The company must pay this $18,000 in equal quarterly installments during the year. Therefore, on April 15 the Cardoza Corporation had the following transaction.

April 15: *Paid the first quarterly federal income tax installment of $4,500, Check 46.*

In this transaction, the amount of the income tax installment is debited to an expense account called Income Tax Expense. The Cash in Bank account is credited for $4,500. The journal entry for this transaction is shown in Figure 13–1. (This transaction could also be recorded in the cash payments journal.)

	GENERAL JOURNAL			PAGE 4	
DATE	DESCRIPTION	POST. REF.	DEBIT	CREDIT	
19— Apr. 15	Income Tax Expense		4 50 0 00		1
	Cash in Bank			4 50 0 00	2
	Check 146				3

Figure 13–1. Journalizing the Payment of an Income Tax Installment

Similar entries would also be made for the other three installments (in June, September, and December).

Calculating the Adjustment for Income Taxes

At the end of the year, a work sheet is prepared to organize the adjustments and determine the net income for the year. In your study, you have been given the total amount of the income taxes for the year. Knowing that amount, you were able to enter the adjustment on the work sheet along with the other adjustments.

Usually, however, the adjustment for income taxes is determined as the work sheet is being prepared. As an example, let's look at the work sheet for the Cardoza Corporation, shown in Figure 13–2 on pages 296–297. To determine the adjustment for income taxes and complete the work sheet, these steps would be followed.

1. Record the account balances and total the Trial Balance section.
2. Record all adjustments *except* the adjustment for corporate income taxes. Do *not* total the Adjustments columns.
3. Extend all amounts *except* that of Income Tax Expense into the Balance Sheet and Income Statement sections.
4. On a separate sheet of paper, total the amounts listed in the Income Statement Debit and Credit columns. Then tentatively determine the net income before taxes by subtracting the Income Statement Debit total from the Income Statement Credit total. (The objective is to determine the net income in advance and then to calculate the exact amount of the income tax.)

Income Statement Credit	$980,000
Income Statement Debit	−883,375
Net income before taxes	$ 96,625

The Cardoza Corporation's net income before taxes is $96,625.

5. Determine the federal income tax on the net income of $96,625. By using the IRS tax rate table, Cardoza found that its total federal income taxes for the year were $24,400. Since Cardoza had already paid $18,000 during the year, it now owes only $6,400 ($24,400 − $18,000).

6. Record the adjustment for federal income taxes in the Adjustments section of the work sheet. The adjustment is recorded as a debit of $6,400 to Income Tax Expense and a $6,400 credit to Corporate Income Tax Payable. Total the Adjustments section.

7. Extend the amount of the income tax expense to the Income Statement Debit column and the income tax payable amount to the Balance Sheet Credit column.

8. Total the Income Statement and Balance Sheet sections.

9. Determine and record the amount of the net income after taxes, $72,225, and complete the work sheet.

The adjustment for income taxes would be journalized with the other adjusting entries. Income Tax Expense is closed—along with the other expense accounts—into Income Summary.

Remember: At the end of the fiscal period, the adjustment for additional income taxes owed is recorded on the work sheet as a debit to Income Tax Expense and a credit to Corporate Income Tax Payable.

Recording the Payment of the Income Tax Liability

The Cardoza Corporation begins the next fiscal period with an income tax liability of $6,400. It pays the liability on March 15, as shown in Figure 13–3.

		GENERAL JOURNAL			PAGE 12
	DATE	DESCRIPTION	POST. REF.	DEBIT	CREDIT
1	¹⁹⁻⁻ Mar. 15	Corporate Income Tax Payable		6400 00	
2		Cash in Bank			6400 00
3		Check 1462			

Figure 13–3. Journalizing the Payment of the Income Tax Liability

Taxable Income

In this discussion, we've been assuming that the Cardoza Corporation determined its income tax for the year by multiplying its net income for the year by the tax rate. The corporation's net income was its taxable income. Taxable income is the amount on which taxes are assessed. Taxable income is usually sales less various exemptions and deductions specified by law and the IRS.

However, the net income shown on the income statement may differ from the taxable income. Here are some of the reasons why.

	ACCOUNT NAME	TRIAL BALANCE	
		DEBIT	CREDIT
1	Cash in Bank	8 830 00	
2	Accounts Receivable	58 250 00	
3	Allowance for Uncollectible Accounts		320 00
4	Merchandise Inventory	180 500 00	
5	Prepaid Insurance	1 220 00	
6	Store Equipment	44 720 00	
7	Accum. Depreciation—Store Equipment		17 250 00
8	Office Equipment	28 920 00	
9	Accum. Depreciation—Office Equipment		8 410 00
10	Organization Costs	3 000 00	
11	Accounts Payable		56 860 00
12	Corporate Income Tax Payable		
13	Interest Payable		
14	Notes Payable		36 000 00
15	Common Stock		100 000 00
16	Paid-in Capital in Excess of Par		10 000 00
17	Retained Earnings		16 975 00
18	Income Summary		
19	Sales		789 064 00
20	Purchases	589 203 00	
21	Purchases Discounts		1 056 00
22	Selling Expenses	77 376 00	
23	Administrative Expenses	22 316 00	
24			
25			
26			
27	Interest Expense	3 600 00	
28	Income Tax Expense	18 000 00	
29		1 035 935 00	1 035 935 00
30	Net Income after Income Taxes		
31			

Figure 13–2. Work Sheet   (Left side)

1. The depreciation method used for income statement purposes may differ from the method used for income tax purposes. For example, the firm might use the straight-line method of depreciation for its income statement, but ACRS for income tax purposes.

ADJUSTMENTS		INCOME STATEMENT		BALANCE SHEET		
DEBIT	CREDIT	DEBIT	CREDIT	DEBIT	CREDIT	
				8830 00		1
				58250 00		2
	(c) 1680 00				2000 00	3
(b) 189880 00	(a) 180500 00			189880 00		4
	(d) 520 00			700 00		5
				44720 00		6
	(e) 4300 00				21550 00	7
				28920 00		8
	(f) 2760 00				11170 00	9
	(g) 1000 00			2000 00		10
					56860 00	11
	(i) 6400 00				6400 00	12
	(h) 120 00				120 00	13
					36000 00	14
					100000 00	15
					10000 00	16
					16975 00	17
(a) 180500 00	(b) 189880 00	180500 00	189880 00			18
			789064 00			19
		589203 00				20
			1056 00			21
(e) 4300 00		81676 00				22
(c) 1680 00		28276 00				23
(d) 520 00						24
(f) 2760 00						25
(g) 1000 00						26
(h) 120 00		3720 00				27
(i) 6400 00		24400 00				28
38716 00	38716 00	907775 00	980000 00	333300 00	261075 00	29
		72225 00			72225 00	30
		980000 00	980000 00	333300 00	333300 00	31

(Right side)

2. A firm may include certain types of revenue in the income statement, but not in the tax return. For example, in the income statement, the firm may account for the total installment sales. On the tax return the firm may list only the cash actually received from installment sales. Also, some items listed in the income statement, such as interest or dividends received on some investments, are not taxable. And some revenues, such as gains on the sale of property, are taxed at different rates.

3. A corporation may record certain types of expenditures as assets and, consequently, not include them on the income statement. These same expenditures may be listed on the tax return as expenses. For example, a company might not list expenditures for research and development on its income statement, but would list them as expenses on the tax return.

Before reading further, do the following activity to check your understanding of corporate income taxes.

Check Your Learning

On a sheet of notebook paper, indicate whether the following statements are true or false.

1. All forms of business organization are subject to federal income taxes.
2. Corporations are required to estimate the amount of their net income and income taxes and to pay the estimated tax in four equal installments during the year.
3. The income tax adjustment is usually calculated as the work sheet is prepared.
4. Income Tax Expense is credited for the amount of the additional income taxes owed at the end of the fiscal period.
5. Taxable income is always the same as net income.

Check your answers with those in the answers section. Re-read the preceding part of the chapter to find the correct answers to any questions you may have missed.

Declaration and Payment of Dividends

A *dividend* is a distribution—either in the form of cash or shares of stock—that a corporation makes to its stockholders. Dividends are allocated to stockholders according to the number of shares they own and according to whether the stock is preferred or common.

Three dates are important in the declaration and payment of a dividend.

1. Date of declaration: Date on which the board of directors votes to pay, or declares, a dividend. Dividends are declared separately for each class of stock.
2. Date of record: Date as of which the ownership of shares is determined. This date determines a person's eligibility for dividends and ordinarily is about one or two weeks after the date of declaration.
3. Date of payment: The date the dividend is paid.

Journal entries must be recorded on the date of declaration and on the date of payment. No entry is required on the date of record.

We shall discuss two types of dividends: cash dividends and stock dividends.

Cash Dividends

Most dividends are cash dividends. **Cash dividends** are distributions in the form of cash paid to the stockholders as a reward for their investment. The board of directors declares the dividend and generally pays cash dividends up to a certain percentage of the firm's net income after income taxes. The cash dividend is expressed as a specific amount per share—for example, $1.12 per share. A stockholder who owns 100 shares is thus entitled to $112 ($1.12 × 100 shares).

Before a corporation can pay a cash dividend, however, three things are required.

1. Retained earnings: *Retained earnings* are the profits (earnings) that have been kept (retained) by the corporation and not distributed to stockholders. The Retained Earnings account is a stockholders' equity account and has a normal credit balance. The company must have a sufficient balance in the Retained Earnings account against which to charge the dividends.

2. An adequate amount of cash: A corporation may have earned large profits, but not all profits are in cash. For example, the revenue may be in the form of accounts receivable. The balance of the Cash in Bank account must be high enough to cover the total cash dividend paid out.

3. Formal declaration by the board of directors: The payment of dividends, although it may be a matter of policy, is not automatic. The board of directors must pass the declaration in the form of a motion, which is recorded in a minute book. This minute book is the source document for the accounting entry. It is just like the minute book of a club. It is a written, narrative record of all actions taken at official meetings. A corporation's minute book also contains all details relating to the purchase of plant and equipment, the obtaining of bank loans, the establishing of officers' salaries, and so on.

On January 20, the board of directors of the Cardoza Corporation declared a quarterly cash dividend.

January 20: Declared a cash dividend of $.72 per share (on 5,000 shares of common stock outstanding) to all the stockholders of record as of February 11, payable on March 2, Minute Book p. 241.

The total amount of the dividend is $3,600 (5,000 shares × $.72 = $3,600). In the transaction, Retained Earnings is debited for $3,600. Since the dividend will not be paid until March 2, Dividends Payable, a current liability account, is credited for $3,600. The general journal entry for this transaction is shown in Figure 13–4 at the top of the next page.

	DATE		DESCRIPTION	POST. REF.	DEBIT	CREDIT	
1	19-- Jan.	20	Retained Earnings		3 6 0 0 00		1
2			Dividends Payable			3 6 0 0 00	2
3			Minute Book, p. 241				3

Figure 13–4. Journal Entry to Record the Declaration of a Cash Dividend

Remember, a journal entry is not necessary on February 11, the date of record. An entry is necessary on the date of payment.

March 2: Issued a check for $3,600 in payment of the dividend declared on January 20, Check 1431.

When the dividend is actually paid, Dividends Payable is debited for $3,600 since the liability is being decreased. Cash in Bank is credited for $3,600. The entry for this transaction is shown in general journal form in Figure 13–5 at the top of page 301.

The Cardoza Corporation maintains a separate checking account from which it pays cash dividends. Check 1431 is deposited in this account. A separate check is prepared for each stockholder receiving a cash dividend.

Remember: A cash dividend results in a decrease to both a corporation's assets and retained earnings.

Before reading further, do the following activity to check your understanding of cash dividends.

Check Your Learning

The Sherman Shoe Company was incorporated with authorized capital of 50,000 shares of $50-par common stock. To date, 8,000 shares have been issued. On January 12, the board of directors voted to declare a cash dividend of $.75 (Minute Book, p. 505) to stockholders of record as of January 31, payable on February 20 (by Check 1834). Write your answers to the following questions on a sheet of notebook paper.

1. What is the total amount of the cash dividend?
2. If Paula Hess owns 600 shares of Sherman Shoe Company stock, what is the amount of the cash dividend she will receive?
3. On which dates must journal entries be recorded?
4. In general journal form, record the journal entries required.

Check your answers with those in the answers section. Re-read the preceding part of the chapter to find the correct answers to any questions you may have missed.

DATE	DESCRIPTION	POST. REF.	DEBIT	CREDIT	
19— Mar. 2	Dividends Payable		3 60 00		1
	Cash in Bank			3 60 00	2
	Check 1431				3

Figure 13–5. Journalizing the Payment of a Cash Dividend

Stock Dividends

A **stock dividend** is a distribution by a corporation of shares of its own common stock to its common stockholders. In other words, the dividend distributed to stockholders consists of shares of stock rather than cash. Stock dividends are usually issued by corporations that wish to give their stockholders some return on their investment but that do not wish to distribute cash or other assets that could be used to finance future expansion.

A stock dividend does not result in a decrease to the corporation's assets. It merely transfers a dollar amount from Retained Earnings to the paid-in capital accounts. The amount transferred is the fair market value (usually the current market price of the stock) of the additional shares of stock issued.

Let's look at an example. The Cardoza Corporation has the following balances in its stockholders' equity accounts as of October 11.

Common Stock, $20 par, 5,000 shares outstanding	$100,000
Paid-in Capital in Excess of Par	10,000
Retained Earnings	80,000
Total Stockholders' Equity	$190,000

On October 11, the board of directors declared a 20% stock dividend of 1,000 shares (5,000 × .20) to stockholders of record as of November 1, payable on November 16. The present market value of the stock is $23 per share.

The effect of a stock dividend, remember, is to transfer an amount equal to the market value of the stock from Retained Earnings to the paid-in capital accounts and to increase the number of outstanding shares. Since the market value of the stock is $23, the total amount of the stock dividend is $23,000 (1,000 shares × $23). Retained Earnings is debited for this amount. The total par value of the stock being issued is $20,000 (1,000 shares × $20 par value). This amount is credited to an account called Common Stock Dividend Distributable. This account is a temporary stockholders' equity account, not a liability account. There is no obligation to distribute cash or other assets; the obligation is to distribute additional shares of stock. It appears on the balance sheet in the Paid-in Capital section, just below the Common Stock account. Finally, when the market value of the stock is more than the par value, the difference is recorded in the Paid-in Capital in Excess of Par account. It is, therefore, credited for $3,000, the amount of the difference ($23,000 − $20,000).

The journal entry for the October 11 transaction is shown in Figure 13–6.

	DATE		DESCRIPTION	POST. REF.	DEBIT	CREDIT	
1	19-- Oct.	11	Retained Earnings		23 00 00		1
2			Common Stock Dividend Distrib.			20 00 00	2
3			Paid-in Capital in Excess of Par			3 00 00	3
4			Minute Book, p. 197				4

GENERAL JOURNAL   PAGE 15

Figure 13–6. Journalizing the Declaration of a Stock Dividend

Remember: The capital stock account(s) of a corporation are used to record the par value of the stock issued. Any excess must be credited to Paid-in Capital in Excess of Par.

After this transaction is posted, the balances of the stockholders' equity accounts are as follows. Notice that total stockholders' equity is unchanged, although the balances of the individual accounts have changed.

Common Stock, $20 par, 5,000 shares outstanding	$100,000
Common Stock Dividend Distributable, 1,000 shares	20,000
Paid-in Capital in Excess of Par	13,000
Retained Earnings	57,000
Total Stockholders' Equity	$190,000

No journal entry is required on November 1. On November 16, the stock dividend is distributed to the shareholders. The journal entry for the transaction is shown in Figure 13–7. Common Stock Dividend Distributable is debited for $20,000 to show that the stock due the stockholders has now been issued. Common Stock is credited for $20,000, the par value of the additional shares being issued.

	DATE		DESCRIPTION	POST. REF.	DEBIT	CREDIT	
1	19-- Nov.	16	Common Stock Dividend Distributable		20 00 00		1
2			Common Stock			20 00 00	2
3			Minute Book, p. 197				3

GENERAL JOURNAL   PAGE 16

Figure 13–7. Journalizing the Payment of a Stock Dividend

Remember: The Common Stock Dividend Distributable account is used to record the par value of a stock dividend declared but not yet paid to stockholders.

The total stockholders' equity for the corporation is still unchanged. After this transaction is posted, the stockholders' equity accounts have the balances shown in the following table.

Common Stock, $20 par, 6,000 shares outstanding	$120,000
Paid-in Capital in Excess of Par	13,000
Retained Earnings	57,000
Total Stockholders' Equity	$190,000

The stock dividend has no effect on the proportionate share of ownership of an individual stockholder. For example, Claude Bertrand owned 500 shares of the Cardoza Corporation's stock. This represents a 10% share in the corporation (500 shares owned ÷ 5,000 shares outstanding). When the corporation declared a 20% stock dividend, he received 100 shares (20% of 500 shares). His total stock now amounts to 600 shares; the corporation's total stock outstanding is now 6,000 shares. Claude Bertrand still has a 10% share in the ownership (600 shares owned ÷ 6,000 shares outstanding).

Since a stockholder's proportionate share in a company does not change when the company issues a stock dividend, why does a corporation issue stock dividends? Here are a few reasons.

1. Stock dividends give stockholders a sense of receiving a return on their investments. The corporation in turn does not have to take any cash or other assets out of the business.
2. The board of directors may wish to retain assets permanently in the business. By issuing a stock dividend, the corporation increases its permanent paid-in capital accounts (Common Stock and Paid-in Capital in Excess of Par) and decreases the balance of Retained Earnings, against which cash dividends are charged.
3. Stock dividends are not considered to be income. Stockholders therefore don't have to pay any income tax on them.

Remember: A stock dividend does not have an effect on a corporation's total assets or total stockholders' equity.

Stock Split

A **stock split** is a deliberate split in the par or stated value of a corporation's stock and the issuance of a proportionate number of additional shares. For example, a corporation with 10,000 shares of $50-par stock outstanding may reduce the par value to $25 and increase the number of outstanding shares to 20,000. In this case, the corporation is doubling the number of outstanding shares (called a 2-for-1 split). If you owned 200 shares before the split, you would own 400 shares after it. The company may accomplish the split in shares by calling in all the old shares and issuing certificates for new ones on a 2-for-1 basis. Or, it may issue an additional share for each old share. The journal entry that may be made to record this stock split is shown in Figure 13–8. (The par values are listed only as an explanation.)

This 2-for-1 stock split reduces the market price per share by approximately half. This increases the stock's salability, because it now costs less.

GENERAL JOURNAL   PAGE 12

	DATE	DESCRIPTION	POST. REF.	DEBIT	CREDIT	
1	19-- May 15	Common Stock ($50 par value)		50000000		1
2		Common Stock ($25 par value)			50000000	2
3		Minute Book, p. 1117				3

Figure 13–8. Journalizing a Stock Split

A stock split does not change the balances of the stockholders' equity accounts. The headings of the capital stock accounts in the ledger are changed to show the new par or stated value per share. The stockholders' ledger is also revised to show the new distribution of shares. (In practice, almost all accountants record stock splits with a memorandum entry.)

Treasury Stock

In Chapter 12 we stated that treasury stock is the corporation's own stock that had been issued to stockholders at one time and was later reacquired by the corporation. Corporations often reacquire shares of their own stock through donations from stockholders or by buying them back in the open market. The reacquired stock is held by the corporation and may be reissued to stockholders at a later time. The corporation may hold treasury stock indefinitely.

Treasury stock should not be confused with unissued stock. Treasury stock is stock that has been issued previously and reacquired. Although treasury stock is not entitled to cash dividends, it does participate in stock dividends and stock splits. Treasury stock can be reissued at a price below its par or stated value with no contingent liability. That is, the holders of reissued treasury stock cannot be held liable for the difference between the par value of the stock and the discounted price at which it was reissued. In other respects it is similar to unissued stock. Treasury stock has no voting rights, no pre-emptive right to share in new stock issues, and no right to share in the assets if the corporation should be liquidated.

A corporation may have several reasons for buying back its own stock.

1. To have stock available to reissue to officers and employees under a bonus plan or employee stock-purchase plan.
2. To support the market price of the stock if it is unusually low.

3. To have shares available for exchanges of stock if the company acquires other companies.

Let's use the Windsor Corporation as an example. The stockholders' equity accounts of the Windsor Corporation are as follows: Common Stock, $50 par (10,000 shares authorized and issued), $500,000; Paid-in Capital in Excess of Par, $10,000; Retained Earnings, $100,000.

May 15: Bought 500 shares of treasury stock at $60 per share, Check 4612.

When the company buys its own stock, the account Treasury Stock is debited for the *cost* of the stock. The Treasury Stock account is not an investment account, because technically a corporation cannot own a part of itself. It is a contra stockholders' equity account and has a normal debit balance. It appears on the balance sheet as a deduction from the total paid-in capital and retained earnings. In accounting for the purchase of treasury stock, the par or stated value of the stock is ignored. The total price paid for the reacquired stock, $30,000, is debited to the Treasury Stock account. Cash in Bank is credited for $30,000. This transaction is shown in general journal form in Figure 13–9.

Remember: Treasury Stock is a contra stockholders' equity account. It is used to record the cost of a company's own stock that is reacquired and held.

June 11: Sold 100 shares of treasury stock at $65 per share, Receipt 3171.

	DATE	DESCRIPTION	POST. REF.	DEBIT	CREDIT	
GENERAL JOURNAL					PAGE 71	
1	May 15	Treasury Stock		30 000 00		1
2		Cash in Bank			30 000 00	2
3		Check 4612				3
8	June 11	Cash in Bank		6 500 00		8
9		Treasury Stock			6 000 00	9
10		Paid-in Cap. from Sale of Treas. Stock			500 00	10
11		Receipt 3171				11
20	Aug. 5	Cash in Bank		5 800 00		20
21		Paid-in Cap. from Sale of Treas. Stock		200 00		21
22		Treasury Stock			6 000 00	22
23		Receipt 3267				23
30	Oct. 1	Bonus to Employees		6 000 00		30
31		Treasury Stock			6 000 00	31
32		Memo. 634				32

Figure 13–9. Journalizing Treasury Stock Transactions

When the company resells its treasury stock at a price above its cost, the difference between the cost and the selling price is credited to a stockholders' equity account titled Paid-in Capital from Sale of Treasury Stock. This account appears in the Paid-in Capital section of the balance sheet, below the other capital stock accounts. In this transaction, Cash in Bank is debited for $6,500, the total amount of cash received on the sale of the treasury stock. Treasury Stock is credited for $6,000, the *cost* of stock being reissued (100 shares × $60 cost). Paid-in Capital from Sale of Treasury Stock is credited for $600, the amount of the difference between the cost and the selling price. This entry appears in general journal form in Figure 13–9.

August 5: Sold 100 shares of treasury stock at $58 per share, Receipt 3267.

This transaction is similar to the previous one, except that Paid-in Capital from Sale of Treasury Stock is debited instead of credited, because the stock was sold for less than its cost. The entry for this transaction is shown in general journal form in Figure 13–9.

Remember: **Paid-in Capital from Sale of Treasury Stock is debited when treasury stock is sold for less than its cost. The account is credited when treasury stock is sold for more than its cost.**

October 1: Reissued 100 shares of treasury stock as a bonus to employees, Memorandum 634.

In this transaction, the expense account Bonus for Employees is debited for $6,000, the total cost of the stock being reissued. Treasury Stock is credited for $6,000. The general journal entry for this transaction is shown in Figure 13–9.

After these entries have been posted, the two related treasury stock accounts will appear as shown in the following T accounts.

Paid-in Capital from Sale of Treasury Stock		Treasury Stock	
Dr.	Cr.	Dr.	Cr.
−	+	+	−
Aug. 5 $200	June 11 $500	May 15 $30,000	June 11 $6,000
			Aug. 5 6,000
			Oct. 1 6,000

Treasury stock is reported in the Stockholders' Equity section of the balance sheet as shown in Figure 13–10. Notice that the number of shares of issued stock has not changed. It is still 10,000 shares. The number of outstanding shares, however, has decreased. The Windsor Corporation had 9,800 shares of stock outstanding (10,000 shares issued − 200 shares of treasury stock). In other words, the acquisition of treasury stock does not affect the number of shares issued. But it does decrease the number of shares of stock outstanding.

Before reading further, do the activity on page 307 to check your understanding of transactions involving treasury stock.

Windsor Corporation
Balance Sheet
December 31, 19--

Stockholders' Equity			
Paid-in Capital:			
Common Stock, $50 par			
(10,000 shares authorized			
and issued, of which 200			
shs are in the treasury)	500000 00		
Paid-in Capital in Excess of Par	10000 00	510000 00	
Paid-in Cap from Sale of Treas Stock		300 00	
Total Paid-in Capital		510300 00	
Retained Earnings		100000 00	
Total Paid-in Capital + Ret. Earnings		610300 00	
Less Treas. Stock (200 shs. at cost)		12000 00	
Total Stockholders' Equity			598300 00

Figure 13–10. Stockholders' Equity Section of the Balance Sheet

---

Check Your Learning

Selected treasury stock transactions completed by the Forbes Corporation are listed below. On a separate piece of paper, record the transactions in general journal form.

Jan. 16 Bought 2,000 shares of own stock at $42 per share, Check 5411.
Mar. 19 Sold 1,000 shares of treasury stock at $46 per share, Receipt 1631.
Dec.   8 Sold 1,000 shares of treasury stock for $40 per share, Receipt 2710.

Check your answers with those in the answers section. Re-read the preceding part of the chapter to find the correct answers to any questions you may have missed.

Financial Statements for a Corporation

In this chapter, you have learned about several events that affect retained earnings during a fiscal period. These events—net income and dividends—are reported on the statement of retained earnings. In the statement of retained earnings of the Cardoza Corporation, shown in Figure 13–11 at the top of the next page, the net income for the period and the cash and stock dividends declared are listed.

Figure 13–11. Statement of Retained Earnings

The Cardoza Corporation's balance sheet is shown in Figure 13–12. Notice that the Cardoza Corporation's income tax liability for the year is listed in the Current Liabilities section of the balance sheet. The dividends declared by the company during the year were paid before the end of the fiscal period. As a result, they are not reported on the year-end balance sheet. If, however, a cash dividend had not yet been paid to stockholders, Dividends Payable would appear in the Liabilities section.

Summary of Key Points

1. A corporation, since it is a separate legal entity, is subject to federal corporate income taxes. Many state and local governments also levy income taxes on corporations.
2. A corporation must estimate its federal income taxes for the year and must pay the estimated tax amount in advance in equal quarterly installments.
3. At the end of the year, when the corporation knows the exact amount of its net income, an adjusting entry is made either for the amount of the additional tax owed or for the amount of the tax overpaid.
4. A dividend is a distribution to the stockholders of a corporation as a return on their investment. Dividends may be in the form of cash or shares of stock.
5. Dividends—either cash dividends or stock dividends—decrease the Retained Earnings account.
6. Cash dividends decrease both a corporation's assets and its retained earnings. Stock dividends do not have an effect on a corporation's total assets or total stockholders' equity.
7. A stock split, a reduction in the par or stated value of a stock accompanied by the issuance of a proportional amount of new stock, reduces the market price per share and increases the stock's salability.
8. Treasury stock is a corporation's own stock that had been issued and later reacquired by the corporation.
9. Treasury Stock is a contra stockholders' equity account. Stock reacquired by the corporation is recorded in the account at cost.

Cardoza Corporation
Balance Sheet
December 31, 19--

Assets

Current Assets:			
Cash in Bank		1441000	
Accounts Receivable	6295000		
Less: Allow. for Uncoll. Accts.	216000	6079000	
Subscriptions Receivable		6000000	
Merchandise Inventory		19410000	
Prepaid Insurance		18000	
Total Current Assets			32948000
Property, Plant, and Equipment:			
Store Equipment	5472000		
Less: Accum. Deprec.-Store Equip.	2585000	2887000	
Office Equipment	3892000		
Less: Accum. Deprec.-Office Equip.	1393000	2499000	
Total Property, Plant, & Equipment			5386000
Intangible Assets:			
Organization Costs			100000
Total Assets			38434000

Liabilities

Accounts Payable		2569000	
Corporate Income Tax Payable		660000	
Interest Payable		15000	
Notes Payable		1000000	
Total Liabilities			4244000

Stockholders' Equity

Paid-in Capital:			
Common Stock, $20 par (200,000 shs. authorized, 6,000 shs issued)	12000000		
Common Stock Subscr. (3,000 shs.)	6000000		
Paid-in Capital in Excess of Par	2500000		
Total Paid-in Capital		20500000	
Retained Earnings		13690000	
Total Stockholders' Equity			34190000
Total Liabilities & Stockholders' Equity			38434000

Figure 13–12. Balance Sheet

Review and Applications

Building Your Accounting Vocabulary

In your own words, write the definition of each of the following accounting terms. Use complete sentences for your definitions.

cash dividend	stock split
stock dividend	taxable income

Reviewing Your Accounting Knowledge

1. How does a corporation account for federal income taxes?
2. Why might a corporation's taxable income differ from the net income reported on its income statement?
3. Name and explain the three dates that are important in the dividend process.
4. What are the three requirements that must be met before a corporation can pay a cash dividend?
5. What is the difference between a cash dividend and a stock dividend?
6. What effect does a cash dividend have on the total stockholders' equity of a corporation? What effect does a stock dividend have?
7. What is the difference between a stock dividend and a stock split?
8. Give two reasons why a corporation might buy back its own stock.
9. Classify the following accounts: Corporate Income Tax Payable, Dividends Payable, Retained Earnings, Common Stock Dividend Distributable, Treasury Stock.
10. What information is reported on the statement of retained earnings?

Improving Your Decision-Making Skills

The Atlantic Corporation would like to increase the marketability of its stock. The company wants to increase the number of shares of its outstanding stock without changing the total value of stockholders' equity. Can you name two ways in which the Atlantic Corporation can accomplish its objective? Which method should the company choose if it does not want to change the value of its retained earnings? Which method do you think the stockholders of Atlantic Corporation would prefer? Why?

Applying Accounting Procedures

Problem 13–1

The Salvetti Corporation estimated that, for the year ended December 31, its net income would be $26,500 and that its estimated federal income taxes would be $4,020.

Instructions:

(1) Prepare the journal entries required on April 15 (Check 1113), June 15 (Check 2060), September 15 (Check 3412), and December 15 (Check 4603) to record the income tax installments paid. Record the entries, in general journal form, on page 14 of a general journal.

(2) On December 31, the Salvetti Corporation determined that its total income tax liability for the year was $4,395. Record the adjusting entry.

Problem 13–2

The following information appeared on the December 31 balance sheet of the Oliver Corporation.

Preferred 9% Stock, $100 par (500 shares authorized, 200 shares issued)	$ 20,000
Common Stock, $50 par (10,000 shares authorized, 6,000 shares issued)	300,000
Paid-in Capital in Excess of Par—Common	24,000
Retained Earnings	70,000

On January 4, the board of directors of the Oliver Corporation voted the 9% cash dividend to preferred stockholders and a $1.25 cash dividend to common stockholders, distributable on February 14 to stockholders of record on January 28.

Instructions: Prepare the entries, on page 62 of the general journal, to record the declaration and distribution of the cash dividend (Check 1054). The declaration of the cash dividend by the board of directors was recorded on page 1145 of the minute book.

Problem 13–3

On December 31, the stockholders' equity of Northland Pottery, Inc. is as follows.

Paid-in Capital:	
Common Stock, stated value $20 (20,000 shares authorized, 18,000 shares issued)	$360,000
Paid-in Capital in Excess of Stated Value	61,000
Retained Earnings	206,000

On December 31, when the stock was selling for $34 per share, the board of directors voted a 10% stock dividend, distributable on February 5 to stockholders of record on January 15.

Instructions: Prepare the entries, on page 32 of the general journal, to record the declaration and distribution of the stock dividend. The declaration of the stock dividend was recorded on page 955 of the minute book.

The following information appeared on the December 31 balance sheet of Sanchez Automotive, Inc.

Common Stock, $25 par (20,000 shares authorized, 16,000 shares issued of which 400 shares are in the treasury)	$400,000
Paid-in Capital in Excess of Par	32,000
Paid-in Capital from Sale of Treasury Stock	6,000
Retained Earnings	98,000
Treasury Stock (400 shares at cost)	12,000

The following are some of the transactions that occurred during the next fiscal period.

Jan.   1   The board of directors declared a semiannual cash dividend of $11,700 ($.75 per share on 15,600 shares outstanding) payable on February 7 to stockholders of record on January 16, Minute Book page 443.

Feb.   7   Paid the cash dividend, Check 4617.

      28   Purchased 700 shares of own common stock at $26 per share, Check 4683.

May   15   Purchased 900 shares of own common stock at $27 per share, Check 4962.

July   1   The board of directors declared a semiannual cash dividend of $10,500 ($.75 per share on 14,000 shares) to stockholders of record on July 20, payable on August 3, Minute Book page 516.

Aug.   3   Paid the cash dividend, Check 5201.

Oct. 15   Sold 400 shares of treasury stock (purchased at $30 per share) at $29, Receipt 5711.

Nov. 29   Sold 700 shares of treasury stock purchased on February 28 at $30, Receipt 6316.

Instructions: Record these transactions on page 42 of the general journal.

Problem 13–5

The following information appeared on the December 31 balance sheet of Waters, Inc.

Common Stock, $10 par (15,000 shares authorized, 10,000 shares issued)	$100,000
Paid-in Capital in Excess of Par	25,000
Retained Earnings	325,000

Some of the transactions of Waters, Inc. during this fiscal year are as follows.

Jan.	15	Declared a cash dividend of $1.68 per share on 10,000 shares to stockholders of record as of January 30, payable on February 10, Minute Book page 1163.
Feb.	10	Paid the cash dividend, Check 5963.
Mar.	15	Paid the previous year's federal income tax liability of $7,500, Check 6037.
Apr.	15	Issued Check 6161 for $12,840 for the first quarterly federal income tax installment for the year.
May	20	Declared a 5% stock dividend to stockholders of record as of May 30, payable on June 10, Minute Book page 1361. The present market value of the stock is $14 per share.
June	10	Distributed the stock dividend to stockholders, Minute Book page 1361.
	15	Paid the second quarterly federal income tax installment for this year of $12,840, Check 6333.
July	15	Declared a cash dividend of $1.68 per share on 10,500 shares to stockholders of record as of July 30, payable on August 10, Minute Book page 1396.
Aug.	10	Paid the cash dividend, Check 6502.
Sept.	15	Wrote Check 6618 for $12,840 for the third quarterly federal income tax installment.
Oct.	20	Purchased 900 shares of own common stock at $15 per share, Check 6703.
Nov.	15	Purchased 100 shares of own common stock at $16 per share, Check 6790.
Dec.	15	Issued Check 6899 for $12,840 for the final federal income tax installment for the year.
	31	Recorded the adjusting entry for the additional federal income taxes for the year, $2,800.

Instructions: Record these transactions on page 72 of a general journal.

Problem 13–6

Meredith Mercantile, Inc. has authorized capital of 1,500 shares of $100-par preferred 9% stock and 15,000 shares of no-par common stock with a stated value of $15.

The following balances appeared in Meredith's accounting records on December 31.

Accounts Payable	$147,390
Accounts Receivable	189,540
Accumulated Depreciation—Building	34,200
Accumulated Depreciation—Equipment	37,305
Allowance for Uncollectible Accounts	6,930
Building	135,000
Cash in Bank	8,730

Common Stock	153,000
Corporate Income Tax Payable	21,900
Dividends Payable	7,200
Equipment	69,900
Land	18,000
Merchandise Inventory	356,805
Mortgage Payable (due in 10 years)	63,000
Notes Receivable	18,000
Organization Costs	9,000
Paid-in Capital in Excess of Par—Preferred	1,500
Paid-in Capital in Excess of Stated Value	33,390
Preferred 9% Stock	120,000
Preferred 9% Stock Subscribed (300 shares)	30,000
Prepaid Insurance	1,290
Retained Earnings	151,650
Stock Dividend Distributable (930 shares)	13,950
Subscriptions Receivable—Preferred 9% Stock	15,150

Instructions: Prepare a balance sheet as of December 31. Place the Assets section on the front of the form and the Liabilities and Stockholders' Equity sections on the back of the form.

Problem 13–7

Murdock Lumber, Inc. has authorized capital of 1,000 shares of $100-par preferred 8% stock and 15,000 shares of $20-par common stock. The account balances shown in the table on page 315 appear in the Trial Balance section of Murdock's work sheet.

Instructions:

(1) Complete the work sheet. (The trial balance has already been recorded on the work sheet in the working papers accompanying this textbook.) Data for the adjustments are as follows.
  (a) The ending merchandise inventory is valued at $291,330.
  (b) Using the aging of accounts receivable method, the estimated uncollectible amount is $5,235. Record the bad debts expense under Selling Expenses.
  (c) The ending supplies inventory is valued at $651. Record the supplies expense under Administrative Expenses.
  (d) The estimated depreciation on equipment for the year is $6,195. Record the depreciation expense under Administrative Expenses.
  (e) Organization costs of $2,770 are being written off. Record this expense under Administrative Expenses.
  (f) Accrued interest expense on the note payable is $210.
  (g) The total corporate income taxes for the year are $59,116.
(2) Prepare an income statement for the year ended December 31.

Cash in Bank	$ 5,874	
Accounts Receivable	163,115	
Allowance for Uncollectible Accounts		$ 2,799
Subscriptions Receivable—Common Stock	39,000	
Merchandise Inventory	284,505	
Supplies	945	
Equipment	109,020	
Accumulated Depreciation—Equipment		17,430
Organization Costs	8,130	
Accounts Payable		76,560
Corporate Income Tax Payable		
Notes Payable		15,000
Preferred 8% Stock		60,000
Paid-in Capital in Excess of Par—Preferred		3,000
Common Stock		165,000
Common Stock Subscribed		45,000
Paid-in Capital in Excess of Par—Common		21,000
Retained Earnings		77,400
Sales		1,524,450
Purchases	1,093,650	
Purchases Discounts		7,980
Selling Expenses	201,456	
Administrative Expenses	57,399	
Interest Expense	2,310	
Income Tax Expense	50,215	
	$2,015,619	$2,015,619

(3) Prepare a statement of retained earnings. No dividends were declared during the year.

(4) Prepare a balance sheet.

14 Corporations: Bonds Payable

Corporations have many sources of funds from which to finance their operations and expansion. In previous chapters, you learned that corporations can acquire cash and other assets by selling stock and by earning profits and retaining those profits in the business. Corporations may also borrow the funds they need. In Chapter 3, you learned about one method of borrowing that corporations can use: issuing notes payable.

Promissory notes are usually issued for relatively short periods of time. Corporations can also borrow money on a long-term basis, for periods of up to fifty years.

In this chapter, you will learn about one form of long-term liability of a corporation. You will learn how to journalize transactions involving a corporation's long-term liabilities and how these liabilities are reported on the corporation's financial statements.

Learning Objectives

When you have completed this chapter, you should be able to

1. Explain the difference between a share of stock and a bond.

2. List some of the advantages, disadvantages, and characteristics of a bond.

3. Journalize transactions involving the issuance of bonds.

4. Explain the purpose of a bond sinking fund.

5. Define the accounting terms presented in this chapter.

New Terms

bond / bond certificate / bond issue / bond indenture / leverage / term bonds / serial bonds / registered bonds / coupon bonds / secured bond / debenture / market rate / discount / premium / amortize / sinking fund / investments / callable bonds

Why a Corporation Issues Bonds

A corporation that needs money on a long-term basis has the choice of raising the necessary funds by issuing (1) common stock, (2) preferred stock, or (3) bonds.

A **bond** can be considered to be a long-term promissory note. It is a written promise to repay a certain amount (the principal) at a specified date and to pay interest at set times. Since bonds are long-term liabilities, however, interest is usually paid to bondholders semiannually (twice a year). (Bonds are also issued by the federal government and by other governmental units such as cities, states, and local school districts. In this chapter, however, we will discuss only bonds issued by corporations.)

The holder of a bond receives a **bond certificate** as evidence of the company's debt to the bondholder. In most cases, bonds are issued in denominations of $1,000 or some multiple of $1,000. A **bond issue** is the total number of bonds that are issued at the same time. For example, a $1,000,000 bond issue may consist of a thousand $1,000 bonds.

The bond issue may be bought and held by many investors. As a result, the corporation usually prepares a separate document that defines the rights, privileges, and limitations of bondholders. This document will also generally describe such things as the maturity date of the bonds, interest payment dates, interest rate, and characteristics of the bonds. This document is called the **bond indenture**.

Advantages of Issuing Bonds

Bonds offer these advantages over the issuance of stock:

1. The bond-issuing corporation may be able to earn a greater return on the money it raises than it has to pay out in interest. This is known as **leverage**. For example, suppose that a firm can borrow $100,000 by issuing bonds with an interest rate of 8%. The company must pay the bondholders $8,000 a year in interest. But suppose that the company can use the $100,000 in the business to earn an additional $15,000 a year after taxes. The extra $7,000 ($15,000 − $8,000) available each year can be used for other purposes, such as paying dividends to the holders of common stock.
2. Interest payments to bondholders are tax-deductible expenses.
3. Bondholders cannot vote, so common stockholders can retain control of the company's affairs.

Disadvantages of Issuing Bonds

On the other hand, these disadvantages of issuing bonds relative to stocks have to be considered:

1. Bondholders are creditors of the corporation, so interest payments are fixed expenses. A corporation pays dividends only when it has enough money to do so.
2. The corporation must eventually repay the principal of the bonds it issues. A company does not have to repay the money it receives from issuing stock.

The following table outlines the differences between stocks and bonds.

Bonds	Capital Stock
Bondholders are creditors; they receive interest and are eventually repaid the principal.	Stockholders are owners; they receive dividends.
Interest paid on bonds is an expense, which must be paid year after year.	Dividends are distributions of net income, rather than expenses.
Interest is a business expense deducted before net income is calculated.	Dividends are not deductible before net income is calculated.

Remember: **A bondholder is a creditor of a corporation; a stockholder is an owner.**

Classification of Bonds

To appeal to investors, corporations have created a wide variety of bonds, each with slightly different combinations of characteristics, just as an automobile manufacturer offers different models of cars with various combinations of accessories.

Term or Serial Bonds

If all the bonds within a bond issue have the same term or time period, they are called term bonds. An entire issue of term bonds comes due at the same time. For example, $1,000,000 worth of 10-year bonds issued January 1, 1986, all mature on January 1, 1996.

Serial bonds have a series of maturity dates. For example, $1,000,000 worth of bonds issued March 1, 1986, may mature as follows.

$100,000 on March 1, 1991	$100,000 on March 1, 1996
$100,000 on March 1, 1992	$100,000 on March 1, 1997
$100,000 on March 1, 1993	$100,000 on March 1, 1998
$100,000 on March 1, 1994	$100,000 on March 1, 1999
$100,000 on March 1, 1995	$100,000 on March 1, 2000

Registered or Coupon Bonds

Most bonds issued today are **registered bonds**. When bonds are registered, the names of the owners are recorded with the issuing corporation. Title to such bonds is transferred when the bonds are sold, just as title to stock is transferred. The corporation mails interest checks to the registered owners.

Coupon bonds derive their name from the interest coupons attached to each bond certificate. The interest coupons are payable to bearer, in much the same manner as paper money is. The owner of the bond clips the coupons as they become due and deposits them with a commercial bank for collection. The owners' names may be registered with the bond-issuing corporation.

Secured or Unsecured Bonds

A bond that is covered or backed up by certain assets of the corporation is called a **secured bond**. Such a bond may be called a mortgage bond or an equipment trust bond. If the corporation defaults, or does not pay the principal or interest, the bondholders, acting through a trustee, may take over the pledged assets.

An unsecured bond, also called a **debenture**, is one that is issued just on the corporation's credit standing. It is not backed up by the assets of a corporation. Such unsecured bonds usually succeed only when issued by financially strong firms.

A bond can have characteristics of all three classifications. For example, 20-year mortgage bonds with coupons for the payment of interest may be term bonds, coupon bonds, and secured bonds.

Before you learn how to account for bonds, do the following activity to check your understanding of bonds.

Check Your Learning

On a separate sheet of paper, indicate whether the following statements are true or false.

1. A bond is a written promise to repay a certain amount on a specific date and to pay interest at set times.
2. Bonds are usually issued for relatively short periods of time.
3. A bond issue is the document that serves as proof of the corporation's debt to the bondholder.
4. Bondholders are creditors of a corporation.
5. A debenture is a bond backed up by certain assets of the corporation.

Compare your answers with those in the answers section. Re-read the preceding part of the chapter to find the correct answers to any questions you may have missed.

Accounting for Bonds Payable

When a corporation issues bonds, the transaction is recorded in the Bonds Payable account. Bonds Payable is a long-term liability account. If there is more than one bond issue, the company keeps a separate account for each. The listing on the balance sheet should identify the issue by its interest rate and due date.

Remember: Bonds Payable is a long-term liability account. It has a normal credit balance.

Issuing Bonds at Face Value

In June, the board of directors of the Cardoza Corporation authorized the issuance of $100,000 of 9%, 10-year bonds (face value $1,000). Interest on the bonds is to be paid semiannually on June 30 and December 31. The bonds were sold on July 1 for their face value.

July 1: Received $100,000 cash for the one hundred 9%, 10-year bonds, face value $1,000, Receipt 1631.

In this transaction, Cash in Bank is debited for $100,000, the total amount of cash received. Bonds Payable is credited for $100,000 to show the increase in the liability. The entry for this transaction appears in general journal form in Figure 14–1. (This transaction could also be recorded in the corporation's cash receipts journal.)

		GENERAL JOURNAL			PAGE 41
DATE		DESCRIPTION	POST. REF.	DEBIT	CREDIT
July 1		Cash in Bank		10000000	
		Bonds Payable			10000000
		Receipt 1631			

Figure 14–1. Journalizing the Issuance of Bonds Payable

Recording the Interest on Bonds Payable

The interest on the bonds issued by the Cardoza Corporation is to be paid on June 30 and December 31 of each year. Interest is calculated using the same formula as interest on notes. The interest due on December 31 is determined as follows.

$$\text{Principal} \quad \text{Interest Rate} \quad \text{Time} \quad \text{Interest}$$
$$\$100,000 \times .09 \times \frac{6}{12} = \$4,500$$

December 31: Issued Check 2791 for $4,500 in payment of the semiannual interest on bonds payable.

The amount of the interest, $4,500, is debited to the Bond Interest Expense account. Cash in Bank is credited for $4,500. The entry to record the December 31 interest payment is shown in general journal form in Figure 14–2.

		GENERAL JOURNAL			PAGE 62
DATE		DESCRIPTION	POST. REF.	DEBIT	CREDIT
19-- Dec. 31	Bond Interest Expense			4500 00	
	Cash in Bank				4500 00
	Check 2791				

Figure 14–2. Journalizing the Payment of Interest on Bonds

Bond Interest Rates

When a corporation issues bonds, it specifies a certain interest rate that it will pay. This fixed rate of interest will not change over the life of the bonds. For example, a $1,000, 9% bond will pay $90 a year interest, or $45 every six months until maturity. However, the demand for money changes and, therefore, interest rates change from day to day. Cardoza can receive $1,000 for its bonds only if the current market rate of interest is 9% for similar bonds. The **market rate** is the rate borrowers are willing to pay and lenders are willing to accept for the use of money. If the current market rate of interest for similar bonds has gone up to 10%, Cardoza would not receive $1,000 from investors. In other words, if the market rate of interest is 10%, wise investors will not pay $1,000 for a bond that pays $90 a year interest if they can earn $100 elsewhere. If the market rate goes down to 8%, Cardoza will be able to issue the bonds for more than $1,000. Investors would be willing to pay more for the bond because they would earn $90 interest a year instead of the $80 they would earn elsewhere.

When issuing bonds, most companies try to set the interest rate as close as possible to the current market rate. However, a company must decide in advance what that interest rate will be. It takes time to notify various regulatory agencies, advertise the bond issue, and print the bond certificates. So, on the date the bonds are issued, there is often a difference between the market rate of interest and the rate of interest stated on the bond certificate. The result is that the issue price of the bond, the price that investors are willing to pay on the date of issue, may not equal the face value of the bond. If the issue price is less than the face value, the bonds are said to be issued at a **discount**. If the issue price is more than the face value, the bonds are said to be issued at a **premium**.

Issuing Bonds at a Premium

The corporation may receive a price for its bonds that is above or below their face value, depending on the rate of interest offered and the general credit standing of the company. If a corporation offers a rate of interest that is higher than the market rate for similar bonds, investors may be willing to pay a premium for the bonds.

For example, on January 1, Dellroe Corporation issued $500,000 of 10%, 10-year bonds, with interest payable semiannually on June 30 and December 31. Because the current market rate of interest is 9.6%, Dellroe was able to issue the bonds at 104. (The figure 104 refers to the price of the bonds; it means that investors are willing to pay an amount equal to 104% of the face value of the bonds.) Dellroe, therefore, received $520,000 for the bonds ($500,000 × 1.04 = $520,000). Dellroe's entry to record the issuance of the bonds is shown in general journal form in Figure 14–3.

	GENERAL JOURNAL			PAGE 16
DATE	DESCRIPTION	POST. REF.	DEBIT	CREDIT
19-- Jan. 1	Cash in Bank		520 00 00 00	
	Bonds Payable			500 00 00 00
	Premium on Bonds Payable			20 00 00 00
	Receipt 673			

Figure 14–3. Journalizing the Issuance of Bonds at a Premium

January 1: *Received $520,000 for $500,000, 10%, 10-year bonds, face value $1,000, Receipt 673.*

In this transaction, Cash in Bank is debited for $520,000, the total amount of cash received. Bonds Payable is credited for $500,000, the face amount of the bond issue. The additional $20,000 is credited to an account called Premium on Bonds Payable. The Premium on Bonds Payable account is used to record the amount received in excess of the face value of the bonds. Premium on Bonds Payable appears immediately below the Bonds Payable account in the Long-term Liabilities section of the balance sheet.

Long-term Liabilities:
10% Bonds Payable, due Jan. 1 $500,000
     Plus Premium on Bonds Payable   20,000 $520,000

The $520,000 is referred to as the *carrying value* of the bonds.

When bonds are issued at a premium, the interest expense incurred by the corporation is actually less than the interest rate stated on the bonds. The reason for this is that, over the life of the bonds, the actual interest expense to the corporation consists of the interest payments to the bondholders *minus* the amount of the bond premium. Look at the table on page 323. It shows the total cost to the Dellroe Corporation for the bonds issued at a premium. Notice that the $20,000 premium actually decreases the total interest cost to the corporation. Instead of a yearly interest expense of $50,000 ($500,000 ÷ 10 years), the annual interest expense is only $48,000 ($480,000 ÷ 10 years). To adjust

Cash to be paid to bondholders	
Face value of the bonds at maturity	$ 500,000
Interest payments ($500,000 × .10 × 10 years)	+ 500,000
Total cash to be paid to bondholders	$1,000,000
Less cash received from bondholders on issue date	− 520,000
Total interest expense for 10 years	$ 480,000

the Interest Expense account to reflect the annual interest expense incurred, the company writes off, or **amortizes**, the Premium on Bonds Payable account over the life of the bonds. The adjusting entry, made at the end of the fiscal period, is shown in Figure 14–4.

	GENERAL JOURNAL			PAGE 21

	DATE	DESCRIPTION	POST. REF.	DEBIT	CREDIT
1		*Adjusting Entries*			1
2	19— Dec. 31	*Premium on Bonds Payable*		2 0 0 0 00	2
3		*Bond Interest Expense*			2 0 0 0 00	3

Figure 14–4. Adjusting Entry to Amortize Premium on Bonds Payable

In this illustration, the bond premium amortization is calculated by the straight-line method. That is, the $20,000 bond premium is amortized in equal installments of $2,000 over 10 years. As you can see, this is similar to calculating depreciation by the straight-line method.

After the adjusting entry is posted, the balance of Interest Expense is $48,000, representing the amount of the annual interest expense on the bonds.

Bond Interest Expense		Premium on Bonds Payable	
Dr.	Cr.	Dr.	Cr.
+	−	−	+
$25,000	Adj. $2,000	Adj. $2,000	$20,000
25,000			

Over the years, the Premium on Bonds Payable account will be decreased. When the bonds mature, the carrying value of Bonds Payable will be $500,000, which is also the maturity value.

Remember: **A premium reduces a corporation's total interest expense over the life of the bonds.**

Issuing Bonds at a Discount

A corporation may issue bonds with a stated rate of interest that is less than the market rate of interest for comparable bonds. These bonds are sold at a discount, or for less than their face value.

For example, on January 1, Plainview Dairy Products issued $100,000 worth of 6%, 20-year bonds, with interest to be paid semiannually on June 30 and December 31. Because the current market rate of interest was 6.2%, Plainview issued the bonds at 96. (That is, investors were only willing to pay an amount equal to 96% of the face value of the bonds.) Plainview received $96,000 for its bonds ($100,000 × .96).

January 1: Received $96,000 for $100,000, 6%, 20-year bonds, face value $1,000, Receipt 1963.

The transaction is shown in general journal form in Figure 14–5.

		DATE	DESCRIPTION	POST. REF.	DEBIT	CREDIT	
				GENERAL JOURNAL		PAGE 41	
1	19-- Jan.	1	Cash in Bank		96 000 00		1
2			Discount on Bonds Payable		4 000 00		2
3			Bonds Payable			100 000 00	3
4			Receipt 1963				4

Figure 14–5. Journalizing the Issuance of Bonds at a Discount

In the transaction, Cash in Bank is debited for $96,000, the total amount of cash received. Bonds Payable is credited for $100,000, the face value of the bond issue. The difference between the face value of the bonds and the cash received, $4,000, is debited to an account called Discount on Bonds Payable. Discount on Bonds Payable appears in the Long-term Liabilities section of the balance sheet as a deduction from Bonds Payable.

Long-term Liabilities:
6% Bonds Payable, due Jan. 1	$100,000	
Less Discount on Bonds Payable	4,000	$96,000

As you can see, the carrying value of Plainview's bonds is only $96,000.

Remember: **The carrying value of a bond issue is the face value of the bond issue plus any premium or minus any discount. When the bonds mature, the carrying value will be the same as the maturity value.**

When the bonds mature, Plainview must pay the bondholders the full maturity value of the bonds, $100,000. When bonds are issued at a discount, then, the interest cost incurred by the corporation is actually more than the interest rate stated on the bonds. The actual interest expense to the corporation is the amount of the interest payments to the bondholders *plus* the amount of the bond discount. The table at the top of page 325 shows the total cost to Plainview Dairy Products for the bonds issued at a discount.

Cash to be paid to bondholders	
Face value of the bonds at maturity	$100,000
Interest payments ($100,000 × .06 × 20 years)	+120,000
Total cash to be paid to bondholders	$220,000
Less cash received from bondholders on issue date	− 96,000
Total interest expense for 20 years	$124,000

You can see that the $4,000 discount increases the total interest cost to the corporation. Instead of a yearly interest expense of $6,000 ($120,000 ÷ 20 years), the annual interest expense is $6,200 ($124,000 ÷ 20 years).

Remember: A discount increases a corporation's total interest expense over the life of the bonds.

To adjust the Bond Interest Expense account to reflect the annual interest expense incurred, the corporation amortizes the Discount on Bonds Payable account, as it does the Premium on Bonds Payable account, over the life of the bond issue. Plainview uses the straight-line method to amortize the bond discount. The adjusting entry, taken from the Adjustments section of the work sheet, is shown in Figure 14–6.

	GENERAL JOURNAL		PAGE 47		
DATE	DESCRIPTION	POST. REF.	DEBIT	CREDIT	
	Adjusting Entries				1
Dec. 31	Bond Interest Expense		200 00		2
	Discount on Bonds Payable			200 00	3

Figure 14–6. Adjusting Entry to Amortize Discount on Bonds Payable

After the adjusting entry is posted, the balance of Bond Interest Expense is $6,200. This amount is the total annual interest expense on the bonds.

Bond Interest Expense			Discount on Bonds Payable	
Dr.	Cr.		Dr.	Cr.
+	−		+	−
$3,000			$4,000	Adj. $200
3,000				
Adj. 200				

The Discount on Bonds Payable account now has a balance of $3,800. When the bonds mature, Discount on Bonds Payable will be fully amortized. The carrying value of Bonds Payable will then be $100,000, the maturity value.

Remember: A bond premium or discount must be amortized, or written off, over the life of the bonds by annual adjusting entries.

Bonds are often sold with interest payment dates that do not coincide with the end of the corporation's fiscal year. For example, on March 1, Kolar Systems, Inc., issued $1,000,000 worth of 20-year, 9% bonds at face value. Interest is payable semiannually on August 31 and February 28.

On August 31, a journal entry is made to record the semiannual interest payment of $45,000 ($1,000,000 × .09 × %12). Bond Interest Expense is debited for $45,000 and Cash in Bank is credited for the same amount.

The corporation's fiscal year ends on December 31. The next semiannual interest payment will not be made until February 28. By December 31, however, four months of interest expense has accrued and must be recorded. Kolar Systems, therefore, makes the adjusting entry for the accrued interest expense shown in Figure 14–7.

	DATE	DESCRIPTION	POST. REF.	DEBIT	CREDIT	
1		Adjusting Entries				1
2	Dec. 31	Bond Interest Expense		30 00 0 00		2
3		Bond Interest Payable			30 00 0 00	3

GENERAL JOURNAL — PAGE 49

Figure 14–7. Adjusting Entry for Accrued Bond Interest

After this entry is posted, the two bond interest accounts have the balances shown in the following T accounts.

Bond Interest Expense		Bond Interest Payable	
Dr.	Cr.	Dr.	Cr.
+	–	–	+
$45,000			Adj. $30,000
Adj. 30,000			

On February 28, Kolar makes the next semiannual interest payment to the bondholders. The total amount to be paid is $45,000. Of this amount, $30,000 was incurred as an expense in the previous year; $15,000 was incurred in the current year. The entry to record the February 28 transaction is shown in general journal form in Figure 14–8. Since the liability owed to bondholders from the previous year is now being paid, Bond Interest Payable is debited for $30,000. Bond Interest Expense is debited for $15,000, the interest expense applicable to the current year. Cash in Bank is credited for $45,000, the total amount of cash paid out.

Remember: If the interest payment date does not correspond to the end of a corporation's fiscal period, an adjusting entry must be made at the end of the fiscal period to record the accrued bond interest expense.

	DATE		DESCRIPTION	POST. REF.	DEBIT	CREDIT	
1	19— Feb	28	Bond Interest Payable		3000000		1
2			Bond Interest Expense		1500000		2
3			Cash in Bank			4500000	3
4			Check 5310				4

Figure 14–8. Journalizing the Semiannual Interest Payment to Bondholders

Before reading further, do the following activity to check your understanding of bond interest.

Check Your Learning

On a separate sheet of paper, answer the following questions.

1. On January 1, the Blake Corporation issued $2,000,000 of 7%, 10-year bonds at 103, with interest paid semiannually on June 30 and December 31.
   a. On January 1, what account(s) are debited and what is the amount of the debit? What account(s) are credited and what is the amount of the credit?
   b. What is the amount of the semiannual interest payment?
   c. What is the amount of the adjusting entry to amortize the premium?
2. On March 1, the Ling Corporation issued $800,000 of 9%, 20-year bonds at 94, with interest payable semiannually on August 31 and February 28.
   a. What was the total amount of cash received on March 1?
   b. What is the amount of the adjusting entry to record the accrued bond interest expense on December 31?
   c. What is the amount of the adjusting entry to amortize the discount?

Check your answers with those in the answers section. Re-read the preceding part of the chapter to find the answers to any questions you may have missed.

Bond Sinking Fund

To provide greater security for bondholders, the bond indenture may specify that the issuing corporation make annual deposits of cash into a special fund. This special fund, called a **sinking fund**, is used to pay off the bond issue when it comes due. The company keeps the sinking fund separate from its other assets. Cash deposited in the sinking fund is invested in income-producing securities. When the bonds mature, the total of the annual deposits, plus the earnings on the investments, should add up to approximately the same amount as the maturity value of the bond issue. The sinking fund may be controlled by either the corporation or a trustee—usually a bank.

For example, the Stevens Furniture Company issued $100,000 worth of 6%, 10-year bonds dated January 1. The bond indenture provides that, at the end of each of the 10 years, the company make equal annual deposits in a sinking fund. Stevens, which manages its own sinking fund, intends to invest this money in securities that will yield approximately 6% per year. The money earned from the investments plus an annual deposit of $7,040 will accumulate to $100,000 in 10 years.

The following are a few of the many routine transactions that affect the sinking fund during the 10-year period. The entries are illustrated, in general journal form, in Figure 14–9.

December 31: Made annual deposit of $7,040 in bond sinking fund, Check 4611.

When the corporation deposits cash in its sinking fund, it records the transaction as a debit to Bond Sinking Fund and a credit to Cash in Bank. Bond Sinking Fund is classified as an investment account. Investments are assets, generally long-term, that are not intended for use in the normal operations of the business. The entry for this transaction is shown in general journal form in Figure 14–9.

March 18: Bought $7,000 of Consolidated Steel 7% bonds at 99½, Check 4732.

In this transaction, Stevens was willing to pay an amount equal to 99½% of the face value of the bonds. The actual cash paid out was, therefore, $6,965 ($7,000 × .995). When Stevens Furniture invests the sinking fund cash, the transaction is recorded as a debit to Sinking Fund Investments and a credit to Bond Sinking Fund, as shown in general journal form in Figure 14–9. Sinking Fund Investments is also classified as an investment account.

August 15: Received $420 in interest and dividends on sinking fund investments, Receipt 1734.

When Stevens receives interest or dividend income on its investments, it debits Bond Sinking Fund and credits Sinking Fund Income. Sinking Fund Income is classified as an Other Revenue account on the income statement.

April 25: Received $18,620 on the sale of sinking fund investments, originally purchased for $18,400, Receipt 2911.

Investments may be sold and the profits reinvested. In this transaction, Bond Sinking Fund is debited for $18,620, the total amount received from the sale of the investments. Sinking Fund Investments is credited for $18,400, the original amount invested. The $220 represents a profit on the investment. It is credited to an account titled Gain on Sale of Sinking Fund Investments.

December 31: Issued Check 17324 for $100,000 to retire the bond issue.

When the bonds mature, the company arranges the sale of all sinking fund investments. The cash received from the sale of the sinking fund investments, plus the last annual deposit, should equal $100,000. The entry to record the payment of the bond issue is shown in general journal form in Figure 14–9.

	DATE	DESCRIPTION	POST. REF.	DEBIT	CREDIT	
1	19X1 Dec. 31	Bond Sinking Fund		704000		1
2		Cash in Bank			704000	2
3		Check 4611				3
15	19X2 Mar. 18	Sinking Fund Investments		696500		15
16		Bond Sinking Fund			696500	16
17		Check 4732				17
25	19X2 Aug. 15	Bond Sinking Fund		42000		25
26		Sinking Fund Income			42000	26
27		Receipt 1734				27
31	19X4 Apr. 25	Bond Sinking Fund		1862000		31
32		Sinking Fund Investments			1840000	32
33		Gain on Sale of Sink. Fund Invest.			22000	33
34		Receipt 2911				34
38	19X6 Dec. 31	Bonds Payable		10000000		38
39		Bond Sinking Fund			10000000	39
40		Check 17324				40

Figure 14–9. Journalizing Bond Sinking Fund Transactions

Remember: **Bond Sinking Fund is a long-term investment account. It has a normal debit balance.**

Before reading further, do the following activity.

Check Your Learning

The Lorain Corporation issued $400,000 of 10-year, 10% bonds. The company has a bond sinking fund and invests all of the money placed in the fund. At the beginning of the tenth year of the bond issue, the balance of the company's Sinking Fund Investments account is $370,000. On a separate sheet of paper, prepare the entries in general journal form to record the following.

1. The sale of the investments for $384,000 on February 12, Receipt 623.
2. The final deposit in the sinking fund on February 28, bringing the balance of the account up to $400,000, Check 904.
3. The payment of the bonds on March 1, Check 905.

Check your answers with those in the answers section. Re-read the preceding part of the chapter to find the answers to any questions you may have missed.

Redemption of Bonds

To be able to take advantage of a future decline in market interest rates, a corporation may issue callable bonds. Callable bonds are bonds that the corporation has the right to redeem, or buy back, at a specified figure known as the *call price*. The call price is ordinarily higher than the face value.

The Atlas Crockery Company issued $2,000,000 worth of 10%, 20-year callable bonds, with a call price of 104. The yearly interest expense on these bonds is $200,000. Five years later, interest rates in general had gone down. Under the new market conditions, Atlas could issue $2,000,000 worth of 15-year bonds at face value, with a stated interest rate of 7%. The annual interest expense on the 7% bonds would be $140,000. Atlas could save $60,000 in interest expense per year by buying back the bonds, even though it would have to pay $2,080,000 for them ($2,000,000 × 1.04).

When a corporation redeems its bonds at a price less than their carrying value, it realizes a gain. If it redeems its bonds at a price that is more than their carrying value, it incurs a loss.

For example, Northeast Transit Company has $500,000 worth of callable bonds outstanding, with a call price of 105. There is an unamortized discount of $2,000. The carrying value, remember, is the face value of the bond issue plus any premium or minus any discount. The carrying value of Northeast's bonds is, therefore, $498,000 ($500,000 − $2,000). Northeast makes the December 31 interest payment and exercises its option of redeeming the bonds on the same date. The entry, in general journal form, is as shown in Figure 14–10.

	GENERAL JOURNAL				PAGE 59
DATE	DESCRIPTION	POST. REF.	DEBIT	CREDIT	
Dec. 31	Bonds Payable		500000 00		
	Loss on Redemption of Bonds		27000 00		
	Cash in Bank			525000 00	
	Discount on Bonds Payable			2000 00	
	Check 634				

Figure 14–10. Journalizing the Redemption of Bonds for More than Their Carrying Value

In the transaction, Bonds Payable is debited for $500,000, the face value of the bond issue now being redeemed. Cash in Bank is credited for $525,000, the amount of cash paid out at the call price ($500,000 × 1.05). Since the bonds are being paid, the discount must be removed from the accounting records. Discount on Bonds Payable is credited for $2,000, the amount of the unamortized discount. The difference between the carrying value and the price paid, $27,000, is debited to an account called Loss on Redemption of Bonds. This account appears on the income statement in the Other Expenses section.

Remember: Loss on Redemption of Bonds is an expense account. It appears on the income statement in the Other Expenses section.

Even if its bonds are not callable, a corporation can buy back as many of them as it can find on the open market. For example, the Seacoast Paper Company has $1,000,000 worth of 7% coupon bonds outstanding, on which there is an unamortized premium of $30,000. The carrying value of the total bond issue is $1,030,000 ($1,000,000 + $30,000). On July 1, Seacoast buys $100,000 (one tenth of the original issue) of bonds in the open market at 97. The entry for this transaction, in general journal form, is shown in Figure 14–11.

		GENERAL JOURNAL			PAGE _81_
	DATE	DESCRIPTION	POST. REF.	DEBIT	CREDIT
1	July 15	Bonds Payable		100 000 00	
2		Premium on Bonds Payable		3 000 00	
3		Cash in Bank			97 000 00
4		Gain on Redemption of Bonds			6 000 00
5		Check 2716			

Figure 14–11. Journalizing the Repurchase of Bonds for Less than Their Carrying Value

In the transaction, Bonds Payable is debited for $100,000, the face value of the bonds being redeemed. Premium on Bonds Payable is debited for $3,000, one tenth of the unamortized premium. Cash in Bank is credited for $97,000, the amount of cash paid for the bonds on the open market ($100,000 × .97). The carrying value of the bonds being redeemed is $103,000 (one tenth of the bond issue). The Gain on Redemption of Bonds account is credited for $6,000, the amount of the difference between the carrying value of the bonds and the cash paid out.

You can see that a redemption, in effect, cancels all or a portion of the Bonds Payable account, as well as the premium or discount. Gain on Redemption of Bonds appears on the income statement in the Other Revenue section.

Remember: Gain on Redemption of Bonds is a revenue account. It appears on the income statement in the Other Revenue section.

Recording Bonds Payable on the Balance Sheet

The balance sheet of the Dill Company, Inc., which appears in Figure 14–12 on page 332, shows the placement of the accounts that have been discussed in this chapter.

The bond sinking fund accounts appear in the Investments section of the balance sheet, below the Current Assets section. The due date and carrying value of each bond issue are reported in the Long-term Liabilities section.

Figure 14–12.
Balance Sheet

Dill Company, Inc.
Balance Sheet
December 31, 19—

Assets

Current Assets:

Cash in Bank		$ 32,000
Accounts Receivable	$220,000	
Less Allow. for Uncoll. Accts.	4,000	216,000
Notes Receivable		30,000
Merchandise Inventory		647,000
Supplies		2,000
Total Current Assets			$ 927,000

Investments:

Bond Sinking Fund	$ 5,000	
Sinking Fund Investments	84,000	
Total Investments		89,000

Property, Plant, and Equipment:

Equipment (Net)	$190,000	
Building (Net)	135,000	
Land	70,000	
Total Property, Plant, and Equipment		395,000

Intangible Assets:

Organization Costs		8,000
Total Assets		$1,419,000

Liabilities

Current Liabilities:

Accounts Payable	$ 70,000	
Dividends Payable	12,000	
Corporate Income Tax Payable	8,000	
Total Current Liabilities		$ 90,000

Long-term Liabilities:

8% Bonds Payable, due Dec. 31, 1990	$100,000	
Less Discount on Bonds Payable	3,000	$ 97,000
9% Bonds Payable, due Mar. 31, 1995	$200,000	
Plus Premium on Bonds Payable	2,000	202,000
Total Long-term Liabilities		299,000
Total Liabilities		$ 389,000

Stockholders' Equity

Paid-in Capital:

Common Stock, $10 par (100,000 shares authorized, 40,000 shares issued)	$400,000	
Paid-in Capital in Excess of Par	220,000	
Total Paid-in Capital	$620,000	
Retained Earnings	410,000	
Total Stockholders' Equity		1,030,000
Total Liabilities and Stockholders' Equity		$1,419,000

Summary of Key Points

1. A bond may be considered a corporation's long-term promissory note.
2. Bondholders are creditors of the corporation. As such, they are entitled to interest payments, as well as repayment of the principal at maturity. Interest is usually paid semiannually.
3. Bonds Payable is a long-term liability account.
4. The market rate of interest, the rate borrowers are willing to pay and lenders are willing to accept for the use of money, affects the issue price of bonds.
5. A bond is issued at a premium when the issue price is higher than the face value. A bond is issued at a discount when the issue price is lower than the face value.
6. A corporation amortizes (writes off) the premium or discount on bonds payable over the life of the bond issue. The amortization is recorded through an adjusting entry.
7. The carrying value of a bond issue is the face value plus the premium or minus the discount.
8. A bond sinking fund is established to accumulate assets to repay the principal of a bond issue at maturity.
9. A corporation redeems its bonds when it wishes to eliminate the debt or to refinance the debt at a lower rate of interest.

Review and Applications

Building Your Accounting Vocabulary

In your own words, write the definition of each of the following accounting terms. Use complete sentences for your definitions.

amortize	coupon bonds	premium
bond	debenture	registered bonds
bond certificate	discount	secured bond
bond indenture	investments	serial bonds
bond issue	leverage	sinking fund
callable bonds	market rate	term bonds

Reviewing Your Accounting Knowledge

1. Explain the major differences between a share of stock and a bond.
2. What are two advantages to a corporation issuing bonds rather than stock? two disadvantages?
3. What are two definite obligations incurred by a corporation when it issues bonds?
4. What is the difference between a bond certificate, a bond issue, and a bond indenture?
5. What is the difference between term bonds and serial bonds? registered bonds and coupon bonds? secured bonds and debentures?
6. If the market rate of interest is higher than the rate of interest stated in the bond agreement, will the bonds be sold at a premium or a discount? Why?
7. How is the bond premium reported on the balance sheet?
8. Why might the issue price of a bond differ from the face value?
9. Why does the amortization of a bond discount increase the total interest expense to a corporation? Why does the amortization of a bond premium decrease the total interest expense to a corporation?
10. What is the purpose of a bond sinking fund?
11. How is a bond sinking fund classified on a balance sheet?
12. Why would a company want to call its bonds when it can wait longer to pay off the debt?

Improving Your Decision-making Skills

Midwest Motor Freight wants to raise $1,000,000 to expand its operations. It is looking at three options: (1) Issue 20,000 shares of $50-par common stock, which would increase the outstanding shares from 40,000 to 60,000 shares. (2) Issue 10,000 shares of $100-par, 8% cumulative preferred stock. (3) Issue $1,000,000 of 7% bonds. What factors should the company consider before making its decision?

Problem 14–1

On January 1, the Beacon Corporation authorized the issuance of $2,000,000 of 7½%, 10-year bonds, with interest payable on June 30 and December 31.

Instructions: Record these transactions on page 27 of the general journal.

Jan.   1   Issued $2,000,000 of 7½%, 10-year bonds, face value $1,000, at 97, Receipt 439.
June   30   Paid semiannual interest on the bonds, Check 1167.

Problem 14–2

The General Bicycle Corporation has the following account balances:

8% Bonds Payable	$900,000
Premium on Bonds Payable	27,000

General Bicycle decides to redeem a portion of the bond issue.

Instructions: Record these transactions on page 36 of the general journal.

June   1   Paid semiannual interest on the bonds, Check 947.
        1   Bought $100,000 worth of its own bonds on the open market at 96, Check 948.

Problem 14–3

During two consecutive years, the Metro Van and Storage Company completed the following transactions.

19X1
Jan.   2   Issued $1,500,000 worth of 20-year, 8½% bonds, dated January 1 of this year at 99. Interest is payable semianaually on June 30 and December 31, Receipt 609.
June   30   Paid semiannual interest on bonds, Check 1073.
Dec.   31   Paid semiannual interest on bonds, Check 1761.
       31   Recorded the adjusting entry for the amortization of the bond discount.
       31   Closed the Bond Interest Expense account.

19X2
June   30   Paid semiannual interest on bonds, Check 2061.
Dec.   31   Paid semiannual interest on bonds, Check 2413.
       31   Recorded the adjusting entry for the amortization of the bond discount.
       31   Closed the Bond Interest Expense account.

Instructions: Record the transactions on page 41 of the general journal.

Problem 14–4

Sterling Printers, Inc., completed the following transactions related to bonds.

19X1

Mar. 1   Issued $750,000 of 20-year, 9% bonds, dated March 1 of this year, at 106. Interest is payable semiannually on August 31 and February 28, Receipt 306.

Aug. 31   Paid semiannual interest on bonds, Check 1404.

Dec. 31   Recorded the adjusting entry for accrued interest payable.

      31   Recorded the adjusting entry for the amortization of the bond premium.

      31   Closed the Bond Interest Expense account.

19X2

Feb. 28   Paid semiannual interest on bonds, Check 1690.

Aug. 31   Paid semiannual interest on bonds, Check 1904.

Dec. 31   Recorded the adjusting entry for accrued interest payable.

      31   Recorded the adjusting entry for the amortization of the bond premium.

      31   Closed the Bond Interest Expense account.

Instructions:

(1) Record the transactions in general journal form. Use page 63.

(2) Post the entries to the Bond Interest Expense account.

Problem 14–5

During two consecutive years, the Worthington Products Corporation completed the following transactions relating to its $9,000,000 issue of 30-year, 7% bonds, dated April 1 of the first year. Interest is payable on March 31 and September 30. The corporation's fiscal year ends on December 31.

19X1

Apr. 1   Issued $9,000,000 of 30-year, 7% bonds at 97, Receipt 366.

Sept. 30   Paid semiannual interest on bonds, Check 1919.

Dec. 31   Deposited $115,500 in a bond sinking fund, Check 2090.

      31   Recorded the adjusting entry for accrued interest payable.

      31   Recorded the adjusting entry for the amortization of the bond discount.

      31   Closed the Bond Interest Expense account.

19X2

Jan. 6   Bought various securities with sinking fund cash; cost, $108,630, Check 100.

Mar. 31   Paid semiannual interest on bonds, Check 2411.

Sept. 30   Paid semiannual interest on bonds, Check 2907.

Dec. 31   Recorded receipt of $5,839.50 of income from sinking fund investments, depositing the cash in the sinking fund, Receipt 60.

31   Deposited $169,950 in the bond sinking fund, Check 3104.

31   Recorded the adjusting entry for accrued interest payable.

31   Recorded the adjusting entry for the amortization of the bond discount.

31   Closed the Bond Interest Expense account.

Instructions:

(1) Record the transactions in general journal form. Use page 101.

(2) Post the entries to the Bond Interest Expense and Discount on Bonds Payable accounts.

Problem 14–6

On April 1, Wilson Mall, Inc., whose fiscal year ends on December 31, authorized the issuance of $12,000,000 of 20-year, 9% bonds, dated April 1, with interest payable on March 31 and September 30. The following transactions took place during the first two years.

19X1

Apr.   1   Issued $12,000,000 of 20-year, 9% bonds at 101, Receipt 601.

Sept.   30   Paid semiannual interest on bonds, Check 1390.

Dec.   31   Deposited $240,000 in a bond sinking fund, Check 1463.

         31   Recorded the adjusting entry for accrued interest payable.

         31   Recorded the adjusting entry for the amortization of the bond premium.

         31   Closed the Bond Interest Expense account.

19X2

Jan.   12   Bought various securities with sinking fund cash; cost, $231,900, Check 101.

Mar.   31   Paid semiannual interest on bonds, Check 1667.

Jul.   1   Recorded receipt of $8,085 of income derived from sinking fund investments, depositing the cash in the sinking fund, Receipt 14.

          8   Bought various securities with sinking fund cash; cost, $13,140, Check 102.

Sept.   30   Paid semiannual interest on bonds, Check 1815.

Dec.   31   Recorded the receipt of $16,695 of income from sinking fund investments, depositing the cash in the sinking fund, Receipt 15.

         31   Deposited $300,000 in the bond sinking fund, Check 2007.

         31   Recorded the adjusting entry for accrued interest payable.

         31   Recorded the adjusting entry for the bond premium amortization.

         31   Closed the Sinking Fund Income account.

         31   Closed the Bond Interest Expense account.

Instructions:

(1) Record the transactions in general journal form. Use page 94.

(2) Post the entries to the Bond Interest Expense, Premium on Bonds Payable, and Sinking Fund Income accounts.

Accounting for a Corporation

In the last three chapters of Unit 3, you learned how to record various transactions for a corporation that issues its stock to the general public. Now you will have the opportunity to apply what you have learned by keeping the accounting records for Ryan Furniture Company, Inc.

When you have completed this activity, you will have

1. prepared financial statements
2. analyzed business transactions concerning stocks, bonds, and corporate income taxes
3. journalized business transactions in the general journal
4. posted transactions to selected general ledger accounts

Ryan Furniture Company, Inc.

Ryan Furniture Company, Inc. is a merchandising corporation. The company earns revenue by selling furniture, Oriental rugs, and other home furnishings to the general public and local businesses.

The company was incorporated several years ago with authorized capital of 5,000 shares of $100-par preferred 8% stock and 25,000 shares of $20-par common stock.

Chart of Accounts

The chart of accounts for Ryan Furniture Company, Inc. is shown on the next page.

Preparing End-of-period Financial Statements

You began working at Ryan Furniture Company at the end of the company's fiscal period. The end-of-period work sheet has already been prepared

RYAN FURNITURE COMPANY, INC.
Chart of Accounts

ASSETS	101	Cash in Bank
	105	Accounts Receivable
	110	Allowance for Uncollectible Accounts
	115	Subscriptions Receivable—Preferred 8% Stock
	120	Subscriptions Receivable—Common Stock
	125	Merchandise Inventory
	130	Store Supplies
	135	Bond Sinking Fund
	140	Sinking Fund Investments
	145	Equipment
	150	Accumulated Depreciation—Equipment
	155	Organization Costs
LIABILITIES	201	Accounts Payable
	202	Corporate Income Tax Payable
	203	Dividends Payable—Preferred
	204	Bonds Payable
	205	Premium on Bonds Payable
STOCKHOLDERS' EQUITY	301	Preferred 8% Stock
	302	Preferred Stock Subscribed
	303	Paid-in Capital in Excess of Par—Preferred
	304	Common Stock
	305	Common Stock Dividend Distributable
	306	Common Stock Subscribed
	307	Paid-in Capital in Excess of Par—Common
	308	Retained Earnings
	309	Treasury Stock
	310	Paid-in Capital from Sale of Treasury Stock
	311	Income Summary

REVENUE	401	Sales
	402	Sales Discounts
	403	Sales Returns and Allowances
COST OF MERCHANDISE	501	Purchases
	502	Transportation In
	503	Purchases Discounts
	504	Purchases Returns and Allowances
EXPENSES	601	Advertising Expense
	605	Bad Debts Expense
	610	Depreciation Expense—Equipment
	615	Miscellaneous Expense
	620	Rent Expense
	625	Salaries Expense
	630	Supplies Expense
	635	Utilities Expense
	640	Income Tax Expense
OTHER REVENUE	701	Sinking Fund Income
OTHER EXPENSES	801	Bond Interest Expense

by another accounting clerk. The work sheet appears in the working papers that accompany this textbook.

Instructions: Using the data on the work sheet,

(1) Prepare an income statement for the year ended December 31.
(2) Prepare a statement of retained earnings. The beginning balance of Retained Earnings was $86,954. During the year, the company declared and paid the regular cash dividend to preferred stockholders (total, $4,800). No dividend was paid to common stockholders.
(3) Prepare a balance sheet. The 10% bond issue is due in ten years on January 1. Place the Assets section on one side of the form and the Liabilities and Stockholders' Equity sections on the other side.

Recording Business Transactions

The following are some of the transactions concerning stocks, bonds, and corporate income taxes that took place during the first six months of the following year.

Jan.   5   Sold 100 shares of common stock at par for cash, Memorandum 1161.

        10   Sold 50 shares of preferred stock at par for cash, Memorandum 1173.

        20   Received subscriptions to 500 shares of common stock at $21.00 per share, Memorandum 1180.

        25   Received 40% of the subscription price from all common stock subscribers, Memorandum 1188.

        31   Received subscriptions to 200 shares of preferred 8% stock at $102.00 per share, Memorandum 1197.

Feb.   1   Declared an 8% cash dividend on 650 shares of $100-par preferred stock to stockholders of record as of February 14, payable March 1, Minute Book page 649.

        1   Declared a 5% stock dividend on 8,400 shares of common stock to stockholders of record as of February 14, payable on March 1, Minute Book page 649. The current market price of the stock is $22.00.

        10   Subscribers to 200 shares of preferred stock paid 25% of the subscription price, Memorandum 1215.

        18   Acquired 300 shares of own common stock at $21.00 per share from the estate of a deceased stockholder, Memorandum 1220.

        28   Subscribers to 500 shares of common stock paid an additional 40% of the subscription price, Memorandum 1231.

Mar.   1   Paid the cash dividend to preferred stockholders declared on February 1, Check 1654.

        1   Distributed the stock dividend declared on February 1 to common stockholders, Minute Book page 649.

	15	Issued Check 1675 for the previous year's federal income tax liability of $11,180.00.
	18	Subscribers to 200 shares of preferred stock paid an additional 25% of the subscription price, Memorandum 1259.
	28	Subscribers to 500 shares of common stock paid the remaining 20% of the subscription price; issued the stock; Memorandum 1268.
Apr.	2	Issued 500 shares of common stock at $21.00 per share, Memorandum 1273.
	15	Paid the first quarterly federal income tax installment of $14,487.50, Check 1782.
	20	Subscribers to 200 shares of preferred stock paid the remaining 50% of the subscription price; issued the stock; Memorandum 1301.
	25	Sold 50 shares of treasury stock at $21.00 per share, Memorandum 1309.
May	1	Sold 50 shares of treasury stock at $20.00 per share, Memorandum 1317.
	22	Sold 100 shares of common stock at $22.00 per share, Memorandum 1329.
	23	Sold 50 shares of treasury stock at $22.50 per share, Memorandum 1330.
	31	Received $750.00 in interest and dividends on sinking fund investments, Memorandum 1342.
	31	Sold 25 shares of treasury stock at $21.50 per share, Memorandum 1343.
June	1	Made a deposit of $2,000.00 to the bond sinking fund, Check 1904.
	15	Issued Check 1919 for $14,487.50 for the second quarterly federal income tax installment.
	28	Sold 50 shares of treasury stock at $20.50 per share, Memorandum 1389.
	30	Paid the semiannual interest on bonds, Check 1964.

Instructions:

(1) Journalize the transactions in the general journal, beginning on page 56.
(2) Post the transactions to the general ledger accounts daily. Selected, opened general ledger accounts appear in the working papers accompanying this textbook.

Unit 4
Accounting for Departmental, Branch, and Manufacturing Systems

The accounting system used by any business must be able to provide the information management needs to help plan, control, and evaluate their operations. In this unit, you will learn about the accounting systems used by businesses whose activities are divided into segments such as departments and branches. You will also learn about the accounting system used by a business that manufactures products. This accounting system is set up to accumulate data on all of the costs involved in manufacturing the company's product or products.

The chapters you will study in this unit are listed below.

Oil fields near Houston, Texas

15 Departmental Accounting Systems

Many businesses carry on more than one type of sales or service activity. Most service stations, for example, do repair work in addition to selling gasoline and oil. Grocery stores have separate sections for produce, meat, frozen foods, and other items. Some large stores may sell everything from stationery to furniture to jewelry. When a company carries on a number of different activities, it usually separates these different activities into departments.

By organizing its operations into departments, a company can delegate authority to department managers, who are held responsible for the activities of their departments. The company can also measure the profitability and efficiency of each department.

In this chapter, you will see how companies organize their accounting data by departments. You will learn how to allocate revenue and costs among departments. You will also prepare income statements that report on a business's operations by department.

Learning Objectives

When you have completed this chapter, you should be able to

1. Explain why a business departmentalizes its operations.

2. Determine gross profit by department.

3. Allocate expenses among departments.

4. Prepare a departmental work sheet.

5. Prepare income statements that report departmental net income from operations and department contribution margin.

6. Define the accounting terms presented in this chapter.

New Terms   departmental accounting system / selling expenses / administrative expenses / contribution margin / direct expenses / indirect expenses

Accounting for Departments

When a business has a number of departments, management always wants to know how well each department is doing. They need to know how much of a contribution each department is making to the firm's overall profit (or loss). The accounting system, therefore, must be organized in such a way as to provide information on revenue and expenses by department. An accounting system that provides data for two or more departments is called a departmental accounting system.

Large companies are more likely to use departmental accounting than small ones. However, even a small business—if it carries on more than one type of business activity—may benefit from departmental accounting. For example, the Whitehouse Company is a two-person business that sells insurance and manages property. Separate accounts are kept for insurance commissions and management fees. At the end of the fiscal year, Sylvia and Irving Whitehouse can compare the profitability of each activity with the amount of time and attention they had to devote to it. This comparison may then form the basis for their decision to spend more time on one activity and less on the other.

The accounting reports for departmental operations are generally limited to income statements. These income statements may report just the departmental sales, cost of merchandise sold, and gross profit. They may also be expanded to show each department's share of expenses. Financial statements for the business as a whole are generated using the information obtained for each department.

Gross Profit by Departments

For a merchandising business, gross profit on sales is one of the most important figures on the income statement. Gross profit on sales, remember, is the difference between net sales and the cost of merchandise sold. To be successful, a merchandising business must sell its goods for more than their cost in order to pay expenses and have an adequate income left over.

Department managers are constantly making decisions that affect their departments' sales or cost of merchandise sold. Department managers are responsible for determining, for example, which merchandise to purchase and what price to charge for that merchandise. Since sales and cost of merchandise sold are, to a great extent, controlled by each department, an income statement reporting the gross profit on sales for each department is very useful to management.

To determine gross profit by department, departmental figures must be kept for each element entering into gross profit. There are two methods of doing this.

1. Keep separate revenue and cost accounts for each department. The balances of each department's accounts would be reported on the income statement.
2. Keep only one general ledger account for each item involved in gross profit and maintain supplementary records for the various departments. The information from these records would be reported on the income statement.

Maintaining Separate Departmental Accounts

Keeping separate revenue and cost accounts for each department provides the most accurate accounting data. Separate accounts for each department are set up for Sales, Sales Returns and Allowances, Sales Discounts, Purchases, Transportation In, Purchases Returns and Allowances, Purchases Discounts, and Merchandise Inventory. For example, The Color Center has two departments: the Paint Department and the Wallpaper Department. It has two Sales accounts: Sales—Paint and Sales—Wallpaper. It also has two Sales Returns and Allowances accounts, two Merchandise Inventory accounts, and so forth. The company's special journals contain columns for each departmental account. For example, The Color Center's sales journal is shown in Figure 15–1. At the end of the month, the column totals are posted to the accounts named in the column headings.

		SALES JOURNAL					PAGE 14
DATE	SALES SLIP NO.	CUSTOMER'S ACCOUNT DEBITED	POST. REF.	ACCOUNTS RECEIVABLE DEBIT	SALES TAX PAYABLE CREDIT	SALES—PAINT CREDIT	SALES—WALLPAPER CREDIT
Sept. 1	1698	Nancy Dolan	✓	173 25	8 25	165 00	
3	1699	Arthur Strachan	✓	394 80	18 80	376 00	
3	1700	Randy Sever	✓	751 80	35 80		716 00
30		Totals		15 679 65	744 65	10 246 00	4 687 00
				(115)	(235)	(401)	(402)

Figure 15–1. Sales Journal for The Color Center

Maintaining One General Ledger Account

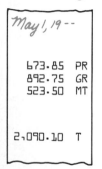

When a company keeps only one general ledger account for each item involved in gross profit, the balance of each account must be distributed among the various departments at the end of the accounting period. To do so, supplementary records are kept to accumulate departmental information. For example, Martin's Grocery has three departments: produce, grocery, and meat. Martin's records sales by department, by having the checkout clerk punch a department key on the cash register for each item purchased. At the end of each day the store's total sales are recorded in a sales journal. The total sales for each department are recorded on a departmental sales analysis sheet like the one shown in Figure 15–2.

MARTIN'S GROCERY
DEPARTMENTAL SALES ANALYSIS SHEET

DATE	PRODUCE DEPT.	GROCERY DEPT.	MEAT DEPT.	TOTAL SALES
May 1	$673.85	$892.75	$523.50	$2,090.10
2	701.40	850.62	676.80	2,228.82

Figure 15–2. Departmental Sales Analysis Sheet

Businesses also use separate analysis sheets for sales returns, purchases, purchases returns, purchases discounts, and so on. At the end of the accounting period, these analysis sheets give departmental breakdowns for each item involved in determining gross profit.

Remember: **In a departmental accounting system, it is necessary to keep separate accounts or supplementary records by department for each account involved in determining gross profit on sales.**

Reporting Gross Profit by Departments

As you can see, it is not difficult to organize the accounting system to report sales and cost of merchandise sold data by departments. Using this information, an income statement that reports gross profit on sales by department can be prepared. Look at the income statement for The Color Center shown in Figure 15–3 on pages 348–349. The income statement has separate sections for reporting data on gross profit for the Paint Department and for the Wallpaper Department. Data from the two departments is combined and reported in the Total section.

Notice too that the accounting information is reported on a departmental basis only through gross profit on sales. Operating expenses are reported in the Total section only. Operating expenses are expenses, other than the cost of merchandise purchased, that are incurred in the operation of the business. They are further classified as either selling expenses or administrative expenses. **Selling expenses** are those expenses incurred to sell or market the goods or services sold by the business. Examples of selling expenses are advertising expense and the salaries of salespeople. **Administrative expenses** are costs related to the management of the business. Examples of administrative expenses are office expenses and the salaries of management personnel. Selling and administrative expenses are generally reported separately on an income statement.

It is not always easy to divide expenses among departments, particularly an expense such as insurance expense. For that reason, some businesses do not departmentalize their income statements beyond gross profit on sales.

Remember: **Gross profit on sales is determined by deducting cost of merchandise sold from net sales.**

		PAINT DEPARTMENT		
1	Revenue:			
2	Sales		560 000 00	
3	Less: Sales Returns & Allow.		14 200 00	
4	Net Sales			545 800 00
5	Cost of Merchandise Sold:			
6	Merch. Inventory, Jan. 1, 19--		96 400 00	
7	Purchases	325 120 00		
8	Less: Purchases Returns & Allow.	9 580 00		
9	Purchases Discounts	5 740 00		
10	Net Purchases		309 800 00	
11	Merchandise Available for Sale		406 200 00	
12	Less: Merch. Inventory, Dec. 31, 19--		110 000 00	
13	Cost of Merchandise Sold			296 200 00
14	Gross Profit on Sales			249 600 00
15	Operating Expenses:			
16	Selling Expenses:			
17	Advertising Expense			
18	Deprec. Exp.-Store Equip.			
19	Misc. Selling Expense			
20	Sales Salaries Expense			
21	Total Selling Expenses			
22	Administrative Expenses:			
23	Bad Debts Expense			
24	Insurance Expense			
25	Misc. Admin. Expense			
26	Office Salaries Expense			
27	Rent Expense			
28	Utilities Expense			
29	Total Admin. Expenses			
30	Total Operating Expenses			
31	Net Income from Operations			
32	Other Revenue:			
33	Interest Income			
34	Other Expenses:			
35	Interest Expense			
36	Net Income			

Figure 15–3. Income Statement Showing Gross Profit by Departments   (Left Side)

	WALLPAPER DEPARTMENT				TOTAL			
1								
2		240 000 00				800 000 00		
3		5 800 00				20 000 00		
4			234 200 00				780 000 00	
5								
6		82 740 00				179 140 00		
7	167 890 00				493 010 00			
8	4 756 00				14 336 00			
9	3 274 00				9 014 00			
10		159 860 00				469 660 00		
11		242 600 00				648 800 00		
12		90 000 00				200 000 00		
13			152 600 00				448 800 00	
14			81 600 00				331 200 00	
15								
16								
17					17 600 00			
18					3 300 00			
19					4 270 00			
20					140 000 00			
21						165 170 00		
22								
23					2 570 00			
24					4 400 00			
25					9 200 00			
26					32 100 00			
27					16 400 00			
28					4 840 00			
29						61 230 00		
30							226 400 00	
31							104 800 00	
32								
33						3 624 00		
34								
35						2 400 00	1 224 00	
36							106 024 00	

(Right Side)

Allocating Operating Expenses

If a business does wish to extend the departmental reporting of accounting data beyond gross profit, it must allocate the various operating expenses among its departments. Some operating expenses can easily be identified as belonging to a given department. For example, suppose that a salesperson only works in one department; that salesperson's salary or commission is then an expense of that department only. However, other operating expenses, such as Rent Expense or Utilities Expense, are not restricted to one department. These expenses must be divided among the departments on some fair basis. Let's look at the operating expenses of The Color Center and see what methods it uses to allocate them between its two departments.

Advertising Expense

The Color Center advertises in newspapers and on the radio. The company's total advertising expense for the period was $17,600. The breakdown between the cost of the newspaper and the radio ads is as follows.

Newspaper advertising	$ 9,600
Radio advertising	8,000
Total advertising expense	$17,600

The Color Center's cost of newspaper advertising is allocated according to the number of column inches each department uses. (Newspaper advertising is billed according to the number of inches a particular ad covers. A company might purchase, for example, a 4-inch ad.) During the past year, The Color Center bought 3,200 inches of newspaper advertising. The Paint Department had 1,920 column inches of advertising, or 60% of the 3,200 inches (1,920 ÷ 3,200). The Wallpaper Department had 1,280 column inches of advertising, or 40% (1,280 ÷ 3,200).

The Paint Department's share of the cost of newspaper advertising is determined as follows.

$$\$9,600 \times .60 = \$5,760$$

The Wallpaper Department's share of the cost of newspaper advertising is calculated as follows.

$$\$9,600 \times .40 = \$3,840$$

For radio advertising, The Color Center allocates the cost to the two departments according to the amount of air time each department used. During the year, The Color Center bought 1,250 minutes of radio time. The Paint Department ran 675 minutes of the ads, or 54% (675 ÷ 1,250). The Wallpaper Department ads ran for 575 minutes, or 46% (575 ÷ 1,250).

The Paint Department's share of the cost of radio advertising is determined as follows.

$$\$8,000 \times .54 = \$4,320$$

The Wallpaper Department's share of the cost of radio advertising is determined as shown below.

$$\$8,000 \times .46 = \$3,680$$

The following table summarizes The Color Center's allocation of advertising expense.

	Paint Department	Wallpaper Department	Total
Newspaper advertising	$ 5,760	$3,840	$ 9,600
Radio advertising	4,320	3,680	8,000
	$10,080	$7,520	$17,600

Depreciation Expense—Store Equipment

The Color Center maintains a plant asset subsidiary ledger that lists the department in which each piece of store equipment is located. The total depreciation expense for the store equipment for the year was $3,300. The depreciation expense for the store equipment located in the Paint Department is $1,840. The depreciation expense for the store equipment located in the Wallpaper Department is $1,460.

Miscellaneous Selling Expense

The balance of the Miscellaneous Selling Expense account tends to vary according to the volume of sales. As a result, The Color Center allocates the expense on the basis of the total sales of each department. The sales by department are as follows.

Paint Department sales	$560,000
Wallpaper Department sales	240,000
Total sales	$800,000

The Paint Department's sales are 70% of the total sales ($560,000 ÷ $800,000). The Wallpaper Department's sales are 30% of total sales ($240,000 ÷ $800,000). The Color Center also uses this basis to allocate some of its other operating expenses.

The miscellaneous selling expense for the year is $4,270. It is allocated as follows.

Paint Department:	$4,270 × .70 = $2,989
Wallpaper Department:	$4,270 × .30 = $1,281

Sales Salaries Expense

The Color Center allocates the salespersons' salaries to the Paint Department or the Wallpaper Department according to the payroll register, which lists each employee by department. Of the $140,000 total sales salaries expense, the Paint Department's share is $88,000 and the Wallpaper Department's is $52,000.

Bad Debts Expense

Bad Debts Expense also varies according to the volume of sales. Like Miscellaneous Selling Expense, it is allocated on the basis of sales.

The bad debts expense for the year is $2,570. It is allocated as follows.

Paint Department:	$2,570 × .70 = $1,799
Wallpaper Department:	$2,570 × .30 = $ 771

Insurance Expense

The Color Center carries insurance policies to cover losses that might result from (1) damage to merchandise or equipment (property insurance, annual premium, $3,600), and (2) injuries to customers while on the premises (liability insurance, annual premium, $800).

The cost of the property insurance on merchandise and equipment is allocated on the basis of the value of the inventory and equipment held by each department at the end of the year, as shown in the following table.

	Paint Department	Wallpaper Department	Total
Merchandise inventory	$110,000	$ 90,000	$200,000
Equipment	19,440	12,960	32,400
	$129,440	$102,960	$232,400

The total value of the company's merchandise and equipment is $232,400. The Paint Department's total of $129,440 is 56% of the total. The Wallpaper Department's total of $102,960 is 44% of the total. Each department's share of the $3,600 property insurance expense is calculated as follows.

Paint Department:	$3,600 × .56 = $2,016
Wallpaper Department:	$3,600 × .44 = $1,584

The cost of the liability insurance (in case of personal injury to customers) is based on sales. The Color Center allocates the $800 liability insurance expense as follows.

Paint Department:	$800 × .70 = $560
Wallpaper Department:	$800 × .30 = $240

The Color Center's total insurance expense is allocated as follows.

	Paint Department	Wallpaper Department	Total
Property insurance	$2,016	$1,584	$3,600
Liability insurance	560	240	800
	$2,576	$1,824	$4,400

Miscellaneous Administrative Expense

Like Miscellaneous Selling Expense, Miscellaneous Administrative Expense is allocated to the two departments according to sales. The expense for the year is $920. It is allocated as follows.

Paint Department:	$920 × .70 = $644
Wallpaper Department:	$920 × .30 = $276

Office Salaries Expense

People who work in the office of The Color Center are paid a total of $32,100 per year. The company allocates the salaries of office workers on the basis of the amount of time the office personnel had to spend on each department. The Color Center's management estimates that 70% of the office staff's time is devoted to the Paint Department and 30% to the Wallpaper Department. The office salaries expense is allocated as follows.

Paint Department:	$32,100 × .70 = $22,470
Wallpaper Department:	$32,100 × .30 = $ 9,630

Rent Expense and Utilities Expense

The Color Center rents 40,000 square feet of floor space. It allocates the expenses for rent and utilities on the basis of floor space occupied by each department. The Paint Department occupies 25,000 square feet, or 62.5% (25,000 ÷ 40,000). The Wallpaper Department occupies 15,000 square feet, or 37.5% (15,000 ÷ 40,000).

The annual rent expense was $16,400. Each department's share of the total expense is calculated as follows.

Paint Department:	$16,400 × .625 = $10,250
Wallpaper Department:	$16,400 × .375 = $ 6,150

The total utilities expense for the year was $4,840. That amount is allocated as follows.

Paint Department:	$4,840 × .625 = $3,025
Wallpaper Department:	$4,840 × .375 = $1,815

Before reading further, do the following activity to check your understanding of how to allocate expenses.

Check Your Learning

The Newburn Drugstore occupies an area of 10,000 square feet. The departments and the floor space occupied by each are as follows.

Pharmacy	1,400 square feet
Camera supplies	600 square feet
Toiletries and cosmetics	6,500 square feet
Greeting cards	500 square feet
Receiving and storage	1,000 square feet

Newburn's annual rent is $16,000. Allocate the rent expense among the five departments.

Check your answers with those in the answers section. Re-read the preceding part of the chapter to find the correct answers to any questions you may have missed.

Net Income from Operations by Department

A company may extend its departmental reporting of income to various points on the income statement, such as net income from operations or net income. Net income from operations is gross profit on sales minus operating expenses. The Color Center keeps separate accounts for each item that enters into gross profit and allocates its operating expenses between the Paint Department and the Wallpaper Department according to the methods described earlier. Once the operating expenses have been allocated, a departmental work sheet can be prepared.

Preparing a Departmental Work Sheet

When the work sheet is prepared, all account balances are first entered in the Trial Balance columns of the work sheet. The adjustments are calculated and entered in the Adjustments section. The amounts are then extended to either the Balance Sheet or Income Statement sections. Finally, the net income (or loss) is calculated and entered. The work sheet is then used to prepare the financial statements, including the income statement.

Look at Figure 15–4 on pages 356–357, the work sheet prepared by The Color Center. Notice that this work sheet has three Income Statement sections. There is an Income Statement section for each department. The third Income Statement section is labeled Nondepartmental. These columns are used to record other revenue and other expense accounts.

By the time the work sheet is prepared, The Color Center has already allocated the operating expenses between the departments. These allocations are the basis for the amounts extended to the departmental Income Statement sections. (Various asset, liability, and ownership equity accounts are not shown, but their balances are included in the totals.) Notice that the net income (or loss) from operations is calculated for each department. The Paint Department had a net income from operations of $105,927, while the Wallpaper Department had a net loss from operations of $1,127.

The combined net income from operations of $104,800 ($105,927 − $1,127) is extended to the Nondepartmental Credit column. The Nondepartmental Income Statement columns are then totaled. The difference between the totals of the two columns represents the net income for the period.

This departmental work sheet can be used to prepare an income statement that reports the accounting data by departments through net income from operations.

Reporting Net Income from Operations by Departments

The income statement showing net income from operations by departments contains a set of columns for each department, as well as a set of columns for the combined total of both departments. The income statement in Figure 15–5 on pages 358–359 is a more representative example of an income statement for The Color Center than the one shown in Figure 15–3 (on pages 348–349). Notice that it follows this format.

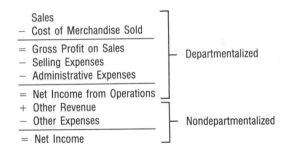

Remember: **Net income from operations is determined by subtracting the total operating expenses from gross profit on sales.**

Contribution Margin by Departments

Some accountants believe that an income statement departmentalized through net income from operations does not realistically report each department's performance. They say that the methods used to allocate operating expenses are arbitrary and that it is difficult to determine each department's "fair share" of the expenses. They also believe that departments should not be held responsible for expenses over which the managers have no control. For these

	ACCOUNT NAME	TRIAL BALANCE DEBIT	TRIAL BALANCE CREDIT	ADJUSTMENTS DEBIT	ADJUSTMENTS CREDIT
3	Accounts Receivable	8204000			
4	Allow. for Uncollectible Accounts		862 00		(f) 2570 00
7	Merch. Inventory – Paint	9640000		(b) 1000000	(a) 9640000
8	Merch. Inventory – Wallpaper	8274000		(d) 9000000	(c) 8274000
9	Prepaid Insurance	554000			(e) 440000
10	Store Equipment	3240000			
11	Accum. Deprec. – Store Equipment		2160000		(g) 330000
16	Income Summary			(a) 9640000	(b) 1000000
17				(c) 8274000	(d) 9000000
18	Sales – Paint		5600000 0		
19	Sales – Wallpaper		2400000 0		
20	Sales Ret. & Allow. – Paint	1420000			
21	Sales Ret. & Allow. – Wallpaper	580000			
22	Purchases – Paint	3251200 0			
23	Purchases – Wallpaper	1678900 0			
24	Purchases Ret. & Allow. – Paint		958000		
25	Purchases Ret. & Allow. – Wallpaper		475600		
26	Purchases Discounts – Paint		574000		
27	Purchases Discounts – Wallpaper		327400		
28	Advertising Expense	1760000			
29	Bad Debts Expense			(f) 2570 00	
30	Deprec. Exp. – Store Equipment			(g) 330000	
31	Insurance Expense			(e) 440000	
32	Misc. Admin. Expense	920 00			
33	Misc. Selling Expense	427000			
34	Office Salaries Expense	3210000			
35	Rent Expense	1640000			
36	Sales Salaries Expense	1400000 0			
37	Utilities Expense	484000			
38	Interest Income		362400		
39	Interest Expense	240000			
40		14718640 0	14718640 0	3894100 0	3894100 0
41	Net Income (Loss) from Operations				
42					
43	Net Income				
44					

Figure 15–4. Departmentalized Work Sheet   *(Left Side)*

Center
Sheet
December 31, 19--

PAINT DEPARTMENT INCOME STATEMENT		WALLPAPER DEPARTMENT INCOME STATEMENT		NONDEPARTMENTAL INCOME STATEMENT		BALANCE SHEET		
DEBIT	CREDIT	DEBIT	CREDIT	DEBIT	CREDIT	DEBIT	CREDIT	
						82040 00		3
							3432 00	4
						110000 00		7
						90000 00		8
						1140 00		0
						32400 00		10
							24900 00	11
96400 00	110000 00							16
		82740 00	90000 00					17
	560000 00							18
			240000 00					19
14200 00								20
		5800 00						21
325120 00								22
		167890 00						23
	9580 00							24
			4756 00					25
	5740 00							26
			3274 00					27
10080 00		7520 00						28
1799 00		771 00						29
1840 00		1460 00						30
2576 00		1824 00						31
644 00		276 00						32
2989 00		1281 00						33
22470 00		9630 00						34
10250 00		6150 00						35
88000 00		52000 00						36
3025 00		1815 00						37
				3624 00				38
				2400 00				39
579393 00	685320 00	339157 00	338030 00					40
105927 00			(1127 00)		104800 00			41
685320 00	685320 00	339157 00	339157 00	2400 00	108424 00	1,119586 00	1,013562 00	42
				106024 00			106024 00	43
				108424 00	108424 00	1,119586 00	1,119586 00	44

(Right Side)

			PAINT DEPARTMENT		
1	Revenue:				
2	Sales			560 000 00	
3	Less: Sales Returns + Allow.			14 200 00	
4	Net Sales				545 800 00
5	Cost of Merchandise Sold:				
6	Merch. Inventory, Jan. 1, 19--			96 400 00	
7	Purchases	325 120 00			
8	Less: Purchases Returns + Allow.	9 580 00			
9	Purchases Discounts	5 740 00			
10	Net Purchases			309 800 00	
11	Merchandise Available for Sale			406 200 00	
12	Less: Merch. Inventory, Dec. 31, 19--			110 000 00	
13	Cost of Merchandise Sold				296 200 00
14	Gross Profit on Sales				249 600 00
15	Operating Expenses:				
16	Selling Expenses:				
17	Advertising Expense	10 080 00			
18	Deprec. Exp.-Store Equip.	1 840 00			
19	Misc. Selling Expense	2 989 00			
20	Sales Salaries Expense	88 000 00			
21	Total Selling Expenses			102 909 00	
22	Administrative Expenses:				
23	Bad Debts Expense	1 799 00			
24	Insurance Expense	2 576 00			
25	Misc. Admin. Expense	644 00			
26	Office Salaries Expense	22 470 00			
27	Rent Expense	10 250 00			
28	Utilities Expense	3 025 00			
29	Total Admin. Expenses			40 764 00	
30	Total Operating Expenses				143 673 00
31	Net Income (Loss) from Operations				105 927 00
32	Other Revenue:				
33	Interest Income				
34	Other Expenses:				
35	Interest Expense				
36	Net Income				

Figure 15–5. Income Statement Showing Net Income by Departments   (Left Side)

Line	WALLPAPER DEPARTMENT			TOTAL		
1						
2		240000 00			800000 00	
3		5800 00			2000 00	
4			234200 00			780000 00
5						
6		82740 00			17914 00	
7	167890 00			49301 00		
8	4756 00			14336 00		
9	3275 00			9014 00		
10		159860 00			469660 00	
11		242600 00			648800 00	
12		90000 00			200000 00	
13			152600 00			448800 00
14			81600 00			331200 00
15						
16						
17	7520 00			17600 00		
18	1460 00			3300 00		
19	1281 00			4270 00		
20	52000 00			14000 00		
21		62261 00			165170 00	
22						
23	771 00			2570 00		
24	1824 00			4400 00		
25	276 00			920 00		
26	9630 00			32100 00		
27	6150 00			16400 00		
28	1815 00			4840 00		
29		20466 00			61230 00	
30			82727 00			226400 00
31			(1127 00)			104800 00
32						
33					3624 00	
34						
35					2400 00	1224 00
36						106024 00

(Right Side)

reasons, income statements are often prepared that report each department's contribution margin. **Contribution margin** is the contribution that a given department makes to the net income of the firm. It is determined by subtracting from gross profit on sales only those expenses that are identified with each department.

Before a company can prepare an income statement showing each department's contribution margin, it is necessary to distinguish between direct and indirect expenses. **Direct expenses** are expenses incurred for the sole benefit of a given department and thus are under the control of the department head. **Indirect expenses** are expenses incurred for the entire business as a whole, and thus are not under the control of one department head. For example, Sales Salaries Expense is a direct expense, since it is incurred solely for the benefit of one department. On the other hand, property tax on real estate is an expense incurred for the business as a whole; it cannot be charged directly to one department.

Some operating expenses may be partially direct and partially indirect. For example, The Color Center's insurance expense consisted partially of liability insurance, which benefited the company as a whole, and partially of merchandise and inventory insurance, which directly benefited separate departments of the company. The insurance premium for liability insurance is an indirect expense; the property insurance premium is a direct expense. Advertising expense could also be partially direct and partially indirect, if some of the advertising stressed the name and location of the company and some focused on one or both of the departments. When classifying an expense as being direct or indirect, use this guideline: The expense must be directly related to the department. If the department were not in existence, the expense would not be in existence.

The format of an income statement that emphasizes contribution margin is as follows.

	Sales
−	Cost of Merchandise Sold
=	Gross Profit on Sales
−	Direct Expenses
=	Contribution Margin
−	Indirect Expenses
=	Net Income from Operations
+	Other Revenue
−	Other Expenses
=	Net Income

Remember: Direct expenses are those that are incurred for the sole benefit of a department. If the department did not exist, the expense would not have been incurred.

The income statement in Figure 15–6 on pages 362–363 presents the same figures that appear in Figure 15–5. In Figure 15–6, however, the data appear in the contribution-margin format.

The Meaning of Contribution Margin

Contribution margin is the most realistic method of reporting the profitability of a department. If the company does away with the department, the company's net income will decrease by the amount of the contribution margin. For example, in the case of The Color Center, the Wallpaper Department had a contribution margin of $18,229. That is, if The Color Center eliminated the department, its net income would be reduced by $18,229 (assuming that the company didn't create a new department or expand the Paint Department).

On the work sheet in Figure 15–4, in which operating expenses were allocated to departments, the Wallpaper Department showed a net loss from operations of $1,127. The Wallpaper Department had this loss because it was assigned a number of indirect expenses. If the company eliminated the Wallpaper Department, these indirect expenses would still exist and would be assigned entirely to the Paint Department.

Before reading further, do the following activity to check your understanding of how to calculate contribution margin.

Check Your Learning

The following amounts for Milner and Porter's Sporting Goods Department were taken from the work sheet. Determine the amount of the department's contribution margin.

Sales	$492,000
Sales Returns and Allowances	8,000
Merchandise Inventory (beginning)	132,000
Purchases	366,000
Purchases Returns and Allowances	6,000
Merchandise Inventory (ending)	152,000
Direct Expenses	104,000
Indirect Expenses	62,000
Interest Expense	4,000

Check your answer with that in the answers section. Re-read the preceding part of the chapter to find the correct answers to any calculations you may have missed.

The Usefulness of Contribution Margin

A company finds that income statements showing contribution margin are extremely useful when it comes to controlling direct expenses. The company can hold the head of a given department responsible for expenses directly chargeable to the department. If the head of a department reduces direct expenses, the department's contribution margin will increase.

		PAINT DEPARTMENT		
1	Revenue:			
2	Sales		560 000 00	
3	Less: Sales Returns & Allow.		14 200 00	
4	Net Sales			545 800 00
5	Cost of Merchandise Sold:			
6	Merch. Inventory, Jan. 1, 19--		96 400 00	
7	Purchases	325 120 00		
8	Less: Purchases Returns & Allow.	9 580 00		
9	Purchases Discounts	5 740 00		
10	Net Purchases		309 800 00	
11	Merchandise Available for Sale		406 200 00	
12	Less: Merch. Inventory, Dec. 31, 19--		110 000 00	
13	Cost of Merchandise Sold			296 200 00
14	Gross Profit on Sales			249 600 00
15	Direct Expenses:			
16	Advertising Expense		10 080 00	
17	Bad Debts Expense		1 799 00	
18	Deprec. Exp.-Store Equipment		1 840 00	
19	Insurance Expense (property)		1 980 00	
20	Sales Salaries Expense		88 000 00	
21	Total Direct Expenses			103 699 00
22	Contribution Margin by Dept.			145 901 00
23	Indirect Expenses:			
24	Insurance Expense (liability)			
25	Misc. Admin. Expenses			
26	Misc. Selling Expenses			
27	Office Salaries Expense			
28	Rent Expense			
29	Utilities Expense			
30	Total Indirect Expenses			
31	Net Income from Operations			
32	Other Revenue:			
33	Interest Income			
34	Other Expenses:			
35	Interest Expense			
36	Net Income			

Figure 15-6. Income Statement Showing Contribution Margin by Departments   (Left Side)

Center
Statement
December 31, 19--

Line	WALLPAPER DEPARTMENT				TOTAL		
1							
2		2400000 00				800000 00	
3		5800 00				20000 00	
4			2342000 00				780000 00
5							
6		82740 00				179140 00	
7	167890 00			493010 00			
8	4756 00			14336 00			
9	3274 00			9014 00			
10		159860 00				469660 00	
11		242600 00				648800 00	
12		90000 00				200000 00	
13			152600 00				448800 00
14			81600 00				331200 00
15							
16		7520 00				17600 00	
17		771 00				2570 00	
18		1460 00				3300 00	
19		1620 00				3600 00	
20		52000 00				140000 00	
21			63371 00				167070 00
22			18229 00				164130 00
23							
24						800 00	
25						920 00	
26						4270 00	
27						32100 00	
28						16400 00	
29						4840 00	
30							59330 00
31							104800 00
32							
33						3624 00	
34							
35						2400 00	1224 00
36							106024 00

(Right Side)

A company that manufactures various products can also use the contribution margin concept to determine the profitability of a particular product. This, clearly, is one of the most important uses of the contribution margin.

Management can use an income statement reporting contribution margin as a tool for making future plans and analyzing future operations. Sometimes such an income statement may even cause a company to eliminate a department. For example, the Westcott Company has five departments. Its net income last year was $120,000, which is about the same as it has been for the past four years. Westcott's income statement, in which all operating expenses are allocated to the various departments, shows that Department E has a net loss from operations of $9,000. In an abbreviated contribution-margin format, here are the results of the last fiscal year.

	Department E only	Departments A to D only	Total, Departments A to E	Total, Departments A to D (With E eliminated)
Sales	$120,000	$1,480,000	$1,600,000	$1,480,000
Cost of Merchandise Sold	72,000	880,000	952,000	880,000
Gross Profit on Sales	$ 48,000	$ 600,000	$ 648,000	$ 600,000
Direct Expenses	32,000	336,000	368,000	336,000
Contribution Margin	$ 16,000	$ 264,000	$ 280,000	$ 264,000
Indirect Expenses	25,000	135,000	160,000	160,000
Net Income (Loss)	($ 9,000)	$ 129,000	$ 120,000	$ 104,000

Now suppose that Westcott eliminated Department E. Because Department E's contribution margin amounts to $16,000, the net income of the entire firm would decrease by $16,000 ($120,000 − $104,000). Another factor Westcott has to consider is possible "spill-over sales" of Department E; that is, customers of Department E may also buy things in other departments. If Department E were eliminated, those customers might shop elsewhere.

Summary of Key Points

1. A departmental accounting system enables a business to find out how well each department is doing by providing information on revenue, cost of merchandise sold, and expenses by department.
2. There are two ways to account for departmental gross profit: keeping separate revenue, cost, and expense accounts by department or keeping supplementary records on revenue, cost, and expenses for each department.
3. Operating expenses may be classified as either selling expenses or administrative expenses. Selling expenses are incurred to sell or market goods or services. Administrative expenses are the costs of managing the business.
4. Operating expenses can be allocated among the various departments by

various means; for example, sales by department, floor space occupied, number of employees, and so on.

5. Income statements may be prepared showing each department's gross profit on sales or net income from operations. An income statement that shows the contribution margin of each department, however, may present a more realistic picture of each department's performance.

6. Contribution margin is the contribution that each department makes to the net income of the business.

7. Operating expenses may be direct or indirect. Direct expenses are those expenses directly related to the operation of a particular department; indirect expenses are those incurred for the business as a whole.

Review and Applications

Building Your Accounting Vocabulary

In your own words, write the definition of each of the following accounting terms. Use complete sentences for your definitions.

administrative expenses

contribution margin

departmental accounting system

direct expenses

indirect expenses

selling expenses

Reviewing Your Accounting Knowledge

1. In what ways may departmental accounting information be useful to a company?
2. What are the two methods of keeping departmental figures for each element entering into gross profit on sales?
3. What is a departmental analysis sheet and how is it used?
4. Assuming that operating expenses are to be allocated to various departments, what basis would you choose for each of the following expenses: rent, depreciation of store equipment, salaries of office personnel, insurance?
5. In what ways is a departmentalized work sheet different from a non-departmentalized work sheet?
6. What information is entered in the Nondepartmental Income Statement columns of a departmentalized work sheet?
7. What is the difference between a direct and an indirect operating expense? Give an example of each.
8. What is contribution margin? How is it calculated?
9. Give two ways in which the concept of contribution margin may be useful to a business.
10. Contribution margin is considered a more realistic portrayal of the profitability of a department than gross profit on sales or net income from operations. Why is this so?

Improving Your Decision-making Skills

You have just been hired as the new manager of Fujiko's Clothing Store. The store has two departments: clothing and shoes. Previously, the income statement listed revenue, cost of merchandise sold, and operating expenses for the store as a whole. However, you want to know the gross profit for each of the two departments. What changes in the accounting system will be required to provide this information? What benefits do you expect to gain from the departmental information?

Problem 15–1

The various operating expense accounts of Capital Discount Stores are listed below.

Bad Debts Expense	Office Salaries Expense
Cleaning Expense	Rent Expense
Depr. Exp.—Office Equipment	Sales Salaries Expense
Depr. Exp.—Store Equipment	Supplies Expense
Insurance Expense	Utilities Expense
Miscellaneous Expense	

Instructions: Use a form similar to the one that follows. Indicate whether each operating expense can be classified as a selling expense, administrative expense, direct expense, or indirect expense. Place a check mark in each column that applies.

Expense	Selling Expense	Administrative Expense	Direct Expense	Indirect Expense
Bad Debts Expense		✓	✓	

Problem 15–2

Lloyd's Shoe Store has three departments: Women's Shoes, Girls' Shoes, and Accessories. The office salaries expense for the current year was $72,000. The company allocates the office salaries expense among the three departments on the basis of the sales for each department. Sales for the three departments for the current year were as follows.

Women's Shoes	$183,000
Girls' Shoes	159,000
Accessories	18,000
Total	$360,000

Instructions: Determine what share of the office salaries expense each of the three departments should bear.

Problem 15–3

Northland Paint and Glass has two departments: the Paint Department and the Glass Department. Northland maintains separate inventory, revenue, and cost of merchandise accounts for each department. The balances at the top of the next page appeared in the Income Statement section of Northland's work sheet.

Income Summary (paint)	$ 157,856	$ 160,672
(glass)	72,448	74,962
Sales—Paint		952,000
Sales—Glass		408,000
Sales Ret. and Allow.—Paint	24,482	
Sales Ret. and Allow.—Glass	1,652	
Purchases—Paint	621,436	
Purchases—Glass	297,444	
Pur. Ret. and Allow.—Paint		8,452
Pur. Ret. and Allow.—Glass		2,592
Pur. Discounts—Paint		11,768
Pur. Discounts—Glass		8,560
Advertising Expense	32,000	
Bad Debts Expense	4,400	
Depr. Exp.—Store Equipment	31,600	
Insurance Expense	1,680	
Miscellaneous Administrative Expense	1,560	
Miscellaneous Selling Expense	1,040	
Rent Expense	19,200	
Sales Salaries Expense	243,564	
Store Supplies Expense	1,212	
Utilities Expense	7,200	
Interest Expense	3,624	
	$1,522,398	$1,627,006
Net Income	104,608	
	$1,627,006	$1,627,006

Instructions: Prepare an income statement for Northland Paint and Glass for the year ended December 31. Report departmental operations through gross profit on sales. Classify the operating expenses as either selling expenses or administrative expenses.

Problem 15–4

The Franklin Shoe Store has two departments: Women's Shoes and Men's Shoes. Franklin maintains separate accounts by department for each element entering into the calculation of gross profit. On December 31, the end of the fiscal year, the following balances appeared on Franklin's work sheet after all adjustments had been entered.

Income Summary (women's shoes)	$102,060	$ 95,640
(men's shoes)	43,564	47,892
Sales—Women's		374,832
Sales—Men's		147,856
Sales Ret. and Allow.—Women's	9,564	

Sales Ret. and Allow.—Men's	4,012	
Purchases—Women's	223,948	
Purchases—Men's	86,648	
Pur. Ret. and Allow.—Women's		5,280
Pur. Ret. and Allow.—Men's		1,368
Pur. Discounts—Women's		3,960
Pur. Discounts—Men's		1,440
Advertising Expense	8,220	
Bad Debts Expense	3,640	
Depr. Exp.—Store Equipment	6,400	
Insurance Expense	780	
Miscellaneous Admin. Expense	712	
Miscellaneous Selling Expense	748	
Office Salaries Expense	17,200	
Rent Expense	16,800	
Sales Salaries Expense	91,000	
Utilities Expense	2,480	
Interest Expense	1,440	

Instructions: Prepare an income statement showing each department's contribution margin. Allocate the direct expenses as follows.

(1) Advertising Expense is allocated as follows: Women's Shoes, $6,560; Men's Shoes, $1,660.

(2) Department managers are responsible for granting credit on sales made by their respective departments. Therefore, Bad Debts Expense is allocated as follows: Women's Shoes, $2,592; Men's Shoes, $1,048.

(3) Depreciation of store equipment is allocated on the basis of the value of equipment in each department. The value of store equipment in Women's Shoes is $15,000; in Men's Shoes, $5,000.

(4) Sales Salaries Expense (sales personnel work in one department only) is allocated as follows: Women's Shoes, $63,720; Men's Shoes, $27,280.

Problem 15–5

The Fleming Jewelry Store has two departments: the Jewelry Department and the Watch Department. Fleming maintains separate departmental accounts for each element entering into the determination of gross profit. The following amounts appear in Fleming's general ledger accounts on December 31, the end of the business's fiscal year.

Cash in Bank	$ 9,210	
Accounts Receivable	60,180	
Allowance for Uncoll. Accounts		$ 1,590
Merchandise Inventory—Jewelry	62,100	
Merchandise Inventory—Watch	42,300	

Prepaid Insurance	870	
Store Equipment	26,940	
Accum. Depr.—Store Equipment		12,165
Accounts Payable		53,110
Interest Payable		
Notes Payable		5,000
Salaries Payable		
R. C. Fleming, Capital		99,120
R. C. Fleming, Withdrawals	23,250	
Income Summary		
Sales—Jewelry		180,000
Sales—Watch		120,000
Sales Ret. and Allow.—Jewelry	1,880	
Sales Ret. and Allow.—Watch	1,320	
Purchases—Jewelry	89,400	
Purchases—Watch	68,700	
Pur. Ret. and Allow.—Jewelry		961
Pur. Ret. and Allow.—Watch		1,004
Pur. Discounts—Jewelry		727
Pur. Discounts—Watch		508
Advertising Expense	9,900	
Bad Debts Expense		
Depr. Exp.—Store Equipment		
Insurance Expense		
Miscellaneous Expense	1,335	
Rent Expense	10,800	
Salaries and Commissions Expense	63,150	
Utilities Expense	2,130	
Interest Expense	720	

Instructions: Prepare a departmental work sheet for Fleming Jewelry Store.

(1) Data for the adjustments are as follows.
   (a) Ending merchandise inventories are: Jewelry Department, $58,950; Watch Department, $40,050.
   (b) The estimated uncollectible amount (based on an aging of accounts receivable) is $3,660.
   (c) Insurance premium expired is $615.
   (d) Depreciation of store equipment for the year totals $7,290.
   (e) Accrued interest on the note payable is $195.
   (f) Accrued salaries and commissions are $510.
(2) Allocate the operating expenses to the two departments as follows.
   (a) The advertising expense is allocated on the basis of the number of column inches used: Jewelry Department, 3,752 column inches; Watch Department, 938 column inches.
   (b) Bad Debts Expense, Insurance Expense, Miscellaneous Expense, Salaries and Commissions Expense, and Utilities Expense are allocated according to sales.

(c) The depreciation expense according to the equipment ledger is: Jewelry Department, $5,028; Watch Department, $2,262.

(d) Rent Expense is allocated according to the square footage occupied: Jewelry Department, 3,200 square feet; Watch Department, 1,800 square feet.

Problem 15–6

Use the work sheet you prepared in Problem 15–5 to complete this problem.

Instructions: Prepare an income statement for the Fleming Jewelry Store showing departmental data through net income from operations.

16 Branch Accounting Systems

In Chapter 15, you learned that when a company has several different activities, it often divides these activities into departments. By organizing its operations this way, the company can delegate authority to departmental managers and measure the profitability and efficiency of each department.

Businesses can also expand their operations by opening branches or stores in different locations. These multistore businesses are often referred to as chain stores. You may have several types of chain stores in your own community. A few examples of multistore businesses are grocery stores, drug stores, variety stores, fast food restaurants, motels, and service stations.

In this chapter, you will learn about the accounting systems used by these multistore businesses. You'll learn how to journalize transactions and how to prepare financial statements that report the individual and combined operations of the branches.

Learning Objectives

When you have completed this chapter, you should be able to

1. Explain the difference between a decentralized and a centralized accounting system.

2. Journalize transactions for a multistore business that uses a centralized accounting system.

3. Prepare financial statements for a multistore business that uses a centralized accounting system.

4. Define the accounting terms presented in this chapter.

New Terms

multistore business / decentralized accounting system / centralized accounting system / interbranch transaction / combined income statement / combined balance sheet

Multistore Businesses

In order to increase sales and income, to be more competitive, or to offer better services, a business may expand its operations. One way of expanding operations is to open another store—a branch—in a different location. The branch may be located in the same city, in another city, or even in another state. A business that has more than one store or branch is referred to as a **multistore business**. Many nationwide businesses have started as one-unit operations.

Some businesses establish each branch of a multistore business as a separate corporation. The branch corporations share the same name and, usually, the same owner or group of owners. Businesses organized this way—with each branch a separate corporate entity—are sometimes referred to as brother-sister stores.

For example, Discount Tire Center is a multistore business with two branches. One branch is located in the town of Fairfield; the second branch is located in the neighboring town of Hinton. The owners of the Fairfield branch and the Hinton branch are the same. Each branch was organized as a separate corporation. A charter was applied for and received by each branch. Therefore, each branch is considered to be a separate legal entity.

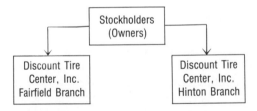

This form of organization has several advantages. First, since each branch is a separate legal entity, the general liability of the multistore business is limited. Each branch is responsible for its own commitments and obligations. Creditors generally cannot look beyond the assets of the individual branch to satisfy their claims. However, when one of the branches needs to borrow money, creditors can examine the combined financial statements of the multistore business. Creditors may then ask the other branch to guarantee the loan.

Within limits, each branch has its own organizational structure. The principal owners of the multistore business maintain control over each branch by owning more than 50% of the stock of each branch. Each branch, however, can sell some shares of stock to employees and individuals in the community in which the business is located, which provides an incentive to those persons.

Accounting Systems for Multistore Businesses

The accounting procedures used vary from one multistore business to another. The system used depends to a great extent on the amount of responsibility and authority allowed each branch by the management of the multistore business. The two basic types of accounting systems used by multistore businesses are referred to as decentralized or centralized although each business may choose variations of each type.

Decentralized Accounting System

An accounting system in which each branch within the multistore business maintains its own accounting records is called a decentralized accounting system. Each branch has its own journals and ledgers, because as a separate corporation it is an independent business. Each branch, however, uses the same accounting procedures and chart of accounts as the others. By using the same procedures and the same classifications of accounts, the owners of the multistore business can easily compare and combine the branches' financial statements at the end of an accounting period.

Centralized Accounting System

The second, and probably more widely used, accounting system for a multistore business is the centralized accounting system. In a centralized accounting system, a central accounting office keeps the accounting records and performs the accounting functions for all the branches. The central accounting office may be located at one of the branches or at a separate location. Each branch sends its source documents—sales slips, purchase requisitions, receiving reports, deposit slips—to the central accounting office. Cash received by each branch is deposited intact in a special branch checking account. A branch may make deposits to but cannot write checks on its account.

The branches do not journalize transactions or maintain ledgers. All accounting functions are performed by the central accounting office. It journalizes all transactions and maintains separate general ledger accounts for each branch. Separate financial statements are prepared for each branch. This centralized accounting system is similar to a departmental accounting system. Each branch is treated like a separate department.

By using a centralized accounting system, a multistore business can decrease its expenses. The company may have lower salary and training costs, or it may need less equipment. Since it is not necessary to maintain an accounting office at each branch, the duplication of activities is eliminated. In addition, the accounting records and procedures are consistent.

Remember: **In a decentralized accounting system, each branch maintains its own accounting records. In a centralized accounting system, all the accounting records are kept and accounting functions performed at one location for all the branches.**

Branch Accounting Functions

Each branch has a manager and an accounting clerk. The accounting clerk assists the manager in all branch matters that concern accounting. The accounting clerk might, for example, prepare purchase requisitions, gather payroll information, batch sales slips, or prepare deposits.

The accounting clerk at each branch works closely with the central accounting office. The accounting clerk collects accounting data and source documents from the various departments at the branch and sends them to the central accounting office daily.

Chart of Accounts for a Centralized Accounting System

In a departmental accounting system, separate revenue, cost of merchandise, and expense accounts are maintained for each department. Since each branch in the multistore business is a separate entity, the central accounting office must separate each branch's operations. Separate accounts for assets, liabilities, stockholders' equity, revenue, cost, and expenses must be maintained in the general ledger. For example, the Discount Tire Center uses a centralized accounting system. The chart of accounts for Discount Tire Center includes a Cash in Bank—Fairfield account and a Cash in Bank—Hinton account. In the partial chart of accounts in Figure 16–1 on page 376, you can see that separate accounts are kept for each branch for all other classifications.

Notice that each branch's account can be identified. The first three digits of the account number identify the account. The last digit identifies the branch. For example, 401 is the code for Sales, 1 is the code for the Fairfield branch, and 2 is the code for the Hinton branch. Therefore, 4011 is the Sales—Fairfield account.

Before reading further, do the following activity to check your understanding of the material you have just read.

Check Your Learning

Write your answers to the following questions on a sheet of notebook paper.

1. The two types of accounting systems used by multistore businesses are __?__ and __?__.
2. In the __?__ accounting system, each branch maintains its own journals and ledgers.
3. In the __?__ accounting system, all accounting functions are performed at one accounting office.
4. Name two advantages of a centralized accounting system.
5. In a centralized accounting system using four-digit account numbers, the first three digits identify __?__ and the last digit identifies __?__.

Check your answers with those in the answers section. Re-read the preceding part of the chapter to find the correct answers to any questions you may have missed.

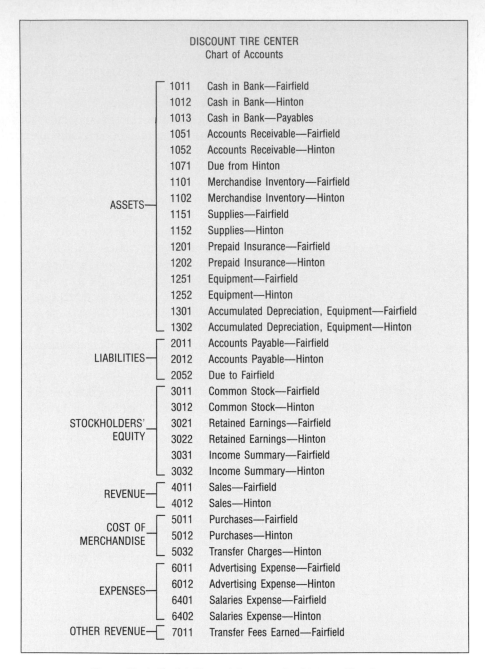

DISCOUNT TIRE CENTER
Chart of Accounts

ASSETS
1011 Cash in Bank—Fairfield
1012 Cash in Bank—Hinton
1013 Cash in Bank—Payables
1051 Accounts Receivable—Fairfield
1052 Accounts Receivable—Hinton
1071 Due from Hinton
1101 Merchandise Inventory—Fairfield
1102 Merchandise Inventory—Hinton
1151 Supplies—Fairfield
1152 Supplies—Hinton
1201 Prepaid Insurance—Fairfield
1202 Prepaid Insurance—Hinton
1251 Equipment—Fairfield
1252 Equipment—Hinton
1301 Accumulated Depreciation, Equipment—Fairfield
1302 Accumulated Depreciation, Equipment—Hinton

LIABILITIES
2011 Accounts Payable—Fairfield
2012 Accounts Payable—Hinton
2052 Due to Fairfield

STOCKHOLDERS' EQUITY
3011 Common Stock—Fairfield
3012 Common Stock—Hinton
3021 Retained Earnings—Fairfield
3022 Retained Earnings—Hinton
3031 Income Summary—Fairfield
3032 Income Summary—Hinton

REVENUE
4011 Sales—Fairfield
4012 Sales—Hinton

COST OF MERCHANDISE
5011 Purchases—Fairfield
5012 Purchases—Hinton
5032 Transfer Charges—Hinton

EXPENSES
6011 Advertising Expense—Fairfield
6012 Advertising Expense—Hinton
6401 Salaries Expense—Fairfield
6402 Salaries Expense—Hinton

OTHER REVENUE
7011 Transfer Fees Earned—Fairfield

Figure 16–1. Partial Chart of Accounts for Discount Tire Center

Remember: In a centralized accounting system, a complete set of accounts is maintained for each branch of the multistore business and all accounting functions are performed at a central location.

Journalizing Transactions in a Centralized Accounting System

Now, let's see how the central accounting office of Discount Tire records the business transactions of the Fairfield and Hinton branches.

Cash Sales

Both the Fairfield and Hinton branches of Discount Tire Center use cash registers to record all cash sales. At the Fairfield branch, for example, cash is removed from the cash registers during the day and at the end of the day and deposited in the branch's checking account. At the end of the business day, the accounting clerk prepares a special cash register report. This report, copies of the deposit slips, and the cash register tapes are sent to the central accounting office.

The central accounting office verifies the cash register report, the tapes, and the deposit slips. A deposit verification report, shown in Figure 16–2, is prepared. As you can see, it lists the sales and sales tax recorded at each cash register. It also lists the two deposits made by the Fairfield branch during the day. The total deposits must equal the total amount reported on the top portion of the form.

Figure 16–2.
Deposit Verification
Report

Discount Tire Center—Fairfield Branch
Cash Register—Deposit Verification
October 10, 19—

Register No.	Time	Sales	Sales Tax Payable	Total
1	1:00 pm	$ 628.44	$31.42	$ 659.86
2	1:20 pm	294.68	14.73	309.41
1	7:00 pm	344.89	17.24	362.13
2	7:10 pm	415.05	20.75	435.80
Totals		$1,683.06	$84.14	$1,767.20

Cash Short or Over	-0-
Total Cash Received	$1,767.20

Deposits	Amount
Deposit slip 2981	$ 969.27
Deposit slip 2982	797.93
Total cash deposited	$1,767.20

The deposit verification report is the source document for the journal entry to record the branch's cash sales. The entry to record the cash sales of the Fairfield branch is shown in Figure 16–3 on page 378.

Figure 16–3. Journalizing Cash Sales

The cash sales for the Hinton branch would be recorded in a similar manner. The Hinton branch accounts, however, would be used.

Sales on Account

When a branch sells merchandise on account to a charge customer, a sales slip is prepared, as in other accounting systems. At the end of each business day, the branch accounting clerk sends all the sales slips to the central accounting office.

Each branch's sales on account are journalized separately. For example, on October 12, the Hinton branch sold $75.00 worth of merchandise on account to C. J. Jones, plus sales tax of $3.75. The journal entry to record this transaction is shown in Figure 16–4. (This transaction could also be recorded in the business's sales journal.)

Figure 16–4. Journalizing a Sale on Account

The central accounting office sends monthly statements to charge customers of both branches. The customers, in turn, send their payments on account to the central accounting office. The central accounting office prepares a receipt for each payment received from a charge customer. The transaction is then recorded in the accounting records. For example, on October 13, the central accounting office of Discount Tire Center received cash on account from A. J. Smith (a customer of the Fairfield branch) and from Mary McFatter (a customer of the Hinton branch). The journal entries to record the two cash receipts are shown in Figure 16–5 at the top of the next page.

DATE	DESCRIPTION	POST. REF.	DEBIT	CREDIT	
Oct. 13	Cash in Bank - Fairfield		25 00		1
	Accts. Rec.-Fairfield/A.J. Smith	✓		25 00	2
	Receipt 487				3
13	Cash in Bank - Hinton		85 00		4
	Accts. Rec.-Hinton/M. McFatter	✓		85 00	5
	Receipt 488				6

Figure 16–5. Journalizing Cash Payments from Charge Customers

Purchases on Account

In Discount Tire Center's centralized accounting system, all purchases must be authorized and placed by the central accounting office. Each branch completes purchase requisitions for needed items (merchandise, supplies, equipment, and so on) and sends them to the central accounting office. The central office then prepares purchase orders to purchase the items from appropriate suppliers. Often, to take advantage of special quantity discounts, the central office combines the requisitions from the two branches and places one large order. The purchasing agent in the central office decides what is to be bought, when it is to be purchased, and how many items are to be distributed to each branch.

When the branch receives the goods ordered, it returns the receiving report to the central accounting office, where it is compared with the creditor's invoice. (The invoice for the goods is sent directly to the central accounting office.) After the invoice has been verified, it is journalized.

As an example, the central accounting office received the following three invoices on October 14.

October 14: *Received Invoice 498, dated October 13, from Ark Tires for merchandise purchased on account for the Fairfield branch, $2,000.00; terms 2/10, n/30.*

October 14: *Received Invoice 259, dated October 12, from Ace, Inc. for supplies purchased on account for the Hinton branch, $284.60; terms net/30.*

October 14: *Received Invoice 601, dated October 13, from City Equipment Co. for store equipment purchased on account for the Hinton branch, $2,641.29; terms n/30.*

The three entries are shown in general journal form in Figure 16–6 at the top of the next page. Notice that each purchase was charged to the accounts of a particular branch.

As mentioned earlier, the central office often combines the purchase requisitions of the two branches and places one large order. When the supplier's

	DATE	DESCRIPTION	POST. REF.	DEBIT	CREDIT	
1	'9-- Oct. 14	Purchases - Fairfield		2 000 00		1
2		Accts. Pay - Fairfield / Ark Tires	✓		2 000 00	2
3		Invoice 498				3
4	14	Supplies - Hinton		284 60		4
5		Accts. Pay - Hinton / Ace, Inc.	✓		284 60	5
6		Invoice 259				6
7	14	Equipment - Hinton		2 641 29		7
8		Accts. Pay - Hinton / City Equip. Co.	✓		2 641 29	8
9		Invoice 601				9

Figure 16–6. Journalizing the Purchase of Merchandise on Account

invoice is received, the central accounting office must allocate the cost of the
items purchased to the two branches. For example, on October 20, the central
office of Discount Tire Center received an invoice from the National Tire Company for $8,672. By checking the original purchase order, it was determined
that, of the $8,672 amount, $3,131 worth of merchandise had been ordered for
the Fairfield branch and $5,541 worth of merchandise had been ordered for the
Hinton branch. The central office ordered the merchandise for the two branches
but received only one invoice. When this happens, an explanation of the allocation is added to the supplier's invoice. For example, the following note was
placed on the invoice from National Tire:

Charge as follows:

Fairfield branch	$3,131
Hinton branch	5,541
Total	$8,672

The transaction is then recorded in general journal form as illustrated in Figure
16–7.

GENERAL JOURNAL   PAGE 29

	DATE	DESCRIPTION	POST. REF.	DEBIT	CREDIT	
1	'9-- Oct. 20	Purchases - Fairfield		3 131 00		1
2		Purchases - Hinton		5 541 00		2
3		Accts. Pay - Fairfield / Nat. Tire Co.	✓		3 131 00	3
4		Accts. Pay - Hinton / Nat. Tire Co.	✓		5 541 00	4
5		Invoice 480				5

*Figure 16–7. Journalizing the Allocation of Merchandise Purchased Between Two
Branches*

Before reading further, do the following activity to check your understanding of the material you have just learned.

Check Your Learning

Thorton's, Inc. is a multistore business with five branches that are organized as separate corporations. Thorton's uses a centralized accounting system and maintains separate accounts for each branch in the general ledger. Listed below are several transactions handled by the central accounting office on June 10. Record the transactions in general journal form on a sheet of notebook paper.

1. Thorton's Branch #5 deposited $7,298.44 in its checking account for cash sales of $6,885.32 and sales taxes of $413.12.
2. Thorton's Branch #2 sold $200.00 worth of merchandise on account plus $12.00 sales tax to Jane Henry.
3. The central accounting office received $630.00 on account from Kim Chin, a charge customer of Branch #3.
4. Received Invoice B16 for $7,944.21 for merchandise purchased on account from the Houston Company for Branch #1.
5. Received Invoice 588 for $725.00 from American Supplies for store supplies purchased for the five branches. The cost is allocated as follows: Branch #1, $200.00; Branch #2, $100.00; Branch #3, $125.00; Branch #4, $200.00; Branch #5, $100.00.

Check your answers with those in the answers section. Re-read the preceding part of the chapter to find the correct answers to any questions you may have missed.

Cash Payments

In a centralized accounting system, all cash payments are made by the central accounting office. The central accounting office of Discount Tire Center maintains a special checking account that is used for all cash payments. This checking account is similar to the payroll checking account.

As you recall, once the employees' total net pay is determined, a check is written on the business checking account for the total net pay amount. That check is deposited in the payroll checking account. Payroll checks are then written to employees, using the payroll checking account. After all payroll checks clear the bank, the payroll checking account has a zero balance.

The special cash payments checking account—called the Payables checking account—is used in the same manner. Money is deposited in the Payables checking account from the checking accounts of the two branches. Checks are then written on this Payables account for various cash payments for *both* branches. A record of the transactions affecting the Payables checking account is maintained in a current asset account called Cash in Bank—Payables.

Cash in Bank—Payables

Dr.	Cr.
+	−
Increase Side	Decrease Side
Balance Side	
(Transfers from Fairfield and Hinton Cash in Bank accounts)	(Payments on account and for expenses for both branches)

Now let's look at how this Cash in Bank—Payables account is used in the centralized accounting system of Discount Tire Center.

Remember: **In a centralized accounting system, all cash payments are made by the central accounting office. A special checking account is maintained for making all cash payments. A record of the transactions affecting this checking account is kept in the Cash in Bank—Payables account.**

Transferring Funds to the Cash in Bank—Payables Account

Once a week, an accounting clerk in the central office prepares a list of the cash payments that must be made for each of the branches. For example, checks might need to be prepared for payments to creditors or payments for such expenses as advertising, utilities, and rent. On October 28, the central accounting office determined that cash payments totaling $7,840.28 had to be made for the Fairfield branch. For the Hinton branch, cash payments totaling $6,295.61 had to be made.

Next, an amount equal to the total cash payments to be made is transferred from each branch's Cash in Bank account to the special Cash in Bank—Payables account. (The amount can be transferred by a check written on the branch's checking account or, more likely, by using an electronic funds transfer system.)

October 28: *Transferred $7,840.28 from the Fairfield branch checking account and $6,295.61 from the Hinton branch checking account into the* Cash in Bank—Payables *account, Electronic Funds Transfer (EFT) 1003.*

Cash in Bank—Payables is debited for $14,135.89 ($7,840.28 + $6,295.61) because the account is being increased by the amount equal to the total cash payments to be made. Cash in Bank—Fairfield is credited for $7,840.28, the total amount transferred for the cash payments to be made for the Fairfield branch. Cash in Bank—Hinton is credited for $6,295.61, the total amount transferred for the cash payments to be made for the Hinton branch.

Cash in Bank—Payables		Cash in Bank—Fairfield		Cash in Bank—Hinton	
Dr.	Cr.	Dr.	Cr.	Dr.	Cr.
+	−	+	−	+	−
$14,135.89		Bal. $10,460.00	$7,840.28	Bal. $8,695.00	$6,295.61

The entry to record the transfer of funds is shown in general journal form in Figure 16–8. As you can see, this transaction simply moves cash from the two branch checking accounts into the special cash payments checking account. The

	DATE	DESCRIPTION	POST. REF.	DEBIT	CREDIT	
1	19— Oct. 28	Cash in Bank—Payables		14135 89		1
2		Cash in Bank—Fairfield			7840 28	2
3		Cash in Bank—Hinton			6295 61	3
4		EFT 1003				4

Figure 16–8. Journalizing the Transfer of Funds

Cash in Bank—Payables checking account now has enough cash to cover the checks that must be prepared that week.

Next, let's see how the cash payment transactions for the two branches are journalized.

Remember: When cash payments must be made, cash is transferred to the Cash in Bank—Payables account at the central accounting office from the Cash in Bank accounts of the branches.

Cash Payments to Creditors on Account

When an invoice must be paid, a check is issued on the Cash in Bank—Payables checking account. Three of the cash payments made on October 28 are discussed below.

October 28: Issued Check 44691 for $275.28 to Duffy Bros. in payment of Invoice 286 for supplies purchased on account for the Fairfield branch.

In this transaction, Accounts Payable—Fairfield and the Duffy Bros.' account in the subsidiary ledger are debited for $275.28. Cash in Bank—Payables is credited for the same amount. Notice that Cash in Bank—Payables is credited rather than Cash in Bank—Fairfield. This $275.28 cash payment is included in the amount credited to the Cash in Bank—Fairfield account earlier (shown in Figure 16–8). This entry is shown in general journal form in Figure 16–9, which appears at the top of page 384.

October 28: Issued Check 44692 for $628.45 to Alost, Inc. in payment of Invoice 441 for equipment purchased for the Hinton branch.

In this transaction, Accounts Payable—Hinton and Alost's account in the subsidiary ledger are debited for $628.45. Cash in Bank—Payables is credited for $628.45. The entry is shown in general journal form in Figure 16–9. As you can see, this entry is very similar to the previous one. However, the Hinton branch's Accounts Payable account and Alost, Inc.'s account are debited in this transaction.

October 28: Issued Check 44693 for $1,057.64 to Lafayette Sales in payment of Invoice 446 for merchandise purchased on account for the Fairfield branch ($689.40) and the Hinton branch ($368.24).

	DATE	DESCRIPTION	POST. REF.	DEBIT	CREDIT	
1	Oct. 28	Accts. Payable-Fairfield/Duffy Bros.	✓	275 28		1
2		Cash in Bank-Payables			275 28	2
3		Check 44691				3
4	28	Accts. Payable-Hinton/Alost, Inc.	✓	628 45		4
5		Cash in Bank-Payables			628 45	5
6		Check 44692				6
7	28	Accts. Payable-Fairfield/Lafayette Sales	✓	689 40		7
8		Accts. Payable-Hinton/Lafayette Sales	✓	368 24		8
9		Cash in Bank-Payables			1 057 64	9
10		Check 44693				10

Figure 16–9. Journalizing Cash Payments on Account

We mentioned earlier that multistore businesses often combine the purchase requisitions from branches and prepare one purchase order. When the invoice is received from the supplier, a notation is added to the invoice indicating how the purchase on account is to be allocated between the two branches. When the invoice is ready to be paid, one check is written (drawn on the Cash in Bank—Payables account).

In the journal entry, the cash payment is allocated between the two branches according to the notation on the invoice. For example, in this transaction, Accounts Payable—Fairfield and Lafayette Sales' account are debited for $689.40. Accounts Payable—Hinton and Lafayette Sales' account are debited for $368.24. The Cash in Bank—Payables account is credited for $1,057.64, the total amount of the cash payment. The entry is shown in general journal form in Figure 16–9.

Remember: In a centralized accounting system, when a cash payment is made, the Cash in Bank—Payables account is credited rather than the Cash in Bank account of the branch.

Cash Payments for Expenses

Expenses incurred in operating the branches are also paid out of the Cash in Bank—Payables account. These expenses include payments for utilities, advertising, and salaries. For example, one of the cash payments that must be made on October 28 is for an advertising bill of $720.16. The Stanley Printing Company printed special advertising circulars for both the Fairfield branch and the Hinton branch. The printing company sent one bill to the central accounting office for the services provided to both branches. Of the $720.16, $375.48 is allocated to the Fairfield branch and $344.68 is allocated to the Hinton branch. The entry to record the payment of the advertising bill is shown in general journal form in Figure 16–10. Notice that Cash in Bank—Payables is credited for the total amount being paid.

	DATE		DESCRIPTION	POST. REF.	DEBIT	CREDIT	
1	Oct.	28	Advertising Expense—Fairfield		375 48		1
2			Advertising Expense—Hinton		344 68		2
3			Cash in Bank—Payables			720 16	3
4			Check 44694				4

Figure 16–10. Journalizing the Cash Payment of an Expense

Interbranch Transactions

The branches of a multistore business occasionally engage in transactions with each other. Transactions between branches of the same multistore business are called **interbranch transactions**. One of the most frequent interbranch transactions is the transfer of merchandise.

For example, the Fairfield branch of Discount Tire Center serves as a warehouse for both branches. When the central accounting office places a large merchandise order, it is shipped to and stored at the Fairfield branch.

When the Hinton branch needs merchandise, it completes a merchandise request form. The requested items are then sent from Fairfield to Hinton. The Fairfield branch charges a 1% transfer fee to cover its handling, storage, and shipping expenses.

The transfer fee is considered to be revenue for the Fairfield branch. Every time merchandise is shipped from the Fairfield branch, the amount of the transfer fee is credited to an other revenue account called Transfer Fees Earned—Fairfield.

Transfer Fees Earned—Fairfield	
Dr.	Cr.
−	+
Decrease Side	Increase Side
	Balance Side

For the Hinton branch, the amount of the transfer fee is considered to be an additional cost of merchandise purchased. In this respect, it is similar to the transportation in charges. Every time Hinton receives merchandise from the warehouse, the amount of the transfer fee is debited to a cost of merchandise account titled Transfer Charges—Hinton.

Transfer Charges—Hinton	
Dr.	Cr.
+	−
Increase Side	Decrease Side
Balance Side	

Two other accounts are also affected when merchandise is shipped from the Fairfield warehouse to the Hinton branch. The two accounts are Due from Hinton and Due to Fairfield. The Due from Hinton account is used to record the total amount the Fairfield branch will receive from the Hinton branch for the merchandise shipped. The amount recorded in the account includes the cost of the merchandise and the amount of the transfer fee. Due from Hinton is a current asset account for the Fairfield branch. Therefore, the "Due from" account has a normal debit balance.

Due from Hinton

Dr.	Cr.
+	−
Increase Side	Decrease Side
Balance Side	

The Due to Fairfield account is used to record the total amount the Hinton branch owes the Fairfield branch for the merchandise shipped. Like the "Due from" account, the amount recorded in the account includes the cost of the merchandise and the amount of the transfer fee. Due to Fairfield is a current liability account for the Hinton branch. Therefore, the "Due to" account has a normal credit balance.

Due to Fairfield

Dr.	Cr.
−	+
Decrease Side	Increase Side
	Balance Side

Now let's look at an interbranch transaction involving the transfer of merchandise between the two branches.

October 29: Fairfield warehouse shipped $20,000 worth of merchandise to Hinton, plus transfer fee of $200, Transfer Request 2826.

When merchandise is shipped from the warehouse to the Hinton branch, *two* journal entries must be made. The first entry records the transaction in the Fairfield branch accounts. The second entry records the transaction in the Hinton branch accounts.

Remember: When merchandise is shipped from one branch to another, a transfer fee is charged. This fee is revenue for the branch shipping the goods and a cost of merchandise for the branch receiving the goods.

Journalizing the Transfer of Merchandise

Three Fairfield branch accounts are affected by this transaction: Due from Hinton, Purchases—Fairfield, and Transfer Fees Earned—Fairfield. Let's look at the entire transaction in T account form.

Due from Hinton		Purchases—Fairfield		Transfer Fees Earned—Fairfield	
Dr.	Cr.	Dr.	Cr.	Dr.	Cr.
+	−	+	−	−	+
$20,200		Bal. $350,000	$20,000		$200

Due from Hinton is being increased. It is, therefore, debited for $20,200, the cost of the transferred merchandise plus the transfer fee. Since merchandise is being transferred from the Fairfield branch, Purchases—Fairfield is being decreased. Purchases—Fairfield is, therefore, credited. The amount of the credit is the cost of the merchandise being transferred, $20,000. Transfer Fees Earned—Fairfield is credited for $200, the amount of the transfer fee.

This transaction is shown in general journal form in Figure 16–11.

		GENERAL JOURNAL			PAGE *38*
	DATE	DESCRIPTION	POST. REF.	DEBIT	CREDIT
1	19-- Oct. 29	Due from Hinton		20 200 00		1
2		Purchases—Fairfield			20 000 00	2
3		Transfer Fees Earned—Fairfield			200 00	3
4		Transfer request 2826				4

Figure 16–11. Journalizing the Transfer of Merchandise (Shipping Branch)

Journalizing the Receipt of Transferred Merchandise

Three Hinton branch accounts are also affected by the interbranch transfer: Purchases—Hinton, Transfer Charges—Hinton, and Due to Fairfield.

Purchases—Hinton		Transfer Charges—Hinton		Due to Fairfield	
Dr.	Cr.	Dr.	Cr.	Dr.	Cr.
+	−	+	−	−	+
Bal. $169,000		$200			$20,200
20,000					

Since the Hinton branch is receiving additional merchandise, its purchases are being increased. Purchases—Hinton is, therefore, debited for the cost of the merchandise being received from the warehouse, $20,000. Transfer Charges—Hinton is a cost of merchandise account. It is, therefore, debited for $200, the amount of the transfer fee. Due to Fairfield, a liability account, is being increased. It is credited for $20,200, the cost of the merchandise plus the transfer fee.

The transaction is recorded in general journal form in Figure 16–12.

		GENERAL JOURNAL			PAGE *38*
	DATE	DESCRIPTION	POST. REF.	DEBIT	CREDIT
1	19-- Oct. 29	Purchases—Hinton		20 000 00		1
2		Transfer Charges—Hinton		200 00		2
3		Due to Fairfield			20 200 00	3
4		Transfer request 2826				4

Figure 16–12. Journalizing the Transfer of Merchandise (Receiving Branch)

Remember: **"Due to"** **means an amount is owed.** **"Due from"** **means an amount will be received.**

Settling Accounts Between Branches

At the beginning of each month, the central accounting office of Discount Tire Center records an interbranch transaction to "pay" for the merchandise shipped to the Hinton branch. Like the interbranch transaction for the transfer of merchandise, two journal entries are required for an interbranch cash payment. The first entry records the payment in the Hinton accounts. The second entry records the receipt of cash in the Fairfield branch accounts.

At the beginning of November, the Hinton branch owes $20,200 to the Fairfield branch (for the merchandise transfer on October 29). Let's now look at the two journal entries required.

Journalizing an Interbranch Cash Payment

As you learned earlier, all cash payments must be made through the Cash in Bank—Payables account. Therefore, before the interbranch cash payment transaction can be recorded, cash must be transferred from the Cash in Bank—Hinton account to the Cash in Bank—Payables account. At the beginning of the week, an accounting clerk in the central accounting office determined that cash payments totaling $24,038 had to be made for the Hinton branch. This amount included the $20,200 the Hinton branch owed the Fairfield branch. In the journal entry to record this transaction, Cash in Bank—Payables was debited for $24,038 and Cash in Bank—Hinton was credited for $24,038. (Cash was also transferred from the Cash in Bank—Fairfield account at the same time.) The interbranch cash payment can now be journalized.

November 5: Paid $20,200 to the Fairfield branch for merchandise transferred to the Hinton branch, Electronic funds transfer (EFT) 1007.

The two accounts affected by this transaction are Due to Fairfield and Cash in Bank—Payables. Since the amount owed is now being paid, Hinton's liability account Due to Fairfield is debited for $20,200. Cash in Bank—Payables is credited for $20,200 because cash is decreasing.

Cash in Bank—Payables		Due to Fairfield	
Dr.	Cr.	Dr.	Cr.
+	−	−	+
Bal. $31,723	$20,200	$20,200	Bal. $20,200

The entry to record the interbranch cash payment is shown in general journal form in Figure 16–13 on page 389.

Journalizing an Interbranch Cash Receipt

The cash received from the Hinton branch must now be recorded in the Fairfield branch accounts. The two accounts affected by the cash receipt from the Hinton branch are Due from Hinton and Cash in Bank—Fairfield. Cash in Bank—

GENERAL JOURNAL   PAGE 40

	DATE	DESCRIPTION	POST. REF.	DEBIT	CREDIT	
1	19-- Nov 4	Due to Fairfield		20 20 0 00		1
2		Cash in Bank—Payables			20 20 0 00	2
3		EFT 1007				3

Figure 16–13. Journalizing an Interbranch Cash Payment

Fairfield is debited for $20,200 because cash is being received. The Fairfield branch account Due from Hinton is credited for $20,200 because the asset is being decreased. The entry is shown in general journal form in Figure 16–14.

Cash in Bank—Fairfield		Due from Hinton	
Dr.	Cr.	Dr.	Cr.
+	−	+	−
$20,200		Bal. $20,200	$20,200

GENERAL JOURNAL   PAGE 40

	DATE	DESCRIPTION	POST. REF.	DEBIT	CREDIT	
1	19-- Nov 4	Cash in Bank—Fairfield		20 20 0 00		1
2		Due from Hinton			20 20 0 00	2
3		Receipt 2841				3

Figure 16–14. Journalizing an Interbranch Cash Receipt

Before reading further, do the following activity to check your understanding of interbranch transactions.

Check Your Learning

On a sheet of notebook paper, record the following interbranch transactions in general journal form.

Apr.   20   Store #1 transferred merchandise to Store #4, $30,000 plus transfer fee of $300, Transfer request 111.

May   2   Store #1 received payment from Store #4 for the merchandise transferred on April 20.

Check your answers with those in the answers section. Re-read the preceding part of the chapter to find the correct answers to any questions you may have missed.

End-of-fiscal-period Procedures

The end-of-fiscal-period procedures for a multistore business using a centralized accounting system are similar to the procedures followed by any other form of business organization. Separate work sheets and financial statements are prepared for each branch. Combined financial statements, which report the results of operations for both branches, are also prepared.

Branch Income Statements

The income statements for the Fairfield and Hinton branches of Discount Tire Center are shown in Figures 16–15 and 16–16, respectively. To save

Figure 16–15.
Income Statement
for Fairfield Branch

Discount Tire Center—Fairfield Branch
Income Statement
For the Year Ended December 31, 19—

Revenue:			
Sales		$626,287	
Less: Sales Returns and Allowances		3,210	
Net Sales			$623,077
Cost of Merchandise Sold:			
Merchandise Inventory, Jan. 1, 19—		$ 61,240	
Purchases	$421,970		
Plus: Transportation In	1,640		
Cost of Delivered Merchandise		$423,610	
Less: Purchases Returns and Allowances	$ 3,720		
Purchases Discounts	8,140	11,860	
Net Purchases		411,750	
Cost of Merchandise Available		$472,990	
Less: Merchandise Inventory, Dec. 31, 19—		64,944	
Cost of Merchandise Sold			408,046
Gross Profit from Operations			$215,031
Operating Expenses:			
Selling Expenses		$ 82,480	
Administrative Expenses		75,268	
Total Operating Expenses			157,748
Net Income from Operations			$ 57,283
Other Revenue:			
Transfer Fees Earned			443
Net Income before Income Tax			$ 57,726
Income Tax			10,568
Net Income after Income Tax			$ 47,158

Figure 16–16.
Income Statement
for Hinton Branch

Discount Tire Center—Hinton Branch
Income Statement
For the Year Ended December 31, 19—

Revenue:			
Sales		$346,921	
Less: Sales Returns and Allowances		1,288	
Net Sales			$345,633
Cost of Merchandise Sold:			
Merchandise Inventory, Jan. 1, 19—		$ 18,294	
Purchases		$232,871	
Plus: Transportation In	$ 620		
Transfer Charges	443	1,063	
Cost of Delivered Merchandise		$233,934	
Less: Purchases Returns and Allowances	$ 300		
Purchases Discounts	1,300	1,600	
Net Purchases		232,334	
Cost of Merchandise Available		$250,628	
Less: Merchandise Inventory, Dec. 31, 19—		17,298	
Cost of Merchandise Sold			233,330
Gross Profit from Operations			$112,303
Operating Expenses:			
Selling Expenses		$ 45,681	
Administrative Expenses		32,188	
Total Operating Expenses			77,869
Net Income from Operations			$ 34,434
Income Tax			5,448
Net Income after Income Tax			$ 28,986

space, selling and administrative expenses are not listed individually. Only the totals are reported on the statements.

As you review the income statement for the Fairfield branch (Figure 16–15), notice that Transfer Fees Earned appears in the Other Revenue section.

On the Hinton branch income statement (Figure 16–16), the Transfer Charges amount is reported in the Cost of Merchandise Sold section.

Combined Income Statement

After income statements are prepared for each of the branches, a combined income statement may be prepared. A **combined income statement** reports the revenue, costs, and expenses of all the branches of a multistore business. Data for the combined financial statements are taken from the individual financial statements of the branches.

The combined income statement for Discount Tire Center appears in Figure 16–17. Notice that the accounting data for the two branches are reported in the first two columns.

The combined income statement also has debit and credit columns labeled "Eliminations." These two columns are used to cancel the results of inter-branch transactions. The combined income statement should not report the revenue earned or additional costs of merchandise from transactions between branches. As a result, the Eliminations columns on the combined income statement are used to cancel the Transfer Fees Earned and Transfer Charges amounts.

Let's examine the Eliminations columns more closely. As you remember, the transfer changes of $443 were added to purchases in the Cost of Merchandise Sold section of the Hinton branch income statement. This amount must be canceled (eliminated) from all affected totals on the combined income statement.

Figure 16–17. Combined Income Statement for Discount Tire Center

			Eliminations		
Discount Tire Center Combined Income Statement For the Year Ended December 31, 19—					
	Fairfield	Hinton	Debit	Credit	Combined
Revenue:					
Net Sales	$623,077	$345,633			$968,710
Cost of Merchandise Sold:					
Merch. Inv., Jan. 1, 19—	$ 61,240	$ 18,294			$ 79,534
Net Purchases	411,750	232,334		$443	643,641
Cost of Merchandise Available	$472,990	$250,628		$443	$723,175
Less: Merch. Inv. Dec. 31, 19—	64,944	17,298			82,242
Cost of Merchandise Sold	$408,046	$233,330		$443	$640,933
Gross Profit from Operations	$215,031	$112,303		$443	$327,777
Operating Expenses:					
Selling Expenses	$ 82,480	$ 45,681			$128,161
Administrative Expenses	75,268	32,188			107,456
Total Operating Expenses	$157,748	$ 77,869			$235,617
Net Income from Operations	$ 57,283	$ 34,434		$443	$ 92,160
Other Revenue:					
Transfer Fees Earned	443	-0-	$443		-0-
Net Income before Income Taxes	$ 57,726	$ 34,434	$443	$443	$ 92,160
Income Tax	10,568	5,448			16,016
Net Income after Income Taxes	$ 47,158	$ 28,986	$443	$443	$ 76,144

The transfer changes amount is included in the amounts reported in the Hinton column for net purchases, cost of merchandise available, and cost of merchandise sold. These amounts represent debit totals. To cancel the transfer charges, $443 must be entered in the Eliminations Credit column on the net purchases, cost of merchandise available, and cost of merchandise sold lines.

If the transfer changes are eliminated from Hinton's cost of merchandise sold, they must also be eliminated from Hinton's reported amounts for gross profit from operations, net income from operations, net income before income taxes, and net income after income taxes. Gross profit from operations, remember, is determined by subtracting the cost of merchandise sold from net sales. If cost of merchandise sold is decreased (by the eliminations), gross profit from operations and all subsequent income totals are increased.

The amounts reported for gross profit from operations, net income from operations, net income before income taxes, and net income after income taxes represent credit totals. To eliminate the transfer charges amount, $443 must be entered in the Eliminations Credit column on each of these four lines.

On the Fairfield branch income statement, the transfer fees earned amount of $443 was reported as other revenue. This amount must also be eliminated on the combined income statement. Since the transfer fees earned amount represents a credit balance, $443 is entered in the Eliminations Debit column on the transfer fees earned line.

If the transfer fees earned amount is eliminated from Fairfield's other revenue, it must also be eliminated from Fairfield's reported amounts for net income before income taxes and net income after income taxes. These amounts represent credit totals. To eliminate the transfer fees earned amount, $443 is entered in the Eliminations Debit column on the net income before income taxes and net income after income taxes lines.

The amounts reported in the Combined column are determined by totaling the amounts reported in the first four columns. Any amount canceled in the Eliminations columns is not reported in the Combined column.

By combining the income statements of the branches, the owners can compare and analyze the operation of all branches. Since the combined income statement reports the total revenue, cost, and expenses of all the branches of the multistore business, the owners see their entire operation as a whole.

Remember: **On a combined income statement, the Eliminations columns are used to cancel the Transfer Fees Earned and Transfer Charges amounts.**

Combined Balance Sheet

Separate balance sheets are prepared for each branch of Discount Tire Center. A combined balance sheet is also prepared. A combined balance sheet reports the total balances of the asset, liability, and stockholders' equity accounts of all the branches of a multistore business. The combined balance sheet for the Discount Tire Center is shown in Figure 16–18 at the bottom of the next page.

The combined balance sheet also has an Eliminations section. The Eliminations Debit and Credit columns are used to cancel the Due from Hinton and Due to Fairfield accounts. As you can see, these amounts are the same, $15,000. The "Due to" amount offsets the "Due from" amount. The combined balance sheet of a multistore business should not report an amount to be received from or paid to itself. The Eliminations columns of the combined balance sheet, therefore, are used to cancel the interbranch receivables and payables.

The amounts recorded in the Combined column are determined by adding the totals of the first four columns. Notice that the $15,000 balance of Due from Hinton is canceled by the $15,000 entered in the Eliminations Credit column.

Remember: A combined balance sheet should not include amounts to be received or paid that result from interbranch transactions. The Eliminations columns are used to cancel the Due to and Due from accounts.

Figure 16–18. Combined Balance Sheet for Discount Tire Center

	Fairfield	Hinton	Debit	Credit	Combined
Discount Tire Center **Combined Balance Sheet** **December 31, 19—**					
			Eliminations		
Assets					
Cash in Bank	$ 19,240	$ 7,484			$ 26,724
Due from Hinton	15,000	-0-		$15,000	-0-
Accounts Receivable	50,400	21,260			71,660
Merchandise Inventory	64,944	17,298			82,242
Supplies	5,820	2,421			8,241
Prepaid Insurance	960	521			1,481
Equipment (net)	125,000	137,000			262,000
Building (net)	460,000	484,000			944,000
Land	30,000	46,000			76,000
Total Assets	$771,364	$715,984		$15,000	$1,472,348
Liabilities					
Accounts Payable	$ 41,300	$ 13,200			$ 54,500
Notes Payable	70,000	245,000			315,000
Due to Fairfield	-0-	15,000	$15,000		-0-
Total Liabilities	$111,300	$273,200	$15,000		$ 369,500
Stockholders' Equity					
Common Stock	$500,000	$380,000			$ 880,000
Retained Earnings	160,064	62,784			222,848
Total Stockholders' Equity	$660,064	$442,784			$1,102,848
Total Liabilities and Stockholders' Equity	$771,364	$715,984	$15,000		$1,472,348

Summary of Key Points

1. In order to increase sales and income, to be more competitive, or to offer better service, a business can expand its operations by opening branches in different locations. The branches may be incorporated as separate legal entities.
2. A multistore business can use either a decentralized accounting system or a centralized accounting system.
3. In a decentralized accounting system, each branch maintains its own accounting records. The same procedures and chart of accounts, however, are used by all branches.
4. In a centralized accounting system, all accounting functions for all branches are handled by a central accounting office. Separate asset, liability, stockholders' equity, revenue, cost, and expense accounts are maintained for each branch.
5. In a centralized accounting system, all cash payments are made from a special Payables checking account. Cash is transferred to the Payables checking account from the branch checking accounts.
6. Transactions between branches of the same multistore business are called interbranch transactions. When an interbranch transaction occurs, two journal entries are required.
7. Transfer fees represent revenue to the branch shipping the merchandise. Transfer fees are an additional cost of merchandise purchased for the branch receiving the merchandise.
8. A "Due from" account is a current asset similar to Accounts Receivable. The "Due to" account is a current liability similar to Accounts Payable.
9. At the end of the fiscal period, both separate and combined financial statements are prepared for the multistore business.
10. Transfer fees earned and transfer charges are eliminated on the combined income statement. "Due to" and "Due from" balances are eliminated on the combined balance sheet.

Review and Applications

Building Your Accounting Vocabulary

In your own words, write the definition of each of the following accounting terms. Use complete sentences for your definitions.

centralized account-
ing system
combined balance
sheet

combined income
statement
decentralized
accounting system

interbranch
transaction
multistore business

Reviewing Your Accounting Knowledge

1. Name three advantages of incorporating the branches of a multistore business.
2. What are the two basic types of accounting systems that can be used by a multistore business? How do they differ?
3. How does the chart of accounts used in a decentralized accounting system of a multistore business differ from the chart of accounts used in a centralized accounting system?
4. How are purchases for the branches of a multistore business handled in a centralized accounting system?
5. Explain the purpose of the Cash in Bank—Payables checking account used in a centralized accounting system.
6. What is the difference between the Transfer Charges and Transfer Fees Earned accounts?
7. When merchandise is shipped from one branch of a multistore business to another branch, why are two journal entries required?
8. Classify the following accounts: Cash in Bank—Payables, Transfer Fees Earned, Transfer Charges, Due to Store #1, Due from Store #2.
9. What is the source of the data needed to prepare a combined income statement for a multistore business?
10. What is the purpose of the Eliminations columns on the financial statements of a multistore business?

Improving Your Decision-making Skills

The Tri-City Auto Parts Company has three branches located in three neighboring cities. Tri-City currently uses a decentralized accounting system. Each branch has its own accounting department and maintains its own journals and ledgers. Because of several problems that have occurred, the company is thinking about switching to a centralized accounting system. What things should Tri-City consider before deciding whether to change to a centralized accounting system?

Problem 16–1

The Lee Company is a multistore business with two branches in the towns of Easton and Hudson. The company plans to switch from a decentralized accounting system to a centralized system. Listed below are some of the accounts currently being used.

Cash in Bank	Equipment	Retained Earnings
Accounts Receivable	Building	Income Summary
Merchandise Inventory	Accounts Payable	Sales
Supplies	Sales Tax Payable	Purchases
Prepaid Insurance	Common Stock	Advertising Expense

Instructions: Using the accounts just listed, prepare a chart of accounts for the centralized accounting system of the Lee Company. The Easton branch will be the warehouse for both branches. The company plans to use a special Payables checking account for all cash payments. Use a four-digit account number.

Problem 16–2

The Bayou Sales Company is a multistore business with three branches: Adams, Baker, and Canton. The company uses a centralized accounting system. The following transactions took place during April.

Apr.   3   The Adams branch had cash sales of $4,860 plus sales tax of $243, Deposit Verification 43.

       8   The Baker branch sold merchandise on account to May Crawford, $400 plus $20 sales tax, Sales Slip 498.

     10   The central accounting office received $840 on account from John Paul Hixson, a charge customer of the Canton branch, Receipt 209.

     15   The central accounting office received Invoice 2874 from Benson's for $87,200 worth of merchandise purchased on account for the Adams branch.

     20   The central accounting office received Invoice B62 from Reid Supplies for $740 in store supplies purchased on account for the Canton branch.

     25   Received Invoice C116 for $1,400 from Modern Offices for a new cash register (Office Equipment) purchased on account for the Baker branch.

     30   Received Invoice 8478 for $25,680 from Andrus Supply for merchandise purchased on account. The total cost is allocated as follows: Adams, $12,800; Baker, $7,230; Canton, $5,650.

Instructions: Record, on page 19 of the general journal, the entries for the Bayou Sales Company.

Problem 16–3

International Products is a multistore business with two branches: Madison and Ogden. The company uses a centralized accounting system with a Cash in Bank—Payables account. On July 12, the following cash payments were made.

(a) A $673.30 advertising bill from Central Printers was allocated as follows: Madison branch, $384.90; Ogden branch, $288.40; Check 1268.
(b) Paid Midland Construction $850.00 on account for work performed at the Madison branch, Check 1269.
(c) Wrote Check 1270 for $2,400.00 to Northwest Insurance for the premiums on 2 six-month insurance policies (Madison branch, $1,400.00; Ogden branch, $1,000.00).
(d) Issued Check 1271 for $738.50 to The Hobbyshop for equipment purchased on account for the Ogden branch.
(e) Paid $3,000.00 to Price Realty for the April rent for the Madison branch, Check 1272.
(f) Purchased store supplies from Lynn Supply Co. for the Ogden branch for $248.00 cash, Check 1273.
(g) Issued Check 1274 for $11,250.00 to Jones Wholesale for the cash purchase of merchandise for the Madison branch.

Instructions:

(1) Determine the amount that must be transferred from each branch's checking account to the Cash in Bank—Payables account. Record the entry in general journal form (Electronic Funds Transfer 2819). Use page 14.
(2) Record, in general journal form, the July 12 cash payments.

Problem 16–4

Colt Enterprises is a multistore business with branches in Stowe and Wayland. Listed below are some of the accounts used in the company's centralized accounting system.

Cash in Bank—Stowe	Due from Wayland	Purchases—Wayland
Cash in Bank—Wayland	Due to Stowe	Transfer Fees Earned—Stowe
Cash in Bank—Payables	Purchases—Stowe	Transfer Charges—Wayland

Colt Enterprises had the following interbranch transactions.

Jan. 26 Transferred $9,250.00 worth of merchandise from the Stowe warehouse to the Wayland branch, Transfer Request 109. There was a 1% transfer fee.

Feb. 2 Transferred $32,698.50 from the Cash in Bank—Wayland account to the Cash in Bank—Payables account, EFT 11.

3 Issued Check 422 to the Stowe branch in payment for the merchandise transferred on January 26.

Instructions: Record the entries, in general journal form, for the interbranch transactions. Use page 67 of the general journal.

Problem 16–5

Townhouse Restaurants, a multistore business with two branches, uses a centralized accounting system. The following balances appeared in the Adjusted Trial Balance columns of the work sheets for the year ended December 31.

Income Summary—Harper	$ 8,000	$ 7,200
Income Summary—Leon	3,700	2,400
Sales—Harper		240,000
Sales—Leon		175,000
Purchases—Harper	120,000	
Purchases—Leon	70,100	
Transfer Charges—Leon	18,100	
Selling Expenses—Harper	60,000	
Selling Expenses—Leon	34,000	
Administrative Expenses—Harper	12,000	
Administrative Expenses—Leon	5,200	
Transfer Fees Earned—Harper		18,100
Income Tax Expense—Harper	12,840	
Income Tax Expense—Leon	7,584	

Instructions: Using the above information, prepare an income statement for the Harper branch and an income statement for the Leon branch of Townhouse Restaurants.

Problem 16–6

The balance sheets of the Harper and Leon branches of Townhouse Restaurants are included in the working papers accompanying this textbook.

Instructions: Use the income statements you prepared in Problem 16–5 and the balance sheets included in the workbook to complete this problem. Prepare a combined income statement and a combined balance sheet for Townhouse Restaurants.

17 Manufacturing Accounting

In your study of accounting, you have learned about various accounting procedures as they apply to service and merchandising businesses. In the remaining two chapters of this unit, you will learn about the accounting procedures for a third type of business: a manufacturing business.

Manufacturing businesses carry on the same kinds of administrative activities as any business. In addition, they are involved in actually making a product as well as selling that product to other companies or to individuals. The accounting system of a manufacturer must include procedures to account for all of the costs that go into the production of a finished product.

In this chapter, you will learn how manufacturers determine the cost of the goods they manufacture and the cost of the goods they sell during an accounting period. You will also learn how to prepare the financial statements for a business that manufactures products.

Learning Objectives

When you have completed this chapter, you should be able to

1. Identify the three major elements in the cost of a manufactured product.

2. Calculate the value of the ending inventories for a manufacturing business.

3. Complete a work sheet for a manufacturing business.

4. Prepare financial statements for a manufacturing business.

5. Journalize the adjusting and closing entries for a manufacturing business.

6. Define the accounting terms presented in this chapter.

New Terms

manufacturing business / direct materials / direct labor / factory overhead / indirect labor / factory supplies / work in process / finished goods / statement of cost of goods manufactured

Manufacturing Operations

Most of the discussions and examples in this textbook have centered around merchandising businesses. As you know, a merchandising business buys goods—such as clothing, books, furniture, and so on—and then resells those goods to customers for a profit. A merchandising business doesn't have to do anything more to the goods before selling them. In contrast, a **manufacturing business** buys raw materials, such as wood or iron ore, and transforms them into finished products through the use of labor and machinery. A manufacturing business *makes* goods to sell; it does not buy finished goods to resell.

A merchandising business can determine the cost of the merchandise it has bought by simply looking at its Purchases account. A manufacturing business, however, must keep track of a whole series of costs to determine the cost of the goods it produces.

Determining the cost of goods sold for a manufacturing business is also more complex. Instead of the one inventory account used by a merchandising business, a manufacturing business has three inventory accounts.

In other respects, merchandising and manufacturing businesses are similar. Both earn revenue by selling their products. Many of the same asset, liability, and stockholders' equity accounts are used by both types of businesses. Finally, merchandising and manufacturing businesses have similar selling and administrative expenses.

As you can see, the major difference between accounting for a merchandising business and for a manufacturing business lies in accounting for the cost of merchandise or goods sold. (Merchandising businesses refer to their products as "merchandise"; manufacturing businesses refer to their products as "goods.")

Elements of Manufacturing Costs

Regardless of the type of product a manufacturing business makes, its cost is made up of three basic elements: direct materials, direct labor, and factory overhead.

Direct Materials

All manufactured products require certain basic ingredients. These ingredients are called direct materials. **Direct materials** are the materials that are used to make and can be easily traced to a finished product. Direct materials are also called raw materials. As an example, suppose you decide to manufacture pencils. The direct materials you need to manufacture those pencils include wood, graphite, paint, glue, erasers, and metal bands.

The direct materials of one manufacturer may be the finished goods of another manufacturer. For example, flour may be the finished product of a miller but part of the direct materials used by a baker.

Direct Labor

The wages paid to employees who actually work on a product—with either machines or hand tools—are called **direct labor**. Direct labor includes only the wages paid to workers who convert the direct materials into finished products. It does not include the wages and salaries paid to supervisors, office workers, managers, maintenance personnel, or others who are not directly involved in the production process.

Factory Overhead

All other manufacturing costs that cannot be easily or directly traced to the products being manufactured are referred to as **factory overhead**. Factory overhead includes a number of different types of production-related costs. Some examples of factory overhead costs are listed below.

- Indirect labor
- Supervisory salaries
- Heat, light, and power for the factory
- Depreciation of factory equipment and factory buildings
- Repairs and maintenance of factory equipment and buildings
- Insurance on factory equipment and buildings
- Factory supplies used
- Payroll taxes on the wages and salaries of factory personnel
- Property taxes on factory equipment and buildings
- Cost of small tools

Separate accounts are kept for each type of factory overhead cost. In some manufacturing businesses, there are so many factory overhead accounts that the businesses use a Factory Overhead controlling account. Individual accounts for each cost item are maintained in a factory overhead subsidiary ledger.

Remember: Factory overhead costs are those production-related costs that cannot be easily or directly traced to the products being manufactured.

Most of the items listed above are self-explanatory. Two items that need further discussion are indirect labor and factory supplies.

Indirect Labor

As explained earlier, direct labor is the wages paid to employees who actually convert the raw materials into finished products. However, a factory could not operate without the services of other types of employees. These other employees include maintenance personnel, timekeepers, security guards, fork lift operators, and so on. The wages paid to these factory employees who do not physically work on the products are called indirect labor.

Indirect labor is different from the salaries paid to supervisors. Salaries are set amounts paid each pay period to employees. Wages are the amounts paid to employees at a specified rate per hour. Wages can vary greatly, depending upon the number of hours worked by employees. Salaries do not vary; salaried employees receive the same amount each pay period regardless of the number of hours they work. Because of this difference, separate accounts are maintained for indirect labor and for supervisory salaries.

Factory Supplies

Direct materials are the materials that can be easily traced to a finished product or group of products. However, other materials are used in the production process. These materials include such items as the grease and oil for machinery, cleaning supplies, or the sandpaper used by a furniture maker. These other indirect materials are referred to as factory supplies.

Before reading further, do the following activity to check your understanding of manufacturing costs.

Check Your Learning

Write your answers to the following questions on a sheet of notebook paper.

1. The sheet metal, glass, and tires of an automobile manufacturer are considered to be __?__.
2. __?__ labor is the wages paid to the employees who actually produce a product; __?__ labor is the wages paid to such employees as repair and janitorial workers.
3. Examples of __?__ include depreciation of factory equipment, factory supplies, and indirect labor.
4. __?__ are often referred to as indirect materials.

Compare your answers with those in the answers section. Re-read the preceding part of the chapter to find the correct answers to any questions you may have missed.

Classifying Manufacturing Costs

Some people further classify manufacturing costs by combining two of the three basic elements. When direct materials and direct labor costs are combined, they are referred to as *prime costs*, since they are the two major costs of producing a product. When direct labor and factory overhead costs are combined, they are referred to as *conversion costs*. These two elements are the costs of converting the third element—direct materials—into a finished product.

Remember: The cost of a manufactured product consists of the costs of direct materials, direct labor, and factory overhead.

Manufacturing Inventories

For a merchandising business, the balance of the Merchandise Inventory account represents the cost of all the merchandise a business has on hand and available for sale at the end of a fiscal period. In a manufacturing business, however, the company's products may be in various stages of completion at the end of the period. Some products may be completed and available for sale, some may be in the process of being completed, and still others may not yet be started.

As a result, a manufacturing business cannot allocate its costs (direct materials, direct labor, and factory overhead) to just one inventory account. Instead, a manufacturing business has three inventory accounts: Raw Materials Inventory, Work in Process Inventory, and Finished Goods Inventory.

Raw Materials Inventory

The raw materials inventory consists of the cost of the direct materials that are still unused at the end of a fiscal period. The balance of the Raw Materials Inventory account is determined by taking a physical inventory and then assigning a value to the materials on hand.

Work in Process Inventory

At the end of a fiscal period, almost all manufacturing businesses have some products that are only partially completed. These partially completed products are called work in process. The Work in Process Inventory account, then, consists of the costs of uncompleted products still in the production process at the end of the period. The balance of the Work in Process Inventory account includes the cost of the direct materials, direct labor, and factory overhead that have already been used.

Finished Goods Inventory

The goods that a manufacturing business has completed and available for sale are its finished goods. The balance of the Finished Goods Inventory account, therefore, consists of the costs of all completed but unsold products. The Finished Goods Inventory account is very similar to the Merchandise Inventory account of a merchandising business.

Remember: A manufacturing business maintains three separate inventory accounts: Raw Materials Inventory, Work in Process Inventory, and Finished Goods Inventory.

Determining the Cost of Manufacturing Inventories

At the end of a fiscal period, a manufacturing business, like a merchandising business, must assign a cost to its ending inventories. It is fairly easy to do this for the raw materials inventory. The items in the inventory are still in the same form as when they were purchased. A physical inventory is taken of the direct materials on hand at the end of the period. The cost of the ending inventory is then determined using one of the inventory costing methods: lifo, fifo, or weighted average cost. A manufacturing business may also apply the lower-of-cost-or-market rule to the ending raw materials inventory.

However, assigning a cost to the work in process and finished goods inventories is generally not as easy. Remember, these inventories consist of the costs of direct materials, direct labor, and factory overhead. A manufacturing business can easily determine its total direct materials cost, total direct labor cost, and total factory overhead cost. The problem lies in allocating these totals between the work in process inventory and the finished goods inventory.

It is usually fairly easy to trace and allocate the costs of the direct materials and direct labor to the work in process or the finished goods. That's why these are called "direct" costs. For example, the Windsor Corporation manufactures fine furniture. At the end of the fiscal period, the company determined that its total direct materials, direct labor, and factory overhead costs were as follows.

Direct materials	$220,000
Direct labor	565,000
Factory overhead	405,000

The company also determined that the following direct materials and direct labor costs could be assigned to its work in process and finished goods.

	Work in Process	Finished Goods
Direct materials	$30,990	$ 63,036
Direct labor	51,750	108,700

(The remaining portion of the direct materials and direct labor costs, $125,974 and $404,550 respectively, can be assigned to goods that were completed *and* sold during the period.)

Factory overhead costs, however, cannot be easily traced. Therefore, manufacturers must estimate the amount of the factory overhead allocated to the work in process and finished goods inventories.

Factory overhead costs can be allocated by several methods. One of the most common methods is to allocate the costs on the basis of a percentage of the direct labor costs assigned to the two inventories. Direct labor costs are used because they vary directly with the level of production. In other words, the more products that are produced, the more hours of direct labor (and, therefore, wages) are required. Many of the factory overhead costs also vary directly with the level of production. As production increases, the costs of indirect labor, utilities, factory supplies, and so on also increase. Let's look at an example of the allocation of factory overhead costs.

To allocate the factory overhead costs to the work in process and finished goods inventories, the factory overhead rate must first be determined. It is calculated by dividing the factory overhead costs by the total direct labor costs. The factory overhead rate for the Windsor Corporation is calculated as follows.

$$\text{Factory overhead rate} = \frac{\text{Factory overhead}}{\text{Direct labor}} = \frac{\$405,000}{\$565,000} = .72$$

The direct labor costs assigned to the two inventories are then multiplied by this factory overhead rate. The resulting amounts are the factory overhead costs to be allocated to the work in process and finished goods inventories. The direct labor costs Windsor allocated to the work in process and finished goods inventories are $51,750 and $108,700, respectively. The factory overhead costs allocated to the two inventories are calculated as follows.

Work in Process Inventory = $ 51,750 × .72 = $37,260
Finished Goods Inventory = $108,700 × .72 = $78,264

Remember: Factory overhead costs cannot be easily or directly traced to the products being manufactured. The costs must be allocated to the work in process and finished goods inventories using the predetermined factory overhead rate.

Manufacturing Accounts

Before we examine the financial statements prepared by a manufacturing business, let's look at the accounts that are unique to a manufacturing business. A partial chart of accounts for the Windsor Corporation appears in Figure 17–1. Many of the accounts that would also appear on the chart of accounts for a merchandising business have been omitted. For example, Figure 17–1 does not include such asset accounts as Cash in Bank, Accounts Receivable, and Land. Nor does it show the corporation's liability, stockholders' equity, and selling and administrative expense accounts. Most of the accounts that are listed are those that are normally found only in the general ledger of a manufacturing business.

As you can see, Raw Materials Inventory, Work in Process Inventory, and Finished Goods Inventory appear in the Assets section of the chart of accounts. The Factory Supplies account also appears in this section. When a manufacturing business purchases such items as oil or grease for lubricating machinery, the cost of these items is debited to the Factory Supplies account. At the end of a fiscal period, the account is adjusted to reflect the cost of supplies still on hand. Factory Supplies is, therefore, very similar to the Office Supplies account.

A manufacturing business, like service and merchandising businesses, also has an Income Summary account. This account is used only at the end of the period during the adjusting and closing process, as for a merchandising business.

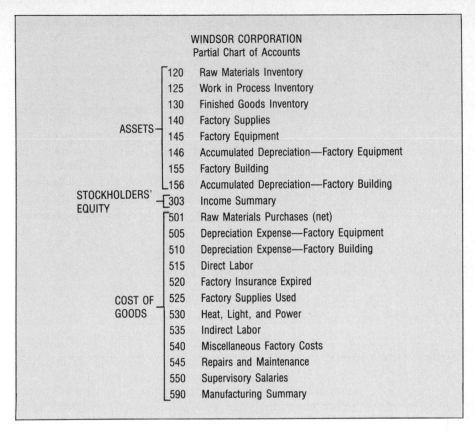

WINDSOR CORPORATION
Partial Chart of Accounts

ASSETS

120 Raw Materials Inventory
125 Work in Process Inventory
130 Finished Goods Inventory
140 Factory Supplies
145 Factory Equipment
146 Accumulated Depreciation—Factory Equipment
155 Factory Building
156 Accumulated Depreciation—Factory Building

STOCKHOLDERS' EQUITY

303 Income Summary

COST OF GOODS

501 Raw Materials Purchases (net)
505 Depreciation Expense—Factory Equipment
510 Depreciation Expense—Factory Building
515 Direct Labor
520 Factory Insurance Expired
525 Factory Supplies Used
530 Heat, Light, and Power
535 Indirect Labor
540 Miscellaneous Factory Costs
545 Repairs and Maintenance
550 Supervisory Salaries
590 Manufacturing Summary

Figure 17–1. Partial Chart of Accounts for a Manufacturing Business

The Cost of Goods section for a manufacturing business contains many more accounts than the Cost of Merchandise section for a merchandising business. These accounts are all *costs* of producing the company's finished products. Most of the cost of goods accounts are self-explanatory. The Raw Materials Purchases account is similar to the Purchases account of a merchandising business. Whenever direct materials are purchased by a manufacturing business, the cost of those materials is debited to the Raw Materials Purchases account.

The Manufacturing Summary account is similar to the Income Summary account. It too is used only at the end of the fiscal period during the adjusting and closing process. The balances of the Raw Materials Inventory and Work in Process Inventory accounts are adjusted through this account. (Finished Goods Inventory is adjusted through the Income Summary account.) Also, the balances of the cost of goods accounts are closed into the Manufacturing Summary account. The balance of the Manufacturing Summary account, which represents the cost of goods manufactured during the period, is then closed into Income Summary.

Remember: The Raw Materials Inventory and Work in Process Inventory accounts are adjusted through the Manufacturing Summary account at the end of the fiscal period.

Before reading further, do the following activity to check your understanding of the material you have just studied.

Check Your Learning

On a separate sheet of notebook paper, write your answers to the following questions.

1. The three inventories of a manufacturing business are __?__, __?__, and __?__.
2. __?__ are the products that have not yet been completed.
3. The goods that a manufacturer has available for sale are called __?__.
4. __?__ costs cannot easily be traced to the work in process or finished goods.
5. At the end of a fiscal period, the raw materials and work in process inventories are adjusted through the __?__ account.

Compare your answers with those in the answers section. Re-read the preceding part of the chapter to find the correct answers to any questions you may have missed.

End-of-fiscal-period Work

At the end of a fiscal period, a manufacturing business completes the same end-of-period activities as does a merchandising business. These activities include the following.

1. Preparing a trial balance (in the first two columns of a work sheet).
2. Completing the work sheet, including adjustments.
3. Preparing the financial statements.
4. Journalizing and posting the adjusting entries.
5. Journalizing and posting the closing entries.
6. Preparing a post-closing trial balance.

The work sheet is completed before the financial statements are prepared. However, so that you might better understand the desired end results and the flow of costs in a manufacturing business, we will look first at the financial statements and then at the work sheet.

Financial Statements for a Manufacturing Business

A manufacturing business usually prepares four financial statements at the end of a fiscal period. You are already familiar with three of them: the income statement, the statement of retained earnings, and the balance sheet. The fourth statement prepared by a manufacturing business is the statement of cost of goods manufactured.

The statement of retained earnings for a manufacturing business is just like that prepared by a merchandising business. As a result, it will not be discussed in this chapter.

The balance sheet prepared by a manufacturing business differs very little from that prepared by a merchandising business. The only difference occurs in the Assets section. For a manufacturing business, the balance sheet reports the balances of the three inventory accounts (Raw Materials, Work in Process, and Finished Goods); Factory Supplies; and the various factory property, plant, and equipment assets.

In the next two sections, we will look more closely at the statement of cost of goods manufactured and the income statement.

Statement of Cost of Goods Manufactured

The statement of cost of goods manufactured is prepared before and as a supporting statement for the income statement. The statement of cost of goods manufactured, as its name indicates, summarizes all the costs of the goods completed during the fiscal period. The statement of cost of goods manufactured for the Windsor Corporation is shown in Figure 17–2 at the top of the next page.

The three basic elements of manufacturing costs are direct or raw materials, direct labor, and factory overhead. The statement of cost of goods manufactured is organized to emphasize these elements. The amounts reported on this statement are taken from the Statement of Cost of Goods Manufactured section of the work sheet.

First, the beginning work in process inventory is recorded on the statement. Next, the cost of direct materials used is determined. The cost of direct materials used is determined in the same way as the cost of merchandise sold is. That is, the beginning raw materials inventory is added to the raw materials purchases amount ($90,000 + $230,000). The result, $320,000, is the cost of all raw materials available for use during the period. Next, the ending raw materials inventory is deducted ($320,000 − $100,000). The resulting amount is the cost of raw materials used, $220,000.

The next "section" of the statement reports the direct labor costs for the period.

Factory overhead costs are reported in the next section. As you can see, each factory overhead account is listed separately on this statement. If, however, there are very many factory overhead costs, they may be listed on another,

$ 220,000
565,000
+ 405,000
$1,190,000

separate statement. In that case, only the total factory overhead cost would be reported on the statement of cost of goods manufactured.

The costs of direct materials used, direct labor, and factory overhead are totaled to determine the total manufacturing costs, $1,190,000.

In the final section of the statement, the cost of goods manufactured is calculated. The beginning work in process inventory is added to the total manufacturing costs ($130,000 + $1,190,000). The result, $1,320,000, is the total cost of work in process during the period. Finally, the ending work in process

Windsor Corporation
Statement of Cost of Goods Manufactured
For the Year Ended December 31, 19--

Work in Process Inventory, Jan. 1, 19--			130 000 00
Direct Materials:			
Raw Materials Inv., Jan. 1, 19--		90 000 00	
Raw Materials Purchases (net)		230 000 00	
Cost of Raw Materials Available		320 000 00	
Less Raw Materials Inv., Dec. 31, 19--		100 000 00	
Cost of Direct Materials Used		220 000 00	
Direct Labor		565 000 00	
Factory Overhead:			
Deprec. Expense–Factory Equip.	32 000 00		
Deprec. Expense–Factory Bldg.	25 000 00		
Factory Insurance Expired	22 000 00		
Factory Supplies Used	14 000 00		
Heat, Light, and Power	42 000 00		
Indirect Labor	120 000 00		
Miscellaneous Factory Costs	16 000 00		
Repairs and Maintenance	24 000 00		
Supervisory Salaries	110 000 00		
Total Factory Overhead Costs		405 000 00	
Total Manufacturing Costs			1,190 000 00
Total Cost of Work in Process in Period			1,320 000 00
Less Work in Process Inv., Dec. 31, 19--			120 000 00
Cost of Goods Manufactured			1,200 000 00

Figure 17–2. Statement of Cost of Goods Manufactured

inventory is subtracted to determine the cost of goods manufactured: $1,320,000 − $120,000 = $1,200,000.

It is this last amount that is carried over to and reported on the Windsor Corporation's income statement.

Remember: The statement of cost of goods manufactured is prepared before and as a supporting statement for the income statement.

Income Statement for a Manufacturing Business

The income statement of a manufacturing business looks very much like the income statement of a merchandising business. The Revenue, Expenses, Other Revenue, and Other Expenses sections are very similar. The main difference appears in the Cost of Goods Sold section. To see the difference between the two sections, look at Figure 17–3 on page 411.

The cost of goods or merchandise sold is calculated as follows for the two types of businesses.

Windsor (Merchandising) Corporation
Income Statement
For the Year Ended December 31, 19--

Revenue:		
Sales (net)		2,000 000 00
Cost of Merchandise Sold:		
Merchandise Inventory, Jan. 1, 19--	400 000 00	
Purchases (net)	1,200 000 00	
Merchandise Available for Sale	1,600 000 00	
Less: Merchandise Inventory, Dec. 31, 19--	250 000 00	
Cost of Merchandise Sold		1,350 000 00
Gross Profit on Sales		650 000 00

Windsor (Manufacturing) Corporation
Income Statement
For the Year Ended December 31, 19--

Revenue:		
Sales (net)		2,000 000 00
Cost of Goods Sold:		
Finished Goods Inventory, Jan. 1, 19--	400 000 00	
Cost of Goods Manufactured	1,200 000 00	
Goods Available for Sale	1,600 000 00	
Less: Finished Goods Inventory, Dec. 31, 19--	250 000 00	
Cost of Goods Sold		1,350 000 00
Gross Profit on Sales		650 000 00

Figure 17–3. Comparison of Income Statements for a Merchandising Business and a Manufacturing Business

Merchandising Business	Manufacturing Business
Beginning merchandise inventory	Beginning finished goods inventory
+ Purchases (net)	+ Cost of goods manufactured
= Merchandise available for sale	= Goods available for sale
− Ending merchandise inventory	− Ending finished goods inventory
= Cost of merchandise sold	= Cost of goods sold

The complete income statement for the Windsor Corporation is shown in condensed form in Figure 17–4 on page 412.

As you can see from the discussion of these two financial statements, determining the cost of goods sold requires the use of the three manufacturing inventory accounts: raw materials, work in process, and finished goods. The basic elements of manufacturing costs flow through these three inventories as shown in the chart in Figure 17–5 on page 412.

Windsor Corporation
Income Statement
For the Year Ended December 31, 19--

Revenue:			
Sales			2,000 000 00
Cost of Goods Sold:			
Finished Goods Inventory, Jan. 1, 19--	400 000 00		
Cost of Goods Manufactured	1,200 000 00		
Goods Available for Sale	1,600 000 00		
Less: Finished Goods Inventory, Dec 31, 19--	250 000 00		
Cost of Goods Sold		1,350 000 00	
Gross Profit on Sales		650 000 00	
Operating Expenses:			
Selling Expenses	300 000 00		
Administrative Expenses	152 000 00		
Total Operating Expenses		452 000 00	
Net Income from Operations		198 000 00	
Other Expenses:			
Interest Expense		18 000 00	
Net Income before Income Taxes		180 000 00	
Income Taxes		62 550 00	
Net Income after Income Taxes		117 450 00	

Figure 17–4. Condensed Income Statement for a Manufacturing Business

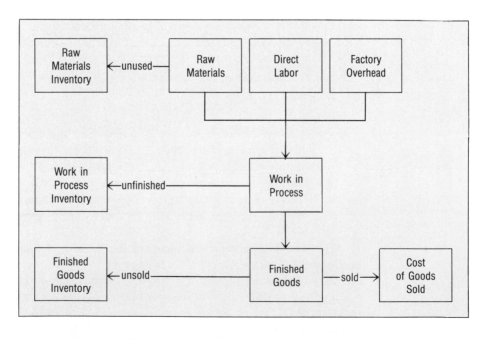

Figure 17–5. The Flow of Manufacturing Costs

Completing a Work Sheet for a Manufacturing Business

The work sheet for the Windsor Corporation for the fiscal period ended December 31 is shown in Figure 17–6 on pages 414–417. The work sheet, as you know, is used to organize all the information needed to prepare the financial statements and to journalize the adjusting and closing entries. As a result, the work sheet completed by the Windsor Corporation has ten columns. However, instead of an Adjusted Trial Balance section, this work sheet contains a section titled Statement of Cost of Goods Manufactured.

All of the accounts that appear in Windsor's general ledger are listed in the Account Name column; their balances are entered in the Trial Balance columns. After this section is totaled, proved, and ruled, the adjustments are entered in the Adjustments section.

Most of the adjustments entered on the work sheet are similar to those of a merchandising business. For example, adjustments are made for estimated uncollectible amounts, supplies used, and insurance expired.

The adjustments to the manufacturing inventories, however, are handled in a slightly different way. Windsor Corporation has three inventory accounts: raw materials, work in process, and finished goods. Since the raw materials and work in process inventories are used to determine the cost of goods manufactured, they are adjusted through the Manufacturing Summary account. The finished goods inventory, since it is used to determine the cost of goods sold, is adjusted through the Income Summary account.

The Raw Materials Inventory account is adjusted first. The beginning inventory amount, recorded in the Trial Balance section, was $90,000. At the end of the period, Windsor determines that the ending raw materials inventory has a value of $100,000. Adjusting the inventory accounts of a manufacturing business, like a merchandising business, involves two steps: (1) The beginning inventory is removed by crediting the account, and (2) the ending inventory is entered by debiting the account. The adjustment for Raw Materials Inventory is shown below.

Raw Materials Inventory		Manufacturing Summary	
Dr.	Cr.	Dr.	Cr.
+	−		
Bal. $ 90,000	(a) $90,000	(a) $90,000	(b) $100,000
(b) 100,000			

The Work in Process Inventory account is adjusted in the same manner. The beginning inventory of $130,000 is first transferred to the Manufacturing Summary account. Then, the ending inventory of $120,000 is entered as the new balance. The adjustment for Work in Process Inventory is shown in the following T accounts.

Work in Process Inventory		Manufacturing Summary	
Dr.	Cr.	Dr.	Cr.
+	−		
Bal. $130,000	(c) $130,000	(a) $ 90,000	(b) $100,000
(d) 120,000		(c) 130,000	(d) 120,000

	ACCOUNT NAME	TRIAL BALANCE DEBIT	TRIAL BALANCE CREDIT	ADJUSTMENTS DEBIT	ADJUSTMENTS CREDIT
1	Cash in Bank	29 150 00			
2	Notes Receivable	50 000 00			
3	Accounts Receivable	180 000 00			
4	Allow. for Uncoll. Accts		2 500 00		(l) 3 500 00
5	Raw Materials Inv	90 000 00		(b) 100 000 00	(a) 90 000 00
6	Work in Process Inv	130 000 00		(d) 120 000 00	(c) 130 000 00
7	Finished Goods Inv	400 000 00		(f) 250 000 00	(e) 400 000 00
8	Prepaid Insurance	25 000 00			(i) 22 000 00
9	Factory Supplies	16 000 00			(j) 14 000 00
10	Factory Equipment	360 000 00			
11	Accum Depr-Fact Equip		218 000 00		(g) 32 000 00
12	Office Equipment	62 000 00			
13	Accum Depr- Off. Equip		40 000 00		(K) 5 000 00
14	Factory Building	500 000 00			
15	Accum Depr-Fact. Bldg		250 000 00		(h) 25 000 00
16	Land	100 000 00			
17	Accounts Payable		82 000 00		
18	Dividends Payable		12 000 00		
19	Corporate Inc. Tax Pay.				(m) 13 800 00
20	Notes Payable		40 000 00		
21	Bonds Payable		300 000 00		
22	Common Stock		300 000 00		
23	Paid-in Cap. in Exc. of Par		100 000 00		
24	Retained Earnings		214 900 00		
25	Income Summary			(e) 400 000 00	(f) 250 000 00
26	Sales (net)		2,000 000 00		
27	Raw Materials Purch (net)	230 000 00			
28	Depr. Exp-Factory Equip			(g) 32 000 00	
29	Depr. Exp-Factory Bldg.			(h) 25 000 00	
30	Direct Labor	565 000 00			
31	Factory Ins. Expired			(i) 22 000 00	
32	Factory Supplies Used			(j) 14 000 00	
33	Carried Forward	2,737 150 00	3,559 400 00	963 000 00	985 300 00

Figure 17–6. Work Sheet for a Manufacturing Business   (Left Side)

STATEMENT OF COST OF GOODS MANUFACTURED		INCOME STATEMENT		BALANCE SHEET		
DEBIT	CREDIT	DEBIT	CREDIT	DEBIT	CREDIT	
				29 150 00		1
				50 000 00		2
				180 000 00		3
					6 000 00	4
				100 000 00		5
				120 000 00		6
				250 000 00		7
				3 000 00		8
				2 000 00		9
				360 000 00		10
					250 000 00	11
				62 000 00		12
					45 000 00	13
				500 000 00		14
					275 000 00	15
				100 000 00		16
					82 000 00	17
					12 000 00	18
					13 800 00	19
					40 000 00	20
					300 000 00	21
					300 000 00	22
					100 000 00	23
					214 900 00	24
		400 000 00	250 000 00			25
			2,000 000 00			26
230 000 00						27
32 000 00						28
25 000 00						29
565 000 00						30
22 000 00						31
14 000 00						32
888 000 00	——	400 000 00	2,250 000 00	1,756 150 00	1,638 700 00	33

(Right Side)

ACCOUNT NAME	TRIAL BALANCE DEBIT	TRIAL BALANCE CREDIT	ADJUSTMENTS DEBIT	ADJUSTMENTS CREDIT
1 Brought Forward	2,737 150 00	3,559 400 00	963 000 00	985 300 00
2 Heat, Light, & Power	42 000 00			
3 Indirect Labor	120 000 00			
4 Misc. Factory Costs	16 000 00			
5 Repairs & Maintenance	24 000 00			
6 Supervisory Salaries	110 000 00			
7 Mfg. Summary			(a) 90 000 00	(b) 100 000 00
8			(c) 130 000 00	(d) 120 000 00
9 Selling Expenses	300 000 00			
10 Admin. Expenses	143 500 00		(l) 3 500 00	
11			(k) 5 000 00	
12 Interest Expense	18 000 00			
13 Income Tax Expense	48 750 00		(m) 13 800 00	
14	3,559 400 00	3,559 400 00	1,205 300 00	1,205 300 00
15 Cost of Goods Manuf.				
16				
17 Net Inc. after Inc. Taxes				
18				

Figure 17–6. Work Sheet for a Manufacturing Business (Continued)   *(Left Side)*

The Finished Goods Inventory is adjusted through the Income Summary account. The same two steps are followed. The beginning finished goods inventory of $400,000 is transferred to Income Summary and the ending finished goods inventory of $250,000 is entered as the new balance. This adjustment is shown in the following T accounts.

Finished Goods Inventory		Income Summary	
Dr. +	Cr. −	Dr.	Cr.
Bal. $400,000	(e) $400,000	(e) $400,000	(f) $250,000
(f) 250,000			

All of the adjustments made by the Windsor Corporation are illustrated in the completed work sheet in Figure 17–6. After all the adjustments are entered on the work sheet, the Adjustments section is totaled, proved, and ruled.

The amounts are then extended to the Balance Sheet, Income Statement, or Statement of Cost of Goods Manufactured section. The cost accounts are

STATEMENT OF COST OF GOODS MANUFACTURED		INCOME STATEMENT		BALANCE SHEET		
DEBIT	CREDIT	DEBIT	CREDIT	DEBIT	CREDIT	
888 000 00	————	400 000 00	2,250 000 00	1,756 150 00	1,638 700 00	1
42 000 00						2
120 000 00						3
16 000 00						4
24 000 00						5
110 000 00						6
90 000 00	100 000 00					7
130 000 00	120 000 00					8
		300 000 00				9
		152 000 00				10
						11
		18 000 00				12
		62 550 00				13
1,420 000 00	220 000 00					14
	1,200 000 00	1,200 000 00				15
1,420 000 00	1,420 000 00	2,132 550 00	2,250 000 00	1,756 150 00	1,638 700 00	16
		117 450 00			117 450 00	17
		2,250 000 00	2,250 000 00	1,756 150 00	1,756 150 00	18

(Right Side)

extended to the Statement of Cost of Goods Manufactured section rather than the Income Statement section. Income Summary and the revenue, operating expense, and other expense accounts are extended to the Income Statement section. Look again at Figure 17–6. Make sure you understand to which section each amount is extended.

$1,420,000
− 220,000
$1,200,000

After all amounts have been extended, the Statement of Cost of Goods Manufactured section is totaled. The difference between the Debit and Credit columns in this section, $1,200,000, is the cost of goods manufactured. The Statement of Cost of Goods Manufactured section is then totaled, proved, and ruled. The cost of goods manufactured amount is extended to the Income Statement Debit column.

The last two sections of the work sheet are totaled and the amount of the net income after income taxes is determined. This amount is the same as that shown earlier on the income statement in Figure 17–4.

Remember: The cost of goods manufactured amount is extended to the Income Statement Debit column on the work sheet.

Before reading further, do the following activity to check your understanding of the material you have just studied.

Check Your Learning

Write the answers to the following questions on a sheet of notebook paper.

1. The financial statements prepared by a manufacturing business are the ___?___, the ___?___, the ___?___, and the ___?___.
2. The main difference between the income statement of a manufacturing business and that of a merchandising business appears in the ___?___ section.
3. Instead of an Adjusted Trial Balance section, the work sheet for a manufacturing business contains a section entitled ___?___.
4. The raw materials and work in process inventories are adjusted through the ___?___ account, while the finished goods inventory is adjusted through the ___?___ account.

Check your anwsers with those in the answers section. Re-read the preceding part of the chapter to find the correct answers to any questions you may have missed.

Journalizing the Adjusting and Closing Entries

At the end of the fiscal period, after the financial statements are prepared, the adjusting and closing entries are journalized and posted.

Adjusting Entries

As shown on the work sheet, the Windsor Corporation had the following adjustments. The adjustments are journalized as shown in Figure 17–7.

- Adjusted Raw Materials Inventory to reflect the ending balance of $100,000 (a) and (b).
- Adjusted Work in Process Inventory to reflect the ending balance of $120,000 (c) and (d).
- Adjusted Finished Goods Inventory to reflect the ending balance of $250,000 (e) and (f).
- Depreciation of factory equipment was $32,000 (g).
- Depreciation of the factory building was $25,000 (h).
- The expired factory insurance premium was $22,000 (i).
- The cost of the factory supplies used during the fiscal period was $14,000 (j).
- Depreciation of office equipment was $5,000 (k).
- The estimated uncollectible amount for the period was $6,000 (l).
- The additional income taxes owed are $13,800 (m).

	DATE		DESCRIPTION	POST. REF.	DEBIT	CREDIT	
			Adjusting Entries				1
(a)	19-- Dec.	31	Manufacturing Summary		90 000 00		2
			Raw Materials Inventory			90 000 00	3
(b)		31	Raw Materials Inventory		100 000 00		4
			Manufacturing Summary			100 000 00	5
(c)		31	Manufacturing Summary		130 000 00		6
			Work in Process Inventory			130 000 00	7
(d)		31	Work in Process Inventory		120 000 00		8
			Manufacturing Summary			120 000 00	9
(e)		31	Income Summary		400 000 00		10
			Finished Goods Inventory			400 000 00	11
(f)		31	Finished Goods Inventory		250 000 00		12
			Income Summary			250 000 00	13
(g)		31	Deprec. Expense–Factory Equip.		32 000 00		14
			Accum. Deprec.–Factory Equip.			32 000 00	15
(h)		31	Deprec. Expense–Factory Bldg.		25 000 00		16
			Accum. Deprec.–Factory Bldg.			25 000 00	17
(i)		31	Factory Insurance Expired		22 000 00		18
			Prepaid Insurance			22 000 00	19
(j)		31	Factory Supplies Used		14 000 00		20
			Factory Supplies			14 000 00	21
(k)		31	Administrative Expenses		5 000 00		22
			Accum. Deprec.–Office Equip.			5 000 00	23
(l)		31	Administrative Expenses		3 500 00		24
			Allow. for Uncollect. Accts.			3 500 00	25
(m)		31	Income Tax Expense		13 800 00		26
			Corporate Income Tax Pay.			13 800 00	27

Figure 17–7. Adjusting Entries for a Manufacturing Business

Closing Entries

Five closing entries are required for a manufacturing business. These entries are as follows.

1. Close the cost of goods accounts into Manufacturing Summary. The cost of goods accounts appear in the Statement of Cost of Goods Manufactured section of the work sheet.
2. Close the Manufacturing Summary account into Income Summary. The amount of this closing entry is the amount of the cost of goods manufactured.
3. Close the revenue account into Income Summary. In our example for the Windsor Corporation, the amount of the closing entry is the amount of net sales.

4. Close the expense accounts into Income Summary. In our example, the amount of the closing entry is the total of the selling expense, administrative expense, other expense, and income tax expense accounts.
5. Close Income Summary into Retained Earnings. The amount of the closing entry is the amount of the net income after income taxes for the period.

The closing entries are illustrated in Figure 17–8.

GENERAL JOURNAL   PAGE 43

	DATE	DESCRIPTION	POST. REF.	DEBIT	CREDIT	
1		Closing Entries				1
2	19-- Dec. 31	Manufacturing Summary		1,200 000 00		2
3		Raw Materials Purchases			230 000 00	3
4		Deprec. Expense – Factory Equip.			32 000 00	4
5		Deprec. Expense – Factory Bldg.			25 000 00	5
6		Direct Labor			565 000 00	6
7		Factory Insurance Expired			22 000 00	7
8		Factory Supplies Used			14 000 00	8
9		Heat, Light, and Power			42 000 00	9
10		Indirect Labor			120 000 00	10
11		Miscellaneous Factory Costs			16 000 00	11
12		Repairs and Maintenance			24 000 00	12
13		Supervisory Salaries			110 000 00	13
14	31	Income Summary		1,200 000 00		14
15		Manufacturing Summary			1,200 000 00	15
16	31	Sales (net)		2,000 000 00		16
17		Income Summary			2,000 000 00	17
18	31	Income Summary		532 550 00		18
19		Selling Expenses			300 000 00	19
20		Administrative Expenses			152 000 00	20
21		Income Tax Expense			62 550 00	21
22		Interest Expense			18 000 00	22
23	31	Income Summary		1 174 500 00		23
24		Retained Earnings			1 174 500 00	24

Figure 17–8. Closing Entries for a Manufacturing Business

The effect of the adjusting and closing entries and the relationship between Manufacturing Summary and Income Summary are illustrated in the following T accounts.

Income Summary

Dr.	Cr.
Adj. Fin. Goods Inv., 1/1 $ 400,000	Adj. Fin. Goods Inv., 12/31 $250,000
Clo. from Mfg. Summary 1,200,000	

Manufacturing Summary

Dr.		Cr.	
Adj. Raw Mat. Inv., 1/1	$ 90,000	Adj. Raw Mat. Inv., 12/31	$ 100,000
Adj. Work in Proc. Inv., 1/1	130,000	Adj. Work in Proc. Inv., 12/31	120,000
Clo. Raw Mat. Purchases	230,000	Clo. to Income Summary	1,200,000
Clo. Depr. Exp.—Fact. Equip.	32,000		
Clo. Depr. Exp.—Fact. Bldg.	25,000		
Clo. Direct Labor	565,000		
Clo. Fact. Ins. Expired	22,000		
Clo. Fact. Supplies Used	14,000		
Clo. Heat, Light, & Power	42,000		
Clo. Indirect Labor	120,000		
Clo. Misc. Factory Costs	16,000		
Clo. Repairs and Maint.	24,000		
Clo. Super. Salaries	110,000		

Summary of Key Points

1. A manufacturing business converts raw materials through the use of labor and machinery into finished products.
2. The major difference between accounting for a merchandising business and a manufacturing business is in accounting for the cost of goods sold.
3. The three elements of manufacturing costs are direct materials, direct labor, and factory overhead. Direct materials are the materials that are used to make and can be directly traced to a finished product. Direct labor is the wages paid to employees who physically convert the raw materials into finished products. Factory overhead consists of all other manufacturing costs that cannot be directly traced to the products being manufactured.
4. Two costs included in factory overhead are indirect labor and factory supplies. Indirect labor is the wages paid to factory employees who are not directly involved in converting raw materials into finished goods. Factory supplies, sometimes called indirect materials, are the costs of materials used in the manufacturing process but that cannot be directly traced to the finished products.
5. A manufacturing business has three inventories: raw materials, work in process, and finished goods.
6. Factory overhead costs can be allocated to the work in process and finished goods inventories on the basis of a percentage of direct labor costs.
7. The Manufacturing Summary account is used only at the end of a fiscal period in the adjusting and closing process. The raw materials and work in process inventories are adjusted through the Manufacturing Summary account. The balances of all cost of goods accounts are closed into the Manufacturing Summary account.
8. The finished goods inventory is adjusted at the end of the period through the Income Summary account.

9. The balance of the Manufacturing Summary account is closed, by the amount of the cost of goods manufactured, into Income Summary.
10. The statement of cost of goods manufactured reports the costs of the goods completed during the period. It is a supporting statement for the income statement of a manufacturing business.

Review and Applications

Building Your Accounting Vocabulary

In your own words, write the definition of each of the following accounting terms. Use complete sentences for your definitions.

direct labor   finished goods   statement of cost of
direct materials   indirect labor   goods manufactured
factory overhead   manufacturing   work in process
factory supplies   business

Reviewing Your Accounting Knowledge

1. How does a manufacturing business differ from a merchandising business?
2. What are the three elements of manufacturing costs?
3. Give five examples of factory overhead costs.
4. What is the difference between direct labor and indirect labor?
5. What three inventory accounts appear in the chart of accounts of a manufacturing business?
6. Which inventory account for a manufacturing business is similar to the Merchandise Inventory account of a merchandising business?
7. Explain one method of allocating factory overhead costs to the Work in Process and Finished Goods inventory accounts.
8. What accounts are summarized in the Manufacturing Summary account of a manufacturing business at the end of the fiscal period? What accounts are summarized in the Income Summary account of a manufacturing business?
9. What four financial statements are prepared at the end of a fiscal period by a manufacturing business?
10. Which inventory accounts appear on the statement of cost of goods manufactured? on the income statement?
11. How does the work sheet of a manufacturing business differ from the work sheet of a merchandising business?
12. Why is the statement of cost of goods manufactured prepared before the income statement?

Improving Your Decision-making Skills

Janet Grayson has just been hired to work in the accounting department of the Hart Manufacturing Company. Hart manufactures children's clothing and sells its products to retail clothing stores in the area. Janet does not understand the difference between cost of goods sold and cost of goods manufactured. How would you explain the difference to Janet?

Problem 17-1

The following items are typical costs incurred by the New England Stove Company, a company that manufactures and sells wood-burning stoves.

(1) Shift supervisors' wages
(2) Exhaust piping
(3) Welders' wages
(4) Sales commissions
(5) Sheet metal

(6) Decorative molds
(7) Welding masks
(8) Administrative salaries
(9) Factory utility bills
(10) Hinges

Instructions: Use a form similar to the one that follows. Classify each of the costs listed above as: direct materials, direct labor, factory overhead, or operating expenses. For factory overhead costs, also indicate whether the item is indirect labor or factory supplies.

Item	Direct Materials	Direct Labor	Factory Overhead	Indirect Labor	Factory Supplies	Operating Expenses
1			✓	✓		

Problem 17-2

At the end of the fiscal period, Caprio Paper Products determined that its total direct labor and factory overhead costs were as follows.

Direct labor costs	$621,000
Factory overhead costs	391,230

The company also determined that the following direct materials and direct labor costs could be assigned to its work in process and finished goods.

	Work in Process	Finished Goods
Direct materials costs	$36,500	$24,800
Direct labor costs	57,000	63,000

Instructions: Use a form similar to the one that follows.

	Direct Materials	Direct Labor	Factory Overhead Rate	Factory Overhead Allocated	Value of Ending Inventory
Work in Process	$36,500	$57,000			
Finished Goods	$24,800	$63,000			

(1) Determine the factory overhead rate.

(2) Determine the amount of the factory overhead costs to be allocated to the work in process and finished goods inventories.

(3) Determine the value of the ending work in process and finished goods inventories.

Problem 17–3

The following amounts appear on the work sheet of the Robbins Manufacturing Company for the month ended May 31.

Raw Materials Purchases	$1,680,000
Raw Materials Inventory, May 1	120,000
Raw Materials Inventory, May 31	200,000
Work in Process Inventory, May 1	600,000
Work in Process Inventory, May 31	800,000
Direct Labor	2,400,000
Factory Overhead (total)	1,800,000

Instructions: Prepare a statement of cost of goods manufactured for the Robbins Manufacturing Company.

Problem 17–4

Foskey Textiles, Inc. is a manufacturing business that processes raw wool into yarn for both knitting and weaving. The Trial Balance section of the company's work sheet has already been completed and is included in the working papers accompanying this textbook.

Instructions: Complete the ten-column work sheet for Foskey Textiles, Inc. Data for the adjustments are as follows.

(1) The ending inventory amounts are as follows.

Raw Materials Inventory	$38,000
Work in Process Inventory	62,000
Finished Goods Inventory	56,500

(2) Estimated annual depreciation on factory equipment is $11,650.

(3) The amount of the expired premium on the factory insurance policy is $13,500.

(4) The ending factory supplies inventory on December 31 is $16,950.

(5) Estimated annual depreciation on office equipment is $1,400.

(6) The company uses the aging of accounts receivable method to determine the estimated uncollectible amount. The company estimates that the total uncollectible amount will be $2,100.

(7) The income tax liability for the year is $41,698.

Problem 17–5

The Farber Products Company, Inc. manufactures glassware. The following amounts appear on the company's work sheet for the year ended December 31.

	Statement of Cost of Goods Manufactured		Income Statement	
Income Summary			$ 362,800	$ 373,440
Sales				2,999,920
Sales Returns and Allow.			24,800	
Sales Discounts			23,600	
Raw Materials Purchases	$ 769,000			
Depr. Exp.—Machinery	31,680			
Direct Labor	965,800			
Factory Ins. Expired	7,600			
Factory Supervision	53,900			
Factory Supplies Used	12,400			
Heat, Light, and Power	53,960			
Indirect Labor	221,240			
Machinery Repairs	31,800			
Misc. Factory Costs	1,360			
Rent—Factory	32,000			
Small Tools Written Off	2,520			
Mfg. Summary (Raw Materials)	138,240	$ 143,200		
(Work in Process)	248,800	252,980		
Selling Expenses			358,980	
Administrative Expenses			145,720	
Interest Expense			13,600	
Loss on Disposal of Equip.			17,200	
Income Tax Expense			95,918	
	$2,570,300	$ 396,180		
Cost of Goods Manufactured		2,174,120	2,174,120	
	$2,570,300	$2,570,300	$3,216,738	$3,373,360
Net Income after Inc. Taxes			156,622	
			$3,373,360	$3,373,360

Instructions:

(1) Prepare a statement of cost of goods manufactured.
(2) Prepare the income statement.

Problem 17–6

The Trial Balance section of the work sheet for the Atwood Products Corporation has already been completed. It is included in the working papers accompanying this textbook.

Instructions:

(1) Complete the ten-column work sheet. Data for the adjustments are as follows.

(a) The ending inventory amounts are as follows.

Raw Materials Inventory	$43,000
Work in Process Inventory	63,400
Finished Goods Inventory	69,250

(b) Estimated annual depreciation of factory machinery is $8,750.

(c) The total factory insurance premium expired is $1,200.

(d) The ending factory supplies inventory on December 31 is $1,000.

(e) The estimated annual depreciation of office equipment is $550.

(f) The total uncollectible amount is estimated to be $2,250.

(g) The income tax liability for the year is $2,205.

(2) Prepare a statement of cost of goods manufactured.

(3) Prepare an income statement.

(4) Prepare a statement of retained earnings. No dividends were declared and paid during the year.

(5) Prepare a balance sheet. Atwood's authorized capital stock consists of 25,000 shares of $10-par common stock.

(6) Journalize the adjusting entries on page 37 of the general journal. Post the entries to the Manufacturing Summary and Income Summary accounts only.

(7) Journalize the closing entries. Post the entries to the Manufacturing Summary and Income Summary accounts only.

18 Manufacturing and Cost Accounting Systems

In Chapter 17, you learned about some of the differences between accounting for a merchandising business and a manufacturing business. You saw that the major difference lies in accounting for the cost of merchandise or goods sold.

Manufacturing costs are composed of three elements: direct materials, direct labor, and factory overhead. In the general accounting system presented in Chapter 17, those costs are allocated at the end of the fiscal period to the three manufacturing inventories: raw materials, work in process, and finished goods. In that system, the periodic inventory system was used.

In this chapter, you will learn about two manufacturing accounting systems that use a perpetual inventory system. You will learn how costs are accumulated in these two systems and how to determine the unit cost of the product.

Learning Objectives

When you have completed this chapter, you should be able to

1. Explain the purpose of cost accounting.

2. Explain the difference between a job order cost system and a process cost system.

3. Journalize entries within a job order cost system and a process cost system.

4. Apply factory overhead to work in process.

5. Account for overapplied and underapplied factory overhead.

6. Determine the unit cost of finished goods.

7. Prepare a cost of production report.

8. Define the accounting terms presented in this chapter.

New Terms   cost accounting / job order cost accounting / process cost accounting / job cost sheet / materials requisition / job order time card / underapplied factory overhead / overapplied factory overhead / equivalent units / cost of production report

Cost Accounting Systems

The purpose of a cost accounting system is to maintain accurate records of manufacturing costs. By using a cost accounting system, a business can maintain more control over the manufacturing process and can determine the unit cost of the product being manufactured.

There are two basic types of cost accounting systems, which usually match the two basic kinds of production operations. The two types of cost accounting systems are job order and process.

Job order cost accounting systems are used by businesses that produce a certain quantity of identifiable items or whose products are easily identifiable as special orders. Job order systems would be used by such businesses as shipbuilders, building contractors, furniture makers, book printers, and shoe manufacturers that produce several distinct styles of shoes. In a job order system, costs are accumulated for each product or batch of products produced.

Process cost accounting systems are used by companies that mass produce products that cannot be distinguished from each other during the production process. Every unit produced is the same. Generally, the products are manufactured in a series of steps, or processes, with each process being handled by a separate department. Costs are accumulated for each process or department. Examples of businesses that use process cost accounting systems are automobile manufacturers, chemical producers, cement makers, food processors, and paint manufacturers.

In some manufacturing businesses, a job order system may be used for some portions of production and a process system for other portions.

In this chapter, we will look first at a job order cost accounting system and then at a process cost accounting system.

Remember: **In a job order cost system, costs are accumulated for each product or batch of products. In a process cost system, costs are accumulated for each process or department.**

Job Order Cost System

A job order cost system is designed to accumulate manufacturing costs for a specific order or batch of products. As a result, each unique product or batch of products is assigned a job number. The costs of materials, labor, and factory overhead are then accumulated and reported according to that job number.

In a job order system, a perpetual inventory system is used. As a result, Raw Materials Inventory, Work in Process Inventory, and Finished Goods Inventory are controlling accounts. Subsidiary ledgers are maintained for each inventory account by type of material (Raw Materials Inventory), by job (Work in Process Inventory), and by work completed (Finished Goods Inventory). The inventory accounts are debited and credited during the year as materials, labor, and factory overhead are used.

Factory overhead costs are summarized in a controlling cost of goods account called Factory Overhead Control. Separate accounts are maintained in a factory overhead subsidiary ledger for the various types of overhead costs. As explained in Chapter 17, factory overhead costs cannot be identified with a specific product or products. Therefore, factory overhead costs are periodically allocated or *applied* to jobs using a predetermined factory overhead rate.

When a cost accounting system is used, the cost of manufacturing a product or batch of products is known as soon as the goods are finished. Therefore, it is possible to record the cost of the goods sold at the time the goods are sold. The cost is recorded in a cost of goods account called Cost of Goods Sold. This account has a normal debit balance.

As you may have guessed by now, it is very important for a business using a job order cost accounting system to have set procedures for handling this flow of manufacturing costs. Let's now look at some of the internal source documents and journal entries of a job order cost accounting system.

Source Documents Used in a Job Order System

The Easton Printing Company manufactures books and magazines according to specifications from various publishing companies. When Easton receives an order from a customer, it assigns a job number to the order. For example, on January 28, Easton Printing Company received an order to print 10,000 copies of a book from the Layton Publishing Company. Easton assigned job order number 301 to this order.

Job Cost Sheets

A **job cost sheet** is a document used to record the various costs incurred for each job. The job cost sheet used by Easton Printing Company is shown in Figure 18–1 on page 431. As you can see, the form has space at the top to record specific information about the job to be completed.

The middle section of the form is used to record the costs of the direct materials and direct labor used and the factory overhead applied in the completion of the job. As materials are needed, they are transferred from the materials warehouse and their cost is recorded in the Direct Materials column. Direct labor costs for the job are recorded in the Direct Labor column of the sheet. When the job is completed, the amount of factory overhead applied to the job is recorded in the Factory Overhead column.

The bottom portion of the job cost sheet summarizes all the costs incurred. It also has spaces to record the selling price for the job. By deducting the total production costs from the sales price, Easton can easily determine the amount of gross profit earned on the job.

JOB COST SHEET

CUSTOMER **Layton Publishing Company**   JOB ORDER NO. **301**

ITEM **Hughes: Advanced Accounting**   QUANTITY **10,000**

DATE ORDERED **January 28, 19--**   DATE STARTED **March 25, 19--**

DATE EXPECTED **April 1, 19--**   DATE COMPLETED **March 29, 19--**

DIRECT MATERIALS	DIRECT LABOR	FACTORY OVERHEAD
3/25 #1704 $6,000.00	3/29 $1,500.00	3/29 $1,125.00
TOTAL $6,000.00	TOTAL $1,500.00	TOTAL $1,125.00

COST SUMMARY

MATERIALS	$6,000.00	SELLING PRICE	$9,200.00
LABOR	1,500.00		
FACTORY OVERHEAD	1,125.00		
TOTAL COSTS	8,625.00	PRODUCTION COSTS	8,625.00
		GROSS PROFIT	$ 575.00

Figure 18–1. Job Cost Sheet

A separate job cost sheet is prepared for each job. All the job cost sheets are maintained in a subsidiary ledger called the work in process ledger.

Materials Requisition Forms

When direct materials are needed for a job, Easton prepares a document called a materials requisition. A **materials requisition** authorizes the materials warehouse to transfer materials to the factory. The materials requisition form used by Easton Printing Company is shown in Figure 18–2.

MATERIALS REQUISITION   NO. 1704

DATE **March 25, 19--**

JOB NO. **301**

AUTHORIZED BY **Ralph Adams**

MATERIALS DESCRIPTION	QUANTITY	UNIT COST	AMOUNT
50# Ecolocote paper	10 rolls	280.00	$2,800.00
Black ink	100 gals.	1.00	100.00
Heavy cardboard backing	20,000	.08	1,600.00
Tyvek coated cover stock	10,000	.15	1,500.00
			$6,000.00

Figure 18–2. Materials Requisition Form

Since each job is identified on the materials requisition form, it is easy to charge the cost of the materials issued to a particular job. For some jobs, materials may be requisitioned several times during the production process.

Job Order Time Cards

Each factory worker has a job order time card. A **job order time card** is a record of the amount of time an employee spent on a particular job. It is also used to calculate the wages to be paid to the employee. The job order time card used by Easton Printing Company is shown in Figure 18–3.

	DATE	IN	OUT	IN	OUT	TOTAL
EMP. NO. 1066	3/25	8:00	11:00	12:00	5:00	8
JOB NO. 301	3/26	7:30	11:30	12:00	5:00	9
NAME LEE BAKER	3/27	8:00	11:00	12:00	5:00	8
WEEK ENDING MARCH 29, 19--	3/28	8:30	11:00	12:00	5:00	7-1/2
	3/29	8:00	11:00	12:00	5:00	8
				TOTAL HOURS WORKED		40-1/2

Figure 18–3. Job Order Time Card

Notice that the time card has a line listing the number of the job the employee is working on. When an employee begins work on a new job, he or she receives a new time card with the new job number printed on it. Employees' wages can, therefore, be charged directly to a specific job.

Employees who do not work directly in the production process also have time cards. Their wages, however, are charged to Factory Overhead Control.

Before reading further, do the following activity to check your understanding of the material you have just studied.

Check Your Learning

Write your answers to the following questions on a separate sheet of paper.

1. An oil refinery would probably use a __?__ cost accounting system.
2. A __?__ system would probably be used by an aircraft manufacturer.
3. In a job order system, a __?__ is used to accumulate the costs incurred in the production of a product or batch of products.
4. When direct materials are needed to produce an item, a __?__ must be completed to authorize the transfer of materials to the factory.

Compare your answers with those in the answers section. Re-read the preceding part of the chapter to find the answers to any questions you may have missed.

When a perpetual inventory system is used with the job order cost accounting system, the Raw Materials, Work in Process, and Finished Goods Inventory accounts are debited and credited as jobs move through the production process.

Journalizing Materials Transactions

When raw materials are purchased, their cost is recorded directly in the Raw Materials Inventory account rather than in a Raw Materials Purchases account. For example, Easton Printing Company had the following transaction.

March 1: *Purchased 100 rolls of 50-pound Ecolocote paper on account from Walters Paper Mill, Invoice 987 for $25,000.*

In this transaction, Raw Materials Inventory is debited for $25,000, the cost of the materials purchased. Accounts Payable and Walters Paper Mill's account in the subsidiary ledger are credited for the same amount. The transaction is shown in general journal form in Figure 18–4. (This transaction could also be recorded in Easton's purchases journal.)

		GENERAL JOURNAL			PAGE 16
DATE		DESCRIPTION	POST. REF.	DEBIT	CREDIT
19-- Mar 1		Raw Materials Inventory		25 000 00	
		Accts Pay/Walters Paper Mill	✓		25 000 00
		Invoice 987			

Figure 18–4. Journalizing the Purchase of Raw Materials

As you learned earlier, when the factory needs materials to complete a job, a materials requisition form is prepared. This form authorizes the warehouse to transfer the needed materials to the factory. The form is also the source document for the entry recording the transfer of materials. On March 25, the factory prepared several materials requisitions as follows.

Requisition No.	Job No.	Amount
1704	301	$6,000
1705	302	4,000
1706	303	5,000

When materials are issued to the factory, the cost of the materials is debited to Work in Process Inventory and credited to Raw Materials Inventory. The journal entry made on March 25 is shown in general journal form in Figure 18–5 on the next page.

The cost of the materials issued for each job is also recorded on the job cost sheet.

DATE	DESCRIPTION	POST. REF.	DEBIT	CREDIT
19-- Mar. 25	Work in Process Inventory		15 00 00	
	Raw Materials Inventory			15 00 00
	Materials Req. 1704-1706			

Figure 18–5. Journalizing the Issuance of Raw Materials

Journalizing Labor Transactions

At the end of each week, the employee job order time cards are collected. Time cards for indirect labor employees are also collected. The total hours worked by each employee are determined and each employee's gross pay is calculated. According to the time cards, Easton's total gross wages for the week ending March 29 are as follows:

Indirect labor		$ 500
Direct labor		
Job 301	$1,500	
Job 302	1,100	
Job 303	1,200	3,800
Total		$4,300

March 29: *Recorded direct labor costs of $3,800 and indirect labor costs of $500 for the pay period, Time cards.*

As you learned earlier, the Work in Process Inventory account is increased for direct labor costs incurred. As a result, Work in Process Inventory is debited for $3,800, the amount of the direct labor costs for the pay period. The Factory Overhead Control account is debited for $500, the amount of the indirect labor costs for the pay period. At Easton, employees are paid for their work on the Friday following the end of the pay period. On March 29, the employees' wages have been earned but not yet paid. Therefore, the total amount of the payroll is credited to the Factory Wages Payable account. The entry for this transaction is shown in general journal form in Figure 18–6.

DATE	DESCRIPTION	POST. REF.	DEBIT	CREDIT
19-- Mar. 29	Work in Process Inventory		3 800 00	
	Factory Overhead Control		500 00	
	Factory Wages Payable			4 300 00
	Time Cards			

Figure 18–6. Journalizing Direct and Indirect Labor Costs

On April 5, Easton had the following transaction.

April 5: Wrote Check 4187 for $4,050 to the Payroll checking account for the net wages to be paid to employees for the pay period ended March 29. The following amounts were withheld: employees' federal income taxes, $109; FICA taxes, $92; and employees' state income taxes, $49.

The entry for this transaction is shown in general journal form in Figure 18–7. Since the wages that had accrued are now being paid, Factory Wages Payable is debited for $4,300. Employees' Federal Income Tax Payable is credited for $109, the total amount withheld. FICA Tax Payable is credited for $92 and Employees' State Income Tax Payable is credited for $49. Cash in Bank is credited for $4,050.

	DATE	DESCRIPTION	POST. REF.	DEBIT	CREDIT	
GENERAL JOURNAL					PAGE 24	
1	Apr. 5	Factory Wages Payable		4 300 00		1
2		Emp. Fed Inc. Tax Payable			1 09 00	2
3		FICA Tax Payable			92 00	3
4		Emp. State Inc. Tax Payable			49 00	4
5		Cash in Bank			4 050 00	5
6		Check 4187				6

Figure 18–7. Journalizing the Payment of Employees' Wages

Remember: In a cost accounting system, direct labor costs are debited to the Work in Process Inventory account. Indirect labor costs are debited to the Factory Overhead Control account.

Journalizing Factory Overhead Transactions

Since it has so many factory overhead accounts, Easton has a Factory Overhead Control account in its general ledger. It also maintains a factory overhead subsidiary ledger, with separate accounts for each type of factory overhead cost. As factory overhead costs are incurred, the Factory Overhead Control account and the appropriate account in the subsidiary ledger are debited. (To simplify the explanations, only the Factory Overhead Control account will be debited or credited in the following discussions.)

On March 29, Easton Printing Company had the following transactions.

March 29: Purchased $500 worth of factory supplies on account from Ace Cleaning Center, Invoice 43.

March 29: Paid the monthly utilities bill of $975, Check 4178.

March 29: Received Invoice 611B from Breton Machinery for replacement parts purchased on account for one of the printing presses, $600.

March 29: Allocated the monthly depreciation of $350 on the factory building, Memorandum 1771.

The entries to record these transactions are shown in general journal form in Figure 18–8. As you can see, the Factory Overhead Control account was debited in each transaction for the amount of the cost incurred.

	GENERAL JOURNAL			PAGE 22	
DATE	DESCRIPTION	POST. REF.	DEBIT	CREDIT	
Mar. 29	Factory Overhead Control		500 00		1
	Accts. Pay./Ace Cleaning Center	✓		500 00	2
	Invoice 43				3
29	Factory Overhead Control		975 00		4
	Cash in Bank			975 00	5
	Check 4178				6
29	Factory Overhead Control		600 00		7
	Accts. Pay./Breton Machinery	✓		600 00	8
	Invoice 611B				9
29	Factory Overhead Control		350 00		10
	Accum. Deprec.–Factory Bldg.			350 00	11
	Memo. 1771				12

Figure 18–8. Journalizing Factory Overhead Costs

It is very difficult, if not impossible, to determine the amount of factory overhead that has been incurred for each job. In addition, some factory overhead costs are not incurred or cannot be determined until the end of the fiscal period, after most of the jobs have been completed and sold to customers. The purpose of a job order cost system is to accumulate job costs as the product or batch of products is being completed. It is therefore necessary to estimate the total factory overhead costs for the year and periodically apply a portion of the estimated amount to the Work in Process Inventory account and the individual jobs. A predetermined factory overhead rate, based on the relationship between direct labor costs and factory overhead costs, is used to allocate the factory overhead costs.

To arrive at the predetermined factory overhead rate, the annual direct labor and factory overhead costs must first be estimated. For example, the production manager at Easton Printing Company estimated that direct labor costs for the year would be $46,000 and that factory overhead costs would be $34,500. The production manager based the estimates on the previous year's actual costs and the estimated production for the coming year.

The predetermined factory overhead rate is found by dividing the estimated factory overhead costs by the estimated direct labor costs. The calculations for Easton are shown below.

$$\frac{\$34,500}{\$46,000} = .75 = 75\%$$

In other words, for every $1.00 in direct labor costs charged to Work in Process Inventory, $.75 in factory overhead costs should also be charged.

At Easton Printing Company, factory overhead costs are applied to the Work in Process Inventory account at the end of each week. The amount to be applied is determined by multiplying the direct labor costs by the predetermined factory overhead rate, as shown below.

Job	Direct Labor Costs	Predetermined Factory Overhead Rate	Factory Overhead Applied
301	$1,500	.75	$1,125
302	1,100	.75	825
303	1,200	.75	900
			$2,850

The entry to record the factory overhead costs applied is shown in Figure 18–9. Work in Process Inventory is debited for $2,850, the amount of factory overhead costs being applied. Although Factory Overhead Control could be credited for the same amount, accountants prefer to use a separate account entitled Factory Overhead Applied. It is, therefore, credited for $2,850.

	GENERAL JOURNAL		PAGE 23	
DATE	DESCRIPTION	POST. REF.	DEBIT	CREDIT
19-- Mar 29	Work in Process Inventory		2850 00	
	Factory Overhead Applied			2850 00
	Memo 1772			

Figure 18–9. Applying Factory Overhead Costs

Remember: In a cost accounting system, a predetermined factory overhead rate is used to periodically allocate factory overhead costs to the Work in Process Inventory account.

Since the predetermined factory overhead rate is only an estimate, the factory overhead applied seldom agrees with the actual factory overhead costs incurred. There may be more or less factory overhead costs incurred than estimated or there may be more or less direct labor costs than had been estimated at the beginning of the year.

At the end of a fiscal period, the balance of the Factory Overhead Applied account may be greater or less than the balance of the Factory Overhead Control account. When the balance of Factory Overhead Control is greater than the balance of Factory Overhead Applied, the difference is referred to as **underapplied factory overhead**. In other words, more factory overhead costs were incurred than were applied. When the balance of Factory Overhead Control is less than the balance of

Factory Overhead Applied, the difference is referred to as **overapplied factory overhead**. In other words, more factory overhead costs were applied than were actually incurred. The difference is usually small. However, this difference must be accounted for before a new accounting period begins. The amount of the difference between the two accounts is eliminated through a closing entry. In the closing entry, the amount of the difference is transferred—as either a debit or a credit—to the Cost of Goods Sold account. For example, suppose that, at the end of the period, Easton's Factory Overhead Control account has a debit balance of $35,600. This amount represents the actual factory overhead costs incurred during the period. The credit balance of the company's Factory Overhead Applied account is $34,725. This amount represents the amount of factory overhead costs applied to the Work in Process Inventory account using the predetermined factory overhead rate. The relationship between the two accounts is shown in the T accounts that follow.

Factory Overhead Control		Factory Overhead Applied	
Dr.	Cr.	Dr.	Cr.
+	−	−	+
$35,600			$34,725

The difference between the two accounts is a debit amount of $875. In the closing entry, Factory Overhead Applied is debited for $34,725 and Factory Overhead Control is credited for $35,600. The Cost of Goods Sold account is debited for the difference of $875. This closing entry to eliminate the underapplied factory overhead is illustrated in Figure 18–10.

GENERAL JOURNAL   PAGE _70_

	DATE	DESCRIPTION	POST. REF.	DEBIT	CREDIT	
1		Closing Entries				1
2	19-- Dec. 31	Cost of Goods Sold		875 00		2
3		Factory Overhead Applied		34725 00		3
4		Factory Overhead Control			35600 00	4

Figure 18–10. Closing Entry for Factory Overhead Costs

Remember: **The difference between the actual factory overhead costs and the factory overhead applied is transferred to the Cost of Goods Sold account at the end of the fiscal period.**

Journalizing Finished Goods Transactions

As jobs are completed, the job cost sheets are totaled and the costs are transferred from the Work in Process Inventory account to the Finished Goods Inventory account. For example, on March 29, the Easton Printing Company completed work on jobs 301 and 302. The costs of these two jobs, as indicated by the job costs sheets, are as follows.

	Job 301	Job 302	Totals
Direct materials	$6,000	$4,000	$10,000
Direct labor	1,500	1,100	2,600
Factory overhead applied	1,125	825	1,950
Total costs	$8,625	$5,925	$14,550

Since these jobs have now been completed, their costs must be transferred from Work in Process Inventory to Finished Goods Inventory. The entry to record the transfer is shown in general journal form in Figure 18–11.

GENERAL JOURNAL PAGE 23

DATE	DESCRIPTION	POST. REF.	DEBIT	CREDIT
19-- Mar. 29	Finished Goods Inventory		14550 00	
	Work in Process Inventory			14550 00
	Job cost sheets 301-302			

Figure 18–11. Journalizing the Transfer of Costs for Finished Goods

The job cost sheets for these two jobs are removed from the work in process subsidiary ledger and transferred to the finished goods subsidiary ledger.

Journalizing the Sale of Goods

When a job order cost system is being used, the costs incurred to manufacture or produce a product are known as soon as the goods are finished. As a result, the cost can be recorded in the Cost of Goods Sold account at the time of the sale. For example, on March 29 Easton Printing Company shipped job 301 to its customer.

March 29: Shipped job 301 to Layton Publishing Company, sales price $9,200, Sales Invoice 1156.

This transaction is recorded in two entries. The first entry records the sale of the goods to the customer. Since this transaction is on account, Accounts Receivable and Layton's account in the accounts receivable subsidiary ledger are debited for the sales price of $9,200. Sales is credited for the same amount. This transaction is shown, in general journal form, in Figure 18–12 on page 440.

The second entry records the transfer of the finished goods into the Cost of Goods Sold account. Cost of Goods Sold is debited for $8,625, the total costs incurred by Easton in printing the book. Finished Goods Inventory is credited for $8,625 to show the decrease in the account. This transaction is also shown in general journal form in Figure 18–12. The job cost sheet is removed from the finished goods subsidiary ledger and filed with the sales invoice in the customer's file.

Remember: Cost of Goods Sold is used to record the total manufacturing costs for products completed and sold.

	DATE	DESCRIPTION	POST. REF.	DEBIT	CREDIT	
1	19-- Mar. 29	Accts Rec / Layton Publishing Co.	/	9 20 00		1
2		Sales			9 20 00	2
3		Sales Invoice 1156				3
4	29	Cost of Goods Sold		8 62 50 0		4
5		Finished Goods Inventory			8 62 50 0	5
6		Sales Invoice 1156				6

Figure 18–12. Journalizing the Sale of Finished Goods

Before reading further, do the following activity to check your understanding of the job order cost accounting system.

Check Your Learning

For each transaction listed below, indicate which account(s) would be debited and credited. Write your answers on a sheet of notebook paper.

1. Applied factory overhead costs to the Work in Process Inventory account
2. Recorded the sale of goods for cash
3. Recorded the direct labor costs for the pay period
4. Completed the production of a specific job
5. Paid the monthly utilities bill

Check your answers with those in the answers section. Re-read the preceding part of the chapter to find the correct answers to any questions you may have missed.

Process Cost System

For some manufacturing businesses, it is difficult to distinguish one unit produced from another. One pound of baking powder looks like the next one; all bricks made are the same; one gallon of gasoline produced is just like the previous gallon produced. In addition, these products are usually manufactured in a series of steps, or processes, with each process being handled by a separate department. When more or less identical products are manufactured in a continuous series of steps, a business will usually use a process cost system.

When a process cost system is used, costs are not accumulated for a specific job. Instead, the costs for materials, labor, and factory overhead are accumulated for a particular production step or department. As a result, a separate Work in Process Inventory account is maintained for each department. As a department incurs materials, labor, or factory overhead costs, they are charged directly to the department's Work in Process Inventory account. The flow of costs *into* the Work in Process Inventory account (or accounts) is very much the same in a job order cost system and a process cost system.

The major difference between the two systems is the way costs are assigned to products. In a job order cost system, most costs can be traced to and assigned to specific jobs and products. Since the products are almost identical, this cannot be done in a process cost system. Instead, an average of the total manufacturing costs is determined and assigned to the goods completed by each department. In other words, the total costs accumulated by a department are divided by the number of units processed to determine the cost per unit. This unit cost is used to determine the manufacturing cost to be transferred from one department's Work in Process Inventory account to the next department's Work in Process Inventory account. Let's look at an example.

The Speedy Bicycle Manufacturing Company makes one bicycle model. Three processes are required and handled by three separate departments. Department A welds and paints the bicycle frames. Department B assembles the wheels and attaches them to the frames. Department C completes the assembly by attaching the seats and handlebars.

In January, Department A had the following costs.

Direct materials	$15,000
Direct labor	35,000
Factory overhead applied	17,500
	$67,500

During January, Department A processed 1,800 bicycle frames. The unit cost per frame is determined by dividing the department's total costs by the number of frames processed. The calculations are as shown below.

$$\frac{\text{Total costs for Department A}}{\text{Total bicycle frames processed}} - \frac{\$67,500}{1,800} - \$37.50 \text{ per bicycle frame processed}$$

When Department A completes its work, the bicycle frames are transferred to Department B for processing. The costs accumulated in Department A ($37.50 per frame) must also be transferred to Department B's Work in Process Inventory account.

Remember: In a process cost system, a separate Work in Process Inventory account is maintained for each department.

Equivalent Units

You just learned how to calculate the unit cost of the bicycle frames completed in Department A of Speedy Bicycle Manufacturing Company. The total costs incurred by Department A were divided by the number of bicycle frames processed. However, the number of frames processed was expressed in equivalent units. **Equivalent units** are a measure of the number of units produced in a period of time, expressed in terms of fully completed units. Partially completed units are restated in terms of whole units.

At the end of January, Department A had fully completed and transferred to Department B 1,760 bicycle frames. Department A also had 60 bicycle frames that were only two-thirds completed. These partially completed bicycle frames must also be included when calculating the number of frames processed since costs have been incurred during their processing. The number of equivalent units is determined as follows.

Completed and transferred	1,760 units
Partially completed: 60 × 2/3	40 units
Equivalent units	1,800 units

It is often difficult to determine exactly how "complete" the work in process is. Materials and labor may be added at various stages of a process. As a result, many companies use the 50% rule. That is, the work in process is considered to be 50% complete on the average. Some products are close to being completed; some are just being started; and some are halfway through the process. On the average, however, the work can be said to be 50% complete. If you apply the 50% rule to Department A's work in process, the equivalent units would be calculated as follows.

Completed and transferred	1,760 units
Partially completed: 60 × .50	30 units
Equivalent units	1,790 units

Journalizing Transactions in a Process Cost System

The process cost system is the same as a job order cost system in many ways. Costs, however, are accumulated by department (process) rather than by job. Each department accumulates and accounts for the costs of raw materials, direct labor, and factory overhead. As a product moves from one department to the next, the departmental costs accumulated up to that point are transferred and added to the costs accumulated in the next department.

As you read the following, you may wish to compare the journal entries for a process cost system with the journal entries for a job order cost system. Many of the entries are handled similarly.

Journalizing Materials Transactions

As in a job order cost system, when raw materials are purchased, their cost is recorded in the Raw Materials Inventory account rather than in a Raw Materials Purchases account.

January 4: *Purchased $60,000 of raw materials on account from the Mason Company, Invoice 0191.*

In this transaction, Raw Materials Inventory is debited for $60,000, the cost of the raw materials purchased. Accounts Payable and Mason Company's account in the accounts payable subsidiary ledger are credited for the same amount. This transaction is shown in general journal form in Figure 18–13.

GENERAL JOURNAL			PAGE 16	
DATE	DESCRIPTION	POST. REF.	DEBIT	CREDIT
19-- Jan. 4	Raw Materials Inventory		6000000	
	Accts. Pay./Mason Company	/		6000000
	Invoice 0191			

Figure 18–13. Journalizing the Purchase of Raw Materials

In a process cost system, a materials requisition is also used to transfer direct materials from the warehouse to a production department. At the beginning of January, the three departments of Speedy Bicycle requisitioned direct materials as follows.

Requisition No.	Department	Amount
1041	A	$15,000.00
1042	B	$17,362.25
1043	C	$25,321.00
		$57,683.25

The cost of the direct materials requisitioned is charged to each department's Work in Process Inventory account. The combined entry shown in Figure 18–14 records the transfer of direct materials from the warehouse to the various departments.

GENERAL JOURNAL			PAGE 16	
DATE	DESCRIPTION	POST. REF.	DEBIT	CREDIT
19-- Jan. 5	Work in Process Inventory—Dept. A		1500000	
	Work in Process Inventory—Dept. B		1736225	
	Work in Process Inventory—Dept. C		2532100	
	Raw Materials Inventory			5768325
	Materials Req. 1041-1043			

Figure 18–14. Journalizing the Issuance of Raw Materials

Journalizing Labor Transactions

Time cards may also be used for direct and indirect laborers in a process cost system. There is no need, however, to allocate employees' wages to specific jobs. Most direct labor employees work in only one department; their wages would be charged to the Work in Process Inventory account of that department. The wages of indirect labor employees are charged to the Factory Overhead Control account. For example, during January, Speedy Bicycle had the following labor costs.

Department A	$35,000
Department B	25,000
Department C	15,000
Indirect Labor	3,500
	$78,500

The entry to record the January labor costs is shown in Figure 18–15 below.

GENERAL JOURNAL   PAGE 20

	DATE	DESCRIPTION	POST. REF.	DEBIT	CREDIT	
1	19-- Jan. 31	Work in Process Inventory—Dept. A		35 000 00		1
2		Work in Process Inventory—Dept. B		25 000 00		2
3		Work in Process Inventory—Dept. C		15 000 00		3
4		Factory Overhead Control		3 500 00		4
5		Factory Wages Payable			78 500 00	5
6		Time Cards				6

Figure 18–15. Journalizing Direct and Indirect Labor Costs

When paychecks are written, a check is written to the payroll checking account. Factory Wages Payable is debited for the amount of the monthly payroll. The various tax payable accounts are credited for the amounts withheld. Cash in Bank is credited for the amount of the check written to the special payroll checking account. For example, Figure 18–16 shows the journal entry made for the payment of the January payroll.

GENERAL JOURNAL   PAGE 21

	DATE	DESCRIPTION	POST. REF.	DEBIT	CREDIT	
1	19-- Feb. 7	Factory Wages Payable		78 500 00		1
2		Employees' Fed. Inc. Tax Payable			1 089 00	2
3		FICA Tax Payable			917 00	3
4		Employees' State Inc. Tax Payable			494 00	4
5		Cash in Bank			76 000 00	5
6		Check 6031				6

Figure 18–16. Journalizing the Payment of Employees' Wages

Journalizing Factory Overhead Transactions

In a process cost system, a factory overhead subsidiary ledger is also maintained. The subsidiary ledger contains separate accounts for each type of factory overhead cost. The balances of the individual accounts are summarized in the Factory Overhead Control account.

During January, Speedy Bicycle incurred various factory overhead costs totaling $40,200. As each cost is incurred, it is journalized and charged to the Factory Overhead Control account.

At the end of the month, factory overhead costs are applied to each department's Work in Process Inventory account. The factory overhead rates do not have to be the same for all departments. For example, Speedy Bicycle applies factory overhead costs at a 50% rate for Department A and at a 60% rate for Departments B and C. Speedy Bicycle bases its factory overhead rates on the direct labor costs charged to each department, as shown below.

	Direct Labor Costs	Factory Overhead Rate	Factory Overhead Applied
Department A	$35,000	.50	$17,500
Department B	25,000	.60	15,000
Department C	15,000	.60	9,000
			$41,500

The entry to record the factory overhead costs applied is shown in Figure 18–17. The Work in Process Inventory account of each department is debited for the amount of that department's share of the factory overhead costs.

	GENERAL JOURNAL				PAGE 20
DATE	DESCRIPTION	POST. REF.	DEBIT	CREDIT	
19-- Jan. 31	Work in Process Inventory—Dept. A		17500 00		1
	Work in Process Inventory—Dept. B		15000 00		2
	Work in Process Inventory—Dept. C		9000 00		3
	Factory Overhead Applied			41500 00	4
	Memo. 4523				5

Figure 18–17. Journalizing the Allocation of Factory Overhead Costs

Journalizing Transfer Transactions

When a department completes its assigned work, the processed products are transferred to the next department. At Speedy Bicycle, when Department A completes its work on the bicycle frames, it transfers the frames to Department B. When Department B has completed assembling and attaching the wheels, it transfers the products to Department C. When Department C has completed the assembly process, it transfers the bicycles to the finished goods inventory.

When products are transferred from one department to another department or to the finished goods inventory, the manufacturing costs accumulated are also transferred. Let's look at some transfers that occurred at Speedy Bicycle.

During January, Department A completed its work on 1,760 bicycle frames and transferred them to Department B. Department A must also transfer its manufacturing costs to Department B. This entry is usually made at the end of the month. The unit cost of $37.50 calculated earlier is used to determine the amount of the entry.

$$1,760 \text{ units} \times \$37.50 = \$66,000.00$$

The journal entry to record the transfer of the manufacturing costs from Department A to Department B is shown in Figure 18–18.

		GENERAL JOURNAL			PAGE 20
	DATE	DESCRIPTION	POST. REF.	DEBIT	CREDIT
1	19-- Jan. 31	Work in Process Inventory – Dept. B		66 00 0 00	
2		Work in Process Inventory – Dept. A			66 00 0 00
3		Memo 4561			

Figure 18–18. Journalizing the Transfer of Manufacturing Costs

As you can see, the costs accumulated by one department become part of the costs (recorded in Work in Process Inventory) of the next department.

Department B assembles the bicycle wheels and attaches two of them to each frame transferred from Department A. During January, Department B assembled 3,557 equivalent units of wheels. Its manufacturing costs were $61,358.25. The department's unit cost per wheel is, therefore, $17.25 ($61,358.25 ÷ 3,557 units).

During January, Department B was able to attach a total of 3,520 wheels to the 1,760 frames. The 1,760 frames with wheels were then transferred to Department C for final assembly. An entry must be made to transfer the total manufacturing costs of the 1,760 frames. To determine the amount of the journal entry, the costs incurred per unit by Department B are added to the costs transferred from Department A, as shown below. The unit cost of the units transferred to Department C is $72 ($126,720 ÷ 1,760 completed frames).

Costs transferred from Department A:	1,760 frames × $37.50 =	$ 66,000
Costs incurred by Department B:	3,520 wheels × $17.25 =	60,720
Total costs		$126,720

$$\text{Unit cost} = \frac{\$126,720}{1,760 \text{ frames}} = \$72.00$$

The entry to record the transfer of 1,760 units from Department B to Department C is shown in Figure 18–19 at the top of the next page.

	DATE	DESCRIPTION	POST. REF.	DEBIT	CREDIT	
1	19-- Jan. 31	Work in Process Inventory – Dept. C		126 720 00		1
2		Work in Process Inventory – Dept. B			126 720 00	2
3		Memo. 4562				3

Figure 18–19. Journalizing the Transfer of Manufacturing Costs

Department C completes the assembly of the bicycles by attaching the seats and handlebars. During January, Department C assembled 3,554 equivalent units. The department had manufacturing costs of $52,421. The department's unit cost per bicycle is, therefore, $14.75 ($52,421 ÷ 3,554).

During January, Department C completed the assembly of 2,000 bicycles. This number includes 240 bicycles that had been transferred in December but not completed until January and the 1,760 frames transferred in January. The cost of the completed bicycles must be transferred to the Finished Goods Inventory. The amount of the journal entry is determined by adding the costs incurred by Department C to the costs transferred from Department B. The calculation is as follows.

Costs transferred from Department B:	2,000 units × $72.00 =	$144,000
Costs incurred by Department C:	2,000 units × $14.75 =	29,500
Total costs		$173,500

$$\text{Unit cost} = \frac{\$173,500}{2,000 \text{ units}} = \$86.75$$

The unit cost of the bicycles transferred to the finished goods inventory is $86.75 ($173,500 ÷ 2,000 completed bicycles).

The entry to record the transfer of the 2,000 completed bicycles from Department C to the Finished Goods Inventory is shown in Figure 18–20.

	DATE	DESCRIPTION	POST. REF.	DEBIT	CREDIT	
1	19-- Jan. 31	Finished Goods Inventory		173 500 00		1
2		Work in Process Inventory – Dept. C			173 500 00	2
3		Memo. 4563				3

Figure 18–20. Journalizing the Transfer of Costs for Finished Goods

Remember: In a process cost system, when goods are transferred from one department to another, the accumulated manufacturing costs are also transferred.

Journalizing the Sale of Goods

As you have seen, the cost of finished goods is known as soon as the goods are transferred from the final processing department. As in the job order cost system, the cost of the goods sold can be recorded at the time the products are sold.

February 1: *Sold 1,950 bicycles on account to Westwood Cycle Center at $100 per bicycle, Sales Invoice 2745.*

This transaction is journalized in two entries, as was done in the job order cost system. The first entry records the sale of the bicycles. Accounts Receivable and Westwood Cycle Center's account in the accounts receivable subsidiary ledger are debited for $195,000, the total sales price (1,950 bicycles × $100 sales price). Sales is credited for $195,000. The entry is shown, in general journal form, in Figure 18–21.

The second entry records the transfer of the finished goods to the Cost of Goods Sold account. The unit cost of the bicycles assembled during January was $86.75. The cost of the 1,950 bicycles sold is $169,162.50 (1,950 × $86.75). The Cost of Goods Sold account is debited for this amount. Finished Goods Inventory is credited for the same amount. This entry is also illustrated in Figure 18–21 below.

		GENERAL JOURNAL				PAGE 21
	DATE	DESCRIPTION	POST. REF.	DEBIT	CREDIT	
1	¹⁹— Feb. 1	Accts. Rec./Westwood Cycle Center	✓	195000 00		1
2		Sales			195000 00	2
3		Sales Invoice 2745				3
4	1	Cost of Goods Sold		169162 50		4
5		Finished Goods Inventory			169162 50	5
6		Sales Invoice 2745				6

Figure 18–21. Journalizing the Sale of Finished Goods

Cost of Production Report

At the end of the month, each department at Speedy Bicycle prepares a cost of production report. The **cost of production report** summarizes (1) the units processed by the department, and (2) the costs charged to the department. The cost of production report prepared by Department B is shown in Figure 18–22 at the top of page 449.

The first section of the report summarizes the number of units processed during January. As you can see, the department had 464 uncompleted units in its Work in Process Inventory on January 1. It began work on 3,130 wheels during the month. Of the 3,594 wheels started, the department completed assembling 3,520. That left 74 uncompleted wheels as of January 31. The equivalent units produced during January are calculated as follows.

Speedy Bicycle Manufacturing Company
Cost of Production Report
Department B: Wheels
For the Month Ended January 31, 19—

Quantity Schedule:	
Work in Process Inventory, January 1, 19—	464
New Units Started	3,130
Total Units to be Accounted for	3,594
Transferred to Department C	3,520
Work in Process Inventory, January 31, 19—	74
Total Units Accounted for	3,594

Costs to be Accounted for:		
Work in Process Inventory, January 1, 19—		$ 3,996.00
Costs transferred from Department A (1,760 @ $37.50)		66,000.00
Costs charged to the department:		
Direct materials	$17,362.25	
Direct labor	25,000.00	
Factory overhead applied (60% of direct labor)	15,000.00	57,362.25
Total Costs to be Accounted for		$127,358.25
Costs Accounted for as Follows:		
Transferred to Department C (1,760 @ $72.00)		$126,720.00
Work in Process Inventory, January 31, 19—		638.25
Total Costs Accounted for		$127,358.25
Unit processing cost (per wheel):		
($3,996.00 + $57,362.25) ÷ 3,557 units		$17.25

Figure 18–22. Cost of Production Report

Units completed and transferred to Department C:	3,520
Units in process (74 × .50)	37
Equivalent units	3,557

The second section of the report summarizes Department B's manufacturing costs for January. The value of the department's beginning Work in Process Inventory is $3,996.00. (That amount was determined by applying the 50% completion rule to the number of units on hand: 464 × .50 = 232. That number was then multiplied by the December unit cost of $17.224: 232 × $17.224 = $3,996.)

During January, Department A transferred manufacturing costs of $66,000.00 to Department B's Work in Process Inventory account. Also during January, Department B incurred the materials, labor, and factory overhead costs listed on the report.

All of these costs are totaled to determine the total costs Department B must account for: $127,358.25.

The third section of the report summarizes how those costs were allocated. As you can see, Department B completed and transferred 1,760 units to Department C at a unit cost of $72.00. The value of the ending Work in Process Inventory is determined by applying the 50% rule to the 74 wheels still in process. That number is then multiplied by the January unit cost of $17.25.

$$74 \times .50 \times \$17.25 = \$638.25$$

The final section of the report shows how the department's January unit cost was calculated.

Before reading further, do the following activity to check your understanding of the process cost system.

Check Your Learning

For each transaction listed below, indicate which account(s) would be debited and which account(s) would be credited. Write your answers on a sheet of notebook paper.

1. Applied factory overhead costs to Department A
2. Recorded the cost of finished goods sold to a charge customer
3. Transferred 1,250 units from Department A to Department B
4. Transferred 1,000 units from Department B to finished goods
5. Paid the factory insurance bill for the month

Check your answers with those in the answers section. Re-read the preceding part of the chapter to find the correct answers to any questions you may have missed.

Cost Accounting and Computers

The volume of paperwork involved in a cost accounting system can be quite extensive and costly to control, even in the smallest of manufacturing businesses. Computers, however, have eliminated much of the time-consuming paper transfer problem. Input devices located throughout a factory can reduce the time used by workers to fill out time cards, materials requisitions, and job cost sheets. Each work station or department may have its own input terminal. For example, workers can simply insert a special card into the terminal when they start or finish a job or process. This method is fast, accurate, and efficient. Terminals can also be used to record the transfer of materials. The use of computers provides faster and more accurate information, which can be used when preparing production summaries.

Summary of Key Points

1. The purpose of a cost accounting system is to maintain more accurate records of manufacturing costs. The two basic types of cost accounting systems are job order cost accounting and process cost accounting.
2. The job order cost system accumulates costs for a particular product or batch of products.
3. The process cost system accumulates manufacturing costs for a specific process or department.
4. Both the job order cost system and the process cost system use the perpetual inventory method to determine the value of ending inventories.
5. Three source documents used in a job order cost system are the job order cost sheet, the materials requisition form, and the job order time card.
6. In a cost accounting system, the Raw Materials, Work in Process, and Finished Goods inventory accounts are debited and credited directly as costs are incurred and the products move through the production process.
7. Factory overhead costs are debited to the Factory Overhead Control account as they are incurred. Factory Overhead Control is the controlling account for the factory overhead subsidiary ledger.
8. In a cost accounting system, factory overhead costs are applied, or allocated, to the Work in Process Inventory account or accounts periodically. The costs are credited to the Factory Overhead Applied account.
9. Factory overhead costs may be overapplied or underapplied at the end of the period. The difference between the Factory Overhead Control account and the Factory Overhead Applied account is closed into the Cost of Goods Sold account at the end of the period.
10. When a cost accounting system is used, the cost of goods sold is known as soon as the production process is completed. As a result, when goods are sold, the cost of the goods can be recorded in the accounting records.
11. In a process cost accounting system, when units are transferred from one department to another, the costs incurred are also transferred from one department's Work in Process Inventory account to another's.
12. Equivalent units are a measure of the number of units processed during a period of time. Partially completed units must be restated in terms of whole units.

Review and Applications

Building Your Accounting Vocabulary

In your own words, write the definition of each of the following accounting terms. Use complete sentences for your definitions.

cost accounting
cost of production
  report
equivalent units
job cost sheet

job order cost
  accounting
job order time card
materials requisition
overapplied factory
  overhead

process cost
  accounting
underapplied factory
  overhead

Reviewing Your Accounting Knowledge

1. What is the difference between the two types of cost accounting systems?
2. Explain the three source documents used in a job order cost system.
3. In a cost accounting system, what accounts are debited and credited when direct materials are purchased on account? What accounts are involved when direct materials are requisitioned?
4. In a job order cost system, to what account are direct labor costs debited? indirect labor costs?
5. How is the predetermined factory overhead rate calculated?
6. Why does a business using a job order cost system usually have either over-applied or underapplied factory overhead at the end of the fiscal period?
7. How is the balance of the Factory Overhead Applied account eliminated?
8. What accounts are debited and credited when completed goods are sold?
9. What are equivalent units and how are they used in a process cost system?
10. What is the purpose of the cost of production report?

Improving Your Decision-making Skills

The president of Molltex Manufacturing wants to know why the factory overhead applied, which is based on the direct labor hours, is greater than the actual factory overhead costs for the year. Can you suggest some reasons why the amount applied is greater than the actual costs incurred?

Applying Accounting Procedures

Problem 18–1

Listed at the top of page 453 are several types of manufactured products. Using a form similar to the one that follows, indicate whether the items would likely be produced in a job order costing system or a process costing system.

(1) Sugar	(5) Paper boxes	(9) Airplanes
(2) Leather handbags	(6) Toys	(10) Pianos
(3) Paint	(7) Computers	(11) Racing cars
(4) Oriental rugs	(8) Metal furniture	(12) Baseball bats

Item	Job Order Cost System	Process Cost System
1		✓

Problem 18–2

The Franklin Company uses a job order cost accounting system. The following transactions took place during March.

Mar.   6   Completed a special order of 344 units. Transferred the total costs of $86,624 to finished goods, Memorandum 1113.

20   Sold the 344 units on account to the Greene Corporation for $113,520, Sales Invoice L1110.

Instructions:

(1) Record the transactions on page 58 of a general journal.
(2) Calculate the unit cost and unit selling price.

Problem 18–3

The Snelling Company applies factory overhead costs at the end of each month using a predetermined factory overhead rate of 90% of direct labor costs. In addition, the Factory Overhead Control and Factory Overhead Applied accounts are closed at the end of each month.

Instructions:

(1) Record the entry on page 43 of the general journal to apply the May factory overhead costs, Memorandum 1692. Direct labor costs were $44,000.
(2) Record the entry to close Factory Overhead Control and Factory Overhead Applied on May 31. The balance of Factory Overhead Control is $38,510.

Problem 18–4

The Davis Corporation uses the job order cost accounting system and the perpetual inventory method. The following transactions occurred in January.

Jan.   5   Purchased raw materials for $10,000 cash, Check 1492.
7   Issued direct materials as follows: Job 113, $2,000 (Materials Requisition 206) and Job 114, $1,500 (Materials Requisition 207).
10   Purchased factory supplies on account from Hightower, Inc., $555, Invoice H2114.
15   Recorded direct labor costs as follows: Job 113, $3,000 and Job 114, $2,000, Time cards.

17 Issued Check 1511 for $4,039 for the net pay due employees. The following amounts were withheld: employees' federal income taxes, $419; FICA taxes, $352; and employees' state income taxes, $190.

18 Applied factory overhead costs to Jobs 113 and 114 at 65% of direct labor costs, Memorandum 1719.

22 Completed Job 113 and transferred the costs to finished goods, Memorandum 1722.

25 Sold Job 113 for $7,500 cash, Receipt 1354.

Instructions: Record the transactions on page 45 of a general journal.

Problem 18–5

Presented below, in T account form, is the Work in Process Inventory account for the Molding Department of the Frame World Manufacturing Company.

Work in Process Inventory—Molding

Dr. +		Cr. −
Bal.	$ 31,000	Transferred out $415,000
Dir. Materials	115,000	
Dir. Labor	205,000	
Fact. Overhead	123,000	

Instructions:

(1) Using the information recorded in the T account, prepare the entries on page 36 of the general journal, to record the following:

   (a) The issuance of the direct materials on September 3
   (b) The direct labor costs on September 12
   (c) The application of factory overhead on September 30
   (d) The transfer of the completely processed products to finished goods on September 30

(2) What was the predetermined factory overhead rate used?

Problem 18–6

The Mink Oil Company uses the process cost accounting system and the perpetual inventory method. The following transactions took place during March.

Mar. 2 Purchased $4,320 of raw materials on account from Preston's, Inc., Invoice AB115.

4 Issued direct materials as follows, Requisitions 110–112.

Department A	$1,000
Department B	500
Department C	750

10 Recorded labor costs as follows, Time cards.

Direct labor

Department A	$2,500
Department B	2,000
Department C	1,000
Indirect labor	500

15 Issued Check 2347 for $4,847 for the net pay due employees. Amounts were withheld as follows: employees' federal income taxes, $502; FICA taxes, $423; employees' state income taxes, $228.

17 Paid the utilities bill of $850, Check 2354.

20 Issued Check 2370 for $1,000 for repairs to factory equipment.

31 Applied factory overhead to the three departments at a rate of 50% of direct labor costs, Memorandum 4300.

31 Transferred 1,280 units, at a unit cost of $5, from Department A to Department B, Memorandum 4301.

31 Transferred 1,400 units, at a unit cost of $7, from Department B to Department C, Memorandum 4302.

31 Transferred 1,300 units, at a unit cost of $10, from Department C to finished goods, Memorandum 4303.

31 Sold 1,500 units at $15 per unit (cost, $10 per unit) on account to the Barker Company, Sales Invoice 4205.

Instructions: Record the transactions on pages 67–68 of a general journal.

Problem 18–7

The manager of Department A of the Joint Metal Company compiled the following information for the month of January.

Beginning inventory (100 units @ 50% @ $15)	$ 750.00
Cost incurred:	
Direct materials	16,697.50
Direct labor	20,000.00
Factory overhead applied	15,000.00
Units completed and transferred out	3,000
Units in process (300 @ 50%)	150
Equivalent units	3,150
Work in Process, January 1	100
New units started	3,200
	3,300
Transferred to Department B	3,000
Work in Process, January 31	300
	3,300

Instructions: Using the above information, prepare a cost of production report for Department A of the Joint Metal Company.

Preparing Financial Statements for a Manufacturing Business

In Chapters 17 and 18, you learned about the accounting procedures and financial statements prepared by a manufacturing business. Now you will have the opportunity to apply what you have learned as you complete the work sheet and prepare the end-of-period financial statements for Carson Manufacturing Company, Inc.

When you have completed this activity, you will have

1. calculated and entered adjustments on a ten-column work sheet
2. completed the work sheet
3. prepared a statement of cost of goods manufactured
4. prepared an income statement
5. prepared a statement of retained earnings
6. prepared a balance sheet
7. journalized and posted the adjusting and closing entries

Carson Manufacturing Company, Inc.

Carson Manufacturing Company, Inc. manufactures small office supplies such as pencil holders, letter baskets, and tape dispensers. The company sells its products to retail office supplies stores in the area.

The company has authorized capital of 200,000 shares of $5-par common stock.

Completing End-of-period Work

Before going on vacation, another accounting clerk in the accounting department of Carson Manufacturing prepared the year-end trial balance. It is included in the working papers that accompany this textbook. You have been asked to complete the work sheet and prepare the financial statements. Carson's fiscal year ends on December 31.

Instructions:

(1) Complete the work sheet. Data for the adjustments are as follows.
  (a) Carson Manufacturing uses the periodic inventory system in determining the cost of the ending inventories. The balances of the three inventory accounts on December 31 are as follows.

Raw Materials Inventory	$18,000
Work in Process Inventory	53,000
Finished Goods Inventory	75,000

  (b) Carson Manufacturing uses the straight-line method to determine the annual depreciation amounts. Depreciation for the year is as follows.

Factory building	$ 6,300
Office building	2,700
Factory machinery	30,000
Office equipment	8,000

  (c) The ending factory supplies inventory on December 31 is $3,500.
  (d) The amount of the expired insurance premium is as follows: factory insurance, $800; office insurance, $1,000.
  (e) Carson Manufacturing estimates that its uncollectible accounts will be 6% of the balance of Accounts Receivable.
  (f) On October 1, the company borrowed $100,000 from the Atlantic States Trust Company and issued a 12%, 6-month note payable.
  (g) The December power bill of $1,500 has not yet been recorded or paid. (Record this as a credit to Accounts Payable.)
  (h) Accrued salaries are as follows: direct labor, $2,500; indirect labor, $1,200.
  (i) The federal income tax liability for the year is $51,280.
(2) Prepare a statement of cost of goods manufactured.
(3) Prepare an income statement.
(4) Prepare a statement of retained earnings. During the year, the company declared and paid a cash dividend totaling $15,000.
(5) Prepare a balance sheet.
(6) Journalize the adjusting and closing entries, beginning on page 69 of the general journal. Post the entries to the Retained Earnings, Income Summary, and Manufacturing Summary accounts only.

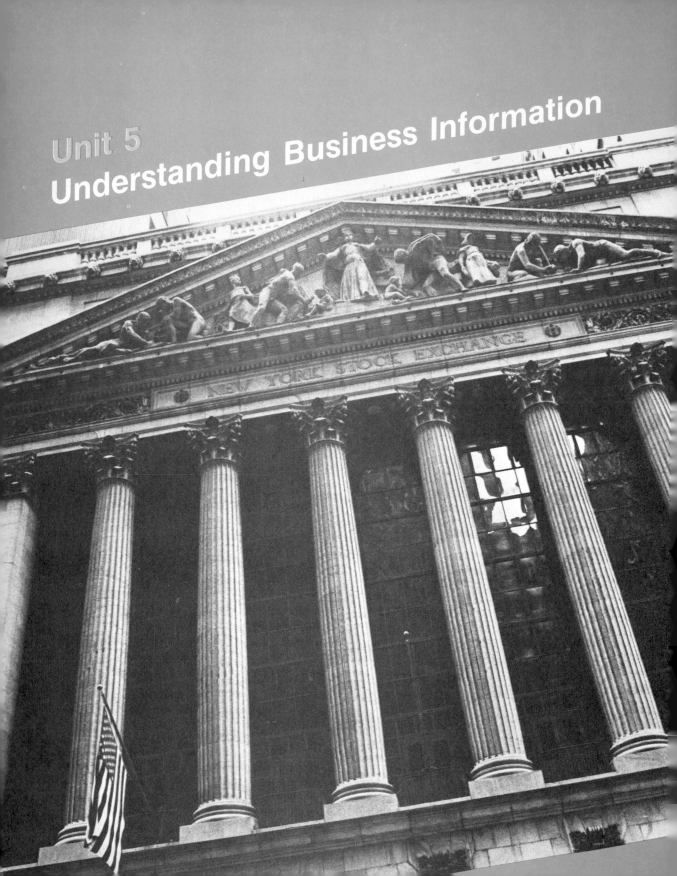

Unit 5

Understanding Business Information

The financial statements prepared by a business are of interest to a variety of different groups. People both inside and outside the business use the information provided in the statements to help them make decisions. If these statements are to be useful, the users must be able to find information that shows important relationships and helps them make comparisons from year to year and company to company. In this unit, you will first learn about the fundamentals on which financial accounting and reporting standards are based. You will also learn several techniques that can be used to examine and explain the information contained on financial statements. Finally, you will learn about a fourth financial statement that is prepared by most businesses.

In this unit, you will study the three chapters listed below.

New York Stock Exchange

19 The Basis of Financial Reporting

To the general public, accounting may seem to be primarily a recordkeeping process that leads to the preparation of financial statements. In reality, those who practice accounting must understand much more than the recordkeeping process. Accountants must understand how accounting standards are developed, what the reporting objectives are, and how the underlying concepts of accounting (rules and principles) influence the actual practice of accounting.

Accounting practice is influenced by "generally accepted accounting principles." These principles form the basis of the rules and interpretations used in accounting practice today. In this chapter, we will look at some of the standards and principles that affect accounting.

Learning Objectives

When you have completed this chapter, you should be able to

1. List some of the organizations that influence accounting standards.

2. Discuss the objectives of financial accounting.

3. List the qualitative characteristics of accounting information.

4. Explain how accounting assumptions, principles, and guidelines affect financial reporting.

5. Define the accounting terms presented in this chapter.

New Terms

generally accepted accounting principles / relevance / reliability / comparability / consistency / economic entity / going concern / unit of measure / time period / historical cost / revenue recognition / matching principle / full disclosure / cost-benefit consideration / materiality / conservatism / industry practices

The Development of Accounting Standards

In the United States' private enterprise system, one of the most important decisions made by any business is the allocation of its capital. Financial data from the business's accounting system are a major source of information that is needed to make such allocation decisions. Accounting information, therefore, must be accurate and reliable for use in the decision-making process. The users of this type of financial data—the managers of the business—are called *internal users*.

Other people also use the financial information that is reported by a business. These people include stockholders, creditors, potential investors, bankers, economists, labor unions, and numerous government agencies such as the Securities and Exchange Commission or the Internal Revenue Service. These people and groups are referred to as *external users*.

To ensure that financial information is accurate and reliable, accounting standards have been developed by a number of professional and governmental organizations. These organizations are described below and on the following page.

American Institute of Certified Public Accountants

The American Institute of Certified Public Accountants (AICPA) is the national professional organization of practicing certified public accountants (CPAs). The views and practices of the AICPA have a great deal of influence on the accounting and auditing standards that are established for use by members of the accounting profession.

Financial Accounting Standards Board

The Financial Accounting Standards Board (FASB) includes members who represent public accounting, industry, education, and investment firms. The FASB issues Statements of Financial Accounting. These statements, along with FASB Interpretations, specify the accounting principles and procedures to be followed on specific accounting issues. The FASB Statements and Interpretations are considered to be authoritative sources and are the basis for generally accepted accounting principles (GAAP, pronounced "gap"). The GAAP are the rules and procedures to be followed in preparing and auditing financial statements.

Securities and Exchange Commission

The Securities and Exchange Commission (SEC) is a government agency that has the power to determine the accounting methods used to prepare the financial reports of companies reporting to it (publicly owned corporations). The SEC regularly issues bulletins that set out the form and content of the financial statements that must be filed with the SEC. The SEC, however, has generally relied upon and supported the accounting standards developed by the AICPA and the FASB.

Internal Revenue Service

The Internal Revenue Service (IRS) is a government agency that regulates the procedures used in the determination of taxable income. Since the expense for income taxes is a major cost for most profit-oriented corporations, the IRS is concerned with the development and application of those procedures.

The IRS derives its authority from the Internal Revenue Code and from other income tax regulations passed by Congress. It is important to note that, although the IRS may be influential, its authority does not govern the accounting standards developed for the determination of net income used for financial reporting.

Other Influences

A number of other organizations have influenced the development of generally accepted accounting principles. The American Accounting Association (AAA) publishes the *Accounting Review,* whose articles include discussions of accounting theory, criticisms of accounting practices, and recommendations for improvements. The National Association of Accountants (NAA) publishes the *Management Accountant,* which emphasizes cost and managerial accounting practices and procedures. The Government Accounting Standards Board (GASB) develops and interprets accounting standards that are applicable to state and local government agencies.

The Conceptual Framework of Accounting

One of the purposes of accounting is to communicate financial information to a variety of users. To that end, periodic financial statements are prepared. The major statements prepared are the income statement, the statement of changes in owner's equity (or of retained earnings), and the balance sheet.

You have learned that accounting consists of a number of rules and procedures that are followed in the recording and reporting of financial information. These rules and procedures are based on the accounting concepts developed by the FASB. In this chapter, we will describe the first two concept statements issued by the FASB. These statements cover the objectives of financial reporting and the qualitative characteristics of accounting information.

Concept Statement 1:
Objectives of Financial Reporting by Business Enterprises

Financial statements are used to communicate important accounting information on the financial position of a business to a wide variety of users. This information is important to both internal and external users in making business and economic decisions. Therefore, the FASB developed the following objectives of financial reporting, standards by which all financial statements should be prepared.

1. Financial statements should provide information that is useful to those persons who must make decisions about granting credit to or investing in a business.
2. Financial statements should provide information to users about cash to be received from dividends and bond interest payments and information on the sale, redemption, or maturity of stocks and bonds.
3. Financial statements should provide information about a business's financial performance during a reporting period.
4. Financial statements should provide information about a business's assets, liabilities, and owners' equity.
5. Financial statements should provide information about how a business obtains and spends cash, about its borrowing and repayment transactions, about its capital transactions (including cash dividends), and about other factors that may affect a business's liquidity or solvency.
6. Financial statements should provide information about how management has used the resources entrusted to it by the stockholders.
7. Financial statements should include explanations and interpretations to help users understand the financial information provided.

Concept Statement 2:
Qualitative Characteristics of Accounting Information

If accounting information is to be useful, it must be understandable. The FASB has described certain qualitative characteristics of accounting information. *Qualitative characteristics* are those characteristics that make information provided by accountants more understandable to users and decision-makers. The four qualitative characteristics are: relevance, reliability, comparability, and consistency.

Relevance

In accounting, **relevance** means that the information being presented must "make a difference" in reaching a decision about the business. Accounting information is relevant if it has predictive value, is timely, and provides feedback. Accounting information has predictive value if it helps the user forecast or predict the results of certain financial events and helps identify the potential risks of certain decisions. Accounting information is timely if it is available to the user in time to make a decision. Accounting information provides feedback if it tells the user something about the accuracy of earlier information and decisions.

EXAMPLE: On March 31, a business reported that its quarterly sales were $550,000 and that the board of directors had declared a quarterly dividend of $.50 per share. This information is relevant to an investor trying to project the next quarter's dividend payment.

Reliability

To be useful, accounting information must be reliable as well as relevant. Reliability relates to the confidence a decision-maker has in the financial information. Reliable information is verifiable (can be proved or confirmed), complete, and free from personal bias.

EXAMPLE: A business reports that an independent consulting firm has determined the value of the firm's inventory and that old and damaged merchandise has been revalued to reflect its current marketability. This information is reliable because it is free from bias, is complete, and can be confirmed by an independent third party.

Comparability

Financial information is more useful if it can be compared from one accounting period to another or from one company to another. Comparability means that the information is presented in such a way that the user can recognize similarities, differences, and trends. Comparability is sometimes difficult to achieve because different accounting methods are permitted. For example, earlier in this text you learned about four methods of determining the value of inventories and four methods of allocating depreciation. Each of these methods is acceptable and permitted.

EXAMPLE: A business reports that its net income after income taxes was $300,000 in one year and $275,000 in the previous year. Since the net income amounts were both reported on the same basis (after income taxes), the information is comparable.

Consistency

Applying the same accounting methods over a number of accounting periods leads to consistency in financial reporting. This consistency helps the user analyze and compare information from a series of reports. It may be necessary, however, to change a particular accounting method in order to provide more relevant or reliable information to users. When this happens, the financial statement should report the change and its effect on the accounting records.

EXAMPLE: A business reports that it continues to use the lifo method to determine the value of its inventory. This information allows a user to compare inventory and cost of merchandise sold over several accounting periods.

Before reading further, do the following activity to check your understanding of the qualitative characteristics of accounting information.

Accounting Assumptions

An assumption is something that is taken for granted as true. The practice of accounting is based on four assumptions about the way in which businesses operate. These assumptions, which affect the way in which financial information is reported, are: economic entity, going concern, unit of measure, and time period.

Economic Entity

Financial reports are prepared for specific economic entities. An **economic entity** is an organization that exists independently of its owner or owners. Thus, for accounting purposes, sole proprietors and partners are considered to be separate from their businesses. (However, they may legally be held personally liable for the debts of their firms.) Corporations are economic entities distinct from their stockholders. Because of this assumption, the transactions of a business and the transactions of its owners are accounted for and reported separately.

EXAMPLE: The personal residence of a sole proprietor, valued at $100,000, is not reported in the accounting records of the business although both the home and the business are owned by the same person. However, a building owned by the business is reported on the business's financial statements.

Going Concern

In accounting, it is assumed that the economic entity will continue to operate indefinitely. In other words, the business is a **going concern**. It is expected to operate long enough to carry out its operations and meet its future obligations. Because of this assumption, financial statements are able to report long-term liabilities and expenses such as depreciation.

EXAMPLE: A business reports that its 9% bond issue, totaling $1,000,000, must be paid in the year 2005.

Unit of Measure

Accounting is based on the assumption that money is the common denominator by which all economic events (transactions) are reported. In the United States, the dollar is the **unit of measure** for business transactions. Accounting also assumes that the dollar is stable over time—that it has a fixed value or buying power. This assumption has created some reporting problems, particularly in periods of rapid inflation. The FASB has only recently experimented with adjusting accounting information for changing prices.

EXAMPLE: A business reports that the value of land that it owns is $50,000.

Time Period

The going concern assumption suggests that an economic entity will continue to operate indefinitely. For decision-making purposes, however, users of financial information need periodic reports. Users want timely and relevant information on a regular basis. In addition, the government requires that income taxes be paid annually. Therefore, the life of a business is divided into segments for reporting purposes. The most common **time period** is the year, although time periods of one month or one quarter are also used.

EXAMPLE: On December 31, a business reports that its sales for the year were $500,000.

Before reading further, do the following activity to check your understanding of accounting assumptions.

Check Your Learning

Write your answers to the following questions on a sheet of notebook paper.

1. The dollar is the __?__ used for reporting accounting information in the United States.
2. The __?__ assumption suggests that a business will continue its operations indefinitely.
3. For reporting purposes, the life of a business is divided into __?__.
4. Financial reports are prepared for specific and separate identifiable units called __?__.

Compare your answers to those in the answers section. Re-read the preceding part of the chapter to find the answers to any questions you may have missed.

Accountants follow certain principles when recording and reporting accounting information. These principles are based on the assumptions just discussed and on the qualitative characteristics of financial reporting. Three of these broad accounting principles are: the exchange principle, the revenue principle, and the matching principle.

The Exchange Principle

The exchange principle states that all transactions should be recorded at their historical cost. Historical cost is the cost or exchange price at the time a transaction is completed. This principle provides the most reliable measurement of financial information. Historical cost is fixed, definite, and can be verified. It is, therefore, the most objective way to account for assets, liabilities, and owners' equity.

EXAMPLE: A business purchases a certain piece of equipment for $5,000. At the end of the period, the business reports the cost of the equipment at $5,000, although its replacement cost is now $6,000.

The Revenue Principle

The revenue principle states that revenue is recognized and recorded when the earning process is complete and title to the goods have been transferred or the services have been performed. According to the revenue principle, revenue recognition occurs at the time of a sale even though, in many cases, no cash has been received. This is often referred to as the point-of-sale revenue recognition method.

EXAMPLE: On September 14, a business sells stereo equipment to a customer on account. The revenue received from this sale is recognized and recorded on September 14, not on the date when the business actually receives cash from the customer.

There are certain exceptions to the revenue recognition method discussed above. These exceptions require other revenue recognition methods.

1. *Percentage-of-completion Method.* Some businesses, such as construction companies, engage in long-term contracts that take several years to complete. When this occurs, revenue may be recognized and recorded periodically when various stages of the project have been completed. The amount of revenue recognized depends on the costs incurred. If 30% of the total project costs have been incurred at the end of one period, 30% of the expected revenue may be recognized and recorded.
2. *Production Method.* Occasionally, a ready market exists for a certain product, such as gold. In this case, revenue may be recognized and recorded as the production process is completed or as the product is grown or mined, but before an actual sale has taken place.
3. *Installment Sale Method.* Merchandise is often sold on the installment basis. That is, the buyer takes possession of the merchandise but pays for

the item in equal payments over a long period of time. When items are sold on an installment basis, revenue is recognized and recorded as each cash payment from the customer is received.

The Matching Principle

The matching principle states that the recognition of expenses should be tied directly to the recognition of revenue. In other words, revenue for an accounting period should be matched against the expenses incurred during the period to earn that revenue. The matching principle requires the use of the accrual basis of accounting, with adjusting entries to update certain revenue and expense accounts at the end of the period.

EXAMPLE: At the end of the fiscal period, a business recorded adjusting entries for depreciation, supplies used, expired insurance, and bad debts. Expenses were then deducted from gross profit on sales to determine the net income from operations of $125,000.

Before reading further, do the following activity to check your understanding of the three broad accounting principles.

Check Your Learning

On a separate sheet of paper, write the letter of the definition from Column B that matches the term in Column A.

Column A	Column B
1. Exchange principle	a. Expenses are recognized and reported in the same period as revenue.
2. Revenue principle	b. Transactions are recorded at the price exchanged at the time the transaction is completed.
3. Matching principle	c. Revenue is recognized and recorded when the earning process is complete and the goods or services have been transferred.

Compare your answers to those in the answers section. Re-read the preceding part of the chapter to find the answers to any questions you may have missed.

General Accounting Guidelines

Accountants are often faced with uncertainties or doubts about how accounting information should be recorded and reported. Costs must be considered; risks are involved; estimates must be made. In reporting accounting information, accountants follow five guidelines. These guidelines are: full disclosure, the cost-benefit consideration, materiality, conservatism, and industry practices.

Full Disclosure

For accounting information to be useful, it must be relevant and reliable. This guideline states that the accountant should make a **full disclosure** of any information that will make a difference to a decision-maker. Additional information that may be useful to the user is usually added in the form of footnotes. You'll learn more about footnotes in Chapter 23. How much and what accounting information should be disclosed in financial reports is, in many instances, a matter of the accountant's professional judgment.

EXAMPLE: A business reports that its net income after income tax includes $75,000 received from the sale of land. Since the sale of the land was an unusual event, a footnote was added so as not to mislead users about the amount of revenue earned from sales, the company's main source of revenue.

Cost-Benefit Consideration

Users of accounting information sometimes assume that the cost of providing additional accounting information is relatively low. This is not always true. According to the **cost-benefit consideration**, the costs incurred to provide new accounting information should not be greater than the benefits of providing the information. After providing a certain, minimum level of information, additional information should be provided only if the benefits derived from the information exceed the costs of providing it.

EXAMPLE: A business reports its research and development expenses by project rather than as one lump sum. Although this involves additional costs, it provides additional information to users concerning the company's areas of concentration for the future.

Materiality

The term "materiality" refers to the relative importance of an item or event. In accounting, the **materiality** guideline suggests that an item or an amount that would make a difference to a user should be included in the financial reports. Whether a particular item or amount is material cannot be determined by examining the item or amount alone. Its relationship to other items or amounts must be considered.

EXAMPLE: In the annual report of a business reporting profits of $10 million, the understatement of profits by $5,000 may be immaterial. The same understatement of profits for a business reporting profits of $20,000 would be material.

Conservatism

In accounting, the concept of **conservatism** means that the accountant should be prudent and use judgment when reporting accounting information. In other words, when faced with several methods of reporting accounting information, the accountant should choose the method that will be the least likely to overstate assets and income.

EXAMPLE: On its financial statements, a business reports the value of its inventory at the lower-of-cost-or-market amount. Under the conservatism concept, if the market value of the inventory is less than the historical cost, the more conservative market value is used.

Industry Practices

The nature of some businesses requires that financial information be recorded or reported in a manner that differs from generally accepted accounting procedures. These different procedures may result from long-standing industry practices or users' past expectations. In some cases, the differences may be a result of government regulations. Examples of businesses that have special industry reporting practices are: oil and gas companies, motion picture firms, cable television companies, real estate brokerages, and banks.

EXAMPLE: In the meat-packing industry, inventories are usually valued at the selling price of the end products (roasts, chops, and so on) less the distribution costs (the costs incurred in getting the products to market). Because of the difficulty of allocating the cost of the raw materials (cattle, sheep, or hogs) to the finished goods, industry practice requires a different inventory valuation method.

Summary of Key Points

1. Accounting standards and practices have been influenced by a number of organizations, such as the American Institute of Certified Public Accountants, the Financial Accounting Standards Board, the Securities and Exchange Commission, and the Internal Revenue Service.
2. Generally accepted accounting principles are the rules and procedures to be followed in preparing and auditing financial statements.
3. Accounting rules and procedures are based on certain characteristics, assumptions, principles, and guidelines.
4. Qualitative characteristics are those characteristics that make accounting information more useful and understandable to users. The four qualitative characteristics of accounting information are: relevance, reliability, comparability, and consistency.
5. The practice of accounting is based on four assumptions about the way businesses operate. These four assumptions are: the economic entity assumption, the going concern assumption, the unit of measure assumption, and the time period assumption.
6. The three broad accounting principles that affect the recording and reporting of financial information are: the exchange principle, the revenue principle, and the matching principle.
7. In recording and reporting accounting information, accountants are often faced with doubts and uncertainties about the importance of the information they provide. Accountants generally follow five guidelines: full disclosure, cost-benefit considerations, materiality, conservatism, and industry practices.

Review and Applications

Building Your Accounting Vocabulary

In your own words, write the definition of each of the following accounting terms. Use complete sentences for your definitions.

comparability	generally accepted	materiality
conservatism	accounting	relevance
consistency	principle	reliability
cost-benefit	going concern	revenue recognition
consideration	historical cost	time period
economic entity	industry practices	unit of measure
full disclosure	matching principle	

Reviewing Your Accounting Knowledge

1. Who are internal users of accounting information? Who are external users of accounting information?
2. What two government agencies have a strong influence on accounting practices and procedures?
3. Name at least four of the objectives of financial reporting developed by the FASB.
4. According to the FASB, what are the four qualitative characteristics of accounting information?
5. What three qualities make accounting information relevant?
6. What is an accounting assumption? What are the four accounting assumptions?
7. What is the unit of measure in use in the United States?
8. Name the three accounting principles that guide accountants in recording and reporting accounting information.
9. Revenue is usually recognized and recorded at the "point of sale." Name and explain three other revenue recognition methods.
10. What are the five guidelines accountants can follow when faced with uncertainties or doubts about how to record or report accounting information?

Improving Your Decision-making Skills

According to the FASB's Concept Statement 1, financial statements should provide information about the economic resources of an entity, the claims to those resources, and the effects of transactions, events, and circumstances on those resources and claims.

How do financial reporting procedures, as you have studied them, meet the FASB objectives?

Problem 19–1

For each of the following items, indicate which accounting characteristic, assumption, principle, or guideline applies.

(1) The owner or owners of a business are separate and apart from the business itself.
(2) Inventory items are recorded at cost.
(3) Sales are recognized and recorded when the earning process is completed and a transfer of goods or services has taken place.
(4) The value of the inventory is reported according to a long-standing practice.
(5) If a choice must be made, amounts should be understated rather than overstated.
(6) Information that will make a difference to a decision-maker should be reported.
(7) The dollar is the common denominator used when recording economic events.
(8) The economic entity is expected to continue operations indefinitely.
(9) The user of accounting information must have confidence in that information.
(10) The costs of property, plant and equipment assets are allocated over the useful lives of the assets.

Problem 19–2

For each of the following accounting procedures or practices, indicate the accounting assumption, principle, or guideline on which the procedure or practice is based.

(1) A building with a market value of $100,000 is reported at its cost of $35,000.
(2) A corporation issues quarterly and annual reports to its stockholders.
(3) The owner of a sole proprietorship maintains a personal checking account and a business checking account.
(4) An inventory item costing $85 was mistakenly omitted from the balance sheet. No correction was made to the balance sheet, nor was a new balance sheet prepared.
(5) The revenue from a sale of merchandise on account was recorded at the time of the sale.
(6) The purchase of low-cost cleaning equipment was charged to an expense account.
(7) The amount of damages being sought in a pending lawsuit against the business ($5,000) was reported in a footnote to the balance sheet.
(8) A debt to be repaid over a ten-year period was classified as a long-term liability on the balance sheet.

(9) An adjustment for accrued salaries was recorded and also reported on the balance sheet.

(10) The value of a company's oil wells was reported in a special way on the balance sheet.

Problem 19–3

For each of the following financial events, determine if an accounting issue is involved. Identify the issue and indicate how the event should be reported.

(1) The warehouse of the Jones Storage Company was recently appraised at a value of $375,000. The original cost of the warehouse was $155,000. The owner insists on reporting the value of the warehouse on the balance sheet at $375,000.

(2) While driving the company's delivery truck, an employee was involved in an accident. The driver of the other vehicle was injured and is suing the company for $300,000. The trial, which the other driver is expected to win, is scheduled for February. The company's accountant wants to report the probable loss in a footnote to the December 31 balance sheet. The owner of the company does not want the lawsuit or the potential loss reported.

(3) For the past five years, the New Market Company has used the fifo method to determine the value of the merchandise inventory reported on the balance sheet. The president of the company has suggested that the lifo method would provide a more relevant value.

Problem 19–4

You are the auditor for the Dixie Company. The accountant of the company has asked for your advice on the appropriate accounting procedure to use for each of the following items. What would you recommend, and why?

(1) The balance of Accounts Receivable at the end of the year is $375,000. However, included in this amount is an unsecured loan to the president (and owner) in the amount of $35,000.

(2) A calculator was purchased for $75. The accountant wants to record the cost as an expense for the period.

(3) The president purchased a new dishwasher for his home and paid for it with a company check for $750.

(4) A physical inventory was taken and the value of the ending inventory was determined to be $100,250. Included in this amount is obsolete merchandise, which cost $2,500.

(5) The company has three cash accounts: a checking account with a balance of $7,500, a petty cash fund of $50, and a change fund of $250. The president would like to combine the amounts and report only one amount on the balance sheet.

20 Analyzing and Interpreting Financial Statements

Accounting is the process of collecting, analyzing, recording, summarizing, reporting, and interpreting business transactions. You are now ready to interpret the results. But just how do you analyze and interpret the financial data that have been reported in the financial statements?

The financial condition of a company and the results of its operations are of interest not only to owners, employers, and managers, but also to creditors and to prospective owners and creditors. All of these groups are interested in two aspects of an enterprise: (1) its ability to pay its debts, and (2) its ability to earn a reasonable profit on the owners' investment.

In this chapter, you will learn about the methods used to analyze and interpret financial statements.

Learning Objectives

When you have completed this chapter, you should be able to

1. Prepare a comparative income statement and balance sheet involving horizontal analysis.

2. Prepare a comparative income statement and balance sheet involving vertical analysis.

3. Calculate commonly used liquidity and profitability ratios.

4. Use liquidity and profitability ratios to analyze the performance of a business.

5. Define the accounting terms presented in this chapter.

New Terms

horizontal analysis / **base year** / **vertical analysis** / **common-size statements** / **trend analysis** / **liquidity** / **profitability** / **ratio analysis** / **working capital** / **current ratio** / **quick ratio** / **merchandise inventory turnover** / **equity per share** / **price-earnings ratio**

Types of Comparison

A given set of facts by itself is not significant. To interpret any facts, you must have something to compare them with. For example, suppose you are told that a certain corporation earned a net income of $56,000 during the past year. What does this mean to you? Does this net income indicate a successful year or a poor year? Does it compare favorably with other years or unfavorably? Does it represent a reasonable return on investment or not? How does it compare with the net income of other firms in the same industry?

As you can see, numbers by themselves generally don't mean very much. It is their relationship to other numbers or their change from one period to another that is more revealing. The techniques of financial analysis are intended to show these relationships and changes. Four common techniques used to evaluate financial statements are horizontal analysis, vertical analysis, trend analysis, and ratio analysis.

Horizontal Analysis

Comparing dollar amount changes and percentage changes for the same items on a company's financial statements for two or more periods is called **horizontal analysis**. As an illustration, we'll examine the comparative income statement (Figure 20–1) and balance sheet (Figure 20–2) of City Builders Supply Company, Inc., for 1986 and 1987. Let's look first at the income statement, Figure 20–1 on page 476.

Notice that, for each item, the increases or decreases of 1987 over 1986 are expressed first in dollars and then in percentages.

Look at the increase in sales. Sales for 1986 were $860,000; sales for 1987 were $980,600. By subtracting the 1986 sales from the 1987 sales, you can see that sales in 1987 increased $120,600.

$980,600	Sales for 1987
−860,000	Sales for 1986
$120,600	Increase of 1987 over 1986

To calculate the percentage of the increase in sales in 1987 over 1986, divide the dollar increase by the amount of sales during the base year and multiply by 100. The term **base year** refers to the year being used for comparison. In this case, the 1987 sales are being compared to the 1986 sales. The base

Figure 20–1.
Comparative
Income Statement
for Horizontal
Analysis

City Builders Supply Company, Inc.
Comparative Income Statement
For the Years Ended December 31, 1987 and 1986

	1987	1986	Increase (Decrease) Amount	Percentage
Revenue:				
Sales	$ 980,600	$860,000	$120,600	14.02
Less: Sales Ret. and Allow.	13,700	11,400	2,300	20.18
Net Sales	$ 966,900	$848,600	$118,300	13.94
Cost of Merchandise Sold:				
Merchandise Inventory, Jan. 1	$ 206,500	$138,700	$ 67,800	48.88
Purchases	817,100	645,700	171,400	26.54
Less: Purch. Ret. and Allow.	12,300	9,100	3,200	35.16
Merchandise Available for Sale	$1,011,300	$775,300	$236,000	30.44
Less: Merch. Inv., Dec. 31	353,600	206,500	147,100	71.23
Cost of Merchandise Sold	$ 657,700	$568,800	$ 88,900	15.63
Gross Profit on Sales	$ 309,200	$279,800	$ 29,400	10.51
Operating Expenses:				
Selling Expenses:				
Advertising Expense	$ 7,900	$ 6,900	$ 1,000	14.49
Delivery Expense	17,700	13,700	4,000	29.20
Depr. Expense—Equipment	6,800	6,600	200	3.03
Sales Salaries Expense	114,650	102,400	12,250	11.96
Store Supplies Expense	750	600	150	25.00
Total Selling Expenses	$ 147,800	$130,200	$ 17,600	13.52
Administrative Expenses:				
Bad Debts Expense	$ 6,200	$ 5,400	$ 800	14.81
Depr. Expense—Building	14,200	14,200	—	—
Insurance Expense	1,100	1,000	100	10.00
Misc. Admin. Expense	860	720	140	19.44
Office Salaries Expense	33,440	27,680	5,760	20.81
Taxes Expense	6,100	5,200	900	17.31
Total Admin. Expenses	$ 61,900	$ 54,200	$ 7,700	14.21
Total Operating Expenses	$ 209,700	$184,400	$ 25,300	13.72
Net Income from Operations	$ 99,500	$ 95,400	$ 4,100	4.30
Other Expenses:				
Interest Expense	8,520	7,860	660	8.40
Net Income before Income Taxes	$ 90,980	$ 87,540	$ 3,440	3.93
Income Taxes	22,142	20,766	1,376	6.63
Net Income after Income Taxes	$ 68,838	$ 66,774	$ 2,064	3.09

year then is 1986. As shown below, sales in 1987 increased 14.02% over 1986 sales.

$$\frac{\$120,600}{\$860,000} = .1402 \times 100 = 14.02\%$$

As another example, look at the increase in net sales in 1987 over 1986.

$966,900   Net Sales for 1987
−848,600   Net Sales for 1986
$118,300   Increase of 1987 over 1986

The percentage of the increase is calculated as follows.

$$\frac{\$118,300}{\$848,600} = .1394 \times 100 = 13.94\%$$

Remember: **To calculate the percentage of increase, divide the dollar increase by the base year amount and multiply by 100.**

People analyzing an income statement often use the percentage increase of net sales as a basis for comparison. In other words, they compare all other percentage changes with the percentage change in net sales. City Builders' net sales increased 13.94% from 1986 to 1987. So long as there have not been any changes in the valuation of any item on the income statement, other than those directly caused by an increase in sales, each item listed should also increase by approximately 13.94%. If they vary considerably from 13.94%, the reasons for the differences should be investigated.

Let's look at the main items on the income statement.

Item	Percentage Change
Net Sales	13.94%
Cost of Merchandise Sold	15.63%
Gross Profit on Sales	10.51%
Total Operating Expenses	13.72%
Net Income after Income Taxes	3.09%

You can see that gross profit on sales and net income after income tax vary quite a bit from the 13.94% increase in net sales. Since gross profit on sales is determined by subtracting the cost of merchandise sold from net sales, the entire cost of merchandise sold section of the income statement should be investigated. This is a starting point in accounting for the rather small percentage increase in net income after income tax (3.09%). The percentage changes of items in the cost of merchandise sold section are as follows.

Item	Percentage Change
Merchandise Inventory, January 1	48.88%
Purchases	26.54%
Purchases Returns and Allowances	35.16%
Merchandise Inventory, December 31	71.23%

The merchandise inventory of January 1 was a carry-over from the previous year. But why was there such a large increase in purchases (26.54%) and purchases returns and allowances (35.16%)? Notice that the ending merchandise inventory in 1987 was 71.23% larger than in 1986. To purchase that quantity of merchandise requires a great deal of cash. To justify such a large increase in merchandise inventory, there should have been a larger increase in sales.

Now let's look at the balance sheet in Figure 20–2 on page 479, which shows the comparison between 1986 and 1987. You will see that changes on this statement are also expressed in both dollars and percentages. Items showing either a large dollar change or a large percentage change stand out immediately. On the balance sheet, negative amounts appear, as indicated by the parentheses. (In accounting, negative amounts—losses or decreases—are enclosed in parentheses so they are easily seen.) Look at the following items.

Item	Dollar Increase (Decrease)	Percentage Increase (Decrease)
Cash in Bank	$(19,100)	(49.35%)
Merchandise Inventory	147,100	71.23%
Accounts Payable	42,600	146.90%

The comparative income statement already indicated the large increase in the Merchandise Inventory account. The changes in the balances of other related accounts should also be examined. For example, the fact that Cash in Bank decreased 49.35% while Accounts Payable increased 146.90% may indicate a pending financial crisis. In order to meet its bills, City Builders may be forced to liquidate some of its merchandise by selling it at cost, or even below cost. The 200% increase in Dividends Payable doesn't look good either because this will mean a large outflow of cash some time in the near future. One good sign, though, is the decrease in Accounts Receivable. However, knowing this, the increase in Allowance for Uncollectible Accounts appears to be unreasonable. The company may want to take a closer look at its charge customers' accounts or its credit-granting policies.

Vertical Analysis

Another tool that can be used to analyze financial statements is vertical analysis. With vertical analysis, every dollar amount reported on a financial statement is restated as a percentage of a certain base amount reported on the same statement. For example, each amount on the income statement is reported as a percentage of net sales. The current year percentages can be compared with percentages of previous years or with the percentages of other businesses within the same industry. These percentages can also be used by the company to prepare future budgets.

Although each percentage applies to one item only, you can quickly see the relative importance of each item in the statement. Let us look first at the comparative income statement (Figure 20–3 on page 480) and then at the comparative balance sheet (Figure 20–4 on page 482) for City Builders Supply Company, Inc. These statements are arranged for vertical analysis.

City Builders Supply Company, Inc.
Comparative Balance Sheet
December 31, 1987 and 1986

Assets	1987	1986	Increase (Decrease) Amount	Percentage
Current Assets:				
Cash in Bank	$ 19,600	$ 38,700	$ (19,100)	(49.35)
Accounts Receivable	76,700	81,400	(4,700)	(5.77)
Less: Allow. for Uncoll. Accts.	3,300	2,600	700	26.92
Merchandise Inventory	353,600	206,500	147,100	71.23
Prepaid Insurance	2,000	2,100	(100)	(4.76)
Total Current Assets	$448,600	$326,100	$122,500	37.57
Investments:				
Bond Sinking Fund	$ 4,100	$ 5,800	$ (1,700)	(29.31)
Sinking Fund Investments	61,700	59,400	2,300	3.87
Total Investments	$ 65,800	$ 65,200	$ 600	.92
Property, Plant, and Equipment:				
Equipment	$ 88,600	$ 86,000	$ 2,600	3.02
Less: Accumulated Depreciation	41,000	34,200	6,800	19.88
Building	160,000	160,000	—	—
Less: Accumulated Depreciation	56,800	42,600	14,200	33.33
Land	40,000	40,000	—	—
Total Property, Plant, and Equipment	$190,800	$209,200	$ (18,400)	(8.80)
Intangible Assets:				
Organization Costs	$ 3,000	$ 4,000	$ (1,000)	(25.00)
Total Assets	$708,200	$604,500	$103,700	17.15
Liabilities				
Current Liabilities:				
Accounts Payable	$ 71,600	$ 29,000	$ 42,600	146.90
Corporate Income Tax Payable	2,392	3,016	(624)	(20.69)
Dividends Payable	12,000	4,000	8,000	200.00
Salaries Payable	4,200	4,000	200	5.00
Total Current Liabilities	$ 90,192	$ 40,016	$ 50,176	125.39
Long-term Liabilities:				
6% Bonds Payable, due Dec. 31, 1998	$100,000	$100,000	—	—
Less: Discount on Bonds Payable	2,200	2,400	$ (200)	(8.33)
Total Long-term Liabilities	$ 97,800	$ 97,600	$ 200	.20
Total Liabilities	$187,992	$137,616	$ 50,376	36.61
Stockholders' Equity				
Paid-in Capital:				
Common Stock, $100 par (4,000 shares authorized, 3,000 shares issued)	$300,000	$300,000	—	—
Paid-in Capital in Excess of Par	86,000	86,000	—	—
Total Paid-in Capital	$386,000	$386,000	—	—
Retained Earnings	134,208	80,884	$ 53,324	65.93
Total Stockholders' Equity	$520,208	$466,884	$ 53,324	11.42
Total Liabil. and Stockholders' Equity	$708,200	$604,500	$103,700	17.15

Figure 20–2. Comparative Balance Sheet for Horizontal Analysis

Figure 20–3.
Comparative
Income Statement
for Vertical
Analysis

City Builders Supply Company, Inc.
Comparative Income Statement
For the Years Ended December 31, 1987 and 1986

	1987		1986	
	Amount	Percentage	Amount	Percentage
Revenue:				
Sales	$ 980,600	101.42	$860,000	101.34
Less: Sales Ret. and Allow.	13,700	1.42	11,400	1.34
Net Sales	$ 966,900	100.00	$848,600	100.00
Cost of Merchandise Sold:				
Merchandise Inventory, Jan. 1	$ 206,500	21.36	$138,700	16.34
Purchases	817,100	84.51	645,700	76.09
Less: Purch. Ret. and Allow.	12,300	1.27	9,100	1.07
Merchandise Available for Sale	$1,011,300	104.59	$775,300	91.36
Less: Merch. Inv., Dec. 31	353,600	36.57	206,500	24.33
Cost of Merchandise Sold	$ 657,700	68.02	$568,800	67.03
Gross Profit on Sales	$ 309,200	31.98	$279,800	32.97
Operating Expenses:				
Selling Expenses:				
Advertising Expense	$ 7,900	.82	$ 6,900	.81
Delivery Expense	17,700	1.83	13,700	1.61
Depr. Expense—Equipment	6,800	.70	6,600	.78
Sales Salaries Expense	114,650	11.86	102,400	12.07
Store Supplies Expense	750	.08	600	.07
Total Selling Expenses	$ 147,800	15.29	$130,200	15.34
Administrative Expenses:				
Bad Debts Expense	$ 6,200	.64	$ 5,400	.64
Depr. Expense—Building	14,200	1.47	14,200	1.67
Insurance Expense	1,100	.11	1,000	.12
Misc. Admin. Expense	860	.09	720	.08
Office Salaries Expense	33,440	3.46	27,680	3.26
Taxes Expense	6,100	.63	5,200	.61
Total Admin. Expenses	$ 61,900	6.40	$ 54,200	6.39
Total Operating Expenses	$ 209,700	21.69	$184,400	21.73
Net Income from Operations	$ 99,500	10.29	$ 95,400	11.24
Other Expenses:				
Interest Expense	8,520	.88	7,860	.93
Net Income before Income Taxes	$ 90,980	9.41	$ 87,540	10.32
Income Taxes	22,142	2.29	20,766	2.45
Net Income after Income Taxes	$ 68,838	7.12	$ 66,774	7.87

The income statement in Figure 20–3 is arranged for vertical analysis. It expresses each item's dollar amount as a percentage of net sales. In other words, the total amount for each item is divided by the total amount of net sales. Look, for example, at the gross profit on sales for the two years. The calculations are shown at the top of the next page.

1987
$$\frac{\$309,200}{\$966,900} = .3198 \times 100 = 31.98\%$$

1986
$$\frac{\$279,800}{\$848,600} = .3297 \times 100 = 32.97\%$$

As you can see, gross profit on sales was 31.98% of net sales in 1987 and 32.97% of net sales in 1986.

As another example, look at the net income from operations.

1987
$$\frac{\$99,500}{\$966,900} = .1029 \times 100 = 10.29\%$$

1986
$$\frac{\$95,400}{\$848,600} = .1124 \times 100 = 11.24\%$$

Net income from operations was 10.29% of net sales in 1987 and 11.24% of net sales in 1986.

Finally, the percentages for net income after income tax are calculated as follows.

1987
$$\frac{\$68,838}{\$966,900} = .0712 \times 100 = 7.12\%$$

1986
$$\frac{\$66,774}{\$848,600} = .0787 \times 100 = 7.87\%$$

In 1987, net income after income tax was 7.12% of net sales; in 1986, it was 7.87% of net sales.

The percentages could be interpreted as shown below.

1987

For every $100 in net sales, gross profit on sales was $31.98.
For every $100 in net sales, net income from operations was $10.29.
For every $100 in net sales, net income after income taxes was $7.12.

1986

For every $100 in net sales, gross profit on sales was $32.97.
For every $100 in net sales, net income from operations was $11.24.
For every $100 in net sales, net income after income taxes was $7.87.

On the income statement in Figure 20–3, you can again see the importance of the increases in purchases (84.51% of net sales) and merchandise inventory (36.57% of net sales) in 1987. In the selling expenses section, the percentage of sales salaries expense declined slightly. Advertising expense as a percentage of net sales remained the same.

When you perform a vertical analysis of a comparative balance sheet as shown in Figure 20–4 on the next page, the dollar amount for each item is expressed as a percentage of total assets or as a percentage of total liabilities and

City Builders Supply Company, Inc.
Comparative Balance Sheet
December 31, 1987 and 1986

Assets	1987 Amount	1987 Percentage	1986 Amount	1986 Percentage
Current Assets:				
Cash in Bank	$ 19,600	2.77	$ 38,700	6.40
Accounts Receivable	76,700	10.83	81,400	13.47
Less: Allow. for Uncoll. Accts.	3,300	.47	2,600	.43
Merchandise Inventory	353,600	49.93	206,500	34.16
Prepaid Insurance	2,000	.28	2,100	.35
Total Current Assets	$448,600	63.34	$326,100	53.95
Investments:				
Bond Sinking Fund	$ 4,100	.58	$ 5,800	.96
Sinking Fund Investments	61,700	8.71	59,400	9.83
Total Investments	$ 65,800	9.29	$ 65,200	10.79
Property, Plant, and Equipment:				
Equipment	$ 88,600	12.51	$ 86,000	14.23
Less: Accumulated Depreciation	41,000	5.79	34,200	5.66
Building	160,000	22.59	160,000	26.47
Less: Accumulated Depreciation	56,800	8.02	42,600	7.05
Land	40,000	5.65	40,000	6.62
Total Property, Plant, and Equipment	$190,800	26.94	$209,200	34.61
Intangible Assets:				
Organization Costs	$ 3,000	.42	$ 4,000	.66
Total Assets	$708,200	100.00	$604,500	100.00
Liabilities				
Current Liabilities:				
Accounts Payable	$ 71,600	10.11	$ 29,000	4.80
Corporate Income Tax Payable	2,392	.34	3,016	.50
Dividends Payable	12,000	1.69	4,000	.66
Salaries Payable	4,200	.59	4,000	.66
Total Current Liabilities	$ 90,192	12.74	$ 40,016	6.62
Long-term Liabilities:				
6% Bonds Payable, due Dec. 31, 1998	$100,000	14.12	$100,000	16.54
Less: Discount on Bonds Payable	2,200	.31	2,400	.40
Total Long-term Liabilities	$ 97,800	13.81	$ 97,600	16.15
Total Liabilities	$187,992	26.55	$137,616	22.77
Stockholders' Equity				
Paid-in Capital:				
Common Stock, $100 par (4,000 shares authorized, 3,000 shares issued)	$300,000	42.36	$300,000	49.63
Paid-in Capital in Excess of Par	86,000	12.14	86,000	14.22
Total Paid-in Capital	$386,000	54.50	$386,000	63.85
Retained Earnings	134,208	18.95	80,884	13.38
Total Stockholders' Equity	$520,208	73.45	$466,884	77.23
Total Liabil. and Stockholders' Equity	$708,200	100.00	$604,500	100.00

Figure 20–4. Comparative Balance Sheet for Vertical Analysis

stockholders' equity, which is the same amount. Suppose you want to find the percentage of total assets represented by Cash in Bank, net Accounts Receivable, and Merchandise Inventory. The percentages for Cash in Bank are calculated as shown here.

1987 $\dfrac{\$19,600}{\$708,200} = .0277 \times 100 = 2.77\%$

1986 $\dfrac{\$38,700}{\$604,500} = .0640 \times 100 = 6.40\%$

The percentages for net Accounts Receivable are as follows.

1987 $\dfrac{\$73,400}{\$708,200} = .1036 \times 100 = 10.36\%$

1986 $\dfrac{\$78,800}{\$604,500} = .1304 \times 100 = 13.04\%$

Finally, Merchandise Inventory has the following percentages.

1987 $\dfrac{\$353,600}{\$708,200} = .4993 \times 100 = 49.93\%$

1986 $\dfrac{\$206,500}{\$604,500} = .3416 \times 100 = 34.16\%$

These percentages could be interpreted as follows.

1987

For every $100 in total assets, $2.77 is in the form of Cash in Bank.
For every $100 in total assets, $10.36 is in the form of net Accounts Receivable.
For every $100 in total assets, $49.93 is in the form of Merchandise Inventory.

1986

For every $100 in total assets, $6.40 was in the form of Cash in Bank.
For every $100 in total assets, $13.04 was in the form of net Accounts Receivable.
For every $100 in total assets, $34.16 was in the form of Merchandise Inventory.

These percentages point out City Builders' poor status with respect to Cash in Bank and Merchandise Inventory, as well as its favorable status with respect to Accounts Receivable. Other items that may need to be examined are:

1. The percentage decrease in the value of plant assets during 1987
2. The percentage increase in the value of Accounts Payable during 1987

Remember: On an income statement arranged for vertical analysis, each dollar amount is usually expressed as a percentage of net sales. On a balance sheet arranged for vertical analysis, each dollar amount is expressed as a percentage of total assets or total liabilities and stockholders' equity.

Financial statements in which all items are expressed as a percentage of another number are called **common-size statements**. All amounts are expressed in a common size; that is, all amounts are expressed as a fraction of 100% and no dollar amounts are given. For example, on a common-size income statement, net sales is assigned a value of 100%. Each income statement item is then expressed as a percentage of net sales. On a common-size balance sheet, total assets is assigned a value of 100% and total liabilities and stockholders' equity is also assigned a value of 100%. Each asset, liability, and stockholder's equity item is then shown as a fraction of one of the 100% totals.

Trend Analysis

Some changes become evident only when data for a number of years are compared. **Trend analysis** is the comparison of the percentage changes in an item or items over a number of consecutive years. Here is the way to calculate the percentages.

1. Select an appropriate year as the base year.
2. Label the base year 100%.
3. Express all other years as percentages of the base year.

For example, let us say that you want to examine the following amounts from the income statements for City Builders Supply for the years 1983 through 1987.

Item	1983	1984	1985	1986	1987
Net Sales	$714,200	$782,380	$806,400	$848,600	$966,900
Cost of Merchandise Sold	466,150	519,180	540,300	568,800	657,700
Gross Profit on Sales	248,050	263,200	266,100	279,800	309,200

The base year for your calculations is 1983. The trend percentages for net sales are calculated by dividing the net sales of each year by the net sales for 1983, as shown below.

1984	$782,380 ÷ $714,200 = 109.54%
1985	$806,400 ÷ $714,200 = 112.90%
1986	$848,600 ÷ $714,200 = 118.81%
1987	$966,900 ÷ $714,200 = 135.38%

Trend percentages for cost of merchandise sold and gross profit on sales are determined in the same way. Here are the results, with the percentages rounded off to the nearest whole percent.

Item	1983	1984	1985	1986	1987
Net Sales	100%	110%	113%	119%	135%
Cost of Merchandise Sold	100%	111%	116%	122%	141%
Gross Profit on Sales	100%	106%	107%	113%	125%

Notice that over the five-year period, the trend of net sales is upward. Cost of merchandise sold is also increasing, but at a more rapid pace. In other words, over the five years, cost of merchandise sold increased faster than net sales, resulting in smaller increases in gross profit. This is fine if the company plans to greatly increase its sales while "holding the line" on profits. But if this shrinking gross profit percentage is not consistent with company policy, it may be a sign that the company is not passing along its increased costs to its customers.

Before reading further, do the following activity to check your understanding of how to calculate percentages of increase or decrease.

Check Your Learning

On a sheet of notebook paper, calculate the percentage of increase or decrease for the following items.

Item	1986	1987
Cash in Bank	$40,500	$38,250
Notes Receivable	21,000	24,000
Equipment (net)	91,500	99,000
Retained Earnings	57,000	48,000

Check your answers with those in the answers section. Re-read the preceding part of the chapter to find the correct answers to any questions you may have missed.

Ratio Analysis

Management is vitally interested in increasing the company's liquidity and profitability. **Liquidity** refers to a company's ability to pay its debts and meet its current operating needs. **Profitability** is a company's ability to earn a reasonable profit on the owners' investment. Since creditors want some assurance of being repaid, they are also concerned with the company's liquidity and profitability.

In their analysis of a company's financial statements, management and creditors often use ratio analysis. **Ratio analysis** is a comparison of two items on a financial statement, resulting in a percentage that is used to evaluate the relationship of the two items. Ratio analysis is generally used to determine a business's liquidity and profitability.

Bankers and other short-term creditors are mainly interested in the current position of a business: Does the business have enough money coming in to meet its current operating needs and to pay its current debts promptly? (*Current,* to them, means one year. This is consistent with the way accountants refer to "current assets" and "current liabilities.") Let's now look at some commonly used ratios, using data from the comparative statements of City Builders.

Working Capital

The amount by which current assets exceed current liabilities is known as a company's **working capital**. Working capital is an important measure of a company's liquidity, because current liabilities are debts that are expected to be paid within one year and current assets are assets that are expected to be converted to cash within one year. Current liabilities are usually paid out of current assets. Working capital, then, represents the excess assets available to continue business operations. It represents the excess assets available to purchase inventory, obtain credit, and expand operations. Lack of working capital can lead to the failure of the business.

The working capital for City Builders Supply for 1986 and 1987 is calculated as follows.

1987	$448,600	**1986**	$326,100
	− 90,192		− 40,016
	$358,408		$286,084

City Builders' working capital during 1987 was $358,408, while it was $286,084 during 1986.

Working capital is useful when analyzing one company's financial statements. It is, however, difficult to compare one company's working capital with another company's. For example, working capital of $50,000 may be adequate for a small grocery store but totally inadequate for a large grocery chain.

Remember: Working capital is current assets less current liabilities.

Current Ratio

The relationship between a company's current assets and its current liabilities is known as its **current ratio**. A firm's current ratio reveals its ability to pay its bills and repay loans. The current ratio is determined by dividing current assets by current liabilities. Using the data in Figure 20–4, City Builders' current ratios are calculated as follows.

$$\textbf{1987} \quad \frac{\$448,600}{\$90,192} = 5.0\text{:}1$$

$$\textbf{1986} \quad \frac{\$326,100}{\$40,016} = 8.1\text{:}1$$

City Builders' current ratio of 5.0:1 (or 5.0 to 1) in 1987 indicates that it has $5.00 of current assets for every $1.00 of current liabilities. In 1986, however, the ratio was 8.1:1. The company had $8.10 of current assets for every $1.00 in current liabilities.

In the past, a ratio of 2:1 was generally considered to be adequate for most companies. Today, creditors realize that the adequacy of a company's current ratio depends on what type of business the firm is in. For example, the current ratio for a merchandising business whose merchandise is subject to abrupt changes in style should be higher than 2:1.

Quick Ratio

Although working capital and current ratio are two indicators of a firm's ability to meet its current debts, they don't reveal the composition of its current assets—a very important factor. Current assets include merchandise inventory. It usually takes quite a bit of time to convert this inventory into cash. A company with a satisfactory current ratio may be in an unsatisfactory position in terms of liquidity when the inventory makes up a large part of current assets.

A ratio that measures a company's short-term liquidity is the quick ratio. The **quick ratio** is the relationship between a company's "quick assets" and its current liabilities. "Quick assets" are those that can be converted into cash quickly. Examples of quick assets are cash, notes receivable, net accounts receivable (that is, Accounts Receivable less Allowance for Uncollectible Accounts), and marketable securities (short-term investments). The quick ratio is determined by dividing a company's quick assets by its current liabilities. City Builders' quick ratios for 1986 and 1987 are calculated as follows.

1987 $\dfrac{\$19,600 + (\$76,700 - \$3,300)}{\$90,192} = \dfrac{\$93,000}{\$90,192} = 1.03:1$

1986 $\dfrac{\$38,700 + (\$81,400 - \$2,600)}{\$40,016} = \dfrac{\$117,500}{\$40,016} = 2.94:1$

City Builders' quick ratio in 1987 is 1.03:1. That is, the company had $1.03 in quick assets for every $1.00 in current liabilities. In 1986, the company had $2.94 in quick assets for every $1.00 in current liabilities.

A quick ratio of not less than 1:1 is normally considered satisfactory. Therefore, City Builders' 1987 quick ratio is adequate. On the other hand, in 1986 City Builders' quick ratio was too high.

Merchandise Inventory Turnover

The number of times a company's inventory is sold during a given year is its **merchandise inventory turnover**. This is calculated by dividing the cost of merchandise sold by the average merchandise inventory. (The average merchandise inventory is found by adding the beginning and ending inventory amounts and dividing that total by 2.) Here is the calculation for City Builders.

1987 $\dfrac{\$657,700}{\dfrac{\$206,500 + \$353,600}{2}} = \dfrac{\$657,700}{\$280,050} = 2.35 \text{ times/yr.}$

1986 $\dfrac{\$568,800}{\dfrac{\$138,700 + \$206,500}{2}} = \dfrac{\$568,800}{\$172,600} = 3.30 \text{ times/yr.}$

In general, a higher merchandise inventory turnover rate indicates a higher gross profit since more merchandise is being sold. It also means that the company has money tied up in the inventory for shorter periods of time. Storage and insurance costs are lower since the company does not maintain a large inventory. A higher turnover rate also means that there is less chance of the inventory becoming spoiled (if it is perishable) or out of date. A lower merchandise inventory turnover rate may mean that a recession or some other factor is preventing sales from keeping up with purchases.

The merchandise inventory turnover for one company can be compared with figures for the rest of the industry as a test of the company's merchandising efficiency. Note that there has been a serious decline in the merchandise inventory turnover rate for City Builders. This is something to watch.

The merchandise inventory turnover can also be used to determine the number of days that the merchandise was kept in stock. This is calculated by dividing 365 days by the turnover figure.

$$1987 \qquad \frac{365 \text{ days}}{2.35 \text{ times per year}} = 155 \text{ days}$$

$$1986 \qquad \frac{365 \text{ days}}{3.30 \text{ times per year}} = 111 \text{ days}$$

Note that City Builders' merchandise remained in stock 44 days longer in 1987 than it did in 1986. The company should probably investigate its sales and purchasing practices.

Remember: **Ratio analysis is generally used to determine a business's liquidity and profitability.**

Before reading further, do the following activity to check your understanding of the material you have just studied.

Check Your Learning

The following items were taken from the financial statements of the Fiske Company. On a separate sheet of paper, compute the merchandise inventory turnover rate for 1987. Also determine the number of days that the merchandise was kept in stock.

Item	1986	1987
Cost of Merchandise Sold	$680,000	$640,000
Merchandise Inventory, December 31	140,000	132,000

Check your answers with those in the answers section. Re-read the preceding part of the chapter to find the correct answers to any questions you may have missed.

Ratio of Stockholders' Equity to Liabilities

The equity of a corporation is composed of creditors' claims and stockholders' investments. Creditors are concerned with a company's ability to pay its debts. Should a company be unable to repay its obligations, creditors have first claim to the assets of the company. Such a claim takes precedence over claims of the stockholders. Management is also concerned with its company's debt-paying ability. However, the company's ability to maintain its credit standing and to borrow in the future are also important to management.

One of the ratios creditors and management look at is the ratio of stockholders' equity to liabilities. This ratio indicates to creditors how "safe" their loans to the company are and also indicates the company's ability to absorb losses. This ratio is found by dividing total stockholders' equity by total liabilities. Look at this calculation for City Builders Supply.

$$1987 \quad \frac{\$520,208}{\$187,992} = 2.77:1$$

$$1986 \quad \frac{\$466,884}{\$137,616} = 3.39:1$$

In 1987, City Builders had $2.77 in stockholders' investment for every $1.00 of creditors' claims. City Builders' ratio, however, shows a significant decline since 1986, from 3.39:1 to 2.77:1. Creditors like to see a high ratio since stockholders' equity can be used to absorb losses. Also, if their investment is large, owners will think twice about assuming great risks.

Ratio of Property, Plant, and Equipment to Long-term Liabilities

Property, plant, and equipment assets are often used as security when a company borrows money on a long-term basis. As a result, long-term creditors are very interested in the ratio of the value of a firm's total property, plant, and equipment to its long-term liabilities. This ratio also indicates the company's ability to borrow more money on a long-term basis in the future. It is determined by dividing the book value of property, plant and equipment assets by total long-term liabilities. Let's look at the calculation for City Builders Supply.

$$1987 \quad \frac{\$190,800}{\$97,800} = 1.95:1$$

$$1986 \quad \frac{\$209,200}{\$97,600} = 2.14:1$$

In 1987, City Builders had $1.95 in property, plant, and equipment assets for every $1.00 of long-term liabilities. In 1986 there was $2.14 book value of plant, and equipment for every $1.00 of long-term liabilities. Both figures would be acceptable to long-term creditors.

Equity per Share

In addition to being concerned about the liquidity and the profitability of a company, the owners and the managers are also very interested in the value of and return on investment in the company. Among the techniques used to determine the financial health of a company is equity per share. **Equity per share** refers to the amount that would be paid on each share of stock if the corporation liquidated without incurring any expenses, gains, or losses in selling its assets and paying its liabilities. The equity per share increases as a firm retains net income after taxes.

If a corporation has only one class of stock, equity per share is determined by dividing the total stockholders' equity by the number of shares outstanding. Here are the calculations for City Builders Supply.

$$1987 \qquad \frac{\$520,208}{3,000 \text{ shares}} = \$173.40 \text{ per share}$$

$$1986 \qquad \frac{\$466,884}{3,000 \text{ shares}} = \$155.63 \text{ per share}$$

Rate of Return on Common Stockholders' Equity

Many corporations exist to earn a net income for their stockholders. Therefore the rate of return on the common stockholders' equity is an important means of measuring how well the investment is doing. This rate can be determined by dividing the net income after income taxes by the average value of stockholders' equity. The calculation for City Builders Supply is shown below.

$$1987 \qquad \frac{\$68,838}{\dfrac{\$466,884 + \$520,208}{2}} = \frac{\$68,838}{\$493,546} = .1395 \times 100 = 13.95\%$$

$$1986 \qquad \frac{\$66,774}{\dfrac{\$422,100 + \$466,884}{2}} = \frac{\$66,774}{\$444,492} = .1502 \times 100 = 15.02\%$$

As you can see, the rate declined from 1986 to 1987. Management may want to uncover the possible causes.

Earnings per Share of Common Stock

Earnings per share of common stock is one of the most frequently reported financial measures. Earnings per share information is often used to judge the performance of a company. It can also be used to compare one company's performance with those of other companies. As a result, earnings per share is usually reported on the income statement, just below the net income amount. If a corporation has only one class of capital stock, earnings per share of common stock is computed by dividing net income after income taxes by the number of outstanding shares of common stock. If the company also has preferred stock, any dividends on preferred stock must first be deducted from net income after income taxes. If you recall, dividends on preferred stock are paid before those on common stock. Here are the calculations for City Builders Supply.

$$1987 \qquad \frac{\$68,838}{3,000 \text{ shares}} = \$22.95$$

$$1986 \qquad \frac{\$66,774}{3,000 \text{ shares}} - \$22.26$$

Any change during the year in the number of shares outstanding has an effect on the earnings per share. That's why a company must disclose any stock dividend or stock splits on its financial statements.

Price-earnings Ratio

A measure commonly used to determine whether the market price of a corporation's stock is reasonable is the **price-earnings ratio**. The price-earnings ratio of a company's stock is calculated by dividing the market price per share by the earnings per share. At the end of 1987, the market price of a share of common stock of City Builders Supply was $132; at the end of 1986, it was $120. The price-earnings ratio is calculated as follows.

$$1987 \qquad \frac{\$132.00}{\$22.95} = 5.8:1$$

$$1986 \qquad \frac{\$120.00}{\$22.26} = 5.4:1$$

The price-earnings ratio indicates how much investors are willing to pay for every $1.00 of a company's earnings per share. What is considered a "reasonable" price-earnings ratio varies from one industry to another. In some industries, a 15:1 price-earnings ratio is normal. In other industries, an acceptable ratio may be more than 30:1.

Summary of Key Points

1. Among the techniques used to analyze and interpret financial statements are horizontal analysis, vertical analysis, trend analysis, and ratio analysis.
2. Comparative financial statements are used to compare financial data over two or more years. These statements can be prepared using horizontal or vertical analysis.
3. Trend analysis indicates changes that become apparent only over a period of years.

4. Liquidity refers to a company's ability to meet its debts. Profitability refers to the earnings performance of a business.
5. Ratio analysis is a means of showing the relationship between two items on a financial statement.
6. Many ratios can be used to analyze and interpret financial data. Among these are the following: working capital, current ratio, quick ratio, merchandise inventory turnover, ratio of stockholders' equity to liabilities, ratio of property, plant, and equipment to long-term liabilities, equity per share, rate of return on common stockholders' equity, earnings per share of common stock, and price-earnings ratio.

Review and Applications

Building Your Accounting Vocabulary

In your own words, write the definition of each of the following accounting terms. Use complete sentences for your definitions.

base year	liquidity	quick ratio
common-size statements	merchandise inventory	ratio analysis
current ratio	turnover	trend analysis
equity per share	price-earnings ratio	vertical analysis
horizontal analysis	profitability	working capital

Reviewing Your Accounting Knowledge

1. Name the four techniques commonly used to analyze financial statement information.
2. What is the difference between horizontal analysis and vertical analysis?
3. How are the percentages of increase or decrease calculated on financial statements organized for horizontal analysis?
4. When an income statement is prepared for vertical analysis, to what amount are all other amounts compared? What amount is used as the base on a balance sheet prepared for vertical analysis?
5. Why are changes given in both dollar amounts and percentages on comparative financial statements?
6. A firm has a gross profit percentage of 34%. What does this mean?
7. Why would someone want to use trend analysis?
8. What is the difference between liquidity and profitability?
9. Of the ratios presented in this chapter, which measure a company's liquidity and which measure its profitability?
10. How does the quick ratio differ from the current ratio? How are they similar?
11. Why is a high merchandise inventory turnover considered to be a benefit to a firm?
12. What ratio can stockholders use to help determine how well their investment is doing?

Improving Your Decision-making Skills

The Hightower Corporation and Matheson's, Inc. are both department stores. During the past year, they reported net income after income taxes of $800,000 and $600,000 respectively. Does this mean that the Hightower Corporation is a more profitable company than Matheson's? What ratios or percentages would help you answer this question?

Applying Accounting Procedures

Problem 20–1

The following data appeared on the income statements of the Desmond Company over a four-year period.

Item	1983	1984	1985	1986
Sales (net)	$600,000	$660,000	$726,000	$774,000
Cost of Merchandise Sold	360,000	423,000	480,000	492,000
Merchandise Inventory	63,000	69,000	78,000	90,000

Instructions:

(1) Calculate trend percentages for the items listed, using 1983 as the base year.

(2) What do these percentages reveal about the Desmond Company?

Problem 20–2

The following data appeared on the balance sheet of the Stanley Company.

Cash in Bank	$144,000
Marketable securities	62,000
Accounts Receivable (net)	472,000
Merchandise Inventory	168,000
Prepaid expenses	6,000
Accounts Payable	240,000
Notes Payable	22,000
Salaries Payable	2,000

Instructions:

(1) Determine the company's working capital.
(2) Calculate the current ratio.
(3) Calculate the quick ratio.

Problem 20–3

The following data were taken from the income statement of the Morgan Company.

Merchandise Inventory, January 1	$ 49,000
Net Purchases	385,000
Merchandise Inventory, December 31	53,000

Instructions:

(1) Calculate the merchandise inventory turnover.
(2) Determine the number of days the merchandise was kept in stock.

Problem 20-4

The following data were taken from the financial statements of the Wright Corporation.

Current Assets	$227,700
Property, Plant, and Equipment (book)	137,550
Current Liabilities	35,250
Long-term Liabilities	120,000
Stockholders' Equity	210,000

Instructions:

(1) Calculate the current ratio.
(2) Determine the ratio of stockholders' equity to liabilities.
(3) Determine the ratio of property, plant, and equipment assets to long-term liabilities.

Problem 20-5

The Stockholders' Equity section of the balance sheet of the Barkley Corporation is shown below. In addition, net income after income tax for the year is $128,000. The present market price of the stock is $48 per share.

Paid-in Capital:		
Common Stock, $10 par (50,000 shares authorized, 40,000 shares issued)	$400,000	
Paid-in Capital in Excess of Par	120,000	
Total Paid-in Capital	$520,000	
Retained Earnings	280,000	
Total Stockholders' Equity		$800,000

Instructions:

(1) Calculate the equity per share.
(2) Calculate the earnings per share.
(3) Determine the price-earnings ratio.
(4) Calculate the rate of return on stockholders' equity.

Problem 20-6

During 1987 Robert's Shoe Store put on a big sales promotion campaign that cost $10,000 more that the store usually spent for advertising. A portion of the partial comparative income statement for the fiscal years ended December 31, 1986 and 1987 appears on the next page.

Instructions: Using horizontal analysis, prepare a comparative income statement for the two-year period. Round off percentages to two decimal places; for example, 33.33%. A form to complete this statement is provided in the working papers accompanying this textbook.

Robert's Shoe Store
Comparative Income Statement
For the Years Ended December 31, 1987 and 1986

	1987	1986
Revenue:		
Sales	$427,680	$324,000
Less: Sales Returns and Allowances	35,040	24,000
Net Sales	$392,640	$300,000
Cost of Merchandise Sold:		
Merchandise Inventory, Jan. 1	$ 28,682	$ 21,887
Net Purchases	225,362	178,428
Merchandise Available for Sale	$254,044	$200,315
Less: Merchandise Inventory, Dec. 31	31,024	23,315
Cost of Merchandise Sold	$223,020	$177,000
Gross Profit on Sales	$169,620	$123,000
Operating Expenses:		
Selling Expenses:		
Advertising Expense	$ 18,010	$ 7,855
Depr. Exp.—Store Equipment	3,450	3,450
Supplies Expense	9,730	7,970
Sales Salaries Expense	43,706	41,125
Total Selling Expenses	$ 74,896	$ 60,400
Administrative Expenses:		
Depr. Exp.—Store Equipment	$ 786	$ 786
Insurance Expense	282	243
Miscellaneous Expense	330	227
Office Salaries Expense	20,682	17,944
Total Administrative Expenses	$ 22,080	$ 19,200
Total Operating Expenses	$ 96,976	$ 79,600
Net Income from Operations	$ 72,644	$ 43,400
Other Expenses:		
Interest Expense	750	600
Net Income	$ 71,894	$ 42,800

Problem 20–7

The partial comparative balance sheet for the Lawrence Produce Corporation appears on page 497.

Instructions: Using vertical analysis, prepare a comparative balance sheet for the two-year period. Round off percentages to two decimal places. A form to complete this statement is provided in the working papers accompanying this textbook.

Lawrence Produce Corporation
Comparative Balance Sheet
December 31, 1987 and 1986

	1987	1986
Assets		
Current Assets:		
Cash in Bank	$ 18,000	$ 90,500
Accounts Receivable (net)	68,000	64,000
Merchandise Inventory	90,000	84,000
Prepaid Expenses	5,800	6,000
Total Current Assets	$181,800	$244,500
Investments	$ -0-	$ 80,000
Property, Plant, and Equipment:		
Equipment (book)	$ 21,400	$ 10,500
Building (book)	176,800	28,000
Land	50,000	20,000
Total Property, Plant, and Equipment	$248,200	$ 58,500
Total Assets	$430,000	$383,000
Liabilities		
Current Liabilities:		
Accounts Payable	$ 43,600	$ 55,000
Notes Payable	5,000	-0-
Sales Tax Payable	4,800	5,000
Salaries Payable	800	1,200
Total Current Liabilities	$ 54,200	$ 61,200
Long-term Liabilities:		
Mortgage Payable	$ 60,000	$ 10,000
Total Liabilities	$114,200	$ 71,200
Stockholders' Equity		
Capital Stock	$250,000	$250,000
Retained Earnings	65,800	61,800
Total Stockholders' Equity	$315,800	$311,800
Total Liabilities and Stockholders' Equity	$430,000	$383,000

21 Statement of Changes in Financial Position

Up to this time, you have prepared three financial statements at the end of a fiscal period. The income statement reports the results of a company's operations during a fiscal period. The statement of retained earnings reports the changes that have taken place in the Retained Earnings account during the period. The balance sheet reports the financial position of a business at the end of the fiscal period.

None of these reports, however, shows why and how the financial position of the business changed during the period. And they do not provide answers to questions such as these: Where did the profits go? What happened to the money received from the sale of stock? Did the company enter into any new financing or investing activities during the period? If so, where did the money for the activities come from?

In this chapter, you will learn about a fourth financial statement that is prepared at the end of a fiscal period. This report shows the changes that occurred in the company's financial position during the fiscal period.

Learning Objectives

When you have completed this chapter, you should be able to

1. Explain the purpose of a statement of changes in financial position.

2. Identify the types of transactions that cause changes in working capital.

3. Identify common sources and uses of working capital.

4. Prepare a schedule of changes in working capital.

5. Prepare a statement of changes in financial position.

6. Define the accounting terms presented in this chapter.

New Terms

statement of changes in financial position / source of working capital / use of working capital / schedule of changes in working capital

Financial Position

The financial position of a company can be measured in several ways. Some people evaluate a company's financial position in terms of the balance of its Cash in Bank account. Most transactions that a business enters into affect the Cash in Bank account either directly or indirectly.

Other people measure a company's financial position in terms of its working capital. As defined in Chapter 20, working capital is the amount by which current assets exceed current liabilities. If you remember, current assets represent cash or other items that can be converted into cash within one year. Current liabilities represent debts that must be paid within one year.

Working capital is a basic measure of a company's ability to pay its current debts. It indicates the funds a business has available—after paying those current debts—to buy more inventory, to obtain more credit, and to expand its operations. Working capital is closely related to the operating cycle of a business. Merchandise is purchased (for cash or on account), goods are sold (for cash or on account), cash is received on account, payments are made to accounts payables and for operating expenses, and more merchandise is purchased to renew the cycle. Current assets or current liabilities are involved in all these activities.

Management, creditors, and investors are all interested in the changes in a company's financial position during a fiscal period. They want to know where cash or working capital came from and how it was used. They want to know the reasons for an increase or decrease in cash or working capital.

For these reasons, most businesses prepare a fourth financial statement at the end of the fiscal period. This statement can be prepared on a cash basis or on a working capital basis. Since working capital generally provides a much broader picture of a company's operations, most companies prepare this fourth financial statement on the working capital basis.

Remember: Working capital is the amount by which current assets exceed current liabilities.

Statement of Changes in Financial Position

The financial statement that explains in detail how working capital has changed between the beginning and the end of the fiscal period is the **statement of changes in financial position**. The statement is also referred to as a statement of changes in working capital or a statement of sources and applications of funds. In this case, "funds" is interpreted broadly to mean working capital. A transaction affects working capital (either increases it or decreases it) if one part of the transaction involves a current asset or a current liability account and the other part of it does not.

Although the format for the statement of changes in financial position may vary, most businesses prepare a statement that contains three sections. The first section lists the sources of working capital. Any transaction that increases working capital is a **source of working capital**. Working capital is increased if current assets are increased or current liabilities are decreased. The second section lists the uses of working capital. Any transaction that decreases working capital is called a **use of working capital**. Working capital is decreased if current assets are decreased or if current liabilities are increased. The third section shows the increases or decreases to the current asset and current liability accounts during the fiscal period.

Remember: A transaction affects working capital if one part of the transaction affects a current asset or current liability account and the other part of the transaction does not affect a current asset or current liability account.

Sources of Working Capital

The four most common sources of working capital include: investments by owners, net income, the sale of noncurrent assets, and increases in long-term liabilities.

Remember: Working capital is increased if current assets are increased or if current liabilities are decreased.

Investments by Owners

The sale of stock by a corporation brings working capital into the business in the form of cash, a current asset. Likewise, an investment of cash or other current assets by the owner of a sole proprietorship or by partners increases a business's working capital. In these transactions, Cash in Bank (or another current asset) would be debited and an ownership equity account (either Capital Stock or the owner's capital account) would be credited.

Net Income

A net income occurs when total revenues are greater than the cost of merchandise sold and total expenses. Net income is actually a summary of many transactions—most but not all of which affect working capital.

Revenues generally result in an increase to working capital because they reflect increases to current assets. For example, when merchandise is sold on account, Accounts Receivable (a current asset) is increased and Sales (a revenue account) is increased.

Cost of merchandise sold and expenses usually decrease working capital because they either decrease current assets or increase current liabilities. For example, when the utilities bill is paid, Cash in Bank (a current asset) is decreased and Utilities Expense (an expense account) is increased.

A net income, therefore, represents a source of working capital because the total increases to working capital are greater than the total decreases to working capital. It may be helpful to remember that the revenue, cost of merchandise, and expense accounts are temporary ownership equity accounts that ultimately affect either Retained Earnings or the owner's capital account. A net income then increases working capital and increases ownership equity.

One example of a transaction that affects net income but not working capital is the recording of depreciation. When the adjusting entry for depreciation is recorded, Depreciation Expense (an expense account) is increased and Accumulated Depreciation (a contra property, plant, and equipment account) is increased. No current asset or current liability account is affected. Net income, however, has been decreased by the amount of the depreciation expense. The net income amount must be adjusted for any included transactions that do not affect working capital. Therefore, the amount of the annual depreciation is added back to the amount of the net income.

It may be confusing to think of depreciation as a source of working capital. Keep in mind though that its real reason for appearing in the statement of changes is to adjust net income. Listing it as a source of working capital is simply one of several ways the adjustment could be shown.

Other transactions that result in an adjustment to net income are the amortization of a bond discount or premium and the amortization of a corporation's organization costs.

Remember: **Depreciation is listed in the Sources of Working Capital section of the statement of changes in financial position as an adjustment to the net income amount.**

Sale of Noncurrent Assets

Noncurrent assets include such things as land, buildings, equipment, vehicles, and long-term investments. Working capital is increased when a noncurrent asset is sold since Cash in Bank is increased and a noncurrent asset account, such as Office Equipment, is decreased. The sale of a noncurrent asset, therefore, is always a source of working capital.

Increases in Long-term Liabilities

When a corporation receives cash by issuing bonds or long-term promissory notes, working capital is increased. In such a transaction, Cash in Bank is increased and a long-term liability account—such as Bonds Payable—is increased. Any increase to a long-term liability account, then, is a source of working capital.

Short-term borrowing, on the other hand, does not affect working capital. For example, if a company issues a promissory note, Cash in Bank is increased and Notes Payable is increased. The increase in the current asset is offset by the increase in the current liability.

The four most common uses of working capital are: withdrawals by owners, net loss, the purchase of noncurrent assets, and decreases in long-term liabilities.

Remember: Working capital is decreased if current assets are decreased or if current liabilities are increased.

Withdrawals by Owners

A withdrawal by an owner of a sole proprietorship or partnership is recorded as a debit to the Withdrawals account and a credit to Cash in Bank. This transaction results in a decrease in working capital, because a current asset is decreased.

In the case of a corporation, a withdrawal occurs when a cash dividend is declared. In this transaction, Retained Earnings (a stockholders' equity account) is decreased and Dividends Payable (a current liability) is increased. A cash dividend, therefore, represents a use of working capital. (The payment of the cash dividend does not affect working capital since the decrease to Cash in Bank, a current asset, is offset by the decrease to Dividends Payable, a current liability.)

Net Loss

A net loss occurs when total revenues are less than the cost of merchandise sold and total expenses. A net loss, therefore, represents a use of working capital because the total increases to working capital are less than the total decreases to working capital.

A net loss must still be adjusted for those transactions that do not affect working capital. Any transactions concerning depreciation, amortization of a bond discount or premium, or organization costs must be subtracted from the net loss amount.

Purchase of Noncurrent Assets

When a noncurrent asset such as equipment is purchased, the transaction is recorded as a debit to Equipment and a credit to Cash in Bank. This transaction results in a decrease in working capital, because a current asset is decreased without a corresponding change in a current liability. If a company purchases the equipment on account, the transaction is recorded as a debit to Equipment and a credit to Accounts Payable. This also is a decrease in working capital, because a current liability is increased without a corresponding increase in a current asset.

Decreases in Long-term Liabilities

When long-term liabilities (such as Bonds Payable) are paid, Cash in Bank (and thus working capital) is decreased. The amount of the working capital used to decrease the long-term liability is, therefore, a use of working capital.

The payment of short-term liabilities (such as Notes Payable) does not affect working capital. The decrease to Cash in Bank is offset by the decrease to the current liability account.

The third section of the statement of changes in financial position lists the increases and decreases to all current asset and current liability accounts and the net increase or decrease in working capital.

Before reading further, do the following activity to check your understanding of working capital.

Check Your Learning

What is the amount of the increase or decrease in working capital of each of the following transactions, considered individually?

1. Bought equipment on account, $600.
2. Issued 1,000 shares of common stock for $12 per share ($10 par), receiving cash.
3. Issued a $4,000, 60-day note to a creditor in settlement of the amount recorded as an account payable.
4. Received $5,000 on account from charge customers.
5. Sold merchandise on account, $900 (cost $600).

Check your answers with those in the answers section. Re-read the preceding part of the chapter to find the correct answers to any questions you may have missed.

Preparing a Statement of Changes in Financial Position

Now let's look at the statement of changes in financial position prepared by the Sanders Corporation. The statement of changes in financial position, remember, explains in detail the changes that have occurred in the company's working capital accounts (current assets and current liabilities) during the fiscal period. Information for the statement is taken from the income statement, the statement of retained earnings, and the comparative balance sheet. The condensed financial statements for the Sanders Corporation are shown in Figure 21–1, Figure 21–2, and Figure 21–3 on pages 504–505.

To prepare a statement of changes in financial position, follow the steps listed below:

1. Determine the change in working capital for the fiscal period.
2. Determine the change (increase or decrease) that has occurred in each working capital account during the fiscal period. Then determine the effect (increase or decrease) each change has on working capital.
3. Determine the sources and uses of working capital for the fiscal period.
4. Complete the Changes in Components of Working Capital section of the statement.

Sanders Corporation
Income Statement
For the Year Ended December 31, 1987

Revenue:		
Sales (net)		900 000 00
Cost of Merchandise Sold:		
Merchandise Inventory, Jan. 1, 1987	128 000 00	
Purchases (net)	698 000 00	
Merchandise Available for Sale	826 000 00	
Less: Merchandise Inventory, Dec. 31, 1987	126 000 00	
Cost of Merchandise Sold		700 000 00
Gross Profit on Sales		200 000 00
Operating Expenses:		
Bad Debts Expense	3 000 00	
Depreciation Expense — Building	8 000 00	
Depreciation Expense — Equipment	5 200 00	
Miscellaneous Expense	4 000 00	
Salaries Expense	103 200 00	
Supplies Expense	2 000 00	
Total Operating Expenses		125 400 00
Net Income from Operations		74 600 00
Other Expenses:		
Interest Expense		15 000 00
Net Income before Income Taxes		59 600 00
Income Taxes		11 130 00
Net Income after Income Taxes		48 470 00

Figure 21–1. Income Statement for the Sanders Corporation

Sanders Corporation
Statement of Retained Earnings
For the Year Ended December 31, 1987

Retained Earnings, January 1, 1987		50 400 00
Net Income after Income Taxes	48 470 00	
Less: Cash Dividends	36 270 00	
Increase in Retained Earnings		12 200 00
Retained Earnings, December 31, 1987		62 600 00

Figure 21–2. Statement of Retained Earnings for the Sanders Corporation

Sanders Corporation
Comparative Balance Sheet
December 31, 1987 and 1986

	1987	1986
Assets		
Current Assets:		
Cash in Bank	3 1 3 8 0 00	2 0 2 8 0 00
Accounts Receivable (net)	3 0 9 0 0 00	3 6 8 0 0 00
Merchandise Inventory	1 2 6 0 0 0 00	1 2 8 0 0 0 00
Supplies	4 0 0 0 00	4 8 0 0 00
Total Current Assets	1 9 2 2 8 0 00	1 8 9 8 8 0 00
Property, Plant, and Equipment:		
Equipment	1 1 6 8 0 0 00	1 0 0 0 0 0 00
Less: Accumulated Depreciation	2 4 4 0 0 00	1 9 2 0 0 00
Building	3 2 0 0 0 0 00	3 2 0 0 0 0 00
Less: Accumulated Depreciation	2 4 0 0 0 00	1 6 0 0 0 00
Land	8 0 0 0 0 00	8 0 0 0 0 00
Total Property, Plant, and Equipment	4 6 8 4 0 0 00	4 6 4 8 0 0 00
Total Assets	6 6 0 6 8 0 00	6 5 4 6 8 0 00
Liabilities		
Current Liabilities:		
Accounts Payable	6 6 8 0 0 00	7 8 4 0 0 00
Salaries Payable	9 0 0 00	8 0 0 00
Notes Payable	9 0 0 0 00	8 0 0 0 00
Corporate Income Tax Payable	1 3 8 0 00	1 0 8 0 00
Total Current Liabilities	7 8 0 8 0 00	8 8 2 8 0 00
Long-term Liabilities:		
Bonds Payable	2 0 0 0 0 0 00	2 1 6 0 0 0 00
Total Liabilities	2 7 8 0 8 0 00	3 0 4 2 8 0 00
Stockholders' Equity		
Common Stock, $100 par (4,000 shares		
authorized, 3,200 shares issued)	3 2 0 0 0 0 00	3 0 0 0 0 0 00
Retained Earnings	6 2 6 0 0 00	5 0 4 0 0 00
Total Stockholders' Equity	3 8 2 6 0 0 00	3 5 0 4 0 0 00
Total Liabilities and Stockholders' Equity	6 6 0 6 8 0 00	6 5 4 6 8 0 00

Figure 21–3. Comparative Balance Sheet for the Sanders Corporation

Determining the Change in Working Capital

The first step is to determine the amount of working capital at the beginning of the fiscal period and at the end of the fiscal period. (The beginning working capital for the period is the ending working capital for the previous period.) The amounts are taken from the comparative balance sheet. To determine the amount of the working capital, subtract the total current liabilities amount from the total current assets amount as shown on the next page.

	1987	1986
Current assets	$192,280	$189,880
Current liabilities	− 78,080	− 88,280
Working capital	$114,200	$101,600

During the fiscal period, working capital increased by $12,600 ($114,200 − $101,600).

Determining the Changes in Working Capital Accounts

The second step in preparing a statement of changes in financial position is to prepare a schedule of the increase or decrease in each working capital account for the fiscal period. This document is called a schedule of changes in working capital

Using the data on the comparative balance sheet, the beginning and ending balances of each current asset and current liability account are listed. Next, the amount of the increase or decrease in each account is calculated. Then, the effect of the change on working capital (increase or decrease) is determined for each account. Remember, working capital is *increased* if a current asset account is increased or a current liability account is decreased. Working capital is *decreased* if a current asset account is decreased or a current liability account is increased. Finally, the increases and decreases to working capital are totaled to determine the change in working capital. The following table shows the current asset and current liability accounts of the Sanders Corporation.

	1987	1986	Increase (Decrease) in the Account	Increase (Decrease) in Working Capital
Increase (decrease) in current assets:				
Cash in Bank	$ 31,380	$ 20,280	$11,100	$11,100
Accounts Receivable (net)	30,900	36,800	(5,900)	(5,900)
Merchandise Inventory	126,000	128,000	(2,000)	(2,000)
Supplies	4,000	4,800	(800)	(800)
Increase (decrease) in current liabilities:				
Accounts Payable	66,800	78,400	(11,600)	11,600
Notes Payable	9,000	8,000	1,000	(1,000)
Corporate Income Tax Payable	1,380	1,080	300	(300)
Salaries Payable	900	800	100	(100)
Increase in working capital				$12,600

The increase in working capital is the same as determined in Step 1.

This schedule will be used later to complete the Changes in Components of Working Capital section of the statement of changes in financial position.

Before reading further, do the following activity to check your understanding of how to calculate changes in working capital.

Determining the Sources and Uses of Working Capital

Earlier we listed the various sources and uses of working capital. Some of these items appear regularly on the statement of changes in financial position. For example, net income is a regular item that is listed as a source of working capital; conversely, a net loss is a use of working capital. Depreciation expense is always listed as a source of working capital. Finally, cash dividends or withdrawals are always listed as uses of working capital.

Other items, such as an additional investment, a purchase of equipment, or a payment of the principal of a mortgage, occur less often. The clues to detecting these transactions are found in the changes in the balances of the *noncurrent* accounts (property, plant, and equipment; investments; long-term liabilities; and stockholders' equity). The noncurrent accounts are examined for two reasons: (1) fewer transactions affect these accounts, and (2) almost every transaction to a noncurrent account either increases or decreases working capital.

Next, the specific accounts in the ledger are examined. The transaction is traced back to the journal to determine two things: why the transaction took place and its effect upon working capital. In the case of the Sanders Corporation, the following changes took place in the noncurrent accounts.

1. Equipment increased from $100,000 to $116,800. The original entry was a debit to Equipment and a credit to Accounts Payable. This transaction resulted in a decrease in working capital.
2. Accumulated Depreciation—Equipment increased from $19,200 to $24,400. The adjusting entry reveals that Depreciation Expense—Equipment was debited and Accumulated Depreciation—Equipment was credited. This transaction resulted in an adjustment to net income.
3. Accumulated Depreciation—Building increased from $16,000 to $24,000. The adjusting entry reveals that Depreciation Expense—Building was debited and Accumulated Depreciation—Building was credited. This transaction resulted in an adjustment to net income.

4. Bonds Payable decreased from $216,000 to $200,000. The original entry was a debit to Bonds Payable and a credit to Cash in Bank. This transaction resulted in a decrease in working capital.
5. Common Stock increased from $300,000 to $320,000. The original entry was a debit to Cash in Bank and a credit to Common Stock. This transaction resulted in an increase in working capital.
6. Retained Earnings increased from $50,400 to $62,600. By examining the Retained Earnings account, it was determined that the net income was added to the account and dividends were deducted from the account. These transactions resulted in both an increase and a decrease in working capital.

Of these items, the following are sources of working capital:

1. Net income after income taxes of $48,470
2. Depreciation expense for the building of $8,000 and depreciation expense on equipment of $5,200
3. Sale of common stock in the amount of $20,000

The following items are uses of working capital:

1. The purchase of $16,800 worth of equipment
2. The repayment of $16,000 worth of bonds
3. The declaration of a cash dividend in the amount of $36,270

With this information, the first two sections of the statement of changes in financial position can be prepared. Look at Figure 21–4. The first section lists

Sanders Corporation Statement of Changes in Financial Position For the Year Ended December 31, 19--				
Sources of Working Capital:				
Operations:				
Net income		48470 00		
Add exp. not req. decr. in work. cap.:				
Deprec. Exp.–Bldg.	8000 00			
Deprec. Exp.–Equip.	5200 00	13200 00		
Work Capital from Operations			61670 00	
Other Sources:				
Sale of common stock			20000 00	
Total Sources of Working Capital			81670 00	
Uses of Working Capital:				
Purchase of equipment		16800 00		
Decrease in bonds payable		16000 00		
Cash dividend		36270 00		
Total Uses of Working Capital			69070 00	
Increase in Working Capital			12600 00	

Figure 21–4. Sources and Uses Section of the Statement of Changes in Financial Position

the sources of working capital. The two depreciation expenses are described as "expenses not requiring decreases in working capital." After the total increase to working capital is determined, the top portion is double ruled.

Remember: Any transaction that increases working capital is a source of working capital. Any transaction that decreases working capital is a use of working capital.

Completing the Statement of Changes in Financial Position

The bottom portion of the statement lists the changes to the various working capital accounts. The schedule of changes in working capital prepared earlier is used to complete this section. Look at Figure 21–5. As you can see, the current

Sanders Corporation Statement of Changes in Financial Position For the Year Ended December 31, 19--				
Sources of Working Capital:				
Operations:				
Net income			48 470 00	
Add exp. not req. decr. in work cap:				
Deprec. Exp. – Bldg.	8 000 00			
Deprec. Exp. – Equip.	5 200 00		13 200 00	
Work. Capital from Operations				61 670 00
Other Sources:				
Sale of common stock				20 000 00
Total Sources of Working Capital				81 670 00
Uses of Working Capital:				
Purchase of equipment			16 800 00	
Decrease in bonds payable			16 000 00	
Cash dividend			36 270 00	
Total Uses of Working Capital				69 070 00
Increase in Working Capital				12 600 00
Changes in Components of Work. Capital:				
Increases (decr.) in Current Assets:				
Cash in Bank			11 100 00	
Accounts Receivable (net)			(5 900 00)	
Merchandise Inventory			(2 000 00)	
Supplies			(800 00)	2 400 00
Decreases (incr.) in Current Liabilities:				
Accounts Payable			11 600 00	
Corporate Income Tax Pay.			(300 00)	
Notes Payable			(1 000 00)	
Salaries Payable			(100 00)	10 200 00
Increase in Working Capital				12 600 00

Figure 21–5. Completed Statement of Changes in Financial Position

assets and the amount of change for each current asset account are listed first. Decreases are shown enclosed in parentheses. Current liabilities are listed next. The total increase in working capital on the bottom portion of the statement must match the amount determined in the top portion of the statement.

Remember: **In accounting, parentheses are used to indicate decreases or negative amounts.**

Reporting Financing and Investing Activities

The Accounting Principles Board of the American Institute of Certified Public Accountants has stated that the statement of changes in financial position should list all important financing and investing transactions—even if current assets or current liabilities are not involved. For example, suppose a company bought a building and issued a mortgage. The entry to record the transaction would debit Building (property, plant, and equipment) and credit Mortgage Payable (long-term liability). Or, suppose a company received land and issued common stock. That entry would be a debit to Land (property, plant, and equipment) and a credit to Common Stock (stockholders' equity). Neither of these transactions affects a current asset or current liability account. Neither of these transactions, therefore, affects working capital.

However, according to the AICPA opinion, both transactions should be reported on the statement of changes in financial position. The issuances of the mortgage and common stock would be listed as sources of working capital. The acquisition of the building and land would be listed as uses of working capital. In these cases, the sources cancel out the uses; there is no change in the amount of working capital.

Summary of Key Points

1. A change in financial position is a change in the amount of working capital between the beginning and the end of a fiscal period.
2. An increase in current assets or a decrease in current liabilities increases working capital. A decrease in current assets or an increase in current liabilities decreases working capital.
3. Sources of working capital include net income, depreciation, owners' investments, long-term borrowing, and the sale of noncurrent assets.
4. Uses of working capital include net loss, purchase of noncurrent assets, payment of long-term debt, and withdrawals or declarations of dividends.

Review and Applications

Building Your Accounting Vocabulary

In your own words, write the definition of each of the following accounting terms. Use complete sentences for your definitions.

schedule of changes
in working capital
source of working
capital

statement of changes
in financial position
use of working capital

Reviewing Your Accounting Knowledge

1. What is working capital? Why is it important?
2. What information is contained in a statement of changes in financial position that is not readily apparent in the other financial statements?
3. What are the principal sources of working capital?
4. What are the principal uses of working capital?
5. Why is depreciation expense considered to be a source of working capital?
6. Why does an increase in a current liability result in a decrease in working capital?
7. Give three examples of noncurrent assets.
8. Equipment costing $14,000, having accumulated depreciation of $14,000, is discarded. A junk dealer agreed to remove and dispose of the equipment in exchange for any salvage rights. How does this transaction affect working capital?
9. What are the sources of information used in preparing a statement of changes in financial position?
10. Why are the noncurrent accounts examined to discover changes in working capital?

Improving Your Decision-making Skills

For the current year, a company reported a net loss of $11,000 on its income statement and an increase of $5,000 in working capital on its statement of changes in financial position. Explain the apparent contradiction between the net loss and the increase in working capital.

Applying Accounting Procedures

Problem 21–1

Listed at the top of the next page are the current asset and current liability amounts for several different businesses.

| | Current Year | | Previous Year | |
	Current Assets	Current Liabilities	Current Assets	Current Liabilities
Stanwood Company	$ 93,146	$ 14,081	$ 89,496	$ 16,936
Jensen, Inc.	106,591	31,107	110,946	42,155
Graham & Sons	156,000	112,400	124,800	89,600
Center City Products	73,000	27,000	77,000	26,000
Davis, Inc.	181,800	54,200	244,500	61,200

Instructions: Use a form similar to the one that follows.

(1) Determine the working capital amount for the current year and the previous year for each of the five companies.

(2) Determine the increase or decrease in working capital for each company.

Company	Working Capital, Current Year	Working Capital, Previous Year	Increase (Decrease) in Working Capital
Stanwood Company	$79,065	$72,560	$6,505

Problem 21–2

The following are some of the transactions completed by the Sellers Company during the fiscal period.

(1) Declared a dividend of $.25 per share on 10,000 shares outstanding.
(2) Collected $87,000 in accounts receivable during the period.
(3) Purchased store equipment for $5,000 cash.
(4) Issued a $5,000, 30-day, 9% note payable to a creditor as settlement for an account payable.
(5) Depreciation expense for the year totaled $12,000.
(6) Issued 5,000 shares of $25-par common stock for cash.
(7) Purchased land for $25,000, paying $10,000 cash and issuing a mortgage for the balance.
(8) Issued $100,000 in 8%, 5-year bonds at 103, receiving cash.
(9) Net income for the period after income taxes was $24,900.
(10) Salaries expenses for the period were $49,000.

Instructions: Use a form similar to the one that follows. For each transaction, indicate whether the transaction increases, decreases, or has no effect on working capital. Place a check mark in the appropriate column.

Transaction Number	Effect on Working Capital		
	Increase	Decrease	No Effect
1		✓	

Problem 21-3

At the end of the current fiscal period, Florida Sea Tours examined its accounting records. The following changes took place in the noncurrent accounts of the business during the year.

(1) The company reported a net income after income taxes of $300,000 for the year.
(2) Reduced the mortgage principal by $100,000.
(3) Received $60,000 cash for bonds issued at face value.
(4) Bought deck chairs (Equipment) on account for $30,000.
(5) Depreciation expense for the year was as follows: Excursion boats, $100,000; equipment, $20,000.
(6) Cash dividends declared and paid totaled $50,000.

Instructions: Prepare the sources and uses of working capital section of a statement of changes in financial position. Florida Sea Tours' fiscal period ends on December 31.

Problem 21-4

The following data appeared on the comparative balance sheet of the Lantern Shop for the fiscal years ended December 31, 1987 and 1986.

	1987	1986
Cash in Bank	$12,000	$10,000
Accounts Receivable (net)	30,000	25,000
Notes Receivable	3,000	5,000
Merchandise Inventory	50,000	55,000
Prepaid Insurance	1,000	2,000
Accounts Payable	20,000	18,000
Notes Payable	8,000	10,000
Corporate Inc. Tax Payable	5,000	4,000
Salaries Payable	1,000	2,000

Instructions: Prepare a schedule of changes in working capital for the fiscal period. Use the form provided in the working papers that accompany this textbook.

Problem 21-5

The comparative balance sheet for the Matthews Company for the fiscal years ended June 30, 1987 and 1986, appears on the following page in condensed form.

Additional data for the current year concerning the company's operations and transactions in the noncurrent general ledger accounts are also reported on the following page.

(a) Net income was $46,100.
(b) Depreciation expense for the year was $5,500.
(c) Additional equipment was purchased for $25,600 cash in May.
(d) The company paid the $16,000 mortgage.
(e) Cash withdrawals by Matthews during the year were $19,000.

Assets	1987	1986
Cash in Bank	$ 22,000	$ 24,600
Accounts Receivable (net)	32,100	30,900
Merchandise Inventory	83,400	86,200
Supplies	2,700	3,100
Equipment	98,000	72,400
Accumulated Depreciation—Equipment	(42,000)	(36,500)
Total Assets	$196,200	$180,700
Liabilities and Owner's Equity		
Accounts Payable	47,300	38,900
Notes Payable		4,000
Mortgage Payable		16,000
D. R. Matthews, Capital	148,900	121,800
Total Liabilities and Owner's Equity	$196,200	$180,700

Instructions: Prepare a statement of changes in financial position for the Matthews Company for the year ended June 30, 1987.

Problem 21–6

The comparative balance sheet of the Bagwell Corporation for the years ended December 31, 1987 and 1986, appears on the following page in condensed form.

Additional data for this year concerning operations and transactions in the noncurrent accounts in the ledger are as follows.

(a) Net income after income taxes was $44,700.
(b) Depreciation of equipment and building for the year was $14,000 and $4,000, respectively.
(c) A cash dividend of $27,000 was declared and paid during the year.
(d) An addition to the building was constructed at a cost of $10,000, paid in cash.
(e) One hundred shares of preferred 8% stock were repurchased and canceled at a cost of $105 per share.

Instructions:

(1) Prepare a schedule of changes in working capital for the fiscal period ended December 31, 1987.
(2) Prepare the statement of changes in financial position for the fiscal period ended December 31, 1987.

Assets	1987	1986
Cash in Bank	$ 36,000	$ 44,000
Notes Receivable	3,000	4,000
Accounts Receivable (net)	60,000	55,400
Merchandise Inventory	140,000	126,000
Supplies	600	500
Equipment	69,000	69,000
Accumulated Depreciation—Equipment	(42,000)	(28,000)
Building	(100,000)	(90,000)
Accumulated Depreciation—Building	36,000	32,000
Land	30,000	30,000
Total Assets	$360,600	$358,900

Liabilities and Stockholders' Equity		
Accounts Payable	$ 41,000	$ 47,000
Corporate Income Tax Payable	4,000	3,100
Salaries Payable	2,000	2,400
Preferred 8% Stock, $100 par	80,000	90,000
Common Stock, $100 par	160,000	160,000
Paid-in Capital in Excess of Par	6,400	6,400
Retained Earnings	67,200	50,000
Total Liabilities and Stockholders' Equity	$360,600	$358,900

Unit 6
Accounting for Not-for-profit Organizations

The preceding chapters in this textbook have been devoted to the procedures used by entities that are organized to earn a profit for their owners. However, not all organizations are profit oriented. Some are established to provide services to their members or the general public. These nonprofit organizations must also maintain accounting records and prepare reports on the results of their activities. In this unit, you will learn about the procedures these nonprofit organizations use to plan for, control, and report on their operations.

The chapters you will study in this unit are listed below.

Examining printed currency, U.S. Treasury, Washington, D.C.

22 Budgeting and Control in Not-for-profit Organizations

In earlier chapters, you learned to classify, record, and report accounting information for businesses organized to earn a profit. In this unit, you will learn about a different type of accounting system—one used by not-for-profit organizations. Not-for-profit organizations include governmental agencies and organizations such as civic groups, professional associations, and social clubs. Unlike business organizations that are organized to earn a profit for their owners, the typical not-for-profit organization is organized to provide services.

In this chapter, you will look at the accounting system used by not-for-profit organizations. You will also learn about one tool used by not-for-profit organizations to plan for and manage their funds.

Learning Objectives

When you have completed this chapter, you should be able to

1. Explain the difference between a not-for-profit organization and a profit-oriented business.

2. List the five principles of budgeting.

3. Name two methods that can be used to develop the revenue and expenditure projections for a budget.

4. Explain how a budget summary report can be used to control an organization's funds.

5. Prepare a budget summary report.

6. Define the accounting terms presented in this chapter.

New Terms

not-for-profit organization / fund / fund accounting / budget / budget period / revenue projection / expenditure projections / zero-base budgeting / budget summary report / free balance / budget adjustment

Characteristics of Not-for-profit Organizations

Every business needs money to start and maintain operations. To start a business, the owner or owners must have a sufficient amount of capital. To stay in operation, a business must earn a profit. The success of a business is usually measured by the amount of profit that it earns.

Not all organizations are profit-oriented, however. Some organizations have other goals. For example, an organization's primary goal may be to provide services to its members or to the general public. Examples of service-oriented organizations include civic groups, schools, libraries, museums, professional associations, and public broadcasting stations. An organization with goals other than earning a profit for its organizers is called a **not-for-profit organization**.

It takes money to start and maintain the operations of a not-for-profit organization, just as it does in a for-profit business. Its success is measured differently, though. Its success is measured not by the profits the organization makes but by the services it provides and how well those services are received by the public.

Fund Accounting

The word *fund* has several meanings in accounting. A change fund is an amount of money used for making change in cash transactions. A petty cash fund is an amount of money set aside for making small, incidental cash payments. A bond sinking fund consists of the cash and other securities set aside to pay off a bond issue when it comes due. *Fund* can also be used to refer to a corporation's working capital. In not-for-profit organizations, *fund* has another meaning.

In accounting for not-for-profit organizations, a **fund** is a set of accounts (asset, liability, equity, revenue, and expense) used to record the transactions for a particular activity. A not-for-profit organization usually has a number of funds. For example, a university may have several scholarship funds, an investment fund, and a building fund. A university, and other not-for-profit organizations, also has a general fund. The general fund is used to account for all other, nonspecific activities. **Fund accounting**, then, is the accounting system used by not-for-profit organizations to account for the transactions of their various funds.

Basic Principles of Budgeting

To be successful and meet its goals, a not-for-profit organization must carefully plan for and manage its funds. Goals must be set, objectives established, and the purposes of the organization clearly defined. Part of the planning process includes preparing a budget.

A **budget** is a formal written statement of expected revenue and expenditures for a future period of time, called the **budget period**. A budget period is usually twelve months. A budget is one of the most important financial tools a not-for-profit organization can use. First, it forces the managers or directors of the organization to look at the goals of the organization. Second, it requires the cooperation of everyone in the organization to work toward and carry out those goals. Finally, by comparing the budget with the actual results, the organization can evaluate its performance and, if necessary, revise its goals.

There are five basic principles involved in the budgeting process.

1. Develop long-term goals.
2. Develop short-term goals.
3. Define budgeting responsibilities.
4. Establish budgeting guidelines.
5. Establish follow-up procedures.

To see how the budgeting process works, we will look at the operations of the Carson Recreation Center. The Carson Recreation Center is a community center that provides facilities and activities for the general public. These activities include swimming, golf, softball, baseball, basketball, tennis, exercise programs, and crafts.

Develop Long-term Goals

Long-term goals are those goals that the organization wishes to accomplish over a long period of time, such as five or ten years. An organization's long-term goals are like roadmaps. They point out the general directions that the organization can take. For example, a long-term goal for the Carson Recreation Center might be to build a swimming pool in five years. To meet this goal, the organization must develop plans to raise the money needed, to estimate expenditures, and to hire personnel. An organization's long-term goals are used to develop its short-term goals.

Develop Short-term Goals

If an organization's long-term goals are like roadmaps, its short-term goals are like street signs. They are the specific ''routes'' an organization can take to meet its long-term goals. Short-term goals are goals that the organization wishes to accomplish within a short period of time, usually one year. For example, one of the Carson Recreation Center's short-term goals may be to raise $5,000 from a raffle. All of an organization's short-term goals are used to prepare its annual budget.

Define Budgeting Responsibilities

Developing the budget for an organization such as the Carson Recreation Center requires the cooperation of a number of people. Each person involved in the budgeting process must know what her or his responsibility is. For example, the director of the Center's summer softball program must estimate the program's revenue and expenditure needs. The director may, in turn, ask the summer league manager to estimate the program's revenue from entry fees or a fund-raising project.

Establish Budgeting Guidelines

No task can be accomplished without certain guidelines. In the budgeting process, it is important to set up methods for sharing information and to establish realistic deadlines for reporting budgeting data. Preparing a budget requires detailed planning, organization, and the cooperation of many people. As a result, the Carson Recreation Center begins its budgeting process in January, six months before the beginning of its fiscal year on July 1.

Establish Follow-up Procedures

Follow-up is very important in budgeting. Once the budget has been prepared and approved, it should be compared periodically with the actual revenue and expenditures for the period. For example, the actual revenue received and the expenditures made for one quarter (three months) should be compared with the estimates for the same period. Adjustments may need to be made if revenue is lower or expenditures higher than expected.

Before reading further, do the following activity to check your understanding of the material you have just studied.

Check Your Learning

Write your answers to the following questions on a sheet of notebook paper.

1. An organization whose primary goal is to provide services to its members or the general public is called a(n) __?__.
2. A(n) __?__ is a set of accounts used to record the transactions of a particular activity of a not-for-profit organization.
3. One of the most important tools used by a not-for-profit organization is the __?__, a formal written statement of the expected revenue and expenditures for a future period.
4. __?__ goals are those goals that an organization hopes to accomplish within one year or less.

Compare your answers to those in the answers section. Re-read the preceding part of the chapter to find the correct answers to any questions you may have missed.

Preparing a Budget

A not-for-profit organization uses its budget to maintain control over its funds and their uses. The budget is a one-year plan for the organization. It sets forth the specific short-term goals, the sources of revenue, and the uses of that revenue. In a not-for-profit organization, once funds have been set aside or budgeted for a specific purpose, those funds cannot be used for any other purpose.

The budget for the Carson Recreation Center is actually composed of the budgets for all the individual programs offered by the Center. To see how a budget is developed, let's look at the budget prepared for the summer softball program. (The complete budget for the program appears in Figure 22–1.)

Two important estimates must be made during the budget preparation period: revenue and expenditures. Let's look first at how the director of the summer softball program estimates the revenue to be received.

Revenue Projections

Estimates of the funds to be received during a budget period are called **revenue projections**. One common method of making revenue projections is to base those projections on the previous year's budgeted and actual revenue amounts.

For example, the previous year's budgeted and actual revenue amounts for the Carson Recreation Center's summer softball program are as follows. The difference between the budgeted and actual amounts for each revenue source is also listed.

Revenue	Previous Year's Budget	Previous Year's Actual	Over (Under) Budget
Entry Fees—Teams	$ 2,000	$ 2,000	$ -0-
Entry Fees—Tournaments	1,000	468	(532)
Fund-raising Projects	5,000	4,924	(76)
Gifts	2,000	2,420	420
General Fund Contributions	2,000	1,845	(155)
Totals	$12,000	$11,657	$(343)

The revenue actually received last year from team entry fees was $2,000, the same amount as had been budgeted. The program, however, received only $468 from tournament entry fees, $532 less than had been estimated. This decrease was a result of cancelling two tournaments because of rain. The program received $4,924 from its fund-raising projects, $76 less than expected. However, the program received $420 more than expected from gifts (donations). Finally, the program received $1,845 from the general fund, $155 less than budgeted. (Money is contributed to each program by the Center's general fund. The amount contributed is the difference between the program's expenditures and the program's revenue from other sources.)

The total actual revenue received was $343 less than the budgeted amount. As a percentage of the total revenue, the $343 is a small amount. Therefore, the program director can assume that the softball revenue projections for the previous year were realistic. If there are no major changes planned for the program for the coming year, the program director could use the previous year's revenue projections for the coming year's budget.

If the program for the coming year is going to be expanded or changed in some way—or if there is reason to believe that enrollment will change—it may be necessary to adjust the revenue projections. In this case, revenue projections should be based on the previous year's actual amounts. The revenue projections should be increased or decreased by the amount of the expected change.

Let's look at the revenue projections, shown below, developed by the director of the summer softball program. During the previous year, 50 teams participated in the program. Since the entry fee was $40 per team, the summer softball program actually received $2,000 in entry fees. During the coming year, the Center plans to increase the entry fee to $45. As a result, the revenue projection for team entry fees is $2,250 ($45 × 50 = $2,250). This projection is $250 over the previous year's actual revenue amount.

Revenue	Previous Year's Actual	Current Year's Budget	Over (Under) Actual
Entry Fees—Teams	$ 2,000	$ 2,250	$250
Entry Fees—Tournament	468	1,000	532
Fund-raising Projects	4,924	5,000	76
Gifts	2,420	2,000	(420)
General Fund Contributions	1,845	2,000	155
Totals	$11,657	$12,250	$593

The revenue projection for tournament entry fees is $1,000. This projection is the same as the budgeted amount for the previous year, but $532 more than was actually received. The program director may be asked to justify this rather large increase.

During the coming year, the program director plans to hold the same fund-raising activities. As a result, the program director estimates that the fund-raising revenue will be $5,000.

During the previous year, the softball program received $2,420 in gifts (by "passing the hat" at each game). However, members were asked to donate more last year because of the decreased revenue from tournament entry fees. Since the director expects to receive more entry fees this year, the gifts revenue projection is again set at $2,000.

The summer softball program receives contributions from the Center's general fund to make up the difference between the revenue actually received and the expenditures actually made. During the previous year, the program had expenditures of $11,657 and revenues of $9,812. Therefore, $1,845 was contributed to the softball program from the general fund. This year, the director estimates that $2,000 will be needed from the general fund.

As you can see, the program director estimates that the total revenue for the coming year will be $12,250. In order to balance the budget, the summer softball program's expenditures can be no more than $12,250.

Expenditure Projections

Once the revenue projections have been determined, the expenditures for the budget period are determined. Estimates of the expenditures to be made during a budget period are called **expenditure projections**. Expenditures are the costs incurred for goods and services used to carry out the goals of a program or organization.

The expenditure projections for the summer softball program are determined in the same way as the revenue projections. That is, the expenditure projections are based on the budgeted and actual expenditure amounts for the previous year. Expenditure projections, however, must equal or be less than the revenue projections. For the summer softball program, the expenditure projections can be no more than $12,250.

The first step is to compare the previous year's budgeted and actual expenditures. For example, the previous year's budgeted and actual expenditures for the summer softball program are listed below and on the next page.

Expenditures	Previous Year's Budget	Previous Year's Actual	Over (Under) Budget
Wages			
Umpires—League Games	$ 4,320	$ 4,320	$ -0-
Umpires—Tournaments	1,000	650	(350)
Scorekeepers—League Games	1,080	1,080	-0-
Scorekeepers—Tournaments	300	200	(100)
Field Maintenance	1,000	1,200	200
Total	$ 7,700	$ 7,450	$(250)
Operating Services			
Postage	$ 100	$ 94	$ (6)
Utilities	650	985	335
Miscellaneous Repairs	450	544	94
Other	200	107	(93)
Total	$ 1,400	$ 1,730	$ 330
Supplies			
Scorebooks	$ 100	$ 96	$ (4)
Paint	250	187	(63)
Softballs	300	186	(114)
Trophies	800	829	29
Awards	700	605	(95)
Lightbulbs	250	210	(40)
Other	200	145	(55)
Total	$ 2,600	$ 2,258	$(342)

Expenditures	Previous Year's Budget	Previous Year's Actual	Over (Under) Budget
Equipment			
Umpires' Equipment	$ 100	$ 79	$ (21)
Home Plates	100	52	(48)
Bases (1st, 2nd, 3rd)	100	88	(12)
Total	$ 300	$ 219	$ (81)
Total Expenditures	$12,000	$11,657	$(343)

Let's look at the differences between the budgeted and actual expenditures.

Wages

The total wages expenditures were $250 less than budgeted. As you can see, the actual expenditure for wages for umpires and scorekeepers during tournaments was $850, $450 less than the budgeted amount. Since two tournaments were rained out, the program had lower wages costs. However, wages for field maintenance personnel were $200 over the budgeted amount.

Operating Services

The total operating services expenditures were $330 over budget last year. The major reason for this was the expenditure for utilities. If utilities costs are expected to increase, the expenditure projection for utilities should be increased in the coming budget period.

Supplies

The actual supplies expenditures were $342 less than the budgeted amount. As you can see, only the expenditure for trophies was over the budgeted amount. The actual expenditures for all other supplies items were less than the budgeted amounts. At first glance, it looks as if the previous year's expenditure projections for supplies were too high. However, the budget director may have cancelled the purchase of some supplies to offset the higher utilities costs.

Equipment

The expenditures for equipment are fairly low. The total actual expenditures for equipment for the previous year were $219, $81 less than the budgeted amount.

Preparing the Expenditure Projections

After examining the previous year's expenditures, the softball program director can develop the expenditure projections for the coming year. Expenditure projections, like revenue projections, are based on the actual amounts for the previous year. The expenditure projections for the summer softball program's budget are shown at the top of page 526.

The total expenditure projection for wages is $8,475, an increase of $1,025. The increase is a result of the plan to increase the number of league

Expenditures	Previous Year's Actual	Current Year's Budget	Over (Under) Actual
Wages			
Umpire—League Games	$ 4,320	$ 4,620	$ 300
Umpire—Tournaments	650	1,000	350
Scorekeepers—League Games	1,080	1,155	75
Scorekeepers—Tournaments	200	300	100
Field Maintenance	1,200	1,400	200
Total	$ 7,450	$ 8,475	$1,025
Operating Services			
Postage	$ 94	$ 100	$ 6
Utilities	985	1,000	15
Miscellaneous Repairs	544	300	(244)
Others	107	100	(7)
Total	$ 1,730	$ 1,500	$ (230)
Supplies			
Scorebooks	$ 96	$ 100	$ 4
Paint	187	200	13
Softballs	186	200	14
Trophies	829	800	(29)
Awards	605	550	(55)
Lightbulbs	210	200	(10)
Other Supplies	145	100	(45)
Total	$ 2,258	$ 2,150	$ (108)
Equipment			
Umpires' Equipment	$ 79	$ 50	$ (29)
Home Plates	52	25	(27)
Bases (1st, 2nd, 3rd)	88	50	(38)
Total	$ 219	$ 125	$ (94)
Total Expenditures	$11,657	$12,250	$ 593

games and the number of tournaments over those held last year. Wages for field maintenance personnel must also be raised because of the increased use of the playing fields.

The total expenditure projection for operating services is $1,500, $230 less than last year's actual expenditure. The major reason for this decrease is that the program director expects fewer miscellaneous repairs during the coming budget period.

The total supplies expenditure projection is $2,150, a decrease of $108. The supplies budget has to be decreased in order to offset the higher wages expenditures for the year.

The total expenditure projection for equipment is also being decreased. The program director does not plan to purchase as much equipment during this budget year.

Carson Recreation Center
Summer Softball Program
Budget Request
January 15, 19—

Revenue	Previous Year's Actual	Current Year's Budget	Over (Under) Actual
Entry Fees—Teams	$ 2,000	$ 2,250	$ 250
Entry Fees—Tournaments	468	1,000	532
Fund-raising Projects	4,924	5,000	76
Gifts	2,420	2,000	(420)
General Fund Contributions	1,845	2,000	155
Total Revenue Projections	$11,657	$12,250	$ 593

Expenditures			
Wages			
Umpires—League Games	$ 4,320	$ 4,620	$ 300
Umpires—Tournaments	650	1,000	350
Scorekeepers—League Games	1,080	1,155	75
Scorekeepers—Tournaments	200	300	100
Field Maintenance	1,200	1,400	200
Total Wages	$ 7,450	$ 8,475	$1,025
Operating Services			
Postage	$ 94	$ 100	$ 6
Utilities	985	1,000	15
Miscellaneous Repairs	544	300	(244)
Other	107	100	(7)
Total Operating Services	$ 1,730	$ 1,500	$ (230)
Supplies			
Scorebooks	$ 96	$ 100	$ 4
Paint	187	200	13
Softballs	186	200	14
Trophies	829	800	(29)
Awards	605	550	(55)
Lightbulbs	210	200	(10)
Other Supplies	145	100	(45)
Total Supplies	$ 2,258	$ 2,150	$ (108)
Equipment			
Umpire Equipment	$ 79	$ 50	$ (29)
Home Plates	52	25	(27)
Bases (1st, 2nd, 3rd)	88	50	(38)
Total Equipment	$ 219	$ 125	$ (94)
Total Expenditure Projections	$11,657	$12,250	$ 593

Figure 22–1. Completed Summer Softball Program Budget

As you can see, when projections are based on the actual amounts of the previous year, the program director must carefully examine the previous year's budget before increasing or decreasing any amounts for the coming budget year. The budget committee may ask the program director to justify any increases or decreases in the budget amounts.

After the projections for revenue and expenditures have been determined, the program director prepares the complete summer softball program budget. This budget, shown in Figure 22–1 on page 527, is then presented to the budget committee for review and approval.

Remember: Budget expenditure projections cannot be higher than the revenue projections.

Zero-base Budgeting

Another fairly new method of developing budget projections disregards the previous year's budget. The coming year's projections are developed as though they were being done for the first time. This method is called zero-base budgeting.

In developing the revenue projections, the program director must prepare an itemized list of the expected revenue from each source. The summer softball program's itemized revenue projections could be presented as follows.

Notice that for each revenue source a goal has been established. For example, the goal for the number of softball teams is 50. Five tournaments are

Entry Fees—Teams (50 teams @ $45 per team)		$ 2,250
Entry Fees—Tournaments (5 tournaments, 10 teams per tournament, $20 entry fee; 5 × 10 × $20)		1,000
Fund-raising Projects		
Fruitcake Sale (500 cakes @ $3 profit each)	$1,500	
Spaghetti Dinner (500 meals @ $3 profit each)	1,500	
Car Wash (5 car washes; total of 1,000 cars washed @ $2)	2,000	
Total Fund-raising Projects		5,000
Gifts (A hat will be passed at each game until target goal is met.)		2,000
General Fund (A request will be made for $2,000 in funding from the General Fund of the Carson Recreation Center)		2,000
Total Revenue Projection		$12,250

planned with ten teams at each tournament. Goals were also set for each fund-raising project. In order to meet the goals, everyone involved in the summer softball program must work together. If the goals cannot be met, the program will receive less revenue. This could cause a reduction in the activities planned for the coming year.

Expenditure projections are developed the same way as revenue projections. Each expenditure projection is prepared as if for the first time. The program director must usually justify each expenditure item with a brief, concise explanation.

Let's look at three expenditure projections under the zero-base budgeting method.

UMPIRES FOR SOFTBALL LEAGUE GAMES

Request: $4,620
The softball league games will be held over a ten-week period. During this time, 385 games will be scheduled. Two umpires are required for each game, and each umpire receives $6 per game.

Number of Games	385
Cost of umpires per game ($6 × 2)	×$12
Total cost for league umpires	$4,620

PAINT

Request: $200
Each of the four fields must be painted once a week for ten weeks. Field paint is $5 a gallon and a gallon will paint one field.

Number of times fields will be painted (10 weeks × 4 fields)	40
Cost of paint to stripe one field	×$5
Total cost for paint	$200

UMPIRE EQUIPMENT

Request: $50
This year four umpire protection masks must be purchased at the cost of $12.50 per mask.

Cost per mask	$12.50
Number of masks needed	×4
Total cost for masks	$50.00

These are just a few examples of zero-base budgeting for expenditures. As you can see, each expenditure item projection must be justified by facts and figures.

Remember: Revenue and expenditure projections can be based upon the previous year's budgeted and actual amounts or they can be developed using zero-base budgeting.

Summarizing the Program Budget Requests

After each program's budget is approved, the budget director of the Carson Recreation Center prepares a cover sheet that summarizes all the program budgets. The budget request summary combines the revenue and expenditure projections of all the Center's programs into one listing. The entire budget for the Carson Recreation Center appears on this one page. Specific details about each program can be found by examining the program budgets, which follow the summary page.

The budget request summary for the Carson Recreation Center is shown in Figure 22–2.

Notice that during the previous year the actual revenue received was $64,043, while actual expenditures totaled $63,461. The difference of $582 represents a surplus to the Center, which was carried over into the current budget period. A surplus occurs when the funds received are more than the expenditures made.

Before reading further, do the following activity to check your understanding of the material you have just studied.

Check Your Learning

Write your answers to the following questions on a separate sheet of notebook paper.

1. A budget is composed of __?__ projections and __?__ projections.
2. __?__ are the costs incurred for goods and services used to carry out the goals of an organization.
3. The two methods that can be used to develop budget amounts are __?__ and __?__.
4. If there are 240 softball games scheduled and if the two umpires required for each game are paid $6 each, the expenditure projection for umpire wages is __?__.

Compare your answers to those in the answers section. Re-read the preceding part of the chapter to find the correct answers to any questions you may have missed.

Budget Control

Once the budget has been approved, a not-for-profit organization must turn its attention to controlling the budget. The budget revenue projections represent amounts the not-for-profit organization expects to receive in order to reach its goals. The budget expenditure projections are the maximum expenditures approved for each item. The not-for-profit organization must establish procedures

Carson Recreation Center
Budget Request Summary
For the Fiscal Year Ended June 30, 19—

Revenue	Previous Year's Actual	Current Year's Budget	Over (Under) Actual
Membership Fees	$26,602	$27,000	$ 398
United Way	10,000	10,000	-0-
Entry Fees—Leagues	5,650	6,400	750
Entry Fees—Tournaments	1,581	1,600	19
Concession Stands	6,134	6,000	(134)
Tuition and Fees	5,060	5,300	240
Fund-raising Projects	6,178	6,200	22
Gifts	2,838	2,700	(138)
Total Revenue Projections	$64,043	$65,200	$1,157
Expenditures			
Personal Services			
Director's Salary	$16,905	$18,032	$1,127
Wages	25,580	24,568	(1,012)
Total Personal Services	$42,485	$42,600	$ 115
Operating Services			
Postage	$ 480	$ 500	$ 20
Utilities	9,260	10,000	740
Miscellaneous Repairs	1,240	1,200	(40)
Other	421	500	79
Total Operating Services	$11,401	$12,200	$ 799
Supplies			
Scorebooks	$ 370	$ 400	$ 30
Trophies	1,975	2,000	25
Awards	1,820	1,800	(20)
Instructional Supplies	3,290	3,500	210
Prepaid Supplies	830	1,000	170
Other	640	700	60
Total Supplies	$ 8,925	$ 9,400	$ 475
Capital Outlay			
Acquisitions	$ 650	$ 1,000	$ 350
Total Expenditures Projections	$63,461	$65,200	$1,739

Figure 22–2. Budget Request Summary

to periodically compare the budget amounts with the actual revenue and expenditures for the budget period. By comparing the current year's budgeted and actual amounts with the previous year's actual amounts, the budget director can determine if the revenue and expenditure projections are realistic and within the limits set by the budget.

Like most not-for-profit organizations, the Carson Recreation Center prepares a budget summary report. A **budget summary report** summarizes and compares the current year's budgeted and actual revenue and expenditure amounts with the previous year's actual amounts. The budget summary report prepared by the Carson Recreation Center is shown in Figure 22–3. Notice that this report has been prepared for the first three months of the Center's fiscal period. This report is cumulative; that is, it reports the total amounts that have been received or paid out as of September 30. The Carson Recreation Center prepares a budget summary report at the end of each month. The report prepared on October 31 would report the total revenue and expenditure amounts for the four months ended October 31. Budget summary reports can also be prepared to report and compare revenue and expenditure amounts for a single month. Budget summary reports—either monthly or cumulative—are also usually prepared for each of the Center's programs in addition to the report for the Center as a whole.

Let's now look more closely at this report and the information it presents. The budget summary report has five amount columns.

1. The figures in the Current Year Budget Amount column are the approved budget amounts for each item for the current budget period. These amounts are the same as those reported on the budget request summary (Figure 22–2 on page 531).

2. The Current Year-to-Date (Y-T-D) Amount column reports the actual cumulative revenue and expenditure amounts—the actual amounts received or paid out up to the date the report was prepared. For the budget summary report shown in Figure 22–3, the Current Year-to-Date column summarizes the revenue received and expenditures paid out for the months of July, August, and September.

3. A **free balance** is the budgeted amount that remains to be collected or spent as of a specific date. The free balance for each budget item is determined by subtracting the current year-to-date amount from the current year budget amount.

Current year budget amount
− Current year-to-date amount
= Free balance

As you can imagine, the Free Balance Amount column can be used to control the organization's—or a particular program's—expenditures. If a program has a $25 free balance for awards, that is the maximum amount that can be spent on awards for the rest of the budget period. The program's director may have to eliminate some planned awards purchases in order to stay within the budget limit.

4. The Previous Year-to-Date Amount column reports the actual revenue and expenditure amounts for the same period during the previous budget year.

Carson Recreation Center
Budget Summary Report
For the Three Months Ended September 30, 19—

	(1) Current Year Budget Amount	(2) Current Y-T-D Amount	(3) Free Balance Amount (1−2)	(4) Previous Y-T-D Amount	(5) Over (Under) Previous Y-T-D (2−4)
Revenue					
Membership Fees	$27,000	$22,780	$ 4,220	21,800	980
United Way	10,000	2,500	7,500	2,500	-0-
Entry Fees—Teams	6,400	4,250	2,150	3,950	300
Entry Fees—Tourn.	1,600	720	880	700	20
Concession Stands	6,000	3,985	2,015	4,005	(20)
Tuition and Fees	5,300	1,400	3,900	1,290	110
Fund-raising Proj.	6,200	3,800	2,400	3,960	(160)
Gifts	2,700	1,240	1,460	840	400
Total Revenue	$65,200	$40,675	$24,525	$39,045	$1,630
Expenditures					
Personal Services					
Dir. Salary	$18,032	$ 4,508	$13,524	$ 4,226	$ 282
Wages	24,568	8,260	16,308	8,430	(170)
Total Per. Serv.	$42,600	$12,768	$29,832	$12,656	$ 112
Operating Services					
Postage	$ 500	$ 140	$ 360	$ 128	$ 12
Utilities	10,000	2,760	7,240	2,489	271
Misc. Repairs	1,200	348	852	364	(16)
Other	500	76	424	62	14
Total Op. Serv.	$12,200	$ 3,324	$ 8,876	$ 3,043	$ 281
Supplies					
Scorebooks	$ 400	$ 150	$ 250	$ 125	$ 25
Trophies	2,000	680	1,320	635	45
Awards	1,800	560	1,240	585	(25)
Inst. Supplies	3,500	925	2,575	849	76
Repair Supplies	1,000	175	825	166	9
Other Supplies	700	156	544	143	13
Total Supplies	$ 9,400	$ 2,646	$ 6,754	$ 2,503	$ 143
Capital Outlay					
Acquisitions	$ 1,000	$ -0-	$ 1,000	$ 450	$ (450)
Total Expenditures	$65,200	$18,738	$46,462	$18,652	$ 86

Figure 22–3. Budget Summary Report

By comparing the previous year-to-date amounts with the current year-to-date amounts, the budget director can spot major differences or trends.

5. The Over (Under) Previous Year-to-Date column reports the difference between the Current Year-to-Date Amount column and the Previous Year-to-Date Amount column. This column serves as a warning light to the budget director. If there is a large difference between the year-to-date amounts for the two periods, the budget director may want to investigate the cause of the difference. If the actual revenue received to date during the current year is less than the amount received to date during the previous year, there may be cause for concern. For example, the Center has received $3,800 from fund-raising projects this year. This amount is $160 less than had been received during the same period last year. If that trend continues, the Center will not reach its goal of $6,200. The budget director will want to determine exactly why less money has been received this year. If an expenditure is running ahead of, or over, the previous year's expenditure, the budget director will also want to investigate the causes for the difference. For example, utilities costs to date are $2,760, $271 more than for the same period last year. If utilities use cannot be adjusted, it may be necessary to decrease the budgeted amounts for other expenditure items.

Before reading further, do the following activity to check your understanding of the material you have just studied.

Check Your Learning

Write your answers to the following questions on a sheet of notebook paper.

1. Budget expenditure projections are the __?__ amounts that the organization can pay out for each item.
2. The __?__ is used to summarize and compare the actual revenue and expenditure amounts with the budgeted revenue and expenditure amounts.
3. If the budgeted amount for wages is $20,000 and the current year-to-date amount is $14,950, the free balance amount is __?__.
4. The __?__ amount is the total amount received or paid out as of the date the budget summary report was prepared.

Compare your answers with those in the answers section. Re-read the preceding part of the chapter to find the correct answers to any questions you may have missed.

Budget Adjustments

After reviewing the budget summary report, the budget director may decide that the budget amounts for certain items are not adequate. When this occurs, budget adjustments should be made. A budget adjustment is a change made to a current budget amount to account for decreased revenue or increased expenditures. Budget adjustments must usually be approved by the budget committee.

Let's look at an example of a budget adjustment. The actual expenditures for utilities as of September 30 are $2,760. Using this amount, the budget director estimates that the total expenditure for utilities for the year will be approximately $11,040. The budgeted amount, the maximum amount the Center is authorized to spend, is only $10,000. The budget director must make a budget adjustment to increase the utilities budget by $1,040. It may be possible to increase the Center's revenue by $1,000 by asking for additional donations or holding an additional fund-raising activity. If this is not possible, decreases must be made in the budgeted amounts of other expenditure items in order to provide for the increased utilities cost.

Budget adjustments are essential in the budgeting procedure. Remember that budgets may be prepared as much as a year before the budget period. During that time, many changes can occur that affect the budget estimates. Those changes and their effects cannot be ignored. If budget amounts are unrealistic or actually in error, it is important to recognize this fact and adjust the budget rather than live with an inaccurate, unrealistic budget. Any adjustment to the budget must be approved. A procedure for handling budget adjustments is usually established by the budget committee.

Summary of Key Points

1. An organization with goals other than earning a profit for its organizers is called a not-for-profit organization.
2. Not-for-profit organizations use a fund accounting system. A fund is a set of accounts used to record the transactions for a particular activity.
3. One tool used by a not-for-profit organization is a budget. A budget is a formal written statement of expected revenue and expenditures for a future period of time, the budget period. The most common budget period is twelve months.
4. The five basic principles involved in the budgeting process are: (a) develop long-term goals, (b) develop short-term goals, (c) define budgeting responsibilities, (d) establish budgeting guidelines, and (e) establish follow-up procedures.
5. A budget consists of two estimates: revenue projections and expenditure projections. Expenditure projections must be equal to or less than revenue projections.
6. Revenue and expenditure projections can be based on the previous year's actual amounts or developed from scratch, using zero-base budgeting.
7. Once a budget has been approved, the not-for-profit organization must set up procedures to monitor the actual revenue and expenditure amounts. A budget summary report can be prepared to summarize and compare the current year's budgeted and actual revenue and expenditure amounts with the previous year's actual amounts.

8. The free balance is the budgeted amount that remains to be collected or spent as of a specific date. It is determined by subtracting the current year-to-date amount from the current year budgeted amount.
9. It is sometimes necessary to adjust budget amounts if revenue is lower or expenditures higher than expected. Budget adjustments must usually be approved by the budget committee.

Review and Applications

Building Your Accounting Vocabulary

In your own words, write the definition of each of the following accounting terms. Use complete sentences for your definitions.

budget   expenditure projection   not-for-profit
budget adjustment   free balance   organization
budget period   fund   revenue projection
budget summary report   fund accounting   zero-base budgeting

Reviewing Your Accounting Knowledge

1. How is the success of a not-for-profit organization measured?
2. What type of accounting system is used by not-for-profit organizations?
3. What is the usual length of a budget period?
4. What are the five basic principles of budgeting?
5. Why is it so important to develop follow-up procedures in the budgeting process?
6. What two types of estimates must be made during the budget preparation period?
7. What two methods can be used to develop the projections for revenues and expenditures?
8. What purpose does a budget summary report serve?
9. How is the free balance amount for each item on a budget summary report determined?
10. Why is it sometimes necessary to make budget adjustments?

Improving Your Decision-making Skills

Case 1

Fran Jeffries has just started work as an accounting clerk at the Fernwood Recreation Center, which has just entered its budget preparation period. Fran does not understand why the budget is so important to the Center. What explanation can you give Fran?

Case 2

The Smithville Day Care Center is having financial problems. One of the major causes of the difficulty is that the staff has not been able to follow the budget that the director has prepared. The director has asked for your help. What suggestions can you offer the director to help the staff stay within the approved budget?

Problem 22–1

A budget must be prepared for the Johnson City Park Commission. The revenue projections and actual receipts for the previous budget period are as follows.

	Previous Year's Budget	Previous Year's Actual
Entry Fees—Leagues	$ 3,700	$ 3,640
Entry Fees—Tournaments	1,950	1,800
Donations	1,200	1,400
Tuition and fees	1,000	950
Concession stand	2,400	2,200
General fund contributions	4,000	4,000
Total revenue	$14,250	$13,990

The directors of the Park Commission made the following decisions.

(a) All entry fees will be raised 10% (based on actual receipts).
(b) A fund-raising campaign is expected to increase donations by 25%.
(c) Tuition and fees revenue projections are expected to be the same as the previous year's budgeted amounts.
(d) Concession stand prices will be increased 20%.
(e) General fund contributions are expected to be the same as in the previous year's budget.

Instructions: Prepare the Revenue section of the budget request summary for the Johnson City Park Commission. Use April 1 as the date.

Problem 22–2

The Carlyss Youth Center uses zero-base budgeting. The revenue projections and actual receipts for the previous budget period are as follows.

	Previous Year's Budget	Previous Year's Actual
Membership fees	$38,000	$40,200
Donations	4,600	5,100
Entry fees	3,000	2,500
Crafts tuition	6,000	6,800
Racquet ball court rental	3,000	3,400
Skate rentals	2,400	2,140
Locker rentals	1,200	970
United Way contributions	5,000	5,000
Total revenue	$63,200	$66,110

The director of the Carlyss Youth Center has made the following revenue estimates for the coming budget period.

Membership fees	100 individuals @ $120 per person
	150 families @ $200 per family
Donations	$500 for the budget period of one year
Entry fees	
Basketball	20 teams @ $25 per team
Softball	30 teams @ $50 per team
Baseball	10 teams @ $30 per team
T-ball	20 teams @ $20 per team
Crafts tuition	30 classes of 25 persons each; tuition $10 per person per class
Racquet ball court rental	$300 per month
Skate rentals	$200 per month
Locker rentals	25 lockers @ $4 per month
United Way contributions	$5,000 requested

Instructions: Prepare the Revenue section of the budget request summary for the Carlyss Youth Center. Use March 15 as the date.

Problem 22–3

The budget committee of the Bayou Country Health Care Center has been working on next year's budget for the past three months. The expenditure projections are based on the expenditure projections and actual expenditures for the previous year.

The budgeted and actual expenditure amounts for the previous year are shown in the following table.

	Previous Year's Budget	Previous Year's Actual
Salaries and wages	$125,300	$122,800
Employee benefits	15,036	14,736
Travel	8,000	7,140
Lab expenses	35,000	34,800
Supplies	15,000	14,820
Repairs and maintenance	8,000	9,240
Electricity	12,000	11,810
Water	600	544
Dues and subscriptions	1,200	1,200
Contracted services	10,000	12,400
Lab equipment	25,000	22,800
Miscellaneous	2,000	1,240
Total expenditures	$257,136	$253,530

The budget committee made the following decisions about the coming year's expenditures.

(a) Employees' salaries, wages, and benefits are expected to increase by 5%. In addition, one new employee will be hired at a salary of $12,000, with estimated employee benefits of $1,440.

(b) Expenditures for the following items are expected to increase 10%: lab expenses, supplies, repairs and maintenance, contracted services, and miscellaneous.

(c) Electricity costs are expected to be 25% more than the previous year's actual amount.

(d) The lab equipment budget was approved at $25,000 and the travel budget at $8,000.

(e) Expenditures for water and dues and subscriptions are expected to be the same as the previous year's budgeted amount.

Instructions: Prepare the Expenditures section of the budget request summary for the Bayou Country Health Care Center. Use January 15 as the date and round all amounts to the nearest whole dollar.

Problem 22–4

The Lynnwood Community Center uses zero-base budgeting. The director of the center has asked you to prepare the expenditure projections for the swimming pool. The pool is indoors and is used all year.

Expenditure information from the previous year's budget is as follows.

	Previous Year's Budget	Previous Year's Actual
Salaries—Director	$ 14,000	$ 14,000
Salaries—Maintenance personnel	12,000	12,000
Wages—Life guards	15,000	14,200
Wages—Instructors	10,000	9,600
Employee benefits	5,000	4,480
Repairs and maintenance	3,000	2,940
Electricity	30,000	34,290
Water	2,400	2,160
Pool supplies	5,600	6,200
Equipment	2,500	2,150
Miscellaneous	1,000	240
Total expenditures	$100,500	$102,260

Additional budget information for the coming year that you have collected appears on the next page.

Instructions: Prepare the Expenditures section of the budget request summary for the Lynnwood Community Center. Use July 15 for the date.

Salaries	
Director	To receive a $2,000 raise
Maintenance personnel	To receive a 5% raise
Life guards	4,000 hours @ $4 per hour
Instructors	50 classes @ $250 per class
Employee benefits	Estimated at 9% of total wages and salaries
Repairs and maintenance	
Filter system	$700
Pool	$1,000
Heater for pool	$1,200
Miscellaneous	$500
Electricity	Estimated to increase 10%
Water	No change from previous year's budgeted amount
Pool supplies	$7,100
Equipment	$3,000
Miscellaneous	$600

Problem 22–5

The budget committee of the Active Club of America has been discussing the coming year's budget for several weeks. The following information has come out of those discussions.

The previous year's budgeted and actual amounts are shown in the table on the following page.

Information concerning the revenue projections is as follows.

(a) The goal of this year's membership drive is $15,000.

(b) The club plans to discontinue the pizza sale fund-raising project in the coming year. Three car washes will be held; each is expected to raise $700. The club expects to raise $3,500 from the spring dance.

(c) The club has a surplus (the difference between the previous year's actual revenue and actual expenditures) of $326.

(d) The club has requested $15,000 from the United Way.

(e) The amount projected for gifts is the difference between the projected expenditures of $43,259 and the projected revenue from other sources of $35,926, or $7,333.

Additional information about the expenditure projections is as follows.

(a) Salaries for maintenance personnel are expected to increase 10%.

(b) The estimates for office services is $3,000 and $1,500 for Social Security.

(c) Projections for the following expenditures should be the same as the previous year's budgeted amounts: travel, refreshments, water, dues and subscriptions, and miscellaneous.

(d) The following expenditures are expected to increase 10%: craft supplies, office supplies, and repair supplies.

	Previous Year's Budget	Previous Year's Actual
Revenue		
Membership fees	$12,000	$11,800
Fund-raising projects		
Car wash	2,000	1,752
Pizza sale	1,000	845
Spring dance	3,000	3,860
Surplus	1,000	1,000
Gifts	8,000	9,420
United Way contributions	15,000	15,000
Total revenue	$42,000	$43,677
Expenditures		
Maintenance services	$14,000	$14,000
Office services	2,000	2,620
Social Security	1,100	1,247
Travel	1,000	789
Craft supplies	3,000	2,879
Refreshments	1,000	1,088
Office supplies	800	940
Repair supplies	2,500	2,144
Electricity	6,000	6,790
Water	300	275
Equipment	8,000	8,000
Insurance	1,200	1,200
Dues and subscriptions	700	745
Miscellaneous	400	634
Total expenditures	$42,000	$43,351

(e) Electricity costs are expected to increase 18% over the previous year's actual expenditures. The club will budget $8,000 for electricity for the coming year.

(f) The insurance company stated that the premium for the insurance policy would be $900.

(g) The equipment list prepared by the director totaled $4,500.

Instructions: Prepare the complete budget request summary for the Active Club of America for the fiscal year ending June 30. Round all amounts to the nearest whole dollar.

Problem 22–6

The table on the following page lists actual revenue and expenditure amounts for the Great Lake City Chamber of Commerce for the first two months of its fiscal year. The table also lists the current year's budget amounts and the year-to-date amounts for the previous budget year.

	Current Year's Budget Amount	Current Y-T-D Amount	Previous Y-T-D Amount
Revenue			
Dues	$ 73,420	$40,201	$42,768
Interest	3,000	327	314
Sale of services	9,000	122	105
Projected income	5,000	160	147
Contributions	10,000	2,710	2,401
Total revenue	$100,420	$43,520	$45,735
Expenditures			
Salaries	$ 36,000	$ 6,000	$ 5,333
Payroll taxes	2,400	400	357
Employee benefits	3,600	600	533
Travel	2,700	550	550
Rent	6,000	1,000	900
Electricity	4,800	870	761
Telephone	3,600	598	588
Office cleaning	1,200	200	200
Insurance	6,000	1,000	1,000
Conferences	720	314	384
Membership development	1,000	245	362
Dues	5,500	195	214
Printing	2,400	998	1,840
Office supplies	5,000	634	828
Postage	4,000	1,260	1,140
Office equipment	12,000	7,980	3,820
Audit	3,000	-0-	-0-
Miscellaneous	500	84	77
Total expenditures	$100,420	$22,928	$18,887

Instructions: Prepare the budget summary report for the Great Lake City Chamber of Commerce for the two months ended February 28. Determine the free balance amount and the amount the current year's amounts are over or under the prior year's actual amounts.

23 Financial Reporting for Not-for-profit Organizations

In Chapter 22, you learned that some organizations are not established to earn a profit. Organizations whose main goal is to provide services for their members or the general public are called not-for-profit organizations. Not-for-profit organizations use an accounting system called fund accounting. One of the most important financial tools of a fund accounting system is the budget.

Like profit-oriented businesses, not-for-profit organizations prepare financial statements that summarize the financial activities of the organization. The financial statements of a not-for-profit organization communicate information to present and potential contributors and users to help them evaluate the services provided and the ability of the organization to continue to provide these services. In this chapter, you'll learn about two financial statements that are prepared by a not-for-profit organization. You will also learn that these financial statements often include explanations and interpretations to help users understand the financial information provided.

Learning Objectives

When you have completed this chapter, you should be able to

1. Name and explain the purpose of two financial statements commonly prepared by a not-for-profit organization.

2. Prepare a statement of revenue, expenditures, and changes in fund balance.

3. Prepare a fund balance sheet for a not-for-profit organization.

4. Explain the purpose of notes to the financial statements.

5. Define the accounting terms presented in this chapter.

New Terms

fund balance / **statement of revenue, expenditures, and changes in fund balance** / **self-generated revenue** / **support revenue** / **capital additions revenue** / **program expenditures** / **object expenditures** / **notes to financial statements**

End-of-period Reporting for Not-for-profit Organizations

At the end of a fiscal period, a profit-oriented business prepares financial statements that summarize the financial condition of the business and the results of its operations. These statements are of interest to owners, employees, management, creditors, and others.

The financial statements prepared by a not-for-profit organization are also used by many different people to evaluate how the organization carried out its responsibilities. They can be used to evaluate how well the organization used the revenue and other resources available to it. Creditors are interested in the financial performance of the organization; they want to know whether the organization can pay its debts.

The financial statements of a not-for-profit organization can also be used to measure the organization's service efforts and accomplishments. They also provide information about the organization's ability to continue to provide existing services. Management, contributors, and users of the organization study the financial statements when discussing and planning for future activities. The financial statements can be used to determine if existing services need to be expanded or discontinued.

As you can see, the financial statements of a not-for-profit organization are used by those who provide money to the organization, by users of the organization's services, by creditors of the organization, and by management. The major purpose of the financial statements is not to measure profit, but to measure performance. The financial statements can answer such questions as: Did the organization stay within its budget? Were contributions used for the purposes for which they were intended? How well did management carry out its financial responsibilities? Did management make the best use of funds available? Are the services rendered by the organization worth the cost?

Most not-for-profit organizations prepare two types of financial statements at the end of a fiscal period: a statement of revenue, expenditures, and changes in fund balance and a balance sheet.

Statement of Revenue, Expenditures, and Changes in Fund Balance

The users of the financial statements of a not-for-profit organization are interested in measuring the operating performance of the organization. In a profit-oriented business, the main measure of performance is the amount of profits earned. The not-for-profit organization's effectiveness is measured by the services it provides for the money available. Obviously, a not-for-profit organization tries to wisely use the money it receives to meet its goals.

In Chapter 22, you learned that a not-for-profit organization usually has a number of funds, or sets of accounts that summarize the transactions for particular activities. For example, a university might have, among others, a scholarship fund; a student loan fund; and a property, plant, and equipment fund. The university will also have a general fund, a set of accounts that is not restricted to a specific purpose. The resources of the general fund can be used for any purpose designated by the director of the organization. The normal operations of the organization—its day-to-day transactions—are usually recorded in the accounts of the general fund.

Users of a not-for-profit organization's financial statements also want to know the financial condition of the organization's various funds. They want to know about the changes that have affected the fund balances. A **fund balance** is the difference between the assets and liabilities of a particular fund. The fund balance is similar to the owner's equity of a profit-oriented business.

The financial statement that reports a not-for-profit organization's revenue and expenditures for a budget period, as well as the change in the fund balance, is called a **statement of revenue, expenditures, and changes in fund balance**. This statement is prepared for each fund of a not-for-profit organization. A combined statement, which reports the total revenue and expenditures for all of an organization's funds, can also be prepared at the end of the fiscal period.

Let's look at the statement prepared by the Thompson Memorial Library for its general fund. The library's statement of revenue, expenditures, and changes in fund balance is divided into three parts: sources of revenue, expenditures (by program and object), and changes in fund balance.

Remember: The fund balance is the difference between the assets and the liabilities of a particular fund.

Sources of Revenue Section

As you recall, a for-profit business earns revenue by providing services or selling goods to customers. A not-for-profit organization usually has several sources of revenue. The Thompson Memorial Library has three sources of revenue: self-generated revenue, support revenue, and capital additions revenue.

Self-generated revenue for a not-for-profit organization is the revenue earned from delivering or producing goods, rendering services, or other activities. Examples of self-generated revenue are membership dues; rental, entry, or tuition fees; taxes; interest on investments; and the money received from fund-raising projects or the sale of services.

Support revenue for a not-for-profit organization is the contributions received from individuals, businesses, or other organizations. Examples of support revenue include gifts, donations, grants, money left to the organization by a deceased person, and the contribution of services or facilities. Support revenue can be used for any purpose by the not-for-profit organization. As a result, it is sometimes called *unrestricted funds*.

Capital additions revenue is the money received by a not-for-profit organization that is restricted to a particular use by the contributor. For example, a gift of $100,000 that must be used to build an art gallery is considered to be capital additions revenue. Money given to a college to be used for student loans is another example. The revenue was received and is to be used for a specific purpose outlined by the person donating the money.

Now let's look at the sources of revenue section of the Thompson Memorial Library's statement of revenue, expenditures, and changes in fund balance, shown in Figure 23–1.

Thompson Memorial Library
Statement of Revenue, Expenditures, and Changes in Fund Balance
General Fund
For the Budget Period Ended June 30, 19—

Sources of Revenue

Self-generated:			
Fees for services		$16,400	
Book rentals and fines		22,240	
Investment income		1,460	
Total self-generated revenue			$ 40,100
Support:			
Grants			
Government	$50,000		
Other	10,000		
Total grants		$60,000	
Contributions		24,000	
Contributed services of volunteers		28,000	
Contributed use of facilities		18,000	
Total support revenue			130,000
Capital additions:			
For books		$21,000	
For art work		17,000	
Total capital additions revenue			38,000
Total Revenue			$208,100

Figure 23–1. Sources of Revenue Section of a Statement of Revenue, Expenditures, and Changes in Fund Balance

Notice that the Thompson Memorial Library has three sources of self-generated revenue: fees for services (media center usage, copy machine usage, rental of computer time, or library loan services), book rentals and fines, and investment income.

There are four sources of support revenue. The library received a government grant of $50,000 and other grants of $10,000 during this fiscal year. These funds are unrestricted and can be used for whatever purpose the director chooses. The director may want to improve the library's services by increasing circulation or by buying new media equipment or computer terminals.

The contributions support revenue was received from a fund drive in which individuals were asked to pledge and give a certain amount. This revenue is also unrestricted. However, many organizations specify how the contributions from fund-raising projects will be used.

The contributed services of volunteers represent the time donated by various individuals to the library. Although the persons work without pay, their services represent a $28,000 donation to the library. The amount reported is the fair market value of the volunteers' services.

The contributed facilities support revenue of $18,000 is the amount of rent the library would have had to pay if it had rented its facilities. Since the owner allows the library to use the building free of charge, the library is receiving an $18,000 donation. This revenue is also reported at the fair market value.

During the fiscal year, several individuals gave money to the library to buy books and art work. Since this revenue is restricted, it is reported as capital additions revenue. Notice that the specific purposes of the capital additions revenue are listed on the statement.

Remember: Self-generated revenue is the revenue earned from delivering or producing goods, rendering services, or other activities. Support revenue is the unrestricted contributions from individuals, businesses, or other organizations. Capital additions revenue is the restricted contributions received from individuals or groups.

Before reading further, do the following activity to check your understanding of sources of revenue.

Check Your Learning

Match each revenue source in Column A with its proper revenue classification in Column B. Write your answers on a sheet of notebook paper.

Column A	Column B
1. Interest from investments	A. Self-generated
2. Unrestricted cash contributions	B. Support
3. Land restricted by the donor	C. Capital additions
4. Unrestricted government grant	
5. Book rental fees	
6. Tuition for classes	
7. Entry fees	
8. Contributed services of volunteers	
9. Cash contributions	
10. Use of contributed facilities	

Compare your anwers to those in the answers section. Re-read the preceding part of the chapter to find the answers to any questions you may have missed.

In Chapter 22, you learned that expenditures are the costs incurred for goods and services used to carry out the goals of an organization. Not-for-profit organizations often classify their expenditures by program or by object. Program expenditures are all of the expenditures made for a particular program of the organization. The various programs of the Thompson Memorial Library include the circulating library, research library, collections and exhibits, educational services, community services, fund raising, and general administration.

Object expenditures are the expenditures of an organization classified according to the type of cost. The object expenditures for the Thompson Memorial Library include personnel costs (wages, salaries, and the cost of fringe benefits), travel costs, purchased services (utilities, rent, insurance, and so on), the cost of supplies and equipment, and the costs of the books and art work purchased for the library.

Remember: **Program expenditures and object expenditures are two different methods of reporting the same expenditures.**

On the statement of revenue, expenditures, and changes in fund balance, some organizations report their expenditures on a program basis, while others use the object basis. The Thompson Memorial Library reports its expenditures both by program and by object. The Expenditures section of the library's statement of revenue, expenditures, and changes in fund balance is shown in Figure 23–2 on page 550.

Notice that the program expenditures include the costs of specific programs as well as management (general administration) and fund-raising costs. Costs for each program can be reviewed easily. For example, the total costs for the library's collections and exhibits program for the period was $24,200.

The object expenditures include all the different types of costs incurred by the library. A user looking at this part of the statement can tell at a glance exactly how much was spent during the budget period for, say, insurance or utilities.

The object expenditures include wages of $28,000 and rent of $18,000. These are the same amounts reported as support revenue in the first section of the statement (as contributed services of volunteers and contributed use of facilities). The amounts are also reported in the Expenditures section of the statement to give a truer picture of the operations of the library. They are the amounts the library would have had to pay out if the volunteers' services and the library facilities had not been donated.

Notice also that the total program expenditures and total object expenditures are the same, $206,000. This occurs because the program expenditures and object expenditures are two different ways of classifying the same costs. The program expenditures include the object expenditures. The object expenditures are allocated to the various programs, just as the business expenses were

Program expenditures:		
Circulating library		$ 31,500
Research library		62,800
Collections and exhibits		24,200
Educational services		31,300
Community services		10,400
General administration		41,600
Fund raising		4,200
Total program expenditures		$206,000
Object expenditures:		
Personnel:		
Salaries	$20,000	
Wages	28,000	
Related benefits	2,488	
Total personnel		$ 50,488
Travel		2,000
Purchased services:		
Rent	$18,000	
Utilities	15,240	
Maintenance contracts	6,800	
Subscriptions	18,210	
Insurance	3,000	
Other	7,762	
Total purchased services		69,012
Supplies		4,100
Equipment		2,400
Library books		40,000
Capital additions:		
Library books	$21,000	
Library art work	17,000	
Total capital additions		38,000
Total object expenditures		$206,000

Figure 23–2. Expenditures Section of a Statement of Revenue, Expenditures, and Changes in Fund Balance

allocated to the departments in Chapter 15. For example, personnel costs are allocated to the library's programs according to the time a staff member spends on that program. If a staff member spends 20% of his or her time dealing with circulation services, 20% of that staff member's salary would be allocated to the circulation program.

Before reading further, do the following activity to check your understanding of the material you have just studied.

Changes in Fund Balance

The statement of revenue, expenditures, and changes in fund balance contains a section that reports the effect that the current year's operations have had on the fund balance. This section of the statement reports: (1) the beginning fund balance, (2) the net increase or decrease in the fund balance for the budget period, and (3) the ending fund balance.

Earlier in this chapter a fund balance was defined as the difference between the assets and liabilities of a particular fund. The current operations of the not-for-profit organization either increase or decrease the fund balance. To determine the amount of the change in the fund balance for the budget period, the difference between revenue and expenditures must be calculated. In a profit-oriented business, if revenue exceeds expenses, the ownership equity of the business is increased. If expenses exceed revenue, the ownership equity of the business is decreased. Likewise, in a not-for-profit organization, if revenue exceeds expenditures, the fund balance is increased. If expenditures exceed revenue, the fund balance is decreased. (The fund balance, remember, is similar to the ownership equity of a for-profit business.)

The revenue for the general fund of the Thompson Memorial Library for the budget period was $208,100. As you've just seen, the fund's total expenditures were $206,000. For this budget period, revenue exceeded expenditures by $2,100 ($208,100 − $206,000). Therefore, there is an increase in the fund balance of $2,100. The final section of the statement of revenue, expenditures, and changes in fund balance reports this increase, as shown in Figure 23–3 at the top of the next page.

The beginning fund balance, $67,600, is listed on the first line of this section of the statement. Then, the increase in the fund balance is listed and added to the beginning balance amount. The resulting amount, $69,700, is the ending fund balance amount for the budget period.

Figure 23–3.
Reporting an
Increase in the
Fund Balance

Beginning fund balance, July 1, 19—	$67,600
Increase in fund balance	2,100
Ending fund balance, June 30, 19—	$69,700

Suppose, for example, that the total expenditures of the general fund for the budget period had been $211,900. In this case, expenditures exceed revenue by $3,800 ($211,900 − $208,100). This results in a decrease in the fund balance. The decrease would be reported in the final section of the statement as shown in Figure 23–4.

Figure 24–4.
Reporting a
Decrease in the
Fund Balance

Beginning fund balance, July 1, 19—	$67,600
Decrease in fund balance	3,800
Ending fund balance, June 30, 19—	$63,800

The complete statement for the Thompson Memorial Library is shown in Figure 23–5 below and on the next page. As you have seen, a not-for-profit

Figure 23–5.
Completed State-
ment of Revenue,
Expenditures, and
Changes in Fund
Balance

Thompson Memorial Library
Statement of Revenue, Expenditures, and Changes in Fund Balance
For the Budget Period Ended June 30, 19—

Sources of Revenue

Self-generated:		
Fees for services	$16,400	
Book rentals and fines	22,240	
Investment income	1,460	
Total self-generated revenue		$ 40,100
Support:		
Grants		
Government	$50,000	
Other	10,000	
Total grants	$60,000	
Contributions	24,000	
Contributed services of volunteers	28,000	
Contributed use of facilities	18,000	
Total support revenue		130,000
Capital additions:		
For books	$21,000	
For art work	17,000	
Total capital additions revenue		38,000
Total Revenue		$208,100

Figure 23–5.
Completed State-
ment of Revenue,
Expenditures, and
Changes in Fund
Balance (Continued)

Expenditures

Program expenditures:		
Circulating library		$ 31,500
Research library		62,800
Collections and exhibits		24,200
Educational services		31,300
Community services		10,400
General administration		41,600
Fund raising		4,200
Total program expenditures		206,000
Object expenditures:		
Personnel:		
Salaries	$20,000	
Wages	28,000	
Related benefits	2,488	
Total personnel		$ 50,488
Travel		2,000
Purchased services:		
Rent	$18,000	
Utilities	15,240	
Maintenance contracts	6,800	
Subscriptions	18,210	
Insurance	3,000	
Other	7,762	
Total purchased services		69,012
Supplies		4,100
Equipment		2,400
Library books		40,000
Capital additions:		
Library books	$21,000	
Library art work	17,000	
Total capital additions		38,000
Total object expenditures		$206,000
Beginning fund balance, July 1, 19—		$ 67,600
Increase in fund balance		2,100
Ending fund balance, June 30, 19—		$ 69,700

organization reports the results of its current operations and the effects of those operations on its fund balance. The statement of revenue, expenditures, and changes in fund balance, then, is like a combined income statement and statement of changes in owner's equity (or statement of retained earnings).

Balance Sheet for Not-for-profit Organizations

The balance sheet reports the balances of the asset, liability, and fund balance accounts of a particular fund as of the end of the fiscal period. A balance sheet is prepared for each fund of the not-for-profit organization. Most not-for-profit organizations prepare several balance sheets. A combined balance sheet, which reports the balances of all the organization's funds, can also be prepared. In this chapter, you will learn about two balance sheets prepared by the Thompson Memorial Library: the general fund balance sheet (Figure 23–6) and the property, plant, and equipment fund balance sheet (Figure 23–7).

General Fund Balance Sheet

An organization's general fund represents the resources available to the organization that have no external limitations placed on their use. (External limitations are those placed on the use of the donated funds by the contributors themselves.) The general fund can be used for any purpose designated by the library's director or governing board. For example, the general fund could be used for current operations or to purchase certificates of deposit.

Figure 23–6.
General Fund
Balance Sheet

Thompson Memorial Library
General Fund Balance Sheet
June 30, 19—

Assets

Cash in Bank		$ 1,860
Certificate of deposit (Note 2)		50,000
Grants receivable (Note 1)		
Government	$25,000	
Other	3,000	28,000
Prepaid expenses		2,480
Total Assets		$82,340

Liabilities

Accounts Payable		$12,640

Fund Balance

Designated by governing board		
Investment	$20,000	
Purchase of shelving	15,000	
Total restricted fund balance	$35,000	
Undesignated fund balance	34,700	
Total fund balance		69,700
Total Liabilities and Fund Balance		$82,340

The governing board of the library (similar to a board of directors) may decide to set aside a portion of the general fund balance for specific purposes. For example, the governing board of the Thompson Memorial Library decided to invest $20,000 in a 12-month certificate of deposit and to purchase $15,000 in shelving equipment. These internal designations of the fund balance should be reported on the general fund balance sheet.

The general fund balance sheet for the Thompson Memorial Library is shown in Figure 23–6. As you can see, it is organized much like the balance sheet of a for-profit business. You will learn more about the two notes listed on the balance sheet later in the chapter.

Property, Plant, and Equipment Fund Balance Sheet

The Thompson Memorial Library prepares a separate balance sheet for its property, plant, and equipment fund. If you recall, the purchase of several property, plant, and equipment assets were reported as expenditures on the statement of revenue, expenditures, and changes in fund balance of the general fund.

Equipment	$ 2,400
Library books (unrestricted)	40,000
Library books (restricted)	21,000
Art work	17,000
Total	$80,400

Since these assets will be used for more than one year, they should also be recorded in the property, plant, and equipment fund accounts and reported on

Figure 23–7.
Property, Plant, and Equipment Fund Balance Sheet

Thompson Memorial Library Property, Plant, and Equipment Fund Balance Sheet June 30, 19—			
	Previous Year's Balance	Current Year's Capitalization	Current Year's Balance
Assets			
Library Books	$389,460	$61,000	$450,460
Library Equipment (net)	95,700	2,400	98,100
Art Work	62,840	17,000	79,840
Total Assets	$548,000	$80,400	$628,400
Liabilities and Fund Balance			
Liabilities	-0-	-0-	-0-
Fund Balance	$548,000	$80,400	$628,400
Total Liabilities and Fund Balance	$548,000	$80,400	$628,400

the fund's balance sheet. The process of transferring the general fund expenditures to the property, plant, and equipment fund is called *capitalizing an expenditure*.

For this budget period, $80,400 in general fund expenditures must be capitalized and reported as assets on the property, plant, and equipment fund balance sheet. The balance sheet that was prepared for the property, plant, and equipment fund of the Thompson Memorial Library is shown in Figure 23–7.

Notice that the current year expenditures for property, plant, and equipment assets are listed in the second column of the balance sheet. Those amounts are then added to the beginning account balances reported in the Previous Year's Balance column. The new account balances are reported in the Current Year's Balance column.

The current year's capitalization amount is also added to the beginning fund balance amount. (The increase in the asset accounts results in an increase in the fund balance.) Since there are no liabilities, the total assets amount equals the ending fund balance amount.

Before reading further, do the following activity to check your understanding of the material you have just studied.

Check Your Learning

Write your answers to the following questions on a sheet of notebook paper.

1. In addition to the funds set up for specific activities, a not-for-profit organization always has a __?__ fund, which can be used for any purpose designated by the organization's director.
2. The __?__ is the difference between the assets and liabilities of a particular fund.
3. The governing board of a not-for-profit organization may designate a part or all of the __?__ for a specific purpose.
4. The process of transferring general fund expenditures to the property, plant, and equipment fund is called __?__.

Check your answers with those in the answers section. Re-read the preceding part of the chapter to find the correct answers to any questions you may have missed.

Notes to Financial Statements

In order to adequately disclose accounting information, most not-for-profit organizations present additional useful information on a separate sheet accompanying the financial statements. Additional information that explains significant matters not disclosed in the financial statements and the accounting policies followed by the organization are called **notes to financial statements**. These notes support the financial statements and are considered to be an important part of the organization's reporting system.

The notes to the financial statements of the Thompson Memorial Library are shown in Figure 23–8.

Thompson Memorial Library
Notes to Financial Statements
For the Budget Year Ended June 30, 19—

Note 1: Summary of Significant Accounting Policies

The financial statements of the Thompson Memorial Library have been prepared on the accrual basis.

The assets, liabilities, and fund balances are reported on two balance sheets.

General fund sources of revenue restricted by donor, grantor, or other outside party for particular purposes are reported as revenue in the year the money is spent.

Property, plant, and equipment acquisitions are accounted for as general fund expenditures and then added to the property, plant, and equipment fund and reported on that fund's balance sheet.

Plant and equipment assets are depreciated over their estimated useful lives by the straight-line method.

The library occupies without charge a building owned by the City of Cameron. The estimated fair rental value of the building is reported both as support revenue and as an expenditure for the budget period.

The library reports capital additions revenue from grants and donations in the Revenue and Expenditures sections of the financial statement.

The values of donated books and art work are based on the fair market value at the time the donations are received.

Contributed services of volunteers are reported as support revenue and as expenditures at the fair market value.

Note 2: Investments

Investments are composed of certificates of deposit. A listing is found below.

Lake City National Bank (10.5%)	$20,000
First National Bank (9.8%)	20,000
National Bank of Commerce (6.0%)	10,000
Total	$50,000

Note 3: Pension Plans

The library withholds FICA taxes and contributes the employer's share as required by law. No other pension plan is in effect.

Note 4: Classification of Expenditures

The cost of providing library services is summarized by program and by object. Certain library program costs are allocated by actual expenditures and time devoted.

Library books, equipment, and art acquisitions are reported as general fund expenditures. These expenditures are added to the property, plant, and equipment fund during the same budget period.

Note 5: General

The library received a substantial amount of its support from federal, state, and local governments. A significant reduction in the level of their financial support would affect the library's programs and activities.

Figure 23–8. Notes to Financial Statements

Summary of Key Points

1. The financial statements issued by a not-for-profit organization are used by many different people to evaluate an organization's performance.
2. The two financial statements usually prepared by a not-for-profit organization are the statement of revenue, expenditures, and changes in fund balance and the balance sheet.
3. The fund balance represents the difference between the assets and liabilities of a particular fund. It is similar to the ownership equity of a for-profit business.
4. The statement of revenue, expenditures, and changes in fund balance reports the total revenue and expenditures of a particular fund for a budget period, as well as the change in the fund balance.
5. A not-for-profit organization generally has three types of revenue: (1) self-generated, (2) support, and (3) capital additions.
6. The expenditures of a not-for-profit organization may be classified by program or by object.
7. If revenue for a budget period exceeds expenditures, there is an increase in the fund balance. If expenditures exceed revenue, there is a decrease in the fund balance.
8. The balance sheet of a not-for-profit organization reports the balances of the asset, liability, and fund balance accounts of a particular fund.
9. Part or all of the fund balance of a not-for-profit organization can be designated for a certain purpose by the organization's governing board. The designation of the fund balance should be reported on the balance sheet.
10. Capital additions are first reported as general fund expenditures on the statement of revenue, expenditures, and changes in fund balance. Each expenditure is capitalized and reported on the property, plant, and equipment fund balance sheet.
11. Notes to the financial statements explain significant matters not disclosed and the accounting policies followed by a not-for-profit organization.

Review and Applications

Building Your Accounting Vocabulary

In your own words, write the definition of each of the following accounting terms. Use complete sentences for your definitions.

capital additions
  revenue
fund balance
notes to financial
  statements

object expenditures
program expenditures
self-generated
  revenue

statement of revenue,
  expenditures, and
  changes in fund
  balance
support revenue

Reviewing Your Accounting Knowledge

1. What two statements are prepared by a not-for-profit organization?
2. What is a general fund?
3. What is the purpose of the statement of revenue, expenditures, and changes in fund balance?
4. Name three major sources of revenue for a not-for-profit organization and give an example of each.
5. What is the difference between support and capital additions revenue?
6. What are the two methods of classifying the expenditures of a not-for-profit organization?
7. How is the change in fund balance determined? When is the fund balance increased? When is the fund balance decreased?
8. What is meant by capitalizing an expenditure?
9. How does the balance sheet for the property, plant, and equipment fund differ from the balance sheet for the general fund?
10. Why are notes to financial statements prepared?

Improving Your Decision-making Skills

Lorraine Fazzio was examining the financial statements for the past two years of the Jones County Boys Club. She noticed that the sources of revenue amount had increased 30% last year. She also noticed that, for the same period, the fund balance decreased 10%. Can you suggest some reasons why the revenue increased but the fund balance decreased? List as many reasons as you can.

Applying Accounting Procedures

Problem 23–1

The table at the top of the next page lists the general fund revenue received by the Peachtree Community Center for the year ended August 31.

Tuition and fees	$ 6,945
Concession stand income	2,489
Contributed services of volunteers	28,670
Entry fees	740
Fund-raising projects	22,000
Grants for equipment purchases (restricted)	30,000
Interest on investments	3,945
Donation of land (restricted)	28,500
Federal government grant (unrestricted)	10,000
Use of contributed facilities	15,000
Donation for land improvements (restricted)	3,000
State grant (unrestricted)	5,000

Instructions: Prepare the Sources of Revenue section of the statement of revenue, expenditures, and changes in fund balance for the Center's general fund. Classify the revenue as self-generated, support, or capital additions.

Problem 23–2

The following expenditures were made by the Greater Leesville Chamber of Commerce during the fiscal year ended December 31.

Office equipment	$ 1,250
Telephone	1,245
Utilities	3,600
Insurance	2,800
Salaries	56,200
Wages	12,900
Related benefits	8,290
Dues	2,400
Rent	6,000
Travel	5,600
Supplies	3,200
Capital Additions	
Computer equipment	14,000
Conference table and chairs	9,700
Postage	8,460
Printing	7,200
Miscellaneous	568

These expenditures can be allocated to the various programs as follows.

Community development	$28,240
Fund-raising	4,800
General administration	64,829
Education support	12,674
Industrial development	20,850
Research	12,020

Instructions: Prepare the Expenditures section of the statement of revenue, expenditures, and changes in fund balance for the Greater Leesville Chamber of Commerce. Classify the expenditures by program and by object (Personnel, Travel, Purchased Services, Supplies, Office Equipment, Capital Additions).

Problem 23–3

The beginning fund balance of the general fund of Smithfield Community College was $87,246. The beginning fund balance of the college's scholarship fund was $74,250. Total revenue and expenditures for the two funds during the past year were as follows.

	General Fund	Scholarship Fund
Total sources of revenue	$489,625	$295,845
Total expenditures	510,146	288,888

Instructions: Prepare the Changes in Fund Balance sections of the statement of revenue, expenditures, and changes in fund balance for the general fund and for the scholarship fund. The college's fiscal year ends on June 30.

Problem 23–4

The following balances appeared in the general fund accounts of the Longview Civic Center on November 30.

Cash in Bank	$ 12,845
Certificates of Deposit	85,000
Grants Receivable—Government	40,000
Grants Receivable—Other	10,000
Accounts Receivable	2,640
Prepaid Expenses	6,250
Accounts Payable	9,868
Wages Payable	684
Fund Balance	146,183

During the November board meeting, the directors of the Center voted to designate a portion of the fund balance as follows.

(a) $50,000 for a six-month certificate of deposit that would mature on May 28
(b) $25,000 for a new sound system for the Center

Instructions: Prepare a balance sheet for the general fund of the Longview Civic Center.

Problem 23–5

The amounts on page 562 appeared on the balance sheet for the property, plant, and equipment fund of the Reston Pavilion for the previous year.

Land	$ 80,000
Land Improvements	20,000
Building	1,000,000
Sound Equipment	18,000
Fixed Equipment	400,000
Movable Equipment	190,000
Liabilities	-0-
Fund Balance	1,708,000

During the current year, the following property, plant, and equipment items were purchased.

Land	$30,000
Tables (Movable Equipment)	2,900
Chairs (Movable Equipment)	5,000
Additional auditorium seats	70,000

Instructions: Prepare the balance sheet for the property, plant, and equipment fund of the Reston Pavilion. The organization's fiscal year ends on June 30.

Problem 23–6

The Baldwin County Society for the Performing Arts had the following revenue and expenditures for its general fund for the fiscal year ended December 31.

Admissions	$70,468
Income from investments	8,429
Tuition and fees	24,218
Concession stand income	16,800
Unrestricted contributions	25,000
Government grants (unrestricted)	15,000
Other grants (unrestricted)	5,000
Contributed services of volunteers	35,000
Use of contributed facilities	24,000
Donation for the purchase of production equipment (restricted)	16,000
Donation for the purchase of land (restricted)	30,000
Salaries	45,000
Wages	39,000
Related benefits	5,400
Travel	1,000
Rent	24,000
Maintenance contracts	6,298
Subscriptions and dues	3,420
Insurance premiums	2,400
Utilities	8,640
Miscellaneous expenditures	968
Supplies	18,964

Lighting equipment (capital addition)	55,000
Production equipment (capital addition)	16,000
Land (capital addition)	30,000

The balances of the general fund accounts on December 31 are as follows.

Cash in Bank	$ 10,698
Certificates of Deposit	100,000
Accounts Receivable	15,200
Grants Receivable—Government	8,000
Grants Receivable—Other	2,000
Prepaid Expenses	1,600
Accounts Payable	6,900
Fund Balance, January 1	116,773

Instructions:

(1) Prepare a statement of revenue, expenditures, and changes in fund balance for the organization's general fund. The expenditures can be allocated to the various programs as follows.

Ballet school	$53,230
Neighborhood productions	34,890
General and administrative	62,400
Production	80,970
Little Theater	24,600

The object classifications are: Personnel, Travel, Purchased Services, Supplies, and Capital Additions.

(2) Prepare the general fund balance sheet. The governing board of the organization voted to make the following fund balance designations.
  (a) Invest $75,000 in a six-month certificate of deposit
  (b) Purchase $50,000 worth of production equipment

(3) Prepare the notes to the financial statements. The following information should be included in the notes.
  (a) The society uses the accrual system of accounting.
  (b) Sources of revenue restricted by the donor are recognized whenever the expenditure is made.
  (c) The society occupies, without charge, a building owned by the county.
  (d) A number of volunteers contribute their time and services.
  (e) The $100,000 balance of the Certificates of Deposit account can be broken down as follows.

| Gulf National Bank (11%) | $75,000 |
| American Bank of Commerce (9½%) | 25,000 |

  (f) Expenditures are classified by program and by object.
  (g) Revenue is classified as self-generated, support, or capital additions.
  (h) The society must continue to receive local support and assistance from volunteers.

Glossary

a

account a record of the increases and decreases for a specific asset, liability, or owner's equity item

accounting cycle the activities a business completes within a fiscal period to keep its accounting records in order

accrual the recognition of an expense or revenue that has gradually increased over time but has not yet been recorded

accrual basis of accounting an accounting method that recognizes revenue when it is earned and expenses when they are incurred

accrued expense an expense that has been incurred in one fiscal period but will not be paid until a later period

accrued revenue revenue that has been earned in one fiscal period but not yet received and recorded

accumulated depreciation the total amount of depreciation that has been recorded for an asset up to a specific point

adjusting entries the journal entries made to update the balances of all general ledger accounts affected by adjustments

adjustment an amount that is added to or subtracted from an account balance to bring that balance up to date

administrative expenses those costs related to the management of the business (for example, the salaries of administrative personnel or insurance expense)

aging accounts receivable a technique for estimating the total amount of uncollectible accounts in which each customer's account is examined and classified by age, the age classifications are multiplied by certain percentages, and the total estimated uncollectible amounts for the categories are added to determine the balance of Allowance for Uncollectible Accounts

allowance method a method of accounting for uncollectible accounts in which an estimate is made of the amount of sales on account for which payment will not be collected during the fiscal period

amortize to write off either the Discount on Bonds Payable or Premium on Bonds Payable account over the life of the bond issue

appraisal value the estimated worth of an asset

articles of incorporation

articles of incorporation the application made by a corporation to incorporate in a particular state

assets items of value owned or controlled by a business or individual

authorized capital stock the maximum number of shares of stock a corporation may issue according to its charter

b

balance sheet a report of the final balances in all asset, liability, and owner's equity accounts at the end of a fiscal period

bank discount the interest charge deducted from the face value of a non-interest-bearing note payable at the time the note is issued

base year the year being used as a basis for a comparison

basic accounting equation assets = liabilities + owner's equity; shows the relationship between assets and total equities

beginning inventory the merchandise a business has on hand at the beginning of the fiscal period

bond a written promise to repay a certain amount (the principal) at a specified date and to pay interest at set times; can be considered a long-term promissory note

bond certificate a document that serves as evidence of the company's debt to the bondholder

bond issue the total number of bonds issued at the same time

book value the value of an asset at a specific point in time; for a plant asset, it is the original cost less the accumulated depreciation

book value of accounts receivable the amount a business can reasonably expect to receive from its charge customers; it is determined by subtracting the balance of Allowance for Uncollectible Accounts from Accounts Receivable

budget a formal written statement of expected revenue and expenditures for a future period

budget adjustment a change made to a current budget amount to account for decreased revenue or increased expenditures

budget period the time period for which revenues and expenditures are being planned

budget summary report a report that summarizes

and compares the current year's budgeted and actual revenue and expenditure amounts with the previous year's actual amounts

c

callable bonds bonds that the corporation has the right to redeem, or buy back, prior to maturity at a specified amount known as the call price

capital additions revenue the money received by a not-for-profit organization that is restricted to a particular use by the donor

capital stock the total amount of investment in a corporation by its stockholders

cash basis of accounting an accounting method in which revenue and expenses are recognized only when cash is received or paid out

cash dividends distributions in the form of cash paid to the stockholders as a return on their investment

cash payments journal a special journal used to record all transactions in which cash is paid out

cash receipts journal a special journal used to record all transactions in which cash is received

centralized accounting system an accounting system for a multistore business in which the accounting records are kept and accounting functions are performed at one location for all the branches

charter the articles of incorporation that have been approved by the state; it defines how the business may operate

check register a book of original entry used to record checks written; it replaces the cash payments journal in a voucher system

closing entries entries made at the end of the fiscal period to close out the balances of the temporary accounts and to transfer the net income or loss for the period to the Capital or Retained Earnings account

combined balance sheet a balance sheet that reports the assets, liabilities, and stockholders' equity of all the branches of a multistore business

combined income statement an income statement that reports the revenue, costs, and expenses of all the branches of a multistore business

common-size statements reports in which items are expressed as a percentage of another number and no dollar amounts are reported

common stock the type of capital stock representing the basic rights to the ownership of a corporation; it includes voting rights at the corporation's annual meeting

comparability presenting financial information in such a way that the user can recognize similarities, differences, and trends

conservatism a guideline that states that, when faced with several methods of reporting accounting infor-

mation, the accountant should choose the method that will be the least likely to overstate assets and income

consistency the application of the same accounting methods over a number of accounting periods

contingent liability a situation in which the endorser of a discounted note agrees to repay the note at maturity if it is not paid by the maker; the liability of the endorser depends upon the possible dishonoring of the note by the maker

contra account an account whose balance is a decrease to another account's balance

contribution margin the contribution that a given department makes to the net income (or loss) of the firm

controlling account a general ledger account whose balance must equal the total of the balances in a subsidiary ledger

corporation an artificial legal being that may own property, enter into contracts, sue and be sued, and so on, and that has an existence apart from that of its owners, the stockholders

cost accounting an accounting system in which the records are organized to maintain accurate, up-to-date summaries of manufacturing costs

cost-benefit consideration the accounting guideline that the cost incurred to provide new accounting information should not be greater than the benefits provided by that information

cost of merchandise the accounts that are involved in determining the actual cost to the business of merchandise to be resold to customers

cost of merchandise sold the actual cost to the business of the merchandise sold to customers during the fiscal period

cost of production report a report that summarizes the units processed by and the costs charged to a department

coupon bonds bonds that have interest coupons payable to bearer attached to each bond certificate

credit an amount entered on the right side of a T account

current assets those assets that are expected to be used up or converted to cash within one accounting period (for example, cash, notes and accounts receivable, merchandise, supplies, prepaid insurance)

current ratio a liquidity ratio that expresses the relationship between a company's current assets and its current liabilities; calculated by dividing the dollar amount of current assets by the dollar amount of current liabilities

d

debenture an unsecured bond issued only on the corporation's credit standing

debit an amount entered on the left side of a T account

decentralized accounting system an accounting system for a multistore business in which each branch within the business maintains its own accounting records

deferral the postponement of the expense or revenue recognition of a bill already paid or cash already received

departmental accounting system an accounting system that provides data for two or more departments

depreciable cost the total amount of the plant asset to be depreciated; calculated by subtracting any disposal value from its original cost

depreciation a systematic procedure for allocating the cost of plant assets to the accounting periods in which the firm receives service from the assets

direct expenses those expenses incurred for the sole benefit of a given department and, therefore, under the control of the department head

direct labor the wages paid to those employees who physically work on a product, with either machines or hand tools

direct materials the raw materials that are used to make and can be easily traced to a finished product

direct write-off method a procedure in which an uncollectible account is removed from the accounts receivable subsidiary ledger and the controlling account in the general ledger when a business determines that the amount owed is not going to be paid

discount the amount by which the face value of a bond exceeds the issue price of the bond

discount period the amount of time between the date a discounted note is given to the bank and the maturity date of the note

discounting notes receivable a situation that occurs when a business sells its notes receivable to a bank for cash rather than holding them until maturity

dishonored note a note that has not been paid or renewed by the maker at the maturity date

disposal value the estimated value of a plant asset at the time of its disposal; often called trade-in value or salvage value

dissolution a situation in which the original partnership is dissolved but the business continues to operate

dividends the share of the corporation's earnings distributed to stockholders as a return on their investments

double-declining-balance method a method of depreciation in which the book value of the asset at the beginning of the year is multiplied by twice the straight-line depreciation rate to determine the depreciation expense; it is a form of accelerated depreciation

double-entry accounting a financial recordkeeping system in which every business transaction affects at least two accounts; for every debit there must be an equal credit

double taxation taxation as personal income of the dividends paid to stockholders out of income already taxed at the corporate level

e

economic entity an organization that exists independently of its owner or owners

ending inventory the merchandise a business has on hand at the end of the fiscal period

equity per share the amount that would be paid on each share of stock if the corporation liquidated without incurring any expenses, gains, or losses in selling its assets and paying its liabilities; calculated by dividing total stockholders' equity by the number of shares outstanding

equivalent units a measure of the number of units produced in a period of time, expressed in terms of fully completed units

expenditure projection the estimate of expenditures to be made during a budget period

expense the cost of goods and services used to operate a business

f

face value the amount written on the "face" of a promissory note; in most cases, it is the same as the principal

factory overhead all manufacturing costs other than the costs of direct labor and direct materials, which cannot be easily or directly traced to the products being manufactured

factory supplies those materials used in the manufacturing process that cannot be easily traced to a product; often referred to as indirect materials

finished goods those products that have been completed and are available for sale

first in, first out method a method of assigning costs to inventory in which it is assumed that the items purchased first were also the first items to be sold

free balance the budgeted amount that remains to be collected or spent as of a specific date

full disclosure the guideline that, in reporting accounting information, an accountant should make a full disclosure of any information that will make a difference to a decision-maker

fund a set of accounts used to record the transactions for a particular activity (for example, scholarship fund, building fund, general fund)

fund accounting the accounting system used by not-for-profit organizations to account for the transactions of their various funds

fund balance the difference between the assets and liabilities of a particular fund (assets − liabilities = fund balance)

g

general journal a two-column, all-purpose journal in which all types of business transactions can be recorded

general ledger a book containing all permanent and temporary accounts used in the business

generally accepted accounting principles the rules and procedures to be followed in preparing financial statements

going concern the assumption that a business or economic entity will continue its operations indefinitely

gross profit method a method of estimating the cost of inventory in which the percentage of gross profit of the firm, based on the firm's experience over some period of time, is used as the basis for estimating the value of the inventory

gross profit from operations net sales minus the cost of merchandise sold

gross profit on sales the amount of profit made during the fiscal period before expenses are deducted

h

historical cost the cost or exchange price at the time a business transaction is completed

horizontal analysis a comparison of dollar amount and percentage changes for the same item in a company's financial statement for two or more periods

i

income statement a report of the net income or loss earned by a business during the fiscal period

indirect expenses expenses incurred for the entire business as a whole and, therefore, not under the control of one department head

indirect labor the wages paid to factory employees who do not physically work on a product

industry practices the expectations or previously used methods that result in financial information being reported in a manner that differs from generally accepted accounting principles

interbranch transactions transactions between the branches of the same multistore business

interest a charge made for the use of money

interest allowance an allocation of net income (or loss) to a partner in a business; it is calculated as a certain percentage of the balance of the partner's capital account

interest-bearing note a promissory note that requires the maker to pay the principal plus interest at maturity

investments assets, generally long-term, that are not intended for use in the normal operations of a business

issued shares shares of stock sold to stockholders

j

job cost sheet a form used in job order cost systems on which the various manufacturing costs incurred for each job are recorded

job order cost accounting system an accounting system that is designed to accumulate manufacturing costs for a specific order or batch of products

job order time card a record of the amount of time an employee spent on a particular job; it is used in the job order system

journal a chronological record of a business's transactions

l

last in, first out method a method of assigning a cost to inventory in which it is assumed that the items purchased last were the first items to be sold

legal capital the minimum amount of the capital contributed by the stockholders that must be retained by the corporation in order to give some protection to the creditors

leverage the ability of a bond-issuing corporation to earn a greater return on the money it raises from a bond issue than it has to pay out in interest to the bondholders

liabilities the creditors' claims to the assets of a business; amounts owed to creditors

liquidation a situation in which both the partnership and the operation of the business are ended

liquidity a measure of a company's ability to pay its debts

lower-of-cost-or-market rule a method of reporting the cost of the ending inventory in which the inventory is reported at the replacement cost if that cost is lower than the original cost

m

maker the person or business who borrows money and promises to repay the principal and interest

manufacturing business a business that transforms raw materials into finished products through the use of labor and machinery

market rate the rate borrowers are willing to pay and lenders are willing to accept for the use of money

markup the amount a retailer adds to the cost of merchandise to arrive at the selling price

matching principle the principle that states that revenue for an accounting period should be matched against the expenses incurred during the period to earn that revenue

materiality a guideline that suggests that an item or an amount that would make a difference to a user or a decision-maker be included in the financial reports

materials requisition a form used in a job order cost system that authorizes the materials warehouse to transfer direct materials to the factory

maturity date the due date of a promissory note

maturity value the amount to be paid on the due date of a note; the principal plus interest

merchandise inventory turnover the number of times a company's inventory is sold during a given year; calculated by dividing the cost of merchandise sold by the average merchandise inventory

multistore business a business that has more than one store or branch

mutual agency the right of any partner to enter into valid contracts in the name of the firm for the purchase or sale of goods or services within the normal scope of business

n

net purchases the total of all costs related to the merchandise purchased during the fiscal period

net sales the amount of sales for the period less any returns, allowances, and discounts

no-par stock stock that does not have a value printed on the stock certificate

non-interest-bearing note payable a promissory note on which the interest is paid (deducted) at the time the note is issued rather than at the maturity date; a note that has no stated rate of interest on its face

not-for-profit organization an organization with goals other than earning a profit for its owners; usually these goals include providing a service to members or the general public

note payable a promissory note issued by a person or a business to a creditor

note receivable a promissory note accepted by a person or business

notes to financial statements additional information that explains significant matters not disclosed in the financial statements themselves and the accounting policies followed by an organization

o

object expenditures the expenditures of an organization classified according to the type of cost

other expenses expenses that are incurred but not in the normal operations of the business

other revenue income received or earned but not in the normal operations of the business

outstanding stock stock that is actually in the hands of stockholders

overapplied factory overhead a situation that occurs when more factory overhead costs were allocated than were actually incurred

owner's equity the owner's claim to or investment in the assets of a business

p

paid voucher file a file that contains the paid vouchers, filed in numerical order

par-value stock stock that has a face value printed on the stock certificate

partnership an association of two or more persons to carry on, as co-owners, a business for profit

partnership agreement a written document that sets out the terms under which the partnership will operate

payee the person or business to whom a promissory note is payable

percentage of accounts receivable a method for estimating the amount of uncollectible accounts in which the balance of Accounts Receivable is multiplied by a certain percentage

percentage of net sales method a method for estimating the amount of the adjustment for bad debts expense in which a business assumes that a certain set percentage of the current period's net sales will be uncollectible

periodic inventory system an inventory system in which the number of goods on hand is determined by periodically counting them

perpetual inventory system an inventory system in which a constant, up-to-date record of the amount of merchandise on hand is maintained

post-closing trial balance the trial balance prepared after all adjusting and closing entries have been journalized and posted

posting the process of transferring amounts from a journal to ledger accounts

pre-emptive right the right of existing stockholders to subscribe to (purchase) new shares, when they are issued, in proportion to their present holdings

preferred stock a type of capital stock that has two preferences over common stock: (1) the corporation pays dividends to preferred stockholders before it pays them to common stockholders, and (2) the corporation pays the dividends at a stated, uniform rate; preferred stockholders, however, cannot vote

premium the amount by which the issue price of a bond exceeds the face value of that bond

prepaid expense an expense paid in advance

price-earnings ratio a ratio that is used to determine whether the market price of a corporation's stock is reasonable; calculated by dividing the market price by the earnings per share

principal the amount being borrowed when a promissory note is issued

privately held corporation a corporation whose ownership is confined to a small group of stockholders

proceeds the amount of cash that the maker of a non-interest-bearing note actually receives; the difference between the face value of a note and the bank discount

process cost accounting system an accounting system that is designed to accumulate costs for a particular production step or department rather than for a specific product or batch of products

profitability a company's ability to earn a reasonable profit on the owners' investment

program expenditures all of the expenditures made for a particular program of an organization

promissory note a written promise to pay a certain sum of money on a fixed or determinable date (the maturity date)

property, plant, and equipment long-term tangible assets that are used for more than one accounting period in the production or sale of goods or services (for example, equipment, furniture, vehicles, machinery, tools, buildings, land)

protest fee the bank charge to the endorser of a discounted note that is dishonored; it must be paid along with the maturity value

publicly held corporation a corporation whose stock is publicly traded on a stock exchange or over the counter

purchases journal a special journal used to record all transactions in which items are bought on account

q

quick ratio a liquidity ratio that expresses the relationship between a company's quick assets and its current liabilities; examples of quick assets include cash, notes receivable, net accounts receivable, and marketable securities

r

ratio analysis the comparison of two items on a financial statement, resulting in a percentage that is used to evaluate the relationship between the two items

realization the sale of assets of the business for cash

registered bonds bonds for which the names of the

bondholders are recorded with the issuing corporation

relevance presenting accounting information that "makes a difference" to a user in reaching a decision about the business; relevant information has predictive value, is timely, and provides feedback

reliability the confidence a decision-maker has in the financial information being reported; reliable information is verifiable, complete, and free from bias

retail method a method of estimating the cost of inventory in which the cost of the ending inventory is based on the ratio of the cost value of the goods to the retail value of the goods

retained earnings the profits that have been kept by the corporation and not distributed to stockholders as dividends

revenue the income earned from the sale of goods and services

revenue projection the estimate of the funds to be received during a budget period

revenue recognition revenue is recognized at the time the earning process is complete and title to the goods has been transferred or the services have been rendered

s

salary allowance an allocation of net income (or loss) to a partner in a business; used as a means of recognizing and rewarding differences in ability and time devoted to the business

sales journal a special journal used to record the sale of merchandise on account

schedule of changes in working capital a work paper on which the increase or decrease in each current asset and current liability account during the period is calculated

schedule of unpaid vouchers a list of all unpaid vouchers as of a certain date by creditor and the amount owed; it is similar to the schedule of accounts payable

secured bonds bonds that are backed up by certain assets of the corporation

self-generated revenue for a not-for-profit organization, the revenue earned from delivering or producing goods, rendering services, or other activities of the organization during a period of time

selling expenses the costs incurred to sell or market the goods or services sold by the business

serial bonds a bond issue that has a series of maturity dates

sinking fund a special fund into which annual deposits are made by a corporation; it is used to pay off a bond issue when it becomes due

source document a paper prepared as evidence that a transaction actually occurred

source of working capital any transaction that increases working capital; working capital is increased if current assets are increased or current liabilities are decreased

specific identification method a method of assigning a cost to inventory in which the actual cost of each item in the ending inventory is determined and assigned

stated value the value of no-par stock that has been assigned to the stock by the corporation's board of directors

statement of changes in financial position the financial statement that explains in detail how working capital has changed between the beginning and the end of the fiscal period

statement of changes in owner's equity a report that shows the changes that have occurred in the Capital account during the fiscal period

statement of cost of goods manufactured a report that summarizes all the costs of the goods completed during the period; prepared as a supporting document for the income statement

statement of retained earnings a report that shows the changes that have taken place in the Retained Earnings account during the fiscal period; prepared as a supporting document for the balance sheet

statement of revenue, expenditures, and changes in fund balance the statement prepared for each fund of a not-for-profit organization that reports the revenue and expenditures for a budget period along with the change in the fund balance

stock the shares of ownership in a corporation

stock certificate a document that shows how many shares of corporation stock are owned by a particular stockholder

stock dividend a distribution by a corporation of shares of its own common stock to its common stockholders

stock split a deliberate splitting of the par or stated value of a corporation's own stock and the issuance of a proportionate number of additional shares

stock subscription a stockholder's contract to buy shares of stock on an installment basis for an agreed-upon price

stockholders the owners of a corporation

stockholders' equity the ownership equity in a corporation

stockholders' ledger a subsidiary ledger that lists the names and addresses of individual stockholders, the number of shares they own, and the value of their stock at the date of purchase

straight-line method a method of calculating depreciation in which an equal amount of the depreciable cost of an asset is charged off, or expensed, for each year of its estimated useful life

subsidiary ledger a ledger that is summarized in a controlling account in the general ledger

sum-of-the-years'-digits method a method of calculating depreciation in which the depreciation expense is calculated using fractions based on the number of years of the asset's estimated useful life

support revenue for a not-for-profit organization, the unrestricted contributions received from individuals, businesses, or organizations during a period of time

t

taxable income the amount of income on which income taxes are calculated

term the amount of time between the issue date of a note and the maturity date

term bonds a bond issue with the same maturity date

time periods the segments into which the life of a business is divided for reporting purposes; the most common time period is one year

treasury stock issued stock that has been reacquired by the corporation either by buying it back or by receiving it as a donation

trend analysis the comparison of the percentage changes in an item or items over a number of consecutive years; all amounts are expressed as and compared to an appropriate base year

trial balance a proof of the equality of debits and credits in the general ledger

u

uncollectible account an account receivable that cannot be collected because a charge customer is unable or unwilling to pay

underapplied factory overhead a situation that occurs when more factory overhead costs were incurred than were allocated

unearned revenue revenue received in advance but not yet earned

unit of measure the standard unit of measure by which all economic events (transactions) are reported; the dollar is the unit of measure used in the United States

units-of-production method a method of calculating depreciation in which the depreciation expense is calculated according to the asset's actual use; the asset's useful life may be expressed, for example, in units produced or miles driven

unpaid voucher file a file that contains all unpaid vouchers, filed according to the dates on which they should be paid

use of working capital any transaction that decreases working capital; working capital is decreased if current assets are decreased or if current liabilities are increased

V

vertical analysis a method of analyzing financial statements in which each dollar amount on the statement is restated as a percentage of a base amount on the same statement

voucher a written authorization for each cash payment made by a company; it serves as the source document for recording the transaction

voucher check a special check that has an attached stub that lists the details of the cash payment

voucher register a book of original entry in which all vouchers are recorded in numerical order; it expands and replaces the purchases journal

voucher system an accounting system to control all purchases and cash payments by a business; a voucher is prepared for every bill or invoice to be paid

W

weighted average cost method a method of assigning a cost to inventory in which an average unit cost is assigned to all like articles in the ending inventory

withdrawals the cash or other assets withdrawn from the business for the owner's personal use

work in process those products that have not yet been completed at the end of the fiscal period

work sheet a working paper used to collect information from the general ledger for use in completing end-of-period work

working capital the amount by which current assets exceed current liabilities

Z

zero-base budgeting a method of developing budget projections in which the previous year's actual revenue and expenditures are disregarded and the coming year's projections are developed independently

Answers to "Check Your Learning" Activities

Chapter 1, page 9
1. credit
2. asset
3. basic accounting equation
4. liabilities
5. journal

Chapter 1, page 16
1. Accounts Receivable
2. cash receipts journal
3. Debit Purchases; credit Accounts Payable
4. check stub
5. Entries include: a purchase return or allowance, a sales return or allowance, employer's payroll tax liabilities, correcting entries, bank service charges, and bank card fees

Chapter 1, page 18
1. A controlling account is a general ledger account whose balance must equal the total of the balances in a subsidiary ledger.
2. accounts receivable subsidiary ledger; accounts payable subsidiary ledger
3. daily

Chapter 1, page 23
1. Special journals save time in posting because the totals of the special amount columns are posted to the general ledger accounts named in the headings. The individual entries are not posted.
2. After posting, the account number of the general ledger account is entered in parentheses below the total of a special amount column. A check mark is entered in parentheses below the total of a General Debit or Credit column.
3. The accuracy of the subsidiary ledgers is proved by preparing a schedule of accounts receivable and a schedule of accounts payable. The totals of the schedules must match the balance of the controlling account.

Chapter 2, page 36
1. credit

2. $735.47; debit Supplies Expense; credit Supplies
3. $35,496.06

Chapter 2, page 42
1. $51,193.00
2. $9,852.04
3. $10,028.10

Chapter 2, page 49
1. Merchandise Inventory; Income Summary
2. Insurance Expense
3. Income Statement section of the work sheet
4. the Capital account; the Withdrawals account

Chapter 3, page 67

19—

Feb.	7	Bad Debts Expense	170.00	
		Accts. Rec./A. Almond		170.00
		Memo. 22		
	18	Accts. Rec./B. Moreno	64.00	
		Bad Debts Expense		64.00
		Memo. 23		
	18	Cash in Bank	64.00	
		Accts. Rec./B. Moreno		64.00
		Receipt 1786		

Chapter 3, page 76
1. Not yet due, $600.00; 1–60 days past due, 280.00; 61–120 days past due, 300.00; 121–365 days past due, 600.00; more than 365 days past due, 600.00
2. $2,380.00
3. $1,280.00

Chapter 4, page 86
1. $9.86
2. $16.27
3. $35.51
4. $30.26
5. $10.10

Chapter 4, page 87
1. May 27
2. January 16
3. July 26

4. March 12
5. October 29

Chapter 4, page 94
1. a. Debit Notes Receivable for $1,200; credit Accounts Receivable and Norman C. Hobson's account for $1,200.
   b. interest-bearing note
2. a. Debit Cash in Bank for $1,228.11; credit Notes Receivable for $1,200.00 and Interest Income for $28.11.
   b. $1,228.11

Chapter 4, page 98
1. 22 days
2. 68 days
3. $1,000.00
4. $1,022.19
5. $1,006.96
6. $6.96 interest income

Chapter 5, page 107
1. Cost of Merchandise Sold; Current Assets
2. periodic
3. perpetual

Chapter 5, page 111
1. 27 units
2. $82.20
3. fifo, $84.50; lifo, $81.00

Chapter 5, page 116
1. retail
2. markup
3. gross profit

Chapter 6, page 127
1. $73,142
2. Land, $72,000; Building, $168,000

Chapter 6, page 132
1. $1,575
2. $1,575
3. $3,360
4. $2,520

Chapter 7, page 159
1. voucher
2. Vouchers Payable account
3. Purchases; Vouchers Payable
4. check register
5. unpaid voucher file

Chapter 7, page 165
1. Apr. 6: voucher register; Apr. 9: general journal;

Apr. 15: check register
2. The debit memo number is entered in the Payment columns on the upper half of the line used to record the original voucher.
3. $8,996.40

Chapter 8, page 181
1. cash
2. accrual
3. deferral
4. prepaid expenses
5. liabilities

Chapter 8, page 188
1. a. $2,000.00
   b. Debit Salaries Expense, credit Salaries Payable
2. a. January 30
   b. $36.99
   c. Debit Interest Receivable; credit Interest Income

Chapter 9, page 204
1. $100.00; Income Tax Expense; Corporate Income Tax Payable
2. Depreciation Expense—Delivery Equipment; Accumulated Depreciation—Delivery Equipment
3. Interest Receivable; Interest Income
4. Interest Expense; Discount on Notes Payable
5. $3,000.00; Unearned Rent; Rental Income

Chapter 9, page 208
1. Income Statement
2. Other Revenue
3. Other Expenses
4. Balance Sheet
5. statement of retained earnings

Chapter 10, page 233
19—

May 7	Equipment	$18,000.00	
	Accounts Receivable	16,000.00	
	J. LeBrand, Capital		34,000.00
	Memo. 247		

Chapter 10, page 241
1. $36,000 loss
2. Pearson, $42,000; Wong, $62,000

Chapter 11, page 253
Aronson, $32,000; Bullock, $24,000

Chapter 11, page 255
Milo, $20,200; Bower, $17,800

Chapter 12, page 270
1. Corporations are subject to federal income taxes on their annual net income. Stockholders must pay

personal income taxes on the dividends they receive from the corporations.

2. 100 shares
3. Common Stock account; Retained Earnings account

Chapter 12, page 276

19—

Jan. 2	Cash in Bank	250,000	
	Common Stock		250,000
	Memo. 10		
6	Organization Costs	5,000	
	Cash in Bank		5,000
	Check 21		
Mar. 5	Cash in Bank	206,000	
	Common Stock		200,000
	Paid-in Cap. in Exc. of Par		6,000
	Memo. 50		

Chapter 12, page 283

1. Common stock was issued for cash at a price above stated value. The difference between the stated value and the issue price was credited to the Paid-in Capital in Excess of Stated Value account.
2. Subscriptions to shares of common stock were received at a price above the stated value.
3. A portion of the subscription price was received from subscribers.
4. The remaining portion of the subscription price was received from subscribers.
5. The common stock subscribed to was issued.

Chapter 13, page 298

1. False
2. True
3. True
4. False
5. False

Chapter 13, page 300

1. $6,000
2. $450
3. January 12 and February 20
4.

19—

Jan. 12	Retained Earnings	6,000	
	Dividends Payable		6,000
	Minute Book, p. 505		
Feb. 20	Dividends Payable	6,000	
	Cash in Bank		6,000
	Minute Book, p. 505		

Chapter 13, page 307

19—

Jan. 16	Treasury Stock	84,000	
	Cash in Bank		84,000
	Check 5411		

Mar. 19	Cash in Bank	46,000	
	Treasury Stock		42,000
	Paid-in Cap. from Sale		4,000
	of Treasury Stock		
	Receipt 1631		
Dec. 8	Cash in Bank	40,000	
	Paid-in Capital from Sale	2,000	
	of Treasury Stock		
	Treasury Stock		42,000
	Receipt 2710		

Chapter 14, page 319

1. True
2. False
3. False
4. True
5. False

Chapter 14, page 327

1. a. Debit Cash in Bank for $2,060,000; credit Bonds Payable for $2,000,000 and Premium on Bonds Payable for $60,000.
   b. $70,000
   c. $6,000
2. a. $752,000
   b. $24,000
   c. $2,400

Chapter 14, page 329

19—

Feb. 12	Bond Sinking Fund	384,000	
	Sink. Fund. Invest.		370,000
	Gain on Sale of Sink.		14,000
	Fund Invest.		
	Receipt 623		
28	Bond Sinking Fund	16,000	
	Cash in Bank		16,000
	Check 904		
Mar. 1	Bonds Payable	400,000	
	Bond Sinking Fund		400,000
	Check 905		

Chapter 15, page 354

Pharmacy, $2,240; Camera supplies, $960; Toiletries and cosmetics, $10,400; Greeting cards, $800; Receiving and storage, $1,600

Chapter 15, page 361

$40,000

Chapter 16, page 375

1. centralized accounting; decentralized accounting
2. decentralized
3. centralized
4. Advantages include: may be less costly, no duplication of accounting activities, more efficient,

accounting records and procedures and consistent for each branch

5. the account; the branch

Chapter 16, page 381

1.	Cash in Bank—Branch 5	7,298.44	
	Sales		6,885.32
	Sales Tax Payable		413.12
2.	Accts. Rec.—Branch 2/J. Henry	212.00	
	Sales		200.00
	Sales Tax Payable		12.00
3.	Cash in Bank—Branch 3	630.00	
	Accts. Rec.—Branch 3/K. Chin		630.00
4.	Purchases—Branch 1	7,944.21	
	Accts. Pay.—Branch 1/Houston Co.		7,944.21
5.	Store Supplies—Branch 1	200.00	
	Store Supplies—Branch 2	100.00	
	Store Supplies—Branch 3	125.00	
	Store Supplies—Branch 4	200.00	
	Store Supplies—Branch 5	100.00	
	Accts. Pay.—Branch 1/Amer. Supp.		200.00
	Accts. Pay.—Branch 2/Amer. Supp.		100.00
	Accts. Pay.—Branch 3/Amer. Supp.		125.00
	Accts. Pay.—Branch 4/Amer. Supp.		200.00
	Accts. Pay.—Branch 5/Amer. Supp.		100.00

Chapter 16, page 389

19—

Apr. 20	Due from Store 4	30,300		
	Purchases—Store 1		30,000	
	Transfer Fees Earned—Store 1		300	
	Transfer request 111			
20	Purchases—Store 4	30,000		
	Transfer Charges—Store 4	300		
	Due to Store 1		30,300	
	Transfer request 111			
May 2	Due to Store 1	30,300		
	Cash in Bank—Payables		30,300	
2	Cash in Bank—Store 1	30,300		
	Due from Store 4		30,300	

Chapter 17, page 403

1. direct materials
2. Direct; indirect
3. factory overhead costs
4. Factory supplies

Chapter 17, page 408

1. Raw Materials Inventory, Work in Process Inventory, Finished Goods Inventory
2. Work in process
3. finished goods
4. Factory overhead
5. Manufacturing Summary

Chapter 17, page 418

1. statement of cost of goods manufactured; income statement; statement of retained earnings; balance sheet
2. Cost of Goods Manufactured
3. Statement of Cost of Goods Manufactured
4. Manufacturing Summary; Income Summary

Chapter 18, page 432

1. process
2. job order cost accounting system
3. job cost sheet
4. materials requisition

Chapter 18, page 440

1. Debit Work in Process Inventory; credit Factory Overhead Applied
2. In the first entry, debit Cash in Bank and credit Sales; in the second entry, debit Cost of Goods Sold and credit Finished Goods Inventory
3. Debit Work in Process Inventory and credit Factory Wages Payable
4. Debit Finished Goods Inventory and credit Work in Process Inventory
5. Debit Factory Overhead Control and credit Cash in Bank

Chapter 18, page 450

1. Debit Work in Process Inventory—Department A and credit Factory Overhead Applied
2. In the first entry, debit Accounts Receivable and the customer's account and credit sales; in the second entry, debit Cost of Goods Sold and credit Finished Goods Inventory
3. Debit Work in Process Inventory—Department B and credit Work in Process Inventory—Department A
4. Debit Finished Goods Inventory and credit Work in Process Inventory—Department B
5. Debit Factory Overhead Control and credit Cash in Bank

Chapter 19, page 465

1. d
2. b
3. a
4. c

Chapter 19, page 466

1. unit of measure
2. going concern
3. time periods
4. economic entities

Chapter 19, page 468

1. b   2. c   3. a

Chapter 20, page 485

Cash in Bank, 5.56% decrease; Notes Receivable, 14.29% increase; Equipment (net), 8.2% increase; Retained Earnings, 15.79% decrease

Chapter 20, page 488

Merchandise inventory turnover rate, 4.71 times/yr.; Number of days in stock, 77 days

Chapter 21, page 503

1. $600 decrease in working capital
2. $12,000 increase in working capital
3. No change in working capital
4. No change in working capital
5. $300 increase in working capital

Chapter 21, page 507

$2,800 decrease in working capital

Chapter 22, page 521

1. not-for-profit organization
2. fund
3. budget
4. short-term goals

Chapter 22, page 530

1. revenue; expenditure
2. expenditures
3. basing estimates on previous year's budgeted and actual amounts; zero-base budgeting
4. $2,880

Chapter 22, page 534

1. maximum approved
2. budget summary report
3. $5,050
4. year-to-date

Chapter 23, page 548

1. A
2. B
3. C
4. B
5. A
6. A
7. A
8. B
9. B
10. B

Chapter 23, page 551

1. program
2. program
3. object
4. object
5. object
6. object
7. program
8. object
9. object
10. object
11. program
12. program
13. object
14. program
15. object

Chapter 23, page 556

1. general
2. fund balance
3. general fund
4. capitalizing an expenditure

Appendix A
Applications for Spreadsheet Software

Spreadsheet software turns the computer into a tool that can perform calculations and analyze relationships among numbers. Some software for spreadsheet applications allows the user to perform mathematical calculations only. Other software, called integrated software, allows the user to perform calculations using the spreadsheet, create documents using a word processing program, and create and access databases using a database management program. With integrated software, these functions can be merged to create reports, for example, that use elements from all three programs.

The capabilities of the electronic spreadsheet are especially useful in accounting. Spreadsheets can be used to calculate a variety of financial reports, such as budget summaries, salary reports, income statements, balance sheets, and so on. With its speed of operation and its capability for recalculating numbers quickly, a spreadsheet program can be most helpful in situations where the user wants to test a number of different financial variables.

Characteristics of a Spreadsheet

A spreadsheet is composed of many cells that are used to store data. Collectively, the cells are called a work sheet. Other names for the work sheet are template or matrix. The work sheet varies in size from one software program to another, although all of them are large enough so that only a portion of the work sheet shows on the display screen. The screen can be scrolled vertically and horizontally to see the other parts of the work sheet.

A common work sheet size is 64 columns wide by 256 rows deep. Most programs label the columns with letters and the rows with numbers. Each cell in the work sheet is identified by a letter (or letters) of the alphabet and a number. For example, the cell in column D, Row 4, is labeled D4.

Each cell stores a *value rule* that tells the computer how to use the data stored in that cell. Each cell can store one of three types of data: a label, a number, or a formula. A *label* consists of alphabetic characters and is used to identify the items in the work sheet, just as column heads in a table identify the information in the table. A *number* can be a whole number or a decimal or a combination. A *formula* is usually an instruction to perform a calculation.

Cells that store numerical data can be used in calculations; cells that store alphabetic data (labels) cannot. Most spreadsheet programs read the first character entered in a cell and decide whether the entry is a label (alphabetic input) or a number or formula (numeric input).

Each cell also has one or more *format rules* that determine how the value in the cell is to be displayed. For example, a format rule may cause the value 298.678 to be displayed as $298.68.

Spreadsheet Formulas

A spreadsheet is useful because its cells can store formulas, which are the instructions for performing calculations. Spreadsheet programs can add, subtract, multiply, and divide. In spreadsheet formulas, the plus and minus mean add and subtract. An asterisk indicates multiplication, while a diagonal(/) means division.

Spreadsheet programs carry out mathematical operations in different ways. Some programs add first, while others multiply and divide before adding and subtracting. *When developing formulas for calculations for the activities that follow, use the instructions in the user's guide for your software. Formula notation varies from one software package to another.*

Spreadsheet Activities

For each of the activities that follow, you will need to set up a work sheet using your spreadsheet software. For these activities, use your program's default column width unless otherwise instructed. You should be familiar with the operation of that software before using these activities. *Follow the instructions in your software user's guide for inputting data and for using the special functions of your software.*

Activity 1   Payroll Report

Prepare a work sheet for the information that follows. Center column heads as shown. Input the data and write the formulas to calculate FICA tax (use a rate of 7.15%), net pay for each employee, and totals for all columns. Format the program for two decimal places for all amounts.

	A	B	C	D	E	F
1	EMPLOYEE	TOTAL		DEDUCTIONS		NET
2	NAME	EARNINGS	FICA	FED. W/H	OTHER	PAY
3						
4	BARNES, J	146.30		13.60	5.38	
5	COX, L	176.30		20.70	8.56	
6	ELIAS, C	197.80		20.80	8.96	
7	LYNN, R	142.20		6.90	5.00	
8	LUCAS, S	157.50		14.80	—	
9	PEREZ, E	199.50		13.20	3.65	
10	ROSS, J	164.50		16.30	3.65	
11	WONG, L	223.15		20.20	—	
12						
13	TOTALS					
14						
15	ASSUMPTION: FICA RATE 7.15%					

Print a copy of your completed payroll report.

Activity 2   Salary Schedule

Prepare a work sheet for the information listed at the top of page 580. For this activity, change the pre-set column width to 12 spaces. Each employee is paid a base salary of $300 per week plus a commission amounting to 5% of his or her weekly sales. Input the formulas for calculating the sales commission and the estimated annual earnings for each employee. Then input the formula to calculate the totals for those two items. Print a copy of the completed salary schedule.

	A	B	C	D	E	F
1			YEARS OF	AVERAGE	SALES	ESTIMATED
2	EMPLOYEE		EMPLOY-	WEEKLY	COMMIS-	ANNUAL
3	NAME	AGE	MENT	SALES	SION	EARNINGS
4						
5	ANG	38	14	1380		
6	CARR	28	4	1280		
7	DAVIS	32	6	2294		
8	FRYE	44	10	2355		
9	GATES	31	2	1295		
10	PETERS	48	7	1398		
11	ROWE	53	17	2460		
12						
13	TOTALS					
14						
15	ASSUMPTIONS: $300 BASE SALARY, 5% COMMISSION					

Activity 3   Employee Earnings Report

Set up a work sheet for the following information. Center the headings in each column. Center the "Earnings" head in Column E.

Next, determine and input the formula to instruct the computer to calculate the amount of regular pay, overtime pay, and the total earnings for each employee. All employees are paid overtime ($1\frac{1}{2}$ times the hourly rate) for all hours worked in excess of 40. Then determine and input the formula to calculate totals for the three earnings columns. Print a copy of the finished report.

	A	B	C	D	E	F
1	EMPLOYEE	HOURS	HOURLY		EARNINGS	
2	NAME	WORKED	RATE	REGULAR	OVERTIME	TOTAL
3						
4	ADERS, J	40	3.80			
5	DREW, L	42	4.20			
6	GREEN, H	44	4.60			
7	LOPEZ, J	38	4.50			
8	MARTIN, N	40	5.00			
9	MORA, R	46	5.20			
10	POST, D	38	4.90			
11	ROBERT, K	40	4.60			
12	TSAU, L	40	4.60			
13						
14	TOTALS					
15						
16	ASSUMPTIONS: 40-HOUR WEEK, OVERTIME = $1\frac{1}{2}$ HOURLY RATE					

Activity 4 Annual Bonus Report

Prepare a work sheet, setting column widths at 12 spaces. Calculate the bonus for each employee, total sales, the total bonus amount, and the average bonus. Employees are paid a half percent bonus on the first $500,000 in sales and one percent for all sales over a half million. Print the report.

	A	B	C	D
1			SALES	
2	NAME	TERRITORY	AMOUNT	BONUS
3				
4	ABRAMS	NORTHWEST	850000	
5	ADAMS	WEST	740000	
6	BEST	NORTHEAST	920000	
7	DANAU	SOUTHEAST	680000	
8	HENRY	SOUTH	720000	
9	KANE	NORTH	695000	
10	KODA	SOUTHWEST	612000	
11	LANZA	EAST	922000	
12	RICCI	MIDWEST	980000	
13	TAM	CENTRAL	774000	
14				
15	TOTAL SALES			
16	TOTAL BONUS			
17	AVERAGE BONUS			
18				
19	ASSUMPTIONS: BONUS = $\frac{1}{2}$% FOR 500,000, 1% OVER 500,000			

Activity 5 Sales Report

Prepare a work sheet to calculate the net sales for each day of the week, total sales, returns, discounts, and net sales. Calculate the total returns as a percentage of total daily sales. Calculate the average daily sales and print a copy.

	A	B	C	D	E
1	DAY	SALES	RETURNS	DISCOUNTS	NET SALES
2					
3	MONDAY	2428.00	112.14	24.28	
4	TUESDAY	3217.00	48.26	32.17	
5	WEDNESDAY	4094.00	281.88	40.94	
6	THURSDAY	3876.80	116.28	58.14	
7	FRIDAY	3998.40	119.94	59.97	
8					
9	TOTALS				
10	RETURNS AS % OF TOTAL SALES				
11	AVERAGE DAILY SALES				

Activity 6 Loan Schedule

Set up a work sheet for the table below. Calculate the total interest to be paid on each loan. Use 365 days in your calculations. Also calculate the total interest. When inputting data, convert the interest rate to a decimal (for example, .095) and the time to days (for example, 6 months equals $365 \div 12 \times 6 = 183$). Print a copy of the finished schedule.

	A	B	C	D	E
1	LOAN	LOAN	INTEREST	TIME	
2	NUMBER	AMOUNT	RATE	DAYS	INTEREST
3					
4	104	1200.00	$9\frac{1}{2}$	60 DAYS	
5	105	1000.00	$10\frac{1}{4}$	90 DAYS	
6	106	2000.00	11	1 YEAR	
7	107	3500.00	$11\frac{1}{2}$	6 MTHS	
8	108	2800.00	$10\frac{3}{4}$	1 YEAR	
9	109	4000.00	$10\frac{1}{4}$	18 MTHS	
10	110	3000.00	$9\frac{3}{4}$	9 MTHS	
11	111	2600.00	$10\frac{1}{2}$	6 MTHS	
12					
13	TOTAL INTEREST				

Activity 7 The Accounting Work Sheet

Using your spreadsheet program, set up a work sheet for the column heads in a 10-column work sheet. Input the account titles and balances shown in Problem 2–3 on page 53 of this textbook. Input the adjustment amounts in the adjustments column. Write formulas instructing the computer to calculate the new balances for the adjusted trial balance columns and to transfer the appropriate amounts to the income statement and balance sheet columns. Calculate totals and complete the work sheet. Print a copy of the completed work sheet.

Activity 8 The Adjusted Trial Balance

Set up a work sheet following the format shown below. Input the account titles and the adjusted trial balance amounts from Problem 9–3 on pages 214–215 of this textbook (you may want to use the work sheet from your *Chapter Reviews and Working Papers* if you have already completed this problem manually). Write formulas instructing the computer to transfer balances to the income statement and balance sheet columns and to total and complete the work sheet. Print a copy.

	Adjusted Trial Balance		Income Statement		Balance Sheet	
Account Title	Debit	Credit	Debit	Credit	Debit	Credit
Cash in Bank	3268.49					

Activity 9   The Income Statement

Set up a work sheet for an income statement using the format shown below.

INCOME STATEMENT
FOR THE YEAR ENDED DECEMBER 31, 19--

REVENUE:
  SALES

Change the width of Column A to accommodate the longest entry. Use Columns B through E to enter amounts. Leave a blank row on the work sheet to separate sections of the income statement. The account titles and balances at the end of the fiscal period are listed below. Print a copy of the completed income statement.

Merchandise Inventory:		Advertising Expense	9,600.00
January 1, 19--	25,480.00	Bank Card Fees Expense	1,540.00
December 31, 19--	32,590.00	Insurance Expense	900.00
Sales	208,750.00	Miscellaneous Expense	2,150.00
Sales Returns & Allow.	2,540.50	Payroll Tax Expense	4,128.00
Purchases	102,780.00	Rent Expense	8,400.00
Transportation In	7,250.80	Salaries Expense	39,184.68
Purchases Ret. & Allow.	1,187.40	Supplies Expense	4,200.00
Purchases Discounts	1,840.00	Utilities Expense	2,328.00

Activity 10   The Balance Sheet

Set up a work sheet for use in preparing a balance sheet. Use the format shown below.

BALANCE SHEET
DECEMBER 31, 19--

ASSETS:
  CASH IN BANK

LIABILITIES:

Change the width of Column A to accommodate the longest entry. Use Columns B and C to enter amounts. Leave a blank row on the work sheet to separate sections of the balance sheet. The account titles and balances at the end of the fiscal period are listed below. Print a copy of the completed balance sheet.

Cash in Bank	18,200.60	Employees' Fed. Inc. Tax Pay.	252.00
Accounts Receivable	5,280.00	FICA Tax Payable	418.20
Merchandise Inventory	28,392.00	Employees' State Inc. Tax Pay.	338.00
Supplies	1,034.00	Insurance Premium Payable	60.00
Prepaid Insurance	1,000.00	Fed. Unempl. Tax Payable	70.30
Equipment	12,188.00	State Unempl. Tax Payable	242.80
Accounts Payable	5,178.00	Lynn Burton, Capital	58,400.30
Sales Tax Payable	1,135.00		

Appendix B
Optional Chapter Activities

Chapter 1, Problem 1A

Shown below is a sales slip used by Harrison's Cards and Gifts.

HARRISON'S CARDS AND GIFTS				
61 Boston Post Road				
Sudbury, MA 01776				

Date	*June 30* 19—		No. 419	

SOLD TO	019 56 048 B A BAXTER 27 AMES ROAD SUDBURY MA 01776

Clerk	Cash	Charge ✓	Terms *net 30*

Qty.	Description	Unit Price	Amount	
2	Cranberry glass vases	19.99	39	98
5	Dried flower arrangements	7.95	39	75
5	Cards	1.25	6	25
2	Cards	1.50	3	00
		Sub Total	88	98
Thank you!		Sales Tax	4	45
		Total	93	33

Instructions:

(1) Record this sales slip in the sales journal included in the working papers accompanying this textbook.
(2) Total, prove, and rule the sales journal.

Chapter 1, Problem 1B

The bookkeeper for the Kellogg Company made some errors while posting from the special and general journals.

Instructions: Answer the following questions about each error. Use plain paper or the space provided in the working papers for your answers.

(1) In the cash receipts journal, the cash sale of an old calculator was not posted to the Office Equipment account in the general ledger.
   (a) Will the general ledger accounts balance?
   (b) In the Trial Balance section of the work sheet, will the total of the debit column or the credit column be larger?
   (c) Will the schedule of accounts receivable agree with the controlling account?
   (d) Will the value of the office equipment be overstated or understated?

(2) An entry in the Accounts Payable Debit column of the cash payments journal was not posted to the creditor's account in the subsidiary ledger.
   (a) Will the general ledger accounts balance?
   (b) Will the total debits and total credits in the cash payments journal prove equal?
   (c) Will the schedule of accounts payable agree with the balance of the controlling account?

(3) In the general journal, a debit amount for a sales return was not posted to the Sales Tax Payable account.
   (a) Will the general ledger accounts balance?
   (b) Will the schedule of accounts receivable agree with the controlling account?
   (c) Will the net income for the period be correct?
   (d) Will the balance of the Clark Kellogg, Capital account be affected?

Chapter 2, Problem 2A

In the workbook are abbreviated income statements for three different businesses. Determine the missing amounts for each of the question marks.

Chapter 2, Problem 2B

For each of the companies listed in Problem 2A, determine the ending balance of the owner's capital account using the information in the working papers. Determine the missing amounts for each of the question marks.

Chapter 3, Problem 3A

The Lang Company opened for business four years ago. It used the direct write-off method of accounting for uncollectible accounts during the first three years of operation. With net sales this year of $209,640, the company decided to switch to the allowance method.

The company plans to use the percentage of net sales method to estimate the amount of the adjustment for bad debts expense. The accounting records for the past three years show the following.

	Net Sales	Total Actual Bad Debt Losses
Year 1	$ 86,428	$1,296
Year 2	98,360	1,426
Year 3	132,076	2,047

Instructions:

(1) Based on the figures for the first three years, what percentage of net sales would you suggest be used?

(2) Can the Lang Company use the same accounts under the allowance method as it used under the direct write-off method? Explain.

(3) What should the amount of the adjustment for bad debts be?

(4) If Accounts Receivable has a year-end balance of $14,362, what will the book value of accounts receivable be?

(5) Record the December 31 adjusting entry for bad debts expense on page 53 of the general journal.

Chapter 3, Problem 3B

The Breyers Company uses the accounts receivable aging method to estimate its uncollectible accounts. At the end of the fiscal period (December 31), a co-worker began to prepare the accounts receivable aging schedule. When that person became ill, you were asked to complete the schedule. The following customer accounts remain to be aged:

Account	Amount	Due Date
M. Wilson	$ 62	Jan. 4 (next year)
J. Wolfe	317	Oct. 12
P. Yang	1,362	Nov. 5, $601; Dec. 16, $761
K. Young	443	Dec. 3
S. Zeoli	271	Aug. 9

Instructions:

(1) Complete the accounts receivable aging schedule included in the working papers.

(2) Calculate the total estimated uncollectible amount using the percentages listed below.

Time Past Due	Percent Estimated Uncollectible
Not yet due	2%
1–30 days	4%
31–60 days	20%
61–90 days	30%
Over 90 days	45%

(3) Determine the amount of the adjustment if Allowance for Uncollectible Accounts has a credit balance of $79.42.

Chapter 4, Problem 4A

You are the bookkeeper for the Stratford Office Furniture Company. On February 10, the LaRosa Company purchased merchandise totaling $2,850, terms 2/10, n/30 (Sales Slip 385). On March 17, Stratford accepted a 30-day, 12% note for $2,850 from LaRosa Company in place of the amount that was past due (Note 16). On March 23, LaRosa's note was discounted at the Second National Bank at 10% (Receipt 2716).

On April 19, Stratford received notice that LaRosa Company had dishonored its note and that the bank was charging a protest fee of $10 (Memo. 173).

On September 30, it is determined that LaRosa will not pay its note. The note is, therefore, written off as uncollectible (Memorandum 195).

Instructions: Record the transactions for February 10, March 17 and 23, April 19, and September 30 on page 19 of the general journal.

Chapter 5, Problem 5A

In order to prepare interim financial reports, Jetson House decided to estimate the value of its ending inventory. The company's accounting records provided the following information.

Net Sales	$181,000
Beginning Inventory at Cost	140,400
Beginning Inventory at Retail	216,100
Net Purchases at Cost	77,500
New Purchases at Retail	119,500
Gross profit as a percentage of net sales	34%

Instructions:

(1) Use the retail method to estimate the cost of the ending inventory. Use plain paper or the form provided in the working papers.
(2) Use the gross profit method to estimate the cost of the ending inventory.
(3) Which method would yield a higher cost of merchandise sold?
(4) Which method would yield a higher gross profit on sales?

Chapter 6, Problem 6A

You are the accountant for Welch, Inc., a company that manufactures small hand tools. The company plans to purchase a new machine that costs $3,720. The machine has an estimated disposal value of $80 and an estimated life of five years. You have been asked to supply some information.

Instructions:

(1) Determine the annual depreciation, accumulated depreciation, and book value of the machine for the first three years using the straight-line method, the double-declining-balance method, and the sum-of-the-years'-digits method. Use plain paper or the table provided in the working papers.

(2) Determine the answers to the following questions.
   (a) Which depreciation method would yield the highest book value after three years?
   (b) Which depreciation method would allow the maximum amount of depreciation over the three years?
(3) Assume that, three years from now, the company can sell the machine for $750. Answer the following questions.
   (a) Would any of the depreciation methods provide for a gain on the disposal of the machine? If so, which method(s) and how much of a gain?
   (b) Would any of the depreciation methods result in a loss on the disposal of the machine? If so, which method(s) and how much of a loss?
   (c) If the company wants to choose the method that results in the largest gain at the end of the three years, which depreciation method would you recommend be used?

Chapter 7, Problem 7A

The Bork Company uses the voucher system of accounting. The following list includes typical transactions that occur during an accounting period.

1. Received the monthly telephone bill.
2. Recorded the company's biweekly salary expense and the deductions for FICA taxes and federal income taxes.
3. Recorded the net amount due on the biweekly payroll.
4. Received an invoice for merchandise purchased on account from the Tucker Company.
5. Paid the net amount of the payroll.
6. Returned a portion of the merchandise purchased on account from the Tucker Company.
7. Received a bill for freight charges on merchandise purchased.
8. Canceled a voucher because the totals on the original invoice (for merchandise) and on the voucher were incorrect.
9. Paid the amount owed to the Tucker Company less the discount allowed.
10. Received a bill for supplies purchased on account.

Instructions: For each transaction, indicate the following:

(1) The book of original entry in which the transaction would be recorded.
(2) The accounts that would be debited and credited.
(3) Whether the debit and credit amounts would be posted individually or as part of a column total.

Use plain paper or the form provided in the working papers. In addition to a General Debit column, Bork Company's voucher register has the following special amount columns:

Vouchers Payable Credit	Supplies Debit
Purchases Debit	Miscellaneous Expense Debit
Transportation In Debit	

Chapter 8, Problem 8A

The Lang Company uses the accrual basis of accounting. When the fiscal period ended on July 31, certain adjustments had to be made. These adjustments are shown in the following T accounts.

Interest Receivable			Supplies			Prepaid Rent		
36		Bal.	3,176	1,438	Bal.	5,400	3,600

Interest Payable			Corp. Inc. Tax Pay.			Unearned Adv. Inc.		
	18			1,354		2,500	Bal.	3,000

Rent Expense			Supplies Expense			Advisory Income		
3,600			1,438				Bal.	22,000
								2,500

Interest Income			Interest Expense			Income Tax Expense		
	Bal.	56	18			Bal.	2,335
		36					1,354

Instructions: Record the adjusting entries on page 19 of the general journal.

Chapter 8, Problem 8B

The biweekly payroll at the Heather Shop is $15,980. When the fiscal period ended on December 31, salaries had accrued for 8 days.

On January 3, Check 781 was issued to the payroll bank account for the biweekly payroll. The following total amounts were withheld: Employees' federal income taxes, $1,258.00; FICA taxes, $1,126.59; employees' state income taxes, $631.00; and insurance premiums, $35.00.

Instructions: Record the December 31 adjusting entry and the January 3 transaction on page 43 of the general journal.

Chapter 9, Problem 9A

You are one of the accounting clerks at Ryan, Incorporated. A co-worker started preparing the work sheet for the fiscal period ended December 31. The Trial Balance section has been totaled, proved, and ruled. However, there are some mistakes in the Adjustments section. You have been asked to help. The accounting records show the following information.

1. Ryan, Inc., uses 2% of the balance of Accounts Receivable to estimate its uncollectible accounts.
2. The ending merchandise inventory is $13,722.00.
3. The ending supplies inventory is $222.00.
4. On May 1, the company paid $900.00 for a one-year insurance policy.
5. Estimated depreciation on equipment is $2,050.00.

6. On December 1, the company borrowed $11,569.00 from the First National Bank, issuing a 90-day, non-interest-bearing note discounted at 9½%.
7. Of the $8,500.00 in subscriptions income that was collected this year, $4,000.00 has been earned.
8. Salaries totaling $579.04 have accrued since the last payroll was issued.
9. Total corporate income taxes for the year are $3,545.00.

Instructions: Find and correct the errors in the Adjustments section of the work sheet, which appears in the working papers. Cross out any incorrect amounts and enter the correct amounts above or where appropriate.

Chapter 9, Problem 9B

Errors made while calculating or recording the adjustments on the work sheet may affect the amounts reported on the financial statements. Listed below are several different types of errors. These errors may affect certain amounts on the financial statements.

Instructions: Indicate what effect each error will have on the reported financial statement amounts. Complete the chart provided in the working papers by entering "O" for overstated, "U" for understated, and "N" for not affected.

(1) The ending merchandise inventory was understated by $2,000.
(2) Uncollectible accounts are estimated using a percentage of net sales. When making the calculation, a net sales amount of $12,986 was used rather than the correct amount of $21,986.
(3) Supplies used during the period was calculated at $1,889; the correct amount was $1,789.
(4) The additional $1,116 owed in corporate income taxes was omitted.
(5) In November the company accepted a 90-day, 8% note receivable. When calculating the accrued interest income, a 9% interest rate was used.
(6) The adjustment for prepaid insurance expired was omitted.
(7) When making the adjustment for other income, Unearned Rent was credited and Rental Income was debited.
(8) The adjustment for accrued salaries was omitted.
(9) When adjusting for the annual depreciation, the Equipment account was credited rather than the Accumulated Depreciation—Equipment account.
(10) Uncollectible accounts are estimated using a percentage of Accounts Receivable. The $600 estimate of uncollectible accounts (3% of the balance of Accounts Receivable) was the amount added to the $100 credit balance of Allowance for Uncollectible Accounts.

Chapter 10, Problem 10A

Lynn Abbott, James Austin, and Clarence Butler are partners in the Boca Company. Since sales have been very poor, the partners agree to liquidate the business. The balances of the partnership accounts are shown at the top of page 591. The partners share profits and losses in a 2:1:1 ratio.

Cash in Bank	$38,496	Other assets	$ 9,385
Accounts Receivable	3,290	Accounts Payable	13,804
Merchandise Inventory	72,943	Lynn Abbott, Capital	62,400
Equipment (net)	21,890	James Austin, Capital	41,800
Delivery Truck (net)	11,300	Clarence Butler, Capital	39,300

Instructions: Journalize the following entries to liquidate the partnership. Use page 47 of a general journal.

Nov. 15 Sold the entire merchandise inventory for $75,000, Receipt 2364.

Dec. 5 Collected 85% of the accounts receivable, Receipts 2365–2373.

6 Sold the equipment to a competitor for $20,000, Receipt 2374.

8 The delivery truck was sold for $12,600, Receipt 2375.

12 The other assets were sold for $9,000, Receipt 2376.

14 The gain or loss from realization was allocated to the partners' capital accounts, Memorandum 1436.

15 Paid all creditors the full amount owed, Checks 2453–2462.

18 The remaining cash was distributed to the partners, Checks 2463–2465.

Chapter 11, Problem 11A

Joyce Fritch, Suzanne Jacobson, and Barbara Torres are partners in the firm of Town Line Draperies. The partnership had a net loss of $1,400 for the year.

The balances in the partners' capital accounts at the beginning of the year were $86,500, $81,000, and $85,000, respectively. During the year, Joyce Fritch invested an additional $3,000 in the business. At the end of the year, the balances of the partners' withdrawals accounts were $12,300, $10,000, and $11,700, respectively.

The partnership agreement provides for salary allowances as follows: Fritch, $13,000; Jacobson, $12,000; and Torres, $11,000. The partnership agreement also provides for an interest allowance of 3% on the balances of the partners' capital accounts at the beginning of the year. Any remainder is to be divided equally.

Instructions:

(1) Record the December 31 closing entry for the division of the net loss with salary allowances and interest allowances. Also prepare the closing entries for the partners' withdrawals accounts. Use page 74 of the general journal.

(2) Prepare a statement of changes in partners' equity for Town Line Draperies for the year ended December 31.

Chapter 12, Problem 12A

The Hooper Corporation is authorized to issue 10,000 shares of $50-par preferred 8% stock and 40,000 shares of no-par common stock with a stated value of $20. The account balances as of May 1 are as follows.

Common Stock	$600,000
Common Stock Subscribed	30,000
Paid-in Capital in Excess of Par—Preferred	3,500
Paid-in Capital in Excess of Stated Value	28,384
Preferred 8% Stock	200,000
Preferred 8% Stock Subscribed	10,000
Retained Earnings	193,000
Subscriptions Receivable—Common Stock	3,000
Subscriptions Receivable—Preferred 8% Stock	1,000

On May 8, the Hooper Corporation received subscriptions to 2,000 shares of preferred 8% stock at $54 per share. A down payment of 30% of the subscription price was made at the same time. The journal entries that were made appear in the working papers.

Instructions:

(1) Answer the following questions.
   (a) What effect will this error have on the Preferred 8% Stock account?
   (b) What effect will this error have on the Subscriptions Receivable—Preferred 8% Stock account? Explain.
   (c) What effect will this error have on Total Stockholders' Equity on the May 31 balance sheet? Explain.
(2) Prepare a correcting entry for the error(s) that were made in the May 8 entry. Use May 12 as the date of the entry and Memorandum 467 as the source document. Record the entry on page 125 of the general journal.

Chapter 12, Problem 12B

Prepare the Stockholders' Equity section of the balance sheet for the Hooper Corporation as of May 31. Use the information provided in Problem 12A, as well as the correcting entry you made in that problem.

Chapter 13, Problem 13A

The Weiss Corporation is authorized to issue 5,000 shares of $50-par preferred 8% stock and 75,000 shares of no-par common stock with a stated value of $10. The following account balances appeared on the December 31 balance sheet.

Common Stock	$560,000
Common Stock Subscribed	50,000
Paid-in Capital in Excess of Par—Preferred	5,000
Paid-in Capital in Excess of Stated Value	22,000
Preferred 8% Stock	105,000
Preferred 8% Stock Subscribed	45,000
Retained Earnings	157,400
Subscriptions Receivable—Common Stock	20,000
Subscriptions Receivable—Preferred 8% Stock	15,000

The following transactions took place during the next six months.

Jan. 26 Subscribers to 400 shares of preferred 8% stock paid the remaining $11,000 of the subscription price, Receipt 1144; issued the 400 shares, Memorandum 274.

Feb. 15 The board of directors voted to pay the cash dividend to preferred stockholders, payable on March 5 to stockholders of record on February 20, Minute Book page 635.

Mar. 5 Paid the cash dividend to preferred stockholders, Check 5647.

8 Subscribers to 1,000 shares of common stock paid the remaining $8,000 of the subscription price, Receipt 1340; issued the 1,000 shares, Memorandum 395.

Apr. 13 Declared a 5% stock dividend to common stockholders of record as of April 10, payable April 28, Minute Book page 692. The present market value of the stock is $12 per share.

28 Distributed the stock dividend to common stockholders, Minute Book page 692.

May 14 Purchased 500 shares of own common stock at $12 per share, Check 6736.

June 28 Sold 125 shares of treasury stock at $12.50, Receipt 1731.

Instructions: Record these transactions on page 45 of the general journal.

Chapter 13, Problem 13B

Shown in the working papers are the net income and corporate income taxes paid to-date for several different companies.

The federal income tax rates for corporations are as follows.

If Taxable Income Is		Tax Is	
Over	But less than		Of amount over
0	$ 25,000	15%	0
$ 25,000	50,000	$ 3,750 + 18%	$ 25,000
50,000	75,000	8,250 + 30%	50,000
75,000	100,000	15,750 + 40%	75,000
100,000		25,750 + 46%	100,000

Instructions: Use the IRS tax rate table to determine the following for each corporation. Use plain paper or the form provided in the working papers.

(1) Total corporate income tax for the year.
(2) Amount of the adjustment for additional income taxes owed.

Chapter 14, Problem 14A

Five years ago, the Kardos Company issued $6,000,000 worth of $11\frac{1}{2}$%, 20-year callable bonds with a call price of 105. The interest payments have been made each year for the past 5 years. There is an unamortized bond discount of $16,000.

The company wants to redeem these $11\frac{1}{2}$% bonds and issue $6,000,000 worth of 9%, 15-year bonds.

Instructions:

(1) Answer the following questions.

    (a) Over the next 15 years, how much interest would be paid on the original bond issue?

    (b) How much would it cost the company to redeem the original bond issue?

    (c) How much interest would be paid over the next 15 years for the new bond issue?

    (d) How much interest would be saved over the next 15 years if the company redeems the old bonds and issues the new bonds?

    (e) Considering the premium the company would have to pay for redeeming the existing bonds, how much would the company save over the next 15 years?

(2) Record the following transactions on page 37 of the general journal.

Mar.   7   Redeemed the entire issue of $11\frac{1}{2}$%, 20-year callable bonds, Check 4634.

      15   Issued $6,000,000 worth of 15-year, 9% bonds at 101, Receipt 2641.

Chapter 14, Problem 14B

The Clayton Corporation is authorized to issue 50,000 shares of $25-par common stock. The following balances appeared on the Clayton Corporation's work sheet for the year ended December 31.

Accounts Payable	$ 13,208	Dividends Payable	$ 46,250
10% Bonds Payable	400,000	Paid-in Capital in Excess of Par	192,000
Common Stock	925,000	Retained Earnings	413,000
Corporate Income Tax Payable	1,392	Salaries Payable	4,200
Discount on Bonds Payable	8,000	Sales Tax Payable	1,952

The corporation earned a net income after income taxes of $95,167 for the year. The 10% bond issue is due on January 1, 1995.

Instructions: Prepare the Liabilities and Stockholders' Equity sections of the corporation's balance sheet. Use plain paper or the form provided in the working papers.

Chapter 15, Problem 15A

The Party House has four departments: Department A sells cards, stationery, paper products, and other related items; Department B sells toys and small gift items; Department C sells paperback books and magazines; and Department D sells plants and gardening supplies.

The company is considering whether to eliminate one of the departments. The accounting records show the following. (Note: The company allocates its indirect expenses to each department.)

	Dept. A	Dept. B	Dept. C	Dept. D
Net Sales	$80,200	$110,287	$62,936	$27,706
Cost of Merchandise Sold	41,704	57,349	32,382	14,407
Direct Expenses	18,381	26,283	17,294	7,500
Indirect Expenses Allocated	13,843	18,364	12,237	6,330

Instructions:

(1) Calculate the contribution margin and net income (or loss) for each department. Use plain paper or the form provided in the working papers.
(2) If the Party House eliminates Department D, what would the store's total net income for the period be?
(3) If the indirect expenses allocated to Department D are evenly distributed among the other three departments, what would each department's net income or loss be?
(4) If the indirect expenses allocated to Department D are distributed to Departments A, B, and C using a 2:2:1 ratio, what would each department's net income or loss be?

Chapter 16, Problem 16A

The O'Brien Company is a multistore business with branches in Norwalk, Bridgewater, and Woodbury. The Woodbury store is the warehouse for the other two branches.

On May 5, the Woodbury branch shipped $80,300 worth of merchandise to the Norwalk branch, charging a transfer fee of $803 (Transfer Request 5367). It also shipped $26,400 worth of merchandise to the Bridgewater store, with a transfer fee of $264 (Transfer Request 5368). These entries were recorded as follows.

	GENERAL JOURNAL			PAGE 307
DATE	DESCRIPTION	POST. REF.	DEBIT	CREDIT
19-- May 5	Due from Norwalk	1071	81103 00	
	Purchases-Woodbury	5013		81103 00
	Transfer Request 5367			
5	Due from Bridgewater	1072	26664 00	
	Purchases-Woodbury	5013		26664 00
	Transfer Request 5368			

On May 9, the Bridgewater store paid the amount owed for the merchandise. The transaction was recorded as follows.

DATE	DESCRIPTION	POST. REF.	DEBIT	CREDIT	
1	19-- May 9	Cash in Bank—Woodbury	1013	26 66 4 00		1
2		Due from Norwalk	1071		26 66 4 00	2
3		Receipt 4104				3

Instructions: Prepare three correcting entries, dated May 14, to correct the errors made in the May 5 and May 9 entries (Memorandum 34673). Use page 309 of the general journal.

Chapter 16, Problem 16B

The Hayward Furniture Center is a multistore business with branches in Concord, Duxbury, and Grafton. The company uses a centralized accounting system, with a Cash in Bank—Payables account.

On September 14, the central accounting office received a $4,500 bill from the *Bay State News* for several recent advertisements. The ads feature sale items and list the locations of all three branches. The central accounting office allocates the advertising expense among the three branches according to the square footage occupied by the branches, which is as follows: Concord 5,000 square feet, Duxbury 6,500 square feet, and Grafton 3,500 square feet.

Instructions: Allocate the advertising expense among the three branches. Record the cash payment of the bill on September 14 on page 101 of the general journal (Check 1409).

Chapter 17, Problem 17A

Shown in the working papers are abbreviated statements of cost of goods manufactured for three different companies. Determine the missing amounts for each of the question marks.

Chapter 17, Problem 17B

The Kelly Company manufactures bookcases in various styles. At the end of the fiscal period, the accounting records showed the following information.

All materials are issued when the bookcase is started. The direct materials cost, which is the same for all styles, is $46.50. The direct labor cost for the period totaled $132,400 and the factory overhead costs were $108,300.

During the fiscal period 3,127 units were started. At the end of the fiscal period, 152 units had not yet been completed and 480 units were in the finished goods inventory. The total direct labor cost assigned to the work in process was $7,250 and the total direct labor cost assigned to the units in the finished goods inventory was $21,200.

Instructions: Based on this information, answer the following questions.

(1) What is the total direct materials cost for the period?
(2) What is the direct materials cost for work in process?
(3) What is the direct materials cost for the finished goods inventory?
(4) What is the factory overhead rate?
(5) What is the factory overhead cost for the work in process inventory?
(6) What is the factory overhead cost for the finished goods inventory?
(7) What is the direct materials cost for the units completed and sold during the period?
(8) What is the direct labor cost for the units completed and sold during the period?

Chapter 18, Problem 18A

The Piedmont Company manufactures small sailboats. The company has four departments: Department A makes the hull, Department B paints the hull and attaches the hardware, Department C makes the sails, and Department D inspects the final product and packages it for shipping.

Department B recently had a fire in its office. Several of the monthly financial statements and other production reports were destroyed. You have been asked to help reconstruct one of these statements.

The following information was obtained from other departments and from documents not destroyed in the fire.

1. On December 1, the work in process inventory consisted of 68 units. The Piedmont Company uses the 50% rule to determine equivalent units for work in process.
2. During December, 479 units were completed and transferred to Department C.
3. On December 31, 46 units were still being processed in Department B.
4. Manufacturing costs charged to the department during December were:
   a. Direct materials of $4,500.00.
   b. Direct labor of $12,200.00.
   c. The factory overhead applied was estimated at 55% of the direct labor cost for the month.
5. The costs transferred from Department A totaled $122,145.00 (479 units @ $255.00).
6. The costs transferred to Department C were $145,941.72 (479 units @ $304.68).

Instructions: Based on this information, recreate a cost of production report for the month ended December 31.

Chapter 19, Problem 19A

The Benemore Company uses the fifo method to assign a cost to its ending merchandise inventory. The accounting records show the following information about the beginning and ending inventories and the purchases made for two of its inventory items.

	Item 4610	Item 7954
Beginning Inventory, Jan. 1	47 units @ $31	16 units @ $14
March 5 Purchase	50 units @ 31	29 units @ 15
May 9 Purchase	25 units @ 32	
July 16 Purchase	30 units @ 32	11 units @ 16
August 23 Purchase	60 units @ 31	15 units @ 17
October 25 Purchase	25 units @ 31	20 units @ 16
November 28 Purchase	10 units @ 30	10 units @ 17
Ending Inventory, Dec. 31	42 units	19 units

Using the accounting guideline of conservatism, the Benemore Company reports its ending inventory at the lower-of-cost-or-market amount.

Instructions: Based on this information, answer the following questions. Use plain paper or the space provided in the working papers.

(1) What is the value of the ending inventory of the two items using the fifo method?

(2) If the current market price of Item 4610 is $29 and the current market price of Item 7954 is $18, what is the value of the ending inventory of the two items based on their market prices?

(3) Which amounts should be used on the financial statements for the two items?

(4) If the accounting guideline of conservatism is not used,
  (a) Will the cost of merchandise sold on the income statement be overstated or understated?
  (b) Will the gross profit on sales on the income statement be overstated or understated?
  (c) Will the net income be overstated or understated?

Chapter 20, Problem 20A

Country Casuals is a clothing store selling both men's and women's clothing. You are interested in purchasing a large number of shares of the company's stock for investment purposes. In order for you to make a thorough financial analysis of the business, the following information covering the past three years has been supplied.

	1985	1986	1987
Current Assets	$645,000	$710,000	$725,000
Total Liabilities	$249,500	$276,500	$291,000
Current Ratio	6.1:1	6.5:1	6.3:1
Quick Ratio	1.15:1	1.70:1	1.95:1
Ratio of Stockholders' Equity to Liabilities	3.94:1	4.20:1	4.25:1

Instructions: Based on this information, answer the following questions. Use plain paper or the form provided in the working papers. Round your answers to the nearest whole dollar.

(1) What are the current liabilities for each of the three years?
(2) What are the quick assets for each of the three years?
(3) What are the long-term liabilities for each of the three years?
(4) What is the total stockholders' equity for each of the three years?
(5) What is the working capital for each of the three years?
(6) By what amount did the quick assets increase from 1985 to 1987?
(7) By what amount did working capital increase from 1985 to 1987?

Chapter 21, Problem 21A

The December 31, 1987, balances of the current asset and current liability accounts of the Lopel Corporation are shown below. Also indicated is whether that balance is an increase or decrease over the previous year's ending balance.

Cash in Bank	$172,284, a decrease of $13,294
Accounts Receivable (net)	92,273, an increase of $4,375
Merchandise Inventory	237,374, an increase of $16,283
Supplies	7,485, a decrease of $1,936
Accounts Payable	92,843, an increase of $7,439
Notes Payable	23,930, a decrease of $4,700
Corp. Income Tax Payable	3,945, an increase of $840
Salaries Payable	2,730, an increase of $795

Instructions: Using the form provided in the working papers, prepare a schedule of changes in working capital. Also calculate the percent of increase or decrease in each account from 1986 to 1987. Round the percent to the nearest tenth of a percent.

Chapter 21, Problem 21B

Use the information in Problem 21A and the following additional information to prepare a statement of changes in financial position for the Lopel Corporation for the year ended December 31, 1987.

(1) Net income after income taxes was $34,554.
(2) Depreciation expense for the year was $9,000 on the building owned and $4,200 on equipment.
(3) The company purchased new equipment during the year totaling $20,000.
(4) A cash dividend of $1.25 per share was declared and paid during the year on 15,000 outstanding shares.
(5) The company paid off the remaining $7,950 of the mortgage.

Chapter 22, Problem 22A

The Hayo Teen Center is a neighborhood center that provides services and recreational activities for teenagers. The center offers arts and crafts, dances, vocational instruction, counseling, and organized sports.

The center's budget director prepares an annual budget. Every three months, a budget summary report is prepared and analyzed. The budget summary report for the six months ended June 30 is presented below.

REVENUE	Current Year Budget Amount	Current Y-T-D Amount	Free Balance Amount	Previous Y-T-D Amount
Membership Fees	$25,600	$11,370	$14,230	$12,840
United Way	7,500	3,750	3,750	3,000
Athletic Fees	14,100	8,300	5,800	7,900
Donations	9,500	5,200	4,300	3,750
Dances	8,200	2,700	5,500	3,925
Fund-Raising	12,700	8,100	4,600	7,450
Total Revenue	$77,600	$39,420	$38,180	$38,865
EXPENDITURES				
Personal Services				
Director's Salary	$26,500	$13,250	$13,250	$12,800
Wages	19,300	8,100	11,200	8,900
Total	$45,800	$21,350	$24,450	$21,700
Operating Costs				
Utilities	$ 4,350	$ 2,940	$ 1,410	$ 2,700
Office Supplies	2,800	1,150	1,650	1,170
Repairs	3,700	1,400	2,300	1,165
Postage	950	345	605	425
Insurance	800	400	400	375
Total	$12,600	$ 6,235	$ 6,365	$ 5,835
Supplies				
Awards	$ 850	$ 300	$ 550	$ 395
Repair Supplies	3,850	1,385	2,465	935
Sports Items	2,400	1,500	900	1,150
Misc. Supplies	1,200	350	850	585
Dance Supplies	1,750	600	1,150	825
Total	$10,050	$ 4,135	$ 5,915	$ 3,890
Capital Expenditures				
Equipment	$ 6,000	$ 3,650	$ 2,350	$ 1,200
Furniture	3,150	2,200	950	550
Total	$ 9,150	$ 5,850	$ 3,300	$ 1,750
Total Expenditures	$77,600	$37,570	$40,030	$33,175

The budget director projects that revenue from membership fees is now expected to be approximately 85% of the original budget amount and that the revenue from dances will only be 70% of the original budget amount. The amount received from donations is expected to be 10% higher than originally projected.

The budget director has asked you to prepare a revised budget. Some of the expenditure projections will have to be adjusted to accommodate the revised revenue amounts.

Instructions: Prepare a revised annual budget, including the projected revenue changes and your recommendations for expenditure changes. Use the form provided in the working papers.

Chapter 23, Problem 23A

Taft Craft Center's final budget summary report for the year ended June 30 appears below. You have been asked to provide a breakdown of the various line items.

Taft Craft Center
Budget Summary Report
For the Year Ended June 30, 19—

REVENUE	Budget Amount	Actual Amount
Membership Fees	$12,300	$12,150
United Way	5,500	5,000
Athletic Fees	17,250	16,850
Center Store	6,500	6,795
Dances	10,400	9,700
Fund-Raising	10,000	10,950
Total Revenue	$61,950	$61,445

EXPENDITURES		
Personal Services		
Director's Salary	$21,500	$21,500
Wages	17,800	19,160
Total	$39,300	$40,660
Operating Costs		
Utilities	$ 6,600	$ 5,824
Office Supplies	1,600	1,380
Repairs	3,400	2,685
Postage	750	530
Insurance	800	800
Total	$13,150	$11,219
Supplies		
Awards	$ 850	$ 795
Repair Supplies	2,900	2,340
Sports Items	2,650	2,835
Miscellaneous Supplies	1,200	1,260
Dance Supplies	1,900	1,575
Total	$ 9,500	$ 8,805
Total Expenditures	$61,950	$60,684

Instructions: Using the form provided in the working papers, calculate the difference between the actual revenue and expenditure amounts and the budget amounts. Then calculate the percentage the difference amount was over or under the budget amount. Round percentages to the nearest tenth of a percent.

Index

Credits

Cover: Ligature Publishing Services, Inc.
Book Design: Richard Bartlett
Technical Art: Jan Rapp
Calligraphy: Nancy Edwards

Photographs:
Pages 2–3: © 1982 Milton & Joan Mann/THE MARILYN GARTMAN AGENCY
Pages 62–63: Edward Klamm/BLACK STAR
Pages 224–225: © Barbara Alper/STOCK BOSTON
Pages 342–343: Owen Franken/STOCK BOSTON
Pages 458–459: © 1982 Stanley Rowin/THE PICTURE CUBE
Pages 516–517: © 1978 Bruce L. Wolfe/UNIPHOTO